In Plain Sight:
Felix A. Sommerfeld,
Spymaster in Mexico, 1908
to 1914

Heribert von Feilitzsch

To Karen with best wishes, Heribert

Henselstone Verlag

First published in the United States of America in 2012 by Henselstone Verlag, LLC.

First Edition

Every effort has been made to locate and contact all holders of copyright to material reproduced in this book.
For information about permission to reproduce selections from this book, write to Permissions, Henselstone Verlag LLC, P.O. Box 116, Amissville, Virginia 20106.

Library of Congress Control Number 2012913352
Keyword Data
von Feilitzsch, Heribert, 1965-
    In Plain Sight: Felix A. Sommerfeld, Spymaster in Mexico, 1908 to 1914 / Heribert von Feilitzsch.
    p. cm
    Includes biographical references and index.
    ISBN 978-0-9850317-1-8 (alk. Paper)

    1.   Mexico – History – Revolution, 1910-1920 – Diplomatic History
    2.   United States – Foreign Relations – Mexico
    3.   United States – Foreign Relations - Germany
    4.   Mexico – Foreign Relations – United States
    5.   Mexico – Foreign Relations - Germany
    6.   Germany – Foreign Relations – Mexico
    7.   Germany – Foreign Relations – United States
    8.   Mexican-American Border Region – History – 20th Century
    9.   Smuggling – Mexican-American Border Region – History – 20th Century
    I.   von Feilitzsch, Heribert. Title.

Cover Design by Mach:-)werk Kommunikation und Design, www.machwerk.com

Title picture courtesy of the El Paso Public Library, Aultman Collection
Visit www.In-Plain-Sight.info

Printed in the United States of America

For Berkley

"I had over six years of nerve raking[sic] excitement and felt that I need[ed] a more peaceful occupation. But I wish to add here that during these years of participation in Mexican political affairs I have at all times used, whatever influence I had, to maintain peace and friendly relations with the United States…That is all I have to say at this time."

Felix A. Sommerfeld to Sherburne G. Hopkins in 1919, commenting on his claim of having retired from Mexican affairs in the fall of 1915.[1]

For years I have hoped that someone would disentangle Sommerfeld's role in the Mexican Revolution. You have done that and much more – utilizing a most impressive range of archival sources. "In Plain Sight" is a splendid work.

Charles H. Harris III
Professor Emeritus, New Mexico State University

You have a winner!

Louis R. Sadler
Professor Emeritus, New Mexico State University

This current work is not only a must-read for people interested in history but also highly recommended for those who like to get a glimpse into the causes and motives of human activity and historical events. Rarely has it been possible to document the motivation of secret agents in such detail and so accurately. This fact alone pays tribute to the author and makes this work so significant.

Günter Köhler
Professor Emeritus, Humboldt Universität, Berlin

TABLE OF CONTENTS

Prologue

~

On June 6th 1911, a special train rolled slowly into the main station of Mexico City. Francisco Leon De La Barra, the provisional president of the country, his entire cabinet, the diplomatic corps, and countless dignitaries waited on the platform to pay homage to the man who had unseated the symbol of a generation of repression and corruption, Dictator Porfirio Diaz. As the assembled crowd cheered, Francisco I. Madero, "the Apostle of Democracy" and his entourage of one hundred fellow revolutionaries, friends, politicians, dignitaries, family members, and military commanders stepped off the Pullman cars and wound their way through the crowd, waving, saluting, and greeting. "The bells of the Cathedral and of ninety other churches pealed the joyous message. Factory sirens shrieked, and the whistles of locomotives in the various stations shrilly joined the din. It seemed as though the pent-up feelings of an entire people had been released in a momentous explosion of emotion."[2] Next to the revolutionary leader, a man with a stern look on his face, unfazed by the ecstatic energy of the crowd, pushed a pathway through the masses for his chief. Felix A. Sommerfeld worried about Madero's safety. At 5' 3" and one hundred and forty pounds, Madero threatened to be swallowed by the towering masses. As the drove of people with the revolutionary chieftain in its midst flowed into the streets of the capital, Sommerfeld calmly scanned the crowd for a hint of threat. "An estimated one hundred thousand people cheered deliriously," everyone trying their best to gain - if not a faint glimpse of the hero - maybe a chance to touch him.[3] Felix Sommerfeld, a thirty-two-year-old German-born Boxer War veteran, struggled as the recently appointed head of Madero's personal security detail to keep his charge safe. Understandably, despite the grandiose welcome, Sommerfeld longed for Madero to finish the procession and pass through the gates into the security of the Presidential Palace.

The revolution had started slowly and unnoticed. Here and there a flicker of discontent as far back as 1906 lit the political horizon only to disappear again into the deceptive calm of Porfirio Diaz' iron rule. However, as the aging dictator and his elite administrators, the "Cientificos," refused to plan for an orderly transition of power, as a younger generation of middle class Mexicans remained without a political voice, and as a perfect storm of financial and natural disasters threw the country into an economic tailspin, violence broke out in the fall of 1910. To many observers the quick demise of Diaz' control over the country was a surprise. Madero emerged as the moderate voice of a broad coalition of entrepreneurs, landowners, industrialists, the military, labor, and rural masses. His goal was to establish a democratic system, which would extend political representation to all Mexicans and create an equitable legal system from which land reform and social justice would evolve. In those ecstatic days of May 1911 only a few sharp observers questioned whether this type of slow reform would satisfy the hunger for a better life for seventeen million Mexicans. As time would tell, too many diverse interest groups had been awakened by Madero's revolution and it would take another nine years and over a million deaths to settle for a new social contract, the last paragraphs of which would not be written until the 1940s. The revolution that Madero in his victory march to the center of Mexico City considered to be concluded actually had only just begun.

None in the crowd or even in the close circle of confidantes around Madero had any inkling of the role Sommerfeld would play in their revolution in the decade to come. Madero's victory over the dictator had been won mostly on the battlefield but also in a suite of New York's Astor Hotel and various other negotiation sites in Mexico and the United States. Deposing the old dictator was to be a single battle in a long, drawn out war. Felix Sommerfeld, not by chance but careful design, would play a pivotal role in almost every battle of that war. Unbeknownst to his peers, Sommerfeld had worked for the German naval intelligence service since at least 1908. German agents had maneuvered him close to the future president. From that position, Sommerfeld managed to climb to become the highest placed German intelligence asset in the Mexican government. While working for President Madero, and most likely with his tacit approval, the German army reservist acted as the liaison for the German ambassador in Mexico, Rear Admiral Paul von Hintze, and provided him with valuable intelligence on Mexico, Europe, and the United States. His clout helped focus German foreign policy towards Madero and his successor Huerta. No other foreigner wielded more influence and amassed more power in the Mexican Revolution. From head of security, Sommerfeld took on the development and leadership of Mexico's Secret Service. Under his auspices, the largest foreign secret service organization ever to operate on U.S. soil evolved into a weapon that terrorized and decimated Madero's enemies. His organization proved so effective that the U.S.

government later absorbed and integrated major parts of it into the Bureau of Investigation.

Sommerfeld could not prevent the demise of Francisco Madero, the revolutionary leader he so idolized. The president's Chief of Staff of the Army, General Victoriano Huerta, usurped the presidency in February of 1913 and caused the murder of Madero in a bloody coup d'état. After narrowly escaping arrest and the firing squad Sommerfeld reactivated his secret service organization along the U.S.-Mexican border to join the battle against the usurper president.

The resulting struggle to remove the reactionary forces from Mexico's presidential chair raged not only on the battlefield where Venustiano Carranza, Emiliano Zapata, Alvaro Obregon, and Pancho Villa led hundreds of thousands of Mexicans in the second social revolution of the century.[4] Success or defeat hinged upon the supplies and finances of these revolutionary forces. With the help of his connections in Germany and the United States, Sommerfeld became the linchpin in the revolutionary supply chain. His organization along the border smuggled arms and ammunition to the troops in amounts never before thought possible, while his contacts in the highest echelons of the American and German governments shut off credit and supplies for Huerta. As a German agent working on behalf of the Mexican revolutionaries his activities coincided with the interests of the U.S. and German governments. Surprising to most but not illogical, the U.S. government fully cooperated with Sommerfeld and turned a blind eye to the many flagrant violations of U.S. laws. While certainly not deserving sole credit for the defeat of the man who had murdered Francisco Madero, Sommerfeld's role in Huerta's demise was critical.

This book is not designed to provide a complete analysis of the causes and course of the Mexican Revolution. Rather, the following pages tell a fascinating and forgotten story which is but a sliver of the total. Understood as an all-encompassing treatise the narrow focus of this work would do a great injustice to the sacrifice and struggle of an entire people against the yoke of dictatorship and social injustice. There are many great works on the Mexican Revolution, many of which appear as secondary sources in this treatise. However, there was an element of foreign intrigue that impacted and influenced the causes, course, and conclusion of the Mexican Revolution. Foreign investments had partially created the fertile soil of social discontent and political disenfranchisement upon which Mexico's masses planted their aspirations. Once Madero unleashed the civil war, international financial organizations and corporations, with support of their governments, clearly tried their best to influence events, improve their positions, and protect their employees and other assets. Sometimes foreign governments attempted to turn back the clock, sometimes to advance it to the setting they desired. Felix A. Sommerfeld certainly was not the only secret agent working in Mexico. However, by any standard he was the most influential, the least understood, and the most effective, carefully weaving together Mexican, German, and U.S. interests for his purpose. This amazing ability caused scholars to question Sommerfeld's true loyalties and accuse him of being a double, even triple agent. Nothing could be more misleading. This German agent traded information and favors, not loyalties.

Sommerfeld created and maintained a cadre of characters who joined him in the struggle as the revolution progressed and finally became a battleground in the First World War. All of them seemed to be unaware of the German's true masters. As is the case with all successful spymasters, Sommerfeld decided who played which part in his script and showed his companions only the portion of the script he deemed necessary. Sherburne G. Hopkins, lawyer, lobbyist, and power broker, became Sommerfeld's principal contact in the United States and his boss from 1911 to 1914. Through Hopkins, Sommerfeld gained access to the inner circle of President Wilson's administration. Wilson's Army Chief of Staff, General Hugh Lenox Scott, became his friend, Secretary of War Lindley Garrison would have tea with Sommerfeld when he passed through Washington, Senators William Alden Smith and Albert Bacon Fall invited him to the Select Committee on Mexican Affairs to testify. Hopkins also opened doors for Sommerfeld in New York's financial circles. As a lawyer and lobbyist for industrialist Charles Ranlet Flint and oil tycoon Henry Clay Pierce, Hopkins enabled Sommerfeld to hold the entry keys for American businessmen trying to gain access to the Madero, Carranza, and Villa administrations. Occasionally, Sommerfeld even acted on behalf of President Wilson and the colorful group of amateur diplomats the White House confided in. This role allowed him to manage crucial information flowing to the U.S. government thus manipulating U.S. foreign policy for his ends.

Of all his fellow travelers, Frederico Stallforth stayed close to Sommerfeld the longest. Born in northern Mexico of German parents Stallforth's life before and through the revolution illustrates in many ways the experience of foreign businessmen and expatriates in Mexico. As a mine owner and banker in his Mexican hometown of Hidalgo del Parral, Chihuahua, he, his family, and his businesses suffered greatly. For most of the revolution

Chihuahua became the key battleground of an ever-shifting front. Despite Stallforth's contacts to the Mexican government (through his friend Sommerfeld) and the American government, Wall Street, as well as the German business and diplomatic community, Stallforth's family fortunes and investments melted away in the searing heat of Mexico's revolutionary battles. To a large degree through no fault of his own, the economic and social environment that precipitated the Mexican Revolution held him and his family hostage. For most foreigners in Mexico the story would end with the family business' failure. However, Stallforth's career only started where most others ended. Broke and disillusioned Stallforth joined Sommerfeld in New York before the Great War and became one of the most important German agents in the United States. As is the case with Felix Sommerfeld, Stallforth's role in the historiography is largely undefined and murky.

Sommerfeld's name appears in almost every work on the Mexican Revolution. Historians Harris and Sadler remarked, "...Sommerfeld would move through the Mexican Revolution like a wraith."[5] While Harris and Sadler are the only scholars naming Sommerfeld a "Spymaster," other historians such as Friedrich Katz and Michael Meyer accorded him an enigmatic yet undefined role.[6] Other scholars such as Jim Tuck described him as a "conman," "adventurer," "shady character," and "double agent." In order to paint a three-dimensional portrait of the man and his times, this book correlates Sommerfeld and Stallforth's statements to the U.S. Department of Justice with private and public collections. Declassified and available to historians for years have been the Justice Department and FBI files on Mexico and Germany from 1908 to 1922, the Mixed Claims Commission files, files of U.S. Naval Intelligence and the U.S. army's Military Intelligence Division, and extensive collections contained in the U.S. National Archives under the title "Captured German Documents." Also available are the personal papers of Pancho Villa's financial agent Lazaro De La Garza, of Villa's main strategist and Governor of Chihuahua, Silvestre Terrazas, of General Hugh Lenox Scott, of President Woodrow Wilson and his cabinet members, and of Soldier-of-Fortune Emil Holmdahl. Never seen before are the personal papers of Frederico Stallforth. This book resulted from the minute correlation of American, Mexican, and German archival sources. Not available are the German Secret Service and Military Intelligence files, which were destroyed by fire in 1945. Also Felix Sommerfeld's personal papers have yet to be discovered.

Despite the central role Felix Sommerfeld played in the course of the Mexican Revolution, and despite the many references to his activities in the historical record, the German agent successfully obscured his tracks. Neither his contemporaries nor scholars throughout the past hundred years have been able to piece together a clandestine career that relegates the exploits of James Bond to mere child's play. A spymaster in the Mexican Revolution and a master spy in World War I, to his contemporaries and scholars alike, Sommerfeld remained hidden in Plain Sight.

ACKNOWLEDGEMENTS

ᴧ

*I*n the summer of 1990, while a graduate student at the University of Arizona, the late Professor Michael C. Meyer handed a folder to me and said, if I found any more information on this man I would have a great topic for a thesis. I held in my hands the Military Intelligence file on Felix A. Sommerfeld. It was actually a folder that two of Dr. Meyer's colleagues and friends had given to him: Charles H. Harris III and Louis R. Sadler, two scholars, whose work I admire beyond any other historical scholarship. After Sommerfeld's MID file took a twenty-year journey through research in the United States, Germany, and Mexico, I showed up at their doorstep with a book. Charles Harris III and Louis R. Sadler reviewed my early manuscript and their comments more than any other feedback encouraged me to stay the course.

There are many other people who supported me on this endeavor, certainly my beautiful and understanding family who had to suffer through periods of absolute preoccupation with "my spies." My friend and business partner Ruediger Eder discovered the first picture of Felix Sommerfeld. He spent many an afternoon online to help me track a complete enigma. Jutta Körner, who is the most informed specialist on anything Stallforth, helped me look for several needles in haystacks and gave me lots of energy with her great encouragement to keep writing. Thank you.

I thank my great friends Marc Cugnon and Alaina Love, whose *The Passion Profiler*^{TM} instrument opened my mind to a thorough understanding of Stallforth and Sommerfeld's personalities, motivations, interaction with other players in the story, and their strengths and weaknesses resulting from their personalities. Roby Fields helped me with many an article and his wonderful friendship. My friend and renowned artist Otto Conner tirelessly listened to my theories about what really happened. In a conversation with him I realized how Sommerfeld pulled off the Columbus attack. Otto also thoroughly edited my work. All the commas you see in this book are his. Thank you! There are no words that can describe the deep gratitude, admiration, and respect I have for my great friend Dr. Günter Köhler. He has the sharpest mind I know, the strongest willpower, and the most supportive and patient attitude that a young historian can hope for. His example is one of the driving forces in my intellectual life. To my late friend Dieter and countless other close friends who sat through sheer endless dinner conversations and thesis testing, I owe a deep gratitude.

I will never be able to repay the great and dedicated educators and intellectuals who sharpened my skills as a historian and businessman throughout college, graduate school, and beyond. Without the brilliant minds of George Brubaker, University of Arizona, John Rossi, Pennsylvania State at Erie, Leonard Dinnerstein, University of Arizona, and Melvin Leffler, University of Virginia, my research would have ended in the many dead ends that I maneuvered out of in the years of writing this book. Equally as important as my training in history was the MBA program I attended at Wake Forest University in Winston-Salem, North Carolina. Special thanks to Professors Bern Beatty and Jack Meredith who worked hard on sharpening my strategic thinking and thorough understanding of the inner workings of corporations. These skills allowed me to trace the various money trails so crucial in understanding the Mexican Revolution.

There is a group of people who work tirelessly in the halls of our libraries and archives. Their knowledge of the nooks and crannies of tons of files in the National Archives, Library of Congress, Deutsches Bundesarchiv, and Archivos Municipales Chihuahua provide the keys to successful research. I can never repay the selfless kindness I have been shown over the years. I would like to especially mention Michael Hieronymus, curator of special collections at the Benson Library of Latin American Studies in the University of Texas at Austin. His kindness, incredible knowledge, and experience with all kinds of crazy historians who roam through the materials are unsurpassed. I wish for Michael and for the great collections that the Benson Library offers to historians to always receive the funds and support necessary to continue the great work. In my mind, the rare books collection at Benson is one of best-kept secrets of Latin American studies. I also want to thank David Kessler of the Bancroft Library at the University of California at Berkeley. The Bancroft Library acquired the papers of Silvestre Terrazas in the 1960s. This collection and many more, such as the Holmdahl Papers and German Diplomatic Papers, contribute to the valuable documentation of the Mexican Revolution. David not only guided me along he also helped me edit some of my Germenglish writing. Thank you! In the National Archives in Washington, D.C., I met what must be the most dedicated, motivated, and knowledgeable archivists in the world. I owe immeasurable gratitude to Richard Peuser and his staff that assisted me tirelessly when I asked them to pull rabbits out of the various record group hats.

Acknowledgements

One other acknowledgement is due because of our advanced technological state: the Internet has drastically transformed research capabilities of historians in recent years. Suddenly, digitalized FBI files, excerpts from books mentioning a certain name or fact, and catalogues of archives worldwide are at one's fingertip in the office. An especially valuable tool is the Google books program. Free of charge, at my fingertips, I found the most incredible and interesting histories, PhD theses, diaries, and data collections such as the Prussian army lists digitized by Google. Thank youuuuuu!

I have been able to find the great grandchildren of Frederico Stallforth because of You Tube. Believe it or not, but Frederico Stallforth is available on You Tube, lighting a cigarette, courtesy of Mary Prevo of Hampton Sydney University to whom I owe special gratitude. She allowed a total stranger to spend weeks on end in her upstairs' study and sort through her great grandfather's personal papers. We bounced ideas and impressions back and forth. I shared my drafts and opinions on Frederico Stallforth with her and her aunt Lawrence Webster who remembers Frederico all too well. Their insight, historical sensitivity, and above all, Mary's incredible patience focused my research and sharpened my understanding of a very complex and colorful character.

There are many others whose patience, intellect, and support have accompanied my journey. Please forgive me for not mentioning you by name. Thank you.

Cast of Characters

Ángeles, Felipe — Mexican army general, specialized on artillery, served under Porfirio Diaz, supported ascent of Francisco Madero, became commander of the Collegio Militar (Mexico's West Point) under Madero, briefly Secretary of War under Carranza before joining Villa as Chief of Artillery and most influential military advisor.

Ballin, Albert — Director of HAPAG, influential advisor of the German Kaiser, inventor of modern pleasure cruise ships.

Beltran, Teódulo R. — Hardware store owner in San Antonio, Sommerfeld's employee.

Benton, William S. — British cattle rancher in Chihuahua who confronted Pancho Villa about cattle rustling and was executed (murdered).

Bielaski, Alexander Bruce — Second director of the Bureau of Investigation (later Federal Bureau of Investigation) 1912 to 1919, succeeded Stanley Finch.

Boy-Ed, Karl — Naval captain, German Naval Attaché in the United States, 1913 to 1915, commander of the naval intelligence assets in the U.S.

Bruchhausen, Peter — German Commercial Attaché in Mexico 1908 to 1913, Sommerfeld's secret service handler before the revolution, retired in Argentina.

Bryan, William Jennings — American politician (Democrat) and lawyer, presidential candidate and nominee on several occasions, Secretary of State 1913 to 1915.

Calero, Manuel	Mexican Foreign Secretary 1911 to 1912, ambassador to the United States 1912.
Canova, Leon J.	Journalist from Florida, American diplomat in Mexico, headed the Latin American desk in the State Department 1914 to 1917, implicated in Pancho Villa's attack on Columbus, NM in 1916.
Carranza, Venustiano	State deputy of Coahuila under Porfirio Diaz, Secretary of War in first Madero cabinet 1911, Governor of Coahuila 1911 to 1913, First Chief of the Constitutionalist forces 1913 to 1915, Dictator of Mexico 1915 to 1917, President of Mexico 1917 to 1920, assassinated.
Carothers, George C.	American businessman from Torreon, Mexico, American consul 1913 to 1915, assigned by President Wilson to Pancho Villa as special envoy, worked closely with Felix Sommerfeld.
Chao, Manuel	Mexican revolutionary general, former schoolteacher, Governor of Chihuahua 1914.
Cobb, Zach Lamar	American politician (Democrat), U.S. customs collector in El Paso, Texas 1912 to 1920.
Cowdray, Lord	see Pearson, Weetman.
De Kay, John Wesley	American entrepreneur and self-made millionaire, "Sausage King" of Mexico with the famous brand "Popo," playwright, eccentric socialite.
De La Barra, Francisco L.	Mexican ambassador to the United States under Porfirio Diaz, Mexican President from May to November 1911, Foreign Secretary 1913 to 1914.

De La Garza, Lazaro — Pancho Villa's Secretary of Finance, head of procurement for the Division of the North, businessman and partner of Felix Sommerfeld, Alberto and Ernesto Madero.

Dernburg, Bernhard — German Secretary of Colonial Affairs from 1907 to 1910, leader of Germany's propaganda effort from 1914 to 1915, German Secretary of Treasury in 1919.

Diaz, Felix — Mexican army officer, nephew of the Mexican dictator Porfirio Diaz, involved in the ousting of President Madero as well as multiple conspiracies thereafter.

Diaz, Porfirio — Mexican general and dictator, Mexican President 1876 to 1880 and 1884 to 1911.

Dreben, Samuel — Polish-born Jewish immigrant, famous soldier-of-fortune, machine gunner in Central America and Mexico, decorated World War I veteran, Sommerfeld's employee.

Edwards, Thomas D. — American consul in Ciudad Juarez, Mexico during the Mexican Revolution.

Eversbusch, Richard — HAPAG employee in Tampico, Mexico, German Consul of Tampico in World War I.

Fall, Albert Bacon — Republican Senator from New Mexico 1912 to 1921, Secretary of Interior 1921 to 1922, led a group of American politicians who favored U.S. military intervention in Mexico.

Fletcher, Frank Friday — American admiral, commander of U.S. naval forces in the Gulf of Mexico in 1913 and 1914, led the American occupation of Veracruz in 1914, U.S. Chief of the Navy in World War I.

Flint, Charles Ranlett	American businessman and investor, nicknamed "father of trusts," founder of the Computing Tabulating Recording Company (the company that later became IBM), American Chicle; Also owner of Flint and Company, which supplied arms and ammunition to Mexican revolutionaries; Partner of Henry Clay Pierce in Mexican ventures.
Gadski, Johanna	Famous German soprano before and during the First World War, married to Hans Tauscher.
Goeldner, Ernst	German consul in Chihuahua after Pancho Villa expelled Otto Kueck in 1914.
Gonzalez, Abraham	Mexican revolutionary, Secretary of Interior in the Madero administration, Governor of Chihuahua 1911 to 1913, assassinated in 1913.
Gray, Newenham A.	German agent born in Great Britain, served in the Indian army before Mexican Revolution, specialist on munitions, worked with Felix Sommerfeld and as a Krupp representative in Mexico and New York, was never exposed during World War I, retired in Tucson, Arizona.
Hale, William Bayard	American journalist and writer, friend of President Woodrow Wilson, special envoy to Mexico in 1913 to investigate President Madero's murder, became member of German propaganda effort in 1915, widely discredited spent the years after World War I in Europe until his death in 1924.
Hernandez, Rafael	Francisco Madero's cousin, lawyer, Secretary of Justice in the Madero administration, organizer of Pancho Villa's supply chain.

Heynen, Carl	Businessman in Mexico, German vice consul in Tampico, HAPAG representative in Mexico, German agent in World War I in New York.
Holmdahl, Emil	Swedish-American soldier-of-fortune, mercenary in the Mexican Revolution in multiple factions, suspected of having stolen and sold Pancho Villa's head in the late 1920s.
Hopkins, Sherburne G.	American lawyer and lobbyist, clients included Henry Clay Pierce, Charles R. Flint, Gustavo and Francisco Madero, Venustiano Carranza.
Huerta, Victoriano	Mexican general under Porfirio Diaz and Francisco Madero, President of Mexico 1913 to 1914.
Ketelsen, Emil	German immigrant to Mexico and businessman, father-in-law of Otto Kueck, Ketelsen and Degetau store was major merchant house in El Paso until torched by Pancho Villa.
Knox, Philander	American politician, lawyer, Attorney General 1901 to 1904, U.S. Senator (Republican) 1904 to 1909 and 1917 to 1921, Secretary of State 1909 to 1913.
Krakauer, Adolph	German-Mexican businessman, main investor of the Krakauer, Zork and Moye merchant house in El Paso, supporter of reactionary forces in the Mexican Revolution.
Kramp, Henry	Thiel Detective Agency agent, employee of Sommerfeld.
Kueck, Otto	German consul in Chihuahua City, expelled by Villa in 1914 because of his support of Huerta, succeeded by Ernst Goeldner; Kueck was the German Secret Service handler of Sommerfeld from 1908 to 1912.

Cast of Characters

Lascurain, Pedro	Mexican Foreign Secretary 1912, President of Mexico for 56 minutes in February 1913.
Letcher, Marion	American consul in Chihuahua City, Mexico.
Lawrence, David	Influential American journalist and editor, worked for AP News in Mexico and El Paso in the beginning of the Mexican Revolution, worked for multiple newspapers as editor, founded and was editor-in-chief of U.S. News (later U.S. News and World Report).
Limantour, José Ives	Cientifico and Mexican Secretary of Finance from 1893 to 1911, credited with Mexico's economic boom under Dictator Porfirio Diaz.
Lind, John	Governor of Minnesota 1899 to 1901, friend of President Woodrow Wilson, served as Wilson's special envoy to Mexico from 1913 to 1914, was recalled under a cloud of suspicion for negotiating with Carranza on behalf of U.S. oil interests.
Llorente, Enrique	Mexican diplomat, Consul in Genoa, Italy under Porfirio Diaz, Mexican consul in El Paso 1911 to 1913, Mexican Consul in New York 1915 to 1916, Sommerfeld partner.
Madero, Alberto	Francisco Madero's uncle, businessman and supporter of his nephew as well as Pancho Villa.
Madero, Alfonso	Francisco Madero's uncle, businessman and supporter of his nephew as well as Pancho Villa.
Madero, Ernesto	Francisco Madero's uncle, Secretary of Finance in Madero administration, business partner of Alberto Madero in New York, supporter of Pancho Villa.

Madero, Francisco I.	Mexican politician and revolutionary leader, President 1911 to 1913, murdered in the Decena Tragica on General Huerta's orders.
Madero, Gustavo	Francisco Madero's brother, revolutionary leader, and the President's chief of staff, assassinated in 1913.
Madero, Raul	Brother of Francisco Madero, joined the Constitutionalist army and became General in Pancho Villa's Division of the North.
Mayo, Henry Thomas	American admiral and commander of naval assets along the Mexican gulf coast, precipitated American occupation of Veracruz in 1914 with exaggerated demands on the Mexican federal commander in Tampico.
Meloy, Andrew	American businessman with investments in and around Parral, Mexico, became business partner of Frederico Stallforth, rented office space to infamous German sabotage agent Franz Rintelen and was implicated in his activities.
Mondragon, Manuel	Mexican general, Secretary of War under Porfirio Diaz, conspirator against President Madero, supporter of various plots to defeat revolutionary forces in Mexico.
Obregon, Alvaro	Mexican revolutionary general, took up arms for Francisco Madero, lost one arm in a battle against Pancho Villa, President of Mexico 1920 to 1924.
Olin, Franklin W.	Founder and president of the Western Cartridge Company, supplier and business partner of Felix Sommerfeld, purchased Winchester Repeating Arms Company in 1931.

Olin, John — Son of Franklin W., also business partner of Felix Sommerfeld.

O'Reilly, Tex — American soldier-of-fortune, newspaper editor and author.

Pearson, Weetman — British oil tycoon, built portions of the Mexican railroads, founder of El Aguila Oil Company in Mexico, competitor of Henry Clay Pierce, ennobled to First Viscount (Lord) Cowdray in 1910.

Pierce, Henry Clay — Oil tycoon, first business partner then competitor of Standard Oil Company, purchased majority interest in Mexican railways under Diaz, president of the Waters-Pierce Oil Company.

Rasst, Leon — Jewish-Russian immigrant to Puebla, Mexico, disreputable merchant and arms dealer, moved to New York and cheated Sommerfeld in one of his deals.

Ratner, Abraham Z. — Jewish-Lithuanian immigrant to Mexico and editor of the Tampico News, with his brother José became principle arms buyer for Huerta government in New York, nemesis of Felix Sommerfeld in the business of arms procurement.

Reyes, Bernardo — Mexican general under Porfirio Diaz, opposed the Mexican dictator and was sent to Europe, rebelled against Francisco Madero twice and was killed in Mexico City in the Decena Tragica.

Roberts, Powell — Former policeman, Sommerfeld employee.

Rockefeller, John D. — Oil tycoon, American businessman and founder of Standard Oil Company.

Scott, Hugh Lenox
U.S. army general, West Point superintendent from 1906 to 1910, stationed in the western United States on various assignments, specialized on Indian and Mexican affairs, was highly respected by Pancho Villa, on friendly terms with Felix Sommerfeld 1913 to 1919, became Army Chief of Staff for President Wilson in 1914.

Smith, William Alden
Senator from Michigan (Republican) 1907 to 1919, member of the Fall Committee Hearings on Mexican Affairs, joined Senator Fall and other government officials in calls for military intervention in Mexico.

Stallforth, Alberto
Frederico Stallforth's younger brother, reserve officer in the German army, German vice consul in Parral, Mexico.

Stallforth, Frederico
German-Mexican businessman from Hidalgo del Parral, Chihuahua, friend of Sommerfeld, German agent in the U.S. in World War I.

Steever, Edgar Z.
U.S. army general, assistant professor of mathematics at West Point in the 1890s, combat veteran in the Spanish-American War, commander of 4th cavalry regiment in Fort Bliss at the outbreak of the Mexican Revolution in 1910, retired with rank of General in 1914.

Tauscher, Hans
Wealthy German businessman, representative of German arms manufacturers such as Krupp and Mauser in the United States, married to Johanna Gadski, a world-famous soprano and diva, both lived in New York.

Vasconcelos, José C.
Mexican intellectual, philosopher, politician, and educator, lawyer for Henry Clay Pierce, briefly Secretary of Education in the Gutiérrez

	administration in 1914, Secretary of Public Education in the Obregon administration.
Villa, Francisco "Pancho"	Mexican revolutionary, started as a bandit under Porfirio Diaz, became troop commander in the Madero Revolution, Governor of Chihuahua for a brief period in 1914, general of the Division of the North.
Villar, Lauro	Mexican general, chief of the army under President Madero, wounded on the first day of the Decena Tragica as he defended the Presidential Palace in Mexico City.
von Hintze, Paul	German Ambassador to Mexico 1911 to 1915, German Foreign Secretary 1918.
von Bernstorff, Count J.	German Ambassador to the United States 1908 to 1917, founder of German Democratic Party, member of the German parliament 1921 to 1928, opposed to Hitler, exiled to Switzerland.
von Bethmann Hollweg, T.	German Chancellor 1909 to 1917.
von Bülow, Prince B.	German Chancellor 1900 to 1909, succeeded by von Bethmann Hollweg.
von der Goltz, Horst	Alias for German agent Franz Wachendorf, served under Sommerfeld in 1913/14, moved to New York in 1914 as a sabotage agent, arrested in England in 1914, extradited to the U.S. in 1916, tried in the U.S. in 1917.
von Papen, Franz	German Military Attaché in the United States, 1914 to 1915, member of Prussian parliament 1921 to 1932, German Chancellor 1932.

Weber, Max	German vice consul in Ciudad Juarez, worked for Ketelson and Degetau.
Wilson, Henry Lane	American diplomat and lawyer, ambassador to Mexico 1910 to 1913.
Worcester, Leonard	Assayer in Chihuahua City, American immigrant and roommate of Felix Sommerfeld before the Mexican Revolution.
Zapata, Emiliano	Mexican revolutionary from the State of Morelos, fought for land reform against Porfirio Diaz, Francisco Madero, Victoriano Huerta, and Venustiano Carranza until he was killed in 1919.

PART I

~

THE FORMATIVE YEARS

CHAPTER 1

~

EARLY LIFE IN PRUSSIA

The 28th of May 1879 marked the birth of one of the most fascinating, complex, and enigmatic personalities of his time. Felix A. Sommerfeld's mother, Pauline Sommerfeld, nee Rosenbaum, was delighted to have delivered the fourth healthy son to her husband Isidor. His brothers Hermann, eight years older, Julius, almost exactly six years his senior, and Siegfried, a vibrant four-year-old, all curiously waited to see the baby for the first time.[7] The family lived in Borkendorf, a little village six miles or "half-an-hour away" from Schneidemühl.[8] The Sommerfeld family operated the Borkendorfer Mühle, a grain mill and distribution center.

When Sommerfeld was born, Schneidemühl was a boomtown largely triggered by the expansion of the railway system.[9] Since the opening of the central rail station in 1851, the town gained importance as a transportation hub between Russia to the East and Prussia to the West. Between 1867 and 1879, the town's population grew by more than thirty percent and, for the first time topped ten thousand.[10] The Sommerfeld family took advantage of the opportunities the rail connection offered and expanded their distribution business rapidly. Isidor Sommerfeld also owned several buildings and land along the Küddow River in the city of Schneidemühl. When it came to flour, feed, and seed, the Borkendorfer Mühle and its store on the Hasselort Street were where it came from. As a result of prudent expansion the Sommerfelds were one of the wealthiest families in town, a great success for a Jewish family in 19th century Prussia.

While history books rightfully trace the roots of the Jewish Holocaust to institutionalized anti-Semitism as a black and white issue in the militaristic Prussian state, the history of Schneidemühl from 1815 to 1900 offers some shades of gray. After the Congress of Vienna ceded Schneidemühl to Prussia in 1816, institutional racism focused mainly on the Polish minority. To solidify the reacquired territory next to the Kingdom of Poland, the Berlin government enticed German settlers to move to the East. Jewish citizens of the large Prussian cities in particular moved eastward to take advantage of the tax breaks, affordable land, and economic opportunity. While German and German-Jewish settlers received all kinds of benefits from the state, the Polish language was officially banned from offices and education. By 1896, Schneidemühl had an impressive Jewish community of over one thousand souls, about ten percent of the population.[11] The "eastern frontier" of Prussia allowed Jewish families to become members of the rising bourgeoisie of the industrialized German Reich. In the beginning of the nineteenth century most members of the Jewish community of Schneidemühl consisted of beggars, peddlers, and lower class workers, while the Polish and German protestant communities shared middle class wealth. By the end of the century, around the time of Felix's birth, the Polish upper classes were wiped out and protestant Germans and Jews shared the great wealth the industrialization accorded them.[12]

[13]

The most important stepping stone for climbing the social and economic ladder up to the German middle class was the acquisition of citizenship. Although the Sommerfelds had been residents of Schneidemühl since around 1800, they initially had no chance of advancement because the benefits of citizenship were denied to them. Under Prussian law, the Jewish community represented a colony of foreigners in the fatherland, could not own property and enjoyed none of the protections the state accorded to its citizens.[14] The French Revolution set a new trend for European powers. "Liberté, Egalité and Fraternité" included the Jews of France. Although the status of full citizenship for all Jews was briefly withdrawn, Napoleon codified this right. After the end of the Napoleonic wars, Prussia was the first to confer citizenship upon the Prussian Jews in 1812, though this by no means included full equality with other citizens. The German federal edicts of 1815 merely held out the prospect of full equality; but it was not realized at that time, and even the promises that had been given were modified. By the 1850s Jews "without the need to first acquire citizenship" could participate in their towns' self-government.[15] "Many who excelled in the social and administrative process of the kehillah put their business skills and experiences [sic] willingly at [sic] the service of municipal and other self governing [sic] bodies, many even becoming city councilors."[16]

Certainly, in Schneidemühl that was the case. Prominent Jewish families of the city, the Sommerfelds being one of them, played crucial roles in government and business. When Bismarck consolidated the German empire without Austria in 1871, Jewish emancipation found its legal conclusion in the new constitution. Jews finally became full citizens. By 1874 "Jews were allowed mixed marriages, a luxury embraced by increasingly larger number of Jews."[17] In later life Sommerfeld would often claim to friends that he was "half Jew," or "had Jewish blood."[18] He also changed his middle name from Abraham to Armand.[19] This of course hardly disguised his ancestral roots but certainly hinted at the existence of anti-Semitism in his chosen country of residence, the United States of America.

Anti-Semitism in the German Reich after 1871 was never far from the surface. As Sommerfeld would learn as an enthusiastic teen, Jews could not become officers in the German-Prussian army unless they converted to Christianity. In order to assist integration Jewish families selected non-Jewish names for their offspring. Before the 1850s, Felix' brother Hermann would probably have been Chaim. Father Isidor probably would never have chosen "Siegfried," "Julius," or "Felix" as his sons' names unless trying to please society or accord at least a slight edge in the quest of advancement to his children. Following the assessment of Peter Simonstein in his *History of the Jewish Community of Schneidemühl*, the next Sommerfeld boy's name might have been Friedrich.[20] Incidents of anti-Semitic action dot the history of the German Empire usually following boom and bust cycles of the economy. For example, the stock market crash of 1873 and the resulting depression plunged the German Empire into two decades of economic downturn. Jealous of the recently attained economic and social status of Jews, the German catholic party wanted Bismarck to retract the emancipation of the Jews in 1880.[21] When Felix volunteered for military service in China in 1900, the Jewish newspaper *Allgemeine Zeitung des Judentums* noted in its report on the young man's courage: "It would be interesting," so the paper, "to find out, how many members of the anti-Semitic agitators have volunteered to go to China."[22]

Despite the ups and downs of the economy, Sommerfeld grew up in a wealthy Jewish household with more freedoms for a Jewish citizen than ever before. Not much is known about the early years of Sommerfeld's life in Borkendorf. Throughout the school year one can imagine little Felix driving by coach or riding with his father from Borkendorf to Schneidemühl in the mornings, having lunch at the father's office or in one of his relative's homes, finishing his homework in the afternoon, and joining his father for the journey home at night. In 1889, after grade school, Sommerfeld entered the "Oberrealschule" on the Berlinerstrasse, only a few blocks from his parents' store.[23] The middle – or "real" school taught knowledge usable in „real life," such as science, finance, and one or two living languages such as English and French.

Foreign lands and culture especially fascinated Sommerfeld. The popular magazines were full of fascinating articles about the American frontier. Both the gold rush of 1849 and the Apache wars of the 1880s inspired most youths in the tightly regulated Prussian state. Schneidemühl saw a comparatively large percentage of émigrés with descendants living all over Latin America, United States, and Canada.[24] One can picture the young man lying on his bed and day dreaming about the seemingly endless space of the "Wild West," the lack of rules and freedom to do whatever one chose.[25] Sommerfeld's adventurous youth will be discussed in detail. By the time Sommerfeld graduated from high school both his two older brothers, Julius and Hermann, had already decided to seek their fortune in the United States. Hermann sailed to New York in May 1886 and became an American citizen in October 1892.[26] Not much is known about him other than that he first lived in Brooklyn and then in Long Island, New York. According to Sommerfeld, Hermann exported bicycle parts to Germany, where he assembled and sold them. Since American-made bicycles were booming in Germany around the turn of the century this could have been quite a lucrative import/export business. Hermann died sometime in 1901 on one of the overseas trips.[27] Sommerfeld's second brother Julius arrived in the U.S. in August 1889. The sixteen-year-old Julius listed his occupation as farrier when he entered the United States in 1889.[28] He might therefore not have graduated from high school and evaded the three-year draft when he decided to move to the United States. When Julius became an American citizen in April 1901, his brother Hermann witnessed the ceremony.[29] After years as a manufacturing representative, he became a factory owner in Chicago producing hairnets in the 1920s and died in Chicago in August of 1930. Also living in the United States was Sommerfeld's uncle Ed Rosenbaum, his mother's brother. He was a hat maker and lived in Pittsfield, Massachusetts. In fact, the Sommerfeld family had over forty relatives living in the U.S. by the time Felix chose to make his move.[30]

The Oberrealschule was tough and Sommerfeld probably spent a lot of his "free time" doing homework. Children that disturbed the class or showed disrespect to their teachers received corrective action through the whip. The slightest misstep, such as not getting up fast enough when the teacher entered the room, talking in class, or smeared handwriting in the homework booklet caused a written notification to the parents. Father Isidor probably had some experience with these notifications, "Verweise," from the school after having put three boys through the upper school before Felix. As one can easily surmise, life in the high school was strictly regimented. A high school graduate had not only received a thorough education but he had also learned impeccable manners, proper formal dance, and military discipline in all aspects of life. Even the folded size and appearance of Sommerfeld's starched school uniform shirts was regimented. They had better be all within a quarter inch stacked neatly on top of each other! In the time between classes, students learned how to march in Prussian "Stechschritt" (Goose-step), sing marching songs, and stand at perfect attention while teachers examined the uniform for missing buttons, tears, dirt or missing crease.[31] Physical fitness also played a big role in Prussian life. Felix excelled in horseback riding later on but no record of him playing other sports exists. School classes frequently hiked through the countryside on the specially designated "Wandertag," along the Küddow River or by the Sommerfelds' ancestral home, the village of Borkendorf, just eight kilometers to the north. When the snow got too high to play outside or the temperatures stayed at -20C throughout the day, the youths congregated in the "Turnhalle" and practiced gymnastics, such as parallel bars, horizontal bar, rope climbing, and weight lifting. The Spartan discipline of pre-1900 Prussia left an unmistakable imprint on the development of Sommerfeld's personality. Obedience to authority, precision, punctuality, and toughness all became traits that characterized the grown man. His well-honed manners allowed him to dine with presidents, prominent politicians, and social elites alike.

The winter months in Schneidemühl could be brutal, since the continental climate of the Russian flats influenced that part of Germany. Frequent blizzards and ice cold wind created a deep freeze from October well into March. In the snowy winter months the whole town literally turned black. The common way to prevent slippery surfaces was to pour coal dust and ashes on the roads. In the spring the layers of ashes and dust, the melting snow and ice turned the mostly unpaved roads into a morass of slush throughout the town. In addition, the river would overflow in regular intervals and flood the streets right up to Hasselort Street where the Sommerfelds had their business. In 1892, after frequent Cholera epidemics throughout the century, the city fathers finally decided to build a central drinking water system. While drilling a large well, the workmen disturbed an underground river and caused large flooding in the lower part of town. Forty-two properties were under water and it took until the end of the century to finally plug the well.[32] It is not known whether any of the Sommerfelds' properties were affected, but since they were so close to the low areas of the river, it is very likely.

Sommerfeld graduated from Oberrealschule in May 1895 after finishing tenth grade. His graduation records are not available anymore, most likely because of the thorough cleansing of anything Jewish Schneidemühl received in 1942.[33] He could now have joined the ever-increasing cadre of Prussian government bureaucrats, a solid career leading to accepted middle class status and secure retirement. Instead, Sommerfeld planned to study mining engineering in Berlin. However, before the young Prussian high school graduate could do anything, he was drafted. Prussian military draft law allowed youngsters with a tenth grade degree, such as the one Sommerfeld achieved, to serve only one year instead of the mandatory three.[34] After the one-year service the cadet would be discharged as a corporal of the reserve. A member of the reserve had the opportunity to voluntarily join annual exercises, which led to officer ranks over time. However, since Sommerfeld was Jewish, he could only advance to Sergeant Major which, according to his testimony, he never did.[35] If Sommerfeld had converted to Christianity, which is not documented but possible, he could have become an officer. When American authorities took his statement in June 1918, Sommerfeld claimed to have graduated in 1898 and immediately have joined the military as a volunteer.[36] He had a reason to lie about this time in his life...

CHAPTER 2

~

"BOYISH MISTAKES"

7oo young to join the military after his graduation in 1895, Felix worked at his father's business and saved up his money. He had plans. For years he had dreamt of America. On April 30th 1896, the moment came.[37] Almost seventeen years old, he boarded the Hamburg America Line steamer "Normannia" from Hamburg non-stop to New York, arriving on May 9th at Ellis Island.[38] Since a ticket was more than Felix could have accumulated working for his father, he must have had some help from his family. However, the help did not necessarily come from his parents who had wanted him to study in Germany.[39] Apparently, the sixteen-year-old went without a companion.[40] As occupation or calling he entered "none."[41] The ticket was for "Zwischendeck" or steerage cabin, the cheapest ticket available. Sommerfeld certainly had to give up some of the luxuries he grew up with in Borkendorf to make his journey to the U.S.

"In the early days of emigration the ships [that] used to convey the emigrants were originally built for carrying cargo. In reality the passengers were placed in the cargo hold. Temporary partitions were usually erected and used for the steerage accommodation. To get down to the between-deck the passengers often had to use ladders, and the passageway down between the hatches could be both narrow and steep... It was necessary that the furnishings could be easily removed, and not cost more than absolutely necessary. As soon as the ships had set the passengers on land, the furnishings were discarded and the ship prepared for return cargo to Europe."[42]

Felix stayed with his brother Hermann in New York and worked a "newsstand on the corner of 21st Street and Broadway - he made me work there from five in the morning till late at night and ill treated [sic] me..."[43] After a few months of the "ill treatment" Sommerfeld moved to his brother Julius' apartment who at that time also lived in New York. Sommerfeld went back to Germany sometime in August 1896.[44]

What he did in the next eighteen months is not entirely clear. In his statement to the Bureau of Investigation in 1918, Sommerfeld purposely jumbled dates to hide his escapades. However, it seems likely that he told the truth about having started to study in Berlin in the fall semester of 1896. He told investigators that he studied mineralogy at the "University of Berlin" in Charlottenburg, now one of the districts of Berlin. The only institution of higher learning in Charlottenburg was the Polytechnic Institute founded in 1879, today known as the Technische Hochschule, Berlin. Unfortunately, the Technical University of Berlin does not have any record of him being a student there. This missing documentation does not necessarily exclude the possibility of his being a student since most of their records burned in 1945 as a result of Allied bombings. His degree from the Oberrealschule would not have qualified him to study at the Humboldt University, the other big university in Berlin. The Humboldt University also did not offer mining engineering or metallurgy degrees. The most likely institute of higher learning for mining and metallurgy that accepted his high school degree was the Bergakademie, Berlin, which became part of the Technische Hochschule in 1916. The academy had approximately 7,500 students in 1900. A degree in mineralogy, which Sommerfeld claimed to have earned, would have been a valuable prerequisite for competing in the mining industry for a good job. Other mining academies existed in Freiburg, Dresden, and Clausthal-Zellerfeld, where his famous namesake and physicist Arnold Sommerfeld occupied the mathematics chair.

For unknown reasons he dropped out in the middle of the fourth semester in 1900. His military intelligence file and several references to his person in newspapers alleged that he left Germany "as a result of some sort of scandal..."[45] It is likely that something happened which caused Sommerfeld to drop out of school, but neither he in his various statements, nor the officials alleging a scandal ever described it. Whatever the scandal might have been, it did not rise to enough importance to make it into the press either. An acquaintance of Sommerfeld's started the rumor in 1917, possibly to discredit the German. "There was a story about Summerfield [sic] – and I believe it was framed in Germany – to the effect that Summerfield [sic], who was formerly a German army officer, had to leave the country (Germany) after the odour [sic] of a certain scandal of a political nature permeated official circles."[46] What is clear, is that Felix' brother Hermann visited his parents around Christmas 1897. He had just started his new business of selling American-made bicycles in

Germany. He left for New York in January 1898 and Felix likely was to follow him and, with his brother's help, go to college in the United States.[47]

On February 23rd 1898, Sommerfeld arrived in New York from Rotterdam on the steamship "Amsterdam." His father fronted the $30 fare, around $700 in today's value.[48] Also arriving around the same time from Liverpool was a young Jewish boy from Ukraine named Samuel Dreben, almost exactly one year his senior.[49] Just like Felix, Sam had been lured by the American Dream. Dreben went to visit his relatives in Philadelphia and most likely did not get to know the young German from Posen at that time. Dreben's colorful career as a soldier-of-fortune and World War I war hero made the Ukrainian immigrant, nicknamed "the Fighting Jew," into a legend and earned him a grave at Arlington National Cemetery. Sommerfeld and Dreben's lives would parallel and intersect on many occasions over the next twenty-seven years.

Felix's destination was his brother Hermann's residence on 27th Street in Brooklyn, New York. Hans Zimmermann, who would reenter Sommerfeld's life in a very embarrassing way in 1915, was Hermann's landlord and managed the apartments. Sommerfeld claimed in the immigration documents that he was "born in the USA," maybe to circumvent immigration issues. He also listed his occupation as "Electrician."[50]

Two months after his arrival, on April 25th, the Spanish-American war broke out. Within a week of the declaration of war, rather than pursuing his family's plans to get an education, Sommerfeld joined the 12th Infantry Regiment in New York as a private in Company K on May 2nd 1898. As he signed up, without any apparent reason other than maybe higher pay, he lied about his age, claiming to the recruiter that he was twenty-two rather than eighteen years old.[51] Another enthusiastic youngster from Iowa lied about his age in order to qualify and enlisted in 1898. Just like Sommerfeld, fifteen-year-old Emil Holmdahl followed the call of President McKinley for 125,000 volunteers. Both signed up for two years' service.[52] Holmdahl later became a famous soldier-of-fortune in the Mexican Revolution and one of Sommerfeld's daring rebel rousers on the U.S.-Mexican border. While Holmdahl shipped to the Philippines, Sommerfeld received basic training in Lexington, Kentucky. In the middle of September 1898, the German adventurer changed his mind and took leave. Rather than returning to his unit, the now nineteen year-old German deserted and returned to his bother Hermann in New York.[53] On October 1st 1898, the army listed him AWOL.[54] He later claimed to have received a letter from his mother notifying him that father Isidor had taken ill.[55] Sam Dreben sat

10

out the Spanish-American War in Philadelphia, Pennsylvania as a tailor in his relatives' business.

Lacking the funds to pay for his fare back to Germany, Sommerfeld stole $275 from his brother's landlord, paid for the steamer to Antwerp and came home.[56] Why he stole that much is unknown. The ticket to Germany cost less than $50. He possibly had to bribe someone to issue a passport to him since he was listed as a deserter. Felix' relationship with his oldest brother was injured after the 1898 trip. It is likely that Hermann had a hard time forgiving his brother for "borrowing" $275 from his landlord, a good portion of the man's annual income. Hermann died on the August 13th 1901 on a ship sailing to New York of unknown causes.[57] Sommerfeld did not return to America until 1902 thus never having the chance to reconcile with his older brother.

The two adventures of Felix Sommerfeld in America in 1896 and 1898 illustrate a teenager full of energy, quite reckless, with little respect for authority, and driven to make his mark. He also proved to be a product of his time, paralleling the experiences of many young men who ended up rejecting their parents' world and trying their luck in a country of promise and freedom. While Sommerfeld only joined the U.S. army once, two of the most decorated and most famous swashbucklers of the Mexican Revolution and World War I, Sam Dreben and Emil Holmdahl, began their careers in parallel. These two joined up, then went on their own for a while, joined up again and ended up fighting for the United States in World War I. While Holmdahl and Dreben came from less affluent backgrounds, the parents of all three probably were not all too happy with the youths' escapades. Sommerfeld claimed that he even went to America in 1896 without the permission of his father who wanted to his son go to school and start a respectable career. Especially in pre-1900 Prussia such behavior certainly must have affected the relationship with his father. According to Sommerfeld, Isidor's illness, the reason for his return to Germany, resulted from losing a significant amount of money in a bank crash in 1898.[58] How serious the medical condition was is unknown but Isidor, according to Sommerfeld, ended up in a "sanitarium."[59] Neither one of his older brothers journeyed home at that time. This could indicate that the real reason for Sommerfeld's desertion had more to do with the need for someone to help in the family business. Isidor Sommerfeld already lost his two older sons to emigration. After Sommerfeld's return in 1898, he and his older brother Siegfried managed his father's business until 1900 when Siegfried took over for good.[60] According to Sommerfeld, father Isidor developed a kidney condition, which eventually led to his death in 1907. The depth to which Isidor involved himself in the family business after 1898 is unknown.

The lies to immigration officials about his immigration status, the lie about his age when he joined the army, the desertion, and finally the theft of a substantial amount of money remained "family skeletons" for almost two decades.[61] In the fall of 1915, by a fluke, it all came out. The swindled apartment manager saw Sommerfeld's name in a newspaper report in connection with his deposition to the Grand Jury, which had indicted Franz Rintelen, the notorious German sabotage agent. Hans Zimmermann had waited a full eighteen years to get his revenge. Based on his tip, the police arrested Sommerfeld in the Hotel Astor on the warrant issued in 1898 and hauled him off to jail. The newspapers in New York covered the arrest in embarrassing detail since the German was quite a well-known figure in town in 1915.[62] After posting bail, it took a crack lawyer a few months to have the charge dismissed for lack of evidence.[63]

In the eyes of Sommerfeld the old warrant was a Bureau of Investigation plot. Sommerfeld's Uncle Ed Rosenbaum commented on the episode and told federal agents in 1916: "Felix Sommerfeld was arrested in New York City on an old charge for the purpose of detaining him while they went through his room and searched for his private papers...they were not smart enough for Felix."[64] Sensing what was most likely the real reason for Sommerfeld's arrest, the German Naval Attaché Boy-Ed even tried to get the German embassy to exert pressure on Zimmermann. "Since the possibility exists that ...Zimmermann made his accusations against Sommerfeld with best intentions (because he also erroneously thought that Sommerfeld was an enemy of the German cause), I would like to inquire with the Imperial General Consul whether this private Zimmermann could not be approached tentatively and inconspicuously to suppress this disruptive and for the German reputation unfavorable affair."[65]

The German Consul, who had a less than cordial relationship with the Naval Attaché responded, "[S]ince your Excellency declare that German interests are touched by this case, I assume that over there [the Naval Department] more is known about Sommerfeld... I therefore subserviently suggest informing me in detail about the facts of the case."[66] Of course, the Naval Attaché had no intention to brief the Consul or, for that matter, anyone in the Foreign Department on Sommerfeld's status as a German spy. Whether he informed the Consul or not, Sommerfeld had been "outed" in New York's media. To quiet things down and limit the damage, Sommerfeld paid

Zimmermann off first with $1,000, then $500 then another $500 ($42,000 in today's value). Not only did these "gifts" cost him seven times of what he stole, Zimmermann now proceeded to milk Sommerfeld for what he was worth. [67] After all, by this time Sommerfeld was undeniably rich, lived in a suite in the Hotel Astor, and as a German in the midst of spy panic, he was a ripe target for blackmail. There is no record of how much Zimmermann knew about Sommerfeld's work for the German government. Sommerfeld had no choice but to keep Zimmermann quiet. He helped his former landlord move to a comfortable house on Long Island, gave him furniture, and a stipend of $75 ($1,575 in today's value) per month. [68] When he tried to stop payment in 1917, Zimmermann and at least one co-conspirator sent blackmail letters to Sommerfeld threatening with reopening the case of theft and getting it into the papers. [69] While it already was a huge embarrassment for Sommerfeld to be in the papers in 1915, it obviously was the last thing he needed after America's declaration of war against Germany in 1917 to face another arrest or any publicity on the matter.

Reflecting on this time, Sommerfeld himself excused his behavior as "boyish mistakes." [70] However, he agreed with his interrogator in 1918 that the trip in 1898 was a turning point in his life. [71] The episode propelled him into adulthood, awakened a sense of purpose and instilled a need for responsibility. He became a man seemingly mature, who could stand on his own - 5' 8" tall, broad shoulders, barrel chested, strong muscles, dark brown hair with some curls, "short neck, [and] heavy eyebrows." [72] Despite his decision to return to Germany and work in his father's business, Sommerfeld's daring and often reckless nature never faded. Throughout his career, as a soldier, prospector, revolutionary, businessman and spy, he was a fearless dare devil, but also someone who, according to a German saying, 'one could steal horses with.' Sommerfeld did not respect limitations, either internal or external. "In the golden lexicon of youth," he wrote in Frederico Stallforth's guest book in 1911, "there is no such a word as 'fail'." [73] The end justified the means, which led him as a teenager to "borrow" money for his trip back to Germany. In later life he could vacillate between bullying and polite diplomacy. [74] His daring nature became especially clear in World War I, when the American authorities monitored his every move for three years and came up with nothing to indict him with. He had told his brother Julius, "Let them come, I don't keep my papers in my apartment." [75] When interrogated for three days by the BI he did not crack, unlike many of his co-conspirators under the same circumstances. "Interviewed subject this day for four hours, in an attempt to have him reveal his real activities. So far he has craftily concealed all that he has done," was the frustrated notation in his file. [76] Clearly, the "boyish mistakes" had taught Sommerfeld valuable lessons. He went back to Germany to start a new life, face the military draft, and acquire a profession. However, as he admitted to his interrogators, "Germany is small and opportunities are not prevalent."[77] His childhood dream to one day live in America and try his luck at the frontier never faded but became even stronger.

Sommerfeld never spoke about the time after he returned from his trip and before he went back to the United States. He probably did go back to the engineering school in Berlin for one more year. According to his statement to the American authorities, he did not graduate with a degree. In April 1900, after the end of the spring semester, Sommerfeld joined the Prussian army as a draftee. Not surprisingly, his one-year army service did not pass as one would expect.

CHAPTER 3

〜

SERVICE IN CHINA

*I*n June 1900, Chinese insurgents beleaguered the embassy quarter in Beijing prompting intervention of foreign powers under the leadership of Germany. The Boxer Revolution became the young Germany's chance to prove to the great powers of the world that she was a force to be reckoned with. By the end of the 19th century the colonial powers had basically carved up the world. Germany, which until the end of Bismarck's tenure always had looked to the East for acquiring land and resources, entered the colonial game late. "Above all, the Kaiser wanted 'a place in the sun' for the German people. The problem was the only places left were in the shade."[78] Wilhelm II and his advisors invested huge sums into the establishment of a navy that could compete with that of England. There was really not much territory available: Latin America, besides the fact that its countries had gained independence in the 1820s, was off-limits as a result of the Monroe Doctrine. The United States had shown with the swift defeat of Spain in 1898 that her military, especially navy and marines, had grown into a force to be reckoned with. The richest lands in Africa were firmly under the control of the British and the French empires. The Arabian Peninsula as well did not offer any opportunities for the German Empire. As a result, at a great expense, Germany acquired economically and strategically unimportant colonies in Africa, in the Witu area on Kenya's coast and Uganda, which became German East Africa. Germany also acquired what is today known as Tanzania, Namibia, Cameroon, and Togo. In the Pacific basin, the Empire acquired some islands, such as the Solomons, Samoa, parts of New Guinea, Micronesia and Palau, as well as a base in Antarctica. These islands mainly served as refueling stations for the navy. Otherwise the colonies produced a net loss for the Empire, prompting heated debates in parliament and turning the chair of the Colonial Minister into an ejection seat. However, in line with Prussian discipline, the Kaiser and his cabinet wanted to show the world how much more modern and efficient

16

German colonies would be run. The Empire built railroads, schools, and hospitals, set up economic development programs, while boasting of her "great successes" to the other world powers.

China occupied a special position in the colonial constellation, because here unlike anywhere else in the world, the colonial powers competed economically, not militarily. The interested parties were Japan, England, France, Germany, Austria-Hungary, Italy, Russia, and the United States. Foreign policies for China aimed at the creation of open markets, free and unencumbered trade, and, as a consequence, international cooperation in a delicate balance of power framework. Germany's influence was centered on the northern coast where in 1898 the Chinese government had issued a ninety-nine-year lease for the peninsula of Tsingtao that Germany had occupied by military force a few years earlier. To this day a well-known Chinese beer by that name is brewed in the former German colony. Tsingtao was an important harbor, crucial for successful trade with China. Germany also shared a concession for the harbor and railroad station of Tianjin or Tientsin on the PeiHo River and the harbor of Taku at the mouth of the PeiHo. Tientsin had gained strategic importance in the previous decades because of the railroad connection to Peking, now known as Beijing, the Chinese capital.

In 1898, Britain formalized her seizure of Hong Kong in the Opium Wars with a ninety-nine-year lease as its main naval station and export harbor. Not far to the south, Portugal leased the harbor of Macao. The Americans had been fighting in the Philippines against the nationalists there after Spain ceded the islands to the United States for twenty million dollars in 1898. China represented a crucial market for the newly acquired U.S. colony. In the same year that American forces defeated Spain and acquired the Philippines, the French leased the southern Chinese harbor of Kwang-Chou-Wan as a counterweight to British influence in Hong Kong. The Chinese concession to France did not have much economic use but represented a significant strategic value. The main French colonies were located in Indochina to the south from where this Chinese harbor also was administered. In addition, France maintained an important territory, the French district in the city of Shanghai. Britain and the United States also each owned a part of the most important harbor in China and its largest city. Shanghai's tremendous economic value for the colonial powers consistently gained in importance because it was located on the mouth of the Yangtze River and centered between Beijing and Hong Kong. The Russian Empire kept a lease for the year-round ice-free harbor of Port Arthur. As the Boxer rebellion weakened the Chinese government, the

Czar extended Russian influence throughout Outer Mongolia, Manchuria, and what is today North Korea. Japan, with its burning ambition to become a super power in the Far East occupied Formosa (Taiwan), the harbors of Ningpo and Amoy, as well as South Korea.[79]

The arrangements between the colonial powers and the Chinese government, however, lacked an important consideration: The Chinese population. As foreign influence in China grew significantly in the last years of the 19th century, economic domination was supplemented with cultural imperialism. Scores of American protestant, French catholic, German protestant and catholic, and British Anglican missionaries roamed remote rural areas in an attempt to convert the general population to Christianity. Other powers, such as Japan, also tried to increase their power base using cultural infiltration of Chinese society. The backlash turned out to be formidable. A secret order called I-ho ch'üan ("Righteous and Harmonious Fists"), translated by the Western press into the „Boxers," set out to reverse the march of Christianity and Imperialism in an armed uprising in 1898.[80] The members of the Boxer organizations were initially peasants from the northern regions of China.[81]

Over the next two years the revolt gained strength as the Boxers fought against anything foreign in China. The secret order was a culturally traditionalist, nationalist, anti-foreign, anti-government, and populist insurgency. "It was in essence a loose coalition, spreading organically from village to village using the traditional grapevines of rural life...these new Boxers seemed to offer a lifeline to the poor and destitute of the countryside."[82] The uprising gained significant strength in the Shandong province in the part of China where the concession of Tsingtao and Germany's main sphere of influence were located. Boxer fighters succeeded in interrupting railroad service, which in turn disturbed communications with outlying provinces where foreign missionaries operated. The violence spread quickly across the whole country. Isolated communities of missionaries and its Chinese converts took the brunt of Boxer violence with scores of missionaries attacked, displaced, and on some occasion killed.

The Manchu rulers of China, weakened by foreign influence, initially vacillated on how to deal with the popular uprising. On the surface, the Boxer ideology did not challenge the Chinese government. However, below the surface any popular movement such as this had the potential undo the weak central government. When violence first broke out in 1898, Chinese military units in cooperation with mostly British, American, and German forces fought the insurgency sporadically. However, the Chinese government soon realized that it could not curb the masses by force. Switching alliances, the Chinese Empress Dowager Tzu Hsi and a new group of influential courtiers tacitly supported the rebels. The goal was to co-opt the mass uprising for their purposes. The Empress hoped to use the rebellion as a means to loosen the stranglehold of foreign powers that undoubtedly had their eyes on the ancient empire.

"...the united opinion of Europe was that China would soon disappear as a sovereign entity, dismembered and divided."[83] In the spring of 1900, the country exploded in part as a result of a famine that affected Northern China. Boxer propaganda blamed the "two years of bad weather and bad crops... [which] reduced thousands to a give-and-take existence..." on the foreigners.[84] Like an avalanche the massive uprising swept through the country towards the capital. "There was the riot at Shashih, directed against the British and Japanese, in which 'nothing was spared': the Custom House, Haikwan Bank, Commissioner of Custom's house [sic], China Merchants' property, Jardine, Metheson and Co.'s property (one of the great English trading companies in China), and the Japanese Consulate – all were destroyed. There were the riot in Chihili, the anti-foreign and anti-Christian disturbances in central Szechwan, the Kwangsi insurrection, the anti-missionary riot at Foochow, the trouble in Yunnanfu [sic], the terrible outbreaks in Paotingfu [sic], the Kienning riots, the murder of the British missionary Fleming, of Robinson and of Norman."[85]

In early June 1900, twenty-five thousand rebels attempted to gain access to the foreign compound in Beijing where foreign business headquarters and the embassies were located. The Chinese fighters, whose Kung Fu martial arts training gave them the illusion of invulnerability, dressed in colorful clothes, painted their faces with war colors, and left no doubt in any foreigner's mind, what the result would be if he fell into the hands of the rebels. The use of terrorism made its impact on the beleaguered soldiers, diplomats, and their families. The twenty-one officers and 429 foreign soldiers and male diplomats,[86] as well as 2,100 "rice Christians"[87] barricaded themselves between the wall to the Forbidden City and the legations. Despite significant losses and the scare tactics of the Boxers, the defenders of the foreign compound repelled the repeated attacks.

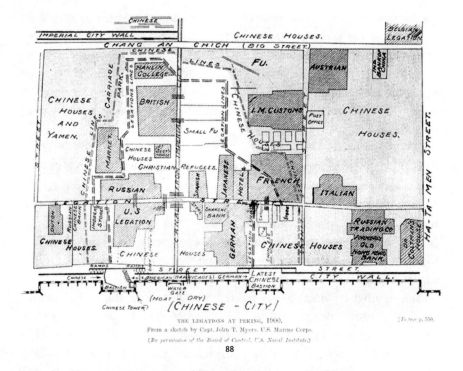

THE LEGATIONS AT PEKING, 1900.
From a sketch by Capt. John T. Myers, U.S. Marine Corps.
(By permission of the Board of Control, U.S. Naval Institute.)

88

The conflict culminated on June 20th 1900, when the German ambassador to China, Clemens Freiherr von Ketteler was murdered on his way to a meeting with the Chinese Empress.[89] The exact circumstances of the killing are unclear. His alleged killer, En Hai, confessed and was beheaded six months later, on December 31st 1900. The Empress had issued a demand for the foreign diplomats to leave Beijing on June 16th, four days before the murder. The diplomatic corps refused to leave and, as a result, the Chinese Empress issued a death warrant for all foreigners that same day. Von Ketteler most certainly suffered from the same illusion of invulnerability as the boxers when he marched (or rather was carried in a litter) through the gate across a bridge into the unprotected part of the capital. The German ambassador stood out among the diplomatic corps as a man of great personal courage. According to eyewitnesses on June 13th, he had attacked two Boxers, "armed and dressed, sash, cap, and boots" with his walking stick.[90] "Where," asked the eye witness of this daring attack, "but in China could a Foreign Minister assault such a one and drag him by the pig tail into his own legation and there lock him up to await punishment? It is said that the German Minister refused to give the man

20

up to the Yamên [Foreign Department of the Chinese government] authorities, insisting that he should be executed on the bridge on the following day."[91]

His courage proved his downfall when the Chinese made an example of the brazen Prussian diplomat. The news of his demise caused great excitement in Germany.

"The horrific news from Beijing has stirred the hearts of the entire nation to its innermost depths. At first they did not believe the unbelievable news, but it gradually became a certainty: the German ambassador murdered, thousands of Europeans, women and children slaughtered by fanatical hordes of yellow barbarians! - And at once the anger flamed mightily, and the cry for vengeance was loud. Our Emperor himself framed this wish into vivid words. It is now incumbent to our ... youth to enter the hard battle for Germany's honor. For the first time one has to defend with arms Germany's honor, even far from home when the borders of the motherland are not threatened by the enemy."[92]

Germany immediately mobilized and organized an international coalition of forces to which the Empire contributed the largest army of 19,200 volunteers. This was just the kind of adventure young Felix Sommerfeld could subscribe to. According to the local section of Berlin's renowned Jewish newspaper on August 20th 1900, the *Allgemeine Zeitung des Judentums* reported: "Felix Sommerfeld, son of the mill owner Isidor Sommerfeld, from Borkendorf which is half-an-hour from here, and who was serving his military [draft] duty in the local infantry regiment in Bromberg, has volunteered to go to China and is already on the way there. Sommerfeld is a private ..."[93] Sommerfeld transferred from his Infantry Regiment in Bromberg, the county his mother Pauline came from, to the East Asian Cavalry Regiment bound for China. The newspaper *Die Woche* described the regiment: "The East Asian Cavalry Regiment assembled in Potsdam. ... Now they have already received the tropical uniforms. Their weapons are lance, carbine, and sword..."[94] It is certain, that he served first as a private, then as a corporal, not officer, as the arresting American authorities, many newspapers and perhaps he himself later claimed.[95]

The German propaganda machine churned in warp speed. Years of frustration with the colonial program, the acquisition of third rate territories, the financial cost, the ridicule from the successful colonial powers all culminated in the battle cry for action. This time, Germany would play a role. She would defend the civilized world against a 'barbarian scourge!' It was the chance the ambitious German emperor had been waiting for. Young Prussian soldiers everywhere signed up to "defend Germany's honor." The Berlin paper *Die Woche* reported on the departure of German forces in the end of July 1900: "The eyes of the whole nation were directed last week at Wilhelmshaven. Quietly and deliberately the mobilization of the Marine Corps was completed. The departure of the battle ready battalion turned out to be a moment of world historical significance. For the first time German soldiers crossed the seas to carry war across the ocean, and to atone for the insult to the German name."[96] The emperor and his wife bid farewell to the troops in Bremerhaven on July 27th 1900. Wilhelm's "Hunnenrede" entered history as one of the most notorious examples of Prussian racism, militarism, and brutality.

"...Prove the tradition of Prussian efficiency, show yourselves as Christians in the joyful endurance of suffering, may honor and glory follow your flags and weapons, give the world an example of manliness and discipline ...You shall fight against a well-armed force, but you also shall avenge not only the death of the ambassador, but also of the many Germans and Europeans. When you confront the enemy you will subdue him, no quarter will be given, no prisoners will be taken. Who falls into your hands, will die by your hands. Just as a thousand years ago the Huns under their King Attila made a name for themselves, one that still today makes them mighty in history, may the name of Germany be confirmed in such a way in China that never again a Chinese would even dare to look askance at a German."[97]

Just as was the case with most German colonial activities, Germany arrived late on the stage. The German troops arrived in China several weeks after Beijing had been freed and order had been restored. Under the command of British Vice Admiral Sir Edward Seymour, the international forces already in China had first attempted to make their way towards Beijing. "The relief column consisted of 900 British, 500 French, 200 Germans, 200 Russians, 120 Americans, 100 Italians, 25 Austrians, and 200 Japanese. Later a party of 65 Frenchmen overtook them by rail."[98] However, when Allied ships bombarded the forts at the mouth of the PeiHo River at Taku, fierce Chinese resistance cut the small Allied force off. "Moving by rail to Tianjin [Tientsin], they were forced to continue on foot as the Boxers had severed the line to Beijing. Seymour's column advanced as far Tong-Tcheou, 12 miles from Beijing, before being forced to retreat due to stiff Boxer resistance. They arrived back at Tianjin on June 26, having suffered 350 casualties."[99] Before a renewed rescue attempt could be undertaken, the now 18,800 Allied forces had to free the harbor of Tientsin, which they achieved in mid-July.[100] Eight powers, England, France, Germany, Russia, Italy, Japan, Austria-Hungary, and the United States were now engaged in an all-out war against not only Chinese rebels but also the Chinese government.

The attacks on Taku without a formal declaration of war prompted the Chinese demand for all foreigners to leave the city on June 16th. The diplomats in the legation quarter of Beijing refused, which triggered the events leading to von Ketteler's death. While Admiral Seymour's relief column and his forces slowly made their way inland, the compound remained under constant attack. The siege was unnerving especially for the female missionaries and wives of diplomats:

"We have had our usual Sabbath service today. This afternoon a very precious experience meeting, telling one another the lessons the Lord had been teaching us during these weeks of storm and stress, and the things for which we thank the Lord. The Chinese had had their meetings as usual, and Miss Evans had a meeting with one group of women. I wanted to meet another group, but it has been so fearfully hot that I thought I would wait until after tea. Later a fierce attack came just after tea, and the bullets were flying so everywhere that I delayed my meeting till the firing stopped. Then it was so far to the group I wanted to reach, and so many sick ones to see by the way, that I was finally obliged to give up my meeting as the darkness was already gathering. Just as I was starting back another terrible attack began and I was rather afraid to come back; but I could not know how long it would last, and dared not wait lest it be dark, so I rushed, and asked the Lord as I went to cover me with his hand, and he did. As soon as I got within the walls of the English Legation (our people are scattered about among all the Legations), I went into the first house I came to, in which were Miss Douw and the ladies of her mission, and waited there until there was a lull in the firing. There have been five distinct attacks today, in one of which the French commander was killed. —Miss Andrews."[101]

Finally, on August 14th, an international force under British Lieutenant General Alfred Gaselee - twenty thousand troops strong - entered Beijing and freed the foreign compound after a fifty-five day siege. The Allied troops found utter destruction bearing witness to the nightmarish experiences and desperate courage of the foreign defenders. According to the American ambassador's report to Secretary of State Hay, "...the Belgian, Austrian, Italian, Dutch, and most of the French Legations had been burned; also the Post Office, three foreign banks, the houses and offices of all the customs officials, and all the missionary compounds except Peitang (Catholic Cathedral). The Legation forces had lost 65 killed, 135 wounded, and 7 deaths by disease."[102]

One of the American infantrymen who on that fateful August day broke through the main gate under a hail of bullets and fought his way to the American compound was Sam Dreben. "The Americans poured through the opening. Inside Peking the fanatical fighting continued. Dreben received the worst scare of his short military career, one that came close to ending right there in China...Sam was slowly advancing along one of the city's narrow streets when a giant lunged at him from behind a building, swinging a mighty two-handed sword around his head and charging like a buzzsaw [sic]. For all his roundness, Sam was agile and he leaped back just as the blade sank into a wall...In the time it took the Boxer to force the sword out of the wood..., Sam had his pistol out and with a single shot sent the enemy off to his ritualistic 'fiery ride.'"[103]

Meanwhile, under the leadership of Feldmarschall Graf von Waldersee, an international force of ninety thousand made its way to China. Among them, the young German recruit Felix Sommerfeld. Sommerfeld testified in 1918 that he served in the East Asiatic Cavalry.[104] The first two squadrons of the Ostasiatisches Reiterregiment under the command of Lieutenant Colonel von Arnstedt, shipped out on the "Dresden" on the 27th of July 1900, bid farewell by the Kaiser with his famous "Hunnenrede."[105] It is unknown, what Sommerfeld thought of the speech when he listened to it as a member of the assembled troops. However, his prompt voluntary service suggests that at the very least he was initially swept up by the pounding German propaganda.

The departure of this wave of ships must have been an exciting scene for anyone participating. On that day in July 1900 the "Rhein," "Halle," "Dresden," "Aachen," "Strasburg," "H.H. Meier," "Batavia," "Phoenicia," "Adria," and "Sardinia" left with twenty generals, nine thousand troops, horses, artillery, trucks, field hospitals and supplies. At the same time, another eight troop transporters had swarms of soldiers, horses, trucks and supplies all over them as they prepared for departure on July 30th and August 2nd.[106] The German "Armada" sailed through the strait of Gibraltar along the coasts of Morocco, Algeria, and Tunisia. After eleven days at sea, the ships refueled at Port Said, Egypt. "Evening 5 o' clock arrival at the port of Port-Seid [sic].

Egyptians and Negroes swam up to our boat and let us understand that we should throw down money for them, which we did, and amused ourselves by watching them diving for the money. We were not allowed ashore because it was said that the plague had broken out."[107]

From Egypt, the fleet shipped through the Suez Canal into the Red Sea where they encountered the French contingent bound for China. To the great excitement of the French soldiers, the Germans played the French national anthem and saluted their Allies. Friedrich Neubert noted in his diary on the 12th of August, that several of his comrades were suffering from the heat, on the 13th a coal trimmer even died of heat stroke with outside temperatures exceeding 50 Celsius (122 Fahrenheit).[108] After crossing the Red Sea, the ships entered the Indian Ocean where they went through a two-day storm that "threw who ever [sic] did not hold tight from one side to the other."[109] On August 27th, one month into the journey, the fleet stopped in Singapore to take on supplies. This second wave of the German Expeditionary Corps arrived in Tientsin on September 6th, three weeks after the capture of Beijing through the Allies.[110] Sommerfeld's unit, one of the four squadrons of cavalry participated initially in "mopping" up operations. By October, the international force had occupied and pacified Beijing, Taku, Tientsin, and other coastal areas in its entirety. The Empress had fled to Xi'an in an oxcart. Feldmarschall Graf von Waldersee, the Allied Commander, arrived in Taku in the beginning of October and immediately moved his headquarters to Beijing.

Although most of the international troops remained garrisoned for much of the following year, some units had plenty of work. The engineers quickly rebuilt the railroads from the coast to Beijing, and small units of international troops moved into the rural areas to guard missionary outposts. The German forces engaged in sporadic punitive expeditions in an attempt to stamp out any remaining resistance. In line with the instructions from their Emperor, some of these expeditions resulted in brutal abuses of the local population.

Little is known about the actual experiences Sommerfeld had in China. However, there are two indications that he did not spend his service in garrison. One indication is the fact that according to his statement to the American authorities in 1918, he spent most of his time in the interior of China and that he learned to speak Chinese "pretty well."[111] The second indication is that he became an expert horseman at the time, which helped him tremendously later in his life when he crisscrossed the Northern Mexican frontier. The picture evolves that he was a "Meldereiter," or horseback messenger, in China. These cavalrymen carried messages from the various headquarters to the outposts. To move around the countryside, they had to speak Chinese and they most certainly had to be excellent horsemen to find their way in a completely foreign land. Sommerfeld also received the promotion to corporal, which indicates that this rise in rank had something to do with the type of service he performed in the cavalry regiment. Whether or not Sommerfeld saw any actual combat is not known. However, it is highly likely that he saw his share of destruction and atrocities.

Already at the onset of liberating the embassy compound Allied troops engaged in widespread looting.

"Three days open ransacking and pillaging ensued ...[The] Imperial Library ... would be looted by the allied forces. Japanese were said to have looted 3 million taels of silver from Manchu "household ministry" ... Allied Forces burnt down all houses with boxer altar, shot Chinese wherever spotted, raped women and imposed incest among family members, ransacked palaces and buildings, and burnt down treasures that could not be transported out of China. ... Residencies of Manchu kings were ransacked by French, Japanese and allied forces as well ... Chinese losses were estimated to be around 100 million taels of silver and more."[112]

Rural settlements, where members of the Boxer organization or their supporters were suspected, did not fare any better. The Allied troops burned down whole villages and looted the already impoverished peasants mercilessly. Soldiers collected braids of executed Boxers, ivory chopsticks, figurines, plates, silver, porcelain, and tapestries, in short, anything that would fit into their luggage in addition to personal effects. After eleven months of service in China, the expeditionary forces received orders for returning home in the spring of 1901. The casualty list had grown over the months of fighting in China. By the end of the German expedition, 115,000 Chinese had died among them around 19,000 civilians, while the Allies had lost 2,500.[113] However, it was not the bullets, lances, or swords of the enemy that killed most Allied soldiers, it was typhoid, malaria, diphtheria, cholera, and many other food and water born sicknesses. The returning soldiers carried many of these diseases home with them causing alarm and minute attention to hygiene on the troop transporters and in the domestic barracks. German propaganda hailed the whole affair a great success. The Chinese government had to sign a peace treaty in September 1901, the Xin Chou Treaty or the Boxer Protocol of 1901. Among other items, Germany as well as the other Allies received substantial reparations amounting to $735 million to be paid over the next thirty-nine years. A member of the Chinese imperial family had to travel to Germany to personally apologize to Kaiser Wilhelm II.

Sommerfeld's unit returned to Germany in the middle of August 1901.[114] According to his recollections he received an honorable discharge at Münster.[115] Every participant of the expeditionary force received a bronze medal from the Emperor. It read "To the victorious fighters - 1900 China 1901-" and featured the imperial crown on one side and the Prussian Eagle slaying a Chinese dragon on the other. Sommerfeld cherished this medal for the rest of his life. Eyewitnesses saw him wear it on holidays and special occasions such as the emperor's birthday.[116] They described the medal to be a "gold medal," which would have indicated that Sommerfeld as a result of bravery or injury received higher honors. However, no Sommerfeld is listed in the Prussian registries of gold medal recipients.

The Boxer Revolution impressed the twenty-one-year-old Sommerfeld thoroughly. For the first time in his life, he witnessed a popular uprising against an unpopular government too weak to reign in foreign influence. As his unit rode up the PeiHo River from Tientsin towards Peking, the destruction along the way must have been impressive. Firsthand he witnessed the brutality of war, decomposing bodies, looting, massacred civilians, displacement of whole communities, and the like. Historian Jim Tuck alleged that Sommerfeld supported the intervention of foreign powers in China.[117] However, there is no conclusive evidence as to Sommerfeld's opinion of the affair. He did like to show off his medal indicating that he at the very least was proud to have served in the German army. However, neither in his letters nor statements to the American government did he ever mention his army service in China in political terms. His later support of Madero and Pancho Villa, as well as his efforts to help foreigners in Mexico escape the turmoil does suggest a sense of humanity and motivation to compromise rather than to fight. He mentioned to his interrogators that he never "carried a rifle or a pistol", even in the midst of fighting.[118] Rather than viewing Sommerfeld as a reactionary thug, as historian Tuck has attempted, it would be fair to assume that the German's absolute loyalty to Madero and his ideology evidenced reform-minded liberalism rather than support of all out revolution. His Prussian upbringing in Schneidemühl, the experiences in the United States, the German army, the Boxer expedition, and his understanding of law and order formed a political character that stood apart from both radical and reactionary forces in the turbulent decade after 1910.

After the Boxer Rebellion was crushed, Sam Dreben and Emil Holmdahl fought in the Philippines under Captain John J. Pershing. Just like Sommerfeld these two young men had received their baptisms of fire, Dreben both in China and the Philippines, Holmdahl just in the Philippines. As was the case for Sommerfeld, both fought repeatedly on the "wrong side," as historians of social revolutions would note. However, they ended up defending the uprising of Mexico's moderate factions both against the radical left and reactionary right. Their politics were mingled with financial ambitions but not devoid of social conscience. All three understood the need for change and all three supported Madero's revolution against the aging dictatorship in Mexico. Certainly not for a lack of opportunity neither one of the trio joined up with reactionary forces in the course of their revolutionary activities. Although on the "wrong" side in China and the Philippines, this social conscience that made the trio so indispensable in the Mexican Revolution, developed on the battlefields of the Orient.

The parallels between the Boxer Revolution and Mexico in the decade to come are inescapable. Both China and Mexico faced rapid industrial growth powered mainly by foreign companies and their governments. In both countries, foreigners had little understanding or interest in local culture and tradition, resulting in alienating the working poor. In both countries, the governments had grown apart from the masses and thus became foreign themselves. In China, the special circumstance of Christian missionaries trampling on millenniums of tradition, beliefs, and faith contributed greatly to the uprising. In both places, a return to traditional values flowered in Mexico with Indigenismo, in China with a return to Confucian tradition. Most significantly, in both places, the initial attempt to harness revolution with modest reform gave way to full blown chaos, anti-foreign ideology, and violence. While China's social transformation would erupt sporadically throughout the early 20th century and culminate in the revolution of 1949, Mexico's revolution took its bloody course in a ten-year period between 1910 and 1920 but simmered well into the forties.

As is the case with the Mexican Revolution, the mass uprising in China is largely misunderstood and underestimated in its historical significance. Diana Preston and other western scholars call the Boxer Revolution an "uprising" or "rebellion" rather than the first phase of a social revolution.[119] China was never to be the same after 1901. The Dowager Empress died in 1908, leaving the country without effective leadership. At the same time in Mexico, Dictator Porfirio Diaz failed to arrange for effective succession and created a huge power vacuum. In 1911, the Manchu grip on power ended in a bloody uprising, just as Diaz's flight into exile plunged Mexico into a decade of revolutionary struggle. Sommerfeld became a close witness of the first phase of this transformational process. Without appreciating the nature of social revolution and certainly not appreciating the resulting disorder and seemingly senseless waves of destruction, he witnessed two of the greatest upheavals of our time, and had a role in both. The experiences in the Boxer Revolution sharpened his political horizon and understanding of the power of popular revolt. It was to be déjà vu in 1910 when he joined the forces of the Madero Revolution in Mexico, phase one of the second social revolution of the 20th century.

CHAPTER 4

ɲ

"A HEALTHY LIFE"

When Sommerfeld returned to Germany from China, he went back to school for a final year. His father gave him an allowance to finish. According to his own statement and matching a realistic time line, Sommerfeld graduated from the Bergakademie with a bachelor's degree in mineralogy in July of 1902. Germany's economy was booming that year. Since the German unification of 1871 under Bismarck's leadership, industrialization that had started in the Ruhr area and Saxony now propelled the country to develop the largest economy in the world. In 1902, Germany's industrial output rivaled that of England and the United States. Railroads and canals between the Main, Rhine, Danube, Elbe, and Oder rivers connected the important production centers of Saar, Ruhr, Saxony, and Silesia with the harbors of Hamburg, Bremen, Kiel and Rostock. German unemployment rates hovered around three percent, which translated into virtual full employment.[120] Production of steel, coal, gas, and oil reached new heights in this period. The economy became a hungry beast that had to be continually fed. The raw materials from the mines and wells of Germany no longer sufficed. Colonial expansion, some effects of which Sommerfeld experienced firsthand in China, increased supplies somewhat. However, it was the rapid expansion of the merchant marine and railroads that allowed German industry to be adequately supplied and finished goods to trade anywhere in the world.

According to Sommerfeld's recollections, he did not seriously look for a job when he traveled around Germany in the summer of 1902.[121] Only an hour to two from Berlin by train, he visited the mining centers of Saxony and Thuringia. The lignite or brown coal of Saxony and what is now the western part of the Czech Republic, fueled power plants in the region and supported the large textile and porcelain industries. The mines of the Erzgebirge (German for Ore Mountains) also produced hard coal that fueled the ironworks of the

Ruhr area. While today most lignite mines use open pit production technology, the coalmines of 1900 almost always were underground because the large, earth-moving technology of today had not yet been invented. Other ores of the region that were in demand in 1902 included tin, lead, silver, zinc, bismuth, and tungsten, the latter constituting the glowing metal in the surging light bulb industry. Despite slightly declining prices for raw materials in 1902, the mines of Saxony were humming. Production of coal had increased from 104 million tons in 1895 to 150 million tons in 1900, while iron ore production increased from 4.8 million tons to 8.5 million tons in the same period.[122]

However, the young mining engineer had other plans than to work in the tightly regulated, highly industrialized and well developed mines of Germany. Many of the graduates of the Bergakademie in Berlin moved to North and South America. While the mining industry of Germany certainly offered opportunities for young engineers, there was no comparison to the booming mining development of Northern Mexico and the Western United States. By 1902, the tremendous growth of the U.S. industrial output demanded rapid expansion of mineral production, especially silver, copper, and iron. Mining journals offered leading management jobs from the onset that would take years of experience to attain in Germany. What especially drew young mining engineers to the frontiers of the United States and Mexico was the possibility to stake their own claims and potentially attain ownership of a successful mine. Just as is the case with any high stakes gamble, the downside was a complete lack of security both financially and with regards to health. Not surprisingly, the dark side of starting ventures in foreign lands hardly found mention in the glowing articles of the time.

After less than two months of travel in Germany, Sommerfeld boarded the steamship "Pretoria" in Hamburg on the 18th of September 1902 and headed for New York for the third time in his life.[123] Just as in 1898, his funds only bought him accommodation in steerage. To his relief, the American immigration officials did not question him about his desertion when he disembarked at Hoboken.[124] His brother Hermann had just passed away less than a year before, so he went on to Chicago, where his brother Julius had moved in the meantime. Julius Sommerfeld had become a naturalized citizen in April 1901 and was well on his way to a share in the American dream.[125] He had started a successful hosiery business when he moved to Chicago. Felix stayed with his brother and worked in the office of the business until June 1903. He used his time to brush up on his English and save up funds to finance his ventures on the frontier.

With a "few hundred dollars" in his pocket, Sommerfeld set out for Arizona.[126] According to the young mining engineer, he went to Yavapai County to search for gold, silver and copper. As a matter of fact, the Jerome District of Yavapai County was the largest producer of gold in the state of Arizona from 1876 all the way to 1959. Yavapai County also contained silver and copper deposits. It is not surprising that the ambitious German wanted to try his luck as a prospector in the Bradshaw Mountains of Yavapai County. He took a job as a driller for $4.50 per day (about $100 in today's value) in the "Oro Mine," most likely the Oro Belle Mining and Milling Company just south of Prescott, the then capital of Arizona.[127] The work was hard and underground. According to Sommerfeld the mine operation was plagued by frequent strikes of "Cornishmen" (British subjects from Cornwall) until the owners brought Irish strike breakers to "finish" the problem.[128] According to his own recollections he did not relate well to the mining community. "I knew the bosses," he answered when his interrogator asked if he mingled with mining men. If he made any acquaintances? "No," was the answer.[129] Clearly, he considered the day laborer job below his social and professional level. Reading into his description of the striking Cornishmen who all belonged to the Federation of Miners, a trade union, their plight or union organizing did not particularly arouse his sympathies. Sommerfeld's ambition was to become one of the bosses.

In the fall of 1903, after working a few months in the Oro Mine, Sommerfeld moved up the valley to take a job at the Mud Hole mine on the Lynx Creek near the town of Walker, Arizona. The Mud Hole mine, which is a tourist attraction today, also produced gold in the early 20th century. He did not specify his job, however it is likely that he upgraded his pay somewhat and took a different job to gain more experience in a mine that had more technology. The accommodations in 1903 were very primitive. Sommerfeld testified that he stayed in a house with a fellow miner and "we all used to eat in a big dining room."[130] He obviously lived on site where the mining operators offered "houses" that more aptly could be called shacks without any of our modern amenities: Electricity, running water, heating, or air conditioning. The "big dining room" was a mess hall somewhere on the grounds. The operators charged for rent, food, and supplies that at best wiped out the meager wages of the miners, and more often, if credit was granted, plunged the workers into debt. Alcohol and other entertainment existed in the next larger town, in Arizona's capital Prescott. Only a few hours to the north on horseback the hard working frontiersmen went there to find brothels, saloons, and casinos to spend whatever funds remained. Larger mining camps also offered their own saloons, a sure way to retrieve the meager earnings of the miners.

Sommerfeld did not fit into the typical mold of the early 20th century miner. He had a university degree and neither drank nor gambled.[131] He also was German in a sea of Irish, Polish, Swedish, English, Mexican, and Yavapai Indian laborers. With keen interest he observed the technology with which mining companies determined a good spot, laid a claim, and went about exploiting the natural treasures. After a few months in Mud Hole, Sommerfeld moved on to Jerome, Arizona, where the United Verde Copper Company operated the largest copper mining operation in the region. Over 15,000 inhabitants made Jerome the fifth largest city in Arizona. "The town became a melting pot for immigrant settlers seeking their fortunes. It also became infamous for gambling, prostitution, and alcohol abuse. Four times in the late 1800's the town was leveled by fires, and in 1903 Jerome became known as the 'Wickedest Town in Arizona.'"[132] The copper mining operation and the lawlessness of Jerome did not capture the twenty-five-year-old mining engineer for long. He was determined to try his own luck.

In the spring of 1904 with his own prospector outfit and a mule, Felix Sommerfeld "went up the hills at Bisbee and that neighborhood looking for mineral."[133] Likely as a result of not drinking and gambling he had saved enough money to set himself up. Bisbee is located just south of the infamous Tombstone, Arizona. Eight miles from the Mexican border, Bisbee is situated just north between the Arizona border towns of Naco and Douglas across from the Mexican hamlet of Agua Prieta, Sonora. Sommerfeld certainly had the right nose for going where the action was. In 1904 Bisbee was the largest city between St. Louis and San Francisco fueled by the largest copper mine in the world: The Copper Queen. Throughout the 1880s exploration companies and individual miners staked claims in the area around Bisbee. In the 1890s, the Phelps Dodge Corporation consolidated the claims and started extracting copper on a large scale. Copper, of course, was in high demand since the world electrified itself using copper wire. It was in these mountains along the Mexican border that Sommerfeld tried his luck.

After six months of searching in vain for the winning ticket Sommerfeld decided to move into Mexico, because, according to other prospectors, "south of the border was the best country."[134] He also probably felt highly uncomfortable in the searing 110 degree Fahrenheit heat of Arizona's summer, interrupted only in the monsoon season by daily torrential rainstorms that woke dry riverbeds to become dreadful, roaring streams full of debris and mud. Sommerfeld jokingly told his interrogators upon the question of whether he got rich, "Well, it was a healthy life."[135]

The next three years of Sommerfeld's life are sketchy and require some conjecture. According to his statements to the American authorities in 1918, he and a recent Irish immigrant from New York, Mark Daly, crossed into Mexico in the summer of 1904.[136] Coming from the area of Bisbee, Arizona and entering Mexico through Nogales, the prospecting partners ventured south. As the Phelps Dodge Corporation controlled Bisbee, another of the largest copper mines in the world dictated economic life in Cananea, Sonora. The Greene Consolidated Copper Company basically owned both mining centers. "Colonel" William C. Greene, an American tycoon, ran a tight ship in his operations.[137] If Sommerfeld really was in the area in 1904, it is not surprising that he did not become employed in Greene's enterprise. Pay was poor. Americans and foreigners received five pesos a day, versus Mexicans doing the same work for 3.50 pesos. The industrialized mining operations resembled what Sommerfeld had seen in Germany a few years earlier. He did not like it then and clearly did not now.

There was another reason, why an ambitious, young German mining engineer would not want to work for Consolidated Copper. In late 1904, socialist and anarchist labor activists became active, fueled in part by Ricardo and Jesús Flores Magon, two of the earliest anti-Diaz agitators. The unequal pay structure and harsh working conditions irked Mexican miners, making Greene's operations fertile soil for organizers. In part as a result of agitation by the Flores Magon brothers, in part as a result of "Colonel" Greene's unwavering attitude towards worker demands, anti-management and anti-foreign sentiment ran high. If Sommerfeld had taken a job as a mining engineer or supervisor at the time, he would have found himself in the middle of this burgeoning labor conflict.

The situation became tense over the course of 1905 and exploded on June 1st 1906. Over three thousand workers went on strike, demanding equal pay for equal work and promotions based on seniority and ability not race and nationality. "Colonel" Greene himself urged his employees to calm down and go back to work. To no avail! The Greene Consolidated Copper Company management refused to give in to the main demands. When strikebreakers from Arizona, the Thiel Detective Agency's specialty, joined with local police forces, violent clashes led to first casualties. In the days following the initial walk out, Mexican and American forces started firing on the strikers. In subsequent fights over thirty workers were killed. Within a few days, Arizona

Rangers together with Mexican Rurales put down the strike. The outrage of Mexican workers being killed by American posses became a rallying cry for the subsequent revolution.

In the boom days of the early 1900s, the only way to make good money was to stake a claim and be lucky, or become a partner in one of the thousands of small mining ventures where a good engineer could make a big difference. So, according to Sommerfeld, he and Mark Daly went through Sonora and headed further south. He wanted to find gold and silver. The hottest silver mines at the time were at the border between Sinaloa and Durango, about 150 miles south of Sonora. The two prospectors ended in San José de Garcia in Sinaloa. According to his testimony Sommerfeld had only $100 in his pocket, not enough to start his own venture.[138] In San José de Garcia the pair split. Sommerfeld considered his companion to lack ambition: "He never liked to work for anybody. He was a rainbow chaser. Daly was the kind who did not do anything as long as he had a grub-stake [sic] and did not care about anything."[139]

After they separated, Sommerfeld told investigators, he negotiated a hefty finders' fee with a desperate superintendent who had "lost" a silver vein. For six thousand pesos in gold ($3,000, approximately $65,000 in today's value) and a manager's salary of $12.50 pesos per day, Sommerfeld took over the mine. The place of this profitable endeavor was the "San Louis [sic]" mine in Sinaloa.[140]

As interesting as Sommerfeld's story sounds, not much of it matches the historical record. There was only one mine named San Luis in northern Mexico at the time. This mine was actually located in the state of Durango, between Torreon and the state capital. According to the Mines Register of 1905, the operator of the mine was the San Luis Mining Co., a New York concern. The listing for the mine showed the following:

'SAN LUIS MINING CO MEXICO Office 27 William St New York Mine office Gabriel Durango Mexico Employs 1,000 men. Walter S. Logan president, W.J. Robinson vice president, Myra B. Martin secretary and treasurer, preceding officers Seymour W. Tulloch, Angel L. Negrete, J. Edward Layne, Walter S. Perry and Col Britton Davis directors, Louis Ross general manager, W. Thomas Moore assistant manager, Lloyd Roby superintendent, Andrew Macfarlane mine superintendent, H.G. Elwes mill superintendent, Sydney D. Tyler engineer."[141]

Although it is not possible to completely discount Sommerfeld's claim that he took over the mine in 1904, the record does not include the young German either as supervisor or engineer, investor, or "in charge," as he had claimed. According to his statement, Sommerfeld stayed in San José until August 1906 when he left for Germany from Veracruz. While he downplayed his successes as a prospector to his interrogators, Sommerfeld testified that he left for Germany with a hefty $12,000 in savings ($252,000 in today's value).[142] Supposedly, he had found the vein, reorganized the mine, staked some of his own claims in Durango and sold them profitably.[143] None of these claims appear to be truthful. The location for the mine is in a different state. He is not listed as an engineer or superintendent. If he really made $12,000 in a twelve month time span, it is hard to understand, why he is not listed in any of the period ownership registers, lists of claims, or as an engineer anywhere, in any mine between 1904 and 1910.[144] What the historical record does show points to a completely different chain of events between 1906 and 1908. Sommerfeld told investigators that after working the San Luis mine, he quit and "went sightseeing" in Mexico City before he boarded a ship from Veracruz to Germany in October 1906.

It is more likely that after trying to work in Durango he did not make any money and returned to Chicago where his brother lived. He is listed as an insurance agent on 3309 Vernon Avenue in Chicago in 1905.[145] Sometime in 1906 Sommerfeld returned to Germany, but not with $250,000 to his name. No record can be found as to the departure point. Most likely he sailed from Canada because his trail in 1907 leads to Montreal. On the second of February 1907, Sommerfeld boarded the "Graf Waldersee" in Hamburg and sailed to New York. In the ship's register, Sommerfeld listed his last residence as "Montreal" and his occupation "Journalist," rather than mining engineer.[146] When he arrived at Ellis Island on February 16th, he is marked as non-immigrant meaning that he proceeded on to another country, namely Canada.[147] In August 1907, Sommerfeld traveled again. This time he arrived in Liverpool from Montreal. He listed his occupation as miner on this occasion. Far from his claim to have made a lot of money mining, he again braved the Atlantic crossing in steerage.[148] Sommerfeld's uncle Ed Rosenbaum told a BI investigator in October 1916 that he and Sommerfeld had a falling out sometime around 1906 or 1907. "That this was the first time [August 1916] he had seen or communicated with his nephew Felix for over eight years, as they had had a falling out over some money that Felix had borrowed from Rosenbaum and his wife's relatives at that time."[149] One can only assume what the true meaning of the word "borrowed" was, another "boyish mistake?"

There is one other fact in the historical record that requires consideration. Both, Sommerfeld's grandfather, Baruch Sommerfeld, and his father Isidor died in 1907. Sommerfeld did mention to his interrogators that one reason for traveling to Germany in 1906 was his father's failing health.[150] Since he arrived in Liverpool in August 1907 as a steerage passenger, it is more likely, if he had money, it came from his father's inheritance rather than as a result of his mining activities. However, this theory does not square with Sommerfeld's own statement, namely that his father was basically bankrupt. Although the record is sketchy at best, several possibilities exist as to how he spent his time between 1906 and 1907.

Sommerfeld most likely did go prospecting in 1903 to 1905 in the Southwest of the United States and Northern Mexico. As was the case with many prospectors of the time, Sommerfeld followed the action, which by 1904 clearly pointed to south of the border. However, his claims of financial success appear to be untrue. Sometime in 1905, Sommerfeld returned to his brother's house in Chicago where he started working in some capacity in the insurance business or journalism. When exactly Sommerfeld returned to Germany is unknown. What also cannot be traced is when exactly he returned to the United States. We can say for sure that Sommerfeld did return to the U.S. sometime in 1908, probably as he claimed to the American interrogators, in the beginning of that year. Again his activities pointed him south of the border. In October 1908 he settled in Chihuahua City, Mexico where his name appeared on a list of residents the German Consulate had assembled.[151] His occupation is defined as "mineur." In 1908, the local Bohemian Club also listed a recent arrival from Germany, Felix Sommerfeld, as a member.[152]

In the interrogation by American authorities in 1918, Sommerfeld claimed that he became the supervisor of "La Abundancia" mine in 1908. His deal with the owners, according to Sommerfeld's testimony, was a seventeen percent share of the claim. While Sommerfeld lied to the BI investigators about the names of the owners of this mine, he described in detail a Mexican-German with a Mexican wife and children. When asked whether he could swear to the fact that this Mexican-German was not a German agent, Sommerfeld evasively said: "To my knowledge, yes."[153] Of course, he was describing the patriarch Friedrich Stallforth of Parral, Chihuahua, whose mines meanwhile belonged to the person who became his friend and co-conspirator in World War I, Frederico

37

Stallforth. Other than the fact that "La Abundancia" did exist and belonged to the Stallforths there is no record of Sommerfeld being the manager there.[154]

There is another possibility that would explain the fact that he lied to American authorities about his activities in the questionable time period 1906 to 1908. According to his statement to American authorities in 1918, Sommerfeld passed through Chicago and San Francisco in 1906 to enter Mexico via Tucson, Arizona. Missing in his explanation are trips that started in 1906 taking him to Montreal, which he listed as his home in immigration documents. He went there again in February of 1907, citing his occupation as "Journalist" and returned back to Germany in August that same year. He did not, as he testified, work in the mines of Chihuahua after a visit to Tucson in 1907.[155] Many of the dare devil frontiersmen of the Mexican Revolution, the likes of Tracy Richardson, Sam Dreben, and Emil Holmdahl, spent those years before the Mexican Revolution as mercenaries for various revolutionaries in Central America. Also lobbyist and future representative of Madero, Villa, and Carranza in Washington, Sherburne G. Hopkins, busied himself with mingling in Central American revolutions. Why did Sommerfeld not mention his return to Germany in August 1907, his occupation as a journalist, and why did he list his residence as Montreal, Canada?

Clearly, Sommerfeld had business to attend to in Germany and Canada. He did not disclose these trips to and from New York and Canada in 1907 to his interrogators for a reason. It is a likely possibility that Sommerfeld went back to Germany in 1906 and enlisted with the "Etappendienst der Deutschen Marine," the German naval intelligence service. By that time the Prussian government had relaxed its discrimination against Jews in the military and public office. For example the Kaiser appointed Dr. Bernhard Dernburg, a Jewish banker, to become Secretary for Colonial Affairs in 1906. Dernburg like most officials engaged in international affairs worked closely with the German press and the "Etappendienst," forerunner of the German Naval Intelligence Service. This organization blurred lines between propaganda, dissemination of misinformation, and intelligence gathering.[156] Dernburg found ample mention in "Nauticus," the official periodical of the Navy's propaganda department.[157] Another publication under Dernburg's direct control with a similar propaganda mission was the *Deutsche Kolonialzeitung*, which sang the praises of German power projection in the colonies. It is unknown but possible that Sommerfeld worked in some capacity in this propaganda and intelligence branch of the German navy. This would explain his "interest" in journalism, his trips to Canada as a newsman for the "Etappendienst," and his subsequent denial to

American authorities. As a member of the Naval Intelligence Service Sommerfeld also would have had a slight chance to meet Dr. Dernburg who seemed to know the German agent in 1915 in a more than just casual way. The *Rangliste der Königlich Preußischen Armee* for 1907, the record of all officers of the Prussian army, showed quite a few members of the armed services with the name of Abraham or Jerusalem and several Sommerfelds, one major, one first lieutenant, and three lieutenants. One of them, first lieutenant Sommerfeld, was attached to a Berlin district, the Landwehrbezirk 2, which included the school for naval intelligence.[158] Regrettably, the listing does not include first names and most of the service records of the Prussian army were destroyed in an aerial attack on Berlin in February 1945.[159] Whether or not he joined the German Naval Intelligence Service in 1906, Sommerfeld's experience on the frontier not only gave him an understanding of "how things worked" in this region. The time as a prospector also widened his horizon and took him further away from the constrictions of his German upbringing. Although he came back to Germany for a brief time, he would never settle there again.

PART II

~

FROM DICTATORSHIP TO REVOLUTION

CHAPTER 5

ᴎ

PRE-REVOLUTIONARY MEXICO

*M*eanwhile in Mexico Porfirio Diaz and his group of ministers and advisors known as "Cientificos" had ruled the country with an iron fist since 1876. The "Cientificos" believed in a technocratic approach to the economy and politics. Steeped in the philosophy of positivism, which held that scientific methods would unveil the processes that explained and controlled human behavior, the "Cientificos" had led the transformation of Mexico's political and economic landscape for nearly four decades. In 1908, not only the dictator himself but most of the members of his governing elite were in their seventies and eighties. The political elite saw itself mired in questions of succession. In March of that year, Diaz in an interview with American journalist James Creelman of Pearson's Magazine announced his plans to embrace democracy, retire, and allow competition in the upcoming elections.[160] This remarkable change in attitude opened a Pandora's Box for the Porfirian regime.

Diaz' administration had actually enjoyed broad based support across large portions of Mexican society for many years. A famous and decorated general who helped defeat the French in 1867, Diaz had seized the presidency in 1876.[161] He united powerful sectors of society into a coalition aiming to grow the Mexican economy, to eradicate crime, and to build a middle class. Of course, in order to enjoy the fruits of the Porfiriato, one had to be on the right side. The centralized power of the Diaz regime would not tolerate dissent while it dispensed favors and office as it saw fit. Within a few years of his grab of power, the government coalition of landowners, industrialists, the church, and the military consolidated, and the Mexican economy stabilized. The infant labor unions were crushed. Diaz' notorious "pan y palo" policy (carrot and whip) wiped out political dissent. The Rurales, the rural police force, received many former bandits into their ranks. Rather than having to earn a living as a robber the Porfirian policeman earned his keep through a small salary and fines he collected. The strategy worked and reported crime rates declined drastically. Corruption, while certainly not extinguished, existed only if sanctioned by the regime. To the great relief and gratitude of the people working on haciendas and mining operations in the northern states of Sonora, Chihuahua, and Coahuila, the Apache wars ended in 1886 with the capture of Geronimo. Governor Luis Terrazas of Chihuahua stood out as a hero in ridding his state of the revolting Indians, consolidating his power base into the 1900s. In 1885, Mexico concluded treaties with the debtor nations of Britain, France, and Spain to consolidate national debt and bring Mexico on a financial path to credit worthiness.[162] In 1888, the first new international loan showed the success of the Porfirian fiscal strategy.[163]

As a result of stability, the government attracted foreign investment. England, traditionally the largest holder of Mexican debt, with Spain and France following close behind, still reeled from the loan defaults of the 1820s and 30s culminating in the 1861 invasion by France. After the defeat of France and the execution of Emperor Don Maximiliano I (Maximilian I) in 1867, Mexican President Juarez unilaterally cancelled service of the debt. As a result Mexico's international credit rating hit a new low point. Several rounds of negotiations designed to revive credit worthiness dragged on into the 1880s. With the ascent to power of Emperor Wilhelm II in 1888 and the retirement of Bismarck in 1890, Germany saw a great opportunity to increase her influence on the American continent. Betting on the stabilizing effect of the Mexican dictator Diaz, Baron Bleichröder of Berlin assembled a syndicate (including the imperial German government) and put together one of the largest international loans ever granted to Mexico. The German bank took on about 50% of the Mexican debt, seriously reducing the British stranglehold on development and economic growth.[164] While being a private banking concern, the Bleichröder family was very close to the German government, and so helped formulate and advance her foreign policy towards Mexico.

In part as a result of Bleichröder's high risk loan, in part as the result of Diaz' successful domestic policies, the resulting stabilization of the Mexican economy and influx of business investors eroded the very competitive advantage the German government had created. A stable economy reduced the financial risks. As a result, more banks, mostly American and French, dared to invest in Mexico. While the economy recovered in the late 1880s, Mexico's northern neighbor, the United States, also experienced an economic boom mostly driven by railroad construction. With efficient transportation to the industrial centers of the East and Midwest in place, a mining boom started in the western states, moved south to Arizona and crossed the border into Sonora and Chihuahua. Rampant growth caused investors to overplay the markets. In 1893, the railroad "bubble" burst and the U.S. economy slid into a serious recession lasting three years. By the end of the downturn, large parts of the U.S. mining industry had been wiped out. However, after the initial shock the economy grew at a steadier pace all the way to 1907. The U.S. economic expansion required fuel, and lots of it: Raw materials, produced cheaper in Mexico than in the west, satisfied the ever greater hunger of American industrial output. From the 1890s to 1908, Mexico experienced the largest expansion of her economy in history, fueled by raw material exports and foreign investment.

Felix Sommerfeld was but one of countless others from anywhere in the world who followed the call of the booming mining industry. American investors came in droves, building the railroads, developing mining, building smelters, and founding highly profitable business ventures. Despite the seemingly obvious assumptions on the origins of the Mexican Revolution, Mexican workers in the northern states preferred working for foreign companies, especially before 1908. The pay and working conditions were usually better than in Mexican companies, although by no means just and fair by today's standards. Historians such as Friedrich Katz credit the revolutionaries' generally lenient attitude to foreign companies in the revolution that started in 1910 partly to the fact that workers would have resented the destruction of their sources of income. [165] The Mexican government worked closely with the foreign businesses. Wages of Mexican workers stayed well below those of their American and foreign counterparts. As time wore on the unequal pay structure caused open resentment. The few strikes that flared up, Cananea Consolidated Copper mine in 1906 and the Rio Blanco textile factory strike in 1907, to name just two, faced brutal and bloody repercussions from the dictatorship. In the Porfiriato, American businesses could count on the help of the Mexican government. With the tacit blessing of the government many foreign businesses also employed their own police forces and strike breakers. To a large extent Porfirio Diaz enjoyed the trust and support of the American administrations of Roosevelt and Taft, as well as of the major European powers.

In the international power game, the United States under Theodore Roosevelt succeeded in keeping European powers from intervening too overtly in Latin America. The Monroe Doctrine and Roosevelt's Corollary now had some teeth since the U.S. had defeated Spain in 1898 and prowled the seven seas with her sizable navy. Neither Britain nor France had any serious ambitions in the American hemisphere, although that did not prevent them from continuously probing American resolve. Germany, as well, enjoyed a harmonious relationship with the United States in the first decade of the 20th century. The German ambassador to the United States and Mexico, Hermann Freiherr Speck von Sternburg, had a very personal relationship with the American President Theodore Roosevelt. Von Sternburg had grown up in England and his wife was born and raised in Kentucky. He knew America well and had participated in international conferences, openly showing his admiration and support for the United States. Roosevelt considered Sternburg a friend and is said to have asked the Kaiser for his appointment.[166] When Sternburg took his assignment as imperial ambassador to the United States, the New York Times reported on him publicly acknowledging Germany's respect for the Monroe Doctrine: "The Monroe Doctrine is an unwritten law with Americans [sic] and President Roosevelt interprets it...as a measure making for peace."[167] Underlying this harmonious U.S.-German relationship, however, was a tension that resulted from Germany's ambitions in the Americas.[168]

In 1902, Germany joined Britain and Italy in a blockade of Venezuela, which had defaulted on international loans. In the course of the blockade, the German Navy sank a Haitian ship. This action posed a direct challenge to the Monroe Doctrine and imprinted itself in the American government's attitude towards Germany. Germany's ambitions were especially pronounced in Mexico, where Porfirio Diaz skillfully manipulated the European powers as counterweights to American influence. Since the German Empire had entered the colonial game late, the far-fetched possibility to gain a foothold in North America made the Emperor salivate. In 1903, German businessmen quietly inquired about the acquisition of Magdalena Bay in Baja California to serve as a German naval station. Just a year before, the Japanese Empire had launched a similar trial balloon. Of course, Porfirio Diaz knew that the United States would never accept such a sale and after leading the Germans on for a while, he dropped the issue. However, Diaz at the same time cancelled an American lease for a coaling station in Magdalena Bay, seriously impacting the bilateral relations between Mexico and the United States. In 1904 and 1905 Germany responded positively to a request from the Mexican government to provide military trainers. Again, Diaz was probably well aware that the American government would never allow the German military to operate in Mexico. However, from his perspective, the mere possibility presented a good counterweight to American influence in Northern Mexico. Whether or not

Germany recognized the fruitlessness of her undertaking is doubtful. Despite strong reservations of the American President, the Kaiser tried to pressure the Mexican dictator up to 1907 to renew his request for German military instructors.[169]

While Germany vied for a larger piece of the economic pie in Mexico, thereby risking the constructive and harmonious relationship with the United States, the sly Mexican dictator in fact managed to reduce German financial influence. The banking house S. Bleichröder und Sohn had provided loans to the Mexican government when other banks refused to take the risk. Since Diaz had stabilized the country and led Mexico through the largest economic expansion in her history, credit worthiness followed the upward pointing economic trends. Rather than expanding business with the renowned banking house from Berlin, the Diaz government approached J.P. Morgan (of New York and London), James Speyer (of New York, Frankfurt, and London), National City Bank (of New York), Teixeira De Mattos Brothers (of Amsterdam), Crédite Lyonnais, Banque de Paris and several others who chomped at the bit. Diaz also brought the Deutsch-Südamerikanische Bank, a dependent of the Dresdner Bank, as well as the Deutsche Bank to the table as a counterbalance to Bleichröder.[170] "In October 1901, the London Firm [J.S. Morgan of London] accepted a $150,000 participation in the Mexican National Railway Re-adjustment Loan, and in February and November 1908, together with the Dresdner Bank, it cosponsored [sic] two issues of debentures for the Interoceanic Railway of Mexico."[171]

By 1900, Bleichröder's exclusive management of Mexican financing needs was waning, drastically reducing the traditionally large influence Germany had on the Mexican government via Bleichröder's loans.[172] While Bleichröder nominally headed the syndicates that Mexican Secretary of Finance José Limantour assembled for new bond issues in 1901 and again in 1907 and 1913, the bank's share in the effort became too small to maintain significant influence with the Mexican government. One of Bleichröder's big German competitors was the Deutsche Bank where the young and ambitious Geheimrat Bernhard Dernburg managed Mexican operations "almost exclusively."[173] Dernburg also visited the United States on a number of occasions and was instrumental in reorganizing and consolidating bad railroad debt after the collapse of 1893.[174] Another large Berlin bank vying for the Mexican market was the Diskonto Gesellschaft. Then Director Friedrich Rintelen sent his son Franz to the United States in 1904, 1905, and 1906 to learn the craft of international finance.[175] He was to become the youngest director of the Diskonto Gesellschaft and the infamous "Dark Invader" in 1915.[176]

The international economic climate in the early nineteen hundreds showed sunshine for the foreseeable future. Just as happens with most business cycles, unforeseen events can suddenly impact the financial summer and initiate a downturn. The profitable days of the new century received a deafening blow at precisely 5:12 a.m. on Wednesday, April 18th 1906. Within forty-two seconds an earthquake somewhere between 7.7 and 8.25 on the Richter scale destroyed the vibrant city of San Francisco and adjacent towns and villages, leaving over three thousand dead.[177] 25,000 buildings in 490 city blocks succumbed to the subsequent fires caused by burst gas lines. Historians estimate the damages caused by the earthquake to have amounted to around $400 Million (8.8 Billion in today's value). While many insurance companies cut corners and did not pay, the hefty insurance payments of the 137 remaining insurers brought the international financial system to the brink.

"In April 1906 the San Francisco earthquake and fire caused damage equal to more than 1 percent of GNP. Although the real effect of this shock was localized, it had an international financial impact: large amounts of gold flowed into the country in autumn 1906 as foreign insurers paid claims on their San Francisco policies out of home funds. This outflow prompted the Bank of England to discriminate against American finance bills and, along with other European central banks, to raise interest rates. These policies pushed the United States into recession which started in June 1907." [178]

As is the case in most economic downturns the retreating levels of cash and liquidity brought to light both legal and illegal financial schemes setting the stage for the Panic of 1907.

The events that led to one of the greatest run on banks in history appear benign and disconnected. On October 16th 1907 the stock of United Copper Company plummeted from a high of $62 per share to $15.[179] It wiped out the fortunes of one F. Augustus Heintze, president of the Mercantile National Bank of New York. The colorful millionaire from Montana had attempted to corner the copper market. John D. Rockefeller, heavily invested in copper commodities, countered Heintze's attempt and unloaded millions of pounds of copper into the market.[180] The price of copper as well as copper shares plummeted. Heintze was finished! The man known on Wall Street as a man whose investments always turned to gold took with him his own savings and loan, the Butte [Montana] Savings Bank and the Mercantile National Bank of New York. Investors quickly learned of the many interconnected schemes of Wall Street players and feared the worst. "Although United Copper was only a moderately important firm, the collapse of Heintze's scheme, exposed an intricate network of interlocking directorates across banks, brokerage houses, and trust companies in New York City. Contemporary observers like O.M.W. Sprague (1910) believed that the discovery of the close associations between bankers and stockbrokers seriously raised the anxiety of already nervous depositors."[181]

Emil Holmdahl (second from right) keeping order in San Francisco 1906[182]

On October 18th 1907, panicking depositors initiated a run on the Knickerbocker Trust Company in New York.[183] John Pierpont Morgan himself entered the fray. He organized a bail out committee including James Stillman (of National City Bank), and George F. Baker (of First National Bank), the most powerful bankers in New York. As Knickerbocker faltered, other banks faced runs on their deposits. The New York Stock Exchange had to cease trading as the bottom fell out. As a committee the three financiers decided on a case-by-case basis whether and with how much to support banks whose deposits faltered. Numerous institutions including the City of New York and the New York Stock Exchange thus survived by the skin of their teeth.[184] By October 24th, J. P. Morgan and the U.S. government decided on a formidable and unprecedented $25 million bailout for New York's financial institutions. John D. Rockefeller, maybe having second thoughts about his role in the panic, seconded the government-backed lifeline with a $10 million commitment of his own. For a while the future of the American financial system hung in the balance. J. P. Morgan asked New York's clergy to pray for "calm and forbearance." Whether with God's or J. P. Morgan's help or as a combination of both, the great bank panic of 1907 ended as quickly as it had come about. Investor confidence recovered within a month and the recession ended in June 1908, almost exactly a year after it had started. The stock market soared to ever-new heights, surpassing pre-panic levels by 1909.[185] However, the shock waves of San Francisco's earthquake of 1906 that combined in catastrophic resonance with the implosion of F. A. Heintze's fortunes in 1907 precipitated the Federal Reserve Act of December 1912.

Although Morgan, Stillman, Baker, Rockefeller, and the American government saved the U.S. financial system in those tense days of October 1907, Wall Street's high-risk gambles had far reaching effects around the world. One of the countries affected most was Mexico. Diaz' regime had successfully rid itself of the dependence on European loans. With the turn of the century American cash had provided the necessary capital for investments in railroads, mining, agriculture, and other industry. Especially the northern states of Mexico, Sonora, Chihuahua, and Coahuila, depended heavily on interstate commerce and U.S. loans. In a matter of months after the recession started in June 1907, the "U.S. depression crippled the Mexican economy."[186] While the crisis of 1907 brought irresponsible financial schemes on Wall Street to the surface, the cash crunch laid bare structural and social deficiencies in Porfirio Diaz' Mexico.

As Wall Street financiers worked to pull the banking system from the brink of collapse, Mexico's economy felt the sting of a tight international credit market. Worried about inflation, the Mexican Finance Minister José Ives Limantour "restricted credit and followed deflationary policies."[187] Between 1907 and 1909, the total revenue of Mexico declined by over fourteen percent.[188] Coinciding with a widespread drought between 1908 and 1909, prices for food and staples increased while real wages decreased. The collapse of metal prices in 1907 left American and Mexican mining operators in Northern Mexico without a viable export market. Thousands of miners lost their jobs while countless others had to stomach pay cuts.

"One of the largest U.S. mining companies doing business in Mexico, the American Smelting and Refining Company (ASARCO), shut down its mines at Santa Eulalia and Santa Barbara in Chihuahua, throwing more than 1,000 people out of work. Most mines in the largest mining center in the state, Hidalgo del Parral, also shut down. The economic empire of William C. Greene, an American tycoon who owned a large number of mines, most of them in Sonora, and had set up vast lumberyards in western Chihuahua, collapsed, greatly increasing the number of unemployed, especially in western Chihuahua."[189]

Greene had already attracted the ire of Mexican workers in 1906 when he "browbeat the governor of Sonora into allowing American irregulars across the border" to break the strike at the Cananea mines.[190] The latest lay-offs and closings of unprofitable pieces in Greene's network of businesses added to the outrage lower and middle class Mexicans felt towards foreign investment in their country. Since the Mexican economy, especially along the northern border, was so tightly linked to that of the United States, there were no jobs for the unemployed miners and impoverished farmers. Widespread discontent with the political leadership of Mexico, which seemed to be out of touch with the economic disaster, increased the clamor for economic and political reform. In Chihuahua the Creel-Terrazas clan who controlled ranches the size of Belgium showed little inclination to ease the suffering.[191] In 1908 the boundless greed of the state's ruling oligarchy reached new heights when robbers stole $300,000 Pesos from the Banco Minero of Chihuahua City, Governor Creel's own bank. After the Chihuahua authorities arrested five suspects, imprisoned and tortured them for the better part of a year, it became clear that it was Creel's own family who had committed the heist.[192] The dire economic situation of workers, farmers, shop owners, and businessmen, the unresolved succession crisis of the aging ruling elite, and the brutal suppression of opposition newspapers and agitators, fomented an explosive mix of discontent among virtually all levels of Mexican society. In this environment three brothers from Germany entered the fray and navigated their late father's business in Parral, Chihuahua in 1908.

CHAPTER 6

~

THE STALLFORTHS IN PRE-
REVOLUTIONARY CHIHUAHUA

*F*ueled by the recession, Chihuahua in the summer of 1908 was buzzing with activity. Laid-off miners tried to find new employment. Thousands of Mexican laborers streamed across the border to return south as the U.S. economy shed jobs. The local newspapers, especially Silvestre Terrazas' El Correo, printed ever-new government scandals involving Enrique Creel and his family. This far related cousin of Luis Terrazas became the voice of the disenfranchised middle classes. Local merchant houses such as Krakauer, Zork and Moye and Nordwald SA worked hard to maintain their businesses in the recession. Worried about their investments American businessmen pressured the Creel government to lower taxes and battle inflation. Mine operators appealed to the local banks for loans. The cash crunch in Northern Mexico had driven cost of capital from an average of twelve percent to eighteen, even twenty-four percent.[193]

In the small town of Hidalgo del Parral in Chihuahua, two German immigrants, the brothers Frederick and Bernhard Stallforth had established a merchant business in 1862 at the onset of the French occupation of Mexico.[194] As the business flourished the Stallforth Y Hermanos Company became the leading regional bank and investment house of the frontier town. The successful colonialists had the right instinct for business. Their investments into the booming mining industry produced huge profits. On April 4th 1882, a Tuesday, Bernardo Stallforth's beautiful wife Emilia gave birth to her first son, Frederico. He had dark brown eyes, just like his mother. Most importantly little Iko, as his mother called him, was born in good health. Emilia, twenty-eight years old, could not have been more relieved. The city of Parral, where she and her husband Bernardo lived, was not exactly a metropolis. 220 miles north of Mexico City and in the far Southwest corner of the state of Chihuahua, the old silver mining town was on the Mexican frontier, the "Wild North of Mexico." However, in comparison to the scant luxuries available to most Mexican citizens, Emilia could not complain. She and her sister Sophia, who was a year older, had married into the most important and wealthy family in town.

By the time of Frederico's birth the Stallforth brothers provided foreign investors, mostly American, British, Spanish and French, the ability to finance mining development, street construction, bridges, the regional power plant, and electrification projects. Presumably for health reasons, the year before Iko's birth, Don Frederico and his wife, Emilia's sister Sophia, had moved back to Wiesbaden, Germany, and left the active management of the business to the younger brother Bernardo, now thirty-nine-years old. Quickly, Stallforth Y Hermanos became the largest trading house in the region with financial connections to one of the most powerful German banking houses, the Deutsch-Südamerikanische Bank, subsidiary of the Dresdner Bank and the up and coming competition to Bleichröder und Sohn. The Stallforths also invested heavily into the social development of their newfound community and were known as great philanthropists. The official government website for Parral describes the Stallforth heritage:

"Don Frederick arrived in Hidalgo del Parral in 1862, close to 28 years old and moved to Wiesbaden, Germany, in 1881. During his short stay of 19 years he worked wonders, creating major industries and thus brought jobs to the regional economy: The Power Parral Mines procuring agency concentrated mineral ore from all the regional mines; the Power Plant which generated enough power for its [Parral's] industries; he donated electric light poles for the downtown; the Factory of Stoves and Heaters Parral; the Factory of Crucibles and Refractory Brick; the Maison Stallforth industrial supply and hardware store; he donated the Botica Charity; the Industrial School for Girls; the school La Esperanza; The Mercado Hidalgo; Guanajuato Bridge; the statue of Don Miguel Hidalgo, the bust of José María Morelos, etc., etc."[195]

La Escuela Frederico Stallforth, donated by Frederico Senior in 1885 still exists today and proudly acknowledges the name of its founder as "el benefactor, quien donó el terreno donde se construyó el edificio."[196] When hunger struck the population of Parral in 1877 as a result of a horrifically bad harvest, Don Frederico bought "large quantities of corn in Durango and afterwards sold it at cost to the entire needy population of the region..."[197] One of the most prestigious buildings in downtown is the Casa Stallforth, today a hotel. Don Frederico financed the construction of this luxurious palace in 1908. Its baroque façade is decorated with Nordic mythological beings. The Casa Stallforth housed the renowned bank Stallforth Y Hermanos until the business finally folded in the 1920s.

It would be unfair to leave out the efforts of other Parral families in the development of the city. There was the Griessen family, Austrian immigrants who also made a fortune in the mining business, the Urquidi family who later intermarried with the Stallforths, and members of the Terrazas family whose patriarch Luis was governor of Chihuahua off and on between 1860 and 1904. Luis Terrazas owned more than seven million acres of ranching land in Chihuahua. The city also had a large immigrant community. French, German, Spanish, Italian, and American all organized their little clubs and get-togethers. The big money could be found in the Masonic Lodge, founded and presided for a long time by Don Frederico Stallforth. Bernardo and later his son Frederico together with his younger brothers Alberto and Alfredo all had a chair.

However, while the wealth of the Stallforth brothers grew, the daily chore of conducting business on the frontier took its first tragic toll when Frederico was three. It was one of many heartbreaking personal tragedies that Frederico suffered throughout his life. In April 1885, Emilia Haase-Stallforth who had just recovered from the recent birth of her third son, Alfredo, suddenly died as a result of a high fever. The three boys, three years, two years, and two months old suddenly found themselves without a mother. Don Bernardo, in charge of the burgeoning business, found little time for the children. Rather than sending the boys to school, Bernardo organized for them to be home schooled. While the brothers were well taken care of, Bernardo still could not close the gaping void only a mother's warmth can fill.

By October 1887, two and-a-half years after Emilia's death Bernardo remarried. His new wife, Anna Haase, was Frederico's aunt (his mother's sister) who knew all about the family and Parral from her many visits. She immediately took charge of the household, the children's education and the needs of her extremely hardworking husband. It was important to Bernardo that his children received a solid humanistic education and that certainly posed some problems in a mining town on the northern frontier of Mexico. By 1890 the Stallforth business had grown tremendously. In addition to dozens of mines, the Stallforths now operated the largest warehousing operation in Parral, collecting, processing, and distributing the many tons of gold, silver, lead, zinc, antimony, copper, and manganese ore that the regional mines produced. In addition to the mining business, the Stallforth bank financed large development projects, electrification of the city, the local power plant, bridges, and roads. However, as a result of increased demand in labor, wages and prices for goods had risen, which gave way to a recession between 1892 and 1894. [198]

The couple also had three more children: Emilia, known as Millie born August 11th 1888, Andrea born November 10th 1890, and Hermann, born January 31st 1893. When Frederico turned eleven, in the midst of economic recession, Bernardo and Anna decided to move the family to Germany. Bernardo wanted to make sure that his six children received a solid German education and experienced German culture and family heritage. They traveled by coach to Chihuahua, from there by train to El Paso then headed to Chicago. It is not clear why the family decided to pass through Chicago instead of proceeding directly to New York via St. Louis. It is probably safe to assume that the 1893 World Fair, which had just opened its doors to the public on May 1st, had something to do with it. The "World's Columbian Exhibition," as the Chicago World's Fair was formally called was the largest world exhibition yet with famous firsts such as AC/DC current, which lit the international exhibition building, and the first hamburger in America, to name but a few. [199] The fair also exhibited the work of the best architects in the world. Particularly interesting to Bernardo might have been the Mines and Mining Building, which exhibited the state-of-the-art mining and metallurgy technology in the world. "Although Mexico planned an extravagant exhibition for the monumental 1893 Chicago Columbian Exhibition, the economic crisis of the 1890s forced the wizards of progress to lower their sights." [200]

While initially planning to create an encore to the very successful Aztec palace in Paris in 1889, the Porfirian government cancelled its own Mexican pavilion and concentrated instead on several, cheaper, yet impressive and successful, exhibits. Mexico's mining exhibit traditionally was one of the most impressive. Visitors could marvel at the extravagant displays of gold, silver, copper, steel, lead, opals, onyx, granites, and marbles. [201] All in all, Mexico won an impressive 1,195 awards for its exhibits in Chicago. "The exposition covered more than 600 acres (2.4 km^2), featuring nearly 200 new buildings of classical architecture, canals and lagoons, and people and cultures from around the world. Over 27 million people (equivalent to about half the U.S. population) attended the exposition during its six-month run. Its scale and grandeur far exceeded the other world fairs, and it became a symbol of the emerging American Exceptionalism." [202]

No one knows the source of Bernardo's illness, but while in Chicago, he fell ill. He developed a high fever. Sadly, after a short sickness, tragedy hit again. On the 3rd of June 1893, at age fifty, while resting in the Hotel Leland in downtown Chicago, Bernardo Stallforth died of acute pneumonia.[203] He was initially cremated at Graceland Cemetery in Chicago, Illinois, but later transferred to the municipal cemetery of Parral where his grave can be visited today.[204] He left six children behind. Anna's three children had lost their father being five, three, and a few months old. The three older boys had now lost both parents. Just as their stepmother, they were looking towards an unknown future on their way to an unknown country, being raised by a stepmother, aunts, and uncles they did not know.

After the funeral Anna continued on to Germany and raised the children there. After finishing school in Germany, Frederico Stallforth drifted around Europe studying languages and dabbling in his uncle's business. In 1907 he married a Bavarian industrialist's daughter, Anita Risse. Stallforth's youth was marked by a chronic shortage of money. His uncle Frederick maintained tight control of his father's inheritance, and recurring health problems hampered Frederico's early business career. His diary shows a response to one of his likely frequent attempts to raise money from family members.

"(Heine) When the leeches have sucked enough blood, one simply has to sprinkle some salt on their backs and they fall off – But you, my friend, how can I get rid of you?

Your despairing cousin"[205]

In 1908 Frederico and his brothers Alberto and Alfredo finally secured a large part of their father's inheritance. On the 9th of November 1908, Frederico Stallforth left for Boston on the steamer "Wilhelm der Grosse" to finalize the founding of a new mining concern, the Mexico Consolidated Mining and Smelting Company. In it, Frederico with his brothers Alberto and Alfredo brought together the properties their father Bernardo had left them. Rather than trying to manage the hodgepodge of mines with Uncle Frederick breathing down their necks, Frederico and his brothers secured a loan in Chicago for $50,000 (over $1 million in today's value), bought out the uncle's interest and started a new venture. Frederico was bursting with pride when the new Board of Directors came together on November 14th 1908 in Boston and elected him "President." Postmarked November 22nd, Anita received a letter from her husband, addressed to "Frau Präsident A. Stallforth." In it he graciously shared his success with her, "...you made me what I am, and my whole family should be grateful that through you I saved the company and the honor of our name."[206] Clearly, Stallforth's need to prove himself to his uncle, and in a larger sense to the world, was his greatest motivation.

Times were tough in Chihuahua in 1908. The Stallforth brothers just like many small and mid-size companies in Chihuahua had to realize that there would be no easy way to obtain a significant loan from a local source. It is in this context one has to view the incredible success that Frederico Stallforth achieved when he obtained the $50,000 loan in Boston and became president of the reorganized Mexican Consolidated Mining Company. The Chihuahua Enterprise reported on the creation of this new company on December 5th.[207] The Manual of Statistics of 1910 listed the company as follows:

MEXICO CONSOLIDATED MINING & SMELTING CO.

A corporation formed under the laws of Maine, July 8, 1904. The company's property, title to which is derived from the Mexican Government, is at San Pedro, Guanacevi Mining District, State of Durango, Mexico. It comprises 21 adjoining claims or about 200 acres, which has been developed and is shipping high grade ore and concentrates.

Stock Par $10 Authorized, $2,500,000 Issued, $2,459,020

The stock is full paid and non-assessable. Transfer Agent, Federal Trust Co., Boston. Registrar, First National Bank, Boston.

Dividends of 50 cents per share were paid quarterly in February (25), May, August and November. The November, 1907, dividend was passed, but 25 cents per share was paid March 10, 1908. To that date the total amount paid in dividends was $660,000. No dividends were paid in 1909.

President, Frederick Stallforth, Parral, Mexico. Vice-President, John C. Fairchild, Boston. Secretary and Assistant Treasurer, W. J. Freeman, Boston. Treasurer, A. Stallforth, Parral.

Directors—John C. Fairchild, Boston. Ambrose I. Harrison, New York. T. Ellett Hodgskin. New York. William S. McCornick, Salt Lake City. Spencer W. Richardson, Boston. William J. Riley, Boston. Samuel S. Rosenstamm, New York. John R. Schermerhorn, East Orange, N. J., A. Stallforth, Parral, Mexico. Frederick Stallforth, Parral. Joseph R. Walsh, New York.[208]

The details of Stallforth's acquisition of the loan illustrate his most important and intrinsic characteristics as a networker and tenacious fundraiser. Alberto Stallforth had already moved to Parral from Germany in May 1907. Initially, he listed his residence in the U.S. immigration papers as El Paso, possibly as a result of the ongoing disputes with Uncle Friedrich. As a reserve officer he had to register with the German Consulate in Chihuahua. Alberto met the German consul in Chihuahua, Otto Kueck, in the summer of 1908. The consul had spent almost two years in Germany to recuperate from a liver illness. For the next years, Alberto helped Kueck with consular duties in Parral.

His dedication to the German community in Parral earned him the title of consular agent. Alberto would retain this responsibility until 1915 and resumed it in 1931.[209] His fulltime job, however, was to manage the Stallforth Y Hermanos operations.

In May 1908, Frederico and stepmother Anna with her two daughters Millie and Andrea took a steamer to New York.[210] While Anna and the girls proceeded to Parral, Frederico scoured the Northeast cities of the United States for the previously mentioned loan. The financially well-connected father-in-law Risse had given Frederico a number of contacts to explore. However, it seemed to be a contact the Stallforths had through their uncle Friedrich that proved to be the winning ticket. In New York, working at 25 Broad Street, the headquarters of the Pierce Oil Company, was an old friend of the family who had "known the Stallforth brothers personally since they came to maturity."[211] Andrew D. Meloy, who will feature prominently in World War I, had organized an investor consortium to invest in the development of public works, mainly railroads, in Mexico.[212] Born in 1867 in Carlyle, Pennsylvania of Irish immigrants, Meloy had made a fortune as a promoter of business in Mexico. Five feet, nine inches tall, high forehead, gray eyes, and brown hair, Meloy projected the image of a tough, even ruthless businessman. His only apparent weakness was his hearing, or lack thereof, which required him to converse in a booming voice with a large funnel held to the side of his head.

When Stallforth approached him about the need for a loan, Meloy concocted the idea of a new company, consolidating the mining properties the Stallforth's held in Guanacevi, Durango. Since Meloy's railroad project connected through Guanacevi, "...it was of the utmost importance to my own interest to conserve the business of the largest potential shipper on the line of my railway."[213] Stallforth immediately took a liking to the idea especially since he would be president and CEO of the new company. Meloy, possibly sensing that his own money would be too much at risk for the time being, took a commission for connecting Stallforth with a group of investors in Boston and New York. What seemed to have escaped the investors was a pattern that accompanied Meloy's business ventures like a foul smell. In a lawsuit in December of 1902, stockholders took Meloy to court claiming that he had purposely misrepresented real estate values.[214] The investment turned out to be worthless, much like the Stallforth business in the middle of a great recession. Following the pattern *The Mines Register* showed the following entry in its 1918 edition:

GUANACEVI TUNNEL CO. MEXICO
Letters returned from 55 Liberty St., New York. Mine at Guanacevi Santiago Papasquiaro, Durango, Mex.
Inc. 1904, in Arizona. Cap., $5,000,000; shares $5 par.
Property: in hands of trustee until conditions in Mexico permit of financing company sufficiently to carry on the extensive development planned.
Lands: 22 properties, about 700 hectares, including timber rights and original concessions, said to possess large bodies of gold and copper ore. The mine has 3 shafts, of 100' depth each, with tunnels of 1,250' and 1,400', the main tunnel, 7x9', planned to be driven about 3 kilometers, management estimating that in this distance a large number of veins carrying lead and copper ores should be cut, the tunnel being estimated as likely to cost about $250,000.
The Mexican Western railroad from Tepehuanes to Guanacevi [Meloy's project] should add materially to value of property.
The L. Diamond Co., of Boston, was never a representative of this corporation, but a number of brokers bought stock and combined to unload on the public at unduly high prices. Debts amounted to $150,000 in 1912 and have since increased.
Idle."[215]

Another worthless project with investors left hanging!

Frederico left again for Germany in July 1908 to return in August for one month with brother-in-law Alfred Risse in tow. After spending September and October with his wife in Munich, Frederico arrived in Boston in November, secured the loan and met up with his brothers in Parral in the beginning of December. His youngest brother Alfredo had meanwhile also arrived in Parral in the summer.[216] In his quest to save the family business in Parral, Frederico had aligned himself with at least two questionable characters: Juan Creel and Andrew Meloy. It is hard to say whether Stallforth consciously sought out those types of characters, or whether he simply did not care. The latter seems to have been the case. Stallforth had no qualms about where funds were coming from in his lifelong pattern of boom and bust. Again and again, he used crooks such as Meloy to receive the benefits of their network without having to do the dirty work himself. Meloy promised the world to the people contributing money to Stallforth's venture and, when it failed, both could shrug off the losses of their investors. Stallforth benefited from networks of people with money who he could excite. Meloy defined his and inadvertently Stallforth's role: "My business ... had been the promotion of important enterprises..."[217]

Promotion! No investment required except networking. Stallforth turned out to be one of the best. He took great care to maintain his contacts to financial circles in New York, Boston, and Chicago in the years to come. This network would prove very handy for him in the next decade when the German government tasked him to raise funds for war-time operations in the U.S. Meloy, his senior brother-in-arms, would be at his side!

Alberto, nominally treasurer of the business took on the actual management of the new company in San Pedro, Durango. Throughout the first year Alberto frequently traveled to Chihuahua City and stayed in the Palacio Hotel. He met with Mexican government agencies, banks, railroads, and other businesses, negotiating taxes, titles, and fees. Stallforth Y Hermanos, the merchant house and small bank of the Stallforth brothers worked closely with Chihuahua's largest bank, Governor Creel's Banco Minero. The Stallforth's also represented the Deutsch Südamerikanische Bank in Parral. This banking connection brought the brothers in contact with most large enterprises of the region, such as the American Smelting and Refining Company ASARCO, businesses of the Maderos, De La Garzas, Creels, and Terrazas. Numerous small local businesses received loans from the Stallforth Bank.

In the course of 1908 repayment of these loans ground to a halt and the Stallforth business slid deeper into the morass of Mexico's recession. The records of Chihuahua's municipal archives show that the Stallforth brothers seemed to hold ever more titles to land and mining properties all over Chihuahua and Durango in 1909.[218] At the same time their business in San Pedro, consisting of mines, mills, and smelters descended deeper and deeper into debt.[219] The logic for this seeming expansion of the ownership of mines and real estate between 1908 and 1910 was that the Stallforth brothers received titles instead of loan repayments. These properties, although on paper representing value, consisted of largely defunct businesses spread all over the region that, rather than helping cash flow, further dragged their financials down. Andrew D. Meloy, Frederico's partner in New York, explained to State Department agents in August, 1915: "The firm [Stallforth Y Hermanos] itself came to be in a very bad way due to the fact that it was carrying as security for great loans mortgages and realty whose negotiable value many times the amount of loans extended had dropped to a fraction of the amount of these loans."[220]

Transporting ore to mills and smelters via railroad and mule trains cost a fortune. By 1910 the Consolidated Mining and Smelting Company had accumulated $362,075 in debt (over $7.5 million in today's value), owing money to among others Creel's Banco Minero and the group of investors in Boston. Juan Creel, who in 1910 still was president of the Banco Minero, negotiated for the Stallforth brothers in New York.[221] He had organized the previously mentioned "great heist" on the Banco Minero in 1908. The fact that two years later Juan still ran the bank shows the degree of disdain and corruption the Creel administration projected to the citizens of Chihuahua.

While Alberto frantically worked on shoring up the business, Frederico's guest book alludes to extensive travels between 1908 and 1910: December 21st 1908, on the "SS Lusitania" back to Germany; April 21st 1909 to Durango via New York; July 12th via El Paso to New York; August 3rd from Boston to New York; August 23rd arrival in Parral. In October Alberto went to Germany to talk to Uncle Friedrich about the situation of the business. In December, Frederico sailed on the "Mauretania" to Germany and spent Christmas with Uncle Friedrich and his family. A highly contentious confrontation with the uncle in 1906 obviously did not keep the two brothers from trying to get the family patriarch to give financial aid. However hard Frederico tried, Uncle Friedrich stayed firm. As Friedrich's monument, the Casa Stallforth, described in Parral's tourist guides as a "majestic residential palace," received final touches in 1909, the business of the two nephews turned sour.[222]

In 1910, Frederico Stallforth pulled all registers in his effort to raise funds for his fledgling company. In April, after conferring with his father-in-law Risse and probably as a result of Risse's connections, Stallforth had an appointment with Albert Ballin.[223] Ballin headed the Hamburg-Amerika Linie as general director. With friendly connections to the Kaiser, Ballin was one of the most successful international businessmen Germany had ever produced. What the young merchant from Parral exactly discussed with the shipping tycoon can only be surmised. Ballin could open doors all over the world, especially in Berlin and New York. Five days after the meeting Stallforth traveled to Berlin. He did not record his meetings there. Whether or not he managed to be received at Bleichröder's or the Deutsche Bank did not change the fact that no new source of finances appeared on the horizon for the Stallforth brothers. However, Frederico could now count Albert Ballin among his growing network of financiers and businessmen in the U.S. and Germany. In May, Stallforth returned to Parral. On June 26th, he reported to his anxious business partners in Boston. Under pressure they agreed to grant the Stallforths another $50,000 loan, secured through a French bank.[224] From Boston Frederico went to the business partners in New York trying to find further financing but to no avail.

On October 15th the Mexico Consolidated Mining and Smelting Company ran out of cash. The troubles started on the 6th of October when auditors, sent as representatives of the Boston investors, took the Stallforth brothers' books apart. The audit showed devastating problems, over $110,000 ($2.3 million in today's value) in inventory discrepancies, some already written off as losses others still open in the books. The commissary store was loaded with "...obsolete merchandise...that ... are old conserves, which, when opened, with a kind of explosion, show some modern sense of areoplanatic [sic] intentions."[225] Expenses had gone through the roof as a result of the "conditions of our business, making rapid communications more necessary than in other periods when a business runs without much [sic] difficulties."[226] The audit showed that the company not only failed as a result of the hostile economic environment and loss of economies of scale, but also because of serious mismanagement. Alberto and Frederico had lost control over the expenses. Rather than managing the outflows of their company as the business contracted, lingering problems such as inaccurate and obsolete inventories obscured a good overview of the situation. It seemed that both Alberto and Frederico were way over their heads in these troublesome days.

On October 11th the Stallforths attempted to cash the $50,000 note that Frederico had negotiated in June. The bank refused. His partners in Boston had withdrawn their support and on October 17th called their note for the original loan of $50,000. Alberto had no choice but to shut down operations. The 3,000 souls of San Pedro saw their largest employer go bankrupt. Company workers had already gone unpaid for a while. Understandably they feared now that they would have to forfeit their owed wages for good. Frederico went with Juan Creel to New York on the 17th to find a solution. Creel proposed reorganization to the stockholders, which they promptly rejected.[227] The situation at the San Pedro office became volatile the next day. Alberto warned Frederico of impending disaster: "I have another telegram from Guanacevi. The workmen threaten to injure the mine and the mill and it will result in an overflow of the water into the mines if their payroll is not paid by management. The management have wired [sic] today to the Board of Directors at Boston."[228] Frederico did his best to pressure the angry business partners to save the drowning business. The choice seemed logical: Either funding found its way to the "animal like, rough worker mob" or the whole business would be destroyed.[229] Whether Alberto Stallforth chose this description of his Mexican labor force to impress the business partners in Boston, or really had such disdain for the angry mob of San Pedro cannot be ascertained. "We strongly advise you," Stallforth notified the Board on October 18th, "in your own interest, if the stockholders do not understand the situation, to provide for funds some way or other...if any debt is committed through riots or through a drowning of the mine, it will be harder, if not impossible to get the mine on a paying basis. We fear this is not properly understood in Boston."[230] The question begs of how volatile the situation really was. The evidence is contained in several frantic telegrams sent between the San Pedro office in Durango and Alberto Stallforth in Parral. On the 18th of October Alberto agreed to pay whatever was necessary in order to prevent the workers from flooding the mine. "Do not cease pumping under no [sic] circumstances whatever Stallforth willing to pay pumping charge but nothing more." He notified Frederico that same day about the "Formation of bandit gangs, managers in danger..."[231] Alberto asked his manager in San Pedro "Wire immediately fully consequences you anticipate if payroll not paid....are workman likely to riot [?]" The answer did not come back. The company shut down. Frederico and Alberto were devastated. On November 2nd an entry in Frederico's guest book shows his friends' attempts to cheer him up:

"A good mine makes a good manager, but it is not always that a good manager makes a good mine, Parral, Nov 2nd, 1910
    Allen T. Rogers"[232]

233

64

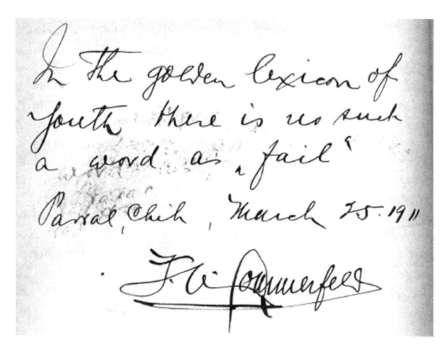

A few months later, Felix Sommerfeld admonished his depressed friend that "In the golden lexicon of youth there is no such a word as 'fail' Parral, Chih, March 25, 1911

F. A. Sommerfeld"[234]

The angry workers of San Pedro, a town of three thousand souls, took whatever they could then flooded the shafts. Mexico Consolidated was the largest employer of the town. When the mine, the mills and the two smelters shut down, the citizens of San Pedro faced a catastrophe. The story of the Mexico Consolidated Mining and Smelting Company is not unique. Next door another investment promoted by Andrew Meloy, the Guanacevi Tunnel Company closed with the same result.[235] Companies throughout the region folded and left whole towns without any means to support their residents. In addition to the economic depression an unprecedented drought in 1909 and 1910 had robbed farming communities in Northern Mexico of their harvests. As if the drought was not enough, a huge earthquake destroyed the ocean front town of Acapulco in July of 1909. Natural catastrophe, the bad economy, vast unemployment, and food shortages, especially among the lower classes of Chihuahua, Durango, and Coahuila, created this unique, volatile mix that fuels social revolutions.

The financial situation remained dire for the three brothers. While the Stallforth Y Hermanos merchant house and bank remained open until 1920, it did not recover from the disastrous end of the mining venture. Frederico had signed for the $50,000 loan in 1908 and it hung over the young entrepreneur like the sword of Damocles. He was personally responsible for repaying it. While the brothers never repaid the loans taken from the Banco Minero, which Pancho Villa confiscated in 1914, they owed money to many other businesses in Chihuahua and Durango. While Alfredo and Alberto continued to run things in Parral, Frederico kept working on finding venture capital in New York. One of the great hopes for their financial recovery was Francisco Madero. While the brothers did not know the revolutionary leader well, they counted on their connection to Felix Sommerfeld. Sommerfeld, within months of the outbreak of the revolution, became one of the most trusted advisors of the future president.

CHAPTER 7

~

APPRENTICESHIP IN SPY CRAFT

A s the Diaz regime slipped deeper and deeper into disfavor with most sectors of Mexican society, Felix Sommerfeld also settled in Chihuahua in the course of 1908. Within the next two years, Sommerfeld would become the most important intelligence asset of the German government in Mexico, and the highest-ranking foreigner in the inner circle of the Mexican presidency. His impact influenced the course of the Mexican Revolution and Mexican-American bilateral relations. Not all details of the German's dramatic rise onto the stage of world politics have been preserved in the historical record. However, one fact, which Sommerfeld tried his best to obscure, will be undeniable: He had help. Whether he arrived from Germany or Canada on orders of the German Naval Intelligence Service, or on his own reconnaissance, the German immediately began building a powerful network comprising the most important players of Northern Mexico.

Within a year Sommerfeld became a spokesman for the German community of Chihuahua. Porfirian leaders such as General Navarro who had charge of the military of Chihuahua, José Ives Limantour, Juan and Enrique Creel, and several members of the Terrazas clan became acquaintances, as did the new generation of revolutionary leaders. By the beginning of the revolution in the fall of 1910, Sommerfeld intimately knew the revolutionary leader Francisco Madero and most if not all his brothers, the future president's uncles Ernesto and Alberto Madero, future governor of Chihuahua and mentor of Pancho Villa, Abraham Gonzalez, military leaders Pascual Orozco and Giuseppe Garibaldi. The German also had the confidence of the German ambassador in Mexico, Rear Admiral Paul von Hintze, diplomats von Richthofen and Rhomberg, the German Commercial Attaché Peter Bruchhausen, German Consul General Rieloff, Vice Consuls Kueck and Weber, and many more. Sommerfeld's network extended to U.S. officials and included the American consul of Chihuahua, Marion Letcher, the customs agent of El Paso, Zach Lamar

Cobb, as well as military commanders along the border such as Colonel Steever and General Pershing. Whether the German agent introduced himself or whether he was presented by German officials does not impact the result, namely that in a very short time with incredible focus and determination Sommerfeld placed himself at the core of economic, military, and political events of the Mexican Revolution. No one could receive, evaluate, and process intelligence better than he. As he saw fit Sommerfeld made Mexican and American officials beneficiaries of his vast knowledge of unfolding events. However, he continuously worked in the interest of his true employer: The imperial German government.

Sommerfeld told the BI agents in 1918 "when I came into Chihuahua I had about $7,000 ($147,000 in today's value)."[236] Considering that Sommerfeld traveled steerage and had to "borrow" money from his relatives in Massachusetts, he grossly overstated his wealth. There is a remote possibility that Sommerfeld received money from inheritance after his father's death in 1907. However, believing Felix' uncle Ed Rosenbaum, he likely arrived in Chihuahua without great financial means. Sommerfeld settled in the Palacio Hotel in downtown Chihuahua, the place where most important travelers stayed on visits. In the lavishly stocked hotel bar, curious observers could overhear bits and pieces of important business being discussed. On August 15th 1908, future Senator for New Mexico, Judge Albert B. Fall of El Paso arrived with his father-in-law, Colonel William Greene, owner of the Consolidated Copper Company in Cananea.[237] Alberto Stallforth arriving from Parral stayed at the Palacio Hotel on August 22nd.[238] On September 5th Colonel Charles Hunt of El Paso, and on September 19th Brigadier General Manual Mondragon, the Secretary of War in the Diaz administration, settled in the hotel.[239] On October 3rd, German charge d'Affairs, Baron Clemens von Radowitz, who "...on visit to the German colony here...[was] met at the train here by Otto Kueck [German Consul], O. Satorius, L. Nordwald [father of Otto], Julio Heyden, and other prominent Germans..."[240]

Von Radowitz had initiated the registration and counting of all German subjects and German owned properties in Mexico on September 2nd 1908.[241] He now toured the country's German consulates to inspect the results of his inquiry. The German community in the State of Chihuahua was quite sizable. The largest German-owned business in the state was Ketelsen and Degetau, a merchant house with branches throughout the state and Texas. Emil Ketelsen, just like many German merchants such as Adolph Krakauer, had settled in Northern Mexico in the late 1800s. By 1892 the merchant firm traded almost anything one could imagine, from Adler sewing machines, glassware, arms and ammunition to real estate. The Ketelsen and Degetau bank, similar to the Stallforth Y Hermanos bank, financed real estate acquisitions, mines, haciendas and the like. Since Chihuahua City had the largest concentration of Germans in the state, Emil Ketelson headed the Vice Consulate there. His business partner and manager of the Ciudad Juarez store, Max Weber was in charge of the vice consulate in that border town. Also employed in the business was Ketelsen's son-in law, a fellow immigrant from Hamburg, Germany, Otto Kueck. When on March 22nd 1905 the well-liked Consul Ketelsen passed away, Kueck took over the diplomatic representation of the German community. He not only inherited the consulate. Through his wife Emilie, Kueck also shared in the sizeable inheritance his father-in-law had left to the three children. The German embassy in Mexico estimated Ketelson to have been worth over one million pesos, almost $11 million in today's value.[242] The German citizenry of the state of Chihuahua in that year consisted of 127 men, of which 87 were merchants, 66 women, and 124 children. Sommerfeld was listed as one of seven German miners in the state.[243]

Quite a few permanent residents stayed at the Palacio Hotel because it had the nicest amenities in the area such as running water. The recession had fathered hosts of transient businessmen, unemployed miners, engineers, and merchants. One such resident of the Palacio Hotel was Leonard Worcester Jr., an assayer and chemist from Leadville, Colorado. He established a good business for himself in the first decade of the new century. Sommerfeld's first engagement in town was to work for Worcester here and there, supplying him with ore samples to be analyzed. A year later, in September 1909, Sommerfeld shared a house with the metallurgist. According to Worcester and numerous other sources, Sommerfeld spent 1908 and 1909, "not engaged in any regular business."[244] The impression Sommerfeld made on Worcester and others in this time, part-time jobs, seemingly aimless wanderings, and the lack of funds all pointed to the early years of a typical soldier-of-fortune, a drifter turned revolutionary. Several historians and the U.S. Justice Department have fallen into this trap. Nothing could be further from the truth. Every single activity of Sommerfeld in those crucial two years before the revolution represented a carefully crafted piece of a plan that led to his meteoric rise.

In his work for Worcester, Sommerfeld came in contact with important businesses such as ASARCO, the largest American owned smelting company in Mexico, the San Troy Mining Company which his friend Donald B. Gillies ran, the Stallforth's Consolidated Mining and Smelting Company, and many more. One of the companies Sommerfeld mentioned in particular was the Exploration Company of England and Mexico. Sommerfeld told investigators in 1918, "...if I found any properties worthwhile....they would give me my commission."[245] While many of his claims about this time do not easily withstand detailed fact checking, his work as a real estate broker on commission seems to be true. On March 26th 1910, while Sommerfeld still roomed with Worcester, the Mining World Magazine mentioned a corroborating article: "The Exploration Co. of England & Mexico, Ltd., is making an extensive examination of the properties of the Santa Eulalia Exploration Co. in the Santa Eulalia camp about 18 miles east of Chihuahua. The properties are among the largest producers in the camp, and are at present shipping about 100 tons daily to the Chihuahua plant of the American Smelting & Refining Co. The examining company lately acquired important holdings in the camp."[246] The company's engineering director R. M. Raymond worked at El Oro in 1903 the same time Sommerfeld did.[247] The corporate effort, the locations of interest, and the time period all match Sommerfeld's claim that he worked in the camps, received commissions, and was able to return to Chihuahua on a weekly basis. A commission based real estate brokerage also did not in any way interfere with any other business he engaged in. The five percent commission agreement could have provided cash for travels and living expenses if Sommerfeld, as he claimed, actually sold properties.

In his interrogation in 1918, the German also specifically mentioned running the mine "La Abundancia" which belonged to the Stallforths.[248] That seemed unlikely. Located in the Baborigame district deep in the Sierra Madre Occidental, this mine was not at all near Cusihuriachic where Sommerfeld claimed to have worked. It is also far away from San Pedro, which is just outside of Torreon, where the Stallforths were running the Mexico Consolidated Mining and Smelting Company. The interrogators did not question Sommerfeld on these details.[249] Sommerfeld wanted the interrogators to believe that he held a full-time job at that time, which he did not. The more likely truth about "La Abundancia" can be assessed from a statement Frederico Stallforth made in 1917. Stallforth testified that he knew Sommerfeld in 1908. "He was in our town in the City of Parral, and at that time he was agent for some mining company and he was trying to sell one of our mines."[250]

How much money he earned in these endeavors remains unknown. Sommerfeld claimed to investigators that he made around 25,000 Pesos (over $250,000 in today's value).[251] This again seems to be a total fabrication designed to portray the image of a settled, successful business life. If

Sommerfeld made his money in real estate the question begs what became of his funds. While he might not have thought of the Stallforth business as a good investment, he had all the connections to get amazing deals anywhere in the mining industry in the recession. A thorough search of all the mining registers and Chihuahua business accounts yielded not a single property, claim, or business share between 1908 and 1913 listed under the name of Sommerfeld. Apparently he invested nothing in mining property, belying further statements he made to the Bureau of Investigation in 1918.[252]

While Sommerfeld worked for Worcester and brokered some real estate, he stayed very active in the social scene of Chihuahua. Within a very short time he became one of recognized leaders of the German community there. This is significant, because especially Germans believe in a hierarchical leadership based on seniority. Sommerfeld neither had seniority nor had he achieved anything worthwhile in the community. The only explanation for his rise in the German community can be that his position was sponsored either by the existing leaders or, more likely, a higher authority, namely the German embassy in Mexico City. On January 30th 1909, the Chihuahua Enterprise mentioned the German organizing a celebration of the emperor's birthday:

"**Germans honor their Kaiser**. Local colony remember their emperor on his birthday…After a patriotic air of the orchestra, Miss Ines Villar recited an appropriate introductory poem composed by F. Sommerfeld…During the supper some of the young men brought around and sold the paper gotten out for the occasion, the 'Deutsche Kolonial Zeitung.' This created no end of fun as practically every German in the colony came in for his share of the 'roast.' F. Sommerfeld got out this paper and deserves much credit therefor [sic]."[253]

Through which connections Sommerfeld was able to secure several copies of the *Kolonialzeitung* leaves room for conjecture. The publisher of this paper was the Department of Colonial Affairs in Berlin headed by Dr. Bernhard Dernburg, the only Jewish cabinet member of the time. In 1914, Dr. Dernburg became head of the German propaganda effort in the U.S. and was in his own words, a close friend of Sommerfeld.[254] When or how this friendship developed between the German reservist and this imperial cabinet member is unknown. Did Sommerfeld know Dernburg in Germany and received an occasional "care package" from him? Whether the paper came from Germany directly to Sommerfeld or via the German embassy in Mexico City is not important. Significant is the fact that in 1909 Sommerfeld, not Kueck or other established leaders of the German community of Chihuahua, had connections that reached further in the German power structure than anyone else's.

Apart from Sommerfeld's activism in the German community, he also pursued other social circles. Immediately after his arrival in 1908, the German joined the Club Bohemio of Chihuahua. Not much is known about this organization other than "...this nice society formed by young members of our first circle was founded on December 21, 1904. As a prerequisite of membership in the Club Bohemio, members have to be single ..."[255] The single men of Chihuahua represented a kind of "Who's Who" in the business world of the state. The club included members such as Agustín Terrazas, Luis Creel, both part of the ruling oligarchy of Chihuahua, Otto Nordwald, son of furniture maker Henry Nordwald, lawyers Pascual Garcia, Salvador Yáñez and Francisco Cordero, mining engineers Luis Bárcenas, Carlos Escobar, José Muñoz, mining entrepreneur Donald B. Gillies, and merchant Federico Moye. There is no indication of this club to ever having engaged in any political activism other than Federico Moye who unsuccessfully challenged the governor's seat in 1911. However, keeping in mind the social and economic status of its members, the group, other than perhaps the Creel and Terrazas men, represented very much the politically and economically disenfranchised middle class of pre-revolutionary Mexico. This group formed the basis of support for Francisco Madero in his coming revolution but had little sympathy for the more radical ideologies of the Flores Magon brothers or Emiliano Zapata.

Through the financial connections of the Stallforth brothers Sommerfeld met Governor Enrique Creel and his brother Juan just around the time of the great Banco Minero scandal that so enraged the Mexican public.[256] Also in town was Alberto Madero, the future president's uncle, with whom Sommerfeld became closely acquainted.[257] Gustavo Madero, Francisco's brother, owned mining properties in Parral and was acquainted both with the Stallforths and Sommerfeld. "In Chihuahua I knew everybody," Sommerfeld boasted to the American interrogators in 1918. The question of whether he "met all the politicos in Chihuahua City" he answered with a clear "yes."[258] His network did not limit itself to the capital of this one state. The Chihuahua Enterprise reported on June 12th 1909 under "local and personal," "F. A. Sommerfeld has gone to Mexico City on business."[259]

Another part-time occupation for which Sommerfeld became known was his work for AP News. While no record exists to show his employment, he did make contact with the Chicago office of the Associated Press sometime before 1910.[260] His contact was Chris D. Haggerty of the Chicago office of AP, not New York, where the Associated Press was headquartered.[261] In 1910 Sommerfeld started working for Haggerty as a stringer. Just like his real estate brokerage, this arrangement allowed Sommerfeld to travel freely, make some money on the side, and not be pressed into a close working relationship. He told investigators that the reason he worked with correspondent Haggerty was that the Chicago journalist could not speak Spanish. Working for the press bore significant advantages for Sommerfeld. He gained easier access to the higher echelons of the political scene in Chihuahua. With a press pass, Sommerfeld could also cross the border between Mexico and the United States without having to register with immigration officials.[262]

There certainly were great stories to cover in Chihuahua. In the summer of 1910, future revolutionary hero Pancho Villa gunned down bandit-companion-turned-police-informer Claro Reza in broad daylight.[263] Pancho Villa's mentor, future revolutionary Governor of Chihuahua, Abraham Gonzalez, headed the office of Madero's anti-reelectionist party in the state capital. Sommerfeld told interrogators in 1918, "I knew [Villa] better than anyone else. I had known him since 1910."[264] It would be a natural for American news organizations to take the pulse of the opposition in interviews with this powerful Madero ally. Although Sommerfeld's work for AP News finds lots of mention in the historiography, he was never mentioned as an author in a single news story that appeared in Chicago papers between 1908 and 1913. According to the German agent, he "sent some telegrams to the Associated Press in Chicago about the Mexican conditions."[265] Haggerty then most likely became the author of resulting articles. Sommerfeld mentioned his initial meeting with Francisco Madero to have been on the occasion of an exclusive interview in the spring of 1911 at Madero's Hacienda of Bustillos near Casas Grandes. Journalist Timothy Turner published the only known exclusive interview with Madero while he was in Bustillos in 1911. Turner never mentioned Sommerfeld and AP News. Neither did Chris Haggerty ever publish an interview with the future president.[266] However, Sommerfeld indeed interviewed Madero in April of 1911, although not for Haggerty but rather on behalf of the German government.[267] The German's connections to the rebels at the very least provided Haggerty with a convenient introduction to the future president and his inner circle sometime in the spring of 1911.

Sommerfeld's main occupation in that time period was of a completely different nature than dabbling in a multitude of part-time occupations. While trying his best to hide his links to German authorities, he did slip to the BI interrogators in 1918 that he had a relationship with the German consul.[268]

Sommerfeld's relationship with Kueck was far closer than the German agent cared to admit. It was Felix Sommerfeld in the spring of 1910, still months before the Madero Revolution, who single-handedly elevated the vice consulate of Chihuahua to become a fully accredited consulate. On April 10th 1910, Sommerfeld, as a "leading representative" of the German community of Chihuahua wrote a letter, which the embassy forwarded to the imperial German chancellor. In it Sommerfeld praised the accomplishments of Vice Consul Kueck.[269] The intervention succeeded and Kueck was promoted to full consul on April 28th 1911.[270] Kueck, who on account of his wife was a very rich man, certainly did not need the pay increase. However, the prestige of this diplomatic status was priceless.

As he built his social network around the business and political elites of the state, Sommerfeld honed his influence with the German community, elevated its diplomatic leader to consul, and participated in its festivities. While observers such as Worcester did not recognize the patterns in Sommerfeld's activities, the German embassy in Mexico City and its Chihuahua representatives Kueck and Weber are keys to understanding the seemingly unrelated jobs. Leonard Worcester testified in 1917 that Sommerfeld "...acted during this time [1908 to 1911] as confidential agent for the German consul at Chihuahua [Otto Kueck], and was in the consul's pay."[271] The sudden appearance in Chihuahua of Felix Sommerfeld, the Stallforth brothers, Consul Otto Kueck, and Commercial Attaché Peter Bruchhausen within a few months of each other was not by chance.[272]

There is only one interpretation of what Sommerfeld was paid to do for Kueck: Espionage. A report Consul Kueck sent to the German Charge d'Affairs von Richthofen only months before the arrival of Ambassador von Hintze in Mexico is a telling testimony to Sommerfeld's true occupation between 1908 and 1910. Kueck reported on the outbreak of hostilities in the end of November 1910, the start of Madero's push to oust Porfirio Diaz. He mentioned reports that he submitted on November 23rd, 26th, 28th, December 9th, and 22nd. For November 23rd and 28th the archival record contains handwritten reports from none other than Felix Sommerfeld.[273] They were not addressed to Consul Kueck but to Peter Bruchhausen, the German Commercial Attaché in Mexico City. Obviously, Sommerfeld reported directly to Bruchhausen, but copied the consul on his assessments. Peter Bruchhausen finds no mention in the historiography as a member of German Naval Intelligence. He came from the Coblenz region of Germany. As a fraternity brother in a "schlagenden Gesellschaft" Bruchhausen purposely received a scar across one cheek in a fencing competition. [274] Like Sommerfeld he had studied mining engineering and served in the Prussian military before joining the diplomatic corps. Without a doubt, Bruchhausen engaged in intelligence gathering operations in Mexico until his departure in 1913. Sommerfeld was one of his prized assets. In his intelligence report dated November 23rd 1910, Sommerfeld began with the following hint: "Our business will have to rest for a while because the political situation up here is such that no man has the motivation to undertake anything..." [275] What business the German agent referred to can only be surmised. Considering that the German embassy had mainly commercial interests in Mexico and that Bruchhausen was the commercial attaché, Sommerfeld was likely engaged in gathering economic and political intelligence. Sommerfeld's trips to Mexico City, mentioned in the Chihuahua Enterprise periodical, fit this theory. As with any task the ambitious German took on, he must have done a good job. So good, indeed, that when Kueck had to admit that he lacked detailed information on the Insurrectos, he reported to the German charge d'Affairs in Mexico City on December 22nd that he had put the right man in charge: "Felix Sommerfeld, who your Excellency knows, is in the field since 14 days and I have expected reports from him daily, which regrettably as a result of disruption of cables have not come forth. As soon as I receive the reports, I will not fail to submit them to your Excellency..."[276]

Sommerfeld's reports contained intimate details concerning government and insurgent troops, their state of readiness, movements, strategy and tactics, casualty counts and the like.[277] His work for AP News also could have served his mission. In 1905 the German ambassador to Mexico wrote to then Reichskanzler von Bülow, "if the relationship of Mr. Weber [Max Weber, German vice consul at Ciudad Juarez] with the representatives of the 'Associated Press' are indeed so close as he mentioned, the possibility should not be excluded to use the same [relationship] on occasion to float news in the American press which we want to see publicized in a way that would make authorship undetectable."[278]

This statement, although dating back five years from Sommerfeld's employment with AP News, clearly indicates that German diplomats used tools such as news organizations for the purpose of propaganda. This clandestine method became a major tool in World War I. Without any clear evidence but existing throughout his files, the U.S. Justice Department accused Sommerfeld of being engaged in propaganda efforts in Mexico. "[Sommerfeld] formerly associated with Frederico Stallforth and in 1914 he was in Mexico where he was associated...in propaganda work." [279] It seems that his work for AP News just around the outbreak of the Mexican Revolution supports this charge.

Also reporting from the front was Frederico Stallforth who submitted similar reports on the situation in and around Parral. Kueck forwarded the weekly reports to the German Consul General Rieloff. [280] Charge d'Affairs von Richthofen in turn received the reports from the consul general, which undoubtedly made their long administrative journey to the German chancellor. [281] It is impossible to pinpoint the exact day when Sommerfeld started to work as a secret agent for Germany. Very possibly the German came to Chihuahua as part of an intelligence team that comprised Bruchhausen, Kueck, and the Stallforths. If he joined up while living in Chihuahua, his intelligence career started sometime between the fall of 1908 and 1909, when according to Leonard Worcester, he received regular payments from Kueck.

Sommerfeld, the Stallforth brothers, and Kueck became the core of a German intelligence organization that proved to be a crucial asset in World War I. Under the umbrella of what convicted German spy Horst von der Goltz called the "Secret Diplomatic Service," German consuls in every major city in North America gathered and forwarded military, political, and economic intelligence on Mexico and the United States before and during World War I. [282] The information passed through the German embassies of Washington and Mexico City to the Foreign Office and the Department of War. There are some well-known agents in the Great War who came from this cadre of consuls. Most notably Carl Heynen, consul in Tampico and representative of the Hamburg-Amerikanische-Paketfahrt-Aktien-Gesellschaft (HAPAG) in Mexico who transferred to New York in the fall of 1914 and became a key personality in Commercial Attaché Heinrich Albert's organization. The consul of Torreon, Sommerfeld's close friend Otto Schubert, was rumored to have promulgated the Plan de San Diego. The plan attempted to incite Mexican and Mexican-American residents in the U.S. Border States during World War I. However, historians Harris and Sadler have unraveled the origins of the uprising and proved beyond doubt that Germany, while certainly profiting from the mayhem, had nothing to do with creating it. [283] Franz Bopp, the German consul in San Francisco, hired Kurt Jahnke and other German sabotage agents, and engaged in attacks on Canada. He was indicted, convicted, and received serious penitentiary time for his activities. [284] Consul Kueck's role has already been mentioned earlier. The existence of this "Nachrichtendienst" or intelligence service finds mention here and there in surviving historical sources. The German military attaché in Washington, Franz von Papen, received permission from the Abteilung IIIB of the German General Staff (Secret Service) in March 1914 to recruit one of the three vice consuls in Mexico for the "Kriegsnachrichtendienst."[285] Papen's choice became Carl Heynen, the HAPAG aforementioned executive for Mexico and vice consul for the Tampico region. In July 1914, one month before the outbreak of the war, von Papen asked the embassy's Naval Attaché Boy-Ed to manage the intelligence service covering the United States and Mexico while he was traveling.[286]

The assumption of historians on German-American relations always has been that Germany had no intelligence assets to speak of in the U.S. or Mexico before the outbreak of the war.[287] This persistent claim originated from the German chief intelligence officer, Walter Nicolai, in his post-World War I writings.[288] This clearly was not the case. Barbara Tuchman in her book *The Zimmermann Telegram* described a plot by the German Kaiser in 1908 creating the so-called Japanese Panic.[289] According to information from German intelligence sources, ten thousand well-equipped Japanese soldiers had assembled in Mexico in order to intervene in the construction of the Panama Canal and attack the United States. The German Foreign Secretary received word from the German consul in Chihuahua that "2,000 to 3,000 Japanese in Khaki uniforms were there at the moment."[290] Kueck's temporary replacement actively promoted the unrealistic scare of an impending Japanese attack on the United States. William Bayard Hale, American journalist, special envoy of Woodrow Wilson, German propagandist, and personal friend of Felix Sommerfeld, broke the story to the U.S. public when the Kaiser granted him an interview in 1908. The resulting outcry in the United States prompted a call up of reserves along the U.S.-Mexican border. The scare waned as Washington and Tokyo concluded the Root-Takahira Agreement on November 30th 1908, which defined spheres of influence for both countries. Precisely around the time of Sommerfeld and Kueck's arrival, the U.S.-Mexican border was ablaze with military maneuvers.

The German government needed to understand who the next Mexican leaders would be and how to estimate their predisposition to German interests, maybe even find ways to influence their politics. The two candidates contesting Mexico's presidential elections were Bernardo Reyes and Francisco Madero. Clear front-runner was Madero, scion of one of the wealthiest families in Mexico. His support base spanned most of the border states, especially Chihuahua, Durango, Coahuila, and Sonora. In December of 1908, Madero's campaign took on steam, fueled with the publication of his bestselling book, *La Sucesión Presidencial en 1910*, in which he declared his candidacy.[291] The motto of Madero's campaign echoed the people's demand for "no reelection" of President Diaz. Francisco Madero and his inner circle, Abraham Gonzalez, Gustavo, Alberto, Ernesto Madero, and Pascual Orozco became prime intelligence targets for the German government as a result.

How and when Sommerfeld met Francisco Madero remains somewhat unclear. The German agent told American interrogators in 1918, that he met with Madero as a journalist for the first time in the spring of 1911. As a matter of fact, he was with Madero in March and April of 1911, but it is possible that this was not the first visit.[292] The interview Sommerfeld referred to was on behalf of the German government, not AP News. It will be discussed in detail in the next chapter. In his statement to the Bureau of Investigation in 1918, Sommerfeld entangled himself in contradictions. To the question of when he first became mixed up in Mexican politics, Sommerfeld answered in the "latter part of 1910." He also inadvertently affirmed that he did become involved in the anti-reelectionist party at that time. Abraham Gonzalez, who became Madero's governor for Chihuahua in 1911, headed the Chihuahua party headquarters. Sommerfeld also alluded to having seen "him [Francisco Madero] on a train once," even admitting "I knew all the Maderos for years."[293] Sommerfeld freely affirmed that he had been part of the revolutionary effort and that he "was in from the beginning of the revolution – at Pedernales, Mal Paso..."[294] The Battle of Pedernales occurred on November 27th 1910 with Pascual Orozco leading the rebel army. According to his own testimony, Sommerfeld, with Haggerty in tow, attached himself to Orozco in the beginning of hostilities in November 1910. "I went out as a correspondent of the Associated Press of Chicago, with Mr. Haggerty ... I stayed in the field for a short time with the revolutionary side. Orozco was the commander."[295] As we know from the reports Sommerfeld sent to German Commercial Attaché Bruchhausen, he was in the "field" on orders from the German embassy. Haggerty provided the cover for his true occupation.

The German agent admittedly knew the Madero clan well. He testified to having known Alberto Madero early on in Chihuahua, although, according to Sommerfeld, he "had nothing to do with politics."[296] Not quite! Alberto Madero sold properties for his nephew to help him raise funds for his presidential run. Later in the revolution Alberto became one of the principle purchasing agents for the Madero government, and the Villa administration in particular. Through his interaction with Gonzalez and Alberto Madero it is very possible that Sommerfeld got to know Francisco Madero much earlier than he admitted to his interrogators. The colorful Soldier-of-Fortune Emil Holmdahl told the

Bureau of Investigation in 1919 that he thought Sommerfeld gave riding lessons to Madero sometime between 1908 and 1910.[297] Sommerfeld was an excellent horseman, particularly after his training and deployment with the Prussian cavalry in China. Rather than being acquainted through business transactions, Holmdahl's version of events certainly lays the foundation for a more personal relationship that, by all accounts, Sommerfeld had developed with Madero by 1911. In testimony before the Fall Committee on Mexican affairs in 1912, Sommerfeld stated that he "became close friends" with the President.[298] The American Consul in Chihuahua, Marion Letcher, who did not have any sympathies for the German, stated to the Secretary of State Philander Knox in 1912, "Sommerfeldt [sic] seems to have been chosen to serve as the constant companion and bodyguard of Mr. Madero, and in such capacities he appears to have gained a hold upon the confidence of the present Chief Magistrate of Mexico to such an extent which has caused considerable surprise among the old acquaintances of Sommerfeldt [sic] in this section."[299]

Reporters of the San Antonio Light newspaper accorded Sommerfeld a crucial role in those early days of the revolution. Madero seemed to have charged the German with public relations responsibilities. "In the opening of hostilities, while Madero was an outcast both from his own country and from the United States, and was hiding with his few men in the mountains, a German miner, Felix Sommerfeld, who once took a course in a German school of journalism in Berlin, made several daring trips to American towns on the border and sent dispatches to the United Press and the Associated Press. It was these dispatches that first attracted the attention of the American press to the gravity of the situation in Mexico...."[300] It was this work for Madero that brought Sommerfeld in contact with the newsmen, especially Chris D. Haggerty, Timothy Turner, William A. Willis, David Lawrence, and Jimmy Hare.[301] Most of these reporters made huge careers, giving Sommerfeld great connections as a spy in World War I. Under the protection of the German government the German agent was uniquely equipped to take great risks in the news (and intelligence) gathering efforts while at the same time providing public relations for the Madero camp.

Felix Sommerfeld's sky rocketing career baffled most who knew him. He achieved his success not as a result of "conning" his way into Madero's favor, as Consul Letcher asserted in 1914.[302] Rather he was sincere, reliable, hardworking, and fully committed to Madero's cause. It would have been impossible to hide a conviction that did not coincide with Madero's. Night after night in the onset of the revolution the two talked.[303] When Madero needed someone to execute missions of the most delicate diplomatic nature, he entrusted the German agent with them. Sommerfeld never let him down. Working at the same time for the German secret service posed no ethical problem for the German agent. As a matter of fact, Sommerfeld hoped that he could convince the German government to support the efforts of Madero, which he eventually did. To his mind, Madero was the only choice to lead Mexico in a way that could bring stability, slow social reform, and an atmosphere open to business from anywhere in the world. Clearly, Sommerfeld believed that a successful Madero revolution would be in the interest of Germany. To update the imperial government on Madero's progress was not only an option, it was a necessity. Sommerfeld was right in this opinion. It is highly likely that Madero either knew outright or at least suspected that Sommerfeld maintained contact to German authorities. The future president neither objected nor placed any restrictions on Sommerfeld's responsibilities at that time or later in the conflict.

Sommerfeld took his responsibilities as a secret agent seriously. While his role in the Mexican Revolution and later in the Great War became legendary, he purposely remained in the background. Starting in 1910, he refused to speak German in public and in 1911 even signed Frederico Stallforth's guest book in English.[304] Despite the thousands of pictures produced during the Mexican Revolution, and despite hundreds of newspaper articles that mentioned Sommerfeld by name, only five pictures of his seem to have survived in the historiography. One depicts him at a dinner with Francisco Madero celebrating the success of the Battle of Juarez.[305] Another shows him standing behind Raul Madero and next to Franz Wachendorf alias Horst von der Goltz, who was convicted in 1917 as a German sabotage agent.[306] The third picture shows him in El Paso next to Francisco Madero, Chris Haggerty (of AP news) and Allie Martin.[307] In a fourth, Sommerfeld appears in a picture, where Madero presents his provisional government.[308] Finally, he is captured in the background behind Generals Villa and Scott in January 1915.[309]

CHAPTER 8

ᴕ

THE CHALLENGE TO THE DICTATOR

*A*s Sommerfeld aligned himself with Francisco Madero to advance the ousting of the hated dictator, Mexico's social fever rose to alarming levels. In inflammatory speeches and pamphlets the anti-reelectionist juntas clamored for a violent overthrow of the old guard. Unemployed, hungry masses in towns and villages all over the country organized, some armed themselves and waited for a leader to start the fight. The Porfirian regime was corrupt, repressive, inept, and had outlived its time. The crises of the day, food shortages, unemployment, increasing food prices, and homelessness festered unchecked. Yet, the middle and upper classes also benefited from and relied upon the regime. The Stallforth brothers represented a segment of society that events thrust into a precarious situation. While the need for change seemed inevitable, the question of degree preoccupied the members of the various political clubs in any major city. Revolution or reform? Who would lead an effort for either? The old regime dictated the events in one last effort. Diaz had opened the lid of the political pressure cooker when he promised free elections for 1910 in the Creelman interview published in March of 1908. This fateful interview in Pearson's Magazine reinvigorated earlier attempts to loosen Diaz' grip on power. The opposition against Diaz rallied around the Flores Magon brothers, General Bernardo Reyes, and Francisco Madero and organized in every town and community of Mexico. Hopes ran high in all layers of society that the next generation of leaders would bring changes to the political system to make it more inclusive. The burgeoning middle class needed a voice. The economic woes added to a sense of urgency among the people of Mexico. However, dictators rarely step down voluntarily.

In the course of 1909, realizing the threat to the political, social, and economic system his government of "Cientificos" had so carefully constructed, the old dictator changed his mind. He played straight into the hands of Ricardo

Flores Magon and the more radical opposition leaders who had tried for the last decade to congeal the Mexican public into a viable, revolutionary front. Officially declaring his candidacy for the office of President, Diaz' repressive power apparatus sprang into action. The dictator's most serious opponent was Bernardo Reyes, a popular general in the Mexican army and governor of Nuevo Leon. Reyes was the only politician who in Diaz' eyes could create a coalition of Mexico's middle and upper classes and include the powerful support of both the Catholic Church and the military. Under pressure from Diaz, the opposition leader took on an extended assignment to Europe in November of 1909. The old fox had effectively eliminated Reyes' political influence at home. Madero, although having openly challenged Diaz with the publication of his book in 1908, *La Sucesión Presidencial en 1910 – El Partido Nacional Democrático*, seemed less of a challenge. Neither Diaz nor his principle "Cientificos" took the "little man" from Coahuila seriously.

Francisco I. Madero[310]

Standing only 5' 3", the slightly built, with 140 pounds fragile looking Francisco Ignacio Madero González was an unlikely challenger to the aging strong man of Mexico.[311] Wife of the Charge d'Affairs of the American Embassy in Mexico, Edith O'Shaughnessy, described her first encounter with the "Apostle of Democracy" in 1911: "Madero, seen at close range, is small, dark, with nose somewhat flattened, expressive, rather prominent, eyes in shallow sockets, and forehead of the impractical shape. But all is redeemed by expression playing like lightning over the sallow, featureless face and his pleasant, ready smile."[312]

Born as one of fifteen children on October 30th 1873, in Parras de la Fuente, located between Torreon and Saltillo in the state of Coahuila, Madero grew up in one of the richest families of Mexico.[313] The Portuguese-Jewish Madero family had settled in Northern Mexico in the early nineteenth century.[314] Grandfather Evaristo had founded the Compañía Industrial de Parras. In the later part of the nineteenth century the Madero family business extended from vineyards, cotton, and textiles, to mining, milling, smelting, ranching, and banking. Francisco went to high school at the Colegio San Juan, a Jesuit school in Saltillo. According to his biographer Stanley Ross, the young Madero briefly wanted to join the Jesuits. For further high school studies and to learn English, the two oldest Madero brothers, Francisco and Gustavo attended Mount St. Mary's College in Emmitsburg, Maryland but stayed only for a year.[315]

In 1887, made possible with the financial support of his father, Francisco and his younger brother Gustavo moved to France where they attended the Lycee of Versailles and finally received a baccalaureate. The Maderos went on to study business management at Hautes Études Commerciales in Jouy-en-Josas, near Paris. Whether a reaction to the strict Jesuit education, or as a result of his reading of Allan Kardec's theosophical magazine *La Revue Spirite*, young Francisco developed a keen interest in Spiritism. This philosophy developed mainly in France in the 19th century and postulated that while not denying the existence of God, it was possible to contact the spirits of the dead via a medium. A person could become such a medium by learning to sense the spirit energies that could open a channel to the afterworld. For many years, while a student in the United States and France, Francisco trained himself to become such a medium. According to people close to him, by the time he ran for President of Mexico, Madero believed himself to be a spiritual medium. He based his candidacy on support from the past spirits of Mexican heroes most notably that of President Benito Juarez. Kardec was the first high priest of the movement. Madero is said to have made a pilgrimage to his grave while studying in France. The founder of Spiritism had spent a lifetime documenting conversations with spirits through media and had conducted highly publicized weekly séances where he conversed with spirits he called upon. In 1857, Kardec published *Le Livre des Esprits*, which defined Spiritism as a philosophy and to this day remains the fundamental document for his followers. While the Catholic Church had declared Kardec a charlatan, his four books on Spiritism enjoyed huge popularity in a rapidly industrializing world. Francisco wrote in his memoirs that he "...did not read bur rather devoured [Kardec's writings]...Because their doctrine was so rational, beautiful, and new it captivated me. From that moment I considered myself a spiritist."[316] In an exchange of letters with his uncle Antonio Garza Madero defined his belief as "...the existence of an uncreated, eternal, infinitely great and good God, the soul or spirit exists in eternal life, ... on leaving the body it experiences joys or pains as merited...[and] spirits are capable of communicating with the living."[317] He fully subscribed to Kardec's teachings. He organized and led a spiritual group in San Pedro. While he did not curb his weakness for dancing, he became a lifelong vegetarian and refrained from drinking, smoking, and gambling.

After graduating with a Master in Business Administration, Madero attended one semester at the University of California at Berkeley where he immersed himself into agricultural engineering. Equipped with loads of enthusiasm the twenty-year-old intellectual returned to Mexico in 1893. According to his biographer Ross, Madero's training had mainly been vocational to prepare him for the family business. The intellectual preparation to one day become the leader of his people "...lay in his acquired conviction of the efficacy of Anglo-Saxon democracy, his enthusiastic acceptance of Gallic egalitarianism, and his responsiveness to the spiritist emphasis on human welfare and progress."[318]He took over a family hacienda near the town of San Pedro, Coahuila.[319] Madero immediately applied his technical knowledge of modern industrial agriculture. He improved upon an irrigation system to support the high yielding American cotton plants that he introduced. Rather than discarding cadavers of cattle and horses, or simply leaving them in the open to rot, Madero built a soap factory. While neighboring landowners looked upon the young entrepreneur as a dreamer and hopeless idealist, the hacienda became highly profitable and set the trend for agricultural development in the whole Laguna region.[320] Madero's success piqued the interest of Mexico's Secretary of Finance, José Ives Limantour, whom Madero corresponded with. Limantour, himself a landowner in Northern Mexico was a friend of the Madero family.[321] While peasants in the surrounding haciendas suffered under debt peonage, Madero's agricultural workers were independent, well paid, and received regular medical exams. At the same time, Madero found an interest in homeopathic medicine and acquired significant medical knowledge. As a result he was able to help overcome shortages of medicine and doctors in rural Coahuila, often even himself visiting the sick in his community.[322] He sponsored a hospital for San Pedro. For the children of his hacienda he built and funded schools. Community kitchens offered free food for families of Madero's workers.[323] By all accounts, Madero's employees were highly motivated, healthy, and as a result some of the most productive laborers in Mexico. When the revolution started, the people of the Laguna region joined the military forces of their progressive hacendado. The men of this region would become the most loyal followers of Madero, and, after his assassination, for the revolutionary leaders to come.

Francisco Madero went on the campaign trail in the spring of 1910 that also took him through Hidalgo del Parral and Chihuahua City.[324] By that time, the Mexican government had ratcheted up its repression of the restless public. Police raided Madero's party headquarters several times, confiscated pamphlets and other publications, and arrested scores of anti-reelection party organizers. And then in the eyes of his followers there came a sign: Comet Halley with its bright tail appeared above Mexico on May 18th, 1910. Did the Mexican people need any more signs that a new leader was born? The people's feeling of a divinely chosen leader finds expression in this poem:

"Lighting up the sky;
It is not our fault, God knows
That you were ordered to do it.

Oh, what a man this Madero,
How good are his deeds!
He commands all the wrong-headed ones
To free and release the prisoners.
O Lady of Guadalupe
Bestow blessings upon him!

The world of Don Porfirio...was coming to an end. The Day of Judgment was at hand, and the Lord had sent an Apostle of Democracy called Madero to act as judge and deliverer."[325]

Porfirio Diaz showed little tolerance for this prophetic attack on his power and had Madero arrested on June 15th 1910.[326] Despite the immediate protest of his family, Madero disappeared in the prison of San Luis Potosi. On June 28th 1910, not surprisingly, with the opposition exiled and jailed, Diaz won the presidential elections by a large margin. According to historian Friedrich Katz, Madero received a total of 183 votes.[327] Demonstrations all over the country followed the fraudulent grab of power. Madero watched the outpourings of public disgust from his jail cell in San Luis Potosi. After months of wrangling and the election passed, José Limantour and Francisco Madero Sr. worked out a bail arrangement for the young opposition leader. Madero and his associates were to stay in town.[328] However, on October 6th 1910, just as the troubles of the Stallforth brothers came to a head, Madero jumped bail went to San Antonio, Texas where he issued the Plan de San Luis Potosi.

In it he assumed the provisional presidency of Mexico, demanded free elections, a free press, and separation of powers as envisioned in the liberal constitution of 1857 drafted by his hero and supporting spirit, Benito Juarez. Madero also declared the elections of the previous June null and void. As Katz points out, the Plan de San Luis Potosi "contained few clauses dealing with social reforms." The plan primarily "aimed at securing the support of Diaz' middle- and upper class opponents."[329] The dire need for land reform that fueled the revolution received one paragraph of attention, the labor problem none.[330] Indeed Madero found support in the social circles of the Stallforths and the single bohemian friends of Felix Sommerfeld. Just around the time when workers in San Pedro flooded the Stallforth mines and threatened to kill their managers Madero called for an armed insurrection against the government of Mexico to begin on Sunday, November 20th. This date marked the official beginning of the Mexican Revolution. While not actively participating, the Stallforths with many of Chihuahua's middle and upper classes supported the uprising and hoped to gain advantages if it succeeded.

Madero, while challenging the dictatorship of Diaz, was not a leftist rebel. His political convictions are the key to understanding his rise and fall in Mexican politics. On the left, the Flores Magon brothers, labor activists and unions, as well as peasant leaders such as Zapata envisioned an overthrow of the existing power structures, radical redistribution of land and means of production, and a political system that might or might not have resembled a parliamentary democracy. On the moderate right, there were middle and upper class Mexicans who believed that a generational transfer of power from Diaz and the "Cientificos" might require brief and controlled armed rebellion.

Once Diaz was gone, the new leaders would maintain the old system in general terms with some tweaks such as more control for Mexican entrepreneurs. The anti-foreign element among the Madero followers "held together diverse groups within the country, and gave it a needed focus."[331] Politically, the new generation of Mexican leaders wanted to create a voice for themselves in parliament as well as in the states. Further to the right one could find the group that most benefited from the Porfiriato. The "Cientificos," the Catholic Church, and the military had little interest in rebellion or revolution. This most conservative group included people such as José Ives Limantour, Felix Diaz, Bernardo Reyes, and General Victoriano Huerta. Even this group knew that change was inevitable. However, it had to be controlled.

Madero was somewhere to the left of the moderate right. As such he could attract the support of some of the old guard. People like Limantour silently tolerated Madero's activism as long as they believed they could control him. On the moderate left Madero also received support because this political segment believed that a Madero led administration could be influenced to make serious social reforms. As the country prepared for the eventual end of Diaz' rule, people from all walks of life and social backgrounds made Madero their leader. Everyone transposed his or her vision for a new Mexico into this basically conservative leader. The right saw him as maintaining the basic economic and social structures; the moderates as the one who would give a political voice to the disenfranchised middle classes; the left believed he would institute land reform and social democracy. The Plan de San Luis Potosi as well as Madero's many statements and writings show a political being who clearly abhorred a prolonged and violent social upheaval. He preferred reform to revolution. Limited redistribution of wealth was part of his vision, but the path required the creation of proper legal structures through which fair and lasting reform could take place. The proper legal structures also provided for a fair political system that allowed for a multi-party system, representative democracy and significant rights for the states. Historian John Womack noted Madero's legalistic approach in his biography of Zapata: "Few revolutions have been planned, carried out, and won by men so uniformly obsessed with the continuity of legal order as the high Maderistas of 1910-1911."[332] His closest advisors and his most loyal followers who would fight for his vision long after Madero's demise were moderate conservatives. This group included Abraham Gonzalez, Venustiano Carranza, Miguel Diaz Lombardo, José Vasconcelos, Gustavo Madero, Sherburne Hopkins, and Felix Sommerfeld. Pascual Orozco did not have the backbone to remain faithful to Madero's political vision but he also fit the profile of a moderate conservative in those first days of the revolution.

The armed insurrection scheduled to begin on November 20[th]1910 turned out to be a dud:

"On the morning of Sunday, November 20 he rode down to the banks of the river [Rio Bravo], intending to cross, on the assumption that his uncle Catarino [Benavides] would be waiting for him with 400 well-armed pistoleros from Coahuila. His uncle duly appeared at the rendezvous, but with only ten men. Abandoning his plans for an attack on a northern town, Madero went into hiding for a few days, then, after further vacillation, traveled incognito to New Orleans with his younger brother Raul."[333] Despite the setback and the ensuing ridicule of the Diaz regime, the insurgents and especially their idealistic leader had impacted the pillars of power in Mexico. U.S. ambassador Henry Lane Wilson, who would have a large role in the assassination of Madero, observed, "while apparently unorganized and without responsible leadership, [the uprising] was ramified throughout the republic and was remarkable for its intensity and bitterness showing the deep-seated antipathy and antagonism to the government."[334]

Uprisings and armed unrest spread all over Mexico. While the rebels in Morelos, Tabasco, Sonora, and Chihuahua received one setback after another with federal forces using deadly counter measures, there was no stopping the tide. On November 21st, the day after Madero's embarrassing kick-off of the revolution, Pancho Villa under the command of Cástulo Herrera gave the federals a bloody nose at the old military colony of San Andres. Felix Sommerfeld reported on the attack to the German commercial attaché, "Day before yesterday a train came through on the way to Guerrero on the Chihuahua Pacific Railway. It contained some weapons and material. Revolutionaries attacked the train at the Station San Andres and terribly shot it up... The revolutionists shot from the hills...on the train. One first lieutenant and three soldiers were killed along with two women..."[335]

The charge ended in retreat but Villa showed the would-be revolutionaries in waiting that the regime was vulnerable. Felix Sommerfeld and Frederico Stallforth reported coordinated attacks on Parral and San Isidro on the same day as the attack on San Andres. Although having to retreat in all cases, the rebels followed up with a daring attack on Chihuahua City, which had been left virtually undefended. The civilian population had to support the federals in defending their city. According to German Consul Kueck in the time leading up to the attack (November 29th 1910), "there is great excitement in the city ...The public buildings are occupied by volunteers, who with the help of police and the remaining troops here will repel a possible attack...In Parral there was an attack on the city, but the rebels have been fought back after four hours. One rumors that thirty people died."[336]

Another rebel leader, twenty-eight-year-old Pascual Orozco, also successfully organized an armed rebellion. He took the town of Guerrero about fifty miles west of Chihuahua City, where he had been Madero's political chief. After several successful skirmishes with the federales, Orozco teamed up with Villa to take the strategically important railroad town of Serró Prieto. The numerically superior federales dealt the revolutionary forces a decisive defeat. Villa and Orozco retreated into the Sierra Madre. The Diaz regime seemed to gain an upper hand. However, Villa and Orozco did not need victories. Their strategy of luring the federals into an extended guerilla action created a broad base of support in the largely rural areas of Chihuahua. The ranks of the guerillas swelled with local fighters while the federal forces reinforced with forced conscription from other parts of Mexico. In order to effectively battle the quick attacking and retreating rebels the government had to spend enormous resources. Time was on the side of the rebels. With every hit and run attack Villa and Orozco's forces gained supplies, munitions, horses, and recruits.

By January 1911, the rebels successfully controlled the countryside while federal forces held the cities. The revolutionary leaders aroused raging public support with these dare devil actions. Pancho Villa rode through Hidalgo del Parral in broad daylight and, when recognized, rode out of town in a hail of bullets from the federal soldiers he had mocked. Pascual Orozco sent dead soldiers' clothing to President Diaz with a note: "Ahí te van las hojas, mándame más tamales." ("Here are the wrappers, send me more tamales").[337] Finally, three months after the failed kick off, Madero crossed the Rio Grande on February 14th from a location near El Paso. Rather than the general on a white stallion, the nominal leader of the revolution had to flee from American authorities that had issued a warrant for his arrest. Under pressure from the Diaz government, Madero stood accused for having violated the neutrality laws of the United States. In his entourage of one hundred fighters were fifty Americans. Giuseppe Garibaldi, grandson of Italy's revolutionary hero, became Madero's chief of staff.[338] Among the mercenaries also was a Frenchman, Emile Charpentier, as well as Americans "Tex" O'Reilly and John Madison alias

"Dynamite Slim."[339] Experienced machine gunners traded for top dollar. Mexican recruiters found the best available. Tracy Richardson and Sam Dreben had just returned from filibustering expeditions in Nicaragua and frequented the nightlife of New Orleans wondering what to do next. When the Madero representative and future Vice President of Mexico, José Maria Pino Suarez, asked Dreben whether he was willing to fight, the reply defined mercenary culture of the time: "Sure thing... Who do I fight, where do I go, and when do I get started?"[340] Told who, where and when, Dreben took command of a rag tag brigade of Yaqui Indians, Sam with his machine gun and the Indians with their machetes and deadly bows and arrows. "It was a ragged army of barefoot Indians who had never fired a gun, but it was his army, and as it moved north to join the main rebel force Sam also would be the civilian administrator, judge and court of appeals. He was Sancho Panza, taking over the government of each town he might capture, and Sam bore a marked physical resemblance to Quixote's equerry as he grandly led his troops, largely battling windmills."[341]

Also joining the revolution was Emil Holmdahl. Already in Mexico by the time Madero called for insurrection, the soldier-of-fortune worked for the railroads, battling "bandits." Supposedly switching sides when he realized that the "bandits" were Insurrectos, Holmdahl joined Madero's forces in the spring of 1911. While Holmdahl's biographer, Douglas Meed, saw "a faint ember of the idealist that was touched by the tales of the ragged revolutionists," the experienced machine gunner and dare devil might have had more materialistic reasons to join.[342] The pay exceeded that of other soldiers, even generals by multiples. Whether idealism played a role or not the good pay certainly made the decision easier. In the spring of 1911, the independent bands of revolutionaries fought their way north and east, following the call of their leader to come to Chihuahua for the decisive battle of the revolution. For all to see, Diaz steadily lost his grip on power. As the revolutionaries roamed the U.S. border cities for recruits, weapons, and other supplies, President Taft ordered twenty thousand U.S. troops to the border on March 6th to provide security along the border. "At first the public was informed the move was for the purpose of 'extensive maneuvers to try out organization and equipment' ...Mystery regarding this large military movement was soon removed, however... the troops had been sent to form a solid military wall along the Rio Grande in order to stop filibustering and to see that there was no further smuggling of arms and men across the international boundary."[343] U.S. war ships also appeared in the waters off Veracruz, Puerto Mexico, and Tampico. Not only was the U.S. influence over "poor little Mexico" for all to see, but also the implication of the U.S. move was a vote of no confidence for Diaz. The Taft administration obviously did not trust Diaz to control his country.[344] The mobilization, while non-partisan on the surface, clearly supported the revolutionary cause.

The revolutionary forces had little in common with the idealistic picture Madero had had in mind: An uprising of the educated classes with the support of peasants and workers. Pancho Villa, the former outlaw and bandit, had little education.[345] Standing six feet tall, barrel chested and muscular with a neck as strong as a bull's, and with intense, brown eyes that showed white all around the pupils, he looked like someone you did not want to challenge. Whether or not he understood the Plan de San Luis Potosi and how he interpreted it remains a question for his biographers. According to historian and author of the most comprehensive Villa biography, Friedrich Katz, it was Abraham Gonzalez, the leader of Madero's anti-reelectionist party in Chihuahua who "gave Villa a brief lesson in Mexican history, told him of the aims of the Anti-Re-electionist [sic] Party and of Madero, and asked him to join the planned revolution."[346] Villa followed men he respected. He respected Gonzalez and since Gonzalez followed Madero, Villa supported Madero. Villa is said to have personally met Madero in the Palacio Hotel in Chihuahua in the spring of 1910. While it would be easy to assume that the slender, intellectual Madero did not at the least impress Villa, there are indications that this was not the case.

While both had a stormy relationship Villa professed to adore Madero, especially after the President's violent end. Unlike Orozco who quickly broke ranks with the revolutionary leader, Villa endured prison and demotion, even the imminent threat of a firing squad, yet, still supported the ideals Madero represented for him. Whether these ideals were his interpretations Villa did own the banner of Maderismo for a few years after Madero's death. It is highly unlikely that while Madero was alive and President, Villa's loyalty to the President was so pronounced. After all, Madero came from a very different social stratum. He had none of the Machismo that traditional Latin American caudillos possessed. His ideas were largely foreign to the uneducated classes of Mexican society to which Villa belonged. However, Villa was loyal to a man with lots of Machismo and an ability to speak to the up and coming strongman of the Mexican Revolution. This man was Abraham Gonzalez. When both Gonzalez and Madero died in the violent overthrow of the constitutional government in 1913, Villa assumed the banner of his two heroes. Suddenly, or maybe because Madero was dead, Villa raised him to a martyr and his ideas to religion. With that he translated the hitherto distant ideology of a president who lacked popular support while in office into terms the simple masses could understand. Madero became a symbol for the revolutionary forces of Mexico. Through this symbolism Villa harnessed the forces of social change that Madero and Gonzalez could not control and that eventually caused their deaths. The ideology of Maderismo was born, a belief structure that allowed for interpretation and addition. While the President had not furthered land reform and radical redistribution of wealth, the Maderista forces that Villa assembled instituted exactly that under the name of their martyr. Most of Madero's inner circle joined Villa's movement between 1913 and 1916.

A second leader of Chihuahua's revolutionary forces also did not rise from the educated classes of society. Popular history has characterized Pascual Orozco Jr. as a former "mule driver," just as Pancho Villa is the "bandit."[347] Orozco came from the burgeoning Mexican middle class. He had built a successful business as a storekeeper and entrepreneur. His mule trains transported ore from the mines in the mountains to the sites of mills and smelters. He invested in a gold mine that, according to his biographer Michael Meyer, made him wealthy. However, just like Villa's his education was largely informal. A skilled leader of men, Orozco was tall, slender, with sunken cheeks and half closed eyes behind which burned an intense fire of determination. He had powerful appeal among the peasant class of Chihuahua. His independent spirit made him an important force in Madero's quest to oust President Diaz. However, that same spirit that made him one of Madero's most important commanders also turned him against his erstwhile leader. Neither Villa nor Orozco had been able to foment revolution in the urban centers of Chihuahua as Madero had expected. The support of the armed insurrection came from the countryside.

Afraid that he would lose his claim to lead the revolution to his military commanders, Madero desperately needed to make his mark as a military leader himself. While Orozco moved his forces towards Chihuahua City, Madero decided to attack Casas Grandes, a town sixty miles to the south. As the revolutionary leader moved through Chihuahua's villages, the ranks of his army swelled from one hundred and thirty to around eight hundred soldiers.[348] On the morning of March 6th, the federal army defending Casas Grandes repelled advancing columns of the rebel army. Madero's Chief of Staff Giuseppe Garibaldi described the desperate house-to-house fighting that took place in the little town.[349] The battle continued throughout the morning with costly attacks and counter attacks. By 7:15 a.m. federal reinforcements attacked the Maderistas in the rear. The outcome was a disaster. Madero escaped capture by the skin of his teeth with a bullet in his arm. His brother Raul also barely managed to escape but was severely injured. Garibaldi, nominally in charge of the military strategy, blamed the disaster on everyone but himself. "My proposal was to attack from the north down the main road, after having engaged the enemy on either side of the town in feigned flanking movements designed to induce him to weaken his center. But the President thought otherwise."[350]

Whether Madero had devised the failing strategy or, more likely, the inexperienced group of officers around Madero, Garibaldi, brother Raul, and Eduardo Hay had completely underestimated the federal response is a matter of historical debate. Clearly the revolutionaries had split their forces, lacked proper communications and had no contingency plan. Of the foreign contingent fifteen Americans were killed, fourteen Americans and two Germans captured. Madero lost a total of fifty-eight men, forty-one captured. The revolutionaries also lost eight carts of supplies, 150 horses, 153 mules, and 101 guns.[351] Madero retreated to the Hacienda of Bustillos and nursed his wounded arm and ego. "For many American insurrectos, Casas Grandes took a lot of fun out of participating in a Mexican Revolution. It forcefully brought home to them that one could suffer grievous bodily harm."[352] Thanks to their status as foreigners the captured legionnaires did not face a firing squad, like their Mexican compatriots. For the foreigners, Diaz' commanders reserved cells in Chihuahua's penitentiary.

Despite the many defeats the federal army dealt the revolutionaries, there was no stopping the revolution. Instead of losing support and recruits, stories of Madero's courage made the rounds among the rebels. Bodyguard, Máximo Castillo, wrote about Madero's participation in the firefights, "...this man either does not know that bullets kill or he is extremely courageous."[353] While recovering and resupplying, Madero summoned his military commanders to Bustillos in the beginning of May. He now decidedly established his supreme command over the revolutionary forces. Pancho Villa, promoted to the rank of Colonel, joined Orozco, whom Madero made Brigadier General. One by one local revolutionary leaders pilgrimaged to Madero's headquarters, submitted and integrated themselves and their forces into the revolutionary army. With Chihuahua's countryside basically abandoned by the federal army, there were two grand prizes still to be had: Ciudad Juarez and Chihuahua City. Gustavo and all the major military leaders now planned for the decisive battle.

There were other visitors at Bustillos. "I went out to interview him [Madero] to get the news to Mr. Haggerty," Sommerfeld recalled what he claimed was his first meeting with Madero. As documents of the German embassy reveal, Sommerfeld interceded with Madero on behalf of the German government. At issue were two German soldiers-of-fortune that the federals had captured in Casas Grandes. Charge d'Affairs Rhomberg tried his best to save their lives and engineer their release. The issue took on a whole new dimension when the mother of one of the mercenaries contacted the German Foreign Office in Berlin. The plight of Ferdinand Lieber and Friedrich Oberbüscher received interest from the German chancellor who wrote to Rhomberg that "any information [was] to pass through my hands."[354] After the battle the two prisoners were transferred to a prison in Chihuahua City. There, Consul Kueck monitored their treatment and worked on their release. However, the governor of Chihuahua refused for understandable reasons. The two Germans had been caught as combatants and there was only one penalty for treason: Execution by firing squad. The defense the two mercenaries had concocted sounded desperate: "The above named [Lieber and Oberbüscher] claim, that they are innocent and had been captured by the people of Madero on the way from Juarez to Chihuahua, a certain Valencia and De Lara; the two further claim that this was done by Garibaldi."[355] The governor referred Kueck to the central government in Mexico City and let the consul know that in his opinion the two were guilty as charged.[356] Kueck who did not believe the story sent Sommerfeld to interview both Madero and Garibaldi and determine whether the two Germans were telling the truth. He wrote to the German embassy: "A Mister F. Sommerfeld, a friend of mine and known at your embassy, had stayed frequently with Madero as a representative of the Associated Press and is currently still with him. I will ask him to speak with Madero and Garibaldi about whether the claims of the two arrested Germans, that they have been [drafted] by force, is the truth. A written explanation of Madero and Garibaldi would certainly suffice to free the Germans."[357] Sommerfeld's response is not preserved. However, he seemed to have done as told and reported back that they were guilty as charged. Luckily, the two only remained in prison until Abraham Gonzalez became governor before a trial could have been scheduled. Not only were they freed, but the crafty German consul with Sommerfeld's help even managed to squeeze a 140 Peso ($1,500 in today's value) compensation for each man from the governor's office.[358]

Another correspondent, David Lawrence, also followed Madero's adventures. Lawrence, like all war correspondents of the time, knew

Sommerfeld well.[359] Born in 1888, he started his career with AP News, later became editor of the New York Evening Post. After World War I, Lawrence founded several weekly news magazines and also attempted to buy the Washington Post. In 1946 he founded and published the U.S. News and World Report and remained its editor-in-chief until he died in 1973. The famous newsman had been with Madero on November 20th 1910 when the latter went on his ill-fated mission to start the revolution. While Lawrence tried to get "the goods" on Madero's plans, Sommerfeld by his and all other accounts had now officially joined the Madero camp as a confidential agent. His responsibilities were to expand rapidly in the next year. According to Lawrence the German agent "while...friendly to the United States ...was unquestionably pro-German..."[360] Sommerfeld became the gatekeeper to Madero for the press. News outlets paid him for access. Lawrence described Sommerfeld around this time as "selfish."[361] Selfish might be the wrong word in Sommerfeld's case. Just as all the other acquaintances of the German in that time noticed, Sommerfeld kept his cards close to his chest with good reason. He certainly could not and would not admit that he worked for the German government and that his handlers had assigned him to the man who had the power to remove Porfirio Diaz.

Jimmy Hare working for the Colliers Magazine also embedded himself with Madero's forces. The tall and slender Englishman pioneered action photography and became the driving force behind the rise of Colliers. Hare covered five wars. Taking pictures in the middle of battle with bullets flying all around him made him a legend. "He appeared suddenly between the rebel and federal lines," Garibaldi wrote in his description of the Battle of Juarez, "calmly taking pictures amid the flying bullets. Our repeated warnings were of no avail. Someone telegraphed Collier's that Jimmy was exposing himself recklessly and risking his life. He showed me a wire from his home office advising him that a dead photographer was of no use to the magazine. 'Can you imagine such ingratitude?' he asked indignantly."[362]

There is no credible source that defines to what degree Sommerfeld and Hare worked together.[363] However, Hare covered the battle at Bauche Station, which Sommerfeld witnessed. Sommerfeld, while on the payroll of the German government, was in charge of access of the many journalists and photographers to Madero and his forces. As such he controlled who received which information. Hare like all the other correspondents had to go through him to gain access to Madero and his military commanders. Garibaldi displayed several of Jimmy Hare's pictures in his autobiography, one of them showing

Sommerfeld in the background when Madero assembled his first cabinet in Juarez.[364] An article about a correspondent's dinner in El Paso in May 1911 illustrated Sommerfeld's control over access to Madero and the resulting love/hate relationship with the American press representatives. Timothy Turner, correspondent for the El Paso Herald and Collier's Magazine recounted a telling anecdote:

"A natty little chap tripped up the aduana [government building] steps. 'I represent the U.P.,' he announced. 'May I see the president?' 'The president is enjoying his noon day siesta,' announced the major domo [entry guard]. 'But really, old top,' argued he of the natty clothes, 'It is for tonight's wire, don't you know?' 'Yes he will be sleeping tonight, too,' said the major domo. The U.P. vanished.

'I am with the New York World,' said one of a shaved head, and the major domo never turned to look. 'The World,' repeated he of the head. 'The New York World.' 'The president is very busy,' said the official watch dog. 'He will see you tomorrow.' 'But?' 'Tomorrow!' Vanish!

And then, strange as it may seem, a heavy set youth appeared. He wore a suit of canvas brown, and his face was decked in crimson tan. He walked right past the major domo and into the sanctum of sanctums.

'And pray whom may that be?' inquired a fool stranger standing near. 'Why, that,' came the answer 'that is mister Sommerfeld, graduate of the Munich school of journalism, general manager of the revolution, city editor of the cabinet, and newsboy of the presidential offices.'

'But why, why can he pass?' asked the idiot again. 'Is he not a newspaper man?' 'No,' thundered the answer, 'he is a journalist, as I told you, and what's more, he is not an American. He is a German. Is that not enough?' It was enough."[365]

Madero had not been not idle in the months before he reentered Mexico near in El Paso. "A key figure in the maderista [sic] apparatus in El Paso was Abraham Gonzalez," historians Harris and Sadler contended.[366] In November 1910, Gonzalez attempted to take the Mexican border town of Ojinaga, across from the U.S. border, but failed. In order to evade Diaz' wrath the tall, portly Maderista commander made his headquarters in El Paso. There he set up a strong support network for Madero's efforts. The revolutionaries bought arms and ammunition from the merchant house Krakauer, Zork, and Moye as well as Shelton-Payne Arms Company. Gonzalez hired the Thiel

Detective Agency to monitor the activities of Diaz agents on the American side of the border. The Madero people also hired local gunrunners to smuggle the arms into Mexico. An agent of the Department of Justice reported that the smugglers on one occasion received twenty dollars in gold for their efforts.[367]

Not only did Gonzalez and Madero organize the supply lines with respect to materiel. Madero funded the uprising out of own pockets but, according to Sherburne Hopkins, the cost of the revolution far surpassed the $300,000 mark ($6.3 million in today's value), which is documented as Madero's investment.[368] In a report dated April 25th Agent Cunningham reported to the Justice Department, "[T]he Standard Oil Company desired to furnish the insurrectos with from five hundred thousand to one million dollars on condition that the insurrectos would issue to the company six-percent gold bonds, and grant a certain commercial concession in Mexico. A meeting between this party and J. V. Smith was arranged by the agent, who was later advised by Smith that the proposition had been submitted to Francisco I. Madero, who, it was believed, would act favorably upon it."[369] There are many theories on how Madero financed his revolution. Madero confided to his fellow conspirator Roque Estrada in the weeks leading up to the November 20th "he had exhausted his financial resources."[370] By all accounts, in the spring of 1911 money was tight. Friedrich Katz described Madero's main motivation to take Ciudad Juarez, across the Rio Grande from El Paso: "He ordered all revolutionaries in the state to northern Chihuahua to seize the border city of Ciudad Juarez. Its capture would have allowed Madero to set up his government on Mexican soil. The customs duties would have financed the revolution…Nevertheless the plan failed. The revolutionaries lacked sufficient arms to carry it out."[371] Abraham Gonzalez' desperate and failed attack on Ojinaga in the previous November speaks to the same dilemma.

From the day of Madero's call to arms, the Diaz regime had railed against American influence and financing of the revolutionaries. The old regime had good reasons to suspect American involvement. The main issues of contention with the United States were concessions in the oil region of Tampico, control over railroads, and the use of Magdalena Bay as a strategic U.S. refueling station. In all three issues, Diaz had moved against U.S. interests. In the last years before the revolution, British oil magnate Weetman Pearson, after 1910 ennobled to be Lord Cowdray, received significant, long-term development concessions estimated to have been valued around 125 million U.S. dollars. Pearson also received contracts for expanding the national railway system in the center and south of Mexico while excluding American firms from wielding influence over northern Mexican tracks that favored trade with the U.S. Pearson's oil company, El Aguila, counted among its investors several influential members of the Diaz regime, Luis Terrazas son in law Enrique Creel and Diaz' son, to name but two.[372] The old dictator's preferential treatment of Pearson undermined the large influence of Henry Clay Pierce and the American oil companies. Historian Alan Knight maintained in his work that despite Pearson's progress, U.S. investments kept rising.[373] Knight doubts that U.S. influence waned and that U.S. intervention had been a logical option. In hindsight Knight could be correct. However, politicians and financial magnates do not have the privilege of seeing the future. In the eyes of companies that had billions of future profits at stake, Diaz' game threatened their corporate well-being. Investments had to be secured, the political environment in Mexico had to favor corporate interests, and one should not forget the clout and political power Henry Clay Pierce, J. P. Morgan, John D. Rockefeller or Edward Doheny wielded. Historian John Skirius and several others correctly maintained, "The Standard Oil trust of the Rockefeller family, Edward Doheny's oil company in Mexico, and the Rockefeller/Stillman/Morgan/Pierce group of investors in railroads were discontent with the Diaz policies favouring [sic] W. Pearson and the cientifico group."[374] Sherburne G. Hopkins, a lawyer who represented the Waters-Pierce oil interests in Mexico, testified to the U.S. investor's resentment of Diaz in the U.S. Senate in 1912, "...the Waters-Pierce Oil Co. was operating under a great disadvantage, for the simple reason that the Diaz Government had granted these vast oil concessions to Lord Cowdray..."[375]

The third issue proved to be the most irritating for the U.S. government. Mexico allowed the lease of a U.S. refueling station at Magdalena Bay to expire in 1908. At the same time, rumors ran rampant that either Germany or Japan would receive access to this highly important strategic location. While in hindsight Diaz clearly used the Magdalena Bay issue to gain bargaining power with the Taft administration, the prospect of Japanese or German warships refueling a few hundred miles from the U.S. border outraged U.S. officials. In a famous meeting between President Taft and Porfirio Diaz in the fall of 1909, the American government tried again to negotiate the lease and, again, the Mexican Dictator stayed firm. Whether or not, the U.S. government actively supported the Madero revolution remains a debate among scholars. However, tacit support, even by looking the other way, proved to be sufficient to destabilize the Mexican government.

While U.S. authorities did indict Francisco Madero for violating the neutrality laws, this investigation came to nothing. Clearly, U.S. authorities had to show the Mexican government that they "officially" did not support Mexican revolutionaries to arm themselves in the U.S. and proceed to attack the neighbor to the south. It was a half-hearted application of the Neutrality Laws that fooled no one. When Madero crossed over to Mexico in February 1911, he left behind a formidable organization that procured arms and smuggled them into Mexico under the "watchful eyes" of American authorities. Not only did the revolutionaries arm themselves in the U.S., they did it with American funds. Agent Cunningham's report in which he details negotiations with representatives of the revolutionaries and Madero himself are corroborated in a story whereby Madero's uncle Alfonso actively negotiated with representatives of Standard Oil in the same time period, around the end of April 1911. However, historians Harris and Sadler documented conclusively that no money passed between Standard Oil Company and the Maderistas. According to their research, Washington learned about the plan to give $1 Million in loans to Madero and notified Standard Oil that it did not approve of its "machinations."[376]

While Harris and Sadler correctly assessed the non-existent relationship between Madero and Rockefeller, numerous newspaper articles and historical accounts spoke of lawyer Sherburne Hopkins as the go between of Standard Oil Company and the revolutionaries. The problem, however, was that Standard Oil and Sherburne Hopkins had absolutely nothing to do with each other. Pierce hated John D. Rockefeller who had led a successful hostile takeover bid against him in 1906. Although Rockefeller and Pierce both wanted to oust Lord Cowdray, Hopkins represented Pierce's holdings against Standard Oil and Lord Cowdray's El Aguila Oil Company. When Hopkins arranged for a 650,000 Peso loan for Madero ($6.7 Million in today's money), it was Pierce's money. It has conclusively been documented that those funds were paid out and directly resulted in a $50,000 payment ($1 Million on today's money) for Hopkins' services.[377] The amount of the loan represented the Maderos' investment in the Mexican Revolution between 1909 and 1911. Secretary of the Treasury, Ernesto Madero, who reimbursed the balance of the loan to Gustavo, listed the following expenses:

$154,000	Arms, ammunition, and equipment
$ 53,000	Legal fees
$ 6,000	Confidential agency New York
$ 5,000	Confidential agency in Washington
$ 18,000	Confidential agency in San Antonio

$ 15,000	Confidential agency in El Paso
$ 12,500	Press campaign
$ 56,000	Expeditions, envoys, trips, and minor expenses[378]

Other payments from Pierce to Madero are documented in the Senate testimony of Sloan W. Emery in 1912. Emery had an acquaintance working at Waters-Pierce Oil Company. He "saw among the first checks drawn by the Madero Government a check for $685,000 to the Waters-Pierce Oil Company." He went on to state that these were "moneys they had advanced the Maderos to carry on that revolution."[379] The U.S. Secret Service, according to historian John Skirius, had direct evidence of further payments by Waters-Pierce to Madero.[380]

On March 25th 1911, Sommerfeld had dinner at the Stallforth residence in Parral.[381] Sommerfeld later testified that he helped out Stallforth's fledgling business early in the revolution and Stallforth wrote to his wife about his "Madero connection."[382] From Parral, Sommerfeld went to Bustillos where he officially entered Madero's services. The provisional president charged him among other tasks with becoming the link between Hopkins, who headed the efforts in New York and Washington, and the revolutionary organizations in San Antonio and El Paso. As such, the ambitious German became intimately intertwined with the development of a secret service organization that spanned the revolutionary administration, all major border cities between Mexico and the United States, as well as New York and Washington D.C. Gonzalez' people in El Paso arranged for arms and ammunition to come across the border. Hopkins purchased and paid for the supplies while at the same time covering the smuggling efforts with political support from Washington. He also tried to raise money for Madero. In his Senate testimony he freely admitted to Senator Albert Fall that he tried to raise a loan with a French bank and his client Charles Flint.[383] Hopkins never admitted that he succeeded in the fund raising efforts but estimated the cost of the Madero Revolution to have been somewhere around $1.5 Million. The Maderos personally contributed less than $400,000. Hopkins explained that the rest of the needed funds came from all kinds of sources, all Mexican. While his contention that the money came from Mexican sources is probably true, it is a typical lawyer's answer. Ninety percent of all mining and over eighty percent of all railroad investments were under the control of foreign capital. All this investment was mostly organized in Mexican companies. Strictly speaking, any contribution coming from any of these companies could be called "Mexican."

Judging from Sommerfeld's dramatic rise in the Madero organization he handled the new job very successfully. The future president liked Sommerfeld and so did people who worked with him. Miguel Diaz Lombardo, Secretary of Education under Madero wrote in a letter to the U.S. Justice Department: "As an intimate friend of the President, I saw Sommerfeld frequently [after June 1911] and came to admire his loyalty, his frankness and his honesty. For at the time, had Sommerfeld been in even a remote degree unscrupulous, he could, in his position, have easily made a fortune."[384] Working as a foreigner in a revolutionary environment was a somewhat hazardous occupation. Coordinating the frantic efforts to take over Mexico within a few weeks showed great organizational talent and the ability to focus. Diaz Lombardo described Sommerfeld's role as being Madero's "trusted, personal agent."[385] This role Sommerfeld did not deny, when he was asked if he had been Madero's "chief agent."[386] His proper title was "Chief of Staff" as he told Captain G. F. Bailey of the U.S. army in 1912.[387] Whatever one might want to call him, Sommerfeld held the key of access to Madero for foreigners. The German agent had in fact managed to place himself at the precise point where all pertinent information on the revolution came together. No one other than Hopkins and Madero's innermost circle had more detailed knowledge of the machinations of the revolution than Sommerfeld.

CHAPTER 9

~

SHERBURNE G. HOPKINS:

KING MAKER

Sommerfeld's cultivation of Sherburne G. Hopkins established the German agent at the center of a network of intelligence sources that allowed him to feel the pulse of the Mexican and American governments from 1911 until 1918. Hopkins was one of Sommerfeld's most important intelligence targets. He represented the key to understanding the links between the Maderistas and U.S. political and financial interests. As colorful a character as Sommerfeld and Stallforth, Hopkins came from a privileged background. Born on October 5th 1867 in Washington D.C., he and his baby sister Jessie (born in 1876) could trace their roots to England. Hopkins' father, Thomas Snell Hopkins, had moved to Washington in the 1860s from Maine where the family homestead remains. Sherburne's ancestor Stephen Hopkins (1583-1644) came to Plymouth, Massachusetts on the "Mayflower."[388] Samuel Sherburne, his great grandfather, fought for American independence as a lieutenant in the New Hampshire Militia.[389] Sherburne Hopkins' mother was Caroline Eastman whose family came from England to Massachusetts on the "Confidence" in 1638.[390] Both sides of Hopkins' family tree count among the oldest families in U.S. history.

Hopkins attended school in Washington, D.C. and went on to college at the Naval Academy in Annapolis.[391] After graduation, the young naval officer first tried his luck in journalism. Much to the disdain of his father, the rambunctious young journalist almost instantly became a subject of national headlines, albeit not as an author. On November 5th 1887, Chief Justice Waite received a small package that "upon opening he found to closely resemble an infernal machine."[392] Rather than immediately calling the authorities, the courageous Chief Justice took the "infernal machine" apart and realized it to be a "canard." "He did not feel that he was any more in danger than he would have been in handling a silk handkerchief."[393]

None other than the young and ambitious journalist Sherburne G. Hopkins alerted the press to this sensational attempt on Justice Waite's life…except he forgot a minor detail: The Justice had not alerted the authorities when Hopkins spurted out the details of the attack to journalists on the beat. The police suspicions as to the source of this amateurishly assembled, infernal machine quickly settled on the young journalist. One can only imagine Thomas Hopkins' face when he heard of his son's arrest. Posting $1,000 bail, he retrieved his son that same evening. Very likely because of Thomas Hopkins' stature as a respected lawyer in town, the charge his son faced was minor: "Conspiracy to defraud the country by furnishing the press with bogus news for sensational purposes."[394] On November 11th 1887 even the conspiracy charge was withdrawn and Hopkins charge now read: "Attempting to obtain money from two well-known newspaper correspondents by false pretenses."[395] No mention of the attempted assassination or murder of the Chief Justice of the United States Supreme Court! Whatever one may conclude about the scandal, Thomas Hopkins proved to be one good lawyer! The Batavia New York Daily News reported on January 6th 1888: "Sherburne O. [sic] Hopkins, the young newspaper reporter of Washington who some weeks ago sent a sham infernal machine to Chief-Justice Waite for the purpose of creating a sensation and selling the news, pleaded guilty yesterday to the charge of attempting to obtain money upon false pretenses, and was fined $100."[396] Despite the scandal Hopkins went on with his studies. He graduated with a degree in international law from Columbia University in 1890 and joined his father's practice.[397] Thomas Hopkins so skillfully covered up the story that not even the Military Intelligence agents or any of Sherburne's later clients ever knew of what Sommerfeld would have termed a "boyish mistake."

While establishing himself as a serious lawyer in his father's practice, Hopkins married Hester Davis in 1891. Not much is known about their courtship other that it was brief. Hester had two children, Sherburne Philbrick on December 3rd 1891, and Marjorie on August 5th 1894. Their son, Sherburne Philbrick, later also a lawyer in the family firm, briefly became a social star when he married Margaret Upton, better known as Peggy Hopkins Joyce, a famous stage actress. The press he received, however, was rather negative since the journalists' interest was the result of Peggy's public separation from Hopkins. The New York Times reported on April 8th 1915, "Mrs. Hopkins here to act – says she wearied of Washington society and will sue for a

Divorce...'Where is he now? In Central America. [sic] I understand. He didn't want to face the publicity in Washington that was sure to follow. I shan't go back and later I shall sue for a divorce. I lived with his parents in their beautiful home, I had my own motors, but I wearied of Washington society."[398] Sherburne P. was only the second of six husbands Peggy consumed in her lifetime.

The law firm now called Hopkins and Hopkins became one of the top lobbying outfits for Wall Street in Washington. One of their largest clients was the "King of Trusts," Charles Flint. In 1892, Flint, also from an old Massachusetts family, had merged several rubber companies to form the monopolistic conglomerate U.S. Rubber Corporation. His principle lawyer for this merger was Thomas Snell Hopkins. In another famous merger, Flint organized the main bubblegum manufacturers into American Chicle in 1899. In 1911, Flint founded the Computing Tabulating Recording Company, which later became IBM. His rubber business naturally necessitated large investments in Latin America, Africa, and India. Flint especially had large real estate interests in southern Mexico. He joined with Henry Clay Pierce to become one of the largest investors in Mexican railways and international shipping companies such as the Pierce Forwarding Company of New Orleans. Pierce had purchased a majority share in the Mexican National Railways in 1903.[399] In Mexico, one of Flint's competitors in the rubber industry was Evaristo Madero, the future Mexican president's grandfather. The Maderos sold out to Flint in the very beginning of the Mexican Revolution, which rightfully prompted historians to suspect Flint's financing of the upheaval. Flint also held large interests in Pierce's endeavors helping the oil magnate stay clear of hated rival John D. Rockefeller who owned the Standard Oil Company. "To the question whether Capt. Sherburne G. Hopkins of Washington had represented him [Piece] in negotiations with Carranza he declined to answer, though he said that the law firm of Hopkins and Hopkins had looked after his interests in Washington for the last twenty-five years. His acquaintance with Capt. Hopkins is slight, but his father, Thomas S. Hopkins, has long been his attorney in Washington."[400]

All along the way, Thomas Hopkins and his son Sherburne provided the legal work for Pierce and Flint. On January 3rd 1900, the St. Louis Republic reported that Hopkins and Hopkins negotiated with the State Department on behalf of Flint. The British had confiscated several loads of flour off the coast of what is Mozambique today. The illegally seized freight had belonged to Flint's shipping concern. In the effort to force the English to release the cargo Hopkins had strong support from the State Department as well as from the German

Foreign Office. In addition to Flint's flour, British warships had impounded a German mail steamer bound for home.[401] The flour cargo ended up spoilt but Britain had to reimburse Flint for the damages.

In 1898 Sherburne Hopkins joined the active navy in the Spanish-American War. Just as Felix Sommerfeld and Emil Holmdahl were swept up in the excitement of the time, Hopkins answered the call of duty. In the tradition of his ancestors, the thirty-one-year-old looked the part of an American nobleman: Tall, slender, even facial features, strict mouth with thin lips that in anger became threatening lines, with a straight nose and friendly eyes that portrayed feelings and sympathy but could also drill into someone's soul. Hopkins evaluated his counterparts with intense focus. One had to withstand his probing glare that sought to determine trustworthiness. He would allow access to the club of insiders or keep careful distance. Ever the alert mind the young Washington lawyer always weighed his words. Words had meaning and consequences. Like a chess player thinking of the next ten possible moves of his opponent, Hopkins could choose his words in such a way that one thought to have received an answer while nothing was said. His memory resembled an information trap. A Military Intelligence informant commented, "Hopkins has forgotten more about Mexico than any other American will ever learn."[402] When not donning a naval uniform, Hopkins always wore a perfectly pressed three-piece suit with a pin holding the perfect knot in his silk tie. His short hair, leaving ears and neck exposed, without side burns, was divided in the center. In his early thirties the first strains of gray showed along the edges giving him an air of wisdom and age which helped with the young lawyer's first impression. He was earnest, sincere, also funny and cordial and, above all, projected superiority and power.

It is unlikely that Hopkins saw much action in the Spanish-American War. As the commander of the District of Columbia Naval Militia, Hopkins seemed to have stayed put while Admiral Dewey defeated the Spanish on the other side of the world. Hopkins name is mentioned in a newspaper article in October of 1898, when he took command of the USS "Fern," a twenty-five year old tugboat. However, rather than being dispatched to the war zone, Hopkins' task was to "bring the Fern to Washington."[403] His rank is given as lieutenant. According to his own testimony to the U.S. Senate in 1912, Hopkins' responsibility "was ...in the purchase of some materials of war for our own Government..."[404] Through the years of his service in the naval reserves, Hopkins in fact had risen to the rank of lieutenant commander. When in the fall of 1899 Admiral Dewey returned to the United States a hero, Hopkins found mention in the official program of Dewey's Washington, D.C. rally as "Naval Battalion, Lieut. Commander Sherburne G. Hopkins, Commanding."[405] His nickname among military peers was Sherby.[406] Raised to the rank of Commander, Sherby remained in charge of the Washington, D.C. Naval Militia through 1904.[407] Through his responsibilities as commander both professionally and socially Hopkins came to know the senior military establishment of Washington intricately.

The years after the Spanish-American War saw Hopkins working more prominently for his father who was approaching the age of sixty. His cases involved disputes in international shipping. He took on international law to no one's surprise since his main clients were Charles Flint and Henry Clay Pierce who represented huge global financial interests. While Flint expanded his own financial empire, Pierce struggled to free himself from dependency on Rockefeller's Standard Oil Company.

Pierce's relationship with Standard Oil Company and Rockefeller developed over four decades and was a complicated one. With the Waters-Pierce Oil Company that Henry Clay Pierce and William H. Waters founded in 1873, the St. Louis native Pierce tried to keep Rockefeller's company from taking over the Southwest. However, in 1878 Pierce made a pact with the devil. In order to buy out his partner, Pierce sold a sixty percent majority of his stock to Standard Oil.[408] While remaining president of Waters-Pierce Oil Company, Rockefeller and Pierce divvied up the U.S. market into spheres of influence: the Southwest remained Pierce's domain, Standard Oil of New York and New Jersey (now Exxon-Mobil) covered the East and all exports from Eastern ports, Standard Oil of California (now Chevron) exported from the West Coast.[409] Pierce could only market oil products that Standard Oil produced and refined. In the United States, as a result of the deal with Rockefeller, Pierce did not own a single oil well.[410] He began to invest in the construction of three refineries at the turn of the century, two in the U.S. and one in Mexico. In 1903 he also bought a majority share in the Mexican National Railways together with other New York financiers including his friend Charles Flint. In his move to Mexico, Pierce was not alone. Californian Edward Doheny through his very able lieutenant Harold Walker as well as British investor Weetman Pearson (later known as Lord Cowdray) also developed Mexican oil fields. All three tycoons not only developed the wells but also created vertically integrated oil companies.

Pierce's investment in the railways turned out to be a brilliant move. The railways were important not only because of the ability to efficiently carry oil products in tank cars but they also were a large oil consumer. By 1900, the Mexican railways had two systems. All locomotives north of the city of Torreon, Coahuila, still consumed coal because of the large reserves available in the north. However, south of this central Mexican town all locomotives had oil-burning engines just like the whole U.S. system. This little known fact explains the strategic importance of Torreon that various rebel bands fought over repeatedly in the coming Mexican Revolution. Since the railroads were the logistical prerequisite to move troops and equipment, Torreon represented the gate between northern Mexico, the Capital, and the South.

Initially, Rockefeller did not really have an issue with Pierce's investments in Mexico. With sixty percent stock and a contract tying Pierce to exclusively market Standard Oil products, Rockefeller stood to earn handily from Pierce's ventures without even having to invest in marketing and distribution. In 1901, Pierce built the first large refinery in Tampico. However, at the same time, the Texas oil and lubricants market, once exclusively Pierce's, became more and more competitive. In particular, the Texas Company (now Texaco) developed new oil fields and refineries that quickly out-produced Pierce and Standard Oil. In 1907, the U.S. government in an anti-trust move against Standard Oil Company revoked Pierce's license for oil production in Texas.[411] With competition mounting in both Texas and Mexico Pierce now realized that his once lucrative contract with Standard Oil was dragging his company down and preventing it from vertically integrating. '"Mr. Pierce thought himself so strongly entrenched in the oil business that he 'went to sleep' on the job,' his Tampico refinery manager reported later. 'The competition [with Pearson] for a number of years was of the cut-throat variety, and there was no love lost between the two companies.'"[412] 1908 saw the consolidation of Pearson's interests in Mexico under the El Aguila Oil Company. At the same time Diaz nationalized the railroads, paid out Pierce and stacked the Board of Directors of the Mexican National Railroads with Pearson puppets against the erstwhile majority shareholder. War between Pearson and Pierce became red hot when a large and lucrative oil supply contract went to El Aguila instead of Waters-Pierce.

Pierce blamed his erstwhile competitor then partner Rockefeller for his troubles. In Henry Clay Pierce's eyes the contract that had tied Waters-Pierce to Standard Oil had become a ball and chain. By 1908, with Standard Oil and Pierce in heavy legal battles in the U.S., Pierce feared that Rockefeller would collude with Pearson and take over the Mexican oil market. Pierce negotiated briefly with Pearson but without results. The New York oil magnate could not overcome the limitations placed on him by Standard Oil. The work climate between Rockefeller and Pierce was utterly poisoned when the revolution broke out. In 1911, Pierce officially employed Hopkins to influence the new Madero government at all costs against Pearson on one side, Doheny and Rockefeller on the other. It took Pierce until February 2nd 1913 to finally sever his shackles when Rockefeller allowed him to buy back his shares in the Waters-Pierce Oil Company.[413] Charles Flint largely financed his friend's buy-out. Hopkins' maneuvers in Mexico which reestablished Pierce's sway over the railroads played a huge role in the success of Pierce's overall business strategy. Not only was the Washington lawyer a wise choice - since Pierce knew him and his father for many years - but Hopkins also had gained incredible experience in Central America in the years leading up to the Mexican Revolution.

Sherburne G. Hopkins in 1914[414]

President Roosevelt's "Corollary to the Monroe Doctrine" of 1904 meant that U.S. foreign policy, even more than before, aimed at supporting U.S. investment in the Americas. Hopkins from the beginning of his law practice had been especially interested in applications of international law. "Dollar Diplomacy" directly resulted from Roosevelt's foreign policy. It meant that the U.S. government actively intervened in its area of influence to support American commerce. The guarantee of government intervention on behalf of U.S. commerce produced a large influx of capital into Mexico and Central America. In the time between 1904 and 1909, Hopkins worked closely with the U.S. Department of State and the War Department while lobbying for his clients. A driving force in those years was Philander C. Knox, a lawyer from Pennsylvania. As Attorney General for Theodore Roosevelt until 1904 and as Senator from Pennsylvania between 1905 and 1909 he became a strong supporter of "Dollar Diplomacy." In 1908 Knox attempted to receive the Republican nomination for President but lost to William Howard Taft. When Knox became Secretary of State for Taft in 1909, one of his first official acts was to send U.S. Marines to Nicaragua. Knox was a longtime friend of Thomas Hopkins' and as such also knew Sherburne.

Investments in Central America in the early 1900s had risen sharply. The U.S. government had backed the secession of Panama from Columbia and started to build the Panama Canal in earnest in 1903. When finished, the cost of shipping from the Atlantic to the Pacific oceans would be cut in half. Panama was not the only choice for a trans-isthmian canal. Since the 1840s there had been a plan to build a canal through Nicaragua. The San Juan River connected San Juan del Norte at the Atlantic Ocean close to the border between Costa Rica and Nicaragua with the largest lake in Central America, the Lago Nicaragua. At its narrowest, only fifteen miles separate the lake from San Juan del Sur on the Pacific. American businessman and robber baron Cornelius Vanderbilt had first tried to build the link between the oceans in 1849 to transport men and supplies from the American east coast to California. Starting at Greytown (San Juan) the Accessory Transit Company took passengers by ship to the lake. There the customers had to disembark and transfer across land to the ships waiting in the harbor of San Juan Del Sur. Permanent unrest in the regions prevented Vanderbilt from completing his canal project.[415] By the beginning 1900s, at the height of negotiations between the American government and Nicaraguan dictator José Santos Zelaya, the Central American strongman refused to give the United States extraterritorial rights for the proposed Canal Zone. When the negotiations failed, Panama became the location of choice and Zelaya a decided enemy of the U.S. In 1904 the U.S. government bought out the French company that had been working on the Panama Canal project since the 1880s, Zelaya now approached England, Germany and Japan to invest in a competing canal project. American interests clearly stood to be challenged. The United Fruit Company, as well as Sam "the banana man" Zemurray, owned half the Isthmus for its banana plantations as well as railroads and large fleets of transport ships. Guatemala's strongman and United Fruit Company puppet Manual Estrada retained Hopkins and Hopkins for his services in 1906.

The law firm showed its unparalleled manipulative might when it single-handedly shaped Central American history in the following years. After a skirmish between Honduras and Guatemala in 1906, the two countries and El Salvador had concluded the so-called friendship pact that isolated Nicaragua. In the spring of 1907 Nicaragua invaded Honduras in an attempt to unseat President Bonilla, a puppet of United Fruit Corporation. With the help of U.S. marines the Honduran leader survived. Virtually a protectorate of the United States with marines occupying Bluefields on the Atlantic side of the country, Nicaragua invaded Honduras in 1908 to install a new, less hostile government there. Despite the official support for intervention of the U.S. government, Hopkins and his international clients worked behind the scenes to contain the Nicaraguan Dictator Zelaya. The weapon of choice was to provide money for neighboring countries such as Honduras and Guatemala while denying finance to Zelaya. After years of effort, Nicaragua had finally concluded a loan for 1.25 million pounds Sterling (over $100 Million in today's value) from the Ethelburg Syndicate in London in 1909.[416] Hopkins and Hopkins signed Ethelburg as their client and promptly succeeded in canceling the loan.[417] Apparently, Hopkins leaked crucial information on the impending U.S. intervention to unseat Zelaya to Otto Fuerth, a director of Ethelburg. The loan was cancelled and Zelaya gave up before the Marines landed. Hopkins testified in 1920: "I imparted the information to a friend of mine named Otto Fuerth, whom I had known for a number of years and who had vital interests in that Republic, and I did not want to see him make a loss, and I gave him a little quiet information."[418]

U.S. marines were not the only ones fighting in Central America at that time. In 1906, Sam Dreben had taken a night watch job somewhere along the Panama Canal and partied until he was fired.[419] From Panama he headed to Bluefields, Nicaragua, which was under the control of U.S.-financed rebels. Delighted to find an experienced machine gunner, the rebels hired Dreben on the spot. Serving with him was Tracy Richardson who Dreben quickly trained on handling a machine gun. Richardson became a lifelong friend of Dreben's. Another familiar character had drifted into the mercenary armies of Central America in 1906 was Emil Holmdahl. Fighting under "General" Lee Christmas in Honduras, Holmdahl also manned a machine gun. "It was a golden opportunity for all the footloose veterans of the Spanish American War and the Philippine Insurrection..."[420] Most of the fighting occurred under the auspices of American corporations, who in many cases not only financed the "revolutionaries" but also hired them outright. Counting on the support of U.S. troops under the "Dollar Diplomacy" paradigm, the efforts to remove Nicaraguan Dictator Zelaya in Central America purposely escalated. In the fall of 1909, U.S. intrigue finally succeeded: "In fighting along the San Juan River near Lake Nicaragua, Zelaya's troops captured two American mercenaries, Lee Roy Cannon and Leonard Groce. They were caught in the act of laying mines designed to blow up steamer traffic on the waterway...In spite of protests by the United States consul in Managua, the two were led from their filthy cell...shot...and unceremoniously shoved ... into the graves."[421]

The executions of Cannon and Groce dominated the American headlines of the day. The steamer they had attacked was indeed a Nicaraguan troop transporter. Their execution, albeit brutal, was justified. According to international law the two mercenaries were pirates. However, the New York Times and other dailies turned the two bombers into American heroes. In an article dated November 23rd 1909, the two rose from simple employees in local mining and farming outfits to "large property owners."[422] While Hopkins and his clients worked with the American government to unseat Zelaya, American mercenaries together with forces from Guatemala and Honduras attacked Nicaragua full scale. Everyone expected an imminent invasion of the country by U.S. forces. As Hopkins managed to cancel the loan and American mercenaries began attacking the capital of Managua, the Nicaraguan dictator left. Even before U.S. troops landed, Managua fell. Four hundred American machine gunners supported the attack.[423] Dreben and Richardson both suffered gunshot wounds. "Each had been paid $5,000 [$100,000 in today's value] and was given a tract of banana land, but Sam, as usual had gambled away the land and much of the gold..."[424] Holmdahl "considered discretion the better part of valor and boarded a banana boat bound for New Orleans."[425] How much money he received is unknown but given the going rate, he made out like a bandit!

Hopkins' involvement in the Nicaraguan change of government was critical. He represented his clients and acted on behalf of the U.S. government, especially Philander Knox who had become Secretary of State in 1909. Hopkins also supported Knox's efforts to properly finance and equip the rebel forces. Guatemalan President and puppet for United Fruit Company, Manuel Estrada, received funds from the United States, mainly in the form of loans. The banana fleets of United Fruit and Pierce transported weapons and ammunition to the Central American republics. The main U.S. port from where tramp steamers sailed was New Orleans, a hot bed for mercenaries, revolutionaries, and intrigue of all kind. After Zelaya fled, the American government installed a new puppet regime. "I knew exactly what was going to happen. I knew that nothing could save Zelaya," Hopkins boasted to Senator Smith in 1912.[426] Upon the question of whether Hopkins' intimate information about Nicaragua's troubles came from sources in the government, he replied: "I should not say directly from our Government, Senator. I knew what was going to happen before our Government did, and stopped Zelaya's loan from going through. I am also free to say that I received a great many hints that things were going to happen. I knew the sentiment in the State Department and elsewhere..."[427]

While thousands of Central American soldiers fought alongside hundreds of American mercenaries, Hopkins' conscience was clear. "I never purchased a gun in my life," he responded to Senator Fall upon the question of who bought the weapons for the revolutionaries, "that is, personally."[428] His task was to oust Zelaya and help his international clients retain their investments. That was all. Hopkins freely admitted to his position as a go between of the U.S. government, American business interests, and the "friendly" governments of Central America. Whether Hopkins' relationship with the U.S. government was more than just lobbying, cannot be assessed. He certainly had open doors in the State Department and especially with Philander Knox. The "quiet information" he gave to Otto Fuerth represented confidential State and War Department decisions that Philander Knox leaked to Hopkins in order to unseat Zelaya. In a memorandum for a Lieutenant Colonel in the Military Intelligence Division in 1920, a Major alluded to the fact that Hopkins indeed was considered "to be friendly toward M.I.D...[but] will not give out information which maybe [sic] detrimental to his clients..."[429] Over time, Hopkins did send confidential information to the Military Intelligence staff. While it can be assumed that he really was working at the very least as an informant for this clandestine service, he, just like Sommerfeld, was a master at collecting and disseminating information for his purposes.

Hopkins' obvious success and experience in Central America in the decade prior to the Mexican Revolution made him the prime candidate to orchestrate a successful uprising for the Maderos and American high finance.

On the one hand, American investors, especially Hopkins' client Henry Clay Pierce, wanted to unseat Lord Cowdray (Pearson) and his Cientifico puppets. On the other hand, the Maderistas needed finance and political support from the highest echelons of the U.S. government. Sherburne G. Hopkins' task was to bring these interests together. According to Hopkins, Gustavo Madero and his father Francisco Sr. met with him sometime in October of 1910 in the Hotel Astor in New York. They made a deal. Hopkins received a retainer of $50,000 (over $1 million in today's money) payable upon successful completion of Diaz' overthrow. Since that day in New York, according to Hopkins, he had been in "almost daily" contact with Madero's brother, preparing the revolution. What exactly this responsibility entailed, Hopkins did not elaborate on. Clearly, there were only three areas in which work was required: Procuring loans to finance arms and ammunition purchases; building an organization for the revolutionaries that procured and shipped arms and ammunition; and creating political support in the United States for the rebellion. Showing how much his connections were worth, Hopkins successfully interceded with his friend, Secretary of State Philander Knox, to allow munitions to pass unchallenged from El Paso to Ciudad Juarez.[430]

While working the Washington political circles and New York's high finance on the Maderos' behalf, Hopkins also supplied the U.S. military command with crucial information about the progress of the Mexican uprising. Decidedly understaffed in the early teens, the U.S. military carefully watched what was developing along the southern border. While Hopkins did not "work" for the Military Intelligence Division, he was one of their most important informers on Mexican affairs. Apparently, Hopkins had only a few contacts very high up in the military and political hierarchy who knew him and received information from him. Astonishingly, after many years of working with the State Department, Department of Justice and Department of War, lower-tier employees of these departments seemed to never have heard of him or did not know that he was one of their informants. Even his name is continuously misspelled which makes the researcher's job even harder. Telling of Hopkins' connection with Military Intelligence and other secret service branches of the U.S. government throughout the Mexican Revolution is a confidential letter from the U.S. military attaché in Havana, Cuba, Major Henry A. Barber to Brigadier General and Chief of the War College Division Albert L. Mills in March 1912 with copies to the Chief of Staff of the War Department. General Mills took over as Chief of Militia Affairs in 1912 and as such was Hopkins' direct superior. As Chief of the War College General Mills also commanded the

Military Intelligence Division: "Yesterday 'Captain' Shirley Hopkins, legal advisor to President Madero of Mexico and to President Estrada Cabrera of Guatemala, was here. He said that he met in Guatemala two American officers, Major Cheney and Captain McCoy, and that he met them again in the City of Mexico. I am informed at this Legation that the South American Division of our State Department knows all about Mr. or 'Captain' Hopkins, and I would suggest that if the War College does not know him it might be well to get the information from our State Department."[431]

The Captain McCoy mentioned in the letter, whom Hopkins met first in Guatemala and then in Mexico City, was a Military Intelligence officer.[432] The Military Intelligence Division made a huge effort between the fall of 1911 and the early part of 1912 to assess whether the Madero government had a chance of survival. Under cover as journalists, the two agents tried to understand the opposition to Madero and its effectiveness.[433] It is not surprising that the agency tried to recruit Hopkins. As a naval officer he had the duty to cooperate, and as a lawyer representing Madero Hopkins was better connected than any agent the Military Intelligence Division had in its employ in 1912. With the approval from the highest echelons of the American government, the Secretaries of War, Justice, and Treasury, Hopkins built an organization along the U.S.-Mexican border that provided all the crucial information needed to formulate a policy on how to deal with the Mexican Revolution. The letter from Major Barber clearly suggested to General Mills to hire Hopkins into the Military Intelligence Division (M.I.D.). As is the case in most intelligence matters there is no official letter or acknowledgement that Hopkins became an informer and agent for the Military Intelligence Division in the spring of 1912. However, the evidence is overwhelming. In November 1918, Hopkins wrote a letter to Brigadier General M. Churchill, United States Army, and Director of Military Intelligence:

"Sir:

I have to acknowledge receipt of your circular without date (Mil. Mon. Sub-Sec. M. I. 2.) requesting certain information, which is herewith furnished as follows:

(a) Affirmative.
(b) Mexico and Central America.
(c) Information already supplied to Major Furlong.
(d) I reside in Washington permanently.

Respectfully,

S. G. Hopkins"[434]

On February 13[h] 1919 Colonel John Dunn, Acting Director of Military Intelligence asked Hopkins in a letter, "Captain Huntington hopes to receive from you shortly certain reports on Mexican towns...Kindly note that the offices of the Military Intelligence Division are now located at 7th and B Sts., NW."[435] On December 21st 1920, Colonel Smith of the Military Intelligence Division wrote to the Chief of Military Intelligence, General Dennis E. Nolan, "Capt. Hopkins was not in accord with Carranza during the World War, and M.I.D. was furnished considerable information of value during that period, sometimes voluntarily and at other times upon direct request from M.I.D...Capt. Hopkins was well thought of by many officers in M.I.D. who came in contact with him, and his information was considered reliable though at times tending to prejudice M.I.D. in favor of his friends..."[436]

As the Maderos apparently put the well-connected lawyer in charge of the U.S. representation of their efforts, Hopkins had to find personnel quickly. The success of Madero's uprising depended on immediate financing, munitions shipments, and political support in Washington. Historians friendly to Madero's efforts to democratize Mexico and to institute meaningful social reforms are generally hesitant to admit the Madero-oil connection. An admission of these facts would somehow constitute a compromising situation for Madero. But what did he concede in order to receive this support? The question of influence on politicians is as old as politics existed. History is full of examples of undue influence being exerted to advance selfish goals. This does not mean that history is not also full of examples of politicians using whatever means they can to advance their own goals. Indeed, there is no hard evidence to suggest that the Maderos did anything other than what they could to advance their own goals. Henry Clay Pierce thought that President Madero would create a more favorable political environment for his corporate interests than Diaz. So he supported him. Even without any additional concessions, Pierce and the other U.S. magnates were not idealists. They faced an impossible work environment under Diaz.

When Senator Hitchcock asked Hopkins whether his engagement in Mexico was for "any idealistic purpose," the answer defined the sad reality: "Of course not altogether, Senator."[437] While at the same time an informant for the Military Intelligence Division, a representative of the Maderos and other governments, he also worked for the Flint and Pierce interests. Hopkins was a man who reached his goals and those of his clients. While sometimes balancing conflicts of interest in a gray zone of professional ethics, he probably was a patriotic American in World War I. Despite the M.I.D. misgivings, when Hopkins determined that intelligence could be given without hurting the interests of his clients, it was reliable and valuable. His contacts in the M.I.D. hierarchy are also interesting. Not a single document could be found where Hopkins corresponded with Colonel Van Deman, the de-facto head of the M.I.D. for many years. Hopkins corresponded with people much higher up in the food chain, usually with the Secretary of War and his Chiefs of Staff. As a result it appears more often than not that lower tier staff did not know him. From the evaluations of his M.I.D. handlers it becomes clear that they recognized the essence of his value. Informed like no-one else, Hopkins had to be handled with one caveat aptly defined in 1920 by Major Montague of the Military Intelligence Division. "His loyalty shifts with his fee," he cautioned his superiors.[438]

CHAPTER 10

~

¡VIVA MADERO! ¡VIVA LA REVOLUCIÓN!

While Madero and his staff resupplied at Bustillos in March 1911, the revolution in other parts of the country was in full swing. Emiliano Zapata, leader of the Insurrectos in the south had ousted the governor there and was in control of the state of Morelos by March 22nd 1911. Morelos, just to the south of Mexico City, was mountainous and remote, yet in a geographic position to cut the capital's economic lifelines to the largest harbor, Veracruz. After several successful battles against the federals in April, Zapata now commanded troops well in excess of five thousand strong and threatened the harbor city as well as the capital. While the Zapatistas routed the federal troops in the south, Madero's forces congregated outside Ciudad Juarez. Orozco and Villa had successfully cut the rail lines between the capital of Chihuahua and the border city. The federal troops were effectively cut off. On April 19th 1911 Madero demanded a formal surrender. According to Sommerfeld's testimony in the Senate in 1912, he had been the one to deliver the message to the Federal Commander in Ciudad Juarez. "I knew General [Juan] Navarro...he is a man who will not violate the rules of warfare... so I went in."[439] With Sommerfeld was Roque Gonzalez Garza, a leading member of Madero's and later Pancho Villa's administrations. General Navarro refused. On April 22nd 1911 Mexican rebel troops under the command of Giuseppe Garibaldi led a surprise attack on Bauche Station only a few miles south of Ciudad Juarez. The fierce fighting lasted all night and resulted in the federal forces' retreat. Sommerfeld was with the Italian commander.[440]

The situation around Ciudad Juarez intensified with every day that passed. Newspapermen swarmed the rebel leader Madero who had made his headquarters just across the river west of El Paso. Until Sommerfeld managed their access to Madero getting the news was a daunting task for the representatives of AP, United Press, Colliers, Hearst, New York Times, and the New York World. "...almost every correspondent who entered the camp was arrested and held until he had proved [sic] his identity. The insurrectos had poor memories and more than once one of the newspaper men was arrested daily for several days running...The newspapermen were forced to hire automobiles by the day in order to keep in touch with Madero and the telegraph office on the American side. Wild dashes in both directions at the sound of new alarms and the spreading of wild rumors were hourly occurrences."[441] Revolutionary forces surrounded Ciudad Juarez on three sides, railroad and communication to the city was cut. Yet Madero hesitated. While Orozco and Villa were itching for the fight, Madero attempted to negotiate with the federal commander. Historians have interpreted this hesitation as a sign of Madero's inability to make decisions, contemporaries as weakness. In reality, the hesitation of the future president resulted from very logical reasoning. At issue were American concerns about stray bullets endangering the lives of American citizens across the river in El Paso. Using these concerns as a pretext, American officials threatened both combatant parties.

A few weeks earlier at Agua Prieta American forces indeed did cross the border to prevent further bullets flying across into Douglas, Arizona. The Americans quickly retreated but, as Garibaldi described in his autobiography, caused the federal forces to surrender.[442] A military engagement on the border would have shown to what extent the Mexican Government had already lost control. However, it is questionable that the U.S. actually contemplated any serious action. What Hopkins and others rather alluded to was that the Taft administration attempted to achieve the resignation of Diaz without a blood bath. An engagement between Mexican government troops and American forces certainly could have backfired. Madero's problem in the event of an American military intervention was that he would have lost control over his commanders. Villa and Orozco, fighting the American military, most certainly would have ended in disaster and would have meant Madero's end as a viable successor of Diaz. Both Diaz and Madero had to negotiate. And they did. With the help of the State Department the two opposing forces declared an armistice on April 22[nd]1911.

Madero's father Don Francisco Madero Sr. had been meeting with Mexico's Secretary of Finance, José Ives Limantour in New York on March 11th and 12th. Hopkins refused to admit to Senator Fall in 1912 that he directly attended the meetings. According to a speech Senator Smith gave in in April 1914, Hopkins was present and directed meetings. The senator did not specify the date but alluded to the fact that the delay in attacking Juarez was directly related to ongoing negotiations with Diaz representatives in New York's Astor Hotel.[443] Whether Hopkins presided over any meetings or not he certainly knew all the details of the negotiations. Also documented as present besides Francisco Madero Sr. were Francisco Leon De La Barra, José Vasconcelos, Francisco Vasquez Gomez, Venustiano Carranza, and José Ives Limantour.[444] It is conceivable and very likely that other people attended some of the meetings such as high-ranking members of the State Department. However, the surviving State Department files do not provide any reports to substantiate this suspicion. Henry Lane Wilson, the U.S. ambassador to Mexico, claimed in his memoirs to have been negotiating with Limantour at the same time. Whether he was a member of these meetings is unknown but likely.[445] The meetings took place in a "special suite of rooms" in the Astor Hotel.[446] In light of the disdain the Madero people felt for the members of Diaz' power structure, Hopkins told senators in 1912 that Limantour "was one of the few men among the Cientificos whose skirts were clean."[447] An amazing statement considering that Limantour was the architect of the Cientifico economy! Quite obviously, the Maderos with Hopkins as their go-between wanted to make a deal with Limantour to take over power in Mexico and preserve the existing structures while sacrificing Diaz. These meetings probably also marked the first encounter Hopkins had with the future revolutionary leader Carranza. He saw first-hand Hopkins' negotiation skills and clout with the U.S. government and New York's high finance. This made a lasting impression on Carranza. Hopkins would become his U.S. representative and trusted advisor in 1913 and 1914.

The negotiations concentrated on several issues: Limantour, whom Hopkins was well acquainted with as a result of his work for Flint and Pierce, tried to preserve the influence of the Diaz power structure. According to historian Peter Henderson, the Finance Minister even considered the idea of breaking up the large haciendas in Chihuahua and having them sold "in small plots to the peasants."[448] The Maderos wanted to replace several governors and, above all, insisted that Diaz and his Vice President would resign. Hopkins, State Department officials, and the Madero delegation also negotiated the return of control over the Mexican national railroads to Pierce's people and the de-clawing of Lord Cowdray's influence. The U.S. Department of State either in the person of Philander Knox or one of his senior officials wanted a restoration of order, guarantees for American lives and property in Mexico, and threatened armed intervention for both sides if American lives were lost in the fights along the border. The threat of U.S. military action was a serious one since twenty thousand U.S. troops had been called to the border on March 6th 1911. It was virtually impossible to prevent stray bullets from landing on the American side and even more difficult to prevent combatants of either side from purposely shooting across the river in order to provoke an incident. The exact results of the negotiations are not known. However, the diplomatic efforts of the Madero people were significant. Madero's father left New York for the border after the March 12th meetings while Limantour went to Mexico City. In the end of March, the Diaz representatives and Madero's people engaged in follow up meetings in San Antonio.[449] On the 4th of April 1911, Madero sent his erstwhile presidential running mate, Francisco Vasquez Gomez personally to see German Ambassador Count Bernstorff in Washington, who at the time was also accredited to Mexico.[450] In a letter dated the 15th of February, and addressed to the heads of state of the major powers, Madero reiterated his commitment to the rules of war, the upholding of international agreements, international commerce, the adherence to the constitution, and sanctity of lives and property of foreigners.[451]

Francisco Madero Sr. and his brother Alfonso joined the rebels' camp around the 22nd of April, when the armistice took hold. Intense negotiations followed with representatives of the Diaz people. On May 6th the talks officially broke down. Diaz had refused to resign immediately. Historical accounts vary as to the details about what followed next. However, all agree that Madero ordered the rebel forces to stand down rather than attack the city. What was really going on behind the scenes?

In testimony to both the U.S. Senate in 1912 and the federal investigators in 1918, Sommerfeld insisted that he personally was charged to arrange an understanding with American authorities that safeguarded the Americans across the river. His contact was Colonel Edgar Z. Steever of the 4th Cavalry at Fort Bliss. "Colonel Steever is the only army officer who ever had command of an exploring expedition to the Holy Land, having been in charge of the American Palestine exploring expedition engaged in the survey of Moab, Ammon, Bashan and other regions east of the Jordan and the Dead Sea, from Oct. 1, 1872, to Oct. 1, 1874." A few years later the commander at Fort Bliss had been "Assistant Professor of Mathematics at West Point and in charge of the Engineering Department and cavalry school in 1891."[452]

Steever also commanded combat units in the Spanish-American war. His combat record in the Philippine insurrection accounted for "thirty-four battles and skirmishes with Filipinos during the years 1899 and 1900."[453] After the Philippine assignment Steever took over as commandant of the cavalry and artillery school at Fort Riley.[454] His last assignment was the cavalry command at Fort Bliss from which he retired in 1914. The scars of battles past had taken their toll on the old warrior. The colonel was almost blind. Fort Bliss was an important assignment given the potential of American intervention. It is not surprising that the War Department chose a commander as brilliantly educated and smart, with lots of actual combat experience. A tall man with a huge, white mustache, Steever projected authority and experience. He was an expert horseman who trained his cavalry units relentlessly.

Madero had ordered Sommerfeld to keep Steever abreast of the plans of the revolutionary forces. "That was part of my duty, in order to avoid any trouble, any international complication, you know," he explained to Senator Smith in 1912.[455] Indeed, the German became the link between the U.S. and Mexican forces. While Sommerfeld correctly stated that he acted on Madero's orders, there is no question that he fulfilled a promise that had been given to the U.S. State Department in the negotiations earlier that month. U.S. support of Madero depended on the safeguarding of American lives and property. Sommerfeld's cooperation with the American commander allowed the latter to "string out his guards along the river, his patrols, so that nobody could pass the bridge or pass the river."[456] With the agreement in place to heed the conditions the U.S. Government had placed on the revolutionaries, Madero's negotiation position with the Diaz representatives improved tremendously. Limantour in an interview with New York Times reporter Steven Bonsal on April 21, 1911, claimed that border incidents could not be stopped and intimated that Madero's attack on Juarez would cause an intervention.[457] Madero, employing Sommerfeld as Steever's contact, and using Hopkins in Washington as a contact to Knox, had effectively removed that argument. Sommerfeld was in touch with Steever and the American Consul in Juarez, Edwards, at least a week before the breakdown of the armistice.[458]

The question remains as to why Madero wanted to call off the sacking of Juarez despite the favorable military and political situation. While neither Hopkins nor Sommerfeld allude to Madero's decision not to attack, the truth is that Madero was still negotiating for the resignation of Diaz.[459] On Sunday, May 7th word came from Mexico City that Diaz had agreed to resign. Madero called off the planned attack on Juarez that night, while a "peace commission" from Mexico City brought the latest offer from Diaz.[460] Sommerfeld had already notified Colonel Steever of the pending attack. He now "...went to the swinging bridge with a letter and turned the letter over to one of the orderlies of Col. Steever...'We will not attack to-night, because the peace commission is here, and no attack will be made.'"[461] The importance of this delay became clear in the weeks following the success of Madero's campaign and the exile of Diaz. "Madero clearly believed that Porfirio Diaz's ... resignation ended the underlying reason for the civil war."[462] After the treaty of Juarez, Madero disbanded the revolutionary armies and expected the rebels to disperse and return to civilian lives. This attitude of Madero's was in line with the expectations of the State Department and New York financiers who worried about uncontrollable unrest in Mexico. Hopkins and the State Department had negotiated on that point. The resignation of Diaz would trigger an abandonment of hostilities and peaceful transition of power in Mexico City.

Clearly, Hopkins and the State Department completely underestimated the volatility of the situation. While Madero desperately tried to keep control over his forces under Orozco, Garibaldi, Obregon, and Villa, negotiations kept dragging on. Garibaldi described the situation:

"The interminable discussions led to no conclusion, and we on the sand dunes could only grit our teeth and wait. Our temper was sorely tried when that day federal Colonel Tamburel told American newspaper correspondents that the rebels did not attack because they were afraid. That evening I went with several others to Madero and begged him to release us from our pledge to obey him, since we could not answer the ugly mood of our men. He held us to our promise of loyalty and urged us to be patient and bear with him in this difficult position. But during the night, unknown to Madero, we began to move our troops, gradually enclosing Juarez."[463]

On the morning of May 8th the inevitable happened. It is not known to what extent Orozco knew of the plan to disband the revolutionary forces. However, he likely had an inkling and wanted to assert his military power. Fighting started with rebels hurling insults at the entrenched federals. Not long after, the insults changed to bullets. Whether or not Orozco had ordered the beginning of hostilities or whether there really was no way around it, the assault started along the Rio Grande and quickly spread towards the bullring. Supporting the argument that Orozco and Villa had planned the attack against the will of Madero is Felix Sommerfeld's testimony to federal investigators in 1918: "I telephoned to the Associated Press correspondent, Mr. Lawrence, at El Paso. I had him called to the booth and I telephoned the message to him and he sent the message out about three quarters of an hour before anybody knew of it."[464]

Sommerfeld and in extension Madero were out of the loop. Garibaldi testified in his autobiography to the same point. As a result of the overt insubordination of the three revolutionary commanders, the communication with Steever had broken down as well. All Sommerfeld could do was to notify the press and have them contact the U.S. authorities. It is unknown whether better communication could have changed the fact that in the ensuing battle that lasted for two days, six El Paso citizens were killed by stray bullets and fourteen were injured.[465] It certainly did not help that the curious citizenry of the city occupied rooftops and railroad car roofs to observe the fighting. Garibaldi, who was very critical of Americans expecting a "show," aptly described the scene: "The town of El Paso on the other side of the river was like a gigantic grandstand, crowded with people who had been waiting for days for this battle. It was only with difficulty that the American troops kept them out of the danger zone they had established...But unfortunately during the first day's fighting five of these spectators were killed and twelve wounded by stray bullets which could not be traced. Colonel Stevens [sic] notified us that if this kept up he would be compelled to send his forces across the bridge." [466]

When the shooting started, Madero still held out hope for a peaceful transition of power. After Diaz had agreed in a speech to Congress that he would resign, Madero agreed with the federal commander of Juarez on a cease-fire until 4 p.m. to verify the news. According to eyewitnesses the fighting began around 11:00 a.m. just below the international bridge, which was Garibaldi's command. According to Garibaldi the attack started at one o'clock in the morning, which does not correspond with the known facts of the battle.[467] Several attempts by Madero to control his troops failed. Sommerfeld scurried between the battle lines and Madero's headquarters to relate news.[468] Shortly after noon, a large explosion could be seen from the American side near the international bridge, blowing apart several dozen federals.[469] By 1:00 p.m. the rebels had taken strategic positions along the river and the customs house.[470] Federal defenders shot a horse out from under Madero's messenger who carried a white flag while on the way to General Navarro. Madero addressed his troops again urging an end to the fighting. He tried to explain his attempts to arrive at a deal with Diaz and that maybe no fighting would be necessary. He did not want to break his cease-fire agreement with Navarro. "'Our cause is greater than Juarez, and we cannot afford to dishonor ourselves for any single victory.' His words were greeted with much enthusiasm..."[471] The moment the provisional president turned to go back to his headquarters, the men and their officers went to the frontline and joined the fight. By the evening, Diaz had officially retracted any offer of resignation, and under the urging of his commanders Madero gave orders for a full attack. It was almost comical since heavy fighting had been going on against his orders since the early afternoon. Perched on railroad cars and hotel rooftops, El Paso's curious citizens and journalists watched house-to-house fighting all day on Tuesday. Not wanting to risk heavy machine gun fire on the streets, rebel soldiers punched holes into the adobe houses to move up without being exposed.[472] Jimmy Hare of Colliers Magazine went so far as to "lead the American legion in order to get pictures of the fighting."[473]

On Wednesday afternoon the battle was over. "A crowd of American sightseers flock[ed] into Juarez to collect souvenirs and satisfy their morbid curiosity."[474] The Madero officers had a hard time curtailing looting. The city was a disaster zone with hundreds of buildings damaged, rail, telephone, and water cut. The Ketelsen and Degetau store stood in flames allegedly after Villa's men sacked, looted, and demolished it. Faithful employees of the merchant firm, German Consuls Weber and Kueck never forgave Villa for this act and turned against Villa for the remainder of the revolution.

General Navarro had surrendered to revolutionary Lieutenant Colonel Giuseppe Garibaldi.[475] The Italian legionnaire let it be known to the Mexican leaders Villa and Orozco that he had been the one on the front line and defeating the federals.[476] According to Garibaldi and the famous Colliers Magazine photographer Jimmy Hare, there was no sight of either Villa or Orozco in the house-to-house battle in the middle of Juarez.[477] Hare did shoot a picture of the surrender that showed both Navarro and Garibaldi in the same frame. Villa would never forgive the Italian mercenary for challenging his bravery and, according to Katz, tried to kill him a week later in El Paso. The incident came to the attention of the El Paso mayor as well as the sheriff, which earned Villa an embarrassing expulsion from the city.[478] Garibaldi joked about the incident in his autobiography admitting Villa's fury and expulsion but not that he himself was the target.[479] The suave, educated, arrogant, and affected Italian with a British accent did not have much in common with the much simpler, gun slinging Villa.

Orozco and Villa both had shown the limits of Madero's sway over the revolution. After the Battle of Juarez, Madero decided to save the eighty-year-old Mexican federal commander Navarro from execution. According to his own Plan de San Luis Potosi, the general should have faced court-martial and execution. Villa especially wanted Navarro's head because the general had "burned the houses of rebel sympathizers in Cerro Prieto and executed some twenty persons." [480] In the process Madero briefly faced serious insubordination on the parts of Villa and Orozco. Villa had a detachment of soldiers surround Madero's headquarters. According to several eyewitnesses the confrontation between the revolutionary leader and his commanders almost ended in Madero's arrest, maybe even murder.[481] The situation diffused when Madero bravely confronted the soldiers and spoke to them. Having reestablished his authority, the future president personally accompanied Navarro to safety in El Paso. The Mexican general found refuge in the Popular Dry Goods Company, "...which was owned by Jewish-Hungarian immigrant Adolph Schwartz. Despite the protection of U.S. Secret Service agents, Navarro was whisked away when a group of Popular [sic] employees, most of them sympathetic to the rebels, began to jeer and taunt the general."[482]

On May 11th the negotiations between the Madero faction and Diaz resumed. The position of Madero had now improved significantly. The Maderistas were fully in control of Juarez. As Madero had originally planned, the control over the customs house, and import as well as export duties provided a financial shot in the arm of the revolutionaries. In a telegram to Gustavo Madero, who had made his headquarters in El Paso, Sherburne Hopkins gave an update of his negotiations in Washington and New York: "Knox gave private assurance tonight all munitions would be passed El Paso Juarez if apparently regular commercial business this settles everything so prepare and get busy everything here most favorable and New York Bankers commencing discuss proposing new loan."[483] According to Katz, "the Porfirian Elite and the revolutionary elite shared a fear of 'anarchy.'"[484] One might add the financial elite in New York and the U.S. State Department. On May 21st the warring parties concluded a peace agreement, the Treaty of Juarez. It stipulated that Diaz would resign by the end of the month and leave the country. Interim President would be Francisco Leon De La Barra, Diaz' ambassador to the United States. The revolutionary armies were to disband and the new government would take care to "...re-establish tranquility and public order. As soon as possible the reconstruction or repair of telegraph and railway lines hitherto interrupted shall be begun."[485]

This "treaty" was the result of negotiations that had been ongoing between the U.S. government, New York financiers, Madero and the Diaz administration since March. Rather than disarming the federal forces, dismembering the Diaz political elite, and instituting a revolutionary government, the agreement reflected the will of Washington and New York to establish order and safeguard American property and investments. The choice of Ambassador De La Barra to become provisional president represented a known quantity for the U.S. government. Under the guarantee of order, Gustavo Madero and Sherburne Hopkins managed to secure the financial support of Henry Clay Pierce and Charles Flint. Secretary of State Philander Knox even threw out the enforcement of the Neutrality Laws that allowed Madero's forces to rearm before the Mexican dictator had left office.

While waiting for Diaz to leave the country, Francisco Madero and his inner circle attended banquets in El Paso. On one occasion he sat next to the defeated General Navarro, which further alienated Madero's military commanders Orozco and Villa. Giuseppe Garibaldi, Abraham Gonzalez, as well as Madero's brothers Raul and Gustavo also attended the banquet.[486] Orozco and Villa openly challenged Madero's leadership. Pancho Villa in particular decried the terms of the Juarez treaty, calling Madero's entourage "perfumados," a derogatory expression meaning elegant dandies. According to a story related to General Hugh Lenox Scott in April 1914, Villa had stolen two horses from a railroad engineer named William E. Dudley. When the engineer managed to get Francisco Madero involved, he witnessed the following:

"Mr. Madero begged Villa to give back the horses. He told Villa that he (Madero) had been a guest at Mr. Dudley's camp that day and had been treated royally by Mr. Dudley and his wife, and that they were foreigners. He even told Villa that he would buy and present him with better horses; that Mr. Dudley was his personal friend. Villa threw his hat on the ground and stamped on it and told his Commander-in-Chief to take the horses and with it his resignation...a truce was finally arranged by which Villa stayed with Mr. Madero but only took the horse belonging to W. F. Dudley, but told J. L. Dudley [his wife] that if ever he bothered him again he [Villa] would burn him with green wood."[487]

There are hundreds of bandit stories about Villa. Many of them were exaggerated or even fabricated. This story, however, accentuates the trouble Madero had in keeping Villa in line. In the efforts to bring the revolution into a path of order and legality, Villa clearly became a liability in the days after Juarez. His disagreements with his chief came to a head on May 18th when Villa either voluntarily resigned or Madero forced him out as a commander.[488] Villa received the bullring of Chihuahua and a meat business as compensation for his services. According to people close to the colonel, he had hard feelings for Madero. L. L. Ross, a Bureau of Investigation agent and subsequent Sommerfeld spy reported that Villa "...has bourne [sic] himself with a good deal of malice towards Madero, who is [sic] seems has taken away from him a good deal of his authority, which he resents and is doing a good deal to create dissatisfaction."[489]

Villa was not the only one challenging Madero's authority. Harris and Sadler detailed at least two assassination attempts on Madero while he stayed in El Paso. Orozco was implicated in one of them.[490] Sommerfeld now remained so close to Madero that observers thought he might have become his bodyguard. In a sense he was. According to his testimony in 1912 he took over some of the secret service detail that Gustavo Madero and Abraham Gonzalez had put together in the fall of 1910. Most notably, Sommerfeld stated that he "...took those men because I knew I could rely upon them, because they were true blue. They were Americans, and I knew they would not double cross me..."[491] Francisco Madero's life was threatened and Sommerfeld whom Madero trusted intrinsically used his own agents to safeguard him while over two thousand Mexican troops under Madero's command were available to him. Sommerfeld's instinctive distrust of Orozco and other commanders surrounding Madero at the time saved the rebel leader's life. Senator Fall asked Sommerfeld point blank in 1912, whether he went to Orozco to prevent his killing of Madero. Sommerfeld answered, "Yes."[492]

Sommerfeld's role in these decisive days of the Mexican Revolution cannot be underestimated. As Madero's personal secretary or "confidential agent" as he put it, the German had unprecedented access to information which was of high value to the German government. Historian Friedrich Katz pointed out in *The Secret War in Mexico* that it was not only the movements and inner workings of the Madero faction which Germany was interested in. "After the American troop mobilization on the Mexican border [in March 1911], a section of the American press stated that this step had been directed primarily at Germany."[493] Germany had threatened to act should German lives and property be affected in the violence. Rather than entrusting American forces with providing security, the German statement had rattled American leaders and, according to journalists familiar with the U.S. military leadership, triggered the large mobilization along the Mexican-American border. How serious the Taft administration considered the German threat to be, the unprecedented troop strength of over 20,000 balanced whatever Germany had in mind. Important for this German-American saber rattling is the consideration of the position Sommerfeld found himself in. As a Madero confidante he negotiated with the American commander of Fort Bliss, thus gaining insight into Steever's preparedness, orders, freedom of action, and capability. While in the pay of the German Consul Kueck, under the cover of an AP News press pass, and in the top echelon of the revolutionary command, Sommerfeld gave the German authorities the necessary insight to play their diplomatic cards. By virtue of Madero's victory, Felix Sommerfeld had become Germany's top agent on the American continent.

In the meantime Mexico City erupted with violence. Porfirio Diaz had announced that he would resign by the 25th of May. On the outskirts of the city five thousand revolutionary troops under the command of Emiliano Zapata beleaguered the city. Zapata had promised Madero not to invade the well-defended capital but rather wait for Diaz to resign and allow for a peaceful transition of power. On the night of May 24th a mob armed with rocks and machetes charged the Zócalo (central plaza) and hurled stones into the windows of the National Palace. In a last show of force Diaz ordered his guards to open fire and disperse the crowd. The ensuing street fighting lasted all night. On the 25th the capital crackled with anticipation of Diaz resignation. Finally, at 2 p.m. Diaz entered the Chamber of Deputies. Tens of thousands of demonstrators lined the streets with thousands of heavily armed cavalry and infantry defending the National Palace and Parliament. All but two deputies voted for Diaz' resignation. These two, old comrades relics of the war against Emperor Maximilian and the Battle of Puebla, were the only men willing to stand up for their fallen leader. In his resignation speech Diaz showed no remorse. He hoped that history would judge his leadership of Mexico fairly. "I do not know," Diaz said showing his amazement as to the forces assembled against him, "of any facts imputable to me which could have caused this social phenomenon; but permitting, though not admitting, that I may be unwittingly culpable, such a possibility makes me the least able to reason out and decide my own culpability."[494]

On May 26th the former ambassador to the United States, Francisco Leon De La Barra, assumed the provisional presidency of Mexico. He was to stay in power until elections could be called in October for which he was not allowed to be a candidate. In the early morning hours of May 27th Citizen Diaz and his family left the capital. Guarded by two battalions of infantry and several cavalry detachments, the unscheduled train quickly made its way towards Veracruz. Two hundred Zapatistas camping out near the railroad in Puebla unknowingly stopped the train to check its contents. Only few survived the onslaught of machine gun batteries and Mauser rifle fire when the baggage car doors opened. Near the place where General Diaz had fought his most famous battle resisting the French invasion on May 5th 1862 (Cinco de Mayo), Diaz commanded his last military engagement. With the old General standing next to his officers he directed the cavalry to pursue the hapless Indians who had held up the train. No quarter, no mercy! Once the slaughter was complete, a satisfied Diaz ordered the American engineer to fire up the engines and steam to the coast. Upon reaching Veracruz, the refugees stayed in a heavily guarded house near the harbor. In charge of Diaz' safety was General Victoriano Huerta. On the morning of June 1st the former dictator addressed his military detail for a last time as a commander. He lauded their loyalty and pledged "that if ever sudden danger from without threatens my country I will return, and under that flag for which I have fought much, I, with you at my back, will learn again to conquer." [495] Choking on those words, tears in his eyes, the senile old master of Mexico left on the German Hamburg America steamer "Ypiranga" for Spain never to set foot on Mexican soil again. The women of Veracruz had "filled the cabin of the refugees with flowers, and its men crowded the pier end and with roaring vivas sped Porfirio Diaz to his exile."[496] Whether the flowers and vivas served to ensure his departure or whether there really was appreciation left for the fallen dictator, one can only surmise. Only in February the German Emperor Wilhelm II had bestowed the "Großkreuz des Roten Adlerorden," the Cross of the Order of the Red Eagle, on the President.[497] Now Wilhelm invited the fallen dictator to Bad Nauheim for a thorough cure in the warm springs there.[498] Diaz died a broken man on July 2nd 1915 in Paris, France.

On June 2nd Madero and his "perfumado" entourage of around one hundred followers including Giuseppe Garibaldi, Felix Sommerfeld, and Sherburne Hopkins left for Mexico City. "His train took four days and nights to make a trip that normally averages thirty hours."[499] The special train from Eagle Pass traveled via San Pedro, Madero's home, Torreon, Zacatecas, Aguascalientes, and San Luis Potosi to Mexico City. "At every station, every siding, all along the tracks, the shabby ragged people of Mexico waited to hear him, see him, perhaps touch him. Mothers fought forward with their babies, aged and sick limped over cobblestones to the tracks, rancheros and peons trotted in from miles away." [500] Sommerfeld and Hopkins experienced this incredible ride. A proud Sommerfeld told investigators "Mr. and Mrs. Madero had asked me to come to Mexico City and live with them."[501] Notwithstanding the prophetic comet Halley, another sign shook the superstitions of Mexico's masses. "On the morning the train was due in Mexico City, at dawn, there was an earthquake. For the first time in generations, the spongy ground did not absorb the shock. Walls cracked, buildings crumbled, the crowds that jammed the windows and packed the roofs ran praying into the streets."[502] The wife of American Charge d'Affairs, Edith O'Shaughnessy, woke to "the violent swaying of the house, so violent that as I jumped up I could not keep on my feet. There was a sound as of a great wind at sea and on all sides the breaking of china…"[503] Did the earth tremble in fear of the violence still to come or in joyous anticipation of the apostle of democracy entering the capital?

Madero's arrival in Mexico City as the victorious leader of the revolution triggered one of the largest celebrations the city had ever seen. Provisional President Francisco Leon De La Barra, many Mexican and foreign dignitaries including the diplomatic corps, and the peasant leader from Morelos, Emiliano Zapata, lined up to pay homage. The "little man from Coahuila" had mounted what historian Lloyd Gardner defined as the "first serious challenge to the international order established by the industrial nations after the middle of the nineteenth century."[504] While the city exploded in joy, the revolutionary leaders started to implement first political changes. Madero, while nominally the leader of the Democratic Party, did not hold an office in the new government. Madero's uncle Ernesto became Secretary of Finance (Secretary of the Hacienda). Rafael Hernandez, Madero's cousin became Secretary of Justice. Francisco Vasquez Gomez (Education), Emilio Vasquez Gomez (Interior) and Manuel Bonilla (Communication) rounded out the representation of the Maderistas in De La Barra's administration.

Almost immediately after Diaz' departure, the new administration moved against Lord Cowdray with all barrels blazing.[505] Hopkins' personal friend and client, Gustavo Madero, had arguably become the most powerful behind-the-scenes actor in the new power structure. Asked whether "Madero went to work to do all he could to break down the Cowdray influence in Mexico?" Hopkins answered defiantly: "He [Madero] has followed the law…"[506] Hopkins worked to sack the Board of Directors of the Mexican National Railway. While he claimed in his testimony before the U.S. Senate in 1912, that Pierce only hired him officially in July, the result of Hopkins' work was that virtual control of the railroads reverted to Pierce in October.[507] Ernesto Madero, Francisco's uncle and Secretary of Finance, managed to save the jobs of the president of the company and several officers. Otherwise, Lord Cowdray was finished. After a meeting between the oil magnate and Francisco Madero in the beginning of August 1911, Cowdray decided to get help. On August 23rd, 1911 the Washington Post reported that the British oil tycoon sold all his oil holdings in Mexico to John W. Gates for a pittance, $25 Million in gold ($525 Million in today's value).[508] In reality, the deal was a merger. Gates owned refineries and oil facilities in Texas that ultimately became Texaco years later. Cowdray's hope was that American ownership of El Aguila would enlist the American government as an arbiter in future disputes. After an unsuccessful throat cancer operation in Paris, Gates died within weeks of merging with El Aguila and Pearson's other holdings in Mexico. His widow sold majority interest in the Texas company after her son Charles died in 1912.[509] According to testimony of Sherburne Hopkins, none other than Standard Oil Company bought the Gates and Pearson oil interests.[510] In Lord Cowdray, Madero had made a deadly enemy who would do whatever he could to depose and eliminate the Mexican leader.

PART III

~

THE MADERO PRESIDENCY

CHAPTER 11

r

REVOLUTION UNCHECKED

Emiliano Zapata, the notorious leader of the revolutionary forces of Morelos, precipitated the first crisis that confronted the new government of Mexico. Zapata, like many of the grass roots supporters of the revolution, immediately expected laws mandating land reform, return of confiscated communal lands to villages, and bargaining rights for labor unions. The reality on the ground in Mexico City was completely different from those expectations. Madero had ceded presidential power to De La Barra until the general elections scheduled for November 1911 could be held. The new cabinet only contained moderate conservative Maderistas, such as Ernesto Madero and the Vasquez Gomez brothers. The provisional president and four other cabinet members were carry-overs from the Porfiriato. Madero himself applied strict allegiance to the rule of law. As such, he initiated and supported the disbanding of the revolutionary forces and relied on the Rurales and federal army to maintain order. "Logically the Juarez treaty should have been a blueprint for transition to a revolutionary government," historian John Womack wrote, joining in the chorus of Madero's contemporary critics.[511] Of course, Madero never embraced radical revolutionary change, neither in his call for Diaz not to be reelected, nor in his Plan de San Luis Potosi, nor in the treaty of Juarez.

Madero's supporters as well as historians such as Womack projected their agenda into the new Mexican government and quickly became disillusioned. Hiding behind the De La Barra government and promising in general terms to address everyone's grievances, Madero's broad coalition of radicals, moderates, and conservatives started to crumble, literally on the day Diaz sailed into exile. Worse, instead of reversing the illegality of the Diaz regime - the confiscations, the state terror, and the sell-out of national resources - the De La Barra administration "appeared to restore the situation as it existed under the old regime."[512] Prophetically, Diaz had warned that the tiger, once unleashed, could not easily be controlled. Madero's unhappy compromise with the old elites that gave De La Barra the job of tamer aggravated the disenchantment of the Mexican people with their new leaders. Indeed, Diaz should have been more accurate in his prophecy. It was not one tiger Madero had unleashed – the new leaders faced a jungle with packs of dangerous animals roaming in it.

Not so much a wild animal, but a personality as true to his convictions as Madero was Zapata. He fought the Diaz administration to reverse the land grab of the planters of Morelos. The promise of agrarian reform formed the basis of his support. He never abandoned his roots nor did he compromise on his goals. If any revolutionary leader in Mexico could be called pure, Zapata's name would occupy the top spot. With his peasant troops the "Attila of the South" had created the southern front in the revolution. When the old dictator stumbled and fell, Zapata held his forces at the gates to the capital to allow Madero a triumphal entry. Patiently, he waited at the train station to greet and submit to the new leader. On June 8th 1911, the day after celebrations ceased, the stoic man with the large mustache and even larger sombrero called in his favors in a meeting with the "high ruling circles of the revolutionary coalition".[513] Zapata demanded in no uncertain terms from the new leaders - Francisco and Gustavo Madero, Venustiano Carranza, Abraham Gonzalez, and Emilio Vasquez Gomez - that "right away, lands must be returned to the pueblos, and the promises which the revolution made be carried out."[514] Madero urged patience and cited legal issues that first had to be resolved. From Madero's perspective the agrarian reform question could not be settled with arms and violence. Albeit hated, the plantation owners of Morelos claimed legal titles to their property. In Madero's eyes confiscating this land and returning it to villagers would have been as illegal as the original land grabbing under Diaz. It would also have alienated the moderate and conservative wings of his movement.

While Madero urged patience for the process of elections and legal reforms to take place, Zapata kept pushing for action. To the peasant leader, Madero's resistance to quick action posed a two-fold problem. He had to control his supporters to whom he had promised immediate results in return for their participation in the fighting. Zapata also had to decide whether he had supported a revolutionary cause or had simply helped to unseat one elite for another. With great patience and self-discipline the wild cat from Morelos retracted his claws and agreed to temporarily sacrifice his greatest weapon. In expectation that the new government would act to resolve the land question in his home state, he agreed to disband his forces. Over the resistance of his followers, he agreed to send the villagers home and relinquish control over the state of Morelos to the federal army. In good faith Zapata also relinquished his quest for the governorship of Morelos.

Almost immediately following his grand entry into the capital Madero traveled to many of the southern states. On June 12[th]1911, he visited Morelos ostensibly to further negotiate with Zapata. Rather than showing his support for the villagers who had fought under his banner, Madero committed the same mistake he had already made in Chihuahua. He let himself be entertained by the hacendados of Morelos, so "aggressively élite that Zapata ... refused to attend."[515] Worse, as Zapata kept his word and disbanded the revolutionary army, a power vacuum developed in the countryside. The revolutionary spirit simmered below the surface and erupted in what Diaz used to call - and Madero now called - banditry. The outbreaks of violence in Morelos triggered a legalistic response from the government: restore order and arrest the perpetrators! To the revolutionaries and historians on the left Madero and De La Barra's response to the continued uprisings and lawlessness in Morelos showed a breach of faith with the ideals of the revolution. Federal troops harassed local communities while the new government disbanded the revolutionary forces. Even to Madero's followers this made no sense. In this context Zapata's eventual revolt against the new government seemed a foregone conclusion and justified.

Felix Sommerfeld accompanied Madero on his trips to the south as a staff member. On July 19th 1911, federal troops in the city of Puebla clashed with Maderista forces. In an ensuing bloodbath machine guns mowed down "...several dozens of insurgents and their families. Many of the Maderistas were machine-gunned in the city bullring as they waited to greet Madero who was scheduled to visit the city the following day. In the wake of the infamous battle that lasted until dawn, out-gunned revolutionaries fled to safety in the surrounding countryside."[516] Order was quickly restored, however, sentiments ran deep. Madero arrived in Puebla the day after the clashes and promptly sided with the federal forces. Sommerfeld recalled the incident that followed the Maderista retreat from Puebla. As one of the retreating groups of revolutionaries passed by a textile factory in the town of Covadonga, shots rang out prompting the rebels to attack. In the resulting firefight "three German men and a woman were assassinated by some revolting rebel bands."[517] The murders created an international incident. Since the German Ambassador Rear Admiral Paul von Hintze was aware that the Mexican leader traveled in the region, he met with him in close-by Puebla. Von Hintze adamantly demanded from the Mexican leader that the murderers be caught, tried, and restitution paid to the victim's families.

The German ambassador relentlessly pursued the murderers of Covadonga for years to come. Probably the only foreign government to achieve payments for its murdered citizens, von Hintze's efforts resulted in a restitution of 400,000 German Marks (about $95,000 at the time, $2 million in today's value) to Germany in June of 1912.[518] The perpetrators were tried and executed in the presence of the German ambassador in March of 1913 (by then the Huerta government ruled Mexico).[519] Von Hintze's success with the Madero government remains stunning. While he settled with and received financial restitution from the Mexican government for four German citizens, eighty Americans and forty Spaniards had been killed without their respective governments ever finding an accommodation with the Madero administration.[520] The U.S. and Spain lacked an important ingredient: Von Hintze was in the possession of a personal contact high up in the Madero administration in the person of Felix Sommerfeld who was the President and Finance Minister's friend and confidante.

The "revolting rebel bands" Sommerfeld referred to had, just a month before, helped Madero's ascent to power. In this testimony Sommerfeld clearly reflected the attitude of Madero, who in these months after the unseating of Diaz, alienated many of his followers. The German agent made no mention of the clashes at Puebla that triggered the events at Covadonga. Shocking to his supporters, Madero declared the perpetrators of the attack on Covadonga to be criminals rather than revolutionaries.[521]

The meetings between von Hintze and Madero in Puebla in July 1911 provide a glimpse into the German ambassador's role in Sommerfeld's life. When Sommerfeld moved from Chihuahua to Mexico City, he switched bosses. Rather than reporting to Consul Kueck and Commercial Attaché Bruchhausen, Sommerfeld now seemed to report directly to the German Ambassador von Hintze. The clearest evidence of Sommerfeld's deep involvement with the German embassy in Mexico City appeared in a series of correspondences between the German Chancellor von Bethmann Hollweg and Ambassador von Hintze in 1911. According to Sommerfeld's statement to the American authorities in 1918, he met the rear admiral for the first time when Madero and von Hintze discussed the murders of Covadonga.[522] However, on July 25th, one week after the supposed "first meeting" von Hintze wrote to the German chancellor, "...the local representative of the Associated Press, Mr.

Sommerfeld, is a confidential agent of the Maderos and enjoys a large standing with them. He is German and deserves, as much as others and I have been able to observe him, trust, naturally with certain limitations."[523]

Without specific mention, the ambassador told the head of the German government that he had an agent as high in the Mexican government as one could get. Because the German agent sent his earlier reports to Peter Bruchhausen it is possible that Sommerfeld actually met von Hintze in Puebla for the first time. However, by then he had already been a German naval intelligence asset and von Hintze immediately tasked Sommerfeld with an important mission. On the 22nd of July, just as the supposed "first meeting" took place, von Hintze asked Sommerfeld to approach the Secretary of Finance, Ernesto Madero, and check whether the De La Barra government had indeed signed, or was planning on signing, a reciprocity treaty between the United States and Mexico. The rumor that the United States had been negotiating such an agreement had upset German financial circles, as it would have further reduced German financial influence over the Mexican government. Sommerfeld did as he was told and brought a letter from Ernesto Madero that denied any existence of a treaty or plan to negotiate a treaty. Whether the two knew each other in person or not, von Hintze would not have used Sommerfeld for such a sensitive, clandestine diplomatic mission without prior knowledge of his loyalty and skill. Von Hintze's mention of Sommerfeld to the German chancellor, namely that "He...deserves, as much as others...have been able to observe him, trust..." clearly referred to Kueck and Bruchhausen. Also telling is a small detail that belied Sommerfeld's work as an AP correspondent: Sommerfeld had Ernesto Madero address the letter to him with the address of "German Consulate, 5 de Mayo 32."[524]

When American authorities asked Sommerfeld in 1918, who paid him compensation in Mexico City in those days of 1911, he sidestepped the question. Just as he hid the fact that he was on Consul Kueck's payroll earlier, he now testified that he lived "on my own money."[525] If Madero did not pay him, which Sommerfeld emphatically claimed, and if, as he testified, he only worked very sporadically for AP News, who paid his living expenses? The answer can only be the German embassy. Sommerfeld was worth every penny the German government invested in him. Through Sommerfeld, von Hintze, and by extension von Bethmann Hollweg and the Kaiser himself, had a back door access to the new government of Mexico. The fact that Sommerfeld lied again, just as he had about his employment with Kueck, and did not disclose the obvious connection between him and the German ambassador prior to the

Covadonga incident, can only substantiate his true occupation in Mexico City. Indeed, subsequent events will show the extent to which von Hintze and Sommerfeld cooperated until Madero's death in 1913. As the new government settled in Mexico City, Germany vied for military contracts and political influence. Von Hintze's instructions from Germany were to observe Mexican politics but engage actively in promoting German economic interests.[526] Sommerfeld helped him to achieve both.

It was not surprising that, just when the Madero Revolution unseated Porfirio Diaz, the German Emperor personally sent Paul von Hintze, one of his confidantes, to fill the vacant German ambassador's job in Mexico City. Nominally, the German ambassador to the United States also had responsibility for the embassy in Mexico after Ambassador Karl Gottlieb Buenz left for Germany in 1910. Dealing with significant health issues, Buenz officially retired from the diplomatic corps in January 1911.[527] However, Ambassador Count von Bernstorff and his embassy staff had very limited interaction with the Mexican government. Neither in his memoirs nor in his war reminiscences does Bernstorff even mention Mexico or any interaction with it before 1914. He never traveled to Mexico City, never met with President Madero. The country he had diplomatic responsibility for simply was not on his radar. The unofficial representative of Germany in the time between ambassadors Buenz and von Hintze was a local physician, Gustav Pagenstecher.[528] A pioneer in the field of psychometrics, the wealthy immigrant from Germany also had significant business interests in Mexico. The previously cozy relationship between Ambassador Karl Buenz and Gustav Pagenstecher went so far as to both allegedly making 100,000 Pesos (over $1 million in today's value) in an illegal business scheme under Diaz.[529] After his recall to Germany, Dr. Buenz received a new assignment. HAPAG Director Albert Ballin sent him to New York in 1913 to head the U.S. office of the shipping powerhouse, the Hamburg-Amerikanische-Paketfahrt-Aktien-Gesellschaft.[530] The lack of proper German representation in Mexico for almost two years, especially in view of the political upheavals at the time, worried the German Foreign Office. Once Diaz went into exile, Germany had lost the last important connections to the leadership cadre in Mexico.

The Emperor chose von Hintze for the important task of establishing contact to the new government. Hintze was not a diplomat of the traditional school. When his appointment was announced career diplomats in the Foreign Office politicked against him. Ambassador von Bernstorff certainly would have liked to have had input into the appointment. His career and von Hintze's would cross again as both vied for the appointment to Foreign Secretary towards the end of World War I. Rear Admiral von Hintze was one of the most daring and influential international players in German World War I history. His career spanned an incredible range: He rose from naval officer to become confidante of the German naval chief Grand Admiral von Tirpitz and the Kaiser himself. Then he became an ambassador and diplomat. As such, von Hintze's ascent culminated in briefly becoming Foreign Secretary at the end of the First World War. None other than Secretary Hintze appealed to the Emperor's honor in 1918 and asked him to retire into exile for the sake of Germany. Strange as it might seem, von Hintze joins Sommerfeld and Stallforth as one more player of this crucial time in world history that has not been adequately treated by historians.[531]

Paul Hintze was born in 1864 in the little town of Schwedt approximately eighty miles northeast of Berlin. The Hintze family was part of the hardworking German middle class of the Prussian country towns. Schwedt only had ten thousand inhabitants but because the city is located on the Oder River it benefited from trade. Paul's father owned a tobacco plant, making cigars of the raw tobacco he imported. He also had a seat in the City Council. The Hintze family was one of the best regarded and wealthiest in town. Paul attended the humanistic Gymnasium (high school) and graduated with a baccalaureate in 1882. Rather than serving the mandatory year in the military, he joined the navy as an eighteen-year-old. Paul struck his superiors as very smart and very tough. After basic training on the school ship "Prinz Adalbert," Hintze sailed the seven seas for the next twelve years, in which he saw the coasts of Africa, the Middle East, North and South America. In 1894 the navy lieutenant (Kapitänleutnant) studied at the Naval Academy in Kiel, a school for which very few officers had the honor of admission.

Among the many that trained and studied at Kiel there were several graduates worth mentioning for this story: Grand Admiral Alfred von Tirpitz (then Captain Tirpitz) graduated in 1865, von Hintze (then without noble title) in 1896. Karl Boy-Ed, eight years von Hintze's junior, joined the class of 1894. After serving in active duty in the Far East, Boy-Ed became German Naval Attaché in Washington in 1912 and worked for then Ambassador von Hintze in his partial responsibility for Mexico. Franz Rintelen (never had a noble title), the son of a well-known Berlin banker, graduated in 1905. Rintelen was to become a notorious German sabotage agent in the United States in World War I. All three worked for Grand Admiral von Tirpitz who became the loudest voice clamoring for unrestricted submarine warfare in the Great War. Von Tirpitz' naval high command also had administrative responsibility for all overseas secret service operations. The Department of the Navy and in extension its naval attachés in the German embassies of North and South America had the responsibility for creating, maintaining, and financing secret service operations. The organizational umbrella, the "Nachrichtenbüro," also called Department "N," changed from a propaganda organization, hailing the German navy and its accomplishments, to the naval intelligence service.[532] Karl Boy-Ed served in the Department "N" first under Rear Admiral von Hintze, then as its chief from 1906 to 1909.[533] His intelligence responsibilities and his background as the son of a famous female novelist explain his proclivity for journalism and propaganda when he was naval attaché in the United States and beyond.[534] Army intelligence operations were limited to the European countries or in coordination with the navy, which provided almost all funding. The military attachés attached to such embassies had no reporting requirement to the diplomatic service. As such, the ambassadors had the advantage of complete deniability should clandestine operations be uncovered.

After Paul Hintze completed his studies at the Naval Academy in 1896, he joined the Naval Command in Berlin. His assignment coincided with Emperor Wilhelm's decision to update the German navy en par with the Royal Navy of England. For that purpose he appointed Tirpitz to State Secretary of the Imperial Navy. Tirpitz became rear admiral in 1895 and was ennobled in 1900. Tirpitz oversaw the greatest expansion of the German navy in history. He immediately purged the Naval High Command of most officers who had served under his predecessor, and appointed younger officers into his staff that he personally had vetted for their loyalty to him and his cause. The departmental cleansing swept young naval officers such as von Hintze and, a few years later, Karl Boy-Ed and Franz Rintelen, into Tirpitz' inner circle. The Grand Admiral became the father of the modern German navy that, by the time the Great War broke out, was not quite as powerful but slightly more modern than the British navy.

In 1898, Rear Admiral Tirpitz commissioned navy captain Hintze to join the East Asian battle group as a "Flaggleutnant," the liaison officer to the Naval High Command. In this capacity Hintze faced an outraged Admiral Dewey when the German navy obstructed Dewey's efforts to subdue the Spanish in the Philippines in the Spanish-American War. German ships had operated so close to the U.S. navy that Dewey had to employ searchlights, which gave away the American positions to the Spanish. Dewey also had declared a blockade and accordingly expected any naval vessel to allow search parties to board.

Naturally the proud German navy rejected this infringement on international law. Hintze never commented on his confrontation with Dewey, which must have been so heated that news stories about it could be found twenty years later. According to newspapers, Dewey told the German naval officer "if he [German Admiral von Diederichs] wants a fight he can have it now."[535] Cooler heads prevailed. Rather than shooting out their differences, the German fleet found a way to compromise with the Americans and eventually left the Philippine theater. Ambassador von Bernstorff commented on the affair in his 1920 memoirs. According to the ambassador, the underlying cause of the aggression was that Germany tried to "acquire" the Philippine islands after the U.S. had declared it did not want to hold on to them in the long term. "[A] misunderstanding had occurred, as a result of which the Berlin Foreign Office had acted in perfect good faith. In the public mind in the United States, however, the feeling still rankled that Germany had wished to make a demonstration against their Government."[536] It was unfortunate that Hintze had to find himself in the middle of this "misunderstanding." Karl Boy-Ed also saw the Spanish-American War unfold in front of his eyes as a lieutenant. According to a short autobiographical sketch he witnessed the American occupation of Manila.[537] Paul Hintze's extraordinary career progressed rapidly. In 1901 he became 1st officer on the cruiser "Kaiser Wilhelm." A year later he joined the staff of Admiral von Tirpitz.

In 1903, the navy dispatched their thirty-nine-year-old and experienced naval captain Hintze to the German embassy in St. Petersburg. The German naval officer did not portray the stone-faced, military demeanor one would expect. Rather, his slightly rounded face with a protruding nose and high cheekbones was fatherly and friendly. Certainly not to be underestimated, Hintze's eyes could shoot arrows of hot emotion. But for the most part he was charming, good natured, and funny. With one eyebrow raised above the other he listened to his counterparts without interrupting. When he spoke, his words were carefully chosen and meaningful. Dark rings under his eyes betrayed the long hours of work, reading reports, dictating letters and memoranda. Hintze could be counted on. "His social suaveness...his empathy for the idiosyncrasies of other people made him quickly establish friendly relationships."[538] He was a popular commander at sea. As the new naval attaché to St. Petersburg Hintze occupied a critical position in the embassy: Emperor Wilhelm II became extraordinarily interested in reports from Tirpitz' protégé. Hintze's assessment of Russian politics and the quality of his intelligence soon caused the Kaiser to use Hintze for most sensitive missions between the German government and the Russian Czar. Never trusting of the Foreign Office, the Emperor preferred communication with his cousin "Nikki" to go through naval attaché Hintze. In 1905, Hintze joined the two emperors in a summit meeting in the Swedish city of Bjoerko. A year later Hintze received the title "Flügeladjutant." This promotion, in a roundabout way, made him the direct representative of the German Emperor in Russia, a position that in many ways was more powerful than that of the ambassador. Hintze's close relationship with the two emperors and the circumvention of the Foreign Office by the Kaiser made him a long-term target of career diplomats in the Reich. In 1908, Wilhelm II made Hintze into a nobleman with the title of Baron that could be inherited. As such, the middle class tobacco merchants of Schwedt became nobility. Von Hintze also received the promotion to rear admiral that year.

While several biographers have diminished von Hintze's career in the following years, the truth shows a stellar rise to prominence of the rear admiral. It was neither "an indiscretion" nor a sudden "change of heart" that propelled von Hintze into the Foreign Office. Von Tirpitz and the German Emperor desperately needed someone to take over the embassy in Mexico City. That person had to have several key abilities: First, absolute loyalty to the military authorities, especially the Emperor and von Tirpitz. Second, the new ambassador needed to have intelligence experience. He needed to build a network of agents, gather intelligence, and assemble it into the highly sensible and informed reports the Kaiser and the Admiralty had been acquainted to receive from St. Petersburg. None better than von Hintze could be found. Historian Reinhard Doerries seconded that the ambassador was mainly a spymaster and even alleged that at the outbreak of the Great War, "Paul von Hintze, German minister in Ciudad Mexico and in charge of German agents in Mexico engaged in sabotage across the Rio Grande in the U.S."[539] Mexico in 1911 was not a second rate assignment. The revolution and the competition for influence with the new Mexican leadership necessitated a diplomat of the highest ability. That person was Rear Admiral von Hintze. In Mexico, he was to sow the seeds of a highly efficient intelligence network that would be ready for action when the Great War started. Two years after von Hintze took up his new assignment in Mexico City, his young staff officer from Berlin, Karl Boy-Ed, reported to a new assignment in Washington D.C. as German naval attaché responsible for Mexico and the U.S.[540] Von Hintze would eventually turn his whole spy organization over to his protégé in Washington and in 1915 move on to an assignment in China. As imperial ambassador in Beijing, he was to use the excellent experience he had gained in Mexico from 1911 to 1914. With great success he intrigued against the Entente powers that were trying to engage China for their cause in World War I.[541] His tactics included diplomatic maneuvering, political intrigue, and clandestine operations such as sabotaging Entente supply lines.

Von Hintze arrived in Veracruz on April 25th 1911.[542] As soon as the new ambassador presented his credentials to President De La Barra, von Hintze began to lay the groundwork for a clandestine network in Mexico. The most obvious existing organization was the network of consulates in all major cities of the country. Mexico had one German consul in the capital and official vice consuls in cities with larger German communities such as Puebla, Veracruz, San Cristobal de las Casas, Monterrey, Chihuahua, Guaymas, and Torreon. Vice Consuls were exclusively German subjects. With an official title and a token salary they reported on events in their regions and promoted German businesses in their area. They often were not fully employed by the government and could be businessmen or community leaders. Smaller or more remote towns had honorary consuls that reported to the vice consuls and usually were only paid for expenses. Honorary consuls did not have to be German but in the case of Mexico usually were at least of German descent. Within weeks of taking office, the rear admiral had contacted every one of them and began making a picture for himself as to how connected these people were, whether they could keep secrets, and how well they understood what was going on around them. He also visited the respective regions personally. For example in December 1911, von Hintze asked the Mexican government to provide for protection while he traveled to "the north of the Republic."[543] The two best-connected Germans in his area of responsibility were Carl Heynen and Richard Eversbusch who had offices in Tampico, Veracruz, and Mexico City. Heynen represented the interest of Albert Ballin and the Hamburg Amerika Linie, HAPAG, in Mexico. While von Hintze had a large influence on the activities of the German naval fleet in the Mexican theatre, Heynen controlled the merchant marine and represented a direct link between HAPAG's chairman Albert Ballin and the German ambassador in Mexico. Heynen's cooperation with von Hintze and the German embassy in the United States would prove most fruitful in future clandestine operations. At the onset of World War I, Heynen joined the German secret service operation around Heinrich Albert in New York. He became one of the most influential German agents of the war and worked closely with both Felix Sommerfeld and Frederico Stallforth.

What was missing in von Hintze's organization was a connection that reached deep into the power structure of the new leaders of Mexico. Enter Felix Sommerfeld. Whether the Admiralty had assigned the German agent to the embassy in Mexico City or von Hintze received a recommendation from Consul Kueck to do the same is not known. However, Sommerfeld immediately became von Hintze and the Admiralty's greatest asset in Mexico. Sommerfeld proved his proximity to the new government, both to von Hintze and the German chancellor, with his first assignment, the verification of the Mexican-American reciprocity treaty. Within days, the German agent was able to dispel rumors of such a contract. Apart from Hintze's frequent debriefings of Sommerfeld in the embassy and various clubs in Mexico City, the ambassador's main job was to steer business towards Germany.[544] Among other things, the relationship of the Deutsch-Südamerikanische Bank with the Mexican finance minister was important to recoup some of the financial influence lost to U.S. and French banking concerns under Diaz. As with any business of that type, Sommerfeld probably provided intelligence on the decision-making process and discussions in the inner circle of the new leadership. The Maderos had a very close relationship with the Deutsch-Südamerikanische Bank, which according to many scholars supported the revolution with loans.[545]

Of greatest interest to the German government were arms and ammunition purchases for the federal army. Although the German Krupp concern had been able to supply the Mexican army with Mauser rifles and making the German 7mm cartridge a standard in Mexico, German manufacturers had lost significant contracts for cannon and other hardware to French manufacturers. General Manuel Mondragon was Porfirio Diaz' main arms purchaser and he had decided against German weapons on numerous occasions. Von Hintze with Sommerfeld's help was able to reverse this trend and steer a host of profitable contracts to German manufacturers. In the beginning of February 1912, the German Ambassador wrote to the Foreign Office in Berlin, "...the President of Mexico asked me to telegraph whether the imperial government would be willing to sell 200,000 of the current infantry rifles and carbines with 500 cartridges each? If yes, when can be delivered and how expensive? Speculators in London have offered to arrange this deal for him [the President]; he prefers to arrange directly from one government to another."[546] The positive response of the War Department came a week later. However, the Mexican government had meanwhile placed the order with someone else. Von Hintze kept badgering the Mexican President until the bidding was reopened. After having "prepared the President of the Republic," he took the director of the Vereinigte Deutsche Waffenfabriken to an appointment with Madero. The meeting resulted in an order for 200,000 rifles and 10 million cartridges that, to Hintze's great dismay, the German manufacturer refused to accept. The Mauser representatives claimed to have too much of a backlog. Most likely, the real reason had to do with the financial terms and securities which the fledgling government of Mexico could not provide. This order and several others finally saw deliveries in 1914, long after their placement. This delayed delivery schedule caused the international community to mistakenly allege German government support for Madero's successor, Dictator Victoriano Huerta.[547] The opposite was true.

Von Hintze's activities to boost German arms sales to Mexico in the spring of 1912 contained two fascinating aspects. The personal involvement of the Mexican President in the attempt to boost German exports showed the degree of personal access the ambassador enjoyed with Madero. Sommerfeld, as Madero's personal secretary and Ambassador von Hintze's go to contact within the administration, was likely the key to opening the doors for von Hintze. The other notable aspect was von Hintze's description of corruption this early in the Madero administration. While considering the Mexican President to "...have the inexcusable fault of being honest, one of his brothers [Gustavo] in order to compensate for this folly, monopolizes the most dubious transactions for himself."[548] The ambassador asked the businessmen for whom he intervened not to inform him about under-the-table payments and bribes. Certainly understanding that no business was possible in Mexico without bribes, he wanted to maintain some appearance of higher ground.[549]

While the German ambassador in Mexico established himself, the De La Barra government, which Madero installed until free elections could be conducted, attempted to consolidate its power over Mexico. Madero proposed and De La Barra appointed provisional governors in a host of states. These governors included Madero's friend and revolutionary associate Pino Suarez who took office on the Yucatan peninsula. Venustiano Carranza, Madero's confidante who had spearheaded negotiations with the Diaz government in New York that led to the Treaty of Ciudad Juarez, took over the governorship of Coahuila, Madero's home state. Abraham Gonzalez, the chief organizer and recruiter of Madero's revolution, took over the governorship in Chihuahua. José Maria Maytorena, who had led the Yaqui troops in support of the revolution in Sonora, became provisional governor there. Madero nominated Francisco Naranjo for the governorship of Morelos. Altogether, fourteen governorships changed as a result of Madero's treaty of Juarez. On the surface, it seemed that the new leaders in Mexico City were well on their way to lay the groundwork for democratic change in the republic. However, below the surface, the structure of Diaz' almost forty-year-rule proved hard to change. While provisional governments took over the states, conservative legislators and state judges in effect undermined attempts to change the system. "In Coahuila, Carranza almost lost his freedom of action due to legislative opposition."[550] The conservative legislators blocked any attempt to push through reforms. Other state governments ran into the same issues. Legal disagreements that escalated to the holdover Mexican Supreme Court led to decisions that favored the old guard. The national assembly, while on the surface kowtowing to the new leaders, remained conservative and largely loyal to the old regime. Even the newspapers of the day opposed the Maderistas and contributed to more widespread disillusionment with the revolutionary leadership.

Madero still hoped to gain popular support for the first free and democratic elections in Mexico since 1870. He traveled ceaselessly across the country and rallied his supporters wherever he could. At the same time he was confronted with the brutal suppression of his fighters, whether in the Puebla incident or with the Yaqui Indian tribes in Sonora. While he felt support of the De La Barra government to be crucial, Madero attempted to negotiate settlements and buy time through tempering the opposition. Throughout the summer Madero interacted with Zapata. On August 18th 1911, Madero spoke in the city of Cuautla: "I have come here to bring calm and traquillity [sic], and I will not leave your state...until you have security that your rights will be respected in every sense. Have faith in me, as I have in you, and we will continue marching without any obstacle along the new path of Democracy and Liberty."[551] The weakness of Madero's control of the De La Barra government became painfully obvious in the days following the speech. Madero had promised to cause the retreat of federal forces under Huerta, which De La Barra had sent to pacify the state and disarm the Zapata army by force. He also agreed to change out the current governor of Morelos for Eduardo Hay, one of Madero's closest confidantes and committed revolutionary. Madero's brother Raul was to take over the federal garrison with 250 revolutionary fighters to replace the federal forces. Madero briefly succeeded in halting Huerta's advance with regular armed forces, which allowed the Zapatistas to voluntarily disarm. However, the moment Madero left the state, Huerta under orders from the conservative legislature in Mexico City and President De La Barra moved in. Initially, the federal forces had the initiative. However, the popular uprising that followed the perceived breach of contract with the Mexican government could not be quelled. By October Zapata had reconstituted his army numbering over three thousand fighters.

Huerta employed brutal measures in his quest to capture Zapata and his fighters: Villages burnt, prisoners of war executed, women and children attacked, tortured and killed. The more violence the federals employed the more determined the revolutionaries became. While campaigning for his presidency, Madero continued to attempt to reach an agreement with the Zapatistas. However, trust between Zapata and the Mexican government had evaporated. Madero blamed the De La Barra government and especially generals Blanquet and Huerta, both carry-overs from the Porfirian regime. Madero's public attacks on Huerta's campaign, his leadership, and military conduct would have devastating effects in the not so distant future. Huerta began to hate the little man from Coahuila. Sommerfeld sensed the growing discontent and distrusted the Mexican general unequivocally. In his testimony to American interrogators in 1918, Sommerfeld was asked whether he knew Huerta. He replied: "Yes, sir, very well." Whether he had any dealings with him? "Yes when he was a general under Madero." "As confidential agent, I never trusted him. I warned Madero six months before [the coup d'état] ... to look out for him."[552] Without question, the German agent, who had witnessed the disagreements between Madero and Huerta in person, recognized the old soldier's lack of loyalty to the new government. Zapata as a result of the tragic developments in the summer of 1911 would remain a thorn in the side of Madero until the President's violent end in 1913.

Madero was slightly more successful in the pacification of the Yaqui Indian tribes in Sonora. Here, the Mexican leader was able to keep his word and arrange for the return of communal lands to the tribe. On September 1st 1911 he concluded a contract with eleven representatives of the Yaqui Indian tribes.[553] "By this agreement the government ceded to the tribes national territory in the various ejidal regions to be cultivated on the government's account at a stated daily salary. When all the land had been irrigated and opened to cultivation and when the first successful harvest had been gathered, the lands were to be divided among the inhabitants...The government also committed itself to furnishing provisions until the first harvest, schools, a pair of mules for each family receiving between five and ten hectares, and a tax exemption for thirty years."[554]

It should not be surprising that the Yaqui contingents represented the most loyal and fiercest defenders of Maderismo in the future battles waged on

Madero's behalf. Sommerfeld was with Madero in Sonora and got to know the leaders of the Yaqui tribes. Madero would again send the German agent into Yaqui territory in 1912 to keep the state pacified. Sommerfeld also played a big role in a Yaqui uprising in 1914. In short, with good reason Sommerfeld considered himself an expert on the Yaqui Indians years after Madero had first introduced him to their leaders. In 1917 following a renewed uprising of the Yaquis, Sommerfeld described his intimate knowledge of the issues in Sonora in a letter to the American Department of Justice:

"Of course everybody knows that the principle cause of the Yaqui uprisings and outrages is the unjust, cruel and criminal treatment they received during the Government of General Porfirio Diaz, especially while [Ramon] Corral [Diaz' hated Vice President in 1910] and Gen. …Torres were governors of Sonora…During my investigation I ran across many interesting details, Hundreds [sic] of Yaquis passed continuously [across] the American border to work in the mines of Arizona, Nevada and California and on ranches in Arizona and the Imperial Valley and other parts of Southern California. They work there for a few months -- sometimes weeks only – and with the money they saved out of their wages they buy second hand revolvers, rifles, at times new ones, ammunition and black powder. They then slowly work their way across the Mexican border back into their country and in this way keep their tribesmen – the socalled [sic] bronco Yaquis [bronco in this case means untamed, wild, belligerent] supplied with arms and ammunition. It is a continuous chain of supply carriers, larger than you possibly could imagine."[555]

Sommerfeld should have known because he had supplied the Yaquis with arms and ammunition in previous years when they fought under Pancho Villa. Madero, with the help of these agreements and their implementation by Governor Maytorena, a fierce Madero loyalist, ended the Yaqui uprising in 1911. Disagreements would again flare up in 1912 when Madero dispatched Sommerfeld to take care of it, which he and Maytorena did. In 1913 after the murder of Madero, the Yaquis turned into a fierce fighting force pitted against then President Huerta. Because of their tenacity and natural fighting instincts, Yaqui troops, often only armed with machetes, bows and arrows became the most feared adversaries in the Mexican Revolution. Taking prisoners was not one of their strong points. As Sommerfeld commented, "…Mexicans they never pardon…"[556]

More trouble brewed for Madero in the fall of 1911. As a result of the disagreements over the response to Zapatista uprisings, Madero had a falling out with Emilio Vasquez Gomez, the Maderista Secretary of Interior. Using Gustavo Madero, who behind the scenes ran day-to-day business for his older brother, Madero succeeded in President De La Barra dismissing Vasquez Gomez. The problem was, of course, that Emilio's brother, Dr. Francisco Vasquez Gomez who had been Madero's vice presidential candidate in the 1910 election, could not accept his brother's dismissal. Himself Secretary of Education, Dr. Vasquez Gomez broke with his longtime friend and compatriot. The two brothers aligned themselves with General Reyes who had returned from exile in June of 1911. Reyes had also been a candidate in opposition to Diaz in 1910. As previously mentioned, Diaz had sent the old general on an overseas assignment to get him out of the way. Officially, Reyes and his opposition group, the Reyistas, had supported the Madero uprising. With the first cracks in the Madero faction showing, Reyes declared himself presidential candidate against Madero for the election scheduled for the beginning of October 1911. Dr. Vasquez Gomez who ran for Vice President on the ticket and his brother Emilio joined the Reyista opposition. Supporters of the Vasquez Gomez brothers now called themselves Vasquistas. Madero also chose a new vice presidential candidate, his loyal friend, progressive journalist and governor of Yucatan, José Maria Pino Suarez.

The election had originally been scheduled for December 1911. However, the Maderos thought it wiser to call the election for October 3rd. Reyes who had campaigned vigorously became the target of revolutionary mobs. After being pelted with stones and fearing for his safety, Reyes withdrew his candidacy and left Mexico one month before the election. On his way to Havana, Cuba he announced that he doubted the coming election would be fair. Having a hard time staying on the sidelines Reyes proceeded to take a leaf from Madero's earlier playbook against Diaz. The sixty-one-year-old general left Cuba, stopped over in New Orleans, and finally settled in San Antonio on October 7th 1911. There he declared himself in revolt and gathered likeminded opposition including Emilio Vasquez Gomez and others around him.

The election took place as scheduled on October 3rd. Edith O'Shaughnessy commented, "...you can't tell an election from a revolution here. It's all lively to a degree. I have now seen both."[557] The results were unequivocal: Madero received 19,997 Electoral College votes, his running-mate Pino Suarez 10,245. The turnout was slightly over ten million people of a population of fifteen million.[558] In third place was De La Barra with eighty-seven electoral votes. The international community deemed the election fair and free. Despite the upheavals of the De La Barra administration and despite the disappointment of many revolutionaries with Madero, the Mexican people for the first time in forty-one years had spoken with a clear voice: Viva Madero! To the relief of many the De La Barra interim presidency was over. However, the damage caused in the time between Madero's victorious entry into the capital and the fall election proved to be too large to overcome. Nine months after defeating Diaz, Mexico's ruling elites maintained a firm grip on power. It would take Madero's demise and the likes of Carranza, Villa, and Zapata to clear the slate in the bloodiest period of the Mexican Revolution. Madero remained in power one year and three months before the reactionary forces he had kept in place took his and Pino Suarez' lives.

CHAPTER 12

～

THE "HOPKINS PLAN"

O n November 6th 1911, Francisco Ignacio Madero took the oath of office as the first democratically elected President of Mexico since Benito Juarez. Edith O'Shaughnessy present at the inauguration with her husband, the American Charge d'Affairs, keenly observed the "Apostle of Democracy." She commented in a Harper's Magazine article in 1917:

"The extreme pallor of his face was accented by his pointed, black beard, already the delight of the caricaturists, but his mien was grave and his gestures unusually few. Across his breast was the red, white, and green sash, the visible sign of the dream come true. I could not but ask myself, as I looked about the vast assemblage and heard the roar of the Indian throngs outside, what have they had to prepare themselves for political liberty after our pattern? But then, you know, I have always had a natural inclination for the strong hand and one head. L' appetit oient en mangeant and a taste for revolutions may be like a taste for anything else. Many of these millions have nothing to lose, and hope mixed with desire is rampant. Madero would seem to be President, not because he is a good and honest man and a well-wisher to all, but simply because he is a successful revolutionary leader, and what has been can be."[559]

Trouble did not wait long to bubble to the surface. Bernardo Reyes, the revolutionary general who had challenged both Diaz and Madero, announced from San Antonio that he would not accept the results of the election. Appearing before American journalists with Emilio Vasquez Gomez on inauguration day, the general vowed to oppose the new President. Sommerfeld recalled the affair to his interrogators in 1918: "So a few days after the inauguration of Madero, the President called me to Chapultepec [the presidential residence] and told me that he was informed that General Reyes was preparing a revolution against him. He asked me to go to San Antonio and find out the true situation. Reyes was in San Antonio, Texas. I left for San Antonio and arrived there about the middle [of] November."[560] Sommerfeld's mission went beyond just finding the facts. The German agent arrived with broad authority over the Mexican secret service, diplomatic immunity, and Madero charged him with the elimination of the threat posed by the rebellious general. The subsequent events demonstrate the quick, suave, yet fatal efficiency of the German secret agent that had so rapidly propelled his career with Madero, Hopkins, and von Hintze. The reason why Madero dispatched Sommerfeld to take care of Reyes and Vasquez Gomez was not only because the President trusted the German. With the election and inauguration of Madero, Sommerfeld had become Chief of the Mexican Secret Service.[561] While he nominally reported to the new Secretary of the Interior, Abraham Gonzalez, Sommerfeld considered himself responsible only to the President. In reality, however, he reported to Gustavo Madero, the President's brother. Gustavo did not have an official portfolio in the new government, but everyone in Mexico and beyond knew that he was the closest and most powerful of any advisors to Madero. It was Gustavo who had hired Hopkins, who in turn had provided Madero with the Pierce money to topple Diaz. Gustavo also was the person who accounted for his expenditures in order to be reimbursed. His accounts that caused a mighty scandal in Mexico included the funds he spent on the secret service operations in San Antonio, El Paso, New York, and Washington. Because as a foreigner Sommerfeld could not hold an official post in the Mexican government, he became Gustavo's trusted assistant and as such did indeed have regular contact with the President. When Gustavo could not be around, Sommerfeld also took over responsibilities for President Madero's personal safety. Hence he often traveled with the President.

Sommerfeld appeared on the American scene on November 18th 1911, in the middle of the night, when San Antonio BI agent H. A. Thompson "received a telephone call from Mr. Sommerfeldt [sic], who is a special service agent for the Mexican Government."[562] Another source that does not mention Sommerfeld's name but illuminates his role in the new government is an informant of the Bureau of Investigation in El Paso. On February 15th 1912, Agent Lancaster reported, "...a prominent Mexican from Mexico City now at the Sheldon Hotel informed him confidentially that the important papers of Henry Clay [sic] Wilson, Ambassador at Mexico City would be stolen by an employee who works in his office the first opportunity that presents itself; that the Mexican secret service agents had been opening the mail of Mr. Wilson and claimed that Ambassador Wilson was unfriendly to the Mexican people and was trying to cause intervention."[563] Sommerfeld was in El Paso on that day and while Agent Lancaster personally knew Sommerfeld, his informant obviously did not. The German disdained American officials such as the American Ambassador Henry Lane Wilson and Senator Albert B. Fall of New Mexico both of whom consistently clamored for military intervention. In October 1912, Sommerfeld created a tense situation when refused to answer Senator Fall's questions in a senate subcommittee. "I regard Senator Fall as an enemy of our existing Mexican Government and of President Madero," he justified his lack of cooperation.[564] Sommerfeld's task from the Mexican President was to insure the stability of the Mexican government with all means at his disposal. Opening Ambassador Wilson's mail not only interested the Mexican government but also provided valuable insights into American thinking for the German Ambassador von Hintze.

Once in San Antonio, Sommerfeld immediately went about canvassing the existing secret service organization and connecting with Agent Thompson of the BI.[565] In addition to the detectives of the Thiel Detective Agency he inherited secret service agent Teódulo R. Beltran, the owner of a security company in town.[566] While Beltran and his informants seemed to be reliable, the Mexican consul there was not. In fact, Sommerfeld quickly realized that several other Mexican consuls along the border conspired with the enemy. He had them immediately fired, stating to Senator Fall months later that they were a bunch of "drunkards."[567] In El Paso, where the local consul had openly attended Reyista meetings and was consequently fired, there was a larger Mexican secret service apparatus than in other towns. The head of the organization in El Paso was Abraham Molina, a confidante of Abraham Gonzalez, Secretary of the Interior in Madero's new cabinet. To the BI agents in El Paso Molina was the "Secret Service agent for the Mexican Government here."[568] Also working for the Madero people was the local Thiel Detective Agency under the auspices of Henry Kramp. Sommerfeld called on the Thiel detectives especially when Americans had to be shadowed or questioned. After ridding El Paso of the hostile Mexican consul, Madero dispatched a new consul to El Paso, Enrique C. Llorente.

Llorente was an experienced diplomat whose last assignment had been Genoa, Italy. Born on August 5th 1877 at the Hacienda de Cececapa to the southwest of Tampico, Llorente had been Mexican consul in Galveston, Texas in the early 1900s.[569] While in Galveston he met his wife, the daughter of a wealthy American businessman.[570] Not much else is known about the consul. He had no major role in the Madero revolution, there are no documents that could illuminate his connections to the northern revolutionaries, and there seem to be no other revolutionary credentials in his biography. When Llorente crossed the border in 1914 as a special representative for the Villa government, he indicated to the American border officials in Brownsville that his occupation was "capitalist."[571] Indeed, it seems that Llorente was a protégé of Francisco Leon De La Barra, the Secretary of State under Diaz and provisional President of Mexico between June and November 1911. Clearly, Llorente was not one of Abraham Gonzalez' people. The new consul reported to Sommerfeld, and his real job for the Madero administration was the financial support of the German's clandestine operations in the next years. While Sommerfeld was the spymaster, Llorente, who as a consul enjoyed diplomatic immunity, was the paymaster. The pair remained together through the Great War first in El Paso, then in New York. Sommerfeld needed Llorente for an official cover, a fact that the consul likely was not aware of. Since the German could not hold office in the Mexican government, he pushed Llorente to the fore anytime clandestine schemes bubbled to the surface of public attention.

The role the Mexican consul had to play was not an easy one. Not only did U.S. officials at the border focus their attention on him, which eventually got him into conflict with U.S. law. He also had to withstand brutal attacks from factions within the Mexican government, especially those trying to pin corruption charges on the Maderos and Gustavo in particular. Without the protecting hands of Sommerfeld and Hopkins, as well as the highest echelons of the Madero government, Llorente would not have lasted as long as he did. Violations of the Neutrality Laws as well as investigations of the Mexican parliament into the El Paso office's spending came to nothing, as if the investigations reached a certain level on either side of the border and were squelched.[572] When Llorente received a prison term for embezzlement in Mexico in 1914, he quickly reappeared in New York a few months later as a diplomat working for – who would have thought – Sommerfeld.

Sommerfeld's efforts to demolish Reyes' plans for an uprising began without delay. The situation that presented itself to Sommerfeld was complicated. Bernardo Reyes enjoyed popular admiration not only in certain parts of Mexican society but also among the Mexican-American community of Texas. Texas governor Oscar B. Colquitt, who had opposed Madero launching his revolution from San Antonio a year earlier, viewed Reyes' opposition to the newly elected Mexican President favorably. The border between Texas and

Mexico remained a simmering hotbed for conspiracies, crime, and arms smuggling months after Madero had succeeded in ousting President Diaz and winning the revolution. Reyes seemed the man of the hour to rid the border of unrest. When the general arrived in San Antonio in October 1911, he received a hero's welcome from the local community, Mexican and Anglo alike: "...a crowd of four hundred to five hundred persons, including four delegations from the Grand Lodge of Mexican Masons, gathered...to welcome a distinguished Mexican general...He was General Bernardo Reyes, retired General de Division of the Mexican Army with forty-five years of service to his credit. He was every inch a soldier. He was also former governor of the neighboring state of Nuevo Leon where he had gained a reputation unequaled in Mexico for his honesty and administrative ability. In addition, he was a man noted for his friendliness to Americans..."[573] To Colquitt, Reyes, the pro-American former governor of a border state, decorated general, and most powerful opponent of Madero, seemed best prepared to settle affairs in revolutionary Mexico, and with that pacify the U.S.-Mexican border.

San Antonio had hosted anti-Madero conspiracies since the summer of 1911, virtually without interference of the Texas authorities.[574] With the arrival of the formidable opposition leader on the border, the loosely organized pockets of anti-Madero agitation gelled into a viable movement. Supporters of Ricardo Flores Magon and the Vasquez Gomez brothers threw their lot in with the rebellious general. Despite the clear supposition that the Madero opposition in Texas intended to invade Mexican territory in clear violation of federal and state neutrality laws, Texas authorities did nothing to stop the conspiracy.[575] Historians Harris and Sadler credited Governor Colquitt's friendliness and inactivity towards Reyes in large part to the fact that "two of Reyes's principal conspirators were influential Texas political figures and supporters of Colquitt."[576]

While the local authorities stayed inactive, the Mexican Secret Service as well as the Bureau of Investigation kept a close eye on developments in San Antonio as well as El Paso, Laredo, and Brownsville. For the Mexican government, agents Beltran, Molina, and the Thiel detectives collected intelligence on the rebel movements. Independently, U.S. federal authorities did the same. On November 16th, the week of Sommerfeld's arrival on the scene, a federal grand jury indicted Reyes and several of his co-conspirators in Laredo.[577] According to Sommerfeld, the problems he encountered in Texas were two-fold: Mexican agents and the Department of Justice were not working together. The other problem was that Reyes and his group of dissidents had enjoyed complete freedom of action from the Texas governor and local authorities. Indeed, the glaring difference with which the Texas Rangers, local law enforcement, and the state government treated the armed insurrections of Madero and Reyes worried the new Mexican government.

The first set of problems Sommerfeld identified was simply one of coordination and leadership. Since both groups of agents had been investigating, Sommerfeld outlined the obvious solution: "They [federal agents] knew it [the Reyes conspiracy] already and they [Department of Justice agents] were watching him...It was simply a question of getting in touch [with federal agents] because I believed it was necessary to work hand in hand with the [federal] authorities of the United States."[578] Immediately before Sommerfeld's appearance in San Antonio, Mexican agents started to share important leads with the Bureau of Investigation agents. On November 17th, in a memorandum on Reyista activities, BI agent Louis E. Ross mentioned a lead from the Mexican agents, namely that the El Paso firm Krakauer, Zork and Moye was the source of weapons for the Reyistas.[579] As a result of the federal indictment of Reyes, Governor Colquitt started to feel the pressure to become active. The Mexican government in the person of Felix Sommerfeld also demanded decisive action. "[I went to the Department of Justice] because it was the Mexican government which was threatened and I wanted to know what the Department of Justice was going to do."[580]

Sommerfeld's agitation on behalf of the Mexican government and the federal indictment showed astonishing results. Governor Colquitt not only had a change of heart, he now became an ardent enforcer of the neutrality laws of Texas and the United States. The Texas Rangers, formerly indifferent if not supportive of the anti-Madero activities, now received orders from the governor to canvass the border and assist in smashing the rebel organization. Sommerfeld's idea of Mexican, U.S. federal, and local authorities working in tandem against the conspirators bore fruit within days of his arrival on the scene. On the 18th of November San Antonio law enforcement arrested Bernardo Reyes. He immediately posted bail.[581] On November 19th agent Thompson of San Antonio who had received a phone call from Sommerfeld in the middle of the night, reported that the German agent had told him when and where Reyes and his followers would cross the border into Mexico. The attempt to cross the border armed would have been enough to take the old general into custody and extradite him to Mexico later on. As a result of the notorious leaks in the Marshall's office, double agents en masse, and the loose lips of local law enforcement, the Reyistas got wind of the trap and delayed their plans. Finally, on November 30th, the Bureau of Investigation's special agent Louis E. Ross with a deputy U.S. Marshall, Captain John R. Hughes of the Texas Rangers, and Abraham Molina of the Mexican Secret Service in tow arrested the whole rebel junta of fourteen Reyes co-conspirators.[582] Other arrests and confiscation of weapons and supplies followed in El Paso, Laredo, and Brownsville.

The plotting of the Mexican opposition forces in Texas continued for the remainder of the Madero administration but for all intents and purposes, at least the Reyes uprising had been crushed.[583] Bernardo Reyes ended up jumping bail and fleeing to Mexico where he surrendered to Mexican federal forces on Christmas Day, 1911. He subsequently was tried and went to prison. "That was the first Madero mistake," Sommerfeld mused in 1918, "They should have shot him."[584] The other conspirators received "only a figurative slap on the wrist..." for their activities.[585] Historians Harris and Sadler meticulously detailed the court cases of the main plotters. In some cases the convicted plotters were allowed to leave jail and go home at night. In one case a prisoner, José Bonales Sandoval, whose wife had died in Mexico City, asked the local federal judge Waller T. Burns for a loan to go to Mexico. Agent William Chamberlain complained in a BI report on December 22nd, not only was the work of the Grand Juries corrupted, but the local press colluded with the conspirators as well: "There are leaks here [San Antonio], and at Laredo and Brownsville, especially the secret and solemn work of the Federal Grand Juries. The Reyistas seem to be well posted on inside matters of these Grand Juries. The press has published movement [sic] snad [sic] names of those indicted and not arrested; this handicaps the work of the U. S. officials, who desire to execute their part."[586]

The Justice Department as well as the Mexican government in the person of Felix Sommerfeld did all they could to get Reyes and his men convicted. To the dismay of the Justice Department, rather than getting severe punishments for the indicted plotters, local prosecutors made life for lenient judges easy. Judge Burns stood out as "...a defendant's dream. He was the picture of solicitude for the defendants, from looking after their welfare in jail, to sending a defendant to look for another defendant who had fled, to construing the statutes to mean that violating the neutrality laws was only a misdemeanor and not a felony..."[587] Sommerfeld, in his typical go-getting attitude, increased the manpower of the Mexican Secret Service and trained them in cooperating in a "legal" way with U.S. authorities.[588] His attempts to force conviction, however, transcended "legal" ways. He went so far as to influence court proceedings with bribes. One of the bribery attempts became public in July 1912. Assistant U.S. attorney Noah Allen, assistant to the pro-Reyes prosecutor Lock McDaniel[589] in Judge Burns' notorious court in Brownsville, Texas, had been "...in communication with President Madero, and ...he was the recipient of a valuable scarf pin which had been presented to him by the President through one F. A. Sommerfeldt [sic]."[590]

Sommerfeld went back to Mexico City on December 3rd for a conference with the Maderos.[591] Sherburne Hopkins, who had been on business in Great Britain, had just returned to New York.[592] The German agent had realized that the border was brewing with intrigue, threatening the very existence of Madero's rule. Historians Harris and Sadler compared the atmosphere in the border towns with that of West Berlin in the height of the Cold War.[593] Sommerfeld found that neither the U.S. authorities nor the Mexican secret service organization was in any shape to stand up to the unchecked intrigues. He found the consuls and many of the Mexican informants to be unprofessional and highly ineffective. Mexican agents were well-known to anyone in the border communities, notorious for switching sides as the political winds would dictate. American mercenaries, now unemployed in New Orleans, San Antonio, and El Paso took money from whoever paid them to perform services for whoever asked for them. Those were the findings Sommerfeld reported to Hopkins and Madero.

Realizing his and the American government's impotence vis-à-vis the many conspiracies against the Mexican government, Madero sent Hopkins in December 1911 to confer with the Taft administration. Hopkins posed an all-important question: Could the federal government secure its border and guarantee the enforcement of its own Neutrality Laws? The answer clearly was no! In the end of 1911 the Bureau of Investigation had one special agent in El Paso, who covered all investigations between that city and San Antonio, where another secured the border. The Department of the Treasury had covered Texas and New Mexico with one customs collector in El Paso, and one each in San Antonio, Houston, Eagle Pass, Marfa, and Columbus. In Arizona, the only manned border ports were at Naco and Nogales. The San Diego collector covered the California border. The Texas Rangers and some marshals complemented the assets of the U.S. law enforcement along the Texas border, but, as the Reyes uprising showed, the state and local forces were ineffective at best and supportive of the conspirators and smugglers at worst. After an increase in manpower to quell the Reyes uprising in December 1911, Texas reduced its ranger forces back to the old, insufficient numbers by January

1912.[594] Finally, the U.S. military maintained cavalry forces along the border, Fort Bliss and Columbus being the largest garrisons. After the successful Madero revolution, those forces also had been reduced significantly. In Fort Bliss one military intelligence officer covered the information gathering for the whole of Texas. In short, security and border control were abysmal!

When Hopkins approached the U.S. government, most likely through his close friend and Secretary of State Philander Knox, he proffered the idea that at this junction both governments had the same goals: Prevent further unrest in Mexico, especially the smuggling of arms and men across the border, and restrict formation of various conspiracies on the American side. While the U.S. needed time to tool up for the task of securing the border, Hopkins offered to finance the creation of a Mexican intelligence service that would provide the manpower to do the investigative legwork for the American authorities. Since the American and Mexican interests were literally identical, the Mexican organization would act in complete transparency together with American authorities. The new organization would employ a large number of Americans such as former rangers, deputy marshals, policemen, and private detectives, whose loyalties at the very least trended towards the United States.

Hopkins also lobbied for an amendment to the Neutrality Laws that would put some teeth into a loosely defined set of laws that proved hard to enforce along the Mexican border. Hopkins wanted to mandate increased fines and penalties for violators. In combination with an arms embargo against anyone outside the constitutional government of Mexico, the amendment also was to allow the U.S. government to seize any arms suspected to be contraband.[595] President Taft made a proclamation to that effect on March 2nd 1912 and on March 16th declared an arms embargo against all factions other than the constituted government of Mexico.[596]

While Hopkins worked on his plan to deal with the chaotic border situation, Madero sent Sommerfeld on a new mission, this time to Puebla. According to Sommerfeld he arrived there in early January on a confidential mission. The "...Governor of Pueblo [sic] and the Commanding General of that zone were at logger heads...I went there to settle it. I invited them both to dinner and made them kiss and make up and become friends...They always took about 15 or 20 cogniacs [sic] and also the necessary champagne."[597] The conflict Sommerfeld referred to was quite more complicated than the alcohol induced "kiss and make up" episode would suggest. When Sommerfeld went to the capital of the state of Puebla, Zapata's revolt had taken on previously unimagined dimensions. The rebel leader threatened most of the southern states with an army of over twelve thousand guerillas. Madero had proclaimed a state of emergency for Morelos. At the same time that Zapata continued to gain strength and battled against the forces under Victoriano Huerta in a brutal guerilla war, another revolt broke out in the state of Puebla. Forces loyal to Emilio Vasquez Gomez rose up against the government and threatened the capital of the state. In January 1912, the embattled Madero government permitted Brigadier General Juan Francisco Lucas, a military leader of the Diaz era and twenty-five-year strongman of that region, to fight the rebels in Puebla and surrounding areas. Hardly surprising the de-facto leader of Puebla had no use for Governor Nicolas Melendez, a Madero appointee. Immediately the general proceeded to sabotage the local Maderista governments, which led to vociferous complaints from the new governor and Madero loyalist of Puebla. The President sent Bruno M. Trejo of his personal military staff to negotiate between embattled Governor Nicolas Melendez and Lucas. Although not mentioned in any historical sources, Felix Sommerfeld as head of the Mexican Secret Service clearly had been a member of Madero's delegation. The two factions settled their differences and as a result of pay-offs, Lucas deactivated his forces for the time being.[598] Whether the settlement happened over a few drinks at dinner will not be known. However, the episode shows once more the leading role that Sommerfeld played in the crisis management of the Madero administration in 1912.

The ink on the settlement between Melendez and Lucas had not yet completely dried when the next crisis emerged. On January 31st 1912, the federal garrison of Ciudad Juarez, across from the Texas border town of El Paso, erupted in violence. As part of the ongoing demobilization of the Mexican federal army in part because of the dire financial state of the government, the local commander had two hundred soldiers discharged. Already a tense climate within the armed forces that consisted of soldiers recruited before the revolution as well as Orozco and Garibaldi's irregulars, the disgruntled soldiers declared themselves loyal to Emilio Vasquez Gomez, and sacked the border city. The mutiny presented an opportunity for José Inés Salazar, an officer in the Orozco forces who had fought for Madero but to his great disappointment had not received a commission in the regular army. Under his command, the frontier garrison succumbed to the surprise attack in just a few hours with eight killed and as many wounded. From his headquarters in San Antonio, Vasquez Gomez declared himself provisional President on the 1st of February, and threatened more "bloodshed" should troops be sent to quell the uprising.[599] American newspapers reported nervously on the successful uprisings that now simultaneously flared up along the U.S.-Mexican border, in Morelos, and Puebla. They predicted Madero's quick demise.

Madero immediately dispatched Sommerfeld to the border. Since the Vasquista rebels had severed all communications and transportation between Torreon and Juarez he arrived in El Paso via Eagle Pass on the 6th of February. The trip must have been harrowing for Sommerfeld, who apparently had to sacrifice his otherwise immaculate appearance including a clean shave. The El Paso Herald described what could only have been Sommerfeld's arrival on February 7th, even quoting his awkward German accent: "More mystery was injected into the local situation [referring to the formation of a Vasquista Junta in El Paso] by the arrival of a bewhiskered and bewildered individual who wore a neat tweed suit and mysterious look. He went immediately to his room [at the Hotel Orndorff], which he insisted should be on the front of the hotel where he 'could get the air.' After he had gone to his room, whiskers, mystery and all, a man, said to be one of the Madero family [likely Madero's uncle Alberto] followed him up the stairs and a conference is said to have taken place. His name could not be found on the register."[600]

The clamor for American intervention turned to a roar in those early days of February 1912.[601] Mexican authorities threatened severe repercussions in the case of American troops entering Mexico. They leaked to U.S. agents that in case of intervention, they would "blow up the international railroad bridge across the Rio Grande."[602] Thank goodness cooler heads prevailed when by mistake a detachment of nineteen American soldiers under Lieutenant Benjamin W. Fields "crossed the international bridge into Mexico" on the 15th.[603] The Mexican federal army detained the soldiers for an hour but released them when the American commander, Colonel Steever, officially apologized for the blunder.[604] Sommerfeld and Llorente negotiated the soldiers' release. Fields was subsequently court-martialed.

The Mexican government's response to the revolt was timid at best. At issue was the questionable loyalty of General Orozco, Madero's military commander in the region. Just a few weeks prior Orozco had refused Madero's orders to join the fight against Zapata in the south. In a meeting with Madero on January 19th the revolutionary leader tendered his resignation as commander of the Rurales of Chihuahua rather than fight in Morelos. Madero refused to accept it. However the already strained relationship between the President and his commander tensed as the situation in Chihuahua became critical. Uprisings in Casas Grandes and other rural areas of the state caused the resignation of interim governor Aurelio Gonzalez who preferred exile in the

U.S. to martyrdom for Madero's embattled government. Orozco became the man of the hour. Within a few days troops loyal to Orozco retook the city. On February 7th the El Paso Herald reported that federal troops were on their way and that the Mexican government, namely Llorente and Sommerfeld, were issuing guns to the citizens of Juarez in an attempt to shore up the defenses against the rebels.[605] For a few days it seemed that the Vasquista revolt had fizzled even quicker than the Reyes revolt a month earlier. The wild card still was Orozco. Madero remembered only too well how Orozco tried to arrest and kill him in the beginning of the revolution. In an effort to coopt his commander into the Madero political system, the Mexican President offered the governorship of Chihuahua to him. When the revolutionary commander refused, all alarm bells went off in Mexico City.

According to Sommerfeld's statement in 1918, at that juncture no one in the central government of Mexico had any doubts that Orozco would eventually declare himself in revolt.

"If Orozco would accept [the governorship] I believed then Orosko [sic] should be held on the government side, but if he refused I was absolutely convinced that he was going to rise. When I arrived in El Paso I received a telegram from the President in code saying 'Orosko [sic] offered governorship as suggested. Orosko [sic] refused.' I knew immediately that Orosko [sic] was waiting for his moment. On arriving in El Paso I found Orosko [sic] had been there the day before in Juarez and taken out the forces who had rebelled a few days before and taken them to Chihuahua and with tears in his eyes protested to the Consul [Llorente] his loyalty to the constitutional government. Knowing him as I did I told the governor [Abraham Gonzalez] not to pay any attention to his protestations, [sic] of loyalty and to make the necessary preparations of coping with the situation which would arise in a few days."[606]

Whether Sommerfeld actually was the one who hatched the idea to offer the governorship of Chihuahua to Orozco is unknown and perhaps unlikely.[607] However, he clearly had been part of a faction among the advisors to President Madero who pushed for this final test of Orozco's loyalty. If the commander had accepted, which could have given him a powerful position within the constitutional government to bring about significant social change, he would have proven his willingness to work within the Maderista political system. Orozco, in his Plan de la Empacadora, called for higher wages, agrarian reform, and the abolition of company stores. His biographer, Michael Meyer, clearly believed that these goals reflected Orozco's true convictions. However, his declining the offer left no doubt that Orozco had greater ambitions for himself and his followers in the north of Mexico than heading up political and social reform. In hindsight, Chihuahua's subsequent revolutionary governments under Abraham Gonzalez, Pancho Villa, and Silvestre Terrazas all achieved a tremendous amount of redistribution of wealth and social change. For a historian relying on facts that were created by events, a cause-and-effect conclusion in this case is now almost impossible to make. Were these revolutionary changes implemented in order to coopt the rebellious masses in the years between 1912 and 1919 or did the three revolutionary governors implement the changes because of their revolutionary conscience? In the first case, Orozco's decision not to join the political system pushed for more radical reform than he might have otherwise achieved as governor. In the second case, he threw his revolutionary conscience by the way side in order to acquire power. If that was his motivation, the plan failed miserably and unnecessarily took tens of thousands of Chihuahuans to their violent deaths.

The Mexican government's premonition that Orozco would declare himself in revolt proved logical and right. However, he waited for the most opportune moment. The moment the commander had refused to accept the governorship of Chihuahua, given the powerful position he was cast into in the aftermath of the Vasquista revolt, Madero and his people had to prepare for the worst. Orozco was highly popular among Chihuahuans. He had positioned himself as a viable and powerful alternative to the Madero administration that faced great disillusionment among the masses of Chihuahua. Although Orozco had resigned his position as a commander of the Rurales, he directed thousands of irregular forces and had split the loyalties of the Chihuahuan federal forces.

While Sommerfeld linked the U.S. authorities with Mexican secret service activities, Madero dispatched his trusted friend Abraham Gonzalez to take over the governorship of Chihuahua. Both Sommerfeld and Governor Gonzalez switched into high gear to create defenses against the development of a guerilla force as powerful as the Zapata forces in the South. One of Gonzalez' first moves was to call on his old friend Pancho Villa who had been asked by the Orozco rebels to join their cause. Rather than joining, Villa declared his unequivocal loyalty to Madero. Under a new commission from Abraham Gonzalez, Villa recruited a loyal force of irregulars and Rurales to fight. He would be Orozco's deadly enemy for years to come.

On February 7th, the day after Sommerfeld had arrived in El Paso, bewhiskered and bewildered as he might have looked, American authorities arrested Ricardo Flores Magon and his brother Jesús. For years the two had conspired against the Mexican governments of Diaz and Madero from the U.S. side of the border. American agents had watched their every move until the latest arrest. The Flores Magon brothers represented the far left of the revolutionary spectrum. A worker-based opposition and one of the earliest revolutionary activists in Mexico, the Magonistas had staged their own uprisings and strikes against Porfirio Diaz. In 1911, they briefly integrated their movement with the broader Madero coalition. However, as the De La Barra and Madero administrations did little to address the plight of Mexican workers, the Magonista movement separated and resumed recruiting Mexicans and Mexican-Americans along the U.S.-Mexican border. The brothers' arrest was an important milestone in the U.S. government's effort to establish firmer control over the Mexican communities on the American side of the border in 1912.

The situation in Chihuahua was dire. On the 18th of February, rebels had burned "three long bridges ... on the Northwestern [railroad] ...north of Guzman." They also had cut all wires along the track, effectively cutting off communication between Ciudad Juarez and Chihuahua City.[608] Sommerfeld's strategy to deal with the Vasquistas was the same he had used to undermine the Reyes revolt: Cut off supplies from the U.S. and identify hostile junta members to the U.S. Justice Department representatives and the military for arrest. Under the leadership of Abraham Molina and Mexican military authorities, the conspirators that sacked Juarez on January 31st and prompted the Vasquez uprising were arrested on February 19th.[609] However, the Vasquistas showed no sign of giving up. Chihuahua was ablaze and refugees from all over the state started pouring into El Paso. On the 20th of February, Agent Lancaster reported to his superiors, "I saw Consular Agent of the German Government, Fred [sic] Stallforth, who is stationed at Parral, Mexico, and has just arrived from Parral and does not hesitate in saying that conditions in Mexico are alarming; that he thought intervention would occur. He stated that all foreigners are leaving Parral."[610] Indeed, Frederico Stallforth had come to El Paso to meet with Alberto Madero and Sommerfeld. He needed help for the miserable financial bind he found his company in.[611] Although he had no official function with the German government, using his notorious showmanship, this minor detail did not deter him from representing himself as such to the American authorities. Marie de Günther, wife of Paul Günther who was a wealthy Mexican-German businessman in Chihuahua, wrote in Stallforth's diary reflecting the glum mood of refugees now congregating in El Paso: "Here's to the fellow who makes us laugh; who makes us forget our sorrow. May he have a good, big bank account, and friends who never borrow."[612] American businesses all across Chihuahua had to shut down operations. The American Smelting and Refining Company (ASARCO), the largest American mining concern south of the border, suffered greatly from the unrest. According to G. C. Kaufman, an ASARCO manager, employees were "assaulted, injured, and robbed..." As BI agent Lancaster talked with Mr. Kaufman about the lawlessness in Chihuahua, "...Frederick [sic] Stallforth representative for the German government walked up and told Mr. Kaufman he had just received a telegram that the National R[ailways] had again been cut, bridges burned out just north of Chihuahua...As Mr. Stallforth was about to walk away he remarked 'Well, we will soon go down there now.' Mr. Kaufman answered this by saying 'Yes we will go down together Frederico, if not one way, [then] another.' By this remark he meant that they would probably go down to that part of the country under foreign protection."[613] Foreign protection stood for what American and other foreign businessmen expected from the American government: Military intervention.

Stallforth family lore contains a heart-warming story of this time not because of its embellished facts but because one can imagine the wide-open eyes of Frederico's daughters Gioja and Anita when her Dad told it. When Gioja was a little girl, Frederico explained to her why he had been absent during her birth in El Paso on March 31st 1912. After Stallforth's visit to El Paso, meeting with Alberto Madero, Sommerfeld, and joining the Günthers at the races, he left for New York to meet with banks and find a solution for his company's decrepit financial condition.[614] However, Frederico told his daughters that he was actually captured by Pancho Villa and held for ransom. True, Pancho Villa did roam the Chihuahuan countryside around that time and he was also known to hold foreigners for ransom, although decidedly more frequently after 1915. The Stallforths with many other residents of Parral had to flee the violence of the Orozco uprising in February 1912. Frederico's wife Anita and her namesake daughter, Gioja's sister, traveled to El Paso by coach and rail via Chihuahua in March 1912. Because rebels cut the rail lines between Chihuahua and Ciudad Juarez, which indeed was a frequent occurrence in March of 1912, Frederico had to follow his pregnant wife on horseback. Somewhere on the trail in the mountains he and his servants allegedly faced bandits who forced the little group to follow them to a camp. There they were held until the "jefe" could see them. According to Thornton Jones Blelock who wrote the story down in 2008,

Stallforth thought of Villa a "...fearless leader of men, loyally dedicated to his chief, President Madero; a sincere and honest soldier, who neither drinks nor smokes, and a man of extraordinary native intelligence..."[615] After some small talk over breakfast, Villa demanded ten thousand pesos for ransom. Stallforth was to stay in camp while the servants had to raise the money in three days. If they did not make it back, Villa promised to kill Stallforth. While the general and his captive waited for the ransom, they rode out together hunting and talking. Villa told stories about the revolution, Madero, the plight of the poor, and his dedication to helping them. The revolutionary general also showed his brutal side. He smashed in a soldier's head, settled a fight between two soldaderas, and entertained the ruffian soldiers around him. On the third day, Stallforth finally faced a firing squad since the servants had not materialized before dark. As the soldiers were raising their guns to dispatch Stallforth, the men arrived with the ransom. Three years later, in 1916, as Stallforth sat in a train from Mexico City to Chihuahua, Villa's private caboose attached to the train. Villa and Stallforth met again. After some small talk the general wrote Stallforth a check for the 10,000 Pesos and thanked him for supporting the revolution.[616]

For Gioja, who told the story to her children, and they to theirs, the details are less important than the fact that Frederico Stallforth came out of the dangers of Mexico unscathed. As a matter of fact, Stallforth was not in Mexico in March of 1912, his finances show no trace of a ten-thousand-peso-payment, an amount he certainly did not have at that time, Villa probably did not occupy himself with procuring pheasant and deer for his troops in the middle of the Orozco uprising, and the 1916 happy ending is highly improbable. Villa was on the run, never personally wrote checks, and Stallforth was in New York that entire year. Curious is the admiration for Villa on the part of Stallforth. Villa did his best to protect foreign businesses and, while taking forced "taxes" from entrepreneurs, Chihuahua lived through a period of relative calm when he controlled it between 1914 and 1915. He was a crude but fascinating hero to many an American's imagination. Did Stallforth's sympathies for the colorful general have anything to do with Sommerfeld who worked for him after 1914? Did Stallforth ever meet Villa face to face? He could have met Villa before the revolution when the future general lived in Parral, during 1911 in the Madero Revolution, or in the latter part of 1912, when Stallforth did travel through Mexico and tried to raise money for his business. That meeting would probably not have made such a good story, though.

In the meantime, Vasquista rebels occupied significant parts of the Chihuahua countryside. They publicly wooed General Orozco, asking the commander to join the fight. While up to this point Orozco seemed to do what he could to stop the insurrection, Sommerfeld had his doubts. The American commander at Fort Bliss, Colonel Steever, as well as the American public in the border cities felt that something had to be done quickly to restore order. Sommerfeld confided to his old friend Steever on the 22nd of February that Orozco was "no longer loyal."[617] The German had not forgotten the close call in Juarez almost a year prior, when Orozco had threatened to kill Madero. On February 23rd 1912, Sommerfeld received orders to report back to Mexico City and see the President. Hopkins, who had been in Guatemala when the latest fighting broke out, also rushed to the Mexican capital.[618] When Sommerfeld arrived on the 25th of February, Sommerfeld, Hopkins, Francisco Madero, and his brother Gustavo convened for an emergency session.

Hopkins had hatched a brilliant plan, which he now presented. Since achieving an understanding with the U.S. government for legal cooperation and intelligence sharing in December, Hopkins had also organized further financing through Pierce and Flint.[619] He promised the President, that he could stop the troubles on the border. However, if President Madero really wanted to have an effective secret service, Abraham Gonzalez had to relinquish his influence. Madero was presented with a difficult decision. Gonzalez had built the support structure that led the Madero Revolution to success. The governor of Chihuahua together with Madero's brother Gustavo had also laid the groundwork for the existing secret service organization. However, the organization Sommerfeld had inspected along the border was a disaster. Hopkins, and in extension Sommerfeld, subsequently would not accept compromise. Gustavo had to run the operations of the secret service without Gonzalez in the middle. Hopkins, Gustavo Madero, and Sommerfeld openly clashed with Gonzalez over the question of secret service control. Evidence of this clash came into the open in October 1912, when Senator Albert B. Fall asked Sommerfeld about his relationship with Gonzalez. The German agent's response was at the same time surprising and telling. Surprising, because not many people disliked Abraham Gonzalez, the burly, cordial, fatherly figure of the Chihuahuan Revolution who enjoyed great admiration among the revolutionaries. He also had hired Villa and Orozco. Telling, because the affair offered a glimpse into the internal power struggles that had developed among the Madero cabinet. Sommerfeld stated, "I have been his friend, but lately he has declared that I am his enemy."[620] Gonzalez' relationship with Gustavo has not been examined by historians. The only hint that there might have been static can be found in February 1912 in the sudden departure of Gonzalez from the cabinet and back to Chihuahua. According to Katz and other historians the patriarchic figure of Chihuahua's revolution was not happy in a Mexico City where all strings came together in Gustavo Madero's office.

Hopkins' logic for unifying the intelligence gathering organizations under one umbrella became a recurring theme in U.S. policy in World War I, World War II, and right up to the aftermath of 9/11. In the Mexico of 1912, the Secretary of the Interior was responsible for police forces and the portions of the secret service that dealt with police action and smuggling. The Secretary of State had control over the consulates, which paid the agents. The Secretary of War controlled the military and the collection of information that was of import. The arms smuggling and rebelling juntas all along the U.S. border also presented military threats. Control over secret service organizations meant power. Gonzalez with his power base in Chihuahua and as the primary organizer of the northern revolution in 1910 was in the best position to grab responsibility over secret service activities along the U.S. Mexican border. Not any different from the Mexican situation, the United States' Treasury Department's secret service competed with Military Intelligence, the Justice Department's Bureau of Investigation, and the State Departments Intelligence Service that came out of the embassies and consulates. The result of the competition among intelligence gathering organizations made their operations very expensive and inefficient. Abraham Gonzalez, just like Felix Sommerfeld, realized that unification of effort would result in an organization along the border that could effectively manage threats coming from the United States. They just disagreed on who would be in charge.

While Gonzalez occupied a very powerful position in the new administration of Mexico, Gustavo Madero and Hopkins at this juncture had more power, more clout, and offered a solution to the threatening disorder along the U.S. border that the President could not refuse. The Washington lawyer laid out his requirements: Sommerfeld would be fully in charge of all Mexican intelligence resources, the consulates, any Mexicans on the American side of the border, the secret service men, and had unlimited funds to build an effective and unified organization. Gonzalez would take back the governorship and support Sommerfeld's organization with extradition papers and intelligence from the Mexican side. Gonzalez obviously did not like having his power curbed by Hopkins and his German protégé. Sherburne Hopkins, when asked in September 1912 by Senator Smith about his role in the Madero administration, gave some fascinating answers:

"Smith: 'You were consulted on behalf of the Madero faction?' Hopkins: 'To be frank, I was the legal adviser of the revolutionary party in Washington.' Smith: 'For how long a period?' Hopkins: 'From the beginning until the end.' Smith: 'Can you explain why they desired to consult you concerning claims for service?' Hopkins: 'Yes, sir; because I was in charge of their secret service.' Smith: 'Did you employ the men?' Hopkins: 'Yes!' Smith: 'In that capacity were you thrown in contact with Mr. Sommerfeld at all?' Hopkins: 'I know Mr. Sommerfeld, but I never saw him until after the [Madero] revolution.' Smith: 'And they [Sommerfeld and the Maderos] came to you with all matters that concerned that Republic?' Hopkins: 'Yes, sir; all matters that pertained to the revolution and in connection with which my services were deemed essential.'"[621]

The decision to implement Hopkins' plan was finalized. Sommerfeld received several days of detailed instructions on the legal environment in which he had to interrupt enemy supply lines, have conspirators on U.S. soil arrested and extradited to Mexico, and steer clear of violating any U.S. laws himself. In his testimony to the U.S. subcommittee on Mexican affairs in October 1912, Sommerfeld's grasp of U.S. law is stunning, a credit due Sherburne G. Hopkins.[622]

Historians Harris and Sadler correctly noted that the Thiel Detective Agency in El Paso not only sent their weekly reports to the Mexican Secret Service but also to the Bureau of Investigation, Alberto Madero (the President's uncle), and the Northwestern Railroad Company.[623] This distribution list was not proof of an act of disloyalty or double crossing on the part of Thiel's customer as Harris and Sadler assumed. The Thiel Agency had been hired in 1910 by Hopkins. The money Consul Llorente received to finance the operation came from Hopkins. The man who took over responsibility for secret service work on the border was Hopkins' man Sommerfeld. The distribution of intelligence to Justice, the Mexican government, and the railroads occurred on the order of Hopkins. It was his deal with Justice, his client the Mexican government, and his other client Henry Clay Pierce who had regained his control over the National Mexican Railroads in October 1911. Hopkins' agent, Felix Sommerfeld also worked on helping Pierce's railroad interests, although there was an overlapping interest in doing so. He told Senator Smith in October

1912: "[T]he Mexican Northwestern Railroad tried to get a wire from here to their office in Juarez, so that they could communicate direct [sic] from here through their offices all along the line, and I wired to the minister telling him if he could do it to do it, because we needed that wire ourselves."[624] Referring to what had developed as a consequence of the meetings in Mexico City, historians Harris and Sadler wrote, "...there has never been a case in United States history when a foreign intelligence service has been allowed to operate within American territory as blatantly as during the period under study [1912]."[625] One certainly can observe in astonishment how it could have been possible for the United States to relinquish a portion of her sovereignty to Mexico when it came to border protection in 1911 and 1912. The proposition sounds preposterous, and, of course, it was. The facts tell a different story. Historians Harris and Sadler whose meticulous research created the most comprehensive and brilliant studies of the U.S.-Mexican border just this once missed an important piece to the puzzle.[626] The creation of the intelligence network along the border in 1912 was a virtual partnership between the two countries. As a matter of fact, many of the battle hardened members of Sommerfeld's organization from 1912 eventually merged into the FBI, an irony of history given Sommerfeld's real background as a German agent. No government as determined and strong as the Unites States' would have tolerated a foreign intelligence service roaming freely in its territory. Those who were not under the protection of the U.S. government quickly learned what the U.S. allowed and what it did not. Bernardo Reyes was one of many Mexican rebels who this intelligence organization neutralized as part of the U.S. security operations along the border. It is easy for researchers to get lost in the web of double agents, triple agents, loose lips, changing loyalties, gun slingers, and rip-offs that all worked along the border in seeming endless chaos. However, once the role of Hopkins, Sommerfeld, the U.S. Departments of Justice, War, and State, as well as that of the Mexican government is understood, the chaos turns into recognizable patterns. While many local histories have detailed the activities in the border towns along Mexico's border, Hopkins' plan had never before been identified.

CHAPTER 13

~

THE "SOMMERFELD ORGANIZATION"

Sommerfeld's execution of the Hopkins Plan began in earnest when, on February 27th 1912, Vasquista rebel forces retook Ciudad Juarez. The garrison of three hundred soldiers fell within hours. Civilians, who the Mexican consul in El Paso, Enrique Llorente, had supplied with arms in the previous weeks, could not turn back the massive rebel attack. Within days the whole of Chihuahua was under siege. On March 1st, Orozco made his move. He declared himself in revolt against Madero and sided with the Vasquista rebels. The former Madero commander installed himself as the leader of what would become known as the "Colorado" movement. The name resulted from the red battle flags the revolutionaries carried, often with the inscription "pan y tierra," bread and land.[627] Within days Orozco declared himself supreme leader, sidelined "provisional President" Emilio Vasquez Gomez, and officially took charge of the irregular forces roaming Chihuahua. He occupied Chihuahua City and declared martial law. Governor Gonzalez barely evaded arrest, first hiding in a friend's residence in Chihuahua and then slipping through the lines.[628] Within days he joined the active fight as a commander of Pancho Villa's irregulars.

Meanwhile, the day after Juarez fell, on February 28th, Sommerfeld returned from Mexico City and arrived in San Antonio. Armed with a letter from the President, requesting all Mexican officials to render any assistance he might require, the German agent gave San Antonio agent H. A. Thompson his "private code," with the promise to keep the BI agent fully advised.[629] Thompson reported to his superiors that the Mexican President had ordered Sommerfeld to "endeavor to devise some plan by which they could regain the ports without any imposition to American citizens..."[630] Senator Smith later in the year asked Sommerfeld whether he had "plenary powers" from the Mexican government to which the German replied "I do not wish to disguise that fact."[631] The conditions Hopkins had demanded from Madero in order to

174

implement his plan had clearly been met. The formal head of the Mexican secret service then continued on to El Paso where he settled in the Sheldon Hotel and began directing the shadow war. It would not be long until Agent Thompson left the San Antonio office of the Justice Department and joined Sommerfeld's organization. For now the main intelligence sources were Molina, Beltran, and the Thiel Detective Agency, which employed personnel in El Paso, San Antonio, Houston, Los Angeles, as well as in Chihuahua City, and other places south of the border.[632]

The buildup of the secret service organization proceeded very quickly. Llorente had received between $600,000 and $700,000 ($12.6 Million to $14.7 Million in today's money) to pay for informants, supplies of arms, and ammunition for the federal army in Chihuahua.[633] From the great reservoir of Mexican refugees all along the border, Sommerfeld and Llorente quickly recruited dozens of informants. The human resources were plentiful and cheap. Within days of setting up, there was nothing going on in El Paso or San Antonio that Sommerfeld did not know about. His people covered the entrance of every hardware dealer, suspect's home, bank, and saloon along the border. Even grocery stores had a shadow, in case rebels would come and supply themselves there. However, the rapid increase in personnel also had its downside. Many of the Mexican informants lacked loyalty or simply suffered from loose lips.

Without Orozco knowing it, Hopkins and Sommerfeld had become his most formidable opposition when they devised their brilliant plan to defeat him. He was not only to battle the military forces of the Mexican government. He now faced the combined law enforcement and clandestine forces of the Mexican and U.S. governments. The first salvo came on March 14th 1912, when President Taft announced the ban on the exportation of arms and ammunition, excepting the constitutional government of Mexico. Although the President's declaration was largely unenforceable at first, it became the centerpiece of Hopkins' plan. Sommerfeld's execution of the largest clandestine operation between Mexico and the United States in history received traction in the following months. It became a death grip for Orozco's Colorados, whom the American press called "Red Flaggers."

Clearly, the existence of the Madero administration hung in the balance in February and March 1912. Rumor had it that Orozco was financed by adherents of the old regime to the tune of $2,000,000 ($42 million in today's value).[634] Sommerfeld personally found out about two certified checks from Juan Terrazas to Orozco's group, one amounting to $52,000 and the other to

$12,500. Both checks ($1.35 Million in today's value) were cashed in the first week of March and financed arms purchases for the rebels.[635] Telling of the power behind Orozco's uprising was also an order the rebel leader gave on March 18th "hereafter the property of Gen. Luis Terrazas would be immune, and was not to be touched under any circumstances."[636] None of the Mexican government resources could have matched that level of funding, especially while many customs houses along the border were in the hands of the rebels or closed because of the crisis. However, the efficient use of the U.S. government in the battle eventually drained even those resources and choked off the oxygen any rebellion required: People, arms, and ammunition.

It took Sommerfeld a few weeks to establish his new role among the American officials in the border towns. While he had the authorization from the Mexican President to operate, American law enforcement and military officials had not received any word from higher-ups about Sommerfeld. Right away, the day before Sommerfeld came to San Antonio, he faced his first challenge: Teódulo Beltran, his intelligence chief in town, accidentally landed in jail. Sheriff Johnson of San Antonio had arrested three Mexican rebels and, while searching their belongings, found two Winchester rifles. Without any cause BI agent Charles D. Hebert who, according to historians Harris and Sadler was "disgruntled," urged the Sheriff to "put [Mexican Secret Service Agent Beltran] in jail with them." How the issue resolved itself is not known. Very likely it took a call from Hopkins to the Justice Department in Washington to clear up the misunderstanding. Hopkins had bailed out many a Madero loyalist in 1911, affirming to Senator Hitchcock that his "legal services were employed for the purpose of protecting those revolutionary agents in this country [the USA]."[637] Hebert remained a thorn in the side of Sommerfeld and the BI agents supporting him.

Trouble also came from the inside of Sommerfeld's agency. Abraham Molina, the former head of the Mexican secret service who now reported to Sommerfeld, would not accept the German's authority. Most likely influenced by the misgivings of his former boss Abraham Gonzalez, Molina actively started undermining Sommerfeld's efforts. On March 11th 1912, he informed Agent Ross of the BI in El Paso "confidentially that the Mexican government had smuggled 250 regulars through from Laredo to Ojinaga, that were mostly artillery men and officers." Untrue, the accusations still prompted the Justice agents to investigate Llorente and Sommerfeld under the suspicion that they recruited soldiers for the Mexican army.[638] As expected, the investigation came to nothing. On the 22nd of March, Molina went so far as to reporting

Sommerfeld to Agent Ross for allegedly having ordered "500 rifle scabbards and 300 belts...and that he took these out yesterday and shipped them east – to Marfa...and that they would probably be smuggled into Ojinaga from there."[639] Of course, the rifle scabbards and belts did not constitute banned ammunitions. Sommerfeld actually was legally shipping weapons and ammunition to the federal commander across from Marfa. He certainly had no reason to smuggle since he was the representative of the Mexican government. On the 30th of March he gave a detailed list of his supplies for the Maderista commander José González Salas to Agent Ross:

"2 machine guns, Colts, 7mm
8 ammunition boxes containing 32 small boxes and 32 feed belts for machine guns
1000 cartridge belts (700 canvas and 300 leather)
331 carbine scabbards with straps
2 belt loading machines for machine guns
50,000 rounds ammunition 30-40"[640]

Sommerfeld's trouble with Molina continued for months. He finally heard about Molina's disloyalty when he hired the same former Bureau of Investigation agent that Molina had "confidentially" informed. Molina received his discharge papers. However, the Mexican secret service agent simply refused to be fired.[641] He had a trump card up his sleeves, namely that he knew the intimate details of an embarrassing affair that had the potential to land both Sommerfeld and the Mexican consul in jail.

On March 14th 1912, Peter F. Aiken, a self-proclaimed soldier-of-fortune with an inflated resume so frequently found in the border towns of Texas at the time, approached Sommerfeld and Llorente with a proposal. He wanted to kidnap Pascual Orozco and bring him to the United States' authorities if the money was right. Sommerfeld, doubting that the self-proclaimed Japanese spy[642] and British veteran of the Boer War had any realistic chance to kidnap Orozco, proposed a slightly different mission to Aiken.[643] For $200 up front (about $4,200 in today's value) and 25 Pesos per day (about $250 in today's value) he was to go and blow up railroad bridges between Juarez and Chihuahua City to slow down troop and supply transports for Orozco. With seventy-five pounds of dynamite and two of Molina's men, Angel Schave and José Borjas Ramos,[644] Aiken crossed into Mexico to demolish "every bridge between Agua Nueva and Terrazas."[645] While Aiken claimed that he succeeded in his sabotage mission, the truth was that the endeavor ended in a disaster for Sommerfeld and Llorente. Aiken was arrested on March 20th. The next day Sommerfeld "came to the jail to see me. He told me that he and the Mexican Consul would do everything they could for me."[646] It took serious bribes to keep him from revealing all he knew to the American authorities. Although Aiken complained from time to time while he spent the next six months in jail, the sabotage agent kept his mouth shut for a couple of months.

Supposedly because Sommerfeld stopped paying him the promised twenty-five pesos per day, Aiken finally told his story to Agent Ross two months after his arrest and conviction. Meanwhile Sommerfeld had found out that Aiken never blew up anything while in Mexico. The German agent told Senator Fall a few months later, "instead of going out to execute his commission, he stayed in Juarez drinking and intoxicated, and came back."[647] Aiken's partner Schave testified, "Ramos and I went to Fabens on the morning of the 15th of March, 1912, and from there we crossed to the Mexican side...Ramos got cold feet and refused to carry out the expedition...On the 19th of March I reported to the Consul and he took the $50 away from me."[648] Aiken's statement, although full of lies, so Ross, "...fully confirms my suspicion that Peter Aiken is doing time in order to keep the Mexican Consul, Enrique C. Llorente and Abraham Molina, out of jail themselves. Pressure was brought to bear upon him to plead guilty in order to keep the consul and Molina out of it."[649] While it is somewhat surprising that neither Llorente nor Molina got in trouble, the real jewel of Ross' report is another fact, further cementing the existence of the Hopkins Plan. Aiken clearly implicated Sommerfeld by name in the affair both as being present when the mission was decided and bribing him to be quiet when he was arrested. Yet, Ross' report only mentioned Llorente and Molina. Sommerfeld, who had squared with the BI agent weeks earlier and admitted "Aiken had been sent on a 'mission' of some sort," never came up as a target of the investigation.[650] He clearly was under the protection of Ross' superiors, likely as high up or higher as the Director of the Bureau of Investigation, A. Bruce Bielaski, in Washington, D.C.

Despite the start-up problems, Sommerfeld's powerbase expanded quickly. He had to launch his campaign with only a handful of agents. By the end of April he added Powell Roberts, a former police sergeant in El Paso. The organization now had four chiefs reporting to Sommerfeld: Molina, Roberts, Beltran, and Kramp. In order to assist Roberts Sommerfeld hired Lee E. Hall, also a former member of the police, and Earl Heath, another American citizen. The Thiel office added former BI agent Cunningham, the informer that had implicated the Standard Oil Company in the financing of Madero's revolution. Molina, whom Sommerfeld whole-heartedly mistrusted, had twenty-six agents under him. Roberts had between twelve and sixteen men, while the Thiel office employed an unknown but certainly higher number of detectives.[651] Among Sommerfeld's new hires was also a British pilot, Lee Hedgson, who brought his plane to El Paso to fly reconnaissance and "...to do what damage I could do them with air bombs..."[652] Hedgson was to take off and fly into Mexico under the cover of a one-plane air show, which Sommerfeld had organized in the ballpark of El Paso. However, the American military commander Steever saw through the plan and threatened to shoot the Brit down if he approached the border.[653] Lucky for Orozco's fighters, the one-plane aerial campaign Sommerfeld had planned was grounded.

Sommerfeld and Llorente also paid hundreds of Mexicans who, for the most part, had been federal soldiers and who had fled from the "Red Flaggers" after the conquest of the Chihuahua garrisons. Agent Lancaster reported, "Alberto Madero, Felix Sommerfeld, and General Darey Boldie had about 2,000 Mexicans in and around El Paso ready to cross to Mexico and take Juarez."[654] This number was highly inflated. On April 25th, Abe Molina told Agent Hebert that they were paying about three hundred Mexican soldiers "drawing there [sic] pay through the Mexican Consul at this place every ten days."[655] While these men maybe did not constitute enough manpower to mount an attempt to retake Juarez, as the Orozquista propaganda suggested, Sommerfeld certainly had enough people to spy on their activities. To the amazement of Senator Smith, Sommerfeld admitted in October 1912 that his spies had even thoroughly infiltrated the rebel army in Ciudad Juarez.[656] Orozquista orders for arms and ammunition often reached Sommerfeld quicker than Krakauer, Zork, and Moye, the rebel's main supplier.

The relationship between the Mexican Secret Service and American authorities had grown so close that it caused historians Harris and Sadler to observe, "...the operations of these two organizations became ... virtually indistinguishable."[657] To clear the bad taste the Aiken affair had left with law enforcement, U.S. officials convened a meeting on May 5th 1912 at Fort Bliss. Special agent Louis Ross of the BI, Army Commander at Ft. Bliss, Colonel Steever, Texas Ranger Webster, Sommerfeld, and Powell Roberts spent all day strategizing. Ross reported to his superiors a week later, "We discussed fully the plan of operation with regarding to shutting off the supply of ammunition the rebels are getting through the lines, and other matters pertaining to the work."[658] Again, a clear reference to the Hopkins Plan and Sommerfeld's, not

Consul Llorente's, central role in it. Immediately after the meeting, Sommerfeld tried to fire Molina again. The decision seemed to be connected to a demand from Ross and Steever to that effect. Neither man trusted the Mexican agent. Maybe as a result of a brilliant sidestep, Sommerfeld had blamed the responsibility of the Aiken affair on Molina and promised to fire him. Again, Molina refused to go and told Agent Ross on May 16th of his blackmailing Llorente and Sommerfeld. Ross reported, "...he [Molina] had opened the Consul's [Llorente] eyes this morning in an interview."[659] While Molina stayed on Llorente's payroll, later BI reports a few months later show him procuring foodstuffs for the Mexican army and disappearing from the reports altogether by the fall. Sommerfeld had finally eliminated his competitor.

In concert, the BI agents and Sommerfeld went after the main pillars of Orozco's organization in El Paso. The man in charge of Orozco's U.S. camp in El Paso was Victor L. Ochoa. Born in Ojinaga of Mexican and Scottish parents, the sixty-two-year-old conspirator had a long history of intrigue. A journalist and newspaper editor at the time, he led a revolt against Porfirio Diaz in 1893 and 1894. The attempt to dislodge the dictator failed and Ochoa barely evaded his pursuers with $50,000 Pesos reward on his head. "He saw his men put up a gallant fight, but outnumbered, they fell one by one until Mr. Ochoa alone survived. Through a ruse he managed to obtain the uniform of one of the regular soldiers and while on the retreat was espied and shot at in the belief that he was a deserter. Then started a chase which led through the mountain fastnesses, through treacherous ravines and gullies. It was a long traverse over three hundred miles, but the plucky Ochoa, finally managed to obtain some aid and eluded his pursuers."[660] Losing every one of his fighters he managed to cross into the United States. "On April 11, 1895, Ochoa was arrested in Texas by the United States government for violating the neutrality laws and was sentenced to prison for two years and six months and pay a fine of $1,000. He was taken to Kings county penitentiary, at [sic] Brooklyn [New York] and was discharged on May 10, 1897. On Feb. 15, 1906, President Roosevelt granted his application for a pardon and a restoration of his civil rights."[661]

A powerful man who had survived attacks by Apache raiders and Diaz' Rurales, Ochoa spent the intervening years in El Paso. He is well-known for his patented inventions such as the Ochoa plane, the orinthopter (a magnetically powered aircraft that flies by flapping its wings), a windmill, magnetic rail brakes, a wrench, and a reversible motor. The radical design of the Ochoa plane which calls for wings to be folded away for storage of the plane in a normal garage was many decades ahead of the first air craft carrier or flying car. He died in 1945 in Mexico where he lived in exile after having shot and killed two men in El Paso in 1936.

When the revolution broke out in 1910, Ochoa's company in El Paso manufactured fountain pens rather than airplanes. Like so many who had pinned their hopes on Madero, Ochoa initially supported the revolution. He quickly became disenchanted, especially when his business in Chihuahua suffered as the result of continuing strife. When Orozco took the helm of the rebels in March 1912, Ochoa set up a sophisticated intelligence, recruitment, and arms smuggling network for the new movement. He became the conduit for the large financial support Luis Terrazas and other enemies of Madero funneled to the revolutionaries. This brought him into the crosshairs of Felix Sommerfeld.

Under permanent observation by Mexican secret service agents and with the Juarez garrison infiltrated with Sommerfeld's spies, Ochoa's activities quickly came to light. True to his tough personality he declared himself publicly in support of Orozco. Defiantly he dared the Justice Department to make a move. Sommerfeld and the agents answered the challenge and kept building a stronger and stronger case. On June 21st 1912, Justice Department official Barnes reported that Ochoa had put $5,000 on Sommerfeld's head and contemplated blowing up the Mexican consulate.[662] According to Sommerfeld's testimony, it was his own people who arrested Ochoa in July and turned him over to the American authorities.[663] He was charged with conspiracy but released a few weeks later on bail. Full of hate over the successful dismantling of his organization, Ochoa continued spreading rumors that Sommerfeld and Llorente were recruiting men for the counter revolution.[664] Eventually, Sommerfeld and the BI agents failed to get a conviction in Ochoa's highly publicized trial in 1913. With many of his associates who Sommerfeld and the BI had arrested but could not get convicted he remained a free man after the Orozco revolt had been crushed.

The main target of Sommerfeld's wrath other than Victor Ochoa was the hardware store of Adolph and Julius Krakauer. To Sommerfeld's dismay, the German Jewish immigrants from the same region that Sommerfeld originated from chose profit over ethics. As a result, every person in and out of the store was meticulously shadowed for months. Sommerfeld also tracked checks cashed in the name of the store thus coming upon the Terrazas payments. Any smuggler who dealt with the store faced a great likelihood of arrest as a result of the Mexican secret service agents' legwork. The El Paso jails swelled with Neutrality Law offenders. While convictions remained hard to obtain, $250 to

$1,000 bonds made sure that the suspects stayed away from further action. The BI agents' reports tell the story: March 11th "...Somerfelt [sic] informed me today that Nunez & Son, who run a grocery store on South Stanton St. are making dynamite bombs at this store."[665] On March 17th "Geo[rge] Harold of the detectives said there would be a rebel meeting on South Broadway tonight and he thought he could get a man into it." In the same report: "I saw Somerfelt [sic] and he informed me that the rebels were going to ship arms and ammunition into Mexico consigned to a merchant of Chihuahua...He promised to furnish me the name of the merchant."[666] Information poured in from all along the border, not just El Paso. The agent reports showed the breadth of Sommerfeld's reach. Interesting to note is the clear description of Sommerfeld as the head of the organization, not Llorente or Molina, as many historians have mistakenly interpreted. March 18th: "I saw L. L. Hall and he informed me that he had gone to work for Somerfelt [sic]...He told me that he had information that Thomas Duran left Douglas last night for El Paso to smuggle guns into Mexico. He also stated that Fernando Escaboza is smuggling guns at Douglas and Stark station and is also recruiting men in this vicinity."[667] Sommerfeld and his people actively participated in stopping the smugglers and making arrests. Also on March 18th, Special Agent Ross wrote, "Mr. Kramp [of the Thiel Detective Agency] showed me a telegram he had received from Douglas stating that Francisca Villareal [,] a child and a man on crutches would arrive on the afternoon train in El Paso and that they carried very important revolutionary documents for delivery in El Paso. He also showed the telegram to Alberto Madero. The secret service men were at the station and brought the state rangers with them."[668]

The lines became so blurred that one day an agent worked for the Bureau of Investigation, the next day for Sommerfeld. On April 25th "At 9 P.M. in company with Mr. L. E. Hall who now works for the Mexican Government, I went down on the river front to investigate conditions..."[669] On May 7th "Agent then with the assistance of T. B. Cunningham [former BI informant] of the Theil [sic] Detective Service and L. LL. Hall [sic] of the Madero Secret Service, made a thorough investigation throughout Pirtleville and Douglas, but failed to hear or locate any of the fore said men who had supposed to have crossed from the Mexican side..."[670] Agent Thompson reported on the same day: "I was informed by T. M. Martinez [one of Beltran's men] who has been covering the arms and ammunition purchased by Andres Garza Galan...These supplies are stored at the home of Casanova on South Heights and **we** [emphasis added by author] are having them watched by Mexican Secret Service Agents..."[671] On May 16th

Sommerfeld himself joined the hunt: "In the evening some of the Mexican government men reported to me that they had located Manuel Garza Adalpe. Somerfelt [sic] and I got a machine and chased out there, but it turned out that they did not have the man located."[672]

The Sommerfeld organization's powers indeed included seize and arrest functions within the territory of the United States greatly alarming American officials such as the Mayor of El Paso and Senator Albert B. Fall. In order to prevent smuggling across the border, Sommerfeld had posted agents on the American side of the border that searched people and vehicles. At first, the agents worked in tandem with the U.S. military but after a few weeks the Mexican agents acted independently. Abe Molina described the issue to Agent Ross on March 18th: "...a number of people were carrying ammunition across the river in their clothes; that they went across on the street car, and each one made several trips a day; that there were some women also engaged in this business, carrying cartridges under their clothes..."[673] Needless to say, the American soldiers guarding the bridges did not body search female smugglers. Sommerfeld in his typical straightforward manner took action. He hired female agents. Under the eyes of U.S. border troops and on American soil the Mexican "agenettes" set up little tents on the bridges, took the women crossing into Mexico, whether American, Mexican, or any other nationality off the street cars, searched them, and confiscated the contraband. The smuggling stopped but the residents of El Paso were outraged. When Senator Fall asked Sommerfeld a few months later, "who put them there?" he claimed that he did not know.[674] However, he did cover for all the other authorities involved, Colonel Steever, the Justice Department, and U.S. Customs. Sommerfeld even covered his friend Enrique Llorente. On the question of who employed the women, the German agent responded that the consul only "paid them."[675] The end justified the means, although the female inspectors quickly disappeared from the bridges after the local papers carried the story voicing the intense public outrage on their front pages.

The noose around the Krakauer, Zork and Moye Company tightened in June and July 1912. Millions of rounds of ammunition had fallen into the hands of authorities since the President's arms embargo proclamation of March 14th. By the middle of May, Agent Thompson wrote to his superiors: "You will note by Agent Ross's reports and also reports sent in by myself that we have a case almost complete against Krakauer, Zork, and Moye...who have been connected with conspiring in this and another matter...We are now able to show conclusively ...that these people are still endeavoring to carry on these shipments that they are constantly receiving orders...and these goods will be delivered...The witnesses who have been captured in exporting this stuff have no hesitancy in stating these facts. In addition to this, we have a witness who has seen and read this contract [to supply the rebels] and I think we will be able to prove its contents and existence."[676]

While the BI agents worked on creating the formal indictment of Adolph and Julius Krakauer, Sommerfeld took matters in his own hands on July 3rd. He announced to people who he was certain would inform Adolph Krakauer, "...when what is supposed to be the federal Government or its representatives are again in possession of the City of Chihuahua, that this individual [Sommerfeld] will see to it that we...'will be fixed.'"[677] The American consul in Ciudad Juarez, Marion Letcher, who could not stand Sommerfeld, forwarded a letter from Krakauer on to the Secretary of State Knox. In turn Knox sent a copy to the Justice Department. In it, Letcher decried the power of the German agent in El Paso and warned that threats such as the ones against the merchants showed the potential for American authorities of losing control.[678] Nothing concrete happened as a result of Letcher's letter. Both Philander Knox as well as Bruce Bielaski were fully aware of Sommerfeld's activities. Krakauer had every reason to be upset. Not only was he indicted the same week these threats became known, Sommerfeld subsequently did "fix" him. He black-balled Krakauer and routed all arms business for the Madero government and later Pancho Villa's Division of the North through the Shelton Payne Arms Company, costing Krakauer's firm millions in sales. Despite Sommerfeld's efforts, Krakauer's indictment in 1912 did not produce a conviction. Barely a year later had an El Paso jury the conspiracy charges in the trial against the merchants as well as Ochoa dismissed. These dismissals underlined the corruption that dogged the legal system along the border: The Krakauer brothers had clearly violated the Neutrality Laws when they supported the Reyes revolutionaries, Vasquez Gomez, and Orozco with munitions and supplies.

However, for the time being, Sommerfeld and the American authorities successfully curbed the vast supplies of munitions. Madero had dispatched his most senior commander, Victoriano Huerta, to crush the Colorados. Battle hardened from his campaign against Zapata and with his notorious brutality it took until late June for Orozco's offensive to collapse. Pancho Villa, who now fought under Huerta's command, had retaken control of Parral, Stallforth's hometown. Much to the surprise of the citizenry, Villa's forces kept order, refrained from looting, and, important to the U.S.

government, did not touch American property. Villa's occupation of Parral stood in stark contrast to the outrages committed months earlier by Orozco's Colorados against the city's residents. Certainly, the fact that Abraham Gonzalez exercised significant influence over Villa in that campaign could have been a reason for Villa's sudden civility. Promoted to general by Madero, Villa's offensive proved to be of vital importance to the campaign against Orozco. The Colorados lost control of most of Chihuahua in June with the main fighting force concentrated in Juarez for a last stand.

As a result of Villa's obvious successes, General Victoriano Huerta decided that the bandit-turned-general was becoming too powerful and popular. Villa's campaign also reinstated Abraham Gonzalez back to Chihuahua's capital. Huerta despised the Chihuahuan governor mainly because Gonzalez was a true revolutionary whose goals included fundamental social change.[679] His influence on Madero and his important power base of Chihuahua made him a threat to Huerta. On trumped up charges, Huerta had Villa arrested on June 4th 1912. Only a last minute intervention by Madero saved him from a firing squad.[680] He languished for the rest of 1912 in prison in Mexico City. There are no historical documents that link Sommerfeld in any way to Pancho Villa's situation. While he was certainly aware of the arrest and subsequent imprisonment, he does not seem to have intervened on Villa's behalf either with Huerta or the Mexican President. He was busy in El Paso where he helped prepare the final battle against Orozco's forces.

While the interruption of the supply lines proceeded with great success, the secret service chief also continued his efforts inside the Colorado forces. Sam Dreben, Sommerfeld's old friend from the Madero revolution, had joined the rebel forces in March 1912. According to his biographer, "the fighting Jew," together with machine gunner Tracy Richardson, was roaming the Chihuahuan countryside bar brawling and single handedly holding back anti-American mobs. Local lore memorialized by Tex O'Reilly, Tracy Richardson, as well as recent popular historians such as Douglas Meed, Art Leibson, and Jim Tuck credited Dreben and Richardson with blowing up dynamite packed locomotives into enemy defenses, holding back a federal advance at the Battle of Rellano with a lone machine gun nest, and killing scores of hapless revolutionary peons. The result of the two soldiers-of-fortunes' antics was the suicide of Madero's commander and Secretary of War, Gonzalez Salas. The stories, while certainly containing kernels of truth, unfairly devalue the Mexican soldiers and their officer corps who certainly represented more than brainless masses of cannon fodder for American mercenaries. Leibson's biography of Dreben continues to detail an encounter with the "obviously drunk" General Campa, who hated "gringos." According to the historian an intervention from "higher authorities" saved Dreben and Richardson from the firing squad.[681]

The unbelievable stories of Dreben's escapades in 1912 are largely based on the Orozquista propaganda published in American border dailies. While not many primary documents of Dreben's engagements in 1912 have survived, there are indications that he actually was one of Sommerfeld's moles in the Colorado forces. Dreben was hanging out in El Paso in early March 1912. Like so many mercenaries he was looking for work and certainly must have been approached by Ochoa's men. Sommerfeld, whose informants literally canvassed every pebble in El Paso, knew Dreben well. The machine-gunning maniac and well-known bar fly in El Paso had been a decorated soldier in Madero's forces. There is no possibility that Sommerfeld did not know about Dreben's alleged gun smuggling and employment with the Colorados described by his biographer.

If indeed Dreben had become a traitor to Madero's cause, Sommerfeld's wrath, so painfully felt by Ochoa and his men, would have been certainty. The opposite was the case. Rather than pursuing him, Dreben appeared in the BI records as a Sommerfeld employee in July 1912.[682] Very likely, Dreben had been Sommerfeld's man since March and had infiltrated the Colorado forces under the cover of being a mercenary, which was a strategy Sommerfeld used frequently.[683] When he was found out, Sommerfeld's organization, the "higher authority" Leibson referred to in his book, saved him and brought him back to El Paso. Under this scenario Sommerfeld's claim to have infiltrated the enemy with his spies, Dreben's subsequent employment with the Secret Service, and the impunity with which he allegedly supported the rebels make sense. Pancho Villa, whose troops according to Meed and Leibson died by the thousands as a result of Dreben's antics, also did nothing to punish him.[684] As a matter of fact, Dreben became Villa and Sommerfeld's main representative in El Paso in subsequent years. Agent Ross' report from July 7th illuminated Dreben's true occupation that matches the historical record namely that just like Aiken "Dreben had been employed by Somerfelt [sic] to blow up bridges south of Juarez."[685]

Despite the failed mission of Peter Aiken and his friends, Sommerfeld had continued to hire sabotage agents to disrupt enemy command and control as well as supply lines. While nothing other than the wild stories in Leibson's book is known about Dreben's time in Chihuahua in 1912, Sommerfeld had organized another sabotage expedition in June. Emile L. Charpentier, a mercenary of French descent, played the main role in the attempt. Sommerfeld knew Charpentier well. The Frenchman had played a decisive role in the battles of the Madero revolution in 1911. According to stories published about him he had built and operated cannon that he had assembled from railroad car axles. As such, the Madero revolutionaries had artillery support for their attacks on the federals. While certain aspects of these stories can be discounted as embellishments, Charpentier definitely was of a higher caliber than Aiken. Joined in his efforts were D. J. Mahoney, Jack Noonan, and Robert McDonald, who had been another member of the famed foreign legion in Madero's revolutionary army. The mission failed just like the Aiken expedition had a month earlier. The group took the advance payments and, a few weeks later, came back to El Paso empty-handed. In Charpentier's statement to Agent Ross, Sommerfeld, Llorente, and Alberto Madero were clearly implicated in the plot. Ross wrote to his superiors, "[The] whole conversation [with Felix Sommerfeld] was an open-and-shut admission that he [Sommerfeld] had sent these men out..."[686] As in earlier episodes the Justice Department only investigated Llorente, a token effort to save some appearance of non-partisan upholding of U.S. laws. The four sabotage agents went on trial in October 1912. All four remained free men and rejoined Sommerfeld's cadre for future missions.

Another widely fascinating character that worked for Sommerfeld in 1912 was Newenham A. Gray. An engineer by trade, Gray became a formidable ordinance expert through his military service in the British army. Born in 1877 of Scottish parents in India, he went to school in Zurich, Switzerland. The Military Intelligence Division described him as "...5 feet 10-11 inches; Dark complexion; dark mustache and hair; stocky build of about 190 lbs.; highly educated, well and expensively dressed; Cockney brogue with slight German accent..."[687] He fought with the British army in India from 1898 to 1907 as an officer in the field artillery. In 1907 Gray joined the Indian Secret Service for which he worked in the Persian Gulf. He came to the Mexican-American border region in 1910. Initially, he consulted with railroad companies. Sometime in 1911 he joined up with Sommerfeld who used him off and on for information gathering and sabotage missions.[688] In 1912, Gray joined Guillermo Bach and Company in Mexico City as a consulting engineer. Guillermo Bach was the representative of the Deutsche Waffen- und Munitionsfabriken, Berlin, and the Krupp concern in Mexico.[689] In his work of soliciting and specifying arms contracts, Gray came into frequent contact with the German embassy in Mexico City. Gray fluently spoke English, French, German, Italian, and Spanish.

In 1914, he joined Sommerfeld in New York, where he helped source arms and ammunition for Mexican revolutionaries and worked for the German Secret Service.[690] Nominally he represented Flint and Company, Charles Flint's company in New York City that supplied the Constitutionalist armies. The Military Intelligence Division and Department of Justice identified him as a spy in 1916. However, he evaded capture for the entire First World War. In 1918, he settled in the area around Tucson, Arizona, where he owned and operated mines.[691] A very secretive German agent, Gray's record of activities for Sommerfeld and the German government is sketchy at best. However, given Sommerfeld's need for technical expertise for sabotage and other secret missions, Gray was an important resource.

A soldier-of-fortune who manned a machine gun in the federal forces fighting Orozco and joined Sommerfeld's organization was Emil Holmdahl. Holmdahl later noted on a picture of Orozco: "We knocked the Hell out of him and his troops later while with Villa at San Andres where I earned the Legion of Honor medal."[692] In May 1912, Holmdahl was sent on a secret mission to recover the remains of Captain Lorenzo Aguilar who was President Madero's cousin. Apparently, Aguilar had been killed while retreating with the federal army from the Battle of Rellano. Holmdahl, under cover as a journalist, unearthed Aguilar's remains in a daring nighttime operation and delivered them to federal authorities. Holmdahl's mission received wide coverage in the daily papers of the time showing him attending Aguilar's public funeral.[693] According to Holmdahl's biographer Douglas Meed the order to retrieve the fallen soldier came from General Trevino of the federal forces. However, with Sommerfeld in charge of the secret service and this mission being close to President Madero's heart, it is more likely that it was Sommerfeld who sent the soldier-of-fortune under cover behind enemy lines. An indication that Holmdahl worked as a secret service agent is found in a mysterious note in his papers dated November 11th 1912:

> "Mr Holmdahl, c/o Condr – No 11.
>   Agua Zorea
> Meet me on wire when No 12 gets to Hermosillo – Opr. Nogales can give you time.
>
> H.J. Temple."

Below the note, Holmdahl wrote in his handwriting years later, probably around 1918: "Temple was general manager SO[uthern]. R[ail]R[oad] of Mexico shot himself when confronted by US agents making arrest for selling information to Germans."[694] The significance of this note is that Holmdahl definitely worked for the Mexican Secret Service in November 1912. When his employment commenced is unknown.[695] In November, he reported to Lee L. Hall, the successor of Powell Roberts in Sommerfeld's organization. As a secret service agent he infiltrated the Orozquistas in El Paso under the cover of a mercenary and was instrumental in arresting one of Orozco's senior generals.[696] A December 28th 1912 diary entry reads, "Jesus Orozco who is prop[rietor] of a Barber Shop in the 500 block on South El Paso St. used a back room of his shop as a sleeping place and a place to hold the meeting of the Revolutionary Junta; the following Red Flaggers were his friends and lived in his shop...."[697] The Justice Department agents subsequently smoked out the place. Holmdahl appeared as a witness for the Mexican government in this and several other Neutrality Law trials in the fall of 1912.[698]

Emil Holmdahl around 1918[699]

As the Orozco rebellion fizzled in the summer of 1912, Sommerfeld kept up the pressure on conspiracies north of the border. In September,

Sommerfeld agent Powell Roberts wrote a note to his boss. In it he warned Sommerfeld that BI agent Hebert had found out that Agent Thompson in San Antonio and Agent Ross in El Paso had received "small payments" from the Mexican consulate. According to Roberts, Hebert and the local Sheriff Wheeler sympathized with the Orozquistas who, according to Sommerfeld's agent, thought that the arms embargo of the government was a mistake. Sommerfeld took the report and accompanied with a hand written letter sent it to Thompson:

"Dear friend Thompson.
Enclosed find a report of Powell Roberts. I have nothing further to say about this man Hebert. You know my opinion. I am going away for about 8 or 10 days. With best regards, sincerely yours,
F.A. Sommerfeld"[700]

Hebert pursued both BI agents Ross and Thompson for allegedly having sold confiscated arms to the rebels. Both were fired as a result of the accusations.[701] Sommerfeld knew this not to be true. Whether the accusations had been a rumor started by Ochoa and his people or whether Hebert had other unknown reasons to discredit the two agents is unknown. No formal indictment ever followed. After being fired, the two BI agents joined Sommerfeld as employees making more money than before.[702] Although historians Harris and Sadler cited disagreements between Ross and Sommerfeld's organization, the BI agent seemed to have tried hard to cover up the fact that many months before he was formally employed, Llorente and Sommerfeld had already paid him under the table.

On August 20th 1912, the federal forces under Victoriano Huerta took back Ciudad Juarez. Madero sent Rafael Hernandez, his cousin and Secretary of Justice, to negotiate a truce between Huerta and Orozco that would have prevented further bloodshed. Sommerfeld attended the meetings. On the night of August 20th, Orozco agreed to lay down his arms in return for amnesty. However, he changed his mind overnight. Sommerfeld blamed Senator Fall for the change of mind, which he reported to Madero.[703] Fall's involvement in the failed negotiations is a matter of debate. Historian William H. Beezley identified a power struggle between Abraham Gonzalez and General Huerta to have been the root of the problem.[704] However, Albert Fall did have a vested interest in sabotaging Madero's efforts to solve the problem. The man who Sommerfeld called an enemy of the Mexican President relentlessly pushed for U.S. military intervention. The more turmoil in Mexico the clearer the "ineffectiveness" of Madero could be shown, thus justifying armed intervention. As a result of the failed agreement, Orozco decided to make a last stand at Ojinaga, the Mexican border hamlet across from Presidio, Texas. There the rebels suffered a decisive defeat. Orozco, wounded in the battle, fled to the United States where Sommerfeld and his people hunted him unmercifully but could not catch him. Like a bad dream the rebel leader kept reappearing in the history of the revolution until an American posse finally killed him on August 30th 1915.[705] With Orozquistas on the loose, Ojinaga remained a hotbed of incessant guerrilla activity throughout the winter of 1912 to 1913.

While Sommerfeld's organization succeeded in choking off Orozco's supply lines and caused his eventual defeat, the clandestine campaign was not without fallout. The relationship between the German agent and Governor Abraham Gonzalez reached a low point. Since the U.S. government seemed to be unable to get convictions of the conspirators Sommerfeld chased into their net, the German agent decided to use the extradition law of 1899 on the arrested men. The system functioned in such a way, that Sommerfeld and his people would present evidence of unlawful behavior of a Mexican subject to the BI agents or the local Sheriffs. The persons would then be picked up and jailed. The Mexican government now had forty days to provide an extradition request. Over and over Gonzalez' government in Chihuahua City caused the deadline to go by. The suspects went free, undoing a lot of Sommerfeld's legwork as a result. He vented his frustrations to Senator Fall in October 1912, "It always takes so infernally long before it goes through the different channels." Fall asked: "You know that de la Fuente was discharged after 40 days in jail?" Sommerfeld: "Yes. That is the fault of the governor of Chihuahua." [706] It is not clear whether Gonzalez actually boycotted Sommerfeld's efforts, as the German alleged. After retreating from the Orozco advance in March 1912, it took Gonzalez until July to reenter Chihuahua and resume the governorship. Surely, much was in disarray in the summer of 1912 that would explain why paperwork simply did not make it to El Paso. The friction between Gonzalez and Sommerfeld, however, is documented and whatever the cause, the extradition delays did not help alleviating the problem.

Sommerfeld also made enemies on the U.S. side that would haunt him many years later. In 1919, when he tried to be released from internment as an enemy alien in Fort Oglethorpe, Georgia, Lieutenant Colonel Bailey, who used to work under Colonel Steever, wrote, "I personally knew this man [Sommerfeld] in El Paso in 1912 and accused him of being a German spy at that time. He acknowledged to me that he was either in the German secret service or an officer of the German General Staff, I have forgotten which...It would be an easy matter I believe to trace his operations along the Border [sic], and if my testimony would be of any service [I] shall be very glad to furnish same as he acknowledged to me he was a German officer at the time he was serving with the Mexican revolutionary forces."[707]

There is only one known record that shows Sommerfeld passing intelligence information to the German government in 1912.[708] However, von Hintze seemed consistently well informed about the Orozco uprising. On the day of Orozco's defeat at the Battle of Bachimba, he reported to the Foreign Office in Berlin, "...for all practical purposes this revolution has ended."[709] It is a natural assumption that Sommerfeld, a man of high standing with the German ambassador, would keep him updated on conditions in the field. Records show the brief interlude with Frederico Stallforth in El Paso. However, the accusations of Lieutenant Colonel Bailey seem a bit far-fetched. While Sommerfeld was proud of his military service in the German army, the good colonel seemed to have mixed up the Mexican and the German governments. Sommerfeld was too careful, even in 1912, to admit to an American officer that he indeed was a German spy.

In general, Americans who saw him in action in 1912 were glad for what he had achieved. Colonel Steever and the BI agents held him in high esteem. Yet he remained an enigma to all. Holmdahl testified in 1919, that, while he was acquainted with Sommerfeld in El Paso, the German "...had few intimate friends, that Sommerfeld always attended closely to business, that he lived well and dressed fashionably, and that he preferred only to be seen in the company of those of social prominence." [710] On September 11th 1912, Sommerfeld left for Chicago and New York. Agent Ross reported to Chief Bielaski: "Felix Somerfelt [sic] representing Madero left here today [on the] Golden State Limited for [the] east [coast]. My information is [that he is] going to interview Woodrow Wilson [to] make arrangements [and] endeavor [to] prevent intervention through democratic members Congress. Many Mexican officials here consider intervention very probable in [the] near future..."[711] Woodrow Wilson, governor of New Jersey, was challenging President Taft as the Democratic front-runner in the upcoming elections. Who gave Ross the idea of Sommerfeld meeting the future American President is unclear. Although hard to prove, there were good reasons for Hopkins setting Sommerfeld up to meet with the future president if not only to update him on the latest developments in the Mexican Revolution. Whether Sommerfeld went to see Wilson in September 1912 or whether he just traveled to Chicago and New York on other business, the telegram from Agent Ross to Chief Bielaski shows the level of clout people close to Sommerfeld thought he possessed.

Trouble did not stop for President Madero. However, this time it was not brewing on the periphery but in the capital of Mexico itself. The President had ceased to be the most powerful man in Mexico. The campaigns against Zapata and Orozco had lifted his Army Chief of Staff, General Victoriano Huerta, to a position that Francisco Madero had no means to check. While clouds of disaster brewed over Mexico, the United States readied itself for a historic presidential election.

CHAPTER 14

COUNT VON BERNSTORFF AND THE 1912 U.S. PRESIDENTIAL ELECTIONS

As Sommerfeld boarded the Golden State Limited on September 11th 1912 and headed for Chicago where his brother Julius lived, the headlines of American dailies were preoccupied with reports on the presidential campaigns of William Howard Taft, Theodore Roosevelt, and Woodrow Wilson. President Taft, the former Secretary of War under Roosevelt, battled with his former boss over the direction of the Republican Party. Roosevelt, who led the progressive wing of the party, challenged the conservatives led by Taft. The primary campaign became one of the dirtiest ever fought in U.S. history. "The Taft spokesmen searched Roosevelt's record and laid down a heavy barrage of personal abuse. Roosevelt replied in kind, giving more than he took. So enormous was the intra party bitterness that some of the Republican state conventions were riotous brawls, with fist fights [being] common."[712] Striking a savage tone in his attacks on the sitting President, Roosevelt called Taft "puzzle-wit," "fat-head," and "a flubdub with a streak of the second-rate and the common in him."[713] Roosevelt's enmity affected Taft so strongly that at one point the President broke down in tears in front of a reporter. Taft confided to a friend, "It is hard, very hard, Archie, to see a devoted friendship going to pieces like a rope of sand."[714]

The Republican Convention in June 1912 became a battlefield for the two giants, Taft because of his physical size and Roosevelt as a result of his antics. The nomination went to Taft who received strong support from the southern states. Roosevelt and his followers left the convention in protest. He was not about to quit. In a separate Progressive Party Convention in August, Roosevelt had himself appointed presidential contender as a third party candidate. Feeling "fit as a moose," the progressive Bull Moose Party challenged the conservative Taft in a presidential campaign that split the

Republicans. Roosevelt's agenda included national health care, a social security system, women's suffrage, and the end of child labor. He also favored a constitutional amendment to allow the collection of income taxes, inheritance taxes, and many more stalwarts of modern progressivism.[715] Roosevelt's party championed even more "ridiculous" causes such as a limit on campaign contributions and the requirement for lobbyists to register. To the dismay of some of his followers, Roosevelt decided not to add trust busting to his platform. He vigorously campaigned against the Democrats for what he called "New Nationalism." Wilson's Secretary of the Navy, Josephus Daniels commented on Roosevelt's general campaign strategy: "He plunged into the campaign and kept the country alternately gasping and applauding at the picturesqueness [sic] of his vocabulary and the vigor of his denunciation coupled with the earnestness of an evangelist."[716]

Colonel Roosevelt on the campaign trail on October 14, 1912, just after an assailant shot him in the chest. The speech manuscript in his pocket saved his life.[717]

On the Democratic side, Woodrow Wilson, the governor of New Jersey and former president of Princeton University, had formulated the New Freedom platform with which he captured the nomination. Together with his trusted friend, journalist William Bayard Hale, he published the "New

Freedom" platform as a pamphlet for public consumption.[718] His strongest contender was representative and speaker of the House, Champ Clark of Missouri. Wilson only clinched the nomination in the 46th ballot after William Jennings Bryan and his followers defected from Clark and joined with Wilson. A slight man wearing a bow tie who resembled a boy more than a man was an important voice in the Texas delegation that switched with Bryan. His name was Zachary Lamar Cobb. His important support for Wilson should earn him the job of customs collector in El Paso in the following year.[719] His position proved to be pivotal in the turbulent years to come.

As the leader of the liberal, pacifist wing of the Democratic Party, William Jennings Bryan had been defeated three times in the presidential races against McKinley, Roosevelt, and Taft. However, he still was a major force in party politics "at least to the extent that any man Bryan opposed would be defeated for the nomination."[720] Bryan, the virtual inventor of the stump speech, subsequently campaigned vigorously for Wilson. An accomplished public orator he connected well with the common man, which proved to be an important asset for the more reserved and scholarly Woodrow Wilson. The two progressive party programs, that of the Democrats and that of the Bull Moose Party, seemed so close that journalist William Allen White wrote in 1924, "...Between the New Nationalism and the New Freedom was that fantastic imaginary gulf that has existed between tweedle-dum and tweedle-dee."[721] Historian Arthur S. Link defined the differences: "[Wilson] believed the federal power should be used only to sweep away special privileges and artificial barriers to the development of individual energies, and to preserve and restore competition in business. The idea of the federal government's moving directly into the economic field, by giving special protection to workers or farmers, was as abhorrent to Wilson in 1912 as the idea of class legislation in the interest of manufacturers or ship owners."[722]

The temperature of the presidential campaigns soared in September and October of 1912. Wilson faced serious attacks from Roosevelt on his foreign policy credentials. Wilson had none; neither did his likely Secretary of State Bryan. It is within this framework that Sommerfeld's trip east to "meet Wilson" presents a fascinating possibility. Did the Wilson campaign seek experts on Mexico for briefings? If so, who made the contacts? Was there an early effort on the part of the German government or Sherburne Hopkins and his client President Madero to establish ties with the likely winner of the fall elections? Sommerfeld's resume made him a formidable expert on Mexico, a country on which neither Wilson nor his senior campaign advisors House,

Bryan, and McAdoo had formed a solid opinion. While this theory is pure speculation, Sommerfeld waved off Senator Smith's question in the October hearing about the purpose of his recent trip. If BI agent Ross' telegram to Bielaski described a well-known rumor in El Paso, the Republican senator certainly was aware of it and asked the question with this background in mind:

"Senator Smith: 'You occasionally make trips to New York?' Sommerfeld: 'I made one.' Smith: 'What did you go there for?' Sommerfeld: 'I went to Chicago, and from Chicago I went to my brother's in New York. I did not want to go to New York City. I went to New York City on account of the Associated Press. The contract for their special wire ran out on the 1st of September and had not been renewed, because the Government made some new conditions. Some of them are very intimate friends of mine and one of them wired to me, so I went to New York and was there in the office, and we had a talk in the Associated Press office with the traffic manager....That is what took me. I went along with my brother. I had not been in New York for five years.' Smith: 'Did you perform any special service there for Mr. Madero?' Sommerfeld: 'No, sir...'"[723]

Sommerfeld's brother lived in Chicago, not New York. He had not been working for the Associated Press in a year, and a wire subscription did not require Sommerfeld to travel at all. While Sommerfeld otherwise appeared fully in control of the interview, parrying when Senators Smith and Fall asked uncomfortable questions, this answer seemed rough. Sommerfeld seemed to stumble, repeat himself, and tried a tad too hard to explain away why he had traveled to New York in September of 1912. Coincidence or not, Colonel Edward House, Wilson's confidante and by most accounts most trusted advisor, was at the National Headquarters of the Wilson campaign in New York conducting meetings with Governor Wilson in "the middle of September."[724] Wilson gave a widely quoted speech in the New York Press Club on September 9th. He spoke again in New York on September 22nd, further supporting the likelihood that Sommerfeld actually met Wilson or his advisors.[725] Further evidence of Sommerfeld's meeting with Woodrow Wilson and/or William Jennings Bryan is a note from Sommerfeld to Ambassador von Hintze on September 19th 1912. In excitement he penciled from aboard the Golden State Limited:

GOLDEN STATE LIMITED
CHICAGO · ST. LOUIS · KANSAS CITY
CALIFORNIA
VIA ROCK ISLAND LINES
EL PASO & SOUTHWESTERN SYSTEM
SOUTHERN PACIFIC COMPANY

EN ROUTE Kansas City, Mo
Sept 19. 1912

Hochgeehrter Herr Minister.

Ich bin auf der
Rückreise von New York, Washington
und Chicago, wohin ich in diplomatischen
Angelegenheit gefahren war.
Es war sehr interessant und
hoffe ich die einigen Fragen
persönlich und mündlich darüber

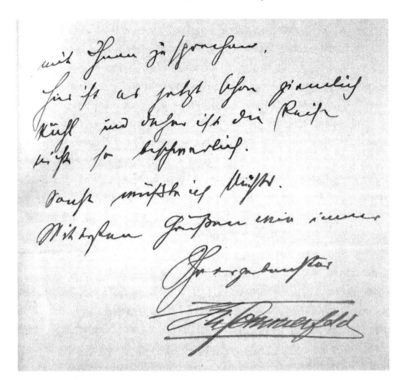

"Kansas City, Missouri, September 19, 1912

Esteemed Minister,

I am on my way back from New York, Washington and Chicago, where I had gone on a diplomatic mission. It was very interesting and I hope to be able to report to you in a few days only verbally. Here it is getting already pretty cold and I was not prepared for that on my trip.
I have to go on now.

With best wishes as always, your subservient F.A. Sommerfeld"[726]

There is no surviving record of Sommerfeld's verbal report. However, his meetings with Wilson's people and the U.S. government seem to have been precipitated by the rapidly declining relationship between Madero and the Taft administration. On the 15th of September 1912, Philander Knox sent a sharply worded note to the Mexican government, accusing it of discrimination against American citizens and property.[727] The note included a long list of cases where

199

Americans had been harmed and the perpetrators had escaped punishment. Only three cases on the list occurred under the Madero government.[728] The note gave voice to the clamor for intervention from conservative senators and newspapers that so worried the Mexican government. Hopkins, as close as he was to Knox, knew how critical the situation was becoming. This explains why Sommerfeld found himself on a mission to push Woodrow Wilson to "make arrangements [to] endeavor [to] prevent intervention through Democratic members [of] Congress."[729] While Hopkins would have faced a conflict of interest to intervene with Wilson and the Democrats against his client and friend Philander Knox on behalf of Madero, Sommerfeld was free to act.

Whether President Taft would have engaged in a military intervention in Mexico only months before his tenure in the White House ended is open to debate. Historian Katz, although not having found a smoking gun in the shape of a plan signed off by the American President, thought it likely that Taft and Knox wanted to create a fait accompli for the incoming Wilson administration by toppling the Madero government.[730] Sommerfeld and the Mexican government were painfully aware of Ambassador Henry Lane Wilson's merciless push for intervention, especially if they looked through his mail. German Ambassador von Hintze who might have made Madero aware of the intrigues of his American colleague reported in December that Taft and Knox had conducted meetings with Henry Lane Wilson and "saw the need to act."[731] While Hopkins and Mexican Foreign Secretary Lascurain worked on the Taft administration to soften its stands, Sommerfeld endeavored on this secret mission to reel in the support of the people who would likely take control of U.S. foreign policy within months.

According to Colonel House's recollections, Wilson had already decided by then that William Jennings Bryan was to become the Secretary of State. Despite him having no prior experience with foreign policy, the agreement had been made when Bryan switched his support to Wilson in July. Von Bernstorff judged Bryan's ability in 1920: "In all political questions, Mr. Bryan followed a much more radical tendency than Mr. Wilson. His opponents call him a dishonest demagogue. I, on the contrary, would prefer to call Mr. Bryan an honest visionary and fanatic, whose passionate enthusiasm may go to make an exemplary speechmaker at large meetings, but not a statesman whose concern is the world of realities."[732] The Mexican situation did concern voters in 1912 and it was important for Wilson's people, especially William Jennings Bryan and the Democrats in Congress to be well briefed on the subject. The meetings have not been documented and none of the participants have ever talked about them. What remains is a circumstantial case, albeit a strong one.

As expected the presidential elections of 1912 clearly favored Wilson who benefited from Roosevelt's split of the Republican vote. The former president of Princeton University received almost forty-two percent of the popular vote and carried forty of forty-eight states.[733] Roosevelt received twenty-seven percent of the vote and carried six states. With twenty-three percent of the vote and carrying only Utah and Vermont, Taft had been thoroughly defeated by both the Democrats and the Bull Moose progressives. Eugene Debs, the candidate for the Socialist Party received six percent of the vote. Despite achieving the highest third party share of the popular vote in the 20th century, the election results represented a crushing defeat for the former President. Roosevelt, who the Republicans blamed for propelling the long-shot Democratic candidate to the presidency, not only carried the scars of an injured self-esteem. Three weeks before the general election Roosevelt barely survived an assassination attempt. His steel spectacle case and the folded manuscript of the speech he had planned for the night saved his life. With a bullet still lodged in his chest and a bloody shirt, Roosevelt insisted on speaking before he allowed doctors to tend to his wound. After the election with Republicans shunning him like a traitor and Democrats in power in Washington, Roosevelt endeavored on a two-year, harrowing expedition to explore a tributary of the Amazon. He returned in 1915, from the brink of death in the jungles of South America, exhausted, skinny, and in bad health. [734] President Taft, whom the race between Roosevelt and Wilson had literally pushed to the sidelines, also retired from politics. He devoted the next decade to his law practice. In 1921, President Harding nominated him Chief Justice of the Supreme Court, where he served until shortly before his death on March 8th 1930.

All eyes now focused on President-elect Wilson who promptly went on a month-long vacation to Bermuda. Colonel House meanwhile canvassed the pool of candidates for the new cabinet. He brought several candidates to the President's attention and endeavored to balance political considerations with the skill and experience required in the executive posts. William Jennings Bryan received the State portfolio. It was Bryan's office to take, one of the most prestigious and coveted, especially for advancing his pacifist agenda. Bryan was a powerhouse in the Democratic Party and thus one of the most important appointments in Wilson's cabinet. However, the new Secretary of State became increasingly unhappy over other appointments that House orchestrated without his input. Secretary of War, Lindley M. Garrison, for example, was an avid interventionist and, thereby, on the opposite ideological spectrum of Bryan.

As Secretary of the Interior, House pushed for Franklin Knight Lane, a conservative Democrat who had served in both the Roosevelt and Taft administrations. He had established the National Park Service and by-in-large supported Roosevelt's conservation policies. The chairman of the Democratic National Committee, William G. McAdoo, who had tirelessly worked on behalf of Wilson's campaign, became Secretary of the Treasury. Wall Street feared that he would translate his trust busting rhetoric into action. However, he proved to be a wise and effective leader through the crises the Wilson administration was about to be confronted with. McAdoo upheld the gold standard, prevented a stock market meltdown at the onset of the Great War, and created the Federal Reserve Bank. He also became President Wilson's son-in-law, when he married Eleanor Randolph Wilson at the White House on May 7th 1914. The only "dyed-in-the-wool" follower of Bryan in the cabinet was Secretary of the Navy, Josephus Daniels, a southern Democrat with strong progressive credentials.[735] House picked him for purely political reasons. James C. McReynolds, another Taft appointee took the Justice portfolio. He served only one year after which he joined the Supreme Court and House's old friend Thomas W. Gregory took over. Gregory, while outwardly professing progressive values, was a staunch conservative who fiercely fought to increase the power of the Bureau of Investigation in World War I.

The German government looked with keen interest and apprehension at the formation of the new cabinet. Ambassador von Bernstorff had established a cordial relationship with the President Taft as well as his predecessor, Theodore Roosevelt. Diplomatic relations with Germany were strong. President Roosevelt had even asked the Kaiser to appoint von Bernstorff's predecessor, Hermann Speck von Sternburg, to be German ambassador in Washington. Roosevelt and von Sternburg, who was married to an American, became good friends. The German ambassador died in 1908 while on a trip to Germany thus creating the void von Bernstorff subsequently filled. With English as his first language and a German-American wife, the Count instantly became a star on the social scene in Washington and New York. "In his callow days Bernstorff was addicted to tennis. A superior, Count Wolff-Metternich, remarked that tennis smacked of the 'dancing age,' and recommended golf. Bernstorff forthwith foreswore the racquet for the driver. He was obviously the right man for the Taft era."[736] Over many consecutive years of Republican stewardship of the White House, German diplomats had cultivated personal relationships with many of the executive cadre in the American government. Bernstorff wrote in his memoir of the war years, "official relations between the German and American Governments were never more cordial than during the years 1909-13...."[737]

Count Johann von Bernstorff was the only possible candidate to follow in the footsteps of Speck von Sternburg. Born in 1862 in London, he was the son of one of the most powerful politicians in the Prussian Empire. While Foreign Minister for Prussia, his father Count Albrecht von Bernstorff had earned the ire of Prince Bismarck in the Prussian constitutional crisis of 1859-1866. Overestimating his political strength, von Bernstorff resigned in a spat over the constitution with the expectation to force his will on the Prussian government. However, the Emperor accepted Bernstorff's miscalculated challenge and appointed Otto von Bismarck chancellor and foreign minister. For the rest of his life, Count Albrecht von Bernstorff would criticize Bismarck's Machiavellian style of governing. In 1862, the elder Bernstorff served as ambassador at the Court of St. James. For the next eleven years young Bernstorff grew up in England until his father's death in 1873.

Von Bernstorff around 1920[738]

After moving back to Germany Johann von Bernstorff went to the humanistic gymnasium in Dresden from which he graduated with a baccalaureate in 1881. While von Bernstorff's dream had always been to pursue a diplomatic career, the family feud with Bismarck made an appointment to the diplomatic service impossible. As a result he joined the Prussian military for the next eight years serving in an artillery unit in Berlin.[739] After being elected a member of the Reichstag he finally succeeded in convincing the Bismarcks to settle the dispute with the long dead father. In 1887, von Bernstorff married Jeanne Zuckmeyer, a German-American. His first diplomatic assignment was Constantinople where he served as military attaché. After a brief assignment to St. Petersburg, von Bernstorff became counselor of the embassy in London. Before he took his assignment in the United States, he served as consul general in Cairo. Despite the problems his family had with the Bismarcks, von Bernstorff basically agreed with Bismarck's policies, in particular with the decision to found the German Reich without Austria in 1871. As a diplomat, von Bernstorff adamantly supported Anglo-German rapprochement and considered the policies of Wilhelm II "reckless."[740]

His World War assignment in Washington will be discussed later in greater detail.[741] Throughout the war years von Bernstorff counteracted the German military strategy, with which he wholeheartedly disagreed. With his stance on the war he aligned himself with the faction in the Prussian government that wanted to keep the U.S. out of the war under any circumstance. His role in the war proved to be crucial in the German government's decision not to institute unrestricted submarine warfare in 1916. After the war, von Bernstorff founded the German Democratic Party, which still exists in Germany under the name Free Democratic Party (FDP). Von Bernstorff stayed a member of the German parliament throughout the tumultuous years of the Weimar Republic from 1921 to 1928. He supported the League of Nations and global disarmament. The rising tide against Democracy in the later years of the Weimar Republic and the Nazi's contempt for his "defeatism" in the war forced von Bernstorff to go into exile to Switzerland in 1933. Virtually unnoticed by the international community, he died in 1939. His opposition to Hitler and his conciliatory role in the First World War earned him posthumous recognition from politicians and historians alike.

Woodrow Wilson was a complete unknown to von Bernstorff and the German government. He certainly appeared to be more anglophile than "Big Bill" Taft from Cincinnati, Ohio. Von Bernstorff wrote about his first impressions of Wilson in his war memoirs: "Woodrow Wilson was a University don and an historian...Even in those days [while President of Princeton] he displayed, side by side, on the one hand, his democratic bias which led him violently to oppose the aristocratic student-clubs, and on the other, his egocentric and autocratic leanings which made him inaccessible to any advice from outside, and constantly embroiled with the governing council of the University. As Governor of New Jersey, The Holy Land of 'Trusts,' Mr. Wilson opened an extraordinarily sharp campaign against their dominion."[742]

Wilson's progressive, anti-imperialist, and anti-trust platform certainly meant the end of "Dollar Diplomacy." What the impact of such a fundamental switch in foreign policy priorities would be, the German Foreign Office did not quite know. Clearly, the Democrats who won the battle for the White House had been out of office so long that they lacked experienced personnel for crucial administrative positions. House advised on the problem of staffing to consider "that the Democratic party [sic] had been out of office for sixteen years, and we had practically no trained men available."[743] On the issue of pushing many of his inner circle, House argued, "...some of my best friends were selected, because, upon analysis, they seemed to be among the best. Every one of those men with whom I was acquainted before the Administration came into power has done splendidly."[744] Von Bernstorff, who in his memoirs counted House as one of his good friends, spoke to the same conundrum:

"The diplomatic corps in Washington thus found itself confronted by an entirely new situation. The Republican Party had been at the helm for sixteen years, and had now to vacate every one of the administrative posts. Even our personal intercourse with the President was governed by different formalities from those which existed in the days of his predecessors. Mr. Roosevelt liked to maintain friendly relations with those diplomats whose company pleased him....My dealings with President Taft were on the same footing...On one occasion he invited me to join him in his private Pullman on a journey to his home in Cincinnati, where we attended the music festival together...President Wilson, who by inclination and habit is a recluse and a lonely worker, does not like company."[745]

In the histories of the period President Wilson's character and personality have been overly simplified and reduced to mere "idealism." Stemming from the word "ideal," the implication was that Wilson believed in "ideals" or "principles" that prevented him from formulating policies that addressed "reality." In terms of foreign policy this characterization exists in juxtaposition to the traditional "Realpolitik" of European governments and the "Dollar Diplomacy" of Presidents Roosevelt and Taft. Without question Wilson made foreign policy decisions that, especially as a result of his withdrawn and misunderstood decision-making processes, were principled and constituted clear departures from the policies of his predecessors. However, "idealism" as the framework of understanding Wilsonian foreign policy leads to dead-end analyses that fill the dusty shelves of today's libraries. Undoubtedly, Wilson was a difficult man to work with. Edward House seemed to be one of the few with unfettered access. It was not William Jennings Bryan who formulated America's foreign policy in the Wilson administration. Neither Wilson nor House trusted Bryan with making informed foreign policy decisions. The de-facto Secretary of State vis-à-vis Europe and Latin America was House who, like Sommerfeld, served the President without portfolio and expectation of compensation. It was power the two men sought and received serving their respective leaders. Just like Sommerfeld had cleaned up the Mexican consulates, in the first months of the new American administration the embassies in Berlin, Rome, and London all came under the leadership of House's men.

Wilson had an "inclination ...to avoid all the human contacts he could, outside the narrow circle of people with whom he felt at ease."[746] According to his friend of whom Wilson said "Mr. House is my second personality. He is my independent self. His thoughts and mine are one," the President's decision-making traits had to be understood. He had a disposition "to avoid any decision which was disagreeable to him, regardless of how important it might be..."[747] His decision-making process was "sluggish" and slow but once he reached a conclusion, he "was capable of working it out ...with lightning speed and precision."[748] Ray Stannard Baker, Wilson's official biographer wrote, "Wilson's method was that of the scholar who goes down into his own mind...The method has vast advantages as a source of power and self-confidence; it has also grave dangers for the man of action, particularly the political leader called upon to face unexpected practical problems."[749] He spoke to the President's alter ego, the passionate, emotional, and impulsive Wilson. "Behind his calm, scholarly features, conveying to the observer an effect of cold self-restraint, lurked a raging, fiery temper, impatient of control and never too safely disciplined."[750] Once his temper was aroused Wilson would not forget. He refused to receive those that he disdained; there were no second chances. It was Colonel House whose job was to limit the damage of "a Wilsonian blasting" whether he had to calm members of Wilson's cabinet, the military, or

Congress. The combination of these character traits and the strange, non-traditional influence of Colonel House on Wilson's decisions made the whole process an enigma to those trying to understand it.

When it came to the roots of Wilson's understanding of the Mexican Revolution, historians have clung to public pronouncements and speeches that sounded far too "idealistic" to be the sources of his actual policies. Wilson had inherited the "Mexican Problem." Colonel House, supported by having lived in a border state, had a fairly detailed understanding of the issues from the American business perspective. It is no surprise that intervention always seemed close to the surface of Wilson's Mexican agenda. It is a tribute to the realism of Wilson's advisors House and Garrison that the two interventions Wilson ordered in his first term did not translate into all-out war with Mexico. With certainty Wilson and House wanted to constructively support the efforts of the democratically elected government of Madero. Historian Thomas Baecker characterized Wilson's understanding of the events in Mexico as being uninformed. "For the most part he conceived of the Revolution in sheerly [sic] political terms, that is, in terms of the Mexican masses struggling for constitutional government and political democracy." [751] The problem with Baecker's criticism, and that of many historians, is the fact that absolutely no western government in 1913 saw the Mexican Revolution as anything other than a political problem. Only the hindsight of the Bolshevik Revolution and other social revolutions in the 20th century allow such a perspective. The real difference between Wilson and House's assessments of Mexico was that they earnestly believed that a Democracy south of the border would lead to prosperity and civil order while their contemporaries in Europe, and indeed his own ambassador in Mexico City, believed that only a strong man could rule of the "half-human, Indian" masses. With this opinion, Wilson stood in stark contrast to conservative forces in American foreign policy including Albert B. Fall and Ambassador Henry Lane Wilson. Under the Taft administration the alliance between Philander Knox and Sherburne Hopkins largely held in check the more sinister forces in the U.S. that supported a return of the old oligarchy. While rattling sabers and touting military intervention as a solution to all problems in Mexico, this interventionist group had little or no impact on actual foreign policy.

The election of Wilson and the expectation of a change in foreign policy empowered these enemies of the Mexican government in the fall and spring of 1912/1913. If any criticism could be hurled against the new administration that did not take power until March 4th 1913, it is the lack of a clear formulation of a Mexican policy in the campaign and the months leading up to the inauguration. As historian Reinhard Doerries rightfully speculated, it was this missing, clear position and "the attitude of a number of other nations, who showed no hesitation to stoke the fire in various ways" that caused the Mexican government to fall under horrible circumstances a week before Wilson's inauguration.[752] The fait accompli of Madero's fall, which an American diplomat engineered, destroyed any possibility that American foreign policy towards Mexico could remain consistent. In line with President Wilson's traits of agonizingly slow deliberation and secretive decision-making, the reaction to the Mexican crisis in the spring of 1913 has been misinterpreted as uninformed, helpless, and "idealistic." Indeed, Wilson had to scramble to devise a wholly reinvented response to the developments in Mexico. It was none other than Felix Sommerfeld and Sherburne Hopkins who were to assist the new government in finding an appropriate response.

CHAPTER 15

~

THE DISMANTLING OF A PRESIDENCY

7he presidential elections in the United States had a huge and immediate impact on the pressing issues of rebellion and unrest that continued to dog Mexico. On October 16th 1912, yet another rebellion in the constant string of challenges to the central government of Mexico broke out. On the surface the revolt led by Colonel Felix Diaz seemed similar to previous uprisings. The nephew of Porfirio Diaz had been chief of police in Mexico City before he became governor of Oaxaca. The revolutionary government replaced Diaz with an interim governor in 1911.[753] It is unclear whether Diaz actually had a commission in the federal army at the time of the uprising, a question that would later save his life. Officially commissioned at the time or not, the colonel came from a different corner of the Mexican opposition. Madero had diligently promoted members of the federal army over those of his revolutionary forces. The decommissioning of the revolutionary forces and the perceived abandonment of revolutionary principles in favor of order had created the core reasons for internal opposition. Indeed, the previous uprisings of Reyes, Zapata, Vasquez Gomez, and Orozco had one common thread: They originated from within the revolutionary movement. All benefited from and utilized the disenfranchised revolutionary fighters of the Madero revolution. Diaz represented a different threat, one that would hasten Madero's demise. Felix Diaz was an officer of the Mexican federal army. His revolt marked the first time since the downfall of his uncle that the military, arguably the most powerful block in Mexican politics, began to rumble with discontent.

The revolt itself was minor and was greatly exaggerated in the American media. On the morning of October 16th 1912 Felix Diaz, leading several detachments of Rurales, marched into Veracruz. One of the three local military commanders quickly abandoned resistance and joined the rebels.[754] Losing only fifteen men, Diaz took control of the port and all-important customs house.[755] Several other units in the immediate area sided with the rebels. However, news reports that all of Veracruz, Oaxaca, Puebla, and Chiapas had risen in support of Diaz were completely untrue.[756] The New York Times published a glorious account on October 20th under the headline "Beginning of the End seen in New Revolt" with a half-page portrait of Diaz titled "General Diaz: Head of the New Revolution." The imperial image of Felix Diaz showed an erect, power-emanating officer in dress uniform, resting his left hand on his sword. His mustache slightly turned up at the tips, he looked over his right shoulder into the distance, as if he had a viable vision for Mexico's future. In this picture, photographers Underwood and Underwood had created the spitting image of ousted dictator Porfirio Diaz, just forty years his junior, and spiced it with a hint of Emperor Wilhelm II. Even the military rank of general referred to the fallen dictator, not to the overweight, spoilt, slow thinking, and opportunistic nephew who never rose to any position of significance in his uncle's regime. Porfirio Diaz certainly never considered him a successor as the New York Time tried to imply a few months later.[757] Felix Diaz was a creation of the American press, Senator Fall, and Ambassador Wilson, a conjured up Porfirio Diaz in his heyday. No one took him seriously in Mexico. None of the senior military brass rallied to his battle cry. Madero's government denied from the onset of the revolt that it saw Felix Diaz as an existential threat to the government.[758]

On the surface, only months after the defeat of Orozco, Colonel Diaz' action proved to be not much more than an inconvenience. Madero sent federal troops to retake the city and after a few days, on October 23rd 1912, Diaz was arrested. Fifty of his troops died as a result of the fighting, the federals lost none.[759] There were no other uprisings and the general who had secured the city, General Beltran, despite reported attempts by Diaz to bribe him, proved his unwavering loyalty to Madero. President Madero, who in an interview had vowed in a self-fulfilling prophecy that "only death can remove me from the Presidency...," seemed fully in control.[760] On the other hand, as early as the 18th of October, the unfavorable press in the United States already openly mused over the personnel in what it hoped would be a new Diaz government. The vicious propaganda brought the sinister machinations of Wilson, Fall, and the American community in Mexico into plain view. Whether Diaz had received any actual support or guarantees from the U.S. government or Henry Lane Wilson in particular is unknown. However, the propaganda and false reports on the uprising clearly had their origin in the American embassy.

In the ensuing weeks after the uprising, Felix Diaz faced court martial. Together with twenty-six conspirators the military tribunal convicted him of treason and sentenced him to death. However, the Mexican Supreme Court granted a stay questioning the authority of the military court. The question arose whether the colonel was a commissioned officer at the time of his treason. Madero did not intervene in this farcical attempt of Porfirio Diaz' holdover judges to undermine him. They clearly used democratic rights achieved in the revolution to overturn the current political system.[761] The conspirators remained in San Juan de Ulua prison in Veracruz pending further judicial action. In January 1913 the government commuted the death sentence and transferred Felix Diaz to a penitentiary in Mexico City. The judge decided that Diaz had not been commissioned. The prisoner therefore transferred to a civilian prison in the capital. Reyes, the other defeated rebel leader of note, served time at the Santiago Tlatelolco military prison also in the center of Mexico City. For several months Pancho Villa also served at Tlatelolco but managed to escape. On Christmas day 1912 Villa in a business suit with a sidearm, flamboyant as ever, took advantage of the intoxicated guards celebrating Christmas. He "simply walked out of the prison, strolling across the courtyard with his assistant as if they were two city lawyers, fresh from visiting their clients and absorbed in discussing the minutiae of a case."[762] Questions quickly arose as to the complicity of the Maderos in the escape. With Huerta being the most powerful general in Mexico, a presidential pardon and release while favored by President Madero, would have been impossible. Gustavo Madero, who had been visiting Villa every day while in Tlatelolco, might have arranged for the helper, the guns, the disguise, and the escape vehicle. He never spoke to the escape neither did his brother, the President. Villa fled to El Paso where he settled quite publicly. Neither the Bureau of Investigation nor Sommerfeld's people investigated the fugitive in exile. This fact, more than any other circumstantial evidence that might exist about Villa's escape, implicated the Madero administration in the prison break.

Bernardo Reyes and Felix Diaz remained imprisoned for the duration, although with broad contacts to the outside world and fellow political prisoners. Historians have criticized Madero's sparing of Reyes and Diaz' lives as examples of the President's hopeless idealism. However, Madero did not consider either Reyes or Diaz to be formidable opponents. Neither one of them had any credentials based on their record of conspiratorial activity. Reyes' revolt wilted as soon as Sommerfeld and the U.S. authorities denied him weapons. Diaz made greater headlines than impact on the battlefield.

Throughout his ascendancy Madero had strived to make legal process the guiding light for a working democracy. How could he now abandon this premise? Killing his opponents in revenge would have strengthened the arguments of the conservative press and the interventionist clique in Washington claiming that Madero was becoming a dictator, albeit an inept one. Felix Diaz had become a figurehead in the games of the conservative opposition to Madero not because of his skill or record, but because he had the right name and looks. None of Diaz' endeavors, whether playing a role in his uncle's regime, the October 1912 uprising, or his efforts to mingle in Mexican politics later on turned out to be successful. Those who dared to align themselves with him usually ended up imprisoned or worse. It is questionable, despite all the allegations of Madero's self-destructive idealism, whether killing Diaz and Reyes would not have hastened the events of his demise, just with different figureheads.

The person who used the events of October to further his agenda was the American Ambassador Henry Lane Wilson. To this day he remains one of the strangest, inexplicably callous, borderline crazy villains of modern Mexican and U.S. history. Born in Crawfordsville, Indiana, on November 3rd 1856, he came from an upper middle class family in the heartland of America. His father, a trained lawyer, served in the House of Representatives as one of Indiana's representatives and also as ambassador to Venezuela. Son Henry attended public high school in his hometown. After graduating from Wabash College in 1879, he apprenticed in a law firm in Indianapolis for one year. After trying his luck at publishing and briefly dabbling in business, Wilson settled in Spokane, Washington and practiced law until 1895. In 1897, the young lawyer, who had meanwhile built up his credentials as a conservative Republican, joined the diplomatic corps. President McKinley appointed him charge d'Affairs for Chile. In 1905, President Roosevelt nominated him minister to Greece. However, before he could be confirmed, Roosevelt reassigned Wilson to head the embassy of Belgium. His conservative credentials and his lifelong membership in the Republican Party brought the Indiana native close to President Taft and Secretary of State Philander Knox.

In 1910 President Taft sent him to Mexico. There the ambassador witnessed the downfall of President Diaz, whose personal friendship he had enjoyed. Wilson's unwavering admiration of President Diaz and the dictator's oppressive methods for governing Mexico brought the ambassador into immediate conflict with the De La Barra and Madero administrations. Behind a veil of concern for American lives and property Wilson actively opposed the two presidents through vicious intrigue both in Washington and Mexico City. In a speech in April 1914 the meanwhile discredited ambassador defined his chauvinistic, racist, and, coming from a trained lawyer, unforgivable assessment of the Mexican dictator Diaz and current political conditions in Mexico:

"Diaz was not a tyrant, but a benevolent autocrat who understood the Mexican people and knew them to be unfitted for self-government. Though not elected by constitutional methods, he governed according to law. He ruled Mexico for thirty years with a hand of iron, but possessed withal undeviating personal honesty, loyalty to obligations and a profound patriotism, together with lofty conception, as to Mexico's needs and future. His foreign policy was clear and fixed from the first days of his power.... At least 80 per cent of the population is of the indigenous races, without an abiding place except by sufferance, with no more than a nominal part or interest in the politics and affairs of the country, unable to read or write, who, while preserving the vices and traditions of their ancestors, have been made infinitely worse by the ingrafting [sic] of the vices of the white man and by the consciousness of a feeling of injustice arising from the realization that they are pariahs and outcasts...Madero...was a dreamer of dreams, and a singer of unknown songs which met no echo. He came into power as an apostle of liberty, but he was the only man who happened to be in the public eye at the psychological moment...Clothed with the chief power of the nation, evil qualities, dormant in the blood or in the race, came to the surface and wrought ruin to him and to thousands upon thousands of the Mexican people...Philosophers should have learned the lesson taught in the pages of Mexico's bloody history, that the practice of democracy, which is a burden at times to the most civilized nations, cannot be successfully imposed upon an illiterate nation clothed only with superficial vestments of modern civilization."[763]

Guiding Wilson's actions was such a deep-seated racism and a disdain for Madero and his followers so emotional that historian Frank McLynn thought the American diplomat might have suffered from mental illness.[764] Thus conflicted, Henry Lane Wilson saw it as his mission to return a strong, dictatorial government to Mexico. His methods remained consistent throughout his time as ambassador. In March of 1911, as Madero's father attempted to negotiate an agreement with Diaz' representative Limantour in New York, Wilson, also in New York, inflated the threat of violence against

American property and lives to such an extent that President Taft ordered twenty thousand troops to the border. The New York Times reported, "Henry Lane Wilson had informed President Taft that conditions in Mexico were far worse that the American people had been led to believe and that the 75,000 American citizens and the $1 billion of property they and other American citizens own would be in great jeopardy in the event of the spread of the revolution...The impression everywhere in Mexico, the active leader of the insurrection, is not the real leader, but has the backing of stronger men and the financial support of a considerable number of rich and prominent Mexicans who resent the activity of American capital in the republic."[765]

According to historian Henderson, the threat of military intervention by the United States became a crucial argument to pressure the Maderistas into compromise.[766] With Madero in power, Ambassador Wilson battered the revolutionary administration relentlessly. It was Wilson who initialized the demand of arming foreigners in Mexico. The protection of American citizens and their property was a major duty of the ambassador. However, when he asked Washington to approve "a thousand rifles and a million cartridges to be sent to the Embassy in Mexico City, so that he could defend the American colony," his request was curtly denied.[767] While there was little danger of intervention from a few hundred Germans or French, the American colony in Mexico was large enough to constitute a threat.[768] American businessmen stood firmly on the side of the remnants of the old regime under which they had prospered. Armed Americans could open a second front in case of an American military intervention. Wilson's influence also likely caused German Ambassador von Hintze's tough stands with respect to arming Germans and bringing the murderers of Covadonga to justice. A proud Prussian, he did not want to appear weak in front of the diplomatic corps and especially the American ambassador. The difference to Henry Lane Wilson was that von Hintze did not push an agenda. His reports to the foreign office seemed balanced. As a whole his interaction with the Madero administration - despite the wrangling - was good.[769]

When Henry Lane Wilson pushed for allowing the Mexican government to arm American expatriates, von Hintze took the opportunity to pressure the Mexican government to allow Germans in Torreon to acquire arms for their self-defense. At the strategic knot between the northern and southern railroad systems and geographically the passage in between the Sierra Madres, Torreon continued to be rife with revolution and counter-revolution. The question of arming German citizens was a sensitive one since the sovereignty of Mexico was concerned. If approved, the Mexican President would instantly create a gray zone for other powers. Once the United States, England, and Spain armed their citizens they suddenly became combatants in the ongoing strife. The whole reason for arming foreign subjects was a perceived and real lack of government protection. Once these foreign communities became belligerents, it would have to be the exact same lacking government resources that had the task to bail them out. In part driven by the belief that Madero's regime was falling further and further behind in its quest to consolidate power, in part to pressure Madero into placing contracts for arms and ammunition with German industry, von Hintze's pursuit of the issue was relentless throughout most of 1912. The German ambassador stressed in his dispatches to the Foreign Office, "...all measures [of arming German citizens] are taken under the premise: Policing, protection of own lives and property, and with the agreement of the Mexican government."[770] The contracts supplying military goods to the Mexican military under Madero, almost without exception, disappeared in a morass of bribery and lack of liquidity of the government.

Starting almost immediately upon von Hintze's arrival in Mexico in April 1911, the consuls of San Cristobal de las Casas, Tuxtla, Puebla, and Torreon asked the ambassador to intervene on their behalf to arm their constituents. To be clear, the German community in all of Mexico amounted to barely four thousand souls of whom two thousand and five hundred lived in Mexico City.[771] The United States colony amounted to around seventy-thousand citizens, of which five thousand lived in the capital.[772] The first request concerned the German community in Mexcalapa in the state of Chiapas. Chiapas had the largest German community of any Mexican state other than the capital where Germans owned a host of large coffee plantations. Mexican Foreign Minister Calero notified von Hintze in November 1911 that the request would be considered by the Secretary of War.[773] The request met with a counteroffer from the War Ministry to provide one hundred federal troops to protect the German farmers, which von Hintze and the German vice consul gladly accepted.[774]

In February of 1912, at the outbreak of the Vasquez Gomez uprising, the German Vice Consul in Torreon Otto Schubert wanted to arm the German community there. The War Department refused to consider the possibility, mainly for the fact that the German consul wanted to source the weapons himself. Von Hintze proposed to Foreign Secretary Calero, that the German government purchased the weapons. The Mexican government relented under the condition that "the embassy controls the sourcing of the weapons and that such armed [citizens] remain personally responsible in case of abuse."[775] On numerous occasions in March 1912, the Madero government allowed von Hintze to arrange for Germans to arm themselves.[776] With Madero's permission Carl Heynen, who as HAPAG representative had the best connections, bought and imported five hundred carbines with fifty thousand cartridges.[777] The only request the President rejected was that the arms were imported tax-free.[778] While Madero obviously refused to accommodate Ambassador Wilson with similar requests, the cooperation between von Hintze and the Madero government with respect to the arming of foreigners seemed close and cordial throughout 1912.

Whether any Germans lives were saved as a result of von Hintze's intervention with the Mexican government is unknown. Both episodes, the murders of Covadonga and the arming of the German colony, show the tenacity with which the German ambassador pressured the Mexican government on issues that served more to show imperial power than physically helping the German community. Much has been made of von Hintze's "sinister plans." American newspapers in the spring of 1911 interpreted the parading of German ships along the Mexican coast and the "secret" arming of German citizens as a covert plan to take over Mexico. The El Paso Times wrote that Taft's reinforcement of the border in the spring was a response to German agitation. Historian Friedrich Katz picks up this thought and cites various Associated Press reports and articles that floated this idea. To his credit he dismissed the American sensationalist articles as what they were: Untrue. The truth should be evident, especially if one considers that the new "German army" standing by in Torreon sported a total of twelve guns. Just like the pursuit of the murderers of Covadonga, von Hintze's strategy was one of deterrence. Should anyone attempt to harm Germans von Hintze's tough attitude insured serious repercussions. As such he succeeded in safeguarding German citizens in the Mexican Revolution. Despite his persistence and often confrontational attitude towards the Madero government, he generally got along well. He complained about corruption and Madero's troubles in maintaining order, but he was under no illusions that a different leader would have had the same problems. By no means a democrat von Hintze realistically recognized that the grievances of the Mexican people had to do with the many poor fighting the few rich.[779] He remarked to the English Ambassador Francis Stronge that looking for another ruthless despot would never resolve the underlying reasons of the revolution.[780]

The American embassy consistently issued reports on violence, discrimination against Americans, and threats against the U.S.-Mexican border. While anti-foreign sentiment undoubtedly existed in revolutionary Mexico, and resulted in damage to lives and property, historians specialized on the Mexican Revolution such as Katz, Knight, Hart, Calvert, McLynn, Henderson, Baecker, and others all agree that the American ambassador purposely inflated these reports. He overstated the facts on the ground with the express determination to force an American intervention. For example, he tricked the Taft administration into sending the USS "Buford" to the coast of Sinaloa in the fall of 1912 to save desperate American citizens from the "life threatening chaos" engulfing the state. When the ship arrived, eighteen Americans waited to be saved. To the London Times they "seemed to be people wanting to travel gratis to San Diego."[781] In his efforts he received wholehearted support from the conservative wing of the Republican Party, mainly in the person of Albert B. Fall. Sommerfeld's testimony to the Fall Committee in October 1912 adds to the overwhelming evidence that this group of Americans who had powerful positions in the formulation of foreign policy conspired to demolish the Madero administration. Wilson kept in contact with Madero's opposition in the military as well as political circles.

Before October of 1912 little is known about the ambassador's contacts with Reyes, Orozco, the Vasquez Gomez brothers, Felix Diaz, and others. However, even if his support of rebellion against Madero was tacit, from the beginning Wilson inserted the threat of U.S. military intervention into the political landscape. Whether President Taft and Secretary Knox understood the distorted character of the information they received from Mexico City is unclear. What is clear, however, is that the agitation of the American ambassador had utterly poisoned U.S.-Mexican relations at precisely the time when Madero had defeated Orozco. The quelling of this formidable rebellion could have precipitated the consolidation of power in Mexico under a constitutional government. The opposite was the case.

The Felix Diaz episode in Veracruz showed a curious synchronicity between U.S. government pronouncements and the American press. Despite the readily available facts, dailies in the United States rallied to the conservatives' hand-wringing demands that "something" had to be done. The American ambassador in Mexico and the voices of the "American colony" there created a misinformation campaign that had the goal of driving public opinion away from Madero towards military intervention. For two years Wilson had written reports to the State Department that historian McLynn characterized as

Sommerfeld's bronze medal from service in the Boxer Rebellion [782]

Porfirio Diaz with his many medals including the red eagle left row, second from bottom[783]

KAISERLICH DEUTSCHES VICEKONSULAT

IN CHIHUAHUA.

Chihuahua, Méx.

CHIHUAHUA (Rein Deutsch)

Name	Beruf	verheiratet	Kinder	total 92
M. Schlensker	Hutmacherin	-	-	1
F. Sommerfeld	Mineur	-	-	1
R. Spiegelberg	Kaufmann	-	-	1
E. Stolze	Kinderfraeulein	-	-	1
K. Winter	Lehrerin	-	-	1
M. Zimmermann	Kaufmann	-	-	1
A. Kniesche	Landwirt	-	-	1
	Deutsch geboren			
E. Passow	Kaufmann	ja	-	2
B. Bucher	"	ja	8	10
A. Buensow	"	ja	3	5
A. Goldschmidt	"	ja	1	3
H. Gosch	"	Witwer	-	1
E. Grimm	"	ja	1	3
M. Gurr	Landwirt	ja	4	6
M. Krakauer	Kaufmann	ja	3	5
E. Linse	Rentier	ja	2	4
C. Maas	Lehrer	ja	3	5
H. Nordwald	Kaufmann	ja	-	2
L. Nordwald	"	ja	-	2
H. Picard	"	ja	1	3
M. Picard	"	ja	1	3
J. Pothast	Rentier	ja	1	3
B. Schneider	Kaufmann	ja	3	5

Listing of the German subjects in Chihuahua in 1908. Courtesy Auswärtiges Amt, Berlin.

Excerpt from a weekly intelligence report Sommerfeld sent to Peter Bruchhausen, dated November 23, 1910. Courtesy Auswärtiges Amt, Berlin.

Presentation of the provisional government of Mexico after the Battle of Juarez in 1911. Felix Sommerfeld is the sixth person from the left, second row. Front row, third person is Villa, fourth is Madero.[784]

Francisco I. Madero, courtesy of the El Paso Public Library, Aultman Collection

Dinner party after the Battle of Juarez in 1911. Felix Sommerfeld is the sixth from left sitting. Second from left sitting is Francisco I. Madero. Courtesy of the El Paso Public Library, Aultman Collection.

Felix Sommerfeld in 1911 first from left standing. Next to him is Horst von der Goltz, a notorious World War I spy. In the front second from the right is Raul Madero, one of Francisco Madero's brothers.[785]

General Hugh L. Scott next to Pancho Villa. Second from right is Felix Sommerfeld. Courtesy of the El Paso Public Library, Aultman Collection

Tracy Richardson, manning a machine gun as one of the American soldiers-of-fortune in the Mexican Revolution. Courtesy of the El Paso Public Library, Aultman Collection

The fire set by Villistas that destroyed the Ketelsen and Degetau store in Ciudad Juarez on May 9th 1911. It turned Ketelsen and much of the German community in Chihuahua against Pancho Villa. Courtesy of the El Paso Public Library, Aultman Collection.

From the left: Felix Sommerfeld, Francisco I. Madero. H. Allie Martin, and Chris Haggerty of AP News. Courtesy of the El Paso Public Library, Aultman Collection

the "gibberings of a crackpot."[786] Despite the efforts of Hopkins, Mexican Ambassador to the United States Calero, and his boss, Secretary of State Lascurain, Madero was clearly losing the battle for public sympathy in the United States. In August 1912, then Mexican Ambassador Calero published an open letter to Henry Lane Wilson in the New York Times, asking the ambassador to confirm or deny outrageous allegations published in the Baltimore Sun a few weeks prior. An editorial had described, "...how American women are passing through the streets of Mexican towns, are practically denuded and made the objects of the insulting ridicule of an immoral populace."[787] Rather than denying the charges outright, Wilson responded that he had no knowledge of such stories. However, he was aware "...of large numbers of Americans abandoning their homes in Chihuahua and Sonora, but understands the exodus to be due to apprehension of violent acts rather than the result thereof."[788] His response showed the viciousness of the propaganda campaign against Madero. Without a doubt, American citizens had been affected by the Orozco uprising. However, it was the very people Wilson and Fall wanted to restore to power who financially supported Orozco and fanned the fires of rebellion. While Wilson sent his inflated reports on violence against American citizens to Washington, Albert B. Fall at the very least had an influence in undoing the peace deal that Madero's Secretary of Justice Rafael Hernandez had reached with Orozco, as Sommerfeld had alleged.[789]

Henry Lane Wilson had a long history of driving foreign policy in Mexico further than the Taft administration wanted it taken. An argument can be made that the American ambassador caused the mass exodus of American citizens from Mexico at the height of the Orozco uprising. On March 2nd 1912, the State Department had directed Wilson, "...in your discretion to inform Americans that the Embassy deems it its duty to advise them to withdraw from any particular localities where conditions...so threaten personal safety as to make withdrawal the part of prudence..."[790] Wilson proceeded to publish a warning so stern and comprehensive that "it was construed as meaning the whole of Mexico."[791] Worse than the burden H. L. Wilson's move placed on the American families, who fled from their homes and businesses leaving their belongings behind, was the impression the exodus created in Mexican political circles. Since none of the other embassies had issued warnings to their citizens, Madero and his advisors suspected an imminent American invasion. Neither Taft nor Knox had intended on this outcome. Consistently, H. L. Wilson had tried to involve the British and German governments in a scheme to intervene militarily in Mexico.

In March 1912, Henry Lane Wilson urged the British and German ambassadors to request troops to protect their citizens. Von Hintze rejected Wilson's request outright and identified Wilson's move as forcing a U.S. military intervention. He wrote to the German Foreign Minister, "International troops landing in Mexico City would stir up the population of the United States and make it possible for the government, as a result of such an atmosphere, to ...wage war against Mexico."[792] The British minister understood and told von Hintze that joining Wilson's scheme "would be making ourselves into a tool of American interests while endangering British life and property."[793] Stronge confessed to von Hintze in March 1912, "...my object is to allay any alarm which may have been caused by distorted versions of the United States notification, and at the same time to best inform British subjects of the real situation here...I have heard nothing from our Foreign Office...[794] Probably unfathomable to either diplomat, Wilson's push had not originated in Washington. When President Taft heard of Wilson's activities from the British, he in no uncertain terms stopped his rogue ambassador: "...on no account make any such suggestion [landing troops] except after consultation and with instruction."[795] Von Hintze as well was much too smart to allow the American ambassador to involve him in his schemes.

As a sideline, von Hintze has been accused of racism governing his actions and furthering the imperialistic goals of Germany in synch with the American ambassador. The German diplomat, just like Edith O'Shaughnessy, British Ambassador Francis Stronge, and others indeed had a low opinion of the aspirations of the Mexican masses. German consuls reported on bandits here and there and everywhere. However, to claim racism as a driving motivation for action is a different proposition. Von Hintze and the rest of the diplomatic corps in Mexico City, as well as the American President, German Kaiser, and English King lacked an intellectual framework with which they could have understood the social upheavals of the time. This lacking framework promoted the search for explanations including with racism.

Only Henry Lane Wilson, however, used racism that in his case included the "white" Mexicans such as Madero, as the overarching intellectual framework guiding political decisions. The rogue ambassador did not have the protection of American lives and property in mind when he sought to arm them. Thousands of Americans in arms as the result of such a strategy could only have ended in disaster, thus the refusal by the State Department to support the plan. Ambassador Wilson's strategy, the involvement of other governments in wild schemes to occupy Veracruz and Tampico, his inflated panic memos to Washington that caused the dispatch of war ships, and the leaking of untrue "facts" to the American press all had only one goal: Create an incident or situation in Mexico that would give the U.S. government no choice but to intervene. This intervention, Henry Lane Wilson knew, would have been the end of the Madero administration he so hated. Von Hintze and the rest of the diplomatic corps in Mexico City were under no illusions with respect to Ambassador Wilson's true objectives.

The ambassador's strategy worked splendidly throughout 1912. The American press, Ambassador Wilson, and the U.S. government with the tough note of September 15th 1912, kept up the pressure on Madero. In response, Madero and his advisors decided that the back of Henry Lane Wilson's strategy had to be broken. After defeating Felix Diaz, Madero sent Sommerfeld and Hopkins to testify in Senator Fall's Foreign Affairs Subcommittee in the end of September and October 1912. Madero also responded to the September note from the U.S. government with a reply in November. Besides economic discrimination against Americans, the note had accused the Madero administration of complicity in murdering American citizens and doing nothing to solve the crimes. The note cited seventeen specific cases. Madero proved to the American government, that of the seventeen cases one was unsolved, three had been tried and the culprits imprisoned, three could not be verified as actual instances reported to the Mexican government, four had occurred prior to the Mexican Revolution under the Diaz regime, three occurred in 1911 and had been investigated. Of course these latter cases fell under the responsibility of the De La Barra government. Only three cases that the note of the American government cited actually occurred while the Madero administration was in power. Two of these cases had been tried and resulted in the dropping of charges for lack of evidence.

By any standard of international diplomacy the tone of the September 15th note stood in no relation to the actual issues that came between the two governments. The choice of wording was a direct result of H. L. Wilson's misinformation campaign. After addressing the "cases" of violence against Americans, Mexican Foreign Secretary Lascurain wrote: "Therefore, the attitude of the Mexican Government with respect to the prosecution and punishment of persons guilty of violence against American citizens is adjusted by law, and it cannot be made subject for reproach except under the suggestion of eminently partial and adverse judgment, which is not in keeping with the proofs of amity previously received and with the course followed by the Government of the United States with reference to crimes committed within its territory against Mexican citizens."[796] Madero and Lascurain felt it to be time for a subtle reminder that Mexico was a sovereign state and that the rule of law existed as documented in the cases that the note had cited. The reply strictly followed the reading of U.S. law, which invites the suspicion that Sherburne Hopkins, at the very least, had advised Madero and Lascurain in drafting the response.

Still on the offensive, Madero dispatched Secretary Lascurain to Washington and New York on December 26th for meetings with Taft and Knox.[797] The American president and his secretary conducted meetings with Henry Lane Wilson at the same time. Ambassador von Hintze reported to the German government a few months later that Wilson had proposed to Taft and Knox, "...either to seize some of their territory and hold it – or to upset the Madero administration (literally)...So they - the three – had decided to upset the Madero administration." [798] Again Ambassador Wilson engaged in threatening propaganda, leaking to the press that he would have an ultimatum for President Madero in his diplomatic pouch when he returned to Mexico in January. Mexico City's newspapers ran amok with the story. [799] In his conversations with the American President, the Mexican Foreign Secretary bitterly complained about the misinformation and disrespect the American representative in Mexico displayed against his government. He asked Taft to recall the ambassador, which the President refused. While not much changed in the immediate term as a result of Lascurain's meetings, Taft and Knox agreed to at least hear the Mexican government's view. Both parties ended the meetings committing to a better working relationship with Madero. [800] Lascurain offered to settle American claims for damages in an attempt to deflate the interventionists' arguments. The Mexican Secretary of State came away from the meetings with the confidence that the clique around Ambassador Wilson was contained. In an interview in Mexico City on January 13th he said, "...Certain political elements interested in an international conflict are the only ones trying to foment a state of feeling adverse to Mexico. Fortunately little has been accomplished as yet."[801]

Secretary Lascurain, while in the U.S., also met with President-elect Woodrow Wilson. This meeting received little attention in the press or the historiography. The only revealing sources are publications in 1913 and 1914 in which H. L. Wilson desperately tried to justify his actions. He wrote of his suspicions that the meeting set the tone of Woodrow Wilson's foreign policy vis-à-vis Mexico in 1913. In excerpts published in the Hearst press, Wilson wrote, "...some months before, the Mexican Minister of Foreign Affairs, Pedro

Lascurain, on behalf of Madero, had sounded out President-elect Wilson and had given him much interesting, but totally false information on Mexican affairs."[802] The information Woodrow Wilson received can easily be surmised. The false reports from Mexico had exaggerated attacks on property and lives of Americans and had resulted in a dramatic poisoning of U.S.-Mexican relations. Lascurain offered clarifications and hard facts to the next American President. Ambassador Wilson had gone as far as directly comparing President Wilson and Madero as being both "apostles of democracy." [803] In clear text, the ambassador felt similar disdain for the new American President as he felt for Madero, a fact that must have given pause to both Wilson and House. Henry Lane Wilson's position likely was one of the subjects of conversation between Lascurain and Woodrow Wilson. Madero wanted the ambassador recalled as soon as the new administration took office, to which Woodrow Wilson acquiesced. [804] Other than removing the intriguing ambassador, Madero additionally wanted to prevent further escalation of U.S.-Mexican tensions, possibly ending in military intervention. With H. L. Wilson as ambassador the Madero administration had clearly given up on their quest to get the Taft administration to abandon its confrontational course. All Madero's people could hope for was to buy time until Woodrow Wilson took the helm.

Efforts to provide breathing room to the embattled Madero administration in the winter of 1912/13 came to nothing. Sporadic uprisings all over Mexico continued. Groups of Orozquistas plagued the north, Zapatistas resurged in Morelos, and bands of Vasquistas roamed the mountains of Puebla. While none of these uprisings had any larger significance, they contributed in the inflated American reporting to a sense that Madero simply could not pacify the country. After the September meetings with Woodrow Wilson, and after the October testimony before the Senate Subcommittee of Foreign Affairs in El Paso, Sommerfeld seemed to have disappeared from the border. BI reports mentioned L. L. Hall as the "Chief of the Mexican Secret Service stationed at El Paso" in January of 1913.[805] Sommerfeld's attention now focused on the interior of Mexico where unrest was fomenting. As the head of Mexico's Secret Service the scare of Felix Diaz' uprising also demanded a tight look over the shoulders of the generals defending the republic. Sommerfeld had long suspected the loyalty of Huerta. He testified to his interrogators in 1918 that he actively warned President Madero of Huerta's treachery in August of 1912.[806] In September, Huerta reportedly boasted in Ciudad Juarez, most likely while intoxicated, that he could take the presidency away from Madero any day.[807] The flap came to the ears of Madero probably via Sommerfeld's organization.

The Secretary of War Peña stripped Huerta of his rank and dismissed him as commander, but not after Madero personally interviewed him. Officially Huerta was relieved of command as a result of his failing eyesight for which he sought treatment in the capital some months later.

Henry Lane Wilson returned to Mexico in the first week of January 1913. Without knowing the extent to which Ambassador Wilson would engage in an active campaign to overthrow the Mexican government, Gustavo Madero, Felix Sommerfeld, and others close to the President saw the clouds of conspiracy thicken. Wilson had resumed the "doom cables" about the Mexican situation immediately after his return. On January 18th Wilson recommended to Secretary Knox to take "...vigorous and drastic action with the purpose of ...the downfall of a Government which is hateful to a vast majority of the people of this country..."[808] Sommerfeld who was monitoring the senior military brass in Mexico told investigators in 1918 that with respect to General Huerta "I never trusted him."[809] It is unclear when the army conspiracy to overthrow President Madero actually hatched. Even less clear is the exact moment when General Huerta switched sides and joined the conspirators.

There are numerous accounts of what happened in Mexico City in February 1913. Several of these accounts mention a story whereby Gustavo Madero received a list of conspirators on February 4th 1913, fully two weeks before the coup d'état. The story of the list first appeared in the New York Times. On July 21st 1914, the paper published a story on the events in February 1913 written by Edward I. Bell, an editor of La Prensa and the Daily Mexican in Mexico City, two independent dailies.[810] The Times was promoting his upcoming book The Political Shame of Mexico, in which the author expanded on the revealing articles in the New York World. He also underscored the investigation of William Bayard Hale that implicated the American government in the events of February 1913. It is Bell who mentioned the "list" Gustavo Madero received on February 4th. The New York Times, which wholeheartedly disagreed with Bell's account, headlined the story with "Says [underlining by author], we helped bring about anarchy in Mexico." It is the only known source of the hearsay list.[811]

Felix Sommerfeld corroborated Bell's account in 1918. According to the German agent, Madero sent him to investigate a rumor that the Zapatistas threatened to attack a munitions depot. The President suspected the information to be another fact twister spread by the American embassy. Intuitively he told Sommerfeld that "there was something wrong" with the reports.[812] Possibly as the result of the list, which, according to Bell ended in

President Madero's hands on February 5th, Sommerfeld visited "some troops outside Mexico City" sometime before the unfolding of the plot. While Bell's account seems embellished and creates some questions as to the timeline of events he suggested that Gustavo Madero as well as the President certainly had been aware of a conspiracy in the making. Suspicion, however, did not fall on Huerta, who, while on the "list," had a question mark attached to it. According to Sommerfeld, the conspiracy reports he received in the field were specific. Given the number of people involved in the conspiracy, it is likely that both Gustavo Madero and Sommerfeld knew of the plan. At the head of the list of plotters was Manuel Mondragon who had returned from Havana a few weeks prior. The former general and Secretary of War under Porfirio Diaz undoubtedly attracted secret service surveillance the moment he set foot into Mexico. His return to Mexico, the significant contacts the old general had to the higher echelons of the federal army, and his public pronouncements against Madero virtually defined his intent. According to William Bayard Hale, "subscriptions towards the overthrow of Madero were passed around almost openly in the capital with only moderate success."[813] For reasons hard to understand from a hindsight perspective, the urgency to protect the President seemed to have been missing.

With newspapers of the day full of conspiracy reports and the constant influx of secret service intelligence on the opposition, it is hard to fathom that the Madero administration did not hole itself up in anticipation of an attack. Instead, virtually unprotected, Francisco Madero could be seen riding his horse through Chapultepec Park in the mornings. The President also did not make any changes to his immediate protective detail that consisted of federal soldiers. The Madero government seemed to be wholly unprepared as to what happened on February 9th 1913. Just like before Pearl Harbor and 9/11, hindsight analysis of all available information revealed the plots. However, Madero had heard true and false plot forecasts for the past year. In January 1913, he felt more confident than at any time before in his presidency that he was following the right path. Reyes was defeated and in jail, Orozco defeated and on the run, Diaz in jail, and Zapata still fighting but confined to Morelos. The Taft administration was on the way out. Ambassador Wilson's days under the new American administration were numbered. Speyer had approved a new loan for Mexico in 1912 and all signs looked good for a larger issue of bonds to be granted in 1913. The financial circles of London, New York, and Berlin seemed to believe more in Madero's ability to create stability than the press. And, Madero was the democratically elected President of Mexico after all.

CHAPTER 16

~

"SHORT OF AN EARTHQUAKE..."

On June 18th 1913, William Bayard Hale transmitted an investigative report to President Wilson, which detailed a fateful military coup in Mexico City in February of 1913. According to Hale, in the early morning hours of Sunday, February 9th 1913, Mexican General Manuel Mondragon surprised the guards of the Mexican capital's penitentiary. Several hundred cadets and officers had marched from the Tlalpan military academy located approximately sixteen miles southwest of the city center.[814] The troops freed Felix Diaz. The commander of the prison had called someone in the government who told him to resist. Who he talked to is unclear. It could have been an officer in the War Department, the Interior Ministry, or Gustavo Madero, the President's brother. With only twenty men guarding the prison, the fight ended before it started. Mondragon, or one of his men, shot and killed the out-gunned and out-manned commander.[815] A second detachment of troops with artillery and heavy machine gun implements from the Tacubaya barracks, just south of Chapultepec Castle, had meanwhile joined them. About seven hundred strong, the troops advanced to the Santiago Tlatelolco military prison north of the Presidential Palace, where General Bernardo Reyes awaited the conspirators in full dress uniform. The two detachments with Reyes leading the spearhead then advanced toward the Zócalo, the central plaza in front of the Presidential Palace.

The guards of the Presidential Palace in the center of the city could not help but notice the rumble of heavy weapons and hundreds of troops from the south right by their location on the way to the prisons. Tlatelolco was situated less than a mile to the northeast. The penitentiary was a bit over one mile due east. According to some reports, Gustavo Madero, who had been roused by the noise of the advancing troops, immediately rushed to the Presidential Palace. Although he lived on Calle Londres close to the Paseo de la Reforma, the thoroughfare used by the advancing troops, the President's brother more likely received a call at the time of the first prison break, or had a messenger apprising him of the situation.[816] However he learned of the attack, Gustavo arrived at the palace in the early morning hours. He gave a fiery speech to the defending troops whose loyalty in those early hours was questionable. Historian Edward Bell credited Gustavo with placing machine guns on the roof and preparing the defense of the building before Army Chief of Staff, General Lauro Villar, arrived at the scene. German Ambassador Admiral Paul von Hintze did not mention Gustavo's presence at all but

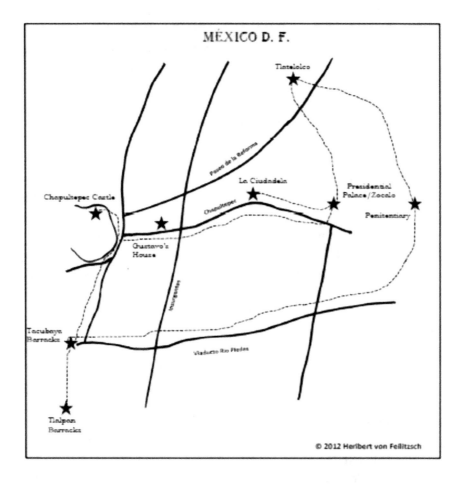

MÉXICO D. F.

© 2012 Heribert von Feilitzsch

remarked that the "Secretary of War [Peña] rushed in his night gown with an overcoat to the Palace."[817] It took Reyes until 7:30 am to advance on the meanwhile bustling market place. Villar met Reyes in front of the gates and

235

commanded the rebelling general to cease and desist. Reyes kept advancing. Suddenly, the machine guns on the roof of the palace let loose and mowed down the assailants. Bernardo Reyes was killed instantly. Four hundred died with him while nearly one thousand were injured, many of them bystanders. The return fire from the rebels seriously injured Villar. A bullet cut through his collarbone.[818] Secretary of War Peña had a bullet wound in the armpit.[819] Felix Diaz and the others retreated. In vicious street fighting which killed more bystanders, they fought their way west through the narrow city streets. Their numbers now having swelled to fifteen hundred troops, the rebels blockaded themselves near the Ciudadela, a fortress about one mile due west. Armed with artillery and heavy weaponry they took the fortress around midday.

At 8:00 a.m. Francisco Madero rode to the Presidential Palace in style: On a gray stallion. According to eyewitnesses, bullets were still flying as pockets of rebels were barricaded in the cathedral and surrounding buildings directly across the Zócalo.[820] In Madero's entourage were cabinet members Rafael Hernandez, Manuel Bonilla, and Ernesto Madero.[821] Also joining him on the way was General Victoriano Huerta, the forcefully retired army chief of staff, in town for his eye treatments.[822] He had a cataract removed but still suffered from poor eyesight. Von Hintze blamed the eye problems on Huerta's excessive drinking.[823] A small detachment of security forces brought up the rear. After the Battle of Casas Grandes in 1911, Máximo Castillo had said of Madero that he either did not know that bullets killed or that he was extremely courageous. Here he rode again, fifteen months later, unfazed by the danger. Waving to cheering crowds, Madero made his way to the palace and surveyed the damage. Von Hintze, who was thoroughly impressed with Madero's bravery, could not believe the time he spent bathing in the crowd's vivas and giving speeches rather than finishing off the remaining rebels.[824]

With General Villar seriously injured and the fighting continuing Huerta offered his services to Madero. He pledged his unwavering loyalty to the President. Madero accepted. According to historian Katz, Huerta had been in contact with Felix Diaz the night of February 8th but had not reached an agreement as to who would succeed the President after a successful coup d'état. The Mexican general did not have any faith in Felix Diaz and firmly resisted the latter's ambition for the presidency.[825] However, another more likely theory describes a course of events that placed Huerta in the role of supreme commander without being one of the conspirators at the time. The injury of General Villar could not have been planned and was the only reason why Madero appointed the general who had fallen from grace just a few months prior. It is only after Huerta found himself in this most powerful position that he succumbed to entreaties made by Ambassador Wilson and his "creation," Felix Diaz.

Meanwhile, the Maderos contemplated their next moves in what they believed to be mop up operations. Felix Diaz, Manuel Mondragon, and approximately fifteen hundred soldiers had barricaded themselves in the Ciudadela, also called the Arsenal, a fortified warehouse with a large repository of arms and ammunition. Rather than immediately following up and assaulting the attackers as they retreated, Huerta stood back and had the building only surrounded. Even worse, as a result of standing down, the federal forces inadvertently allowed the rebel forces to install machine guns on the roof of their fortress and bring field pieces into position in the streets surrounding the Arsenal. Some of the cadets who had attacked the palace with Reyes in the morning were holed up in the cathedral across the Zócalo. These deadly snipers did not get dislodged for the entire ten days of the fighting. In a debatable act of immediate justice, General Ruiz, one of Mondragon's co-conspirators who had been captured on the Zócalo and twelve hapless cadets faced a firing squad in the garden of the palace that afternoon.[826]

Despite the Ciudadela in the hands of Diaz' troops, for all intents and purposes the situation was firmly under the control of government forces for the remainder of the day. The Ciudadela was surrounded by troops under Huerta's command. Unbeknownst to Madero, Huerta's treachery began that day. He allowed supplies for the rebels to get through. Despite American newspaper claims to the contrary, there was no substance to reports of unrest supporting the rebellion anywhere else in the country.[827] The Zapatistas, while still fighting the government, had made no efforts to get close to the capital.[828] In the afternoon, Ambassador Wilson invited the diplomatic corps to an emergency session in the American embassy. As a group they decided on measures to protect their citizens. One of the stated goals was to bargain for a cease-fire allowing foreign citizens to evacuate to safer locations. Towards the end of the meeting, von Hintze reported that a representative of Diaz - to his embarrassment a German citizen - asked the assembled diplomats to demand the resignation of President Madero. The group denied the request and let General Diaz know via his emissary that "he may take great care to honor the lives and properties of foreigners in his military undertakings."[829] Von Hintze was incensed how this German "compatriot" was "insolent" and had a "provocative tone."[830] The presence of this rebel representative was a clear sign of Wilson's active role in the events of the day.

Madero decided that evening to travel personally to Cuernavaca, the capital of Morelos, for a meeting with Felipe Ángeles, his trusted commander currently fighting Zapata's insurrection. According to William Bayard Hale, Zapata had announced that he would suspend his attacks until the government had repelled the forces of reaction from the capital.[831] If that was true then all the dispatches warning of an impending invasion by the "Indian hordes" as a result of the breakdown of order in the capital were part of Ambassador Wilson's conspiracy. Madero traveled in an open car through Mexico City, determined to give the public the impression of self-confidence. Outside the capital the President and his entourage switched to a caboose. Felipe Ángeles met his commander-in-chief at the train station in Cuernavaca. Ángeles had been an officer in the federal army under President Diaz. Born in the state of Hidalgo on June 13th 1869, Ángeles grew up on a livestock farm. When he was only fourteen-years-old, his father sent the extremely bright Felipe to the Heroico Colegio Militar at Chapultepec, an equivalent to West Point in the United States. Ángeles did extremely well in math and sciences. He concentrated his studies on artillery, which brought him into close contact with the chief of artillery and future Secretary of War, Manuel Mondragon. When he graduated, the college offered him various lectureships. In 1898, Ángeles married the German-American Clara Kraus. It did not take long for Ángeles to become fluent in German. In 1904, Mondragon sent the artillery major to the United States to study the newest development in the war industry of the time: Smokeless powder. When the thirty-five-year-old Ángeles returned he was promoted lieutenant colonel. He now spoke English fluently.

In 1908, Mondragon sent him to France where the Mexican army much to German chagrin was now buying most of their heavy guns. Ángeles, as a result of the travels and contact with democratic and parliamentary regimes, had developed a thorough social conscience. He began to publish articles on his ideas for political reform in Mexico. Officers of the federal army were not supposed to have political ideas and especially not mingle in politics. Accordingly, in 1908, he was arrested and charged with sedition. Thanks to his incredible brainpower and the goodwill of General Mondragon, the star officer was released and returned to an assignment in France. For Ángeles there was no turning back. In the autumn of the Diaz regime he clearly saw the need for change. When Francisco Madero surfaced from the sea of anti-reelectionist activists, many of whom were far too radical for Ángeles, he had found his cause. Upon the outbreak of the revolution, the colonel, who was by then studying modern artillery warfare in Paris, requested to return to Mexico. With his political views known to his superiors the request was denied. He had to remain in France where he was to "distinguish himself." In May 1911, Colonel Ángeles became a knight of the Legion of Honor, an award Napoleon Bonaparte had instituted in lieu of nobility titles when France became a republic.

Finally, in January 1912, after the Mexican presidential elections, Ángeles returned home. Madero appointed him commander of Ángeles' alma mater, the Colegio Militar. In June 1912, Ángeles, now brigadier general, received an active command to replace Huerta in the war against Zapata. Huerta had been unable to smash the peasant forces by using the most brutal tactics of mass execution and torture, wiping out whole villages, and terrorizing the civilian population. Ángeles applied a new set of "anti-insurgent" tactics hitherto unknown in Mexico. While he did not defeat Zapata, he introduced rules of engagement, humane treatment of prisoners, prevention of civilian casualties, and a code-of-honor in dealing with the enemy. Despite the fierce fighting, Ángeles succeeded in winning many hearts and minds throughout the population of Morelos. His tactics reduced Zapata's ability to recruit. The development of trust between the warring factions also lends truth to William Bayard Hale's claim that the Zapatistas stood down throughout the "Decena Tragica," the rebellion taking place in Mexico City.

According to historian Ross, it was in Cuernavaca where the President asked Ángeles to become the new supreme military commander and replace Huerta as soon as possible. With the loyal general having agreed to move his forces to the capital Madero returned the next morning. Ángeles, who accompanied Madero to Mexico City, brought one thousand men with sufficient weapons and ammunition to the Presidential Palace.[832] The army staff rejected Madero's request to make Ángeles supreme commander. His promotion to brigadier general had not yet been confirmed in congress, making him theoretically ineligible for the position. However, he took over responsibility for the artillery emplacements in the center of the capital.

All garrisons near Mexico City now mobilized and moved into position in and around the Ciudadela. General Blanquet, an old general and comrade of Porfirio Diaz, committed to move a force of twelve hundred men into the city. It would take him a full week to move four hundred troops for forty miles and join the scene.[833] All other regional commanders also declared their support for the President.

Meanwhile in the capital, foreboding quiet had settled over the usually lively streets. On Monday morning all businesses remained closed. The

American embassy converted its compound into a refugee camp for foreigners seeking shelter. All around them government forces were building up throughout the day. Other than the military, Red Cross vehicles seemed to be the only noticeable traffic. An anxious citizenry that had just watched the carnage on the Zócalo the day before stayed inside not knowing what would happen next. Mexico City had not seen fighting since the American occupation over fifty years earlier. Then brave Mexican cadets had entrenched themselves in Chapultepec and defended their country to the last man. Now, Mexican troops faced each other in the middle of the city. The previous day's skirmishes had left four hundred dead. The Presidential Palace and many buildings in the surrounding streets had been severely damaged. The American consulate had been shelled forcing American Consul General Shanklin to seek refuge in the American embassy. He became an eyewitness to the contacts between Diaz and Huerta, which Wilson arranged through an American agent.[834]

Finally, on Tuesday morning, Huerta's artillery bombarded the Ciudadela and the surrounding streets with great furor. The return fire from the rebels blasted nearby buildings, including the Presidential Palace, and sent scores of civilians scrambling for cover. The psychological effect of war-like conditions in the center of Mexico's capital cannot be understated. Madero and his advisors had no doubt that the shelling of the Ciudadela and massive assault of the federal forces would end the standoff within hours. When nighttime settled over the city, over five hundred casualties and a full day of horrendously destructive battles had not yielded any result. The Diaz forces had held their own. The deceit of the federal commander proved to be the real reason behind the lacking progress.

To this day historians debate on whether Huerta had been a conspirator from the beginning of the revolt. By Tuesday morning, when the government's offensive finally started, there could be no doubt as to the general's treachery. Contacts between Felix Diaz and Huerta had existed as far back as January 1st.[835] Diaz had obviously been unsuccessful in winning Huerta over for his plans. With the rebels holed up in the Arsenal and Huerta having risen to supreme military commander in the city, the general's change-of-heart took shape. As the assault, two days in the making, started to force a resolution on Tuesday morning around 10:00 a.m., Huerta and Diaz met in a house that belonged to Enrique Cepeda. Cepeda worked closely with Ambassador Wilson's agent Harry Berliner. A German Jew under deep cover as a merchant, Berliner in reality worked for the State Department's Secret Service. He personally got to know Sommerfeld in those days in Mexico City, without Sommerfeld ever suspecting Berliner's true occupation. [836] The American agent remained Sommerfeld's most effective shadow throughout the Mexican Revolution and the First World War. Berliner, according to Wilson's recollections "was a messenger of the embassy."[837] Wilson reported to the State Department on the previous day, "...negotiations with General Huerta are taking place." This cable confirmed William Bayard Hale's assessment of the role of Cepeda. Hale interviewed Cepeda's father-in-law and identified the "confidential messenger" between Huerta and the American embassy, while on a subsequent fact-finding mission for President Wilson. He summarized Huerta's treachery:

"'My confidential messenger with Huerta,' 'the confidential messenger between Huerta and myself [H. L. Wilson], a person by whom the President [Huerta] has requested me to reach him whenever I desire,' (Wilson to Knox Feb. 28) – the anonymous figure which moves mysteriously in Wilson's reports and much more prominently in the true story of the Madero betrayal, was Enrique Zepeda [sic], a notorious character who passes as the nephew and is the illigitimate [sic] son of Victoriano Huerta. Enrique Zepeda [sic] is married to the step daughter of an American, Mr E. J. Pettegrew. Pettegrew says that on the Tuesday before the events now occurring [February 11th], that is, on the first day of the battle, he and Zepeda [sic] arranged a meeting between Huerta and Diaz in an empty house in the city. If this is true, it would seem as if the whole bombardment were an elaborate fake, and that the two generals understood each other all the time. Many other things point to this conclusion. It would seem to be the case, if Pettegrew's story is true, that when Zepeda [sic] sought Mr Wilson's offices to bring the two generals together, it was not because his intervention was necessary, but because the conspirators wanted to let the Ambassador believe that he was 'solving the situation' and to secure his promise of Washington's recognition of the government they were plotting to set up."[838]

Hale continued to qualify that this story was based on a single interview and could not be fully substantiated. However, the entire historiography on the fall of Madero has accepted this chain of events as fact. As Huerta, Diaz, and Wilson negotiated an arrangement that involved promise of offices in the new government, outright bribery, as well as threats of American military intervention by Wilson, the bombardment in the heart of Mexico City continued for four more deadly days. Historian McLynn aptly described the scene: "Shopping centres [sic] were palls of smoke, elegant residential areas echoed to the machine gun's hasty stutter, and the once distinguished heart of the capital was like a giant rubbish tip, a tangle of telegraph wire, sandbags and bizarrely skewed lampposts, with the number of human corpses defying the best efforts of improvised ambulances…Soon food grew scarce, prices became hyperinflationary, and many urban myths arose about dinners of roasted cat and dog."[839]

The image of a government unable to restore order intensified in the days of Huerta's "phony war." Huerta sent row after row of infantrymen into the line of fire. Felix Diaz' machine guns mowed them down by the hundreds. The carnage and destruction reached unbearable levels. Ambassador Wilson gleefully manipulated the effects of the bombardment in the streets. On February 12th, the American ambassador with the ministers of Germany, Spain, and Britain in tow demanded an immediate end to hostilities from President Madero. According to Wilson's report to Secretary Knox, "The President was visibly embarrassed and endeavored to fix the responsibility of [sic] Felix Diaz."[840] Wilson blamed the continuing fighting on the President, which, naturally, Madero rejected outright. Madero did, however, authorize the "high-handed, intemperate and totally inappropriate" ambassador to engage the rebels in talks.[841] Hale noted that the American ambassador justified his actions as a spokesman for the entire diplomatic corps in Mexico. The truth was that none of the Latin American representatives or the Austrian and Japanese ambassadors supported Wilson's activism. Indeed, while von Hintze joined Wilson in his audiences with Madero, he also disagreed with Wilson's plans and softened the representations of the ambassador in front of the Mexican President.[842] He wrote to the German Foreign Office a few days later, "Wilson[,] without the slightest attempt to disguise this fact is working on the behalf of Diaz, told Madero in my presence the reason, Diaz was pro-American. Wilson's taking sides makes the activity of the Diplomatic Corps more difficult."[843] Von Hintze's instructions were to keep distance to the American intrigue. He affirmed his pursuit of Germany's goals in the same cable: "keeping restrained towards the many American requests [for support] without causing offense."[844] Ambassador Francis Stronge of Britain weaved in the winds of influence turning alternatively in Wilson and von Hintze's direction. With respect to Wilson's plan to create a united diplomatic front, however, von Hintze seemed to be able to maintain a counter balance with his British colleague's support. About Stronge, Hale said later, quite unfairly as later historians agreed, that he never met "…an individual whose character so absurdly belied his name. Mr Stronge is a silly, stuttering imbecile, the laughing stock of the whole city, which regales itself with nothing more to its perennial delight than daily stories of Mr Stronge and the parrot by which he is constantly attended."[845] It is to von Hintze's credit as a diplomat that he so successfully manipulated his peers towards his ends, no matter how awkward their behavior.

While Wilson pursued his efforts to unite the diplomatic corps behind his actions, he also sent inflamed and utterly false reports to Washington and the American press. On the day of the first attacks, Wilson "...told all comers at the Embassy that the Government had practically fallen and telegraphed to Washington asking for powers to force the combatants [in]to negotiations."[846] On February 11th Wilson cabled to Secretary Knox, "...public opinion, both native and foreign, as far as I can estimate, seems to be overwhelmingly in favor of Diaz [!]... He underestimated federal strength, exaggerated the size of the rebel force, and complained of indiscriminate firing and extensive damage to property." In these cables he asked Washington to give him authority to transmit an ultimatum of "menacing character" to Madero. Knox declined.[847]

The bombardments in the center of Mexico's capital certainly did affect public opinion, especially that of people who were displaced, without food, and threatened by the shelling. The situation was grave but Madero remained confident that the rebels could be beaten quickly. His optimism was well founded. Madero had assembled a force of over six thousand loyal troops to combat the fifteen hundred rebels. Wilson continued his strategy to torment the Madero administration, while negotiating with Felix Diaz and the rebels. Von Hintze reported to his superiors on February 14th, that the American ambassador had received Pedro Lascurain at the embassy and threatened him with military intervention. "...[H]e would have three or four thousand American soldiers at his disposal within a few days and 'that he would restore order here.'...Should Lascurain wish to avoid such a development, 'there was only one way: tell the President to get out..."[848] On the 15th of February, Wilson pushed the "diplomatic corps," Stronge, von Hintze, and Bernardo J. Cologan y Cologan - the Spanish minister - into demanding Madero's resignation. Von Hintze, who had unsuccessfully tried to soften the representations of the American ambassador, finally threw diplomacy aside and told Madero, that the German government "had made no such suggestion."[849] As expected the President rejected the "friendly advice" of the assembled ambassadors outright.[850] Wilson and von Hintze also visited Felix Diaz on the 13th and requested a stop to the "inhumanity" of the fighting. An astute observer, von Hintze came away from the meeting with the impression that Diaz "...seems more impulsive than strong; Mondragon looks suspicious. Relations between them are apparently not good; Mondragon is attempting to dominate Diaz. Result of this visit: Diaz is in trouble, he talks about a thousand men who have rallied on his behalf in various states and who are en route to the capital, but will not say from where."[851]

On February 16th, fully one week since the outbreak of hostilities, the federals and rebels agreed to a twenty-four hour cease fire that Wilson had mediated. Rather than allowing for the evacuation of foreigners from the city, Wilson, without any grounding in fact, suddenly announced a few hours into the cease-fire that the federal army had broken the agreement. All evacuations had to be cancelled. Von Hintze, who according to Hale accompanied the ambassador to the National Palace for those negotiations, came away with disgust at the American ambassador's duplicity. Wilson feared that removing the expatriates would reduce foreign governments' desire for military intervention. The fighting resumed but von Hintze, as a result, had lost all confidence in the American ambassador's good offices.[852] In addition to canceling the cease-fire, Wilson also announced that General Blanquet and his troops had gone over to the enemy and refused to fight Diaz. Von Hintze assumed this to be a fabrication, although it turned out to be more of a self-fulfilling prophecy created through Wilson's intrigue. Throughout the 16th of February Huerta, Diaz, and Wilson remained in contact.

Felix Sommerfeld's role in these trying days is largely circumstantial. His testimony in 1918 is unclear as to the timeline and his activities. However, a cross-reference of Sommerfeld's statements, von Hintze's diary, William Bayard Hale's report, and German embassy records paint a fairly complete picture of his activities in that fateful week in February 1913. For the main part, von Hintze used Sommerfeld for his unofficial communication with President Madero, similar to Wilson using his agents Cepeda and Berliner to shuttle between the traitors, the government, and his office. The German ambassador had done so many times in the past.[853] He was amazingly well informed on the situation and the actions of the Mexican government. Sommerfeld, who was intimately familiar with the inner circles of Madero's government, clearly was one of his critical sources. The agent stayed in the German embassy from the beginning of the attacks until the 13th of February.[854] This means, that Sommerfeld operated out of, and undoubtedly in concert with, the German embassy throughout the unfolding crisis. Incidentally, the embassy listed his occupation as "agent."[855] It is a well-known fact that Gustavo Madero arrested Huerta on February 17th and confronted him about his negotiations with Felix

Diaz in front of his brother, the President. There are two historical accounts explaining Gustavo's taking action against Huerta. One has a loyal officer tipping off the President's brother on the fact that Huerta was secretly supplying the rebels with food. The other claimed that a loyal officer had watched Huerta's negotiations with Diaz and then proceeded to inform Gustavo.[856]

"F.A. Sommerfeldt [sic], Agent stayed 7 days and nights as guest of the Imperial Legation during the "bombardements.""[857]

However, Sommerfeld alluded to a third possibility, namely that it was him who had been tipped off.[858] In his interview with the American investigators in 1918 Sommerfeld tried very hard to cover up any involvement he had with German officials, thus covering up von Hintze's identity as a Mexican official. Similar to Katz' account, the German agent recalled an unnamed Mexican army commander (von Hintze) as the source of his knowledge of the unfolding conspiracy. The possibility presents itself that it was von Hintze who gave the information of Huerta's treachery to the Maderos. In this case the German ambassador had to have used an informal channel, since H. L. Wilson accompanied him to every meeting. Undoubtedly, Wilson would have quickly found out if the German ambassador engaged in independent diplomacy. In his position as head of the secret service, and working for Gustavo Madero, Sommerfeld was the perfect vehicle for von Hintze to sabotage Wilson. As historian Baecker convincingly showed, von Hintze opposed the Wilson plan of installing Diaz as an American puppet. How much information on the dealings of Wilson, which Hintze witnessed and described so accurately in his diary and in the dispatches to Berlin, was Sommerfeld privy to? According to Sommerfeld's own statement he stayed in the German embassy that week. Did von Hintze send Sommerfeld to give pertinent information to the Maderos about Wilson's negotiations with both Diaz and Huerta? An intriguing, yet unprovable thesis.

At 2:00 a.m. on February 17th, Gustavo Madero took Huerta to the President at gunpoint. He confronted Huerta with the evidence of secret negotiations with Diaz. "Huerta raged, blustered and swore up and down that he was not in any plot; he vowed on his scapular that he was loyal, agreeing that his soul should be consigned to the everlasting fires of Hell if he was lying."[859] As the historical record shows, Huerta was lying. His soul probably did make Hell a few degrees hotter when he died in 1915. However, rather than counteracting the treason, the general's representations turned the President's opinion against his brother and those, like Sommerfeld and von Hintze, who knew that Huerta was a traitor. If von Hintze had planned to sabotage Wilson's plan, he now recognized that he had failed. Huerta continued to direct the forces amassed against the rebels and sent scores of soldiers into the line of fire as cannon fodder.

Diplomatic historians Katz and Baecker agree that on the 17th of February, the morning of Huerta's brief arrest, von Hintze changed his tactics. However, both historians misinterpreted the strategy.[860] That morning von Hintze visited the Presidential Palace alone. This is the only time in the whole episode when von Hintze officially acted separately from the "diplomatic corps" led by Wilson. Rather than allowing the American ambassador to install Felix Diaz, who von Hintze considered corrupt and unfit for government, the sly German ambassador had decided to try one last strategy to manipulate the situation against Wilson. The shelling of downtown Mexico City had proceeded unabatedly for a full week. Scores of civilians and thousands of soldiers had perished. Federal troops such as those commanded by General Blanquet had switched sides. The American government, von Hintze knew first hand, did not want Madero to remain in the presidency. The threat of U.S. military intervention loomed large, although, as it turned out later, it was a phantom of Wilson's imagination. Induced by Wilson, a delegation of Mexican senators was now asking for Madero's resignation. Given the overwhelming opposition, von Hintze became convinced that Madero's government was doomed and the President could not stay in power any longer. None of the scholars on the topic have discovered why von Hintze came to that conclusion. Katz wrote that von Hintze "reversed himself," a description that contributed largely to the theory that von Hintze and the German government supported Huerta at this time.[861]

Nothing could be further from the truth. The German ambassador's handwritten diary offers the key facts: Von Hintze knew that a coup was about to happen. While the rear admiral did not say this outright, his actions recorded in the diary are crystal clear. Rather than waiting for the military to make its move, the ambassador proposed for Madero to install Huerta as a successor, while he and his administration would retreat to safety. He pitched the idea first to Foreign Minister Lascurain. The German official maintained that Huerta was the only person who could quickly end the standoff in the city if he were made interim President. This solution would sideline Felix Diaz and upset Ambassador Wilson's plan. Finally, this move also prevented a potential military intervention from the United States. At the same time, Madero would be able to extricate himself, his family, and his administration from the inevitable military coup that was about to happen. From a location of safety, Madero remained free to challenge Huerta in the next election and possibly resume power under more optimal circumstances.

President Madero considered the idea favorably.[862] Immediately after the President met with the German ambassador, the whole Madero family moved into the German embassy. Von Hintze had undoubtedly planned for that to happen. He wrote in his diary that before he went to see Madero he had ordered rooms to be prepared "for seven female members of the Madero family, including the mother."[863] Combining Sommerfeld and Sara Madero's statements with von Hintze's diary, the group most likely consisted of Madero's parents, Francisco and Mercedes, Madero's wife Sara, two of the President's sisters, as well as the wives of Gustavo Madero and José Maria Pino Suarez. Unclear is whether von Hintze had offered sanctuary and safe conduct to President Madero in the transfer of power. Considering that the President brought his whole family to the German embassy, there can be little doubt that that was part of von Hintze's scheme. It is also not surprising that the ambassador did not commit to paper in detail what he had in mind with Madero and his entourage since he almost certainly acted without instructions from Berlin. However, the ambassador's plan was torpedoed from an unforeseen corner. In the afternoon of February 17th President Madero received a message from President Taft, in which the American President affirmed that the United States did not wish to intervene in Mexico.[864] With the threat of intervention off the table, Madero considered his position to be strong enough to master this latest challenge. He made the tragic decision to stay in the Presidential Palace.

In meetings at the American embassy on the morning of the 18th of February, Wilson gave guarantees to conservative Mexican senators that the United States would recognize a new government "...led by De La Barra, Huerta and Diaz...Senator Obregon, one of the delegates, formally asked him [Wilson] whether, if such a government were formed, the United States would abandon its plans for intervention; he [Wilson] answered the question in the affirmative..."[865] It did not matter that President Madero had shown Taft's cable to the senators when they had asked for his resignation. The threat of intervention seemed to have become a trump card in Wilson's hand that could not be beaten, not even by the American President. Huerta meanwhile set the last act of the tragedy in motion. Felipe Ángeles, the trusted and loyal artillery commander who had been in charge of defending the Presidential Palace, received orders to move to another position further way. General Blanquet now took over the responsibility for the President's security. Considering that everyone, including Sommerfeld, Gustavo Madero, and the President knew of the Blanquet's questionable loyalty, it is hard to understand that no one stopped Ángeles' reassignment.

While Gustavo Madero attended a breakfast banquet with General Huerta in the Gabrinus Restaurant, a platoon of soldiers entered around noon and arrested him. The timing of this event is absolutely crucial. Historians Ross, McLynn, and others have written that Gustavo had a lunch appointment. William Bayard Hale who researched the exact timeline for his report to

President Wilson found out that the arrest was at noon but the appointment was in the morning.[866] Huerta was not in the restaurant when the arrest took place. He had excused himself to make a phone call. The detention of both Maderos had been planned to be simultaneous. For unexplained reasons, that did not happen. Huerta most likely had left the restaurant to make a call to inquire about the arrest of the President. Francisco Madero remained in the palace unmolested until 1:30 p.m. At that time a group of soldiers busted into the Salon de Acuerdos and tried to arrest Francisco Madero. According to his statement in 1918, Sommerfeld had talked to the President shortly before the arrest. "I called up Mr. Madero by phone and told him to leave the National Palace, that something was wrong. I didn't know what. I knew something was off. I told him to go quick to the house of Mr. William MacLaren [sic]."[867] If that was a true statement, Sommerfeld had either witnessed or had been notified of Gustavo's arrest. The safe house he referred to belonged to William A. McLaren who was a lawyer in Mexico City. His law firm had a famous partner: Rafael Hernandez, Madero's cousin and Secretary of Justice. It makes sense that Sommerfeld would suggest his place, owned by an American, a lawyer, but also a loyal Maderista supporter. "Madero told me over the phone to go ahead."[868]

The President was not alone when the soldiers came with their guns drawn. A firefight with Madero's guards ensued. Several of the soldiers were killed. Marcos Hernandez, the Justice Minister's brother who was standing next to the President, also died in a hail of bullets. Ambassador Wilson's agent, Enrique Cepeda, who was a member of the arresting party, was shot in the hand. Being promised the governorship of Mexico City as a reward for his treachery, his bleeding hand seemed a small price to pay.[869] Madero, uninjured because Cepeda had orders from Ambassador Wilson to take him alive, slipped by the confused troops and rushed into the adjourning hall.[870] A group of Rurales that had heard the gunfire rushed into the building. Madero opened a window in the hallway and shouted to the soldiers below that everything was under control. Then he entered the elevator. When he exited on the main floor, General Blanquet met him with his pistol drawn. Without any options other than slapping the traitor general, which he did, Madero gave himself up. All but two members of the cabinet were also arrested.[871]

At this juncture Wilson, so sure that everything was going according to plan, implicated himself as familiar with the intricacies of the coup. Not realizing that there had been a delay, Wilson cabled to the State Department one-and-a-half hours before the coup that "the supposition now is that the

Federal Generals are in control of the situation."[872] Finally, at 2:00 p.m., according to Consul Shanklin, Cepeda arrived at the American embassy with his hand bleeding and reported what just had happened in the Presidential Palace.[873] As a result of Cepeda's eyewitness account, Wilson notified Felix Diaz in the Ciudadela and invited him to talks – and a couple swigs of well-aged Kentucky whiskies – at the American embassy.

In a broad sweep with black lists in hand, Huerta's agents went through the city and arrested influential members of the Madero government. General Felipe Ángeles who faithfully continued his artillery fire on the Ciudadela ended up a prisoner within hours. Felix Sommerfeld as well was a wanted man and feared for his life.[874] It is virtually certain that Francisco Madero had advance knowledge of his brother's arrest and that it was Sommerfeld who conveyed the message. William Bayard Hale wrote, "…The plan of seizing the person of the President was delayed for an hour or so…," which referred to the time lag between Gustavo's arrest and the President's.[875] This timeline matches Sommerfeld's testimony. The German agent also told the truth about knowing that something was up. Von Hintze knew of the pending putsch because Wilson had told him so. The German ambassador noted in his diary, "[a]fter the negotiations, which took place yesterday – February 17 – he [Wilson] thinks that the whole affair can be settled today – February 18."[876]

A second indication that Sommerfeld told the truth about those crucial hours is the fact that, when the arresting party surprised Madero, the President was with Marcos Hernandez, the Justice Minister's brother. Madero was not, as most historical accounts claim, in a cabinet meeting. That meeting had ended and, although in the building, the cabinet members were not with Madero when the soldiers came. In addition, Madero had his security detail with him. One would expect armed guards in front of the palace or protecting certain areas, but not next to the President while he conducted a cabinet meeting. Only under the scenario that Madero knew in advance that a putsch was under way would he have surrounded himself with armed guards. Given the timeline with Gustavo's arrest one hour before and the President having been warned, it seemed that Francisco Madero was wrapping up urgent business and prepared to flee the palace just as the soldiers entered. The President quickly ran to the elevator and tried to exit the building. It makes no sense that, before Madero ran, he called out of the window and stopped soldiers who were rushing in to help. The only purpose of this interlude could have been that he had an escape plan. The last piece of circumstantial evidence is that Rafael Hernandez was one of the two cabinet members who escaped that day.

Madero's uncle, Ernesto Madero, was the second escapee. No one knows where the two ministers hid from the searching troops. A good bet is that both went to the house of Hernandez' law partner McLaren or the German embassy. Assuming that Hernandez and Ernesto Madero escaped around the exact time when Madero was arrested, was Madero following his cabinet officers to a car that waited at a side entrance of the Palace?[877] Was Sommerfeld the driver? Another intriguing thought which might never be proven. The German embassy records of visitors and von Hintze's diary do not mention the two cabinet members to have come to the embassy, although the possibility cannot be excluded.

On the morning of the coup, on February 18th, when von Hintze returned from the documented meeting with Ambassador Wilson, the whole group of Madero family members had suddenly left the German embassy after breakfast.[878] According to von Hintze's diary, the Maderos had been in a huff over not being allowed to use the telephone.[879] To von Hintze's express "embarrassment" the Maderos went back to Chapultepec.[880] It was more than embarrassment. Von Hintze now knew of the impending coup and had to realize that the Maderos and possibly his plan to safeguard the President were in jeopardy.

In his statement to the American authorities in 1918, Sommerfeld hinted at the daring role he played in the events unfolding on February 18th. In the early afternoon of the fateful day, after the arrest of Madero and his ministers, a convoy of three cars zoomed out of Chapultepec and made its way through the chaotic streets of the embattled capital to the Japanese legation. Two of the cars displayed the flag of the Republic of Mexico, the third the red dot on white background of the Empire of Japan. In the first two cars were the President's wife, two of his sisters, his parents, Pino Suarez and Gustavo Madero's wives, and Felix A. Sommerfeld. The third car, belonging to the Japanese embassy, contained the wife of the Japanese ambassador and her security detail. Sommerfeld testified that the President had put him in charge of his wife "in case anything happened."[881] That was one of the important tasks of a head of the secret service. He disguised the fact that he also worked on behalf of the German ambassador and used the safety of the German embassy as his base of operations for most of that week. In a list the German embassy kept of "guests" who stayed on the premises, "agent" Sommerfeld is marked down from February 9th to the 13th and again starting on the 18th until he left with the ambassador.[882] In his interrogation in 1918, the German agent recalled the details of the rescue that occurred on February 18th: President Madero's wife, two sisters, and his parents were having lunch at Chapultepec Castle with the Japanese ambassador's wife, Madame Hurigutchi:

> "During lunch hour Madam Huri Gutchi was called out and told that Madero was a prisoner and the Vice President and the whole cabinet were prisoners of Huerta. This was the 18th of February at 2:30 in the afternoon. I then begged Madam Huri Gutchi not to show her excitement. There were lots of officers around…I went and called the officer of the guard and told him to get the automobiles ready as we were going to spend the afternoon in the Japanese legation. I loaded all of the people – the ladies and Madero's father – into the automobiles and we went to the Japanese legation. I stayed there until about seven in the evening. Then I walked over to the German legation. I told Admiral von Hintze…"[883]

Except for one report published in the Washington Post on February 10th 1913, which claimed that Madero's family had taken refuge in the Japanese legation, all available information points to Madero's family remaining in Chapultepec the whole week save for the night of the 17th, which corroborates Sommerfeld's story.[884] Supporting this assumption is an article in the same Washington Post two days later, reporting that Sara Madero was still at Chapultepec. Her own recollections, recorded in 1916, confirmed this important fact: "I never saw my husband since he left the Castle of Chapultepec to go to the National Palace on the morning of the 9th of February. He remained in the National Palace and me at Chapultepec Castle."[885] Why the Maderos left the safety of the German embassy on the 18th is not known. A lack of phone access seemed too petty a reason. A complete lack of appreciation of the pending danger on the part of both the President and his family seems more likely. While von Hintze proclaimed to be "embarrassed" by their departure on the morning of the coup, he still arranged for Sommerfeld to bring them to safety, this time with his Japanese colleague. In the end, he probably breathed a sigh of relief for not having to shelter the President's family. Safeguarding the President and his entourage would have maneuvered him into the crosshairs of Wilson's ire. At the same time he would have had to justify his independent, albeit courageous and humanitarian actions to the German Foreign Office.

Von Hintze and Sommerfeld, and with that also President Madero, were all fully aware of the pending attack on February 18th. The assumption offers itself that Madero asked von Hintze to shelter his family, maybe even himself, and, when this was not possible, to intervene with his Japanese colleague on his behalf. The Japanese ambassador had supported none of Wilson's actions and was decidedly loyal to the constitutional government of Mexico. According to his statement in 1918, Sommerfeld dropped off his refugees and then stayed in the German embassy until the dust settled. While von Hintze approached Madero alone on the 17th, throughout the whole affair up to the daring rescue of the Madero family Sommerfeld seemed to have been the informal connection between Madero and the German ambassador. In his statement in 1918 he almost slipped when he said, "I told Admiral von Hintze –..." then interrupted himself.[886]

Huerta did not waste time either. At 3:00 p.m. he sent a note to the American embassy, which Wilson read to the assembled diplomatic corps confirming that the Mexican President had been arrested. The American ambassador immediately tried to pressure the assembled diplomats into agreeing to his plot and recognizing Huerta as the de-facto head of a new government. Led by von Hintze, the ambassadors refused to give any assurances without instructions from their respective governments.[887] Much had been made of the alleged collusion of von Hintze with the American ambassador. His refusal to commit his government to push Huerta into negotiations with Diaz shows that he was pursuing a different plan. Without openly agitating against Wilson, von Hintze did everything in his power to make lemonade out of lemons. Diaz was Wilson's creation and, if the German ambassador would have had any say in it, he would have made sure that neither Diaz nor Huerta had a future! Huerta also sent a cable to President Taft: "I have the honor to inform you that I have overthrown this Government. The armed forces support me, and from now on peace and prosperity will reign."[888]

Without the support of the rest of the diplomatic corps, Wilson set out to create the new government himself. Huerta accompanied by Lieutenant Colonel Maas and Enrique Cepeda joined Wilson at 9:00 p.m. on February 18th in the smoking room at the American embassy.[889] A few moments later Felix Diaz joined the meeting with Rudolfo Reyes, the slain general's son, after an embassy car flying the American flag had delivered him from the Ciudadela.[890] The three conspirators, Huerta, Diaz, and Wilson talked for three hours. At times the meeting became heated. Huerta who had the might of the army behind him refused to grant Diaz the provisional presidency. Both Diaz and Huerta got up several times to break off the negotiations. When William Bayard Hale interviewed Wilson about that night, the ambassador's chest burst with pride when he recalled how his diplomatic skills kept the meeting afloat.[891]

With Wilson's mediation, the "Pact of the Embassy" concluded that Huerta became provisional President, Diaz had a say in selecting a new cabinet, and could run as a presidential candidate in the next election. Madero's cabinet ministers were to go free. Felipe Ángeles' life also would be spared. However, no agreement covered the future of President Madero and Vice President Pino Suarez. After having interviewed H. L. Wilson, Consul General Arnold Shanklin, General Huerta, Secretaries De La Barra and Lascurain, as well as a host of Mexican military and civilian witnesses, William Bayard Hale concluded: "President Madero was not betrayed and arrested by his officers until it had been ascertained that the American Ambassador had no objection to the performance. The plan for the immediate setting [up] of a military dictatorship would never have been formed except in the American Embassy, under the patronage of the American Ambassador, and with his promise of his Government's prompt recognition."[892]

The coup had succeeded! Much fallout was yet to follow. After the soldiers had removed Gustavo Madero from the Gambrinus Restaurant, they took him to the National Palace where Francisco Madero, José Maria Pino Suarez, and all but two of the other cabinet members awaited their uncertain future. As Wilson met with Huerta and Diaz, guards moved Gustavo to the Ciudadela. Eyewitness accounts collected in Ross' biography of Francisco Madero tell of the horrifying events that followed:

"...around two in the morning, General Mondragon decreed his death. The President's brother was forced with blows and pushes to the door leading to the patio. Bleeding, his face distorted by blows, his clothes torn, Gustavo tried to resist that frenzied, drunken mob of nearly one hundred persons. Holding desperately to the frame of the door he appealed to that sea of faces reflecting the madness of mob violence. Referring to his wife, children, and parents, he pleaded with them not to kill him. His words were greeted by jeers and laughter. One of the crowd pushed forward and, with the mattock from his rifle or the point of a sword, picked out the prisoner's good eye. The blinded Gustavo uttered a single mournful cry of terror and desperation. After that, he made no more sounds, but covering his face with his hands turned toward the wall...Prodding and sticking him with mattock and sword points and dealing him blows with fists and sticks they forced him to the patio...An assailant pressed a revolver to his head...and the shot tore Gustavo's jaw away. He was still able to move a short distance, falling, at last, near the statue of Morelos which, inappropriately, was a silent witness to this scene. A volley of shots was fired into the body...One of the crowd fired yet another shot into the body explaining drunkenly that is was the coup de grâce. The assassins proceeded to sack the body, and Gustavo's enamel eye was extracted and circulated from hand to hand."[893]

The body was unceremoniously dumped in the yard. Gustavo had been Francisco Madero's main advisor. As the go-to person he endured endless accusations of influence peddling and bribery. In a cable to the German Foreign Office von Hintze had sarcastically remarked that for a bribe of a few thousand pesos, Gustavo would have immediately executed the Covadonga murderers.[894] Besides the alleged corruptibility of Gustavo, the complaint alluded to the power of the President's brother. Without question Gustavo, who had to do the President's entire dirty laundry, had racked up quite a number of enemies. Many residents of Mexico City held Gustavo responsible for the hundreds of civilian casualties on the Zócalo on the first day of the revolt. Somehow the victorious putschists that had caused the incredible bloodshed in the center of the capital were able to deflect their responsibility, instead rousing an angry mob to release its anger against a symbol of Maderista rule. The New York Times, true to its policy of supporting the interventionists led by Ambassador Wilson, published a full-length article the next day. In it the paper levied the well-known accusations about Gustavo Madero's corruptibility and incompetence, without a sliver of regret for his horrible end. The article sounded as if Wilson himself had written it.[895]

WHY VICTORS SHOT GUSTAVO MADERO

Powerful Politician Was Generally Regarded as Brother's Evil Genius.

ONCE BANKRUPT, DIED RICH

Accused of Gaining Wealth by Undue Influence and "Strong Arm" Methods.

Special Cable to THE NEW YORK TIMES. [896]

It was obvious to all observers and the diplomatic corps in Mexico City that the fate of the President and his cabinet members hung in the balance. On the eve of their arrest, however, Huerta freed the cabinet members as a sign of good will. Simultaneously, Huerta and Wilson had decided to cross every "t" and dot every "i" in the transition of power as set forth in the Constitution of 1857. On the 19th of February, the day after the coup d'état, Huerta called for the Chamber of Deputies to assemble for a quorum demanding the resignation of the President and Vice President. Not knowing whether the assembly members would be safe only a few representatives showed. Through the use of supplemental representatives the chamber finally declared itself in session in the late afternoon. Meanwhile Huerta sent one of his generals to extract the resignations from the prisoners. Madero negotiated for his family, including Gustavo, whose fate he had not yet learned, Pino Suarez, and Felipe Ángeles to go into exile via Veracruz.

Pedro Lascurain, Madero's Foreign Minister, conducted the negotiations with Huerta. On the following day, February 20th, Huerta gave word that he agreed to Madero's terms. Madero and Pino Suarez signed their resignations, however noting that this was done under duress. The stipulation was that the Cuban and Chilean ambassadors were to hold the agreements until Huerta had signed his commitment for safe conduct of the prisoners and their families. Lascurain took the resignations and, rather than handing them to the ambassadors, went straight to the parliament. Historians still debate whether this was a purposeful act or whether Lascurain did not understand how critical this last trump card was for Madero's safety. The letter from Huerta with the agreed guarantees naturally never appeared. Now the situation looked dim for the two prisoners. For their immediate safety, Carlos Marquez Sterling, the Cuban ambassador, stayed with them. The chamber voted on the resignations and approved them. As the constitution prescribed, Pedro Lascurain, who as secretary of state was next in line, became President. His presidency was the shortest in Mexican history, a mere fifty-six minutes.[897] Huerta was appointed the new Vice President. Lascurain then immediately resigned which the chamber voted on again. Now Huerta became the President of the republic. A sham but legal process!

The situation in Mexico City was still in flux on the day of the inauguration. Huerta had reneged on the promise to guarantee the prisoners' safety. The Cuban Ambassador Marquez Sterling was so worried that he decided to sleep in the President's room on three chairs. The morning after the resignations Madero had no remaining bargaining chip. He now was a civilian at the mercy of Victoriano Huerta and without any guarantees. Pino Suarez, under arrest in the same room with Madero and Felipe Ángeles, prophesized "...to kill us would be equivalent to decreeing anarchy."[898] Madero is quoted as saying: "Will they have the stupidity to kill us? You know, they would gain nothing, for we would be greater in death than we are today in life."[899]

General Huerta knew what he would like to do with the former President. Providing Madero with safe conduct would have undoubtedly started a new revolution against the usurper and with a great likelihood of success. The first indications of trouble ahead poured in when three governors, Abraham Gonzalez, Maria Maytorena, and Venustiano Carranza declared themselves in revolt. All three ran states bordering the United States, namely Sonora, Chihuahua, and Coahuila respectively. Also, these states had been the backbone of Madero's revolutionary movement. The key to Madero's fate was one person: Ambassador Wilson. Huerta asked him for guidance that day. "He then asked me directly whether I thought it better to have Madero impeached by Congress for violation of the constitution or to incarcerate him in a lunatic asylum. I answered, with the concurrence of the German minister, that I ...could only express the hope that he would do what was right and best for the peace of Mexico."[900] Clearly, Huerta had been given a free hand. The usurper general now decided on the deportation option with a secret addendum attached to it.

According to William Bayard Hale, and seconded by Henry Lane Wilson, that evening "...[a] train stood ready at the Railway Station, to take Madero and Pino Suarez with their families down to Veracruz...By nine o'clock the families, hurriedly prepared for departure, were gathered, waiting, on the platform. The Chilean and Cuban Ministers, who had spent the day with Madero, had announced their intention of accompanying the party down to the port, they appeared at the station, announcing that the President and Vice President would soon follow. They did not come..."[901] Victoriano Huerta and Wilson blamed the fact that the deportation did not take place on Madero's wife. According to Wilson's version of the events, Sara Madero had sent advance telegrams to the military commander of Veracruz. The commander replied that he remained loyal to President Madero. Huerta therefore cancelled the transfer fearing that Madero would be freed and would immediately commence a counter-revolution.[902] The more likely explanation was that Huerta had decided to transport the prisoners somewhere away from eyewitnesses, have them taken off the train and shot. This scenario would have given Huerta the appearance of goodwill and, at the same time, the opportunity to blame Madero's murder on the Zapatistas. However, he did not want two ambassadors to be killed in the process.

The distraught wives of Madero and Pino Suarez now decided to enter the lion's den and appeal directly to the American ambassador. In a 1916 interview with American journalist Robert Hammond Murray, Sara Madero recalled the meeting:

"Q: When did you interview with the ambassador and what was his attitude and disposition? [A:] The evening of February 20th 1913. The ambassador showed that he was under the influence of liquor. Several times Mrs. Wilson had to intervene for him to guard his tone of conversation with us. It was a painful interview. I told the ambassador that we were seeking protection for the lives of the President and Vice President. 'Very well, ma'am,' he said 'and what is it you want me to do?' 'I want you to use your influence to save the life of my husband and the other prisoners.' 'That is a responsibility,' said the ambassador, 'for which I can not [sic] lend my name or that of my Government. I'll be frank with you, ma'am. The overthrow of your husband is caused by him never wanting to consult with me. You know, madam, your husband had very peculiar ideas.' I told him, 'Mr. Ambassador, my husband has no unique ideas, but high ideals.' He said that General Huerta had asked what should be done with the prisoners. 'What did you answer?' I asked. 'I told him what was best for the interests of the country,' said the ambassador. My sister-in-law, who accompanied me, could not help but interrupt saying, 'How could you say that? You know very well what kind of man Huerta and his people are, and [he] will kill them all.'

Q: What did the ambassador say to that?

A: He did not answer her, but turned to me and said, 'You know your husband is unpopular, that the people were not happy with your government and president.' 'Well,' I said, 'if that's true, why not set him free and let him go to Europe, where he could not do any harm?' The ambassador replied: 'Do not worry, there is no rush, no one will harm your husband. I knew the details of all that has happened. It was me who suggested that your husband should resign.'[903]

Before the women left the embassy, they handed Wilson a note from Madero's mother Mercedes addressed to the American President. In it she pleaded for the life of her son. Wilson at first refused to transmit the plea but later acquiesced since the diplomatic corps had seen it.

The next morning, Ambassador von Hintze also intervened on behalf of the prisoners. In a first step he visited with Ambassador Wilson and admonished him, "Madero's execution would represent a violation of the conscious agreement [of the embassy] and, further, a blemish upon his [Wilson's] activity in this revolution; if, on the other hand, he prevented the execution of these and for humanitarian reasons, he would add a page of honor to his country's history and to his own achievements."[904] With Wilson in tow von Hintze then went to see Huerta. Wilson made no effort to extract any firm commitment from the general. However, von Hintze, after some tougher prodding, did. He recorded the conversation in his diary: "...he [Huerta] gives his word of honor that F. Madero's life would be spared and protected, no matter what happens. I: That is a valuable assurance, but who will take responsibility for the zeal or excesses of some guard or watchman or some other subordinate? Huerta: I also take responsibility for that with my word of honor. I: We take your word, General, given as it is in the presence of the American ambassador and myself, as a complete guarantee. Huerta: Short of an earthquake, he will be safe."[905]

The day went by without promise of any solution for the prisoners. Wilson busied himself with plotting the de-facto recognition of Huerta as President, which he had promised to the conspirators. Despite a cable from Secretary Knox not to take any steps that would give the impression of recognition, Wilson cabled to the American consulates in Mexico "in the interest of Mexico [I] urge general submission and adhesion to the new government which will be recognized by all foreign states today."[906] Von Hintze refused to be railroaded into any commitment. He knew of Wilson's instructions not to give any recognition to the new government, which is evidenced in a cable he sent to the Foreign Office on February 21st.[907] The German ambassador also caused the rest of the diplomatic corps to stand up to Wilson.

The next day, General Huerta and the diplomatic corps met at the statue of George Washington, which the American government had donated to Mexico in February 1912 in honor of the recent victory of democracy. What could only be understood as a cynical joke of history, Ambassador Wilson and President Huerta laid wreaths on the foot of the statue and gave speeches. Meanwhile in the Presidential Palace, Mercedes Madero was allowed to visit her son. She told him of the murder of Gustavo. He was stricken with grief and sorrow. In Chihuahua, the dark clouds of dictatorship descended on Abraham Gonzalez who also was arrested. That night, according to historian Ross, Felipe

Ángeles thought that Madero hid his head under a blanket and cried. What finally broke this strong, principled, and courageous man was not the coup against him, or the imprisonment. It was the murder of his beloved brother, the lifelong partner in almost every endeavor. Madero blamed his brother's death on himself.

At eleven o'clock that night the prisoners were roused. Major Cardenas, a guard the prisoners had never before met, ordered them to get dressed. They were to be transferred to the penitentiary. Cardenas ordered Felipe Ángeles to stay behind. Then Madero and Pino Suarez left in two cars. The cars drove to the penitentiary only a few blocks away but passed by the main entrance. The motorcade stopped at the far end of the prison where security lights illuminated the wall. Colonel Cardenas opened the door for Francisco Madero to exit. From behind the assassin pulled up a pistol and killed the President with two shots to the back of his head. Then the soldiers pulled Pino Suarez from the car and stood him against the prison wall. He was executed with a 38-caliber pistol. After the execution the soldiers riddled both cars with bullets to simulate an attack. The story, which the world would hear the next morning and which was published in all major U.S. papers, was that the prisoners had died in a crossfire when a rescue party tried to free the ousted President. Despite the cover story and the immediate autopsy, even the staunchly anti-Madero paper. The Washington Post published suspicions of Huerta's potential involvement in the murders. A desperate Mexican consul and close friend of Sommerfeld cabled from San Antonio on the morning of Madero's murder:

"Brother Felix Sommerfeld, I beg you, send me a telegram with anything you know. Felix reply urgently via telegraph.

M. A. Esteva"[908]

That day, at least one American paper reported the death by firing squad of Felix A. Sommerfeld,[909] while others rejoiced upon hearing that he was safe.[910]

On February 24th, the government turned the bodies of Francisco Madero and Pino Suarez over to their families. Scores of citizens had flocked to the site of the murder and spontaneously placed rocks over the spilled blood. As the reality of the enormous loss and demolition of Mexico's first democracy settled in, more and more mourners dared to show their support for the fallen leader. Conducted without official pomp or fanfare, President Madero's funeral on the 24th hardly found mention in the U.S. press or Mexico's for that matter. He was laid to rest at the French Cemetery. Right after the funeral, Madero's wife Sara, his sisters, parents, and uncle Ernesto and his spouse boarded a train bound for Veracruz. From there a Cuban steamer brought them to Havana into safety. Madero's brothers Emilio, Alfonso, and Raul fled to the United States.

Rear Admiral von Hintze did not attend the funeral. Sommerfeld found him that morning "lying on the floor and blood running out of his mouth."[911] Weakened by the around-the-clock demands of the previous weeks, and affected by the horrific conditions in the battered city, the German diplomat suffered from a flame up of amoebic dysentery.[912] The symptoms are debilitating and can lead to more serious complications, such as kidney failure and severe dehydration. Von Hintze had contracted this contagious tropical disease while serving in the navy. The aggressive amoebas attack the walls of the large intestine and cause bleeding ulcers. The symptoms are high fever, vomiting, diarrhea, and abdominal pain. Dysentery takes three to four weeks to subside, which matches the available historical data. However, vomiting blood, as Sommerfeld described, is not an expected symptom.

Ambassador von Hintze's role on the crucial days of February 17th and 18th is one that has been misinterpreted or ignored. Historians such as Katz, Baecker, Henderson, Ross and others correctly understood that the German ambassador was under orders from the Foreign Office not to commit an open affront against Ambassador Wilson. What they did not appreciate sufficiently is that von Hintze was a highly intelligent, perceptive, and courageous player, not at all afraid of or intimidated by Ambassador Wilson. While officially appearing supportive of Wilson, he clearly undermined, softened, and counteracted the American ambassador's reckless schemes. While virtually all American historians have steadfastly maintained that Germany supported Madero's overthrow and Huerta's presidency, the facts support the opposite: Von Hintze generally worked constructively with Madero, concluded trade and arms contracts (which was the most important facet of his instructions from Germany), and even received satisfaction for crimes against German citizens. He only once supported Huerta, namely when the coup seemed a foregone conclusion. From a chess player's point of view, which von Hintze certainly was, propping up Huerta and pitting his power against the influence of Ambassador Wilson and his puppet Diaz appeared to be the only remaining move on the morning of February 17th. If Madero had followed the German ambassador's advice, he would have lived to fight another day or, at least, would have lived which seemed to have been one of von Hintze's immediate humanitarian concerns.

In any case, on the day of the funeral, the ambassador was gravely ill and could not further influence Henry Lane Wilson's machinations. Wilson meanwhile pushed through his agenda for acknowledging all of the demands placed upon Madero in the note of September 15th 1912, which had listed all the "cases" of violence against American citizens. Huerta signed whatever Wilson put in front of him. From his sickbed von Hintze wrote to the Foreign Office on the 28th of February, "Wilson is currently in charge of Mexico, without even trying to hide that appearance. He openly admits: I won't have put on their feet this Government that have [sic] been on their knees without getting my due compensation."[913] In the same memorandum, von Hintze mentioned that not only Wilson received his due compensation. "[T]he current interim President General Huerta on the day of the coup – 18th of February – had his pockets stuffed with 500 peso notes; He [Huerta] handed the head of the American cable service, who informed me on this, three or four of these banknotes and asked him to cable the news of the coup, naturally with a sympathetic twist. Typically Mexican Generals do not carry bundles of 500 peso notes around with them."[914] Considering a bundle of fifty five-hundred-peso-notes to be worth around a quarter-of-a-million Dollars in today's value, the ambassador's information documents Huerta's pay-off for the coup to have been in the millions of Dollars. Von Hintze did not know where the money came from but suspected "American and Cientifico interests."[915]

Huerta publicly promised to order an investigation into the murders. Ambassador Wilson who had cabled the official cover story to Washington also clamored for an inquiry after no one believed the official version. The assassin, Major Cardenas, was briefly arrested and arraigned, then promoted Lieutenant Colonel and sent back to his home in Michoacán. In 1914, he fled to Guatemala before Pancho Villa could arrest and execute him. Felipe Ángeles remained in prison, as did Abraham Gonzalez.

Three days after Madero's funeral, BI agent Blanford in El Paso reported to his superiors that, on the previous day, Pancho Villa had left the city and entered Mexico via Columbus, New Mexico.[916] As a matter of fact, according to his biographer Friedrich Katz, Villa was on the way to Tucson, Arizona. The governor of Sonora, José Maria Maytorena, rather than awaiting arrest by Huerta troops, had fled to the safety of the Arizona town. Villa wanted Maytorena's help to raise an army in Chihuahua. In a separate meeting in Tucson with Mexican general and future president Adolfo de la Huerta, Villa received an invitation to join the resistance in Sonora. He declined on the grounds that his home state was Chihuahua (although he was actually born in Durango). When Maytorena and Villa finally met, the exiled governor, who did not want to see Villa anywhere near Sonora, gave him $1,000 for his venture.[917] Villa returned to Texas and began preparations for an uprising. In his eyes and those of most committed revolutionaries, Abraham Gonzalez was the only revolutionary of national stature left to head a new revolution. However, he remained under arrest in Chihuahua.

As it became clear that the opposition to the new regime would be formidable with Coahuila, Chihuahua, Sonora, and Morelos erupting in violence, Huerta decided to eliminate the most probable leader of the new revolution. He used the playbook that he likely had written initially for President Madero. On the 6th of March,

"...a military detail arrived in Chihuahua to escort the former governor [Abraham Gonzalez] to Mexico City. Three officers, Major Benjamin Camarena, Captain Hernando Limon, and Lieutenant Federico Revilla, presented an order from General Huerta for the transfer of Gonzalez. To comply with the order without exciting popular curiosity, Rabago arranged for the commission to take the prisoner the same night. The escort and Gonzalez boarded a special Pullman car and the train departed at 11:30 p.m. without lights or whistles that might attract attention. They traveled roughly forty miles south to a place near Bachimba Pass, where Camarena signaled a stop with a hand lantern, then ordered Gonzalez to step down from the coach. After the soldiers climbed out, the officer told the engineer to move the train down the tracks three kilometers and wait half an hour before returning....Camarena shot Gonzalez to death. The escort then buried his bullet-riddled body in a shallow grave where he fell."[918]

On Tuesday, March 4th 1913, barely two weeks after the tragic end to the uprising in Mexico City, President Wilson became the 28th President of the United States of America. On a slightly overcast day without precipitation, several hundred thousand American citizens and well-wishers lined the streets of Washington to greet their new leader. It was the celebration of a peaceful transition of power that the American representative in Mexico had just denied its people. President Wilson did not immediately realize the breadth of the ambassador's involvement. However, the nagging questions of who ordered the murder of President Madero lingered. The New York World was the first

American daily to investigate and publish accounts of the ambassador's scandalous behavior. The new American President immediately announced that until all the facts of the coup were on the table there would be no recognition of the Huerta regime. In June, Woodrow Wilson sent his personal friend William Bayard Hale to Mexico to interview all parties involved and report the facts, as he understood them, back to him. Hale concluded,

"...being a man of intense prejudices, he [H. L. Wilson] was so blinded by his hatred of Madero that he honestly mistook it for the hatred of the whole Mexican people...It is hardly a matter of conjecture...that without the countenance of the American Ambassador given to Huerta's proposal to betray the President, the revolt would have failed. On Monday the 17th, the last day of the fighting, Madero was in undisputed possession of the entire city, except the arsenal and three or four houses near it...No sympathetic uprisings had occurred in the country...There was not a moment during the 'Decena Tragica' when it would not have been possible to 'end the distressing situation,' 'put a stop to this unnecessary bloodshed' by stern warning from the American Embassy...President Madero was not betrayed and arrested by his officers until it had been ascertained that the American Ambassador had no objection to the performance...It cannot but be a course of grief that what is probably the most dramatic story in which an American diplomatic officer has ever been involved, should be a story of sympathy with treason, perfidy and assassination in an assault on constitutional government...Trifling, perhaps, in the sum of miseries that have flowed from it, yet not without importance in a way, is the fact that thousands of Mexicans believe that the Ambassador acted on instructions from Washington..."[919]

Without giving any undue sympathy to the activities of the American ambassador, the success of his plan depended on complicity from both the press and the Taft administration. American newspapers were undeniable accomplices in the flawed reporting that emanated from the embassy and led to Madero's fall. Illustrating this point are selective headlines of the Washington Post, the New York Times, and the San Antonio Light. These papers were by no means the only ones featuring tainted facts. They represent the mainstream of American news in that week. The Washington Post had reported throughout the week that the rebels had the upper hand in the situation. On Sunday, the 10th of February, the Post reported, "the president was besieged."[920] The San Antonio Light went even further and reported that same day, that "Diaz controls Capital; Madero flees; Massacre by Zapatistas is feared."[921] On Tuesday, the Post claimed unashamedly that despite being besieged Madero "had gone to Cuernavaca and returned. The rebel reinforcements were gathering in the suburbs of Mexico City, the federal reinforcements were small." [922] On Wednesday, the propaganda machine churned even harder, with the Washington Post reporting on 35,000 troops at the Mexican border "waiting for word" to attack.[923] The paper also reported two American women having been killed, and that the American consulate was wrecked and warships being sent to the region.[924] On Thursday, the Post reported, "Federal troops seized homes of Americans and drove the occupants into the streets." The San Antonio Light carried the same story but revealed its source: "Ambassador Wilson's dispatches today report that many houses occupied by Americans have been seized by federal troops..."[925] On the 15th, the San Antonio Light reported its own wishful thinking: "Madero disappears from Palace."[926] On Tuesday the 18th, before the arrest of Madero, the Post reported, "General Diaz has occupied the Palace." Both the Washington Post and the San Antonio Light reported that two thousand marines were activated and "an expeditionary force prepared." [927] Finally, on Wednesday, the Washington Post headlines read: "Madero is arrested," "Crowd shouts 'Vivas' for Diaz and Huerta."[928] The New York Times, which seconded the barrage of lies spread about the situation in Mexico City, featured a full page spread on Felix Diaz on the 16th, presenting the "favorite of the former President [Diaz]" as the savior of Mexico. The paper speculated that the loyal nephew would step aside for his uncle to resume the presidency of Mexico.[929]

Of course all these reports grossly misrepresented the facts. There were no 35,000 troops, the warships moved up the Mexican coasts ready to take on refugees not to land troops, no marines were heading to Mexico, no Americans had been driven to the streets, or American women shot; the American embassy was safe at all times; even the "Vivas" for the victorious conspirators were muted. Immediately after the arrest of Madero became known, the governors of the northern states declared themselves in revolt and regional outbreaks of violence occurred in fourteen states. The reports of the American press in harmony with the interventionists' efforts to depose the Mexican President also taint the denials of complicity of the Taft government. One single press conference by the American President or his Secretary of State could have rectified the false reporting in that week and would have demolished Henry Lane Wilson's plans. Instead, the White House let it be known that meetings were going on to "determine" what to do with respect to

Mexico, which clearly left intervention on the table as an option. Senators William Alden Smith and Albert B. Fall of the Foreign Relations Committee openly called for intervention thus aiding the coup d'état against a democratically elected President. One can only conclude that most of the American government, including the President himself at least tacitly, more likely actively, supported the coup. Furthermore, the misinformation printed in the largest American papers clearly had the American ambassador's fingerprints all over it. That being the case, the reporting on Mexican affairs in that week was one of the saddest and most shameful performances in the history of the press, the "fifth column of democracy."[930]

The widow of the slain President seconded Hale's opinion and told a reporter for the New York World in 1916, "I have the firm conviction that if the ambassador had made strong representations, as in the interest of humanity he could reasonably be expected to do, not only would this have saved the lives of the President and Vice President, but it would have avoided the responsibility for the actions of the diplomatic representative in Mexico to be placed on the United States."[931] The violent end of the Mexican President, the Vice President, the governor of Chihuahua, generals, politicians, and many civilians in what would be etched into history books as the "Decena Tragica" marked the beginning of the most violent phase of the Mexican Revolution. An estimated one million Mexicans would succumb to violent deaths, fully six percent of the entire population. The choice for government in Mexico had become one of black or white, radical or reactionary. As Pancho Villa told a hacendado years later, "...you did not understand that this government [Madero] would not have disturbed you and you would have continued to be the masters, since Maderito's family and he himself had ties to all members of the high aristocracy, and these ties would have allowed you to remain where you were."[932]

Madero had become a martyr. With Gonzalez murdered, Venustiano Carranza took over the formal leadership of the new revolution calling himself "First Chief of the Constitutionalist Forces." Within days he approached a familiar face in revolutionary matters, Sherburne G. Hopkins. With the customary fee of fifty thousand dollars, Hopkins gladly accepted the job.[933] The inauguration of the Wilson administration released him from any loyalty he had felt towards Secretary Knox. Although not known for his sentimentality, he strongly disagreed with the role of Ambassador Wilson in the overthrow of his client. From his understanding of the situation in Mexico, Hopkins knew that the reactionary forces of Mexico could not succeed in the long run. It is the same assessment that von Hintze communicated to British Ambassador Stronge several weeks before.

Felix Sommerfeld left Mexico City for Havana on the 14th of March. Von Hintze, who had been recalled for recuperation, accompanied him, and gave him diplomatic protection. For the rest of his life, Sommerfeld professed deep gratitude to the German ambassador and credited him with having saved his life.[934] Von Hintze continued on to the city of Baden Baden where he attended to his weakened condition. He returned to Mexico in September. Felix Sommerfeld made his way from Havana to Washington D.C. where he met with Hopkins. Peter Bruchhausen, Sommerfeld's secret service handler had already left Mexico City for a new assignment on February 25th.[935] The German commercial attaché took on an assignment in Buenos Aires, where he became attached to the German embassy until his retirement from the diplomatic corps. Sommerfeld had no known contact with him until May of 1915, when the German naval intelligence agent Franz Rintelen suddenly appeared in New York and contacted Sommerfeld with an introductory letter from Bruchhausen.[936] American authorities had meanwhile indicted Enrique Llorente for breaking the Neutrality Laws. Hopkins arranged for the former consul's defense. As expected, the charges were dropped. Llorente joined Sommerfeld on the border a few weeks later. Carranza stayed in Coahuila but established a revolutionary junta in San Antonio to prepare the offensive against the Huerta regime. The new movement called itself the "Constitutionalists." Felipe Ángeles languished in prison until July 1913. After he made it to safety in the United States he joined the movement and became one of the most influential military tacticians in the Mexican Revolution. On January 23rd 1913, Karl Boy-Ed had stepped off a steamer en route from Hamburg, Germany.[937] The former subordinate of von Hintze, officially the new naval attaché of the embassies of Washington and Mexico City, now also became the new spymaster for the clandestine assets of the German navy on the North American continent. Sommerfeld, who met him in New York a year later, became his most valuable agent.[938]

Ambassador Wilson immediately started on his personal vendetta against President Wilson. In the beginning of March, the New York World and Harper's Weekly Magazine started publishing investigative reports indicting the ambassador for the events in Mexico. In response the "Committee of the American Colony" in Mexico City published the "facts" of the ambassador's "heroic defense" of American and foreign interests in the "Decena Tragica."[939] It did not help. Woodrow Wilson and Secretary of State Bryan were horrified as they learned the details of the ambassador's actions. Bryan recalled him to the United States in August, debriefed, and fired him.[940] Rather than retiring in quiet, the former ambassador went on speaking tours and wrote editorials defending his actions. He filed a massive lawsuit against the New York World and Harper's Magazine for ruining his reputation.[941] Until his death in 1932, he never regretted a single aspect of his activities in Mexico. His racism, utter lack of conscience, low intelligence - maybe even mental instability - did not allow for the slightest accommodation. However, none of the justifications that he summarized in an autobiography in 1927 could change the fact that he had done immeasurable harm to Mexico and American foreign policy. President Taft, Secretary Knox, the large daily newspapers in the United States, Senators Fall, Smith, and others remained untainted despite the overwhelming evidence of their complicity.

PART IV

~

INSURGENCY

CHAPTER 17

~

THE FIGHT AGAINST THE USURPER

The revolt against General Huerta blossomed within weeks of the murder of Madero. Most of the old revolutionary guard who had supported Madero's rise to power reassembled its resources and entered the field united under the Constitutionalist banner. Not joining in was Pascual Orozco who had broken with too many of the revolutionary leaders and who saw a chance to move to the top of the federal military response. While the entire north of Mexico exploded in rebellion, the revolutionary elites in Mexico City, the likes of former President Francisco Leon De La Barra, former Foreign Secretaries Pedro Lascurain and Manuel Calero cautiously joined Huerta. While it is easy to question the moral composition of these former members of Madero's administration, the Constitutionalist's sudden professed loyalty to the murdered President raised the same issue. Forgotten were the criticisms of the Madero government from within his own party, the disillusion of Madero's supporters when governance replaced the revolution. Without a doubt the subtle but relentless passive resistance from his own party that dogged the Madero presidency had encouraged the reactionary forces to make their move. Pancho Villa who now professed unconditional loyalty to his fallen idols Madero and Gonzalez came out of exile to join the fight. Just a few months before Carranza like many of Madero's early supporters had chimed in the chorus of politicians criticizing the government for its inefficiency and indecisiveness. Emiliano Zapata true to his constituency did not formally join the Constitutionalist movement but continued his fight against the Mexican central government that happened to be Huerta's at this juncture.

Quickly filling the void that the murder of Abraham Gonzalez left, Carranza gelled the infant resistance movement into a provisional government and a loosely coordinated fighting force. In Sonora, the rebels under the leadership of Alvaro Obregon quickly dislodged the federal forces and took charge of the important customs houses of Nogales and Agua Prieta. In Chihuahua, schoolteacher turned revolutionary Manuel Chao attacked the federal forces at Parral and, while not winning, decimated the defending force under General Mercado. Pancho Villa who had been in contact with Abraham Gonzalez up to his murder entered Mexico on March 6th 1913 with eight men, a few hundred rounds of ammunition, and what remained of the $1,000 contribution he had received from Maytorena.[942] Taken at face value, Villa's return from exile to join the revolution sounds quixotic. However, a few hundred dollars, a few trusted men, and his ability to focus the rage over his imprisonment and forced exile on the person of Huerta made him a prime candidate to rally the Chihuahuan lower classes behind a charismatic leader.

"Charismatic" is the one description of the First Chief Venustiano Carranza that came to no one's mind. Six foot four inches tall, bespectacled with a long, flowing beard, Carranza was of impressive stature. However, behind the glasses a guarded and stern look dominated the largely obscured features. He was a man who did not like to communicate spontaneously, weighed every word when he did, and seemed utterly devoid of humor or emotion. Similar to Madero, but without the charisma, Carranza was a stickler for rules and process. Anything outside his reading of the law would meet with insurmountable rejection on principle. People who did not understand how to approach the man considered him stubborn, even obstinate and pigheaded. Carranza's personality uniquely served to tear down foreign semi-colonial attitudes towards Mexico. In the face of overwhelming pressure to cave Carranza held his ground, whether against fellow revolutionaries or the American President. As the Mexican ship rocked in the violent storms of the revolution Carranza projected the image of a leader who was courageous, steady, confident, unemotional, and, most importantly, deliberate, and wise. People's loyalty came from the perceived wisdom of the otherwise aloof leader. He paved the way for Mexico to grow its own, indigenous political system largely independent of foreign influence and power.[943]

Born on December 28th 1859, he grew up on a cattle ranch in the desert of central Coahuila. Unlike Madero, Carranza was educated in Mexico only, and never went beyond preparatory school in the capital. The Carranzas, like so many northern landowners, became members of the politically disenfranchised northern middle class that eventually chose Francisco Madero, a fellow Coahuilan, as their leader. Initially, however, Venustiano Carranza supported Porfirio Diaz, which bore fruit for the young politician. Carranza became mayor of his hometown in the 1880s. In a burst of courageous opposition to Porfirian corruption, he and his brother mounted a rebellion against the governor of Coahuila in 1893. Bernardo Reyes, who had the task of settling the upheaval, supported rather than persecuted the young rebels. Thanks to the general's good word, Diaz allowed Carranza to first become a state representative, and, in 1904, senator of his home state. In 1908, while the first voices of opposition to Diaz' candidacy for President became heard, the Coahuilan sought an appointment as governor. He failed and, whether directly related or not, the senator threw his lot in with the leader of the anti-reelectionist party and the man who saved him from the dictator's wrath, General Bernardo Reyes.

With respect to his politics, land reform and radical social transformation constituted a threat rather than a goal for the Coahuilan politician. These political views closely matched Madero's. He differed from Madero in one important aspect: Carranza recognized the corrupting influence of foreign businesses and investment on Mexican politics. While Madero largely ignored, maybe even supported interests of foreign corporations in Mexico, Carranza was a very vocal supporter of indigenous ownership of natural resources and of a political system free from foreign influence. Rather than allowing special rules to apply to foreign capital, he insisted on all corporations to follow existing law. His nationalist rhetoric gained him crucial support from the lower classes of Mexico that otherwise had not much in common with the wealthy landowner turned politician from Coahuila. When Reyes disappeared from the political landscape of the 1910 elections on a European mission, Carranza joined Madero's junta to oust the old dictator. Carranza played a largely undefined but certainly important role in the negotiations with José Ives Limantour in New York in 1911 that led to the quick demise of the dictator.[944]

After Diaz left for Spain, Madero rewarded Carranza's work on behalf of the revolutionary junta with the office of Secretary of War. The assignment turned out to be a blunder since Carranza had never served in any army or military capacity. He was highly unpopular with the federal military and irregular forces alike. A few months into the De La Barra administration, Madero shuffled the cabinet and appointed Carranza provisional governor of Coahuila. In the fall elections of 1911, Carranza won the state office by a majority of the popular vote. When he called on the revolutionaries all across Mexico to come together under the banner of Constitutionalism in March of 1913, he was the only remaining, constitutionally elected governor in the country. On April 19th 1913, an agreement between the rebel forces of Sonora,

Chihuahua, and Coahuila formally created the Constitutionalist government with Carranza as its titular head.[945] As the principle document justifying the uprising against the central government, the group adopted the Plan de Guadalupe, which Carranza had authored.[946]

Although the flames of rebellion flickered and spread all across the country, Huerta was a formidable opponent. The military establishment, which had largely rejected Madero, quickly fell in line behind the new ruler. With Abraham Gonzalez silenced, the irregular revolutionary forces largely dispersed, and the main power brokers of the country firmly behind the new leader, Huerta's consolidation of power seemed a foregone conclusion. The internationally recognized political leaders of Mexico, De La Barra, Lascurain, and Calero lent legitimacy to the new government. For a short while it seemed that international recognition and a few mop up campaigns would be all that stood in the way of pacification and stability - at least in the opinion of Ambassador Wilson who sent the most glowing political reports to Washington. He minimized the amount of resistance developing against the usurper government and predicted the Constitutionalist's quick demise.

While President Taft and Philander Knox might have accepted some of H. L. Wilson's politically motivated and untrue reports at face value, the new administration did not. Secretary Bryan received consular reports from Ciudad Juarez, Guaymas, Saltillo, Torreon, Hermosillo, and Nogales that painted a diametrically opposed picture to the reports from the embassy in Mexico City. According to Consul Edwards in Juarez "the anti-Government faction...are daily growing in number..."[947] The new American administration also signaled a departure from the Dollar Diplomacy pursued by the previous administration. Rather than allowing American financial and business interests alone to narrowly define the course of foreign policy, Wilson signaled the need for long-term sustainability of governments as a guide to his decision-making process. Despite the relentless pressure of Ambassador Wilson to deliver on his promise of U.S. recognition of the new Mexican government, the American President refused to do so. For the first time in U.S. foreign policy a de-facto government would not receive recognition as such. The new American President, in part because of the overt and illegal involvement of his own ambassador, considered Huerta a usurper. In his estimation "...just governments rest always upon the consent of the governed, and there can be no freedom without order based upon law and upon the public conscience and approval. We shall lend our influence of every kind to the realization of these principles in fact and in practice..."[948] These words spoken on March 12th 1913 must have been music to the ears of Sherburne Hopkins and his new client Venustiano Carranza.

As the revolutionary generals Villa, Obregon, Chao, Urbina, Trevino, and others readied themselves for the coming civil war, Hopkins and Sommerfeld prepared the public relations and supply fronts in the United States. A Washington junta manned by Francisco Escudero and Roberto Pesquiera formally represented the Constitutionalists to the American government. However, behind the scenes was the law firm of Hopkins and Hopkins charged by Carranza to raise money and achieve recognition. While few documents have survived that detail the amount of work Hopkins dedicated to the Carranzista cause, one dated July 24th 1913, speaks volumes. In this memorandum officially authored by Escudero, President Wilson received the objectives of the anti-Huerta movement, which "inclined the president towards the Constitutionalists."[949] Of significance is not so much the content of the memorandum but the mode of transmission. Rather than going through the State Department's Latin American desk to the Secretary and perhaps from there to the President, Thomas S. Hopkins, Sherburne's father and law partner, sent it directly to the President's desk via Woodrow Wilson's personal secretary, Rudolph Forster.[950] Carranza had established a direct line of communication between himself and the American President!

Hopkins evidently convinced the President of supporting the Constitutionalists against the Huerta government very early on in 1913. In the wake of Huerta's coup the German Ambassador von Hintze wrote to Berlin "[Henry Lane] Wilson is currently ruling Mexico without even trying to hide the appearance."[951] Huerta, under pressure from the ambitious Wilson, had to agree in writing to American demands for payment of damages in life and property "in principle." [952] Huerta desperately tried to get formal U.S. recognition and therefore offered significant concessions, including elections, by the fall of 1913. However, Hopkins had enough clout with the new American administration to counteract the pressure. Rather than recognizing the new Mexican government, President Wilson sharply criticized Huerta and demanded free elections immediately. In the meantime, Wilson in his March 12th speech had offered to lend a helping hand to the forces of "constitutional rights." It would be up to the lobbying efforts of Sherburne Hopkins to define the extent to which President Wilson was willing to help.

Of utmost importance was the cutting off of funding for Huerta that would be effectively achieved by not recognizing his government. Sommerfeld told American interrogators in 1918, "...when Huerta wanted to make a loan we could protest and say it would not be recognized by the constitutionalist forces."[953] As benign as it sounds, Sommerfeld and Hopkins forced skittish investors in the U.S. and overseas to realize that their loans would not be repaid in case of a victory of the rebellion. Few lenders would take that gamble, as the situation in Mexico grew hotter by the day. Secondly, Hopkins used his old friends and clients, Charles Flint and Henry Clay Pierce, to help in a fund raising campaign for the revolutionary efforts. In an interview with the New York Times on June 30th 1914, Flint told the daily that there was "...nothing surprising about the fact that men interested in affairs in the Southern republic should want to advance money to end the struggle, and to prevent chaos which might follow the fall of the Carranza [sic – meant to be Huerta] Government." The article continued, "Mr. Flint said the financiers were simply acting to preserve their interests."[954] While Charles Flint made these statements eighteen months after Madero's fall, Hopkins had convinced the two financiers early on that Huerta would be bad for business and rallied their support while the U.S. government simultaneously withheld recognition.

Flint's statements and letters about this time are significant in many ways. The Wall Street financier had become a major investor in Henry Clay Pierce's Waters-Pierce Oil Company on the second of February 1913, when Pierce finally bought out John D. Rockefeller's interest in his company for $3 million.[955] As such Flint and Pierce now found themselves free to act and in direct competition with Standard Oil Company in Mexico. Rockefeller and Lord Cowdray saw their chance to get back into the game through Huerta. Thus, they supported the usurper. Pierce and Flint bet on the Constitutionalist horse. Anyone who knew the two tycoons realized that they did not often lose. The extent of the engagement against the Huerta government became clear in a letter Flint wrote to the Department of Justice on May 6th 1919: "I have known Mr. Sommerfeld since 1913, when he was introduced to my firm as an accredited purchaser of ammunition for the Revolutionary Government in Mexico; that is to say, the Carranza Government, which was then engaged in an endeavor to overthrow Huerta. As the law, at that time, permitted the export of munitions of war to Mexico, and as we had been, for many years, dealers in war material, we purchased for Mr. Sommerfeld rifles, ammunition, etc., which were, with the knowledge of the authorities, shipped to Mexico."[956]

In the letter he also alluded to a most amazing achievement of Hopkins in his lobbying efforts to destroy Huerta. Flint, who freely admitted to financing the Carranzista forces with arms as early as 1913, claimed that it was legal and transparent to the authorities. By law, the government of Mexico was the only legal entity that could import arms. Since the United States did not recognize Huerta, there was no legal government in Mexico. Strictly speaking, therefore, any exportation of munitions violated the Neutrality Laws. However, true to his offer to support the constitutional forces of Mexico, President Wilson approved exportation of war material to Carranza's forces while enforcing the arms embargo against Huerta. Agent Matthews of the BI in New Orleans aptly described the "official" attitude of the government vis-à-vis arms smuggling: "Huerta has not been recognized as legal President of Mexico, he is recognized only as the head of the 'defacto [sic]' government of some parts of Mexico but Carranza has only been recognized as such because the US Consuls of Sonora [,] Coahuila and Chihuahua have officials dealing with the officials of the Carranza government. Therefore … from the point of view of the US Authorities Carranza and Huerta are now on equal terms and if it is forbidden to Carranza to send arms and ammunition to Mexico it ought also to be forbidden to do so to [sic] Huerta…"[957]

In the 1919 letter, Charles Flint accurately described Sommerfeld's new job to the attorney general. The German agent became the main arms buyer for the Carranza-led opposition. The initial financing of the new revolution consisted of loans from Flint and Pierce with the stipulation that the war material was purchased from Flint and Co., New York. Sommerfeld also reactivated his organization along the border. With the guarantee from the American government that the arms embargo would not be enforced against the Constitutionalists, Sommerfeld and his people, under the eyes of customs collector Zach Cobb, border agents of the Justice Department, and the U.S. military, smuggled trainloads of arms into Mexico. The munitions factories took orders from Sommerfeld and others in New York, and then sent the supplies as consignments to the local arms dealers, who subsequently delivered them to Sommerfeld's agents for smuggling into Mexico. From his days as Pascual Orozco's nemesis Sommerfeld now reversed his role and used his expertise and the tacit approval of the U.S. government to supply the rebel force against the Mexican government. Saddled with these huge responsibilities, that could mean success or defeat for the rebels, the German agent spent April 1913 shuttling incessantly between Washington, New York, El Paso, and San Antonio.[958]

That month, Bureau of Investigation agents felt the temperature rise all along the border. While Carranza mounted the military resistance against Huerta in Coahuila, his people in Washington were busy setting up the political framework to allow an effective front against Huerta. At the same time,

Madero brothers Raul, Emilio, and Julio organized the junta in San Antonio that would be in charge of military supplies and recruitment. Juan Sanchez Azcona, one of Francisco Madero's oldest friends and compatriots, joined the Madero brothers at the Menger Hotel in San Antonio to help organize. Ernesto and Alberto Madero, the two uncles of the murdered President, worked the Carranza uprising from New York. Of course, the details of the revived Hopkins plan, this time to oust Huerta, remained unknown to the authorities on the ground. The border agents watching the tremendous arms smuggling operation unfold traced the financial source to Sommerfeld. "We have reason to believe that the Maderos [who had few funds of their own in the United States] ... are furnishing money to Carranza through Sommerfeld..."[959] A year later the missing link between the Maderos and the huge financial support became apparent to the BI. "This morning talked with the Chief of Bureau on the phone concerning the shipment of 3,000,000 ball cartridges which had been ordered from the Remington Arms Co. by Flint and Company of New York...Further Mr. Bruff [of the Remington Arms Co.] stated that he did not know for whom Flint and Company were acting, but he was of the belief that it was for General Carranza in Mexico."[960]

All along Flint and Pierce through Hopkins financed the uprising against Huerta. The link between the Carranzistas led by Hopkins in Washington and the San Antonio junta became Felix Sommerfeld. The German shuttled back and forth, reported on progress to both groups, and managed his secret service organization. Despite his super-human efforts, when the rebels finally started to receive resources from New York and Washington in May 1913, it was high time. Until then the conspirators had received little help from Carranza. Federal forces had routed the First Chief's Coahuilan irregulars in short order three times. Just as Sommerfeld and Hopkins succeeded in signing up Flint and Pierce, Carranza was fighting for his survival short of men, money, and material. On the Sonora front, however, maximizing his scarce resources with great tactical skill, Alvaro Obregon continued to expel the federals from the state, which he accomplished by late April. In Chihuahua the federals controlled mainly the Central Railroad corridor and large cities.

First signs of Sommerfeld reestablishing himself on the border became apparent in the last week of April 1913, when his old friend and confidante Sam Dreben screwed up. According to Dreben's biographer, the "Fighting Jew" welcomed the renewed action in Mexico and rejoined Sommerfeld's organization, this time not to prevent but to engage in smuggling of arms and ammunition.[961] Biographer Leibson describes "typical Dreben" escapades, including the daring hijacking of railcar loads of arms and ammunition in downtown El Paso. None of these stories can be verified in the BI records and might be slightly embellished. However, there is strong evidence that the State Department's indecision on whether to allow the importation of arms triggered desperate attempts to supply the fighting forces in Mexico. Sommerfeld this conundrum faced all along the border in April and May 1913.

The BI records document as outrageous a Dreben story as Leibson's, which happened in Piedras Negras. In charge of the Mexican Secret Service in San Antonio was Sommerfeld's chief T. R. Beltran who operated out of the Alamo Safe and Lock Company. Sometime in April, Beltran purchased 3,500 cartridges from a local arms dealer in San Antonio. Dreben had the task of driving the ammunition across the border at nearby Eagle Pass into Piedras Negras, Coahuila.[962] Additional supplies came from another hardware store. The exact amount of ammunition is unknown but several cars hauling significantly more than four cases of ammunition were involved in the operation.[963] Eagle Pass was the closest border crossing to San Antonio and became the crucial supply line for Carranza's forces in Coahuila.

According to the BI, Dreben "...was the man who hired the automobile to haul these supplies, and that the ammunition was loaded at the Alamo Safe and Lock Company's place of business at the corner of Market and Presa Streets..."[964] However, something went terribly wrong. It is unclear whether the BI had not yet received instructions from Washington to allow arms and ammunition to reach the Constitutionalists or whether an overzealous agent arrested the smugglers without authority. In any case, Dreben and four Mexicans, including one J. G. Hermosillo, were caught in the act of smuggling. Agents impounded the cars with the ammunition, while Dreben and his compatriots fled across the border into Piedras Negras. Losing the supplies meant for Dreben and his partners to not receive their commissions, and most likely face legal trouble in the U.S. When Beltran heard of the incident, he immediately went to see Dreben and Hermosillo. The two suspected that it had been Beltran who tipped off the American authorities. Beltran on the other hand accused Dreben of having abandoned the cars unnecessarily. No one accused Dreben of lacking courage without repercussion. In an argument, which played out on Main Street in Piedras Negras, Hermosillo apparently pulled a gun on Beltran. According to eyewitnesses, a firefight ensued between Beltran and Hermosillo that caused quite a commotion.[965] Dreben, whose role in the shootout is not documented, returned to the U.S. and was arrested.

Sommerfeld, who was staying in San Antonio at the time, immediately jumped into the fray. Within a day or two a telegram from BI Chief Bielaski to agent Thompson in San Antonio showed the clout Hopkins and Sommerfeld had with the highest echelons of the U.S. Justice Department. Without further explanation, Bielaski ordered the immediate release of Dreben and the cars.[966] Hermosillo remained in Piedras Negras. Agent Breniman filed papers to have him indicted "in absentia" for conspiracy to export. A grand jury returned the indictment on May 5th. On May 10th Sommerfeld had to go back to New York but returned in the same week.[967] Assuring Agent Barnes that the parties who were involved would stand trial in the United States, Sommerfeld was able to post bail for Hermosillo and the three others.[968] It was important to Sommerfeld to have his agents back for the many tasks ahead. As one could have expected, the indictments had little effect. Dreben and the other driver pleaded guilty and were fined $500 each in January 1914. The judge dismissed the charges against Hermosillo and one other. The remaining three were long gone somewhere in Mexico.[969] Sommerfeld somehow had settled the differences between Beltran, Hermosillo, and Dreben. One can only muse how the tough German agent reinstated discipline among his agents. With the weapons and ammunition returned to their owners, Dreben at the very least made his cut.

Sommerfeld's cozy relationship with the federal U.S. authorities was nothing short of astonishing. Already in 1912, Sommerfeld's agents arrested or caused the arrest of anyone engaged in the Orozco uprising against President Madero. Some of these prisoners were tried or released, but, as an investigative report in the Washington Post on August 11th 1913 revealed, most remained locked up for years. Significant about the Washington Post piece is the fact that the detention of Mexican revolutionaries extended beyond the Orozco uprising and the Taft administration. At the behest of Hopkins and Sommerfeld, the military authorities at Fort Bliss held two hundred and thirty persons without trial beyond the forty-day-limit allowed for extradition papers to be filed. Since Orozco had declared for Huerta, the prisoners in Fort Bliss remained incarcerated indefinitely without legal cause. When a local judge tried to order their release, U.S. military authorities simply moved the prisoners to San Diego where the Texas judge had no authority. There are no sources detailing the final fate of the political prisoners of Fort Bliss, but undoubtedly the U.S. military and Sommerfeld made sure they would not become combatants against the Constitutionalist forces.[970]

The shoot-out episode in Piedras Negras and resulting troubles for Sommerfeld must have been quite a distraction for the busy German. His travels in May can only be described as frantic. He was in San Antonio on May 1st, on May 10th in New York, on May 15th in San Antonio, on May 20th New Orleans, May 24th New York, and on June 5th back in San Antonio. The visits in San Antonio also included "frequent trips to Piedras Negras" with Juan Sanchez Azcona where, according to Agent Thompson of the BI, "they have conferences with Governor Carranza." Thompson in the same memo alluded to his difficulty dealing with the renewed activities on the border, explaining to the Chief, "...you will realize that this [covering the movements of the Constitutionalists in the U.S.] is a difficult matter with no agent for this City and only three men to cover the entire border from Yuma, Arizona to Brownsville, Texas."[971] All the notorious characters that filled the BI reports at the height of Orozco's uprising now reappeared. Sommerfeld's regional chiefs Teódulo Beltran (San Antonio), Henry Kramp and Hector Ramos (El Paso) received reinforcements from Ernesto Fernandez (New Orleans). Also reporting back to the Secret Service were Powell Roberts, H. A. Thompson, Jack Noonan, Emil Holmdahl, Sam Dreben, and a host of lower cadres of agents. They swarmed every city, every border crossing in every state along the border. Missing was Louis E. Ross who after switching from the BI to the Sommerfeld organization in 1912 had committed armed robbery in El Paso in January 1913 and was cooling his heels in jail awaiting trial.[972] Also missing was Abraham Molina, the corrupt former secret service chief who had plotted against his boss in 1912. Molina worked for the Villa purchasing agents in El Paso, procuring miscellaneous supplies.[973]

While the BI could trace a few thousand rounds here and few thousand there, as was the case with the Dreben incident, the floodgates of arms and ammunition for the Carranza troops suddenly flew wide open. Agent Offley from New York reported on May 23rd 1913 that nineteen arms dealers from Galveston, Texas to Los Angeles, California were receiving shipments from the Winchester and Remington factories in Connecticut. He surmised that it was Sommerfeld who ran the logistics. According to BI agent Offley, the revolutionaries had purchased 100,000 rounds of 7mm Mauser cartridges from Remington to support the 50,000 Mauser rifles ordered in Germany. "Summerfield [sic] left San Antonio on the 10th instant for New York City where he will probably communicate with Ed Maurer, Maiden Lane and endeavor to arrange for the further purchase of ammunition."[974] On May 21st agents on the border were trying to watch over the distribution of 63,500 7mm Mauser cartridges which were "consigned to a little gulf port between Galveston and

Corpus Christi, where there is absolutely no demand for anything of this character."[975]

The Shelton-Payne Arms Company quickly became Sommerfeld's preferred dealer to distribute arms and ammunition to the smugglers. The Mexican consulate in Naco, Arizona reported to the U.S. army commander in the city, Lieutenant Colonel A. C. Macomb on June 18th, "...the car of hay with ammunition smuggled through here several days ago, was brought from Benson and it probably went there from El Paso via the S.P. [Southern Pacific] Railroad...the Shelton Payne Arms Co. of El Paso, Texas, is the concern that ships ammunition for the rebels to Douglas."[976] One month later, on July 15th, Shelton Payne was caught with having shipped 446,000 rounds of ammunition "partly covered in coal."[977] As a matter of fact, Sommerfeld's secret service chief Powell Roberts had supervised the shoveling of coal over the munitions boxes at the Badger Fuel Company in El Paso directly under the eyes of military guards.[978] Since Sommerfeld had his run-ins with Krakauer, Zork and Moye who had supported Madero's opposition, Shelton Payne benefited as the recipient of some of the largest arms contracts ever issued to a single dealer. Further attracting the ire of Felix Sommerfeld, Adolph Krakauer continued to ship to the federals, although, when the money was right, they sold to the other side as well.[979] Also clandestinely supporting the Huerta military was Ketelsen and Degetau, the German-owned merchant house in Juarez and Chihuahua. In the Madero revolution Villa troops had looted and then torched the hardware store and warehouse in Juarez. Not surprisingly Ketelsen executives Goeldner and Kueck now supplied arms and ammunition to Villa's nemesis, Victoriano Huerta.[980] In circumstances that are still nebulous, Kueck's involvement with the Huerta government came to light in the summer of 1913. Barely escaping Villa's wrath, Kueck had to flee to the United States never to return to Mexico.[981]

Reports from the commanding officers of the Southern Department along the border speak to the extent of the smuggling effort: "The border is patrolled for more than three hundred miles daily and every effort is being made by the troops to stop the smuggling of arms and ammunition into Mexico. At some points, customs officers are only on duty during the day, leaving their posts vacant at night. Parties doing this smuggling resort to every illegitimate device to get ammunition through, --concealing it in cans, in baled hay, in coal cars covered with coal, etc..."[982] On July 26, Major E. L. Mitchie of the 13th Cavalry regiment reported to his superiors:

"I have no positive knowledge of any...allegations of collusion on the part of any United States civil officers charged with enforcing United States neutrality laws...However, it is well known that public sentiment favors the Constitutionalists, which undoubtedly influences the action of both state and federal officials...Reports from customs officials show that the Shelton-Payne Arms Co., having since January 1st received about two hundred cases rifles and about two million rounds of ammunition. This fact must be known by the officials of the Department of Justice in El Paso, and it must be presumed by all that this ammunition is sold by the Shelton-Payne Arms Co., to parties intending to smuggle it across the border in violation of the United States neutrality laws, as it is far in excess of what could be sold by this firm under normal conditions."[983]

The officer whose troops ostensibly were charged with enforcing the neutrality laws justifiably voiced surprise and frustration with his superiors. Clearly, the major accused the Justice Department, Customs, and local law enforcement authorities of collusion with the smugglers and the dealers supplying the contraband. The Sommerfeld organization was in full swing again, although, as the angry military officer's report shows, not all U.S. government authorities on the border were bought and paid for.

Of note is the BI's knowledge of the orders for Mauser rifles placed in Germany. While many American historians had claimed that Germany actively supported the Huerta government, the facts seem to indicate the opposite. There were two places through which German arms and ammunition could reach Mexico: New York and Mexico City. In New York, a suave and well-connected German reserve officer with the name of Hans Tauscher represented most of the German arms industry, including Mauser. The German arms merchant and German agent in World War I was best known for his wife: He was married to Johanna Gadski, one of the most famous sopranos in history. Gadski performed at the New York Metropolitan Opera from 1898 to 1904 and again from 1907 to 1917 after she had returned from London. Her renditions of Richard Wagner's bombastic operas were legendary, but she also shined in Verdi's Aida and other challenging Italian operas.

Hans Tauscher, in the shadow of his famous wife, established his business in New York around 1900. The German captain of the reserve became increasingly wealthy not only as a result of his wife's career but also because he represented the Friedrich Krupp AG in the U.S. The Washington Post estimated his annual income in 1905 to have exceeded $450,000 (close to ten million

Dollars in today's value).[984] Tauscher's social circle naturally included the German diplomats in the U.S., especially the German military and naval attachés. Tickets to Madame Gadski's star-studded performances were as coveted as were invitations to the after-parties where champagne flowed freely among the social crème de la crème of New York. Ever the connector, Stallforth had met the Tauschers on the Golden State Limited while traveling from New York to El Paso in the fall of 1912. Johanna Gadski's daughter Lotte memorialized the meeting in Frederico's guest book.[985] Thus Frederico Stallforth managed to finagle himself onto the guest lists of these exclusive after-show parties and mingled self-assuredly with New York's high society.

Hans Tauscher, with the help of Sommerfeld and Carl Heynen, took over the efforts of selling arms to Mexico from the stricken German Ambassador Admiral von Hintze. In 1911, the rear admiral had established direct contact with German arms merchants to supply President Madero. Only one of these orders saw actual shipments in Madero's time. All other orders remained on the books of the German suppliers.[986] By 1913, Sommerfeld had two goals: Prevent Huerta from buying arms in Germany and procure arms for Carranza. Preventing Huerta from obtaining financing effectively stopped arms shipments from Germany to Mexico. However, the procurement of arms for Carranza was much more complicated. As long as Huerta controlled the large Mexican harbors, German arms had to be shipped through the United States. Either through his friend Frederico Stallforth, or Carl Heynen, the head of HAPAG in Mexico, Sommerfeld came in contact with Tauscher. The Krupp representative placed orders for Carranza in Germany including the five hundred Mauser rifles mentioned in the BI reports.[987] However, the German government feared negative repercussions should these shipments become public knowledge or fall into the wrong hands. Not willing to ship arms through the United States, the German government impounded the shipment of the five hundred rifles in Hamburg. This shipment would become one of the causes of the U.S. military intervention in Mexico in the spring of 1914.

Sommerfeld received an interesting asset from the German government in March 1913. A deserter from the 19th Cavalry Regiment in Galveston suddenly reported to the German Consul Weber in Ciudad Juarez.[988] His name was Franz Wachendorf alias Horst von der Goltz. According to Frederico Stallforth, it was not Weber who first made contact with Wachendorf but Stallforth's brother Alberto who was the German Consul in Parral. Wachendorf wrote in his memoirs that Weber sent him to Consul Kueck in Chihuahua. Kueck obviously assigned him to Sommerfeld.[989] Alberto Stallforth also would have sent him to Sommerfeld. In his book *My Adventures as a German Secret Service Agent*, Wachendorf told harrowing tales of his activities as a spy for the Constitutionalists, including being captured and sentenced to death. While none of these fantastic stories can be verified, he was a German spy and he clearly worked for the Constitutionalists. In a picture on page 43 in his memoirs, Wachendorf stands behind Constitutionalist general Raul Madero next to his German secret service handler: Felix A. Sommerfeld.[990] Other than the uncorroborated stories in his memoirs, Wachendorf's exploits in Mexico are unknown. What is known, however, is that he borrowed money from the Stallforth brothers in Parral.

"He had been in Mexico at our office at Parral, Chih. Mexico, and he had asked my brother to loan him some money. I believe my brother gave him about 60 or 70 pesos. When in New York von der Goltz told us that he needed some dynamite and if we would be able to get him some. We told him no. A few days afterwards he came back and told us if we could cash a check of $200, this check was signed Capt. Papen, Military Attaché of the German Embassy and drawn on the Riggs National Bank in Washington. I told him I could cash him the check and my brother asked me to get for him the money that he had loaned him, and I retained 30 of $35 out of the money that I gave him back."[991]

992

Clearly Wachendorf became a military spy for Sommerfeld. A hair-raising story of his arrest by federal General Mercado seems to indicate that Sommerfeld had sent him into the federal garrison to find information regarding preparedness and strength of the federal forces. Supporting evidence is a detailed report that Ambassador von Hintze filed with the chancellery in Berlin dated October 27th 1913.[993] In it he relates very specific and detailed intelligence as to the shape of the Mexican federal army. Where he got this accurate information, that led him to a very sober assessment of Huerta's chances against the Constitutionalist opposition, can only be surmised. Placing one or more moles with the federal army certainly would have helped. Additionally, the desperation of Huerta to raise more troops made it very easy for anyone, especially someone with military background, to join up. After being set up with the Carranza opposition, Wachendorf appears to have worked for Sommerfeld until the Great War started and both agents transferred to New York. Wachendorf became a notorious sabotage agent for the German military attaché Franz von Papen in 1914.[994]

There is also no doubt that the German government was actively spying on the Mexican military in this period. There was good reason for doing that. Just as the Empire wanted to know in 1908 who would become the next ruler in Mexico, the same question arose again in 1913. In that year there were multiple accounts of German agents working in and around the border. Historians Harris and Sadler researched a curious swashbuckler with the name of Ivor Thord Gray.[995] Another German agent appeared on the scene in 1913 to work in the Carranza camp, most likely reporting to Sommerfeld. His name was Arnold Krumm-Heller, a colorful German nationalist, born in Westfalen, Germany. He left Germany "with permission of the military authority" at age eighteen and worked in Chile, Peru, and Mexico mostly as a scientist. Between 1907 and 1909 he studied medicine in Paris and transferred to Mexico in 1910. Krumm-Heller became Madero's private doctor in the beginning of 1911.[996] According to the MID, Krumm-Heller worked for Sommerfeld in the Mexican Secret Service in January of 1912. One year later, after Madero's murder, Krumm-Heller became a secret agent for Carranza who sent him on diplomatic missions to Texas. Then-Governor Ferguson, with the prodding from the German secret service agent, was the first U.S. state executive to formally recognize the Constitutionalists as the legitimate government of Mexico. Carranza also dispatched Krumm-Heller on diplomatic missions to Argentina and Chile.[997]

In June 1913, the Huerta government arrested Krumm-Heller, ostensibly for hosting a "meeting of socialists and anarchists."[998] Germany intervened on his behalf and affected his release. Appearing in El Paso in the summer of 1913, the trained doctor then met up again with Carranza and served as a colonel in the Constitutionalist army. He became General Obregon's chief of artillery. [999] In the First World War, Krumm-Heller worked for the German Secret Service. [1000] On a mission to Germany, British authorities arrested him at Falmouth as a spy. Because of his Mexican citizenship he could resume his trip to Berlin where the agent spent the rest of the war as the military attaché for the Mexican embassy.[1001] While in Mexico he also founded the Society of the Iron Cross, a Germanic-imperialist order, with Carranza as head and himself as secretary. While in his published works he presented himself as a "rational nationalist," the German government came to think of him as crazy. Krumm-Heller became fascinated with occultism in Paris in 1908. After he moved to Germany, he became a bishop in the Gnostic Church. He died in Germany in 1949.[1002]

As a result of the investigative reports of the New York World and Harper's Monthly Magazine on the Constitutionalist uprising, as well as the constant barrage of positive information about Carranza from Hopkins, President Wilson had lost all confidence in the State Department's reports about Mexico's current uprising. To both, the President and William Jennings Bryan, the State Department was infested with career diplomats raised in the Roosevelt and Taft years. To the American President this group appeared to enforce Dollar Diplomacy without regards to the ideals of democracy, self-determination, or moral compass. Henry Lane Wilson's reports, especially given his questionable role in the Madero assassination, were but one source of untrustworthy information. In the U.S. Senate the likes of Albert Fall and William Alden Smith continued to push their interventionist agendas, which progressives, including the President, suspected as stemming from Wall Street and high finance. "After discussing Mexico with his cabinet, Wilson concluded that 'they all lacked trustworthy information upon which to base a policy.' At a cabinet meeting of April 18, 1913, 'the advisability of sending a 'confidential man' to Mexico to 'study the situation and get exact facts' was one of the topics of discussion."[1003] The President made the decision to send his friend and campaign supporter William Bayard Hale to Mexico City. His mission resulted in the verification of H. L. Wilson's role in Madero's downfall and the ambassador's eventual firing.

Hale was not to be the only source that helped the new President navigate through the haze of Mexican policy, sidestepping the traditional chain of command of the State Department. John Lind, former governor of Minnesota and member of the House, joined Hale in the summer of 1913 in arranging an understanding with the Huerta government. In later years, lawyer Paul Fuller and Wilson's personal friend, Judge Duval West, negotiated on behalf of the President with Carranza. Wilson and Bryan also very effectively tapped other informal channels that were on a lower level. One such connection was George C. Carothers. Carothers was a consular agent, grocer, and real estate agent from Torreon who developed close relations with the northern revolutionary leadership - especially Carranza, Villa, and influential Mexican businessmen such as Lazaro De La Garza. De La Garza was to become the top financial agent of the Villa faction and wielded crucial influence in the revolutionary movement. Leon J. Canova, a journalist from Florida who was a friend of William Jennings Bryan, reported directly to the Secretary and supported Hale and Lind on their fact-finding missions. In 1915 he was appointed to the State Department and headed the Latin-American desk there. Another journalist who had followed the Madero uprising and became friends with Felix Sommerfeld was David Lawrence. Lawrence worked for AP News with Sommerfeld in 1911. One of the most famous American journalists ever, he ultimately became the founder and editor of US News and World Report. Wilson used him several times on special assignments in Mexico and enjoyed his sharp analyses of the Mexican struggles. Luther T. Ellsworth, American consul at Piedras Negras (across from Eagle Pass, Texas), had been a reliable State Department source of information both on the Madero revolution, Madero's administration, and on the rise of the Constitutionalists. W. J. Bryan noticed him for his steady reporting which had belied much of the misinformation spread by H. L. Wilson and the interventionist group around Senator Albert Fall. Ellsworth also supplied valuable intelligence to the Justice Department during the Orozco uprising. Marion Letcher, the American Consul in Chihuahua, and Thomas D. Edwards with his consular office in Ciudad Juarez supplemented the trustworthy sources of information of the President. The direct line from the consuls to the Wilson administration went through Zachary Lamar Cobb, the El Paso customs collector and political ally of Woodrow Wilson.[1004] Sherburne Hopkins and his father as well served as informal connections to the burgeoning resistance movement in Mexico for President Wilson.

One of the most important links between the American President and the rebels of Mexico was Felix A. Sommerfeld. The public record of Sommerfeld's role in early 1913 remains largely obscured. However, his documented acquaintance with Hale resulted from the aid he gave to Wilson's emissary in the spring and summer of 1913. [1005] Then according to Sommerfeld's testimony in 1918, Hale had a hard time negotiating with Carranza in the fall of 1913. To begin with the First Chief refused to see Wilson's emissary since Hale he did not have official government credentials. Always a stickler for process, Carranza wanted to force Wilson into a de-facto recognition that mandated a diplomatic representative to be dispatched to Carranza. Naturally, not lacking a measure of pigheadedness himself, Wilson did not accept. To prevent the issue from coming to a head, the Wilson administration relied on Felix Sommerfeld in November 1913 to intercede with Carranza. "While in Sonora Mr. William Hale came there and we went to the border and arranged a meeting between Carranza and Hale and acted as a go-between."[1006] It took Sommerfeld from November 2nd until November 12th to get Carranza to grant the audience.[1007] However, Sommerfeld's job had just started. Carranza refused to discuss anything that, in his opinion, touched upon affairs of a domestic nature. At issue was President Wilson's attempt to somehow arrive at a compromise government for Mexico that would be able to allow for and set up national elections. Of course, by November the Constitutionalists had just won several major battles and had no interest in compromise. The talks quickly stalled. According to historian Cumberland, Hale threatened U.S. intervention and Carranza retorted with the threat of war.[1008] Sommerfeld recalled, "...they [Hale and Carranza] were always sparring around and after the meetings I would go and talk to Carranza."[1009] The efforts of the German agent came to nothing. Hale and Carranza split in a huff. The First Chief's mode of operation, being dilatory, delegating, and insisting on written communication, directly contradicted Hale's "go-getter" energy.[1010]

Sommerfeld tried again to bridge the gap. At the urging of Secretary of State Bryan, the German agent rushed to Tucson, Arizona on November 10th 1913, where Hale waited in vain to be received by Carranza:[1011] "I came back because I heard that Dr. Hale had left Carranza in disgust or anger. I met Dr. Hale in Arizona and told him not to lose his patience because Carranza was stubborn and wouldn't let the United States interfere in Mexican politics. He wouldn't discuss politics with Dr. Hale. I told him 'sit still, I am going down to see him.'...I tried to coax him to come off the high horse. He wouldn't...[1012] The problems Hale faced in relating to the First Chief were symptomatic for many who had dealings with the stubborn politician from Coahuila. In part because of his failed attempts to broker an agreement between Hale and Carranza, Sommerfeld realized that he as well could not get along with Carranza. It is unclear whether, as Sommerfeld recounted, Carranza asked him to work with Villa, or whether Sommerfeld was fired as a result of the Hale intervention. However, around Christmas 1913, Sommerfeld switched from the Carranza to the Villa camp. From that moment on Carranza is not known to have ever again personally interacted with Sommerfeld. Historical sources after December 1913 show only Hopkins officially working for Carranza. One other fact, however, became painfully apparent: The American embassy in Mexico City as well as the Latin American desk in the State Department in 1913 and beyond had lost their roles as policy advisors of the American President.

While Sommerfeld busied himself with organizing the supply lines for the Constitutionalists, his friend Frederico Stallforth moved to New York for good. He wrote to his wife in July 1913, "I believe that I will not be able to do anything there [Mexico] within two years."[1013] Business had gone from bad to worse for the Stallforth brothers in the winter of 1912/1913. The Orozco uprising had severely interrupted trade in Chihuahua throughout 1912. After the Madero administration finally suppressed the rebellion, Frederico Stallforth and his brothers had suffered such losses that the business hung in the balance again. The constant fighting in and around Parral caused Stallforth to move his family to El Paso in February 1912 where they stayed until June 1913.[1014] His second daughter, Gioja, was born in El Paso on March 31st 1913. Throughout 1912 and 1913 Frederico Stallforth had attempted to make use of what he called "the Madero Connection."

The Madero connection was, of course, Felix Sommerfeld who, by the fall of 1912, had successfully defeated the Orozco rebels and was the most powerful foreigner in the Mexican power structure. As could be expected Stallforth's investors in New York and Boston wanted to call their loans. His friend Sommerfeld put the hapless businessman from Parral in touch with Alberto Madero and his influential brother Ernesto, the Mexican Secretary of the Treasury, to present a "plan." Stallforth's idea seemed far-fetched and crude but ever the optimist he gambled for high stakes. In a letter to Ernesto Madero, Stallforth explained his scheme:

"Now, when the trouble is practically over, the country is in a very bad shape financially and commercially; business is nearly at a standstill, the fields have not been tilled, the seed and fertilizer are not to be had. Unless people are given immediate assistance with money and materials...they will be driven by hunger into another insurrection...dangerous to the country and business. The Americans and Germans, whose large enterprises in this section have been greatly injured by the insurrection and brigandage, are also in great need of financial assistance. F. Stallforth and Brother stand ready to do as they have done in the past...and advance the necessary money for these purposes, taking, of course, such business security as is proper...If they can succeed in doing this it is clear that prosperity will return to the neighborhood, and prosperity will mean peace, [sic] to the community. It cannot do this, however, unless it receives further financial assistance at once, and therefore asks that the Government make a substantial deposit of funds in its [the Stallforth's] bank, for the purpose of allowing them to continue their assistance to the community...in this way [the financial assistance] will aid in popularizing the Government and will create a feeling favorable to the Government throughout the community..."[1015]

Frederico Stallforth had the highest hopes that this concept would succeed in fending off the creditors in the U.S. He floated his plan with the investors in Boston and New York. He also contacted the U.S. government, as well as the German embassies in Washington and Mexico City. He did not elaborate who in the American government he had interviews with. It would not be surprising if Sommerfeld had put his friend in touch with Hopkins who introduced Stallforth to Philander Knox. Perhaps a coincidence, but still worth considering is the fact that Sommerfeld went to New York for his interview with the Wilson people at precisely the same time Stallforth claims to have contacted the U.S. government.[1016] After he returned from his trip to the East Coast Stallforth spent the last week of October in Mexico City where "the banks showed us great trust, and the [Mexican] Government as well, especially Ernesto Madero."[1017] Again, without offering hard proof of Sommerfeld actively working on Stallforth's behalf, he happened to be in Mexico City in October 1913 around the same time when his friend approached the Secretary of the Treasury and the German embassy.[1018] The feedback from Stallforth's investors in Boston and New York seemed to have been positive. Of course they had no other choice than letting Stallforth try to raise money in any way possible.[1019]

One American Bank, the First National Bank, also tried to jettison Stallforth's defunct mining enterprise, the Mexico Consolidated Mining and Smelting Company. The plan was to get another U.S. concern to take over the mines. True to his endearing optimism, Stallforth wrote to his brother on

December 13th, "If we make this deal, it will mean not only wealth for us but also the complete rehabilitation of our company, our name, and our honor."[1020] Alberto's feedback obviously lacked his brother's optimism. He apparently requested from Frederico to relinquish absolute control over the financial affairs of the business. In the only documented fight between the two, Frederico chastised his younger brother, accusing him of being "petty," "crafty," "unprofessional," and trying to "put a pistol to his chest."[1021] Clearly, Alberto had lost faith and was unwilling to agree to yet another loan on a family inheritance that for all intents and purposes had been destroyed by the Mexican Revolution. Frederico was a gambler - Alberto was not.

Ernesto Madero's response is not documented. However, Stallforth remained positive through the end of 1912 and into 1913. He had every reason to be. Throughout his life, Stallforth consulted fortune-tellers for guidance. Not many of these predictions have survived. However, his files contained one in his 1913 correspondence that is worth mentioning:

"The season of 1913-14 will be quiete [sic] event full [sic] you will have financial trouble about the end of this year [1913], but at the beginning of 1914 things will be brighter and better.- [sic] you must stay in New York for the present at least, if on the contrary you go to Mexico, there will be grave danger physical as well as financial. Madero's connection will be rather beneficial than otherwise, [sic] to you, tho [sic] some disappointment will be encountered by you, this will be over come [sic] later on. Complete order in Mexico is not as yet in sight [sic] in fact the worst is yet to come, a new faction will spring in to [sic] life, beware of the new faction, be neutral when the crisis comes. – You will have to make a trip to Mexico befor [sic] long but you will not stay and return to New York. There is a person, seemingly a friend, about you he will prove himself a traitor. Beware. Box 911 Ocean Park Calf."[1022]

Frederico Stallforth returned only once to Parral in January 1913, not to come back until long after the World War. Of course, a new and powerful faction did rise in Mexico in the person of Pancho Villa who would reach his zenith in 1914. The traitor in New York remains open for interpretation. As will be discussed later, his acquaintance in New York with German sabotage agent Franz Rintelen would cause him tremendous harm and imprisonment. More significant is the mention of the "Madero connection," which Stallforth had obviously discussed with the fortuneteller. However, the plan did not quite evolve as Stallforth had envisioned.

On February 22nd 1913, the house of cards on which Stallforth wanted to re-erect his family business collapsed in a hail of bullets that killed the Mexican President. From El Paso he watched the third revolution in so many years develop in Northern Mexico. However, the "Madero connection," Sommerfeld, put Madero's uncles, Alberto, Alfonso, Ernesto, and Salvador, as well as Madero's cousin Rafael Hernandez, the former attorney general, on the map for Stallforth's eventual salvation. In the end, his friend Sommerfeld proved to be a good choice for financial survival. Hernandez, Ernesto, Alfonso, Salvador and Alberto Madero moved to New York where they opened an import/export firm to supply the Constitutionalist forces. Stallforth moved his family to Santa Barbara, California for the time being and joined the action in New York. The stationary, on which he wrote letters to his wife Anita, showed "115 Broadway, Suite 1600" as his address. That was the new office of the Maderos, whose enterprise he joined in March 1913.

Stallforth's job was to help sell the Madero family real estate to raise funds for the new revolution. Nicholas Lenssen, a business lawyer who dealt with Stallforth and the German secret service throughout the World War, testified in 1918, "...our principle relation with Mr. Stallforth [in 1913] was in connection with properties of the Madero family of Mexico, who were introduced to us by Mr. Stallforth, for the purpose of procuring our advice with regard to a possible sale of these properties. No sale was affected under our advice, and finally the Maderos ceased consulting us."[1023] Although the Madero's sold their vast rubber plantations to Charles Flint, commissions did not materialize for Stallforth. He obviously had not been allowed to represent these valuable assets but rather mining and ranching properties in Northern Mexico. Even a salesman as skilled as Stallforth could not entice investors to buy those properties while the revolution raged in Mexico. "On account of the feeling against any Mexican investment of the banks in the U.S. I did not succeed in doing anything."[1024] Money was obviously so tight that he could not even afford a birthday present for his wife. In a July letter, Stallforth wrote to Anita: "Spent the whole day with Madero. Maybe I can get something out of him in the next days."[1025] A few weeks later he mentioned spending an evening with Zach Cobb discussing the situation in Mexico. He concluded the note with "I am convinced that your mine will make us lots of money as soon as the revolution is over."[1026] Stallforth's meeting with Cobb in July 1913 is significant not because it happened but where it happened. What would the El Paso customs collector come to New York for and whom was he meeting? In April 1915, Lazaro De La Garza, who meanwhile also worked for the Maderos, tellingly wrote to Miguel Diaz Lombardo, Secretary of State of the Convention Government, "Sr. Cobb has been a very good friend of ours who has helped in any way possible."[1027]

Sometime in 1913, probably in the German Club, Stallforth met the German Naval Attaché Karl Boy-Ed who, according to the BI investigators, became his "friend." He mingled with the crowd around the Tauschers, which included the German Ambassador Count Bernstorff and other embassy staff. Hans Tauscher, who established important business connections with the Constitutionalists and the Maderos in 1914, paid Stallforth commissions for acting as a go between. Stallforth also remained closely connected with his business partner and fellow fund raiser Andrew Meloy whose office at 55 Liberty Street he started sharing in 1914. He also made friends with Adolph Pavenstedt, a director at G. Amsinck and Co. that would play a pivotal role in the German World War I strategy in the U.S. G. Amsinck and Co. was the primary trading house and bank the German embassy used in New York. It is very possible but undocumented that Stallforth raised funds through these business and banking contacts to support the Constitutionalists. Meloy and friends of his stature who had mining and railroad interests in Mexico would likely have pitched in when two of the biggest heavy hitters in New York City, Henry Clay Pierce and Charles Flint, declared their support for Carranza.

In his interrogation with American agents in 1918, Sommerfeld talked surprisingly little about the period after Madero's death and about his busy schedule in the spring and summer of 1913. As is the case with most gaps in Sommerfeld's recollections, the unspoken details might have supported the American government's assertion that Sommerfeld was a German spy. However, on a purely objective basis an argument can be made that between the Decena Tragica, which caused the reassignment of Peter Bruchhausen, and the summer of 1914 Sommerfeld had no apparent contact to the German clandestine services. No archival evidence of Sommerfeld reporting to German authorities, especially to von Hintze or Kueck, can be found. However, in 1920, American special envoy to Mexico, John Lind, testified to the Foreign Relations Committee about his diplomatic experiences in Mexico City. Lind said: "Then later [after September 1913] I got in touch with the German minister and found him the best informed of any man in Mexico... He had the situation down to at [a "t"], as we say. He had an accurate estimate of the revolutionary forces and their capacity, and he also had a very accurate conception of the Huertista forces and their weakness. He was the one foreigner in Mexico, who was convinced that Huerta could not win or maintain himself."[1028]

Sommerfeld seemed to be wholly employed by Hopkins and the U.S. interests supporting Carranza, but very likely remained an important informant for Germany. No other foreigner had better connections in the Mexican Revolution. Other agents such as Wachendorf and Krumm-Heller operated in the region and under Sommerfeld's direction. It seems very likely that after Bruchhausen's departure Sommerfeld established a connection with the new North American intelligence chief, German Naval Attaché Karl Boy-Ed. While Boy-Ed later claimed to have met Sommerfeld for the first time in May of 1914, Sommerfeld recalled talking to Boy-Ed on the phone in 1913.[1029] After von Hintze's return to Mexico in September 1913, Sommerfeld returned to von Hintze's stable until the rear admiral assigned his star agent to the naval attaché in Washington. As Lind's testimony illustrates, the German government had great sources of information placed in critical areas around the Mexican conflict. Sommerfeld certainly represented the top asset, personally engaging with the highest echelons of the Wilson administration, acting as go-between for Carranza and Wilson, understanding the mechanics and intricacies of federal and Constitutionalist military strength, finances, and armaments. Sommerfeld had developed and controlled critical secret service assets such as Wachendorf and Krumm-Heller, who complemented the rich sources Germany had for intelligence.

From an ethical standpoint Sommerfeld supplied intelligence to Germany in 1913 without sensing a conflict of interest. In his understanding of the world he could have easily justified working for Hopkins and, at the same time, supporting German business interests in the Mexican Revolution. German and American interests largely coincided. While both countries wanted order and stability, Germany clearly subordinated her interests to those of the United Stated. Huerta was not worth fighting the United States for. Quite in contrast to historians' assessments that Germany wholeheartedly supported Huerta, Germany largely trusted the Wilson administration in its reformulated policy towards Mexico.

It is important to realize that realistically the German Empire could only marginally participate in trade with Mexico. Flint and Co. had locked up the market. Huerta had no money. There were also political reasons why Germany did not want to get involved. Any material sent to Mexico had to pass through the United States and would clearly have been noticed by the authorities as to its origin. This explains why, in order to avoid any potential embarrassment, Germany intercepted and impounded arms shipments in Hamburg before they could proceed on to the United States. Henry Clay Pierce, in July 1913 made a foray to the American government prompted by German investors in Pierce's Mexican National Railways. The Germans wanted to relate to President Wilson that neither Bleichröder nor other German banks supported Huerta.[1030] Just like the German government, these representatives of high finance trusted Wilson's policy towards Mexico to eventually result in stability and positive returns on their investment. Clearly, in 1913, President Wilson, Pierce, Hopkins, and the most influential banks in Germany supported Carranza. Sommerfeld omitted to talk about his efforts in 1913 only because at the time of his interrogation Germany was at war with the United States. It was hard to imagine then that only five years earlier there were no conflicts of interest between Germany and the United States when it came to the Mexican situation.

CHAPTER 18

~

EL GRAL. Y JEFE DE LA DIVISIÓN DEL NORTE, FRANCISCO VILLA

When Pancho Villa crossed into Mexico somewhere near El Paso on March 6th 1913 with eight men and a few rounds of ammunition, his chances of having any impact on the situation in Chihuahua, much less the whole of Mexico seemed slim. His most powerful mentor and political powerhouse Abraham Gonzalez was dead. Manuel Chao, a schoolteacher turned revolutionary, Tomás Urbina, Toribio Ortega, Maclovio Herrera, Domingo and Mariano Arrieta, and others had taken up arms against Huerta, but none of these new leaders had any national standing. Pancho Villa was a national figure in the spring of 1913. However, the arrest and imprisonment by the Madero government several months before had stained his reputation. Villa's forces that had so effectively helped the Maderistas capture Chihuahua had been largely dispersed. Many of his erstwhile brothers-in-arms had either gone back to their civilian lives or had been absorbed into the federal army. The colorful general with the bandit image took a large gamble when he crossed the Rio Grande on that fateful day in 1913. He would return six months later at the head of a formidable army. As the commander of the famed División Del Norte, Pancho Villa was to assemble an army of fifty thousand soldiers at its zenith in late 1914.

Pancho Villa's rise in 1913 stemmed from several factors, not all at his initiative. Despite the imprisonment and exile under the Madero administration, Villa was able to create a veritable religion around the person of Francisco Madero, whose death only he had the power to avenge. As the story of Frederico Stallforth illustrated, people in Chihuahua and Durango suffered greatly in the spring and summer of 1913. The renewed unrest destroyed whatever was left of commerce, mining, manufacturing, and agriculture. Inflationary increases in the cost of basic foodstuffs, clothing, and manufactured goods lifted most anything beyond the reach of common Mexicans. Hunger became widespread. Protestant missionary Alden Buell Case commented, "...These necessities through many weary months were either impossible to obtain, or the prices of the limited supply were beyond reach, hence there was much real suffering..."[1031] Enter Pancho Villa, the charismatic caudillo who as one of his first acts took a Terrazas hacienda, slaughtered whole herds of cattle and distributed meat, corn, flower, and anything else that was not nailed down. While historian Katz explained Villa's feeding of the rural masses a Robin Hood like exploit, the practice had been common ever since Madero fought to overthrow the hated dictator Diaz. Alden Buell Case, wrote about his 1911 experience with the Maderistas: "On taking El Valle the matter of meat supply not only for the soldiers but for the entire population as well was taken in charge by the [revolutionary] military. A drove of fat beeves from these large herds was brought in daily, slaughtered wherever convenient - at first on the main streets – and sold to the townspeople at a very low price. This helped to fill the treasury of the revolutionists and at the same time tended to make them popular with the common people."[1032] Villa also executed hated hacienda superintendents and gave notice to the Chihuahuan elites that any further abuses would be punished unmercifully. Unquestionably, he at the very least continued the strategies that had made Madero's revolution so popular with the common folk of Chihuahua.

At the same time that he rounded up Terrazas' cattle, Villa very effectively battled brigandage, the scourge of rural life. Bandits faced summary execution wherever Villa would find them and by most accounts the crime rate in Chihuahua diminished as Villa's control over the state increased. According to missionary Alden Buell Case,

"...he [Villa] was strongly desirous of retaining the good will of the Washington administration and, perhaps for this reason, he was especially energetic and effective in his hostility to the bandit element wherever encountered. The 'Colorados' [Orozquistas] who refused to accept amnesty in laying down their arms or joining his own troops, were treated as outlaws and hunted down like beasts. Never had Porfirio Diaz in the days of his iron rule exhibited more relentless vigour [sic] or success in the suppression of brigandage than Francisco Villa in the brief era of his supremacy."[1033]

While hunting down the "bandits," Villa also displayed hitherto unknown restraint when he occupied villages and cities. Town folk looked with dread towards efforts of other military leaders especially Tomás Urbina and "Cheche" Campos to take their community from the opposing Huerta forces. The rebel occupiers usually engaged in indescribable feats of plunder, rape, execution, and destruction leaving the townspeople in a state of despair. Cities of relative wealth such as Durango, Torreon, Chihuahua, and Parral had to experience this cycle of violence and theft multiple times as the front lines shifted over the years. In June 1913 Tomás Urbina took the capital of Durango, a great military success for the rebellion against Huerta. Historian Katz quoted an eyewitness who described what happened when the revolutionary forces entered the city:

"Like an avalanche that descends from the mountain, fused their forces with those of the lower classes, full of desires for vengeance, destruction, and plunder, and began to assault stores, carrying out shameful acts of plunder, while other groups, animated by the natural lack of confidence of the peasants, were shooting at fictitious enemies, and dynamite explosions and rifle fire could constantly be heard. The sack of the city was followed by fire, and the night of June 19 was more horrendous than the day of combat, since the city was lighted by the sinister glow of the flames that had engulfed twelve of the main stores in the city."[1034]

Most likely stemming from advice he received from Hopkins, Sommerfeld and others who fought for recognition and support of the Constitutionalists in Washington, Villa showed remarkable restraint when his forces occupied a town or village. Plunderers were summarily executed, order was quickly restored and enforced, and, while prisoners of war faced firing squads, the townspeople were largely left unmolested. Historians argue about Villa's motivation in showing such behavior, which was unusual for revolutionaries. Whether it was solely an effort to prove his civility to the American government or to show to the Mexican population that he was the best choice for restoring order to Mexico, Villa gained an enormous amount of goodwill on both sides of the border. The ranks of his burgeoning army swelled with every village and town he marched through.[1035] With regards to the American government, it received glowing assessments from its consular officers telling of the level of discipline and control Villa exercised over his forces.[1036]

The missionary Alden Buell Case alluded to one more important strategy that quickly formed the basis for the financial success of Villa's campaign. On the surface, Villa did everything in his power to help American citizens - minimize their losses, and prevent any kind of confiscation or taxation. The goodwill he received in return allowed him to quickly build a highly effective organization especially in El Paso, which sold the confiscated cattle, cotton, and anything else he took from the large Mexican-owned estates for cash. The two main power brokers in this "American" side of Villa's revolution were his "little" brother Hipolito and the uncles of Francisco Madero in New York.

A daring heist on April 9th 1913 gave Villa's finances an early boost. With a small force of about two hundred men, the rebels stopped Mexican Northwestern Train No. 7 south of the Chihuahua's capital. The train, which they captured, carried 122 ingots of silver bullion worth about $160,000 ($3.4 million in today's value), which the rebels took. Because the bullion belonged to American smelting companies it would be hard to sell in the United States without risking confiscation. Villa proffered a "strictly confidential" deal to Wells Fargo to return the loot for $50,000 in cash ($1 million in today's value). On top of the "finder's fee," Villa also offered "protection" for future bullion transports. According to documents found at Wells Fargo, Villa received the $50,000. Not surprisingly, the Villistas eventually returned ninety-three of the silver ingots, the rest, according to Villa, had been "stolen by his men."[1037] The savvy methods through which Villa built not only a superior fighting force but also maintained financial independence from Carranza served him well in the years to come.

The final secret to Villa's success and popularity had to do with the mere fact that, while he racked up one military success after another, the federal forces had gained ground on the other revolutionary commanders but lost whatever little popular support they had. In order to satisfy the demands for fresh recruits the central government resorted to forced conscription. As a result federal forces had consistent desertion, discipline, and training problems.[1038] Admiral von Hintze, the German ambassador to Mexico who had returned to his assignment in the beginning of September 1913, authored a telling memorandum with his assessment of the federal forces. The memorandum is dated October 27th and coincided with Huerta's decision to abandon the planned general elections in Mexico. Contrary to many historians, who have tried to paint von Hintze and the German government as big supporters of Huerta, the German ambassador bluntly described why the federal forces were in for certain defeat.

"By decree dated 24th of October...the standing army was increased from 100,000 to 150,000 men...End of February [1913] the army was to be about 40,000 men, but in reality it had barely more than 28,000 men. The troops are mainly recruited from prisons, captured rebels, the accused, through forced conscription (called leva) and a minute part from volunteers...The quality of the soldiers the government has access to is marginal as a result of extraction and qualification; ...In order to evade violence or as a result of expediency, the soldier lets himself be integrated, equipped and drilled, but the thought foremost on his mind is to desert as soon as possible...The officers know the yearning of their troops; as a result the soldiers are locked up in their barracks or camps at sunset and only released at sunrise. As a result the federal army avoids any type of night operations. For that reason guards, outposts, flank protection are not placed as a matter of course, because these men would most likely run away or join the enemy...Another advantage the rebels have over the federals is that their units consist of volunteers, namely revolutionaries by conviction or calling or professional bandits or, finally of deserters of the federal army; without concern the [rebels] can send out their units or bands by night or send them out by day on specific assignments further away, because these people are coming back. Not so the federals..."[1039]

Von Hintze with his assessment of the quality of the understaffed federal officer corps claimed that Huerta was so desperate that he "...promotes waiters, accountants and such from one day to the next to lieutenants and captains -lawyers to generals...The Mexican army has plenty of generals...these are for the most part the type of people which are called 'funeral generals' in Russia, since their only activity is to parade in uniform for funeral processions – for money...one has to expect worse losses than Alviles Canon, Torreon and Durango, since now the generals who so-far remained in their salons are sent into the battlefield."[1040] Villa and Obregon became the two generals that recognized the Achilles' heel Admiral von Hintze so pointedly described. The more pressure the two generals placed on the federal army, the more pronounced this weakness became.

The people already suffering in the countryside flocked to the only man perceived to be able to defeat Huerta: Pancho Villa. In July 1913 Villa's nemesis and Huerta General Pascual Orozco overran the forces of Constitutionalist General Manuel Chao and occupied Chihuahua City.[1041] At the same time Carranza's troops had to retreat first from the capital of Coahuila, Saltillo, then from Monclova. On July 31st the First Chief joined other rebel forces in an attack on Torreon. Badly beaten he retreated for a third time and was forced to leave the whole of the state to the federals. General Scott who did not like Carranza one bit quipped in his memoirs, "Carranza, finding Coahuila too hot to hold him, fled across Mexico to Hermosillo on the Pacific, where he occupied himself in dancing and dining, far out of harm's way."[1042] Whether it was cowardice or strategic thinking that motivated Carranza, his retreat and Orozco's occupation of Chihuahua left no doubt in the Constitutionalist leaders' minds that only a large force under centralized command could effectively oppose the federals. Villa appeared as the man of the hour. He had won the Battle of San Andres earlier in August, which brought the Legion of Honor award to his daring machine gunner, Emil Holmdahl.[1043]

Sommerfeld and his people along the border were busy organizing the supply for the Constitutionalist armies now in excess of fifteen thousand men. Just as he had in the Orozco uprising, Sommerfeld remained a key source for intervention with the revolutionaries on behalf of American citizens. On June 20th 1913, Agent Breniman wrote to his superior in San Antonio: "Am just informed from the American Consul Nuevo Laredo that C. M. Rippeteau and Henry Crumpler, two American citizens and the bearers of messages for Consul Garrett, were arrested yesterday by Carranzistas in vicinity of Nuevo Laredo and have been taken to Hidalgo en route to Piedras Negras where it is feared that they will be summarily dealt with. We [the Bureau of Investigation] are requested to use our influence to protect these citizens. Suggest you see Sommerfeld."[1044]

His organization and he personally channeled important intelligence to the Justice Department agents. On July 5th 1913 Sommerfeld informed BI agent Breniman via the San Antonio BI chief H. A. Thompson "Evaristo Guajardo left here yesterday from Eagle Pass with six men. Guajardo and his brothers intend to immediately start a movement against Carranza from just below or above Eagle Pass."[1045] The German agent asked the BI to investigate the rumor and "ascertain, if possible, the movements of these people, and...to take steps to anticipate them."[1046] The report alludes to the fact that the Sommerfeld organization, again, told the BI what to do and how to do it. Sommerfeld dispatched Agent Jack Noonan from Nogales to Tucson with a companion to scour the desert for federal munitions dumps. "Noonan and Clark intend going out on a still hunt for these deposits of ammunition which they believed to exist." [1047] Of course Noonan also was a well-known smuggler for the Constitutionalist army.[1048]

On October 7th, BI Chief Bielaski directed Agent H. A. Thompson to "...close the bridge at Eagle Pass from 4 p.m. to 8 a.m....it is hoped that a special agent can be stationed permanently at Eagle Pass and that the matter of the closing of the bridge at Eagle Pass will be taken up by you."[1049] Although on the surface one can interpret these instructions as hostile to the resupply efforts of the Constitutionalists, the opposite was the case. Thompson, who left the Department of Justice shortly thereafter to work for Sommerfeld, had allowed Eagle Pass to be virtually open for Constitutionalist supplies to pass through. The State Department wanted to arrange for superficial action to maintain the neutrality laws. In the same telegram Bielaski wrote that the "...Secretary of State has been advised that arrangements are being made to add to the force of special agents now working in Texas and Arizona on neutrality matters."[1050] Of course, adding one man to the main border crossing through which the Villistas received their supplies for the upcoming battles was a joke. The fact that by October 1913 there was not a single agent watching Eagle Pass-Piedras Negras illustrates the U.S. government's tacit support for Villa's fall campaign. The situation at other critical crossings was no different. While the government went after several arms merchants in Nogales and Douglas, Arizona in October, the courts acquitted all of them and the smuggling continued unabated.[1051]

As the most powerful commander in the field, Villa secured the support of most independent rebel leaders, first Ortega and Contreras, finally Urbina, in his bid to establish a unified force. However, Carranza nominated Manuel Chao as the supreme commander over the rebel forces. It was a political move since the First Chief trusted Chao more than the independently minded Villa. In a "Hollywood cowboy movie" showdown Villa succeeded in forcing Chao at gunpoint to withdraw his bid to become commander of the Constitutionalist forces.[1052] The formal recognition of Villa's de-facto command of the División Del Norte followed in September when the Constitutionalist leaders elected the daring commander to take Torreon, the key to supremacy over the north of Mexico.

In three days, the Constitutionalists under Villa's command smashed the defenses of Torreon. Never before had Villa led these many men into battle. His army consisted of eight thousand men, cavalry, and two cannon.[1053] Missing in the fight was Villa's artillery chief Emil Holmdahl. Holmdahl had signed up with the Constitutionalists in March 1913. After fighting in Sonora, the soldier-of-fortune was seriously injured and spent several months recovering in Douglas, Arizona. Still "thin and pale...but ...cheerful," Holmdahl was assigned to Villa's forces around the beginning of November.[1054] Torreon became the largest battle to date. Wave after wave of cavalry charges pounded the three thousand defenders under General Murguía. Finally, after Villa even contemplated breaking off the battle, his charges leapt into the city through a breach in the defense lines. Murguía ordered a hasty retreat and left the city to the rebels. To Villa's credit he had effectively commanded a rebel army that lacked training, discipline, and heavy weaponry. The overwhelming force allowed Villa to charge straight at the enemy. This strategy would gain the self-educated general many victories but would eventually become the main cause for his most disastrous defeats. A well-entrenched defending force with superior weapons and training should have been able to repel Villa's attack. The federal commander and his officers lacked imagination and resolve, its conscripted foot soldiers the motivation to fight. The Battle of Torreon offered a glimpse into the future for the Usurper President Huerta and his forces. Within two weeks of the loss of Torreon, Huerta had fired his Minister of War, General Manuel Mondragon, arrested all representatives in the Chamber of Deputies that he suspected of having rebel sympathies, and called off the planned elections for the end of the month.

The Battle of Torreon became the single most important prize, which propelled Villa to the height of his career. His men captured heavy artillery, half-a-million rounds of ammunition, armored rail cars, eleven cannon including the future division mascot, the three inch El Niño, hundreds of rail cars, and an estimated forty locomotives.[1055] The División del Norte traveled by rail to the battlefields of Chihuahua City and Ciudad Juarez from this time on. Villa also forced loans on Torreon's business elite and the local banks. The "contributions" amounted to three million Pesos (approximately $31.5 million in today's money). With 100,000 Pesos in cash ($ 1 million in today's value) Villa dispatched his brother Hipolito and Lazaro De La Garza, the son of a well-known merchant and industrialist in Torreon, to take over the arms procurement for the División Del Norte in El Paso. De La Garza would handle the finances of the Villa army and its illustrious general until the end of 1915. He also would become Sommerfeld's smokescreen that succeeded in hiding German financial support for Villa from the American authorities in 1914 and 1915. As a result of the victory, the largest insurgent army of its time in Mexico quickly swelled to over 10,000 strong and moved along with a fully equipped hospital train, railcars loaded with kitchen supplies, soldaderas, soldier families, and cooks traveling alongside. The cavalry mounts with loads of alfalfa hay and grain recovered their energy in between engagements riding in the captured cattle cars. The train also included several water cars for the soldiers and the animals. Ammunition and artillery, some of which mounted firmly on the rail stock and heavily guarded formed the rear of this hitherto unseen modern, mobile army.[1056]

To the American public, Pancho Villa became the main attraction in the uprising against Huerta. News reports about the capture of Torreon told of the daring attack of the Villista army, and the brutal execution of foreigners and prisoners in the aftermath. Villa had become a national celebrity, both because of the image that Stallforth related to his daughters in his bedtime stories, and because of his openness to the press. Villa became another rags-to-riches story that so fascinated the American public. While brutal in his dishing out of punishments, he was also seen by Americans as fair and even handed, especially because American property was under his personal protection. Two highly idealistic American characters decided to join Villa's ride to the top after Torreon: Ambrose Bierce and John Reed. While Bierce disappeared without a trace in the chaotic battles of early 1914, Reed wrote a blockbuster description of the Mexican Revolution published that year called *Insurgent Mexico: With Pancho Villa in the Mexican Revolution*.[1057] Another person of great influence on Villa's relationship with the United States came to the fore after Torreon: George C. Carothers, the American consular agent of Torreon was a personal friend of William Jennings Bryan, the U.S. Secretary of State. After Torreon, President Wilson assigned Carothers to stay with Villa. He became the State Department's special envoy to the revolutionary leader. For much of 1914 and 1915 Carothers and Sommerfeld became Villa's direct link to the American government. Carothers eventually evolved into a controversial figure because of the position of power he grew into and of the many accusations of corruption that dogged his brief appearance on the world stage of diplomacy. Thirty-eight years old, Carothers faced harsh criticisms from career diplomats, who envied his success and influence in the Wilson administration. Historian Katz quoted a French diplomat, who wrote in December 1914,

"...all of them [Wilson's special envoys including Carothers] have one aim – the victory of the chief to whom they are accredited. They are similar to election managers going from door to door and from location to location to canvas in favor of their candidates. They have all signed secret pacts with the chieftains to whom they are accredited, which in case of his victory would provide them with substantial profits. They did not even belong to the second set of the United States political world...Mr. Carothers was an agent for an express company...Thus Mr. Wilson's confidential agents might perhaps have been good salesmen for a Chicago canning factory, but they are out of place as diplomats in the great drama taking place in Mexico."[1058]

Carothers and the other "amateurs" President Wilson tapped for special assignments in Mexico certainly offered plenty of broadsides to attack. What the criticisms fail to grasp was that men like Carothers did not have jobs to gather information for the Wilson administration to act upon. Carothers for a brief period in 1914 became the single most important influence on Pancho Villa and thus prevented U.S.-Mexican relations from escalating into war. This aspect of the work of Wilson's confidential men drowned in the noise of jealous righteousness that many historians copied as fact.

Within weeks after Torreon, after having resupplied and absorbed the many recruits flocking to his army, Villa decided to keep the momentum and challenge the federal army in Chihuahua's capital. Using his recently captured rail stock the División Del Norte moved men, women, and equipment to the outskirts of the capital. On November 5th Villa ordered a frontal attack against the numerically inferior defenders. Like in Torreon wave after wave of cavalry challenged the entrenched defensive lines of General Salvador Mercado's federal force and Orozco's irregulars. Holmdahl's artillery was charged with "softening" defensive lines. However, Mercado was ready. He had studied Villa's crude method of attack. Owing to the federals' superior artillery, which Mercado had strategically placed for maximum effect and the deadly machine gun implements along the defensive line, the frontal assaults turned into bloodbaths for the attackers. After three days of heavy losses Villa stood to lose the battle. He ordered a pullback which caused General Mercado to report to Mexico City: "I have the honor to report to you that yesterday [November 8th] at 6 p.m., the enemy was expelled from his last positions and thrown back by our courageous troops..."[1059] Villa seemed to waver as to what to do next. To the defenders of Chihuahua he seemed to have broken off the attacks. However, on November 11th small skirmishes resumed leading Mercado to anticipate a renewed assault on the city.

What happened next was probably the most cunning and brazen military coup devised since the Trojan Wars: Faking a new attack, Villa divided his forces and in the night of November 13th captured two coal trains at the Terrazas Station between Chihuahua and Juarez.[1060] He had the railcars emptied and loaded an elite corps he called Dorados onto the trains. Further cavalry regiments followed at some distance as the Villistas moved north towards Ciudad Juarez. At each train station on the way, the rebels arrested the telegraph operators. Under the threat of death, they had to send fake messages to the garrison in Juarez. The telegrams pretended that Villa had cut the rail lines to the south and that the operators needed urgent instructions on where to direct the threatened trains. As expected the officials at Juarez ordered the operators to retreat north, thus clearing the way for the Villistas to approach Juarez without arousing suspicion. In the early morning hours of November 16th the trains pulled into the downtown of Ciudad Juarez.[1061] When the railcar doors flew open at 2:30 in the morning and Villa's cavalry charged the unsuspecting federal garrison the battle ended almost before it had started.[1062] Disoriented by attacking forces from inside the city as well as from the outskirts, the federals did not stand a chance. With only a few stray bullets pitting some walls and breaking some windows in El Paso[1063], without serious bloodshed, and by complete surprise Villa took Juarez, the jewel customs station for badly needed supplies from the United States. By 8:00 am mop-up operations in the city were replaced by summary executions of federal officers, which lasted for the better part of a week.[1064] To the disgust of the national media in the U.S. and to the horror of the State Department Villa openly rounded up approximately 125 military prisoners, many of them Orozquistas, and had them shot without mercy.[1065] Not all El Pasoans joined in the abhorred outcry for humanity on the part of Villa's troops. "Great numbers of morbidly curious El Pasoans, including some well-dressed women, flocked to Juarez to gawk at the dead bodies, and if lucky they got to witness an execution or two."[1066] One high-ranking officer was allowed to flee to safety in the United States: The federal commander, General Francisco Castro. Villa had not forgotten that this officer interceded on his behalf when he himself faced Huerta's firing squad.[1067] Villa also saved the military band from execution because he wanted more music for his soldiers. The musicians and many federal foot soldiers were offered to join the Division of the North rather than being shot. An easy choice given the circumstances!

The Battle of Juarez coincided with General Hugh Lenox Scott taking command of the Mexican border from Fabens, Texas, to San Diego, California. Scott, a veteran of the Spanish-American War, and former superintendent at West Point had spent the preceding years working with pacifying Indian tribes along the border and commanding the 3rd cavalry regiment in San Antonio. The General had become known for his gift for finding the right tone in negotiations with Native American leaders, and while being a tough negotiator, keeping his word of honor. Scott's reputation as a dedicated and tough officer, as well as his experience in dealing with Philippine rebels, Native American chiefs,

Mexican revolutionaries, and alike made him a perfect candidate for organizing the U.S. military along the Mexican-American border.

The new Pancho Villa image in the El Paso Morning Times after the Battle of Juarez:
Suit and tie, well kempt, civilized, American[1068]

One of General Scott's first acts as the responsible military commander was to deal with the issue of stray bullets hitting Americans any time Mexican battles raged on the other side of the border. Most endangered were the citizens of El Paso because of the strategic importance of Ciudad Juarez just across the river. However, other border communities were threatened as well, such as Laredo, Texas, Eagle Pass, Texas, Presidio, Texas, Columbus, New Mexico, Naco, Arizona, and Nogales, Arizona. Rather than engaging in much diplomacy, Scott ordered immediate defensive moves. In El Paso, Scott had a coal train placed along the river bank and placed heavy artillery in strategic locations to enable the U.S. military to inflict quick and heavy responses to stray bullets. As Scott put it in his memoirs, "I was then ready to act and sent word to both belligerents to keep their bullets on their own side of the Rio Grande or they would be returned with interest."[1069]

According to the general's recollection he sent word to Pancho Villa ahead of his surprise attack on Ciudad Juarez "not to endanger El Paso."[1070] This communication is not documented in the historical record, although there is no reason to doubt it. Villa, while encamped around Chihuahua City, was expected to make a move on Ciudad Juarez in the not so distant future. When the surprise attack came in the night of November 16th Scott was exhilarated: "Villa took my warning...very much to heart. He captured Juarez by a brilliant stroke of genius unlooked for from him, a coup of which any soldier would be proud...There was some little firing in the morning but Villa had so arranged it that his line of fire was up the river and none went across to El Paso."[1071]

While Villa consolidated power and established an effective administration in Ciudad Juarez, the battle for control over Chihuahua raged on. The rebel general decided to challenge the opposing federal army at Tierra Blanca. He preempted the mounting danger of being pinned down in Juarez by federal reinforcements, which were on their way from Chihuahua. The little railway station some thirty miles south of Juarez offered multiple advantages: Moving the battleground away from Juarez, Huerta's forces did not get the chance to create a border incident by firing into El Paso. In addition, the sandy terrain made it harder for the federals to move their heavy artillery into place. On November 23rd the federals under General José Inez Salazar challenged the entrenched Villistas. Typical for Villa's crude planning he "had no reserves, no grand strategy and not even any real tactics; it later transpired that he had not coordinated the movements of his various commanders."[1072] By all military standards the battle should have been a rout for the federal army. For a while it looked that way. The Villistas were short of ammunition, outflanked, and on the brink of disaster. It was a combination of Villa's daring charges with him leading the way against the federal positions and the unbelievable mistakes of General Salazar. Leading three hundred cavalry into the line of fire, Villa managed to push the federals back. Rudolfo Fierro, the crazy-eyed executioner and fighting buddy of Villa, sent a machina loca, a locomotive laden with explosives, into the federal lines.[1073] The tremendous explosion sent the federal soldiers racing for cover in a panic. Now Holmdahl's artillery kicked in gear and opened the lines. A horrendous slaughter followed in which "more than one thousand" Orozquistas fell despite holding up white flags.[1074] The decisive battle for Chihuahua ended in a huge fiesta on the night of November 25th.

Salazar fled to Ojinaga to make his last stand. With him was Holmdahl's old machine-gunning companion from the Central American and Madero days: Tracy Richardson. Generals Mercado and Orozco abandoned

Chihuahua City with the remaining troops on November 29th and also retreated to Ojinaga. On December 8th Villa took control of the capital of Chihuahua. Sommerfeld's fellow member of the Bohemian Club, merchant Federico Moye handed the keys of the city to the rebel general. The federal soldiers that had been left to maintain order were glad to sign up with Villa. He was now truly the master of Chihuahua and the most powerful military commander in the revolution. For the first time in his life, Villa took a political office. He became governor of Chihuahua for one month. "At first I assumed the office of governor of Chihuahua to stimulate public business. But after two weeks of work I transferred it to General Chao in obedience to Carranza's orders and occupied myself with military affairs only."[1075]

One of the thorns in the revolutionaries' side from the time Porfirio Diaz left Mexico City was the power and money of General Luis Terrazas, the largest landholder in Chihuahua and one of the richest men in the history of Mexico. Terrazas had financed the Orozco uprising, allegedly assisted in the plan to assassinate Governor Abraham Gonzalez, and fed the interventionists in the U.S. Senate under Senator Fall all the misinformation they could handle. Huerta also was rumored to be a recipient of Terrazas' financial goodwill. No one in the Constitutionalist movement irked Luis Terrazas more than Pancho Villa. While other rebels confiscated cattle and hacienda stores, Villa converted the destruction of Terrazas' wealth into an art form. He publicly looted banks, and drove tens of thousands of Terrazas' cattle into the U.S. for sale. The relationship between Terrazas and Villa was not just disdain, disrespect, and outright hatred: It was war! The events of December 1913 proved for the first time that Villa was winning this war, hands down.

When Villa took the city Luis Terrazas with the majority of his clan had to flee from Chihuahua for safety in the U.S. One of Villa's first moves was to clear the Banco Minero of its deposits. When the Villistas came to rob the Terrazas bank they made a remarkable discovery. Luis Terrazas Junior, the hacendado's son, had remained behind to safeguard the remaining family including his mother and the bank of which he was a director. For reasons of insanity or overconfidence, the young Terrazas thought that Villa would not touch him. Shortly before the Villistas could nab him, he took refuge in the British Consulate. Whether or not Villa was aware of international law, which designated diplomatic missions immune, or whether he simply did not care less about British sympathies, he ordered the billionaire's son arrested. The British Consul protested vehemently but the Villistas removed Terrazas by force. Villa had learned from a director of the Banco Minero, that a large stash of gold had been removed from the vault and hidden. After a few hours of light torture and a mock execution Terrazas revealed that the gold was hidden in a column inside the bank. He did not know which. Raul Madero, by now a Villista general and Luis Aguirre Benavides, Villa's secretary found the horde: 600,000 Pesos in gold ($6.3 Million in today's value).[1076] For a second time in the history of the revolution, the Banco Minero in Chihuahua City had taken center stage. Where the gold ended up remained Villa's secret. Treasure hunters, including Soldier-of-Fortune Emil Holmdahl, would spend decades after the revolution searching for the famed gold to no avail.

The international community in Mexico City and elsewhere held their breath as they expected the impulsive leader to execute the billionaire's son with pleasure. However, the world underestimated Villa's intelligence. Old cowboy logic dictated, "When the calf is tied, the cow doesn't wander very far."[1077] Luis Terrazas Jr. became his prisoner – for almost two years. In view of the son's predicament his father treaded very carefully when it came to Villa. In the course of the next year, Villa confiscated more than six million acres of Terrazas' land including the largest cattle herds of northern Mexico. The worried father negotiated a deal with Silvestre Terrazas, Villa's Secretary of State (no direct relation to Luis Terrazas), and Lazaro De La Garza, Villa's Secretary of Finance, to account for the confiscations and receive a portion of the compensation received for the land and cattle sales.[1078]

Another well-known member of Chihuahua City society fled to the safety of California ahead of Villa's entry into the city. Otto Kueck, Sommerfeld's contact to the German embassy had compromised himself through a letter, which came to the attention of Villa. The contents are not known, however, Sommerfeld testified in 1918 "We had found out…" indicating that he was part of the team that orchestrated Kueck's downfall.[1079] The accusation was that Kueck had supported the Huerta regime. Considering that Pancho Villa's forces had looted and burned the main Ketelsen and Degetau store in 1911, the likelihood exists that the German merchant had lost his idealism for the revolutionary cause. Sommerfeld also mentioned tensions of Otto Kueck with the American consul Marion Letcher to whom he had allegedly had displayed "strong anti-American feelings."[1080] In any event, the German consul left his good offices to another employee of Ketelsen and Degetau, Ernst Goeldner. Kueck never came back to his home and died on March 19th 1915 in Los Angeles, California of a heart attack.[1081]

The last stronghold of the federal army in Chihuahua beckoned Villa's attention at year's end. All of Sonora was now firmly under Constitutionalist control, Carranza's home state of Coahuila was falling, and Zapata had gained critical ground in the south. Villa now set his eyes on the little border city across from Presidio, Texas. The battle for Ojinaga was different from the other battles the División Del Norte fought in 1913. Villa's army by now could only be described as awesome. Its ranks had swollen to over 20,000 men. Felipe Ángeles, the former chief of the Colegio Militar in Mexico City and Brigadier General under President Madero, took charge of Villa's strategic planning and use of artillery. The might of the rebel army rested on the proper use of artillery fire. Just as the machine gun had transformed military strategy in the first years of the revolution, the development of more accurate artillery and its tactical use to support cavalry charges became the backbone of sound military strategy. The federal army had strong artillery that they used very effectively as a defensive weapon. Just before the revolution started, former Secretary of War under Porfirio Diaz, General Manuel Mondragon, had updated the army with the newest weapons, mainly 75mm and 100mm Schneider-Canet guns from France. The new field guns could accurately fire twenty rounds per minute, each round containing 7.2 kilograms of shrapnel. While the rebels rejoiced every time they captured federal field pieces, nobody knew how to effectively operate them. It took foreigners such as Arnold Krumm-Heller, Emil Holmdahl, and Franz Wachendorf alias Horst von der Goltz to run the artillery units. Using cannon and field pieces in a highly mobile army charging across fluid battlefields required a whole new level of expertise. It was Felipe Ángeles, who had spent years in France to study modern warfare techniques that transformed Villa's artillery into an effective and deadly offensive tool. The field guns lined up as four-gun rapid-fire batteries could mow down fifty to seventy-three percent of attacking cavalry, open a sixty-foot breach in a solid masonry wall with only fifty-eight shells from 1.5 miles distance, and destroy entrenched infantry.[1082]

Also joining the rebel forces were John Reed and Ambrose Bierce, a multitude of photojournalists, a Mutual Film Company crew led by Frank N. Thayer, and several writers.[1083] David Lawrence, Sommerfeld's colleague from the AP News days, imbedded himself with Villa's general staff as a reporter. The rebel general had become a rock star. There was no doubt in anyone's mind when the rebel army congregated outside Ojinaga as to who would carry the day. Rebel detachments under Pánfilo Natera and Toribio Ortega left Chihuahua City with three thousand men. The Battle of Ojinaga started on New Years' day, 1914 when General Ortega surrounded the border city. Villa described the first skirmishes, "...the enemy attacked, dismantled a piece of artillery, caused many casualties, and forced a retreat. The next day the battle continued, and the enemy killed 200 men. On the third day enemy cavalry came out, supported by artillery. There was a furious encounter resulting in great bloodshed, and although the enemy withdrew, driven back by Servin's cannon and the action of our troops, Ortega ceased fire during the combat, and 80 of our men were killed and 130 taken prisoner. Señor! Our forces saw the enemy withdraw without loss or damage, and the 130 prisoners were shot in Ojinaga."[1084] General John J. Pershing, in charge of the American forces protecting the citizens of Presidio, Texas, on the opposite side of the Rio Bravo, impressed in no uncertain terms on the rebel commanders that if bullets were to land on the American side there would be severe consequences. Considering the terrain this requirement severely limited the freedom of movement for the opposing forces. Every time the rebels advanced, the federals would make sure to back right up to the border which caused stray bullets to fly into Presidio. Sometimes, federal soldiers would simply fire into the U.S. in order to halt the enemy advance.

The situation in Ojinaga became surprisingly ugly. Generals Ortega and Natera fought over attack strategy, while the federals very aptly used their combined artillery and cavalry to inflict heavy losses on the Villistas. Much to Villa's chagrin the federals seemed able to resupply themselves from across the border. In Ciudad Juarez an anxious Villa dispatched Sommerfeld to plug the enemy supply line. Sommerfeld told BI Agent John Wren to look for 30/40 ammunition as early as December 23rd. The agents searched the "GH and SA Depot" but found nothing.[1085] On January 7th Sommerfeld approached Agent Wren again with more precise information as to who was supplying the federals at Ojinaga. According to Sommerfeld the munitions were hidden in alfalfa bales.[1086]

After ten days of fighting without being able to dislodge the enemy Villa had enough. With great fanfare he left Chihuahua on the 8th of January and entered the field a few days later with nine hundred additional troops.[1087] The attack started on the 11th of January. "The next day I dictated the following orders for the attack: the troops would be divided in three columns; on the south Hernandez and José Rodriguez with eight hundred men, supported by Servin's artillery; on the right, that is on the east between the Conchos and the Bravo, my headquarters and nine hundred men under Trinidad Rodriguez and Herrera; on the left, Toribio Ortega with seven hundred men and Auxiliaries of San Carlos under Chavarría."[1088] Villa's leadership carried the day. After one hour and five minutes of heavy fighting the federals as well as Orozco's irregulars decided to seek the safety of the United States.[1089] Generals Mercado, Salazar, and Orozco lived to fight another day. Mercado became a prisoner in Fort Bliss, Orozco and Salazar melted into the countryside. On January 12th, General John J. Pershing met Villa for the first time and shook hands with the revolutionary through the border fence. Pershing and the U.S. cavalry had its hands full with the federal refugees, which amounted to "3,352 officers and men as well as 1,607 women."[1090] All had to be fed, guarded, marched to Fort Bliss and interned.

Sommerfeld and his people along the border would hunt José Ines Salazar and Pascual Orozco mercilessly. Salazar was quickly caught and booked in jail. However, Orozco had a better network. A wanted man both in Chihuahua and the United States Orozco tried his best to hide. Huerta's consul in El Paso, Miguel Diebold suddenly departed to San Antonio. Sommerfeld suspected correctly that Diebold was assisting Orozco. The German agent received intelligence on the 19th of January that Orozco was "in Hot Wells or Mineral Wells, near San Antonio."[1091] On that same day Agent Daniel from Marfa confirmed Orozco's whereabouts there.[1092] In the same memo Agent Daniel reported that the British hacendado William Benton knew the whereabouts of Orozco. The BI in El Paso asked Sommerfeld who knew Benton to interview him. Benton had some knowledge of Orozco who had talked to a friend on the 15th in Shafter, Texas but could not confirm having seen him.[1093] Sommerfeld managed to get Diebold indicted and arrested on conspiracy charges.[1094] Despite the efforts of the Department of Justice and Sommerfeld's organization, Orozco slipped away. He lived to see through several more conspiracies, but eventually a posse arranged by a Texas rancher shot him in flagrante delicto rustling cattle on August 30th 1915.

Another famous person disappeared in the Battle of Ojinaga. Ambrose Bierce, who wrote the last known letter to his daughter Helen on December 26th 1913 from Chihuahua City, had been seen as an active participant in the Battle of Ojinaga. "He said that he had ridden four miles to mail the letter and that he had been given a sombrero as a reward for 'picking off' one of the enemy with a rifle at long range. He also told her that he was leaving with the army for Ojinaga, a city under siege, the following day."[1095] After the battle he disappeared and no trace of him was ever found. Bierce's daughter Helen became alarmed after she had not heard anything of her father by January. Most disturbing was the appearance that Bierce had arranged his affairs at home in a way that pointed to his expectation not to return. The seventy-one-year-old writer had been suffering from depression. In a letter to his cousin

313

Laura, Bierce wrote on December 16th 1913: "Good-bye — if you hear of my being stood up against a Mexican stone wall and shot to rags please know that I think that a pretty good way to depart this life. It beats old age, disease, or falling down the cellar stairs. To be a Gringo in Mexico — ah, that is euthanasia!"[1096]

Helen approached the U.S. government to help find her father. Apparently, and quite different from the timeline most historians offer on the efforts of the U.S. government to find Bierce, the request was not made until September 1914. General Scott related the message from Secretary of the Interior, Franklin Lane, to Felix Sommerfeld.

"The Secretary of the Interior, Mr. Franklin K. Lane, is very anxious to get news of a man by the name of Ambrose Bierce, who went to Mexico last year and his friends have heard nothing from him since last December. He is quite a poet and writer, was 71 years of age when he left Washington last fall, was feeling exceedingly strong and healthfull [sic]...He...was accredited to the Villa forces...He had a considerable sum of money with him...In this letter [dated 12-26-1913] he said that his subsequent addresses would be indefinite, that he intended to go [on] horseback and by rail, when possible, through to the West coast of Mexico and from thence to South America...The Secretary would like you to have confidential inquiry made to trace Mr. Bierce. Anything you can do in this direction will be greatly appreciated by him and by the Secretary of War."[1097]

The German agent tracked Bierce from El Paso to Chihuahua City where the writer's presence had been confirmed and the last letter was sent from on December 26th. In this letter Bierce claimed that he was leaving on a troop train from Chihuahua to Ojinaga. The time frame coincides exactly with the dispatch of six brigades under Generals Ortega and Natera to Ojinaga. Of course, the generally accepted story that Bierce somehow attached himself to Villa is untrue given this time frame. Very surprising is the fact that Bierce did not join the movie producers, journalists, and other foreign admirers of Pancho Villa to witness this last battle for control of Chihuahua. At least, none of those remembered Bierce after his disappearance. Tex O'Reilly, the soldier-of-fortune turned writer was one of the few people who claimed to have heard of Bierce coming through El Paso and on to Chihuahua City. "O'Reilly says that several months later, he heard that an American had been killed in a nearby mining camp of Sierra Mojada. He investigated and heard how an old American, speaking broken Spanish, was executed by Federal Troops when they found out he was searching for Villa's troops. The locals told how he kept laughing, even after the first volley of his execution."[1098] Since not many of Tex' stories pass the truth test, it is likely that O'Reilly simply related rumors as his own research.

The most widely accepted stories placed Bierce in Ojinaga in the beginning of January. There, the course of events separate. Some rumors had it that the "old gringo" got in a fight with Pancho Villa and was executed. "Odo B. Slade, a former member of Pancho Villa's staff, recalled an elderly American with gray hair and an asthmatic condition who served as a military advisor to Villa. The American was called Jack Robinson, and he criticized the Mexicans' battle strategies with the accomplished eye of a military expert."[1099] Another claimed that Bierce got lost on the battlefield and was captured by federals that killed him. A more conservative and perhaps more realistic twist was that Bierce "...started out to fight battles and shoulder hardships as he had done when a boy, somehow believing that a tough spirit would carry him through. Wounded or stricken with disease, he probably lay down in some pesthouse [sic] of a hospital, or in some troop train filled with other stricken men. Or he may have crawled off to some waterhole and died, with nothing more articulate than the winds and the stars for witnesses."[1100] George Weeks, a friend of Bierce, traveled to Mexico in 1919 to research the author's disappearance. According to an officer of the Mexican army, Bierce "had collapsed during the attack on Ojinaga and had died from hardship and exposure."[1101]

Sommerfeld's research revealed a potentially different chain of events: Bierce probably never was in Ojinaga or survived the battle and returned to Chihuahua City right after the battle. Sommerfeld found out that the writer left Chihuahua City to the south not to the north where Ojinaga is located. "I investigated in Chihuahua, Mexico and found out that Mr. Bierce left that City some time [sic] in January 1914 for the South, and that is the last anybody [had] ever seen or heard of him. I communicated that information at that time to General Scott on my return to Washington."[1102] Bierce leaving to the south solves several inconsistencies: Villa, who Bierce claimed to have been with, was in Chihuahua City in the beginning of January and had had no plans to come to Ojinaga. If Bierce was with Villa and stayed with him through the battle, why did neither Villa nor anyone else in the Villa camp remember seeing him? If Bierce traveled south towards Durango, he was executing his plan of trying to make it to Mexico's west coast. If he wanted to see fighting, there was plenty of action in January of 1914 in the Laguna region. Also important was the fact that in order to go west, one had to come through Torreon, the railroad hub in central Mexico.

Carey McWilliams, a journalist and Bierce's biographer, seemed to share Sommerfeld's conclusion that the famous writer was alive after the Battle of Ojinaga. Through the good offices of Sherburne Hopkins, McWilliams addressed a letter to Sommerfeld in April 1930 in which he asked for any information about "an ammunition train that was supposed to have been captured by Gen. [Rudolfo L.] Gallegos in the state of Durango in February 1914? It had been rumored that Bierce was attached to this train which was destined for the Huerta forces in Torreon."[1103] Sommerfeld could not offer McWilliams much additional information. The only leads he could provide to the journalist were to check with the Arrieta brothers who were in charge of the Constitutionalist forces in the Laguna and around Torreon in 1914.

The matter of Bierce carrying "a large sum of money" has not been mentioned in the historiography of his disappearance. The Mexican countryside in the early days of 1914 was notoriously infested with rebels of any shape and form, deserted bands of federal soldiers, hapless and homeless peons, and bandits. An old "gringo" traveling with guides, or on a train that had been captured, would have been a prime target for robbery or worse. Conceivably, he was robbed and dumped somewhere along the way without any witnesses. The true story might never see the light of history. Sommerfeld explained the reason why he did not search further for Bierce in 1914. "When I received the letter from General Scott, it was impossible to make any inquiries in the South as I was with the Villa faction and the South was in the hands of the Carranza partisans."[1104] Sommerfeld felt that he satisfied his obligations to General Scott and his superiors in the Wilson administration. Clearly, he did not obsess over the vanished poet. Sommerfeld had more important things to do in the final push against Huerta than to research the disappearance of a suicidal writer in the middle of a war. In a strange twist of history, Sommerfeld's response to Carey McWilliams in May of 1930 from the Hotel Bristol in Berlin is the last known correspondence of the German agent. Just as is the case with Ambrose Bierce, when, where, and how Sommerfeld died remains a under a veil of secrecy that no historian has lifted to this day.

CHAPTER 19

~

VILLA COMES INTO HIS OWN

On February 2nd 1914, several guards led a man out of Pancho Villa's house in Ciudad Juarez, blindfolded him, stood him up against an adjacent adobe wall, and executed him. The man was Francisco I. Guzman. "An effort was made at first to conceal Guzman's summary execution, but [an] inquiry as to a pool of blood in Villa's yard revealed the fact."[1105] He had come to Villa on a secret mission. Felix Diaz, whom Huerta had put on ice after the overthrow of President Madero, wanted to get back in the game. Through emissaries he proposed to Villa to separate from Carranza and form an alliance with him. In the beginning of January 1914, Diaz first sent Bonales Sandoval, a lawyer who had intervened on behalf of Villa when he was in prison. The meeting never took place. Sommerfeld had threatened Sandoval with "a warm welcome awaiting" him if he entered Mexico.[1106] The German agent wrote to Sherburne Hopkins on January 29th: "We are all anxiously waiting for Bonales Sandoval and if he crosses to Juarez we shall give him a reception he never received before. He is a particular friend of mine and I am ready to give him a hot welcome..."[1107] The "particular friendship" stemmed from Sandoval participating in the uprising of General Reyes against Madero in 1912, which Sommerfeld helped defeat. However, Sandoval got away after an American judge allowed him released from prison. The lawyer who seemed in trouble perpetually then served under Felix Diaz in the coup that killed Madero.

On his latest mission Sandoval waited around in El Paso until January 20th then returned to Felix Diaz in Havana.[1108] For unknown reasons Diaz decided to send a second envoy, Francisco Guzman, to sound out Villa's willingness to split with Carranza. On the afternoon of February 2nd there could be little doubt as to Villa's disposition to the offer. Sandoval did not fare any better. His demise just took more time. Diaz sent him a second time to Villa in the fall of 1914 with similar proposals of a Diaz-Villa alliance. This time he had overtaxed Villa's patience. He died by firing squad.[1109]

318

American journalists and the U.S. State Department watched with increasing apprehension the violence with which Villa meted out punishments to those who the Constitutionalists found treasonous. Silvestre Terrazas, Villa's Secretary of the Hacienda, maintained regularly updated blacklists called the "Lista de los enemigos del pueblo."[1110] No quarter was given to anyone on the list or anyone suspected in aiding and abetting the enemy. Guzman was one more "enemy" that received a "just" punishment. Carranza had decreed in 1913, "...anyone who took an active part in the overthrow of Madero must be killed."[1111] Sandoval, Guzman, and others on the payroll of Felix Diaz qualified under that definition. The grounds for these executions had been based on law. "Carranza assumed full responsibility for the executions and declared that it was he who had revived Juarez' law of January 25, 1862, considering all those who were fighting against the legitimate Mexican government as subject to execution."[1112]

Since Villa had taken control of Ciudad Juarez in November, Brigadier General Hugh Lenox Scott, the commander of 2nd Cavalry Brigade headquartered at Fort Bliss, quickly established a good relationship with the rebel leader. Most military men of the time, whether German, American, French, or British considered Villa and many of the revolutionary guard to be "half-tamed beasts." Scott had a similar image of him but also saw in Villa a man who with some coaching would make a reliable and able leader of Mexico. Villa correspondingly liked Scott because of his upright, direct, and concise approach. Evidence from the Battle of Juarez indicated to General Scott that Villa was a man who would ultimately cooperate with the U.S. military authorities. To support his effort, Scott endeavored to raise the Mexican rebel leader out of his "primitive world" and into "civilization:"

"There is nothing that men like Villa respect so much as truthful, direct, forceful statements, no matter how unpalatable. Like a child or a dog these primitive people know well with whom they are dealing and are impressed accordingly...Villa spoke no English and after we had become somewhat acquainted, I told him, 'Civilized people look on you as a tiger or a wolf.' 'Me,' he exclaimed in great surprise. 'Yes,' I told him, 'you.' 'How is that?' he asked. 'Why, from the way you kill wounded and unarmed prisoners. Didn't you kill a hundred and twenty-five unarmed prisoners the other day at Casas Grandes?' 'Why, those were my enemies,' he exclaimed, as if that was what enemies were meant for. 'There it is,' I said. 'Civilized people don't do that. You will only bring down on your own head the execration of civilized people when you do that.' He answered, 'Well, I will do anything you tell me.' 'Stop that, then,' I told him. 'You injure your own cause by it, in the minds of all foreigners.' I gave him a little publication sent me by General Wood, written by the General Staff of the British Army on how to treat prisoners and conquered peoples. He had it translated into Spanish, put it out among his troops, and was guided by it himself to the extent of refraining from killing the next four thousand prisoners that fell into his hands. This shows him susceptible to good influences, even if this was only temporary."[1113]

Villa indeed became a bit more lenient with regards to the execution of prisoners, although most likely not as a result of a newfound humanity but because he strategically needed the goodwill of the American government. In a letter to General Scott dated February 12th 1914, Villa showed how impressed he was with Scott's collegial attitude:

"C. Juárez, Febrero 12 de 1914
Much-esteemed Sir:

It gives me great pleasure to address to you in these lines in order to greet you respectfully, and send you my warmest congratulations for the intelligence and work of the forces under your command and the federal authorities in El Paso, who have proceeded against the group of criminals who tried to invade the territory of our state in order to commit depredations and disturb the order and peace, which happily reigns in this state of Chihuahua.

I present to you my gratitude for the commitment and goodwill that you have demonstrated, to pursue as effectively as justified the wicked sons of Mexico, which blinded by an unhealthy passion, tried to cause damage and discredit to our Fatherland. You know I am entirely at your service and would have very special satisfaction in serving and helping you as I can, being a very nice man of rectitude and intelligence as chief of U.S. forces in this area and I hope that the opportunity will offer itself to demonstrate how much I appreciate the fairness and energy with which the government of the United States is proceeding with respect to the affairs of our unfortunate Fatherland.

I reiterate my respectful greetings, taking this opportunity to subscribe to your stated attention,

Francisco Villa[1114]

For the most part summary executions did not involve American, British, or German subjects. That is not to mean that foreigners in Mexico, especially Spanish and Chinese, did not find themselves victimized by robbery, blackmail, kidnapping, and murder. However, to the relief of the respective governments, those human rights abuses typically spared citizens of the main western powers. From the beginning of the revolution in the fall of 1910, despite the many foreign mercenaries, only one foreign fighter had been publicly executed: Soldier-of-fortune and well-known machine gunner Thomas Fountain, who fell into the merciless hands of the Orozquistas. In general, none of the revolutionary leaders wanted to create an international incident, while depending on weapons and other support from the United States and Europe. However, the wide definition of "enemy," the complete lack of due process, and the seemingly absolute power of the División Del Norte in its territory made the eventual killing of an American, Brit, or German a foregone conclusion. As the execution of Guzman and that of numerous others showed, Villa sensed that neither a Mexican authority nor foreign government had the means to check his power. While generally leaving foreigners alone, Villa had tested the will of the European powers all along. He killed and expelled scores of Spanish citizens from his territory without repercussions. The Chinese, thousands of whom the Villistas rounded up and killed, had no diplomatic representation in Mexico. Finally, when Villa arrested Luis Terrazas Jr. in the British consulate, he purposely created an international incident. Besides some initial outrage nothing happened. Further and further Villa tested the waters of international resolve. He expelled the German consul from Chihuahua with the result that Germany appointed a new one. Indeed, on Silvestre Terrazas' "enemy" list the entire German and French communities of Chihuahua were characterized as "Orozquistas and Huertistas [who] with lots of money assisted in the formation of irregular forces."[1115] The financial support, however, was not meant to support Huerta, but to keep their homes, businesses, and lives. After the Battle of Ojinaga in the first days of 1914, Villa was the single most powerful force in Mexico, master of Chihuahua, and head of its state government.

On February 17th, a rancher named William S. Benton made an appointment with Pancho Villa and met him at his house in Ciudad Juarez. "...Benton was a native of Aberdeenshire, Scotland, and was about 45 years old [he was actually 50]. He went to Mexico from Scotland when about 25 years old. He worked over Northern Mexico as a mining man, rancher, and prospector. He finally settled permanently on the Hacienda Los Remedios, near

Santa Rosalia, in the State of Chihuahua...It is said in Chihuahua that he paid $1.25 an acre for the 100,000 acres which make up the hacienda, and since it has been improved it is estimated to be worth $1,000,000."[1116] The reason Benton wanted to see Villa had to do with a recent order for large haciendas to cut their fences. The reasoning behind this order was manifold. Fencing one's land had never been a tradition in the desert lands of the American Southwest and Mexican North. Cattle were branded and as such could roam until cowboys rounded them up and drove them to market. Smaller ranchers made deals with the large haciendas that allowed their cattle to roam freely. In return, they worked as vaqueros when it came to the large cattle drives in the fall. Fences also prevented the cattle from finding their own water. As a result of fencing, the ranchers who could afford it dug wells while the smaller ranches could not access water. In Texas and the American Southwest barbed wire cattle enclosures precipitated the so-called range wars where smaller ranchers cut wires to keep the traditional open range. However, by the turn of the century enclosure of rangeland became the rule. Not so in Mexico. Benton, who had fenced his hacienda with barbed wire - including what used to be public land -, incurred the ire of the smaller scale Mexican ranches in his neighborhood.[1117] Villa, as soon as he took power, decided for the smaller cattle ranchers and ordered to cut the fences. Hacendados, including Benton, somewhat understandably feared that their cattle would now be rustled as happened to Terrazas' huge herds. According to historian Friedrich Katz, Benton wanted to present Villa with a claim for missing cattle.[1118] This was the issue that Benton wanted to discuss with Villa. However, it is important to note that neither Benton's land nor cattle was ever due to be confiscated.[1119] Benton implied that removing the fences around his pastures, and especially clearing the access to public lands he had fenced, amounted to confiscation of his cattle herds.

The meeting between Villa and Benton turned into an altercation. Villa told Benton that if he did not like it, he would purchase his ranch and evict him. Benton in turn accused Villa of being a bandit.[1120] Then, according to Villa, Benton "reached for his hip pocket. It flashed over me that he intended to kill me."[1121] Benton's family steadfastly claimed that he was unarmed which seemed reasonable since, for obvious reasons, Villa had tight security around him. It is highly unlikely that anyone, especially an armed and hostile hacendado, would be allowed into the office of the then most powerful man in Mexico. Villa's biographer, Friedrich Katz, also supported the theory that Benton was not armed.[1122] Villa's secretary Luis Aguirre Benavides, an eyewitness, told the New York Times in 1915 that when Benton called Villa a bandit he "…did not finish the sentence. General Villa quick as lightning, threw himself, pistol in hand, on the Englishman with the intention of instantly killing him. The woman [Villa's wife Maria Luz Corral] placed herself between th[e] two, thus preventing Villa from firing. The officers of the guard threw themselves on Benton, and, disarming him, led him off immediately to an adjoining room, where he was handcuffed and detained…"[1123]

Exactly how Benton died is not known. Villa and his secretary Aguirre Benavides maintained that Fierro took Benton in a caboose to nearby Samalayuca and smashed his scull thereby killing him.[1124] According to another eyewitness, fellow Englishman Frances Michael Tone, Villa killed Benton in his office and then had Fierro dispose of the body that night.[1125] The British vice-consul of Torreon thought that it was Fierro who killed Benton in Villa's office.[1126] The result, however, is undisputed: Benton was never seen alive after he visited Villa in Juarez that day. According to Villa and many historians who have researched the incident, Benton was an abusive hacendado who had lived and worked in Chihuahua under the protection of Terrazas and Creel. Understandably, Villa and the revolutionary propaganda machine would use these charges to somehow justify the murder. However, the alleged abuses seemed to have transferred into the historiography unchecked. Whether or not the Scottish hothead was more abusive than the American hacendados who were fortunate enough to keep their lands and cattle is unclear. According to historian Katz, Villa and Benton had had an earlier run-in, which had resulted in Villa taking horses and supplies from Benton's ranch.[1127] Benton also had been overheard in the Foreign Club in Chihuahua as supporting the military dictatorship of Huerta. Clearly, the altercation had very personal roots that had little to do with Benton's treatment of Mexican villagers or the supposed confiscation of his ranch.

An added fact that could have exacerbated Villa's hatred for Benton exists in the curious timing of the altercation at Villa's office. As Felix Sommerfeld hunted down the fugitive General Pascual Orozco in the months before, one specific lead pointed to Benton who allegedly knew where Villa's nemesis was hiding. Agent Blanford of the BI asked Sommerfeld to verify the rumor. "Sommerfeld stated that he knows Benton so I requested him to interview him."[1128] The BI agent reported to his superiors on January 19th 1914, "Sommerfeld told me later that he had found Benton and that he had been informed that the friend of young [William S.] Benton is a Mexican and that this Mexican talked with Orozco in Shafter on the 15th instant. The present whereabouts of Orozco was not known to Benton, although he was certain Orozco had left Shafter."[1129] The implication was that Benton somehow had been involved in hiding Villa's most hated opponent. It might never be known what Sommerfeld had reported to Villa with respect to his investigation. However, if Benton indeed had been in any way implicated in the disappearance of Orozco, Villa's wrath would have been boundless.

The murder of William Benton became a huge international incident. The New York Times first broke the story that Benton, who until the 20th of February remained unaccounted for, had been murdered. Villa initially denied that Benton had even been in Juarez to see him. George Carothers, President Wilson's special envoy to Villa supported Villa's denial. When Pancho Villa finally admitted to American Consul Edwards on the 20th that Benton was dead, he refused to go into detail.[1130] On the night of the 20th of February 1914, El Paso's citizens held a mass rally condemning the murder of the rancher.[1131] On the 23rd Villa claimed that Benton tried to kill him, was court-martialed, and executed. Now Secretary of State Bryan sent a hand-written note to Villa via Sommerfeld who stayed at the Sheldon Hotel in El Paso: "Send without delay to this Department [State] a copy of the sentence that formed the basis for the execution of Benton. You can give a copy of the sentence to the press. I am looking forward to receiving this by tonight and advising me of all the facts you have."[1132] Of course, neither a sentence nor any other written documentation existed. In the meantime, British Foreign Minister Grey demanded an investigation. Worse, speculation was abounding that the arms embargo, which had been loosened to aid the Constitutionalists on February 3rd, would be reinstated. The lifting of the ban had been the primary achievement of Hopkins and his friends in Washington. Reinstating it threatened the supply lines for the final push against Huerta. In short, Villa had blundered and the story completely spun out of control.

Sommerfeld's role in the Benton affair is unknown. No record has surfaced to show any directive Sommerfeld received from the German government but he clearly investigated Benton's disappearance. The New York Times reported on the 21st of February that a Brit named Stewart "with Major Holmdahl of Villa's staff, was permitted to search the jails and guard houses of Juarez today, but they found no trace of the missing men."[1133] Holmdahl worked for Sommerfeld's secret service as BI agent Branford had reported to his superiors a week earlier.[1134] Since Villa knew where to find Benton's body, it seems likely that Sommerfeld's agents roamed the jails on behalf of Hopkins, Carranza, or the German government. Naturally, anything of importance

Sommerfeld reported to Hopkins would also reach the American Secretary of State. A week later, two more Britons and a German-American named Gustav Bauch disappeared. Rumors went rampant with stories of Villa's henchmen murdering for pure fun. The El Paso Herald reported on the 24th of February that Bauch was nowhere to be found and probably ended the same way Benton did.[1135] He did. On the 28th the Sausalito News reported, "Storms of Protests follows Villa's Execution of Briton."[1136]

Despite all the real and exaggerated talk of discord between Carranza and Villa, on the 28th of February the First Chief took control of the scandal.[1137] He directed Villa to refrain from any communication with foreign governments or the press. Villa complied only too happily. Then Carranza, in his typical pigheaded manner, gave the international community a bloody nose on purely legal terms. The American government had demanded an investigation into the disappearance and murder of Benton on behalf of the British government. Carranza replied calmly that the British government would have to contact him directly.[1138] Of course this was a ploy. England had recognized the Huerta government and thus did not have any grounds for diplomatic relations with the Constitutionalists. To do so would amount to a diplomatic recognition of Carranza's government. Carranza's Secretary of Foreign Relations, Isidro Fabela, told a New York Times reporter: "Mr. Carranza has officially informed the Department of State at Washington that he could only attend to representations regarding the Benton case if the same were presented to him by a duly authorized representative of the British Government..."[1139] Carranza's delaying strategy worked brilliantly. Within weeks the Benton affair was off the headlines. Villa never turned over the body. An autopsy would have revealed whether Benton had been beaten to death, or was shot at close range, or by a firing squad.

Carranza not only diverted the international attention from Villa onto his provisional government. He also realized that Villa was a loose cannon and needed to be better controlled. The two people up to the task were Felipe Ángeles, Secretary of War in Carranza's administration and brilliant tactician, and Sommerfeld. Villa knew that strategic planning and artillery represented his biggest weaknesses. Ángeles' military career with emphasis on artillery put him in a position to replace the amateurs that operated Villa's cannon and integrate this crucial part of his army into proper attack strategies. Ángeles also had languished in Huerta's prisons after Madero's murder. Villa had the highest regards for this general with untainted Maderista pedigree. The other asset Carranza and Hopkins thought able to "manage" Villa was Felix Sommerfeld.

The German had done an exceptional job mediating between William Bayard Hale and Venustiano Carranza in November, which prevented a total disaster. Carranza now asked him to help. Working on behalf of the First Chief to prevent any attacks on foreigners, Sommerfeld had been in El Paso off and on since December 1913. General Bliss, in charge of the Southern Command, reported to the War Department on December 15th, "General Carranza had dispatched an agent, Felix Sommerfeld, to General Villa, with dispatches directing respectful treatment of foreigners..."[1140] With Villa's army preparing to start the spring campaign against Huerta, Sommerfeld busied himself organizing arms and ammunition to come across the border. The BI agent Scully of New York reported on December 15th, "that one Sommerfield [sic], a soldier of fortune, is said to be in or about New York City ostensibly for the purchase of ordinance supplies."[1141] When Sommerfeld returned from his trip around Christmas 1914, according to the German agent, Carranza asked him to stay with Villa. "...I went back to Carranza and he told me to stay with Villa ...He said 'I need somebody there to guide me.' So I said alright. From that time on I stayed with Villa...[as] advisor and confidential agent."[1142] Sommerfeld, who had experienced his share of problems with the hardheaded Carranza, now had to admit that working with Villa was not much easier. "I had a pretty hard time because he [Villa] was very hard to manage. You never know when he is going to jump."[1143]

Sherburne Hopkins probably orchestrated Sommerfeld's embedding with Villa from behind the scenes. The Benton scandal understandably irked the Washington lobbyist. He had used all his political finesse and connections to finally achieve the lifting of the arms embargo for the Constitutionalists on February 3rd, the day Villa had Guzman executed behind his office in Ciudad Juarez.[1144] The final campaign to oust Huerta was in the making. The cities of Torreon and Zacatecas represented the last obstacles that stood in the way of a march on Mexico City. Considering the advances of the recent months the fall of Huerta seemed virtually certain. For Villa to engage in escapades such as the Benton murder was detrimental to the effort. Sommerfeld, experienced in diplomacy and with the press while also on friendly terms and very familiar with Villa, was a logical choice of someone who could control the rebel general. Hopkins and Carranza sweetened the deal for Sommerfeld with a sizeable monthly income. The German agent wrote to General Scott in July 1914:

"In January [1914] some miners from Chihuahua asked General Villa for the Dynamite concession that is the sole privilege of importing dynamite into Chihuahua through the port of Juarez. This concession has always been in the hands of the dynamite factory in [illegible] Durango, belonging to Limantour and other Cientificos and some Frenchmen. Instead of giving this privilege to the man from Chihuahua General Villa gave it to me. I think some of my friends told Villa, to show me some appreciation for services rendered to him and the cause. I never asked for it [emphasis in the original document]. The import duty on dynamite under the constituted government, that is under Porfirio Diaz and Madero was 24 ½ cts mex per kilo and as duties are paid in U.S. gold at present about 12 cts gold I cut the duty down to 6 cts gold per kilo that is about 1 ¼ cts per lb. From these 6 cts gold I pay about 3 ¾ cts to the federal government, state government and the municipality of Juarez. Since January [1914] about 7 cars of dynamite have passed to Juarez paying me after deduction of all other expenses $1900 net. These 7 cars were paired during march [sic] and beginning of april [sic] since then not a single car of dynamite has been passed across to Juarez and since that time I have not received a single cent for duties on dynamite..."[1145]

Sommerfeld stated to the American authorities in 1918 that this concession actually paid him in "some months $3,000, some months $5,000."[1146] In 1914 that amounted to between $65,000 and $100,000 in today's value, a sizeable monthly income by any standard. These payments to Sommerfeld are not documented in the accounts of the State of Chihuahua.[1147] Most likely they are accounted for in the financial records of the importing companies. An article in the Washington Post on the day that Sommerfeld explained the concession issue to General Scott probably precipitated the German's defensive reaction.[1148] The letter to General Scott represents a clear admission of the facts by Sommerfeld. How long the German agent held this privilege is not known. However, he pushed energetically and, much to the delight of the American authorities, especially of General Scott, he defended American and other foreign citizens and businesses against attack by Villistas or regional revolutionaries. Sommerfeld explained the results of his undertaking: "He [Villa] did not close down any mines...he didn't interfere with the mines. Villa's policy was to let the mines work. So long as Villa was in power mines were working. They [mine owners] had nothing but a letter from Villa [,] 'don't touch any property' and nobody dared to touch it."[1149] With a concession that large Sommerfeld certainly must have been motivated at least in part by the amount of money he made when the mines operated.

The organization that Villa built under the direction of Hopkins and Sommerfeld's other "friends" became a powerhouse in the spring of 1914. Of course it had to since Villa's army was the crucial force in the push to finish off Huerta. The heart of Villa's financial organization was his Department of the Treasury or "Hacienda." Its first manager was Lazaro De La Garza, a wealthy merchant from Torreon. The De La Garza family of Torreon, an old and well-known family that could trace their roots to Spain, was an important player in the region. They engaged in lively business with the U.S. and Europe. Lazaro De La Garza had been the heir apparent of the sizable family fortune. He was born in Laredo, Texas, and had two brothers, José and Vidal. The family engaged in mining and also owned properties in and around San Pedro, the town where Francisco Madero grew up. Lazaro in particular managed the family interests in agriculture. He owned one of the largest cotton gins in San Pedro. Paralleling the experience of the Stallforth brothers, the cotton industry suffered greatly in the years leading up to the revolution. The recession cut down U.S. demand, on top of the severe drought of 1909 that ruined the harvests. By the beginning of 1910, like most middle and upper class Mexicans in the North, the De La Garzas had lost confidence in the ability of the aging Cientificos, the likes of José Ives Limantour, Diaz' notorious Secretary of Finance, to implement meaningful reforms. Lazaro and his brothers knew the Maderos well. For years Francisco's hacienda had sold its harvests to the De La Garzas' cotton gin for processing. Together they had organized exports to the United States. When Madero challenged the dictator in 1910, Lazaro De La Garza headed Torreon's revolutionary junta. Through the time of the Madero administration he and his brothers worked in the family business. After Villa took Torreon in the beginning of October 1913, De La Garza actively joined Villa and headed the infant administration of the hacienda for the División Del Norte.

After Villa controlled Juarez De La Garza transferred his operations to El Paso and turned the department over to Silvestre Terrazas. The hacienda converted rustled cattle from Terrazas' and other ranches into cash, captured cotton from Torreon and the Laguna, and anything else Villa ordered confiscated. It controlled import and export duties and the profits from gambling operations. In charge of the different profit centers were the holders of concessions who, while earning handsome profits, also brought in the cash to finance the huge material requirements of the Villa army. Lazaro De La Garza received the concession for cotton exports from the Laguna region, his erstwhile home.[1150] Francisco Madero's uncle Alberto had the concession for cattle sales in the U.S. and received a "fabulous" commission for this exclusive right.[1151] Hipolito Villa headed one of the most profitable operations of the Villista organization: Ciudad Juarez' extensive gambling and prostitution joints.

Sommerfeld, De La Garza, Madero, and Hipolito Villa worked together very closely and, in an immense logistical effort, supplied the División Del Norte with anything it required: arms and ammunition, clothing, horse hay, rice and beans, coal, horses, and the like. While Silvestre Terrazas and De La Garza before him kept extensive accounts of the transactions, this system depended almost exclusively on the integrity of the concession holders. As it turned out, the temptation and lack of control was too much for some. The most corrupt of Villa's concession holders was the general's little brother Hipolito. He seemed to suffer from sticky hands when it came to counting the hundreds of thousands of dollars his "casas de juego" made. More than once he had to explain serious cases of embezzlement and corruption to his brother who would have immediately shot anyone else for lesser offenses. But Pancho Villa had a soft spot for Hipolito. When De La Garza's office operated out of El Paso, Villa put his former chief of the hacienda in charge of checking on Hipolito. This turned out to be a daunting task. The two almost immediately crossed swords and the relationship went downhill from there. However, as will be discussed later, over time De La Garza's hands became quite sticky also. As a joke of history, the two corrupt Villistas would battle each other in U.S. courts all the way into the 1930s over illegally attained funds.

Alberto Madero and his brothers Ernesto and Alfonso had been in New York since the summer of 1913. As described earlier, their trading business did not really flourish since the family real estate could not be easily converted into cash. This all changed after Villa captured the customs house of Ciudad Juarez in November 1913. Alberto Madero took on the concession for Villa's cattle sales in the U.S. Loads of cash flowed from Ciudad Juarez to New York, and from there to the arms dealers. Rather than selling properties for the Maderos, Sommerfeld and Hopkins set Frederico Stallforth up to be the intermediary between the money and the supplies going to the border. "He [Stallforth] was hard up [for cash], stable tied up, and his wife was ill...so he came here [to New York] and borrowed money [from Sommerfeld]...two hundred dollars, three hundred dollars [at a time]."[1152] Sommerfeld described Stallforth's two to three hundred dollar commission income, not loans, that he now received on a regular basis. Stallforth still had much to be grateful for. He now worked for Sommerfeld with the Madero brothers and Hans Tauscher in New York, forming the link between Charles Flint and the Constitutionalists. As an added benefit, Sommerfeld arranged for his friend's debt to the Mexican government to be settled for 20 cents on the Dollar.[1153] Getting Villa to buy up the remaining promissory notes saved Stallforth and his brothers about $55,000 ($1.15 Million in today's value). This did not mean, however, that the American investors who loaned him money in 1908 and 1910 released Stallforth from his indebtedness to them. Nevertheless, by the end of 1913, Frederico Stallforth suddenly afforded for himself a new house in South Orange, New Jersey, and was able to relocate his wife and two daughters from Santa Barbara to live with him.[1154] Stallforth's commission payments in the spring of 1914 can be found in Lazaro De La Garza's financial records. In February 1914 they show an average of $275 to $336 per week (six to seven thousand Dollars in today's money) paid from Alfonso Madero to Stallforth for arms and ammunition procured from Hans Tauscher.[1155] Stallforth testified in 1917 that he sold one million cartridges to Alfonso Madero in 1913.[1156] He did not mention where the funds for this order came from, about $735,000 in today's value, but Sommerfeld would be a safe bet. The statement to the BI related only to Stallforth's interaction with the Maderos. He was not questioned about his business with Charles Flint, Hans Tauscher, or Felix Sommerfeld that might have yielded a more complete accounting of his involvement in the arms and munitions procurement for Villa.

Contrary to all historical accounts of Germany's role in the Mexican Revolution, the U.S. representative of Krupp and other German arms manufacturers in the person of Hans Tauscher now began to supply Villa's army in earnest. On January 1st 1914, the Huerta government had failed to meet Mexico's international obligations. Huerta officially announced on January 13th that Mexico was not in a position to service its debt in the foreseeable future.[1157] If any American, British, German, or French business and banking interests had been on the fence as to whether to support Huerta or the Constitutionalists, this move by the Mexican government sealed its fate. On the 16th all major German banks addressed a letter to the German Foreign Office. In it Bleichröder und Sohn, the Deutsche Bank, the Dresdner Bank, and other debtors asked the German government to "adopt any appropriate measure it may see fit with highest possible urgency to protect the imperiled rights of the bondholders."[1158] The American government as well rattled its sabers and activated marines to intervene in Mexico if called upon.[1159] The tactical objectives consisted of securing Tampico's oil fields and the customs houses of Tampico and Veracruz that Huerta controlled. Revenue from these three sources would be used to service Mexico's debt independent of who came out on top in the raging civil war.

Both the U.S. and the German governments now threw their full weight behind the Constitutionalists in general, and Pancho Villa in particular.[1160] Historians Meyer, Katz, McLynn, and others steadfastly claimed that Germany supported Huerta against the rebels.[1161] While rumors to that extent were abounding, the opposite was the case. Hopkins and his friends had managed to cut off the money supply for Huerta and thereby nullified most existing arms contracts for lack of funds. The German arms went to where the money was.[1162] On the 7th of February 1914, Tauscher sold one million 7mm cartridges to Alfonso Madero.[1163] On the 9th $9,166 transferred to the German arms dealer for another 300,000 rounds. On the 10th Tauscher signed a receipt for $5,000 down payment on another one-million-cartridge order amounting to $30,555.[1164] On February 17th, Tauscher shipped 300,000 cartridges on SS "El Dia."[1165] On February 27th, the arms dealer shipped 400,000 cartridges on SS "El Valle."[1166] These shipments were "call offs" for a much larger arms contract of twenty or more million cartridges the Maderos had concluded with Tauscher and the Deutsche Waffen- und Munitionsfabriken, Berlin, whose interests he represented. Typically, large orders of millions of cartridges were fixed in a contract that was activated with a down payment of a certain percentage on the gross value, usually ten percent. This payment reserved the production capacity on that contract in the factory. After that, based on the speed of production and the needs of the customer, individual shipments were "called off" and the balances paid, that is the remaining ninety percent of the value of each shipment.

In September 1913, the representative of the Deutsche Waffen- und Munitionsfabriken in Mexico, Guillermo Bach, wrote to the German Ambassador von Hintze "Abraham Z. Ratner...ordered 50 million Mauser cartridges...for $31 per thousand, FOB New York."[1167] The Ratner brothers, Abraham and José, were immigrants from Vilnius, Lithuania, and had settled in Tampico. Under the Diaz administration Abraham Ratner founded the Tampico News in that city and became a wealthy man. When he was found to support the Cientificos under the Madero administration, he was expelled and settled in New York.[1168] When Huerta took power in February of 1913, Ratner took over the purchasing organization for Huerta. He and his brother José worked out of an office in New York. When Huerta had most of Mexico and her customs houses under his control, the Ratners required U.S. factories to relinquish any sales to the Constitutionalists in order to contract with them. While this stipulation worked earlier in 1913, the Hopkins people, mainly in the person of Felix Sommerfeld, almost completely cut the Ratners off as soon as the embargo was lifted in February 1914. U.S. factories received so many orders from the Constitutionalists that their production capacities became filled. As a result, not only the Constitutionalists but also Huerta had to place additional orders in German factories. Whoever activated his contract first would be in the position to claim the production capacity. Huerta, for example, signed a contract for twenty million 7mm cartridges with the Deutsche Waffen- und Munitionsfabriken, Berlin, in September 1913. The Mexican government never made the down payment and, as a result, never received delivery.[1169] Ambassador von Hintze commented in a memorandum to the German Chancellor von Bethmann Hollweg, "...the Mexican Ministry of War [arranged] for the delivery of war materiel with different foreign companies, among them the Deutsche Waffen und Munitionsfabriken...without so far having paid anything on only one of these orders."[1170]

It would be a mistake to conclude, as historian Baecker has, that the munitions in von Hintze's memorandum never made it to Mexico. German arms dealers had transferred these exact contracts, which Historian Baecker listed as not shipped to Mexico, to the Constitutionalists.[1171] The representative of the Deutsche Waffen- und Munitionsfabriken in New York was none other than Hans Tauscher. The German Ambassador in Washington von Bernstorff wrote to the Foreign Office on February 14th 1914, "...American factories are not in a position to satisfy the needs of the Constitutionalists. From our perspective there are no objections to the aforementioned weapons deliveries."[1172] With the support of the German embassy and the German Foreign Office, the contracts were transferred to the benefit of the Constitutionalists since "Money for the payment of these deliveries is existing."[1173] In May 1913, the BI had tracked a Huerta order for fifty thousand Mauser rifles that had allegedly been impounded by the German government in Hamburg.[1174] While the German government could have impounded the weapons in order not to violate the American arms embargo, it is far more likely that Huerta had not paid for the order. The arms were never produced because without a down payment no factory would reserve a production slot. Ambassador von Hintze wrote on December 4th that the German manufacturers were "again" talking about the fifty thousand Mauser rifle and one hundred million 7mm cartridge orders "despite the bad experiences" with the Mexican government in the past.[1175] Whether any portion of this order ever shipped, and to whom, is not clear in the historical record, but most likely it died as a result of lacking funds.

The orders Tauscher shipped to the Constitutionalists in just that one week between February 7th and 13th of 1914 amounted to one million U.S. Dollars in today's value and Stallforth received commissions on all of it.[1176] This volume of shipping from Germany to the Constitutionalists went on for months. The price including commissions of $31 per thousand was exactly what Huerta had negotiated in Mexico City a few months earlier. The key to understanding this issue is one word: shipped. Not "under contract," which is the downfall of historians alleging German support for Huerta. German shipments of guns and American consignments of munitions reached the rebels by sea through the ports of Matamoros and Tampico (after May 14th 1914) via New York, New Orleans, and Galveston.[1177] El Paso received the shipments from the U.S. gulf ports via rail. Virtually none of the Huerta contracts were actually shipped to the federal army but, thanks to the German government's approval and orchestrated through Sommerfeld, Stallforth, and Tauscher, millions of rounds of ammunition and thousands of Mauser rifles arrived at the doorsteps of Villa's army.[1178]

German supplies in the spring of 1914 were crucial. Since the Mexican army used 7mm Mauser rifles and the rebel armies' guns had been mostly captured from the federals, German arms factories were the only one's able to supply replacement rifles. U.S. factories first had to ramp up production of the proper cartridges. In 1914, only a handful of U.S. factories produced munitions and the 7mm Mauser cartridge was a minute percentage of that capacity. In addition, a Spanish-type 7mm cartridge (model 1893, which was used in Mexico) differed from a Russian and Serbian cartridge of the same caliber, which was designed for a more recent Mauser rifle (model 1912). The cartridges were not interchangeable. In the early months of 1914, Sommerfeld intimately got to know this industry as an operative in the Villa supply organization. This knowledge became the basis for his very effective role as an arms merchant in later years.

As the capacities of U.S. manufacturers reached their limits, Hans Tauscher organized shipments from Germany and sold them to Villa's army via Frederico Stallforth and the Madero brothers. In the meantime, with Flint and Co. as the intermediary, Sommerfeld ordered and shipped ammunition from the four largest U.S. manufacturers, Winchester Repeating Arms Company, Union Metallic Cartridge Company, United States Cartridge Company, and Phoenix Metallic Cartridge Company. Only Winchester, and United had the necessary presses and were willing make 7mm cartridges. Through his dynamite concession and Villa's requirements of black powder (for muzzle loaders, older type cannons, grenades, and bombs), Sommerfeld came in contact with a small powder and shotgun shell manufacturer in East Alton, Illinois.[1179] The Western Cartridge Company belonged to Franklin W. Olin who, with the help of his two sons Franklin Jr. and John, was running the rapidly expanding powder and ammunition business. Sommerfeld convinced him to invest in 7mm cartridge capacity and promised Olin solid orders once he could supply the munitions. The demand for Mexico had pushed up prices to very profitable heights. Other U.S. manufacturers did not see a big future for European ammunition. In order to produce this caliber cartridge, manufacturers had to make substantial investments in industrial presses required to make the brass casings. These presses were short in supply, very expensive, and only one U.S. manufacturer produced them.

For the time being, Olin was able to turn out modest amounts of 7mm ammunition in 1914 using the existing equipment. The capacity Sommerfeld was looking for, however, depended on new presses. None of the histories dealing with Olin Industries or Winchester Repeating Arms Company, which are major industrial concerns to this day, mention the role Felix Sommerfeld played in their rise to prominence. Sommerfeld provided his network of German arms dealers, Mexican revolutionaries, U.S. power brokers, and his dedicated marketing and sales efforts to Franklin Olin. Olin, who joined Sommerfeld on occasion for major negotiations, was the brilliant technical genius in the background that dared to invest when no one else would. Working as an inseparable team from 1914 into the 1920s, both men made Western Cartridge Company into a munitions powerhouse. Indeed, the fledgling powder company in East Alton, Illinois came out of the Great War so strong that in 1931 Olin bought his biggest competitor, the Winchester Repeating Arms Company. The Olin-Sommerfeld partnership would pave the way for Franklin Olin and his son John to become two of the most powerful leaders in the U.S. arms industry - and Sommerfeld a very wealthy man.

When Hopkins started Sommerfeld in his career as the main arms and munitions buyer for the Constitutionalist forces, the "Judeo Aleman," as Villa called him, was not automatically accepted. He first had to earn the rebel's trust.[1180] The system of concessions that Villa had set up created a type of peer pressure control system, a feature of Villa's organizational genius. Despite working in concert for the same cause, Villa's concession holders viewed each other with suspicion and jealousy. De La Garza was in charge of basically all the funds to be invested in the U.S. Even Villa's brother Hipolito had to deal with "Lazarito."[1181] De La Garza had no qualms reporting to Villa if anyone in the organization got out of line. On April 14th 1914, he wrote to Villa that General Avila had ruined the meat prices for the Villistas because he sold his loot on the black market for lower prices. General Ortega, he reported, conducted suspicious meetings in his backroom office. Invoking his fellow procurement partners, De La Garza wrote to Villa that Sommerfeld and Alberto Madero agreed that nothing good could come out of these backroom meetings.[1182] Ernesto and Alfonso Madero in New York tried to keep tabs on Sommerfeld with the higher purpose to stay in the very profitable loop. Sommerfeld in turn reported their transgressions to Villa.

Sommerfeld's main tarnish was that he came to the Villa organization as a Carranza man. No one in Villa's inner circle questioned the immense success Sommerfeld has had in neutralizing the largest threat to the revolution: The defeat of Orozco. The German agent also had tight connections to the big money in New York, yet to Villa and his confidantes, Sommerfeld remained an outsider, not "one of them." Historian Jim Tuck interpreted that Sommerfeld's dispatch to Villa was somehow a mission from Carranza to spy on the untamed general.[1183] While Sommerfeld did spy on Villa, it was not at the behest of Carranza but rather the German government. There is no evidence to suggest that Carranza sent Sommerfeld to spy on Villa. Hopkins wrote in 1916 to the Military Intelligence Division, "...Villa has had opportunity to become great, he has ...demonstrated a becoming desire to conform to conventionalities. His association with Gen. Angeles has done much to improve him in this respect..."[1184] Just as Ángeles, who no historian ever characterized a spy, Sommerfeld had been sent to make Villa acceptable as a political leader of Mexico and to check his wild side. All the available evidence suggests that both Ángeles and Sommerfeld showed unwavering loyalty to Villa and worked within his organization to make the general more successful. Carranza had little influence on Villa before Ángeles and Sommerfeld showed up and even less thereafter. While Ángeles straightened out Villa's military organization, Sommerfeld became an integral part in the effort to set up Villa's financial, procurement, and political organizations. Despite his best efforts to instill trust, Sommerfeld's associates De La Garza, Alberto Madero, and maybe even Villa himself initially eyed the powerful German with some suspicion. The day after Villa had murdered Benton De La Garza noted to Alfonso Madero, "Sommerfeld carried fifty thousand [U.S. Dollars] for purchase [of] rifles and wants fifty five thousand more. - Carefully find out what has been purchased as he says fifteen hundred Mauser [rifles] were shipped and wants to buy three thousand 30/40 and two million cartridges at 18 [U.S. Dollars]. - Answer in order to see if we can send money to Sheldon Hotel."[1185] Madero, who quite obviously did not have the connections to investigate the inner workings of the Hopkins-Flint-Tauscher triangle, reported back to De La Garza:

"Very difficult to investigate [.] Best way would be to order them [ourselves.] Not to buy anything without my sanction and furnish the money through me [.] Very best regards,
Alfonso Madero."[1186]

Without the Maderos involvement, two thousand brand new Mauser rifles arrived from Germany on April 15th.[1187] Ostensibly, Madero's plan to control Sommerfeld and to cut him out of the deals had no merit. The German agent very quickly became the most important man in Villa's supply line. After the American government lifted the embargo on February 3rd, train car after train car with supplies began crossing the border to be transferred to Villa's troops. Then the Benton murder became known. Expecting that the arms embargo would be reinstated against the Constitutionalists as a result, customs agent Zach Lamar Cobb refused to clear the shipments. He impounded one million cartridges, which Sommerfeld had purchased for Villa on the 27th of February 1914.[1188] Frantic telegrams between De La Garza and Villa testify to the fear that this was just the beginning. The financial agent told Villa that Sommerfeld, "...advised me that our enemies are working with much insistence on the American government to reinstate the embargo on arms and material..."[1189] The next day, De La Garza tried to calm Villa down telling him that so far there were sufficient supplies to carry out the next campaign.[1190] This might have been one of those days, which Sommerfeld remembered as Villa being "hard to manage." However, reason prevailed and the day after Sommerfeld notified him of the seriousness of the situation, Villa left town and turned the Benton issue over to Carranza. Thanks to Villa leaving the border and the talking to Carranza, shipments resumed until the next international incident. On the 2nd of March, Sommerfeld shipped across a large consignment of black powder, on the 5th Villa ordered 1,300 rifles and 750,000 cartridges, of which Sommerfeld shipped 1,100 rifles and 300,000 rounds on the 12th.[1191]

Hopkins imbedded with Carranza, and Sommerfeld close to Villa had proven their sway over the rogue revolutionary leader and had carried the day. Sommerfeld worked hard at his new job as the chief arms buyer for Villa. As he did when helping Hopkins and the Constitutionalists to set up their front against Huerta, Sommerfeld traveled incessantly between New York and the border in March and April of 1914, this time on behalf of Villa. To his interrogators in 1914 he lied when asked whether Germany supplied any arms: "No, never", was the determined reply. However, after a few more detailed questions came his way, he admitted that the U.S. capacity for 7mm cartridges did not suffice. "I didn't get any arms because we could not get the kind we wanted."[1192] Sommerfeld tried everything in his power to supply the División Del Norte. When De La Garza felt uneasy and sought to investigate him, Sommerfeld had just received $105,000 ($2.2 million in today's value) for arms procurement. In the spring of 1914, that sum bought 3.3 million 7mm cartridges or 3,200 Mauser rifles, model 1893, or any combination thereof. This was but a small fraction of the money Sommerfeld spent in the first half of 1914.

Sommerfeld's relationship with Villa in the beginning of 1914 was nothing short of stormy. In addition to Villa's suspicions that Sommerfeld leaked information to Carranza, the German took the fall for faulty materials. Naturally, Sommerfeld, like anyone else, had to pay some painful dues, while he learned "on the job." In addition to the quality risks inherent in any manufacturing process munitions were highly susceptible to moisture. When a cartridge did not fire it was hard to pinpoint the guilty party. Had the cap or powder been moist? Where did they get wet, in the factory, the various warehouses, the ocean freighter, or the railroad car? Each link in the logistics chain would deny responsibility and refuse to pay for warranties. The buck stopped with Felix Sommerfeld. His mistakes surfaced quickly. On the 12th of March, he reported to Villa that he bought 1,100 rifles and 500,000 cartridges of the caliber 7.65mm.[1193] Villa, of course, did not want to add new calibers to his units, which made resupply that much more complicated. He told De La Garza to admonish Sommerfeld not to source anything but 7mm or 30/40 caliber, the American Springfield rifle cartridge.[1194]

On the 16th of March, Villa's army boarded the trains in Chihuahua and headed south. For the second time since 1911, Torreon stood between the revolutionary armies and Mexico City. With Felipe Ángeles in charge, Villa's forces swooped into Gomez Palacio, severely beating the federal forces.[1195] On March 26th, the División Del Norte surrounded Torreon. The battle lasted a full week. Ángeles' artillery supported 16,000 revolutionary soldiers who pummeled the city with a hail of fire night and day. Especially Villa's famous night attacks caused the federal defenders to become demoralized and sleep deprived. They defected in droves. On April 2nd the city fell. Huerta had sent six thousand fresh reinforcements to nearby San Pedro de las Colonias to no avail.

The newly established federal positions caved and what was left of the Huerta army withdrew to the south. While Villa and his generals celebrated their success, Sommerfeld received severe admonishment. Apparently, Flint and Company had sent bad ammunition. On April 14th, Villa ranted to De La Garza:

"PLEASE IMMEDIATELY solicit two million Mauser cartridges which must arrive within a short time to proceed with the campaign. I much recommend that you pay attention so that we may find no reason for such poor quality cartridges that Sommerfeld bought. I have lost my troops precisely because of not checking which is indispensable when buying this type of material.[1196]

The problems with Sommerfeld's supplies worsened to the level where Villa was ready to fire him. The general sent a telegram to De La Garza on May 30th in which he requested someone else to buy munitions. Of course, this was impossible since no one had the connections that the German agent had. The issue came to a head when De La Garza sent a stinging memo to Charles Flint on May 30th and signed it with Sommerfeld's name:

"Wired you yesterday seventy five thousand [.] Be sure goods ordered through Sommerfeld are new and thoroughly guaranteed, as failure of previous ones caused much damage and bad impression, but are giving you another chance to vindicate. – Ship Monday. – F. A. Sommerfeld"[1197]

The next morning Sommerfeld asked Lazaro De La Garza whether he was out of his mind when he sent the earlier note to Charles Flint:

"You telegraphed Flint and Company yesterday that you are giving them another chance to vindicate themselves. I want to say that Flint has never sold us such merchandize before. Flint is a house of the highest standing and our friend who have [sic] given us advise [sic] and assistance many times. Your telegram is absolutely unjust and therefore I beg you to telegraph Flint telling them that your telegram was sent by mistake. F. A. Sommerfeld"[1198]

De La Garza's response has not been preserved. However, the shipments through Flint and Company from U.S. manufacturers proceeded unabashedly. Most likely all this trouble was caused as a result of shipping munitions by ocean freighter and storing them several times in unsuitable locations before they finally reached the troops. The only chance to eliminate the risks caused by the complicated logistics was local supply. Sommerfeld thus made the decision to develop U.S. suppliers for Villa that could ship directly by rail and without middlemen. The Western Cartridge Company became his pet project for the next years.

The establishment of hegemonic control over the U.S.-Mexico border crossings and especially the important hub of Ciudad Juarez became the baseline for a successful campaign against the embattled central government of Huerta. All international eyes were on Pancho Villa as the man who could accomplish the feat. Just as the international community began to take comfort in the fact that this military genius had lifted himself from the lowest levels of Mexican society to become the savior of Mexico, he killed Benton. It is sheer luck on Villa's part that Huerta had just defaulted on his financial obligations. Without this fact that has largely been ignored by historians, Villa's career as the main general of the Constitutionalist army would likely have been over. The supplies, which Villa received in the early months of 1914, would not have materialized, he would have been indicted in the U.S., and other generals such as Ángeles, Chao, Trevino, or Obregon could have taken charge of the División Del Norte. Instead, Villa survived the scandal, and received the invaluable services of Hopkins, Flint, Sommerfeld, and the German government, while at the same time consolidating an independent and most effective supply organization through De La Garza and the Maderos. This administrative and financial independence from Carranza's administration, which Villa clearly sought, saved him when he challenged the First Chief's power later in 1914. It did not take long for Villa and his inner circle, especially De La Garza and the Maderos, to realize that Sommerfeld was trustworthy. Through his network in the U.S. and Germany, the German supported, and to a large degree made possible, the material independence Villa sought. Starting in the beginning of 1914 and increasing over the next two years Sommerfeld handled fantastic amounts of money. Unbelievably for one lifetime, the German agent resumed for Pancho Villa in 1914 what he had done a year earlier for President Madero: As confidential agent and highest-ranking German he again served in the inner circle of the most powerful man of Mexico. His services became crucial in the next episode of U.S.-Mexican crises that peppered the revolutionary timeline.

CHAPTER 20

N

SOMMERFELD AND THE ARMS OF THE SS "YPIRANGA"

On April 9th 1914, nine sailors from the American navy vessel USS "Dolphin" went ashore in the port city of Tampico. With orders to purchase gasoline the navy tender ran into a routine stop at the Puente de Iturbide (Iturbide Bridge) in a canal across from several warehouses. The Mexican federal soldiers guarding the harbor installations were quite nervous since the Constitutionalists were within a few miles of the defensive positions of the important city. Suspecting that the Americans would spy on their defenses, the federal colonel in charge, Pablo Gonzalez, arrested and detained the sailors. The Mexican commander of Tampico, Ignacio Morelos Zaragoza, immediately realized the folly of his officer and ordered the Americans to be released. The Wilson administration had declared in November that it would depose the Mexican dictator by force if necessary. Since then the relations between the two administrations had even worsened, exacerbated by the recent default of Mexico on its international obligations. By April of 1914, intervention, especially the occupation of some of the large customs houses, which would allow for the debtor nations to confiscate customs revenue, was on everyone's mind. Republican Senators Albert Bacon Fall and William Alden Smith kept up the clamor for taking military action. For all to see, over four thousand U.S. troops at Galveston were ready for deployment to Mexico. Huerta and his advisors knew that the slightest incident could spark an intervention. He therefore had issued orders not to challenge Americans, their properties, or navy ships patrolling in front of Tampico, Puerto Mexico, and Veracruz under any circumstances. As a result, the Mexican commander ordered the American sailors to be released as soon as he heard of their detention. With gasoline on board the tender returned to the USS "Dolphin" after its occupants had been kept for one-and-a-half hours.

Admiral Henry Thomas Mayo commanded the U.S. fleet patrolling the waters off the state of Tamaulipas, which included Tampico, the rich oil city and Mexico's second largest port. In addition to a formal apology from the Mexican commander and the punishment of the arresting officer, Colonel Gonzalez, he demanded to honor the U.S. flag with a twenty-one-gun salute. General Zaragoza acceded to the first two demands but balked at the third. German Ambassador Admiral von Hintze reported a week later, "The Mexican government has arrested the colonel and initiated an investigation against him; it [the government] is prepared to punish him, if the result [of the investigation] pointed to his guilt. The President of the republic personally expressed his regret over the incident: qu'il déplore l'incident. Only with respect to the issue of the salute he is obstinate. He told me, this was as if someone on the street ripped someone else's matchbox from his pocket, threw it on the ground, and demanded that he should pick it up himself and apologize in addition."[1199] The issue escalated in the following week. On the 12th of April Rear Admiral Frank Friday Fletcher, who commanded all U.S. navy assets in the Mexican theatre, offered to salute the Mexican flag one for one, if the Mexicans performed their twenty-one-gun salute. Huerta refused. Von Hintze correctly mused that if Huerta had acquiesced the embattled President would have lost the last bastion for support in the country: the Mexican military.[1200] He could not give in!

On the 13th of April the situation intensified. Wilson ordered all available American forces into Mexican waters. The mission was to create a naval blockade of Mexico as well as an occupation of the ports of Tampico and Veracruz. Marines from Galveston had orders to prepare an invasion of Mexico with the goal of taking the capital. In Mexico this virtual declaration of war (since a naval blockade is an act of war) was regarded as a replay of the Mexican-American War of 1846 to 1848 when U.S. troops entered Mexico City. In that war Mexico lost half of its territory to the United States. How much would the Americans take this time? From the international point of view, the American intervention presented a first class opportunity to seal the fate of President Huerta, while at the same time impounding customs revenues to reverse the default on Mexican bonds. As an added benefit, whichever revolutionary force entered the capital first would be under the scrutinizing eyes of the American military. The U.S. government thus would have created a lever with which to prevent looting and killing of foreigners. Huerta, who had nothing to lose and a lot to gain by invoking Mexican nationalism, did not blink.

Even Villa acknowledged that he would have to join forces with Huerta against the Americans should Mexico be invaded.[1201]

President Wilson gave General Huerta until April 19th, 6:00 p.m. to comply with the U.S. government's demands. The deadline passed.[1202] On the 20th of April 1914, Wilson spoke to a joint session of Congress. He emphasized the fact that the sailors had been taken "...from the territory of the United States."[1203] "The President said, Huerta having refused [the salute of the American flag], he [Wilson] had come to Congress 'for approval and support in the course I now propose to pursue.'"[1204] Congress gave Wilson the green light to use military force as he saw fit. Coincidentally, and not in any way associated with the American action, the German HAPAG steamer "Ypiranga" left Havana on the morning of April 21st and was approaching the Mexican coastline for a routine stop at Veracruz, the largest port in Mexico, three hundred miles to the south of Tampico. Secretary of the Navy, Josephus Daniels, and Secretary of State Bryan roused the President in the West Wing at 2:00 a.m. that fateful day. The American consul at Veracruz, William W. Canada, had transmitted a telegram to Secretary Bryan, informing him that the German ship carried arms and ammunition for Huerta.[1205] Where and how the American consul had learned of the contents of "Ypiranga's" hold is questionable. What can be said with certainty is that some of the weapons had been a consignment originating in Odessa, Russia, and that, for the most part the weapons and ammunition did not come from Germany.[1206] The German involvement consisted only of the consignment's transportation on a HAPAG steamer with regular service to Veracruz. The American President ordered the occupation of the customs house of Veracruz that morning to prevent the landing of the munitions. An order to that effect went to Admiral Fletcher:

"Early on April 21, 1914, General [Joaquin] Mass [sic], the Mexican military commandant, was notified that US forces intended to take charge of the Custom House and was urged to 'offer no resistance but to withdraw in order to avoid loss of life and property of the people of Vera Cruz [sic].' He, for the most part complied, but the commander of the Naval Academy and unorganized pockets of individuals offered resistance. Ships of the Atlantic Fleet started bombardment of Veracruz. By 11:30 AM the first detail of 787 soldiers, of whom 502 were marines, landed and seized the custom[s] house, and an urban battle ensued in which many civilians are said to have taken part. The defense of the city also included the release of prisoners held at the feared San Juan de Ulua prison. In the meantime, the building of the Naval Academy

342

was being bombarded by the USS Prairie. American troops occupied most of the town by that evening. The USS San Francisco and USS Chester continued the bombardment of the Naval Academy building until the following day."[1207]

Nineteen American soldiers died and seventy-two were injured. The Mexican forces lost slightly less than two hundred, most of them cadets of the naval academy. The civilian population, who had resisted in concert with the federal defenders, continued to snipe at U.S. patrols, which forced Admiral Fletcher to impose martial law on the city. Brigadier General Frederick Funston arrived within a week and organized the long-term occupation of the Mexican city.

If the reason for the bombardment and occupation of Veracruz had been to prevent the landing of the "Ypiranga," the operation was hopelessly bungled. The first mishap was that the "Ypiranga" was not at the docks when the marines landed. While the cargo remained on the German steamer it could not legally be seized. Once unloaded the arms would have been under the authority of the custom's house. Seizing the custom's house then would have brought the arms under the control of the Americans. The ownership question thus would be a dispute between Mexico and the U.S., not Germany and the U.S. The timing of the invasion, namely landing troops before the "Ypiranga" had discharged her cargo, botched the seizing of the arms. When she finally approached the harbor around 1:00 p.m., without having been notified of the American action, a U.S. navy captain boarded the HAPAG steamer and ordered it to drop anchor and wait.[1208] Unaware that it was his ship that apparently caused the landing of marines on Mexican soil, the captain of the "Ypiranga," Karl Bonath, cabled to the German naval cruiser SMS "Dresden", anchored in Tampico, and requested instructions.[1209] Captain Erich Köhler of the "Dresden" had no idea about the U.S. interest in the "Ypiranga" freight either. All he knew was that after clearing her freight, the "Ypiranga" would be assigned to take on German refugees. Ambassador von Hintze had asked the German naval authorities to provide a ship in case of war so that German citizens could be evacuated from Mexico.[1210] Captain Köhler of the "Dresden" therefore requisitioned the steamer "Ypiranga" for the German navy.

Meanwhile, all American naval assets assembled at Veracruz to conduct the occupation. As American sailors took the harbor town of Veracruz, angry Mexican citizens in Tampico threatened hundreds of U.S. citizens there. The navy had taken no precautions to safeguard the American colony there. William F. Buckley testified in 1919,

"...neither Admiral Mayo nor the American Government made any arrangements whatsoever for the protection of American citizens in Tampico. As I said before, Veracruz was captured at 11 o'clock. At 1 o'clock a notice to this effect was posted on the doors of the municipal building in Tampico. By 5 o'clock that afternoon a mob of thousands of Mexicans had surrounded hundreds of American men women and children who had taken refuge in the Southern and Victoria Hotels in Tampico and threatened to kill them. Without hearing a word from either the American Government or Admiral Mayo, the captain of the German gunboat Dresden, which was in the river near the custom house, came to the rescue of the besieged Americans and ordered the Mexican authorities in Tampico to disperse the mob within fifteen minutes. This was done, and then the German captain arranged to take the Americans on the German and English gunboats lying near the custom house, and two or three other boats lying in the river under the protection of English and German guns, and the embarkation of the Americans under the protection of English and German guns was begun between 9 and 10 o'clock that night – the night of April 21st – and was concluded before 2 o'clock in the morning."[1211]

With his swift action, albeit unauthorized, Captain Köhler jumped in the fray of another aspect of a completely bungled American operation, and prevented a bloodbath. When the smoke cleared the next morning, several large warehouses owned by Carl Heynen and Richard Eversbusch had been destroyed by fire.[1212] The efforts of saving American lives and transporting hundreds of American refugees to New Orleans and Galveston earned Captain Köhler the appreciation of President Wilson. On May 7th 1914, American Ambassador in Berlin, James Gerard, thanked the German government, "...for the action of the commanders of German warships in Tampico in assisting American refugees to reach the warships of their own country."[1213] A few months later, after the SMS "Dresden" joined the war and roamed the Atlantic as a feared German raider, the American President personally wrote to the German naval commander, again praising "...your action on the night of April 21 last in sending officers to the Southern Hotel at Tampico to offer to take American citizens from that hotel on board the Dresden, for keeping boats running until the late hour of that night, and for sending a boat on April 22 to all of the places between Tampico and La Barra to advise American citizens to go on board the Dresden and to convey those who would go."[1214]

The "Ypiranga" also transported refugees, including Americans, until May 17th.[1215] When the HAPAG steamer weighed anchor on day after the

American invasion, the 22nd of April 1914, the American government was under the impression that the arms and ammunition on board would be returned to Germany.[1216] The New York Times reported that German Foreign Secretary von Jagow had received assurances from HAPAG that the cargo would return to Hamburg.[1217]

In the end, the Americans had to let the ship go because of the botched timing of the invasion. Not knowing the background of the American rationale, Ambassador von Bernstorff in Washington rightfully asked for the release of the ship. The American commander in Veracruz, Admiral Fletcher, now seemed more concerned with American refugees than the arms on board of the German steamer. In charge of the "Ypiranga's" cargo was Carl Heynen, the former German consul and HAPAG representative for Mexico. From his office in Veracruz, Heynen cabled to the HAPAG office in Hamburg, "...the Americans never gave any indication that unloading the arms and ammunition from the Ypiranga would not suit them."[1218] In fact, Military Attaché von Papen reported that the weapons would not have been unloaded if the Americans had voiced any reservations.[1219] On May 31st 1914, Heynen told a reporter of the New York Times: "This is not a matter between the Washington and Berlin Governments, for there was no understanding that we should not land the Ypiranga's cargo elsewhere, the American Admiral commanding at Vera Cruz [sic] having said on April 22 that the ship was free to go where it pleased. We made all arrangements for landing at Puerto Mexico, and the German Government had nothing to do with the matter."[1220]

Much has been made of the fact that the HAPAG rerouted the ship to Puerto Mexico where she ended up clearing her load. However, a secret memorandum from Admiral von Hintze to the German Foreign Office on the 18th of April - three days before the U.S. intervention - sheds some light on the true facts. Von Hintze notified the German government of the brewing trouble between the American navy and the Huerta government. An invasion was imminent. Von Hintze asked and received permission of the German Foreign Office to reroute the "Ypiranga" to Puerto Mexico and the "Dania" to Tampico in order to take on refugees.[1221] Thus the virtually automatic rerouting of the ships proceeded as planned before the invasion ever happened. This also explains the great surprise of German officials when it became public that the invasion happened as a result of the German steamer. The American military and the State Department had not told the German Ambassador in Mexico von Hintze, the Foreign Office in Berlin, the HAPAG representative Heynen, or Ambassador von Bernstorff that the invasion of Veracruz by U.S. forces had anything to do with the German ship. Indeed, German officials had concluded that the military action been planned and executed independent of the arrival of the "Ypiranga." To the German observers the arms of the "Ypiranga" could only have been an excuse for the intervention that would have been executed in any case. On April 26th, von Hintze wrote to the German Foreign Secretary that he fully expected the Americans to march all the way to Mexico City while in a parallel effort the rebels would take Tampico.[1222]

If that was the plan, the Wilson administration made a crucial mistake when it let the ship leave. To the American public the sacrifice of nineteen American sailors had been in vain. When, on the 29th of May, the "Ypiranga" cleared her 1,500 cases of rifles, 15 million cartridges, and various other munitions in Puerto Mexico, one hundred and fifty miles south of Veracruz, emotions ran high.[1223] Also discharging cargo in Puerto Mexico were the HAPAG steamers "Bavaria" with a similar consignment and the "Kronprinzessin Cecilie" with a smaller shipment of arms and ammunition.[1224] William F. Buckley testified to the Senate Committee on Foreign Affairs in 1919, that apparently none other than Carl Heynen desperately tried to prevent the arms to fall into the hands of President Huerta. "...Carl Heynen ...called on the chief of port at Veracruz, Captain [Herman O.] Stickney, an unusually obtuse naval officer, and tried to get him to order him, Heynen, or even ask him, not to permit his boat to land the arms and ammunition in question, as Heynen was anxious for an excuse not to obey Huerta's orders, but this brilliant commander practically ordered Heynen out of his office."[1225] The New York Times seconded Buckley's claim, "Capt. C. Bonath of the Ypiranga, however, said: 'The possibility that our cargo might be landed at Puerto Mexico was not new to the Collector [Captain Stickney]. Before clearance to Puerto Mexico was granted to us, I asked him specifically: 'What would you do if I were compelled [by Huerta] to land these arms at Puerto Mexico?' To this he made no reply.'"[1226]

When the bungle and miscommunications that had caused the arms to circumvent U.S. control became public, the outrage in northern Mexico as well as the U.S. was widespread. Newspapers reported on the supposed German conspiracy to support Huerta against the U.S. government. This idea found treatment for many years to come, with American historian Barbara Tuchman leading the charge, that Germany purposely supported the Mexican dictator in an effort to seek a confrontation with the U.S. government. Of course, the interest of the German government in the months before World War I, as historian Baecker correctly emphasized, was the opposite. The German government and all the major German banks wanted Huerta deposed as much as the U.S. government. German financial circles hoped that a new government, even a U.S. dominated one, would resume servicing Mexico's debt. As the commendation of Captain Köhler in August 1914 showed, the German government supported the U.S. with humanitarian efforts. One of the great ironies of history was the misrepresented role of Carl Heynen who the American press falsely blamed for having orchestrated the "slipping out" of the "Ypiranga."[1227] Among other things, Heynen told Department of Justice investigators in 1918 that he briefly acted as the U.S. consul in Mexico City. According to the German agent, he happened to be in Mexico City when the invasion of Veracruz commenced. When the American Charge d'Affairs Nelson O'Shaughnessy received his passport from Huerta as a result of the attack, he left for Veracruz on the 22nd of April. The diplomat turned the American representation in Mexico over to the Brazilian embassy.[1228] Working at this time as honorary consul for the Brazilian ambassador was Carl Heynen. "In this way Mr. Heynen said it became his duty to act to a certain extent in [sic] behalf of the United States."[1229] Whether Heynen's twisted understanding of this episode withstands thorough legal examination is open to debate. However, he certainly perceived himself to have been the de-facto American consul in town.

Much has been written about the alleged German conspiracy to challenge the U.S. influence in Mexico by supporting General Huerta. To understand the extent of German involvement, a closer look at the financial trail of the arms of the "Ypiranga" clarifies the picture. Historian Michael C. Meyer identified Leon Rasst, a former consular agent for Russia in the city of Puebla, and crook of the first order as one of the financiers of the arms of the "Ypiranga."[1230] Not much is known about Rasst other than he was born around 1867 in Russia. He came to Mexico in the early 1880s and settled in Puebla with his Swiss-born wife Luisa. Rasst became a trader and, through his companies, Rasst, Headen y Compañía and A.M. Davis y Compañía he sold anything from semi-precious stones to liquor to German merchants via New York middlemen.[1231] Court records as far back as to 1887 delineate an odor of dishonesty that followed the commercial activities of the man wherever he went. His first victims were customers of his who paid down money for "six [rail] cars" of Onyx, which were supposedly stored in Veracruz. According to court documents, the Onyx was already sold to someone else. However, Rasst used the value of the Onyx orders to borrow money from a Mexican bank. With that he bought a liquor factory. Through a fraudulent bond scheme, Rasst signed most the loaned money over to his wife and declared bankruptcy for his two front companies.[1232] Despite many trips abroad, he remained a resident of

Puebla. His daughter Helen was born in 1896, his son Benjamin in 1900. The history of Puebla mentions Rasst in the first decade of the 20th century as a Jewish businessman who owned the textile factory with the Teutonic name of "La Prusia."[1233] In 1909, Rasst acquired a railroad commission for the Ferrocarril de Capulac a Chachapa. He is listed as a dealer, meaning that he acted on an investor's behalf.[1234] In his immigration records in the fall of 1913, Rasst claimed to be "Russian General Consul Puebla Mexico," implying that he was a member of the diplomatic corps with a position that did not exist. He lied. Justice Department agent William Doyas reported in 1918, that Rasst "stated that he is a former Russian Consular Agent of Mexico," a position similar to that of Alberto Stallforth with Germany.[1235] There are no records whatsoever that substantiate that Rasst was ever appointed Vice Consul for Russia. Indeed, he most likely did not have any diplomatic status. Rather he dabbled in any "get rich quick" scheme that came his way, whether trading minerals or alcohol, textiles or weapons. BI Agent Berliner wrote in 1918: "Rasst is a Russian Jew of the lowest type and is a very slippery customer. Agent is personally acquainted with him..."[1236]

Rasst and his daughter Helen traveled to New York in November 1913 where, according to Historian Michael Meyer, he purchased arms and ammunition for 1.5 million pesos, which he brought with him from Mexico. This author could not verify a source that substantiated the fact that Rasst carried that much cash with him. It is highly unlikely that Huerta gave $15.8 million in today's value in cash to a Russian businessman whose financial record included fraud and bankruptcy, whose questionable reputation preceded his arrival in New York in 1913, and who had no known connections to arms dealers in New York prior to his arrival. Meyer cites Rasst's partnership with Abraham Ratner, Huerta's official purchasing agent in New York, as the link between Huerta and the so-called Russian consul. Why would Ratner who had handled all of Huerta's international arms deals, not be able to transfer money from Mexico to New York via one of the big banks just like all the revolutionaries had done for years? The scheme of sending Rasst as Huerta's purchasing agent to New York with a vast sum of cash as laid out by Meyer, does not pass the reality check. It would have been too much of a risk for Huerta to smuggle this much cash rather than using the many financial paths that were open to the de-facto Mexican government. Both, the Constitutionalists and the American government all the way up to President Wilson, knew of Rasst's trip.[1237]

Also improbable is the timing of the whole affair. Rasst came to New York on November 29th while the SS "Brinkhorn" left for Odessa on December

7th.[1238] Rasst supposedly had paid for the $607,000 worth of arms and ammunition on board. According to Meyer the shipment contained seventy-five thousand carbines, four million rounds of 7 mm ammunition, twenty rapid-fire machine guns, ten thousand cases (ten million rounds) of 30 caliber cartridges and two hundred and fifty cases of caliber 44 (pistol rounds).[1239] The 7mm ammunition was exactly the type Sommerfeld and others testified was not available. According to German sources quoted by historian Thomas Baecker, the shipment contained only one thousand cases of carbines, twenty cases of machine guns, and fifteen million rounds of miscellaneous ammunition.[1240] Each case of carbines in Baecker's account contained twenty guns not fifty as Meyer had suggested. Consequently only twenty thousand carbines were part of the order. Baecker's account seems more accurate since he consulted the HAPAG registries. So who ordered the munitions and when? Even if the munitions had been ordered months in advance, no U.S. manufacturer would have produced that large an amount of munitions for the Mexican government without a sizeable down payment. Who deposited the initial sixty thousand Dollars or so to activate the production of this order? None of these questions have been addressed in the previous analyses. Without the answers, the odyssey of Huerta's arms, which in the end caused the invasion of Veracruz, makes no sense.

Looking at Rasst's later history, he does have some commercial relations with the Ratners in 1915. However, he does not appear as an arms importer at any time before that. Rasst's connection with Abraham Ratner seemed to be the sole fact that both were Russian Jews. This is hardly enough evidence for a link since one had operated out of Tampico, the other out of Puebla. Other inconsistencies in Meyer's account were minor yet of import for the whole of the story. He wrote "Rasst and his entourage checked in at New York's plush Park Avenue Hotel on November 28th."[1241] Rasst's immigration documentation, however, stated that he was actually headed to the Hotel Lafayette, a third rate hotel on the Lower East Side close to University Park, and he checked in on the 29th.[1242] Compared to the Constitutionalist buyers such as Lazaro De La Garza and Felix Sommerfeld who stayed at the plush Astor Hotel on Times Square when in New York, Rasst's accommodations do not appear to reflect his almost $16 million (in today's value) briefcase.

On April 29th, Agent Scully of the New York Office of the BI reported his understanding of the "Ypiranga" arms to his superiors. Scully had been watching Rasst from the day he arrived in New York. According to the agent Rasst had arranged for the 50,000 rifles and 15 million rounds of ammunition, which Agent Scully had described in detail in December, to be transferred to Odessa, Russia, via the Gans Steamship Line. Rasst was supposed to meet the ship when it arrived in Odessa and clear the consignment through customs. He also had to pay the freight charges of $12,000 ($250,000 in today's value) when the shipment arrived in port. According to Agent Scully, Rasst never made it to Odessa. Instead, the Russian authorities impounded the load. Through the Russian embassy in Washington Rasst negotiated a release of the weaponry from the Russian authorities but the Gans Steamship Line refused to turn the cargo over to him since they had not been paid. Mr. Gans, a successful German-American entrepreneur, finally transferred the freight to a German ship, which delivered it to Hamburg. There the German government impounded the load. "Through a German Banking concern," namely Martin Schroeder of Hamburg, Gans finally received the freight money. The final information Agent Scully had of Rasst was that Huerta had him arrested upon arrival in Veracruz on a charge of theft.[1243] Two facts stand out if Agent Scully's report can be believed: Rasst might have had some money at his disposal but nowhere near the value of the shipment. In all likelihood Rasst had been sent to arrange shipping of the arms, which Ratner had ordered months before. For that purpose Huerta gave him $12,000 (the freight money), which apparently Rasst did not disperse.

In the course of researching the arms of the "Ypiranga," an interesting twist to Rasst's role in the affair surfaced. It appears that Felix Sommerfeld was financially involved with the Russian crook and potentially had a financial stake in the shipment. In a conversation with undercover agent Harry Berliner, Sommerfeld revealed, "...that Rasst obtained a large amount of money in advance ... when Sommerfeld placed a purchase order for ammunition with Rasst ... it developed that the ammunition Rasst was attempting to ship was not of the caliber [sic] ordered by Sommerfeld. In consequence, Sommerfeld resold them to someone else crediting Rasst with the amount he received, thereby leaving a balance due from the original check which Sommerfeld paid Rasst. Rasst never reimbursed Sommerfeld."[1244] It appears that Sommerfeld had a business relationship with the trader in 1914. Both Sommerfeld and Rasst came to New York in the end of 1913. The Russian arrived on November 29th, while Sommerfeld received mention in the BI reports on December 15th, which does not preclude that he arrived a week or two earlier. To his interrogators Sommerfeld confided in 1918, "I heard the vice-president of the National City Bank sold them to the Russian government. I was approached...In 1914, February or March, I dealt in them [the order destined for the Russian

Government], but you couldn't get them by the condition of Congress that you have to export them overseas. You could not bring them back to the United States, so you would have to export them to China and bring them back to Mexico. I tried to get ten or fifteen thousand [30-40 sporting rifles]."[1245]

Sommerfeld's comment on the order for the Russian government is significant in more ways than one. The National City Bank was Rockefeller's bank. Rockefeller supported Huerta against the Constitutionalists to the bitter end. However little credit the Mexican government under Huerta had, in New York it would have been with that institution. Sommerfeld almost certainly mixed up the time frame when exactly the deal with Russia was made. The arms embargo against Mexico ended in the beginning of February, thus eliminating March as the correct month. Routing orders via "China" was unnecessary thereafter. All indications point to Sommerfeld being involved in the Odessa scheme. He was a premier manipulator of men. If Rasst had arrived in New York with some plan to go around the arms embargo via Odessa, he could have talked to Sommerfeld as well as Ratner. Rasst certainly did not have any compunction about dealing on both sides of the fence as long as it was profitable. Sommerfeld paid him money to bring arms to Hamburg via Odessa. From there Sommerfeld's Tauscher connection would have been able to land them in Mexico. By the time Sommerfeld placed the order, the precise timing of the Constitutionalist's campaign was not possible. Certainly Tampico, maybe even Veracruz, was scheduled to be under their control by April.

Sommerfeld's possible role in Rasst's undertakings fits an important puzzle piece into place: Why did Rasst rush back to Veracruz only to be arrested? Huerta certainly would have had a word with him if he had information that Rasst double crossed him and was working with Sommerfeld. This twist in the story also explains how Sommerfeld was beaten out of a large amount of money. Rasst, who never went to Odessa, lost control of the order. Huerta's agents in Europe finally bailed the order out and shipped it with Huerta's other consignments to Mexico. Sommerfeld ended up empty handed. When agents went through Sommerfeld's possessions in his hotel lockbox in 1918, they found three things he considered worthy to keep secure: Two medals from his service in the Boxer rebellion and a note of receivership of $17,000 from Rasst ($350,000 in today's value).[1246]

The person who organized the release of the consignment that the Germans had impounded was John Wesley De Kay. Born on July 20th, 1872 in New Hampton, Iowa, De Kay's family had moved to the frontier in the late 1860s from the Netherlands. According to him he descended from French nobility that could trace its roots to the 10th century. After completing an apprenticeship as a printer, the entrepreneurial teenager moved to South Dakota where he ended owning several local newspapers and a sizeable cattle ranch. In 1899, De Kay moved to Mexico. With the money he had made in his businesses he purchased a concession for operating meatpacking plants in Mexico. He married Anna May Walton in 1907 and had three children.[1247] In 1909, De Kay's company, the Mexican National Packing Company "Popo," was one of the largest slaughtering and meat distribution operations in Mexico with a book value of over $22 Million (Half a billion in today's value). By 1910 he was the "Sausage King" of Mexico.

"DeKay [sic] employed a yankee-style marketing campaign to overcome the Mexican aversion to chilled meat, offering low prices and lottery drawings for inexpensive, handcranked [sic] White Sewing Machines. Crowds grew so large at shops selling Popo products that owners had to call the police to maintain order. In addition, DeKay sought export markets by concluding a contract with Sir Thomas Lipton, who 'also made a substantial investment in...company bonds.' Despite DeKay's best efforts, Popo hemorrhaged capital and was forced into receivership, dragging USBC with it into bankruptcy and forcing [George] Ham [a Popo Director] out of the presidency. Ham was sacrificed to save Popo, which was still in receivership when the 1910 revolution brought Francisco Madero to power. After a bit of nationalist posturing, Madero approved DeKay's plan to reorganize Popo with Canadian capital, but Victoriano Huerta's coup wrecked the plan."[1248]

A self-made millionaire, indeed the American Dream come true for the son of a Dutch immigrant, De Kay decided in 1909 to become a playwright in New York. His first controversial play "Judas" performed in New York's Globe Theatre for only one night in December 1910 before it was banned there, as well as in Boston and Philadelphia.[1249] In New York's art scene of 1910 the storyline of the play was nothing short of scandalous. Mary Magdalene, who at first became a lover of Pontius Pilate, then of Judas, got involved with Jesus. Judas after realizing that Mary Magdalene had given herself to Jesus decided to betray his friend to the Romans.[1250] To top the provocation of New York's theatre lovers, De Kay had Judas played by the voluptuous French actress, Madame Sarah Bernhardt. The eccentric businessman turned playwright obviously had a special attraction to the lovely diva. He showered her with lavish gifts of jewelry, "...a large number of cigarette boxes made from gold nuggets, brooches, nugget buttons and studs, cigar boxes inlaid with ivory, and a large number of other rare articles."[1251] The play, however, bombed.

De Kay craved public attention and flaunted his wealth, which in 1910 included a castle in France, a mansion in England, and a suite in New York's plush Hotel Ansonia.[1252] In January 1914, De Kay negotiated the sale of the majority interest in his meat packing empire to the Mexican government for an estimated $ 5 Million ($105 Million in today's value).[1253] According to Historian Baecker, the German Foreign Office thought that De Kay was "an ill-reputed American businessman." [1254] From all appearances, he was a tough businessman with great success who basked in the sun of his achievements. He had his fair share of lawsuits from investors but it seemed that these had more to do with the havoc the Mexican Revolution wreaked on his company than with unethical behavior on his part. However, he wore long hair and "dresses like a Latin Quarter Bohemian." [1255] His extravagance, eccentricity, showmanship, and nouveau riche behavior certainly did not fit the German ideal of a serious and trustworthy businessman.

De Kay's main value to Huerta was that he had international credit. Sometime in the beginning of 1914, the businessman arranged a badly needed loan with the French government for thirty-five million francs. The loan appears to have been a quid pro quo for the Mexican government bailing out De Kay's defunct meat business. While archival sources on this transaction are missing, the timing and the sizeable price tag of the purchase speak to the quid quo pro theory. According to De Kay himself, he used the French loan and placed arms and ammunition orders with Belgian and French companies.[1256] Von Hintze confirmed the De Kay loan and arms shipments, which were arranged through the Hamburg banking house of Martin Schroeder.[1257] Schroeder, as mentioned previously, bailed out Rasst's impounded shipment from Odessa. The links between these two seemingly unrelated facts are inescapable. Indeed, the third HAPAG ship, "Kronprinzessin Cecilie," which discharged her deadly cargo at the same time the "Ypiranga" and the "Bavaria" did, had carried De Kay's order of seven million cartridges of 7mm Mauser rounds in the beginning of March.[1258] De Kay's role in the procurement of Huerta's arms and ammunition further supports the theory that Rasst never carried that much money when he arrived in New York and that the money that suddenly appeared in Germany in March 1914 came from De Kay.

Two questions beg answering: What caused the alarm over the "Ypiranga's" cargo and why did the American authorities fail to seize the arms when they had the chance to? Despite their best efforts, neither historian

Meyer nor Baecker have found the answers. Obviously, the historical record is not conclusive. Like is the case with any puzzle, there are a lot of pieces and the historian, in the absence of a smoking gun, has the task of finding a framework to accommodate every one of those pieces. Hard evidence suggests that there was an initial order by Huerta, which left New York in December of 1913 headed for Odessa. Leon Rasst at the very least had been selected as the contact between the Mexican and the Russian governments. He had received funds from the Mexican government for the purpose of arranging the shipment of the ammunition. Clearly, Rasst had nothing to do with the ordering process and down payments in the U.S. As all existing evidence supports, the Constitutionalists, who especially sought 7mm cartridges, had the money and the means to buy up the existing U.S. capacities. Unquestionably, Ratner had somehow made the down payments on this order to activate it. As discussed, it is very unlikely that an unreliable character such as Rasst would be given 1.5 Million Pesos ($15.7 million in today's value) in cash by the Mexican government. Huerta and his New York representatives would have easily found a way to transfer the necessary funds to New York via international banking routes. The risk of Rasst, who clearly did not have diplomatic immunity, being robbed or his money being impounded by immigration officials was much higher than wiring the funds.

Using the National City Bank of New York to pay for the munitions and Rasst's supposed connection to the Russian government, the consignment shipped from New York to Odessa. The technical details of the shipment, especially the type of guns and ammunition Huerta bought, are highly suspicious. The Mexican army used mainly 7mm Mauser rifles, model 1896. Why would they buy fifty thousand carbines with ten million rounds of 30 caliber cartridges? From von Hintze's report on December 4th 1913, the day the U.S. shipment left for Odessa, it is clear that German manufacturers had either produced or reserved the production capacity for fifty thousand Mauser rifles and one hundred million rounds of 7mm ammunition. On December 15th 1913, Guillermo Bach informed von Hintze that Huerta had agreed to pay for the first call-off on March 31st. This date is the approximate day the "Ypiranga" left Hamburg for Mexico. Germany also had not placed an arms embargo on Mexico, which meant that shipping this order would have been legal and easy.

The question begs why Huerta and his people chose to order guns that were not prevalent in their army over the Mauser rifles if they had the money to pay for either product. The missing link is Odessa. Clearly, a large portion of the order shipped from New York was indeed destined for Russia. 44 caliber pistol ammunition is a Russian standard, as were the carbines and the 30 caliber rounds. It would make perfect sense that the Huerta buyers purchased available guns and ammunition in the U.S. and shipped them to Russia where they would be sold. The proceeds could then be used to purchase the Mauser rifles and ammunition in Germany for shipment to Mexico. None of the sources historian Meyer and others used detailed the shipment of arms and ammunition that was unloaded in Puerto Mexico. According to historians Baecker and Meyer, approximately fifteen thousand cases left New York and close to eighteen thousand arrived in Mexico.[1259] This is not to say that even if fifteen thousand cases left New York and fifteen thousand cases arrived in Mexico the order contained the same materials. In this case the additional three thousand cases clearly support the thesis that the order had been manipulated. According to Meyer, additional ammunition entered the hold of the "Ypiranga" in Hamburg and Havana. It is more than likely that only the twenty cases of machine guns and four thousand cases of 7mm ammunition transferred from Odessa to Hamburg. As a result of the proceeds from selling the rest of the arms in Odessa and the French loan De Kay had meanwhile organized, Gans could be paid in Hamburg, Huerta's agents in Germany could pay the German manufacturer, and load the Mauser rifles. Franz von Papen, the German military attaché for Mexico and the United States, stayed in Mexico when the German ships cleared their cargo in Puerto Mexico. He had reviewed the official manifests from HAPAG and reported that the "Ypiranga" unloaded ten thousand rifles, 15,750 cases of ammunition, forty machine guns, some grenades and cannon.[1260] The emphasis should be on "rifles," because von Papen in the same report also specified that the SS "Dania" carried "4,000 carbines and 4000 rifles."[1261] The rifles on the "Ypiranga" von Papen reported on were just that, not the original carbines destined to Odessa. The "Ypiranga" clearly only carried a portion of the original consignment. From Hamburg the "Ypiranga" sailed to Le Havre where she picked up more of De Kay's orders. Finally, she headed to Havana, where again cases of ammunition were added to the load, most likely the grenades and cannon Papen reported on. On April 20th, the "Ypiranga" finally steamed to Mexico. The second HAPAG steamer "Bavaria" sailed to Antwerp on April 17th where she loaded further De Kay consignments before she as well headed to Mexico.

The next puzzle piece is the urgency with which American authorities regarded the shipment. Historian Meyer theorized that the invasion of Veracruz was in progress independent of the arrival of the "Ypiranga." The seizing of the arms on the "Ypiranga" would therefore prevent Huerta's forces from using American arms against the American invaders. The U.S. authorities did not know that the arms were American when the "Ypiranga" arrived. It took until the 1970s to at least partially track the order back to New York. However, President Wilson's cabinet members roused him specifically because of the "Ypiranga." This despite Secretary Bryan knew of the "Ypiranga's" cargo and arrival time at least since the 18th. What had created the urgency? There is only one explanation: The State Department had originally underestimated the size of the order. The other important fact was that the U.S. State Department was well aware of the cargo of the "Ypiranga" because the German authorities kept the U.S. abreast. Consul Canada, whose urgent message supposedly caused Secretary Bryan and Navy Secretary Daniels to rouse the President at 2:00 am, had cabled Secretary Bryan already on the 18th of April, three days before the invasion, that the ship and its cargo would arrive in Veracruz on the 21st.[1262]

On the day before America's military action, it took Consul Canada only one look out of the window of his office in Veracruz to see "three trains of ten cars each" waiting for the German ship on Pier 4.[1263] When American marines seized the harbor the next morning, on April 21st, the German captains Köhler (of the cruiser "Dresden") and Bonath (of the "Ypiranga") had no idea that the German ship had anything to do with it. Considering that the State Department had botched the arrival of the "Ypiranga," then had rushed the President to order the attack, and then completely missed informing the German authorities seems odd. Clearly, as Meyer and others have documented, the American attack had been expected after the Huerta government let President Wilson's deadline expire. Since Wilson and the international community supported the Constitutionalists wholeheartedly, the huge arms cache would have been a boon for the rebel army. Again, only a State Department bungle would explain why the cargo of the "Ypiranga" had not been seized that morning. The German government had no reservations about cooperating with U.S. authorities. Ambassadors von Hintze and von Bernstorff wanted Huerta to disappear. A slight diplomatic effort to synchronize the events in Veracruz on the 21st of April would have allowed the "Ypiranga" to land the weapons in Veracruz and have the Americans seize them. Held under American auspices the Constitutionalists could have received the badly needed supplies after their front had advanced into Veracruz. This was only weeks away. Tampico fell on the 14th of May, opening the corridor between the U.S.-occupied Veracruz and the oil fields.

An intervention that severed one of the last supply lines for the federal army certainly was something Hopkins and Sommerfeld supported. They wanted the U.S. to intervene, seize the arms, and give them to the rebels. Indeed, Sommerfeld's investment in some of these munitions could have been recovered under that scenario. Sommerfeld worked hard on managing the reaction of the Constitutionalists to the U.S. intervention. He testified in 1918 that he was in Chihuahua at the time of the U.S. intervention. According to the German agent he shuttled between Villa and Carranza trying to keep them quiet with respect to the U.S. action. Villa, Sommerfeld said, promised to "sit still."[1264] However, Carranza chose a different course of action:

"He [Villa] handed me a telegram from Mr. Bryan to Carranza saying that American forces had landed at Vera Cruz [sic] and 21 were killed...I went immediately to Carranza's house. He was furious. I said 'Listen sleep over it before you answer.' He was going to answer right away. He was going to say this and that. I said 'just say that you as constitutional president protest at [sic] the presence of American troops in Mexico. He said he would think it over...I went to lunch and during my lunch hour Mr. Turner of the Associated Press and Mr. Weeks of the New York Herald came running into the restaurant. He said 'it is all off.' He showed me the message of carranza [sic] to President Wilson...I went to the Foreign Department and said to [Isidro] Fabela, who was in charge, 'who wrote this nonsense.' He said 'not guilty.'...In the meantime Carranza had gotten up from his afternoon sleep and heard I was down stairs. I went up to his room and he said 'what are you so excited about?' I said 'about the message.' ...I said 'tommorrow [sic] morning the embargo will be put on.'"[1265]

In his spontaneous response to President Wilson Carranza asked "...that the president withdraw American troops from Mexico and take up its complaints against Huerta with the Constitutionalist government."[1266] Sommerfeld told German Naval Attaché Karl Boy-Ed in May what he thought about Carranza's handling of the situation:

"The telegram [of Carranza's protesting the invasion of Veracruz which precipitated a renewed arms embargo against Mexico] was a huge misstep, and he, Sommerfeld, had to make clear to Carranza, that the Americans had no choice after Huerta's refusal [to salute the American flag] than to either declare war against Mexico or occupy Vera Cruz [sic]. He, Sommerfeld, had to fix the issue with Carothers by telegraphing immediately that the Carranza protest was 'bull shit' and for the Washington government to promptly send a telegram to Carranza which would allow him to save face in recanting. This precipitated the official message of President Wilson with the emphasis that only Huerta was an enemy of the United States etc."[1267]

The day after the First Chief's belligerent stance became public Sommerfeld asked Hopkins to intercede with Carranza. Hopkins wrote a letter to the First Chief on April 24th. Most interesting is the fact that Hugh Lenox Scott, the Army Chief of Staff, had this letter in his correspondence file. Multiple cross -outs and additions raise the distinct suspicion that Scott (as a representative of the Wilson administration) edited or helped draft Hopkins' letter to Carranza. In the letter, Hopkins pleaded with Carranza to modify his message to President Wilson:

"...I respectfully suggest, as a solution of present difficulties, that the Chief [Carranza] communicate to Mr. Carothers a verbal note...containing the following points: That in view of the new explanations made by Washington relative to the attitude of the American government in respect to the occupancy of Vera Cruz [sic], showing that said occupancy was of a temporary character only, induced by the act of Huerta himself, and considering that, as proof that the American government intends to, and does, respect the sovereignty and dignity of the people of Mexico, the Mexican flag still remains undisturbed over the public buildings of the city of Vera Cruz [sic], the Chief views with satisfaction these practical demonstrations of good faith on the part of the American government, which now happily remove all danger of conflict between the supporters of the Constitutionalist cause and the forces of the United States."[1268]

Carranza did not budge and continued to threaten war with the United States. The U.S. government consequently decided to reinstitute the arms embargo against the Constitutionalists. Sommerfeld and Hopkins' work melted into heap of diplomatic shambles, which, in their opinion, Carranza had created. Full of hope, Lazaro De La Garza reported to Pancho Villa on the 3rd of May that Secretary Bryan had sent a note to Consul Carothers: The weapons ban would be lifted.[1269] While it took several weeks for the borders to reopen to rebel arms, Sommerfeld had told the truth to Boy-Ed. De La Garza told Villa in the same telegram that it had been the efforts of Carothers and Sommerfeld that accomplished the feat.[1270] Despite Sommerfeld's success in reversing the embargo, this episode firmed up his decision to stay close to Pancho Villa, who he considered the only viable leader to bring about peace and prosperity in Mexico. While with the backing of Flint and Pierce Hopkins remained publicly committed to Carranza, Sommerfeld began to work behind the scenes on a political solution for Mexico that included neither Huerta nor Carranza.

Sommerfeld fully supported the American initiative to accelerate the ouster of Huerta. As President Wilson, Secretaries Bryan and Daniels, and probably Consul Carothers all understood, the removal of revenue and supply coming through Veracruz was the death nail in Huerta's reign over Mexico. German Ambassador von Hintze also agreed, writing to Foreign Secretary von Jagow on the 30th of April "military situation for Huerta desperate [;] no soldiers no munitions no weapons."[1271] Whether trying to please the U.S. government and making the Benton scandal disappear, or through the diplomatic efforts of Sommerfeld and Carothers, or maybe as a result of both, Villa stepped out from under Carranza's stated foreign policy. On April 22nd he left Chihuahua City and came to Ciudad Juarez. His presence alone defused a lot of the anxiety in El Paso about impending violence from the Mexican population on both sides of the border. On April 23rd, inviting Woodrow Wilson's emissary George Carothers to dinner and protesting his support for the American President he told the consul to tell "Señor Wilson" that he had no problems with the American occupation of Veracruz. Carothers wrote to Secretary Bryan: "As far as he was concerned we could keep Vera Cruz [sic] and hold it so tight that not even water could get in to Huerta and ...he could not feel any resentment."[1272] A few weeks later, in an interview with American journalists, Villa reiterated his stands, that he would not support a war with the United States. He told the correspondents: "Why war with the United States?...It would be extremely foolish for two reasonable and intelligent men to fight over a drunken man, and would it not be the height of folly for the United States and Mexico to come to blows over a man like Huerta. It seems to me that the entire civilized world would laugh should this come to pass."[1273]

How Villa felt about the appearance of Germany supporting Huerta with arms was a totally different issue. When the news became known that the "Ypiranga" and "Bavaria" had discharged their cargoes in Puerto Mexico, he threatened to expel all Germans from his area of control. Sommerfeld and the German community took Villa's outburst at face value. It had been less than three weeks that the Mexican general had expelled the entire Spanish community from Torreon because they had supported Huerta. The archives contain no record of a communication between the German Ambassador in

Mexico von Hintze and Sommerfeld about this topic. However, Sommerfeld immediately reacted to Villa's threat against the Germans in Chihuahua. On May 29th 1914, he telegraphed Villa and asked him to immediately deny reports he planned to expel Germans as a repercussion of the German arms reaching Huerta.[1274] Villa complied.

Sommerfeld's efforts in the crucial days of April 1914 helped defuse a potential war between Mexico and the United States. The looming armed conflict between the two countries was not some theoretical possibility. Carranza's generals, especially Alvaro Obregon who next to Villa commanded the largest troop contingent in Mexico, united in their call for war against the United States. In response, the U.S. moved additional forces from California to the U.S.-Mexican border on the 29th of April. With the reinforcements came a new commander for Fort Bliss: John J. Pershing.[1275] Sommerfeld and Villa's friend, General Hugh Lenox Scott, had already moved to Washington on April 20th to become Woodrow Wilson's Army Chief of Staff. A total of twenty-one thousand U.S. soldiers stood ready for battle.[1276] Huerta also used the higher purpose of fighting the "Gringos" to try to force a unification of rebel and federal forces. German Naval Attaché Karl Boy-Ed estimated the theoretical strength of federal army, Zapata's fighters, and the Constitutionalist troops in Veracruz to amount to seventeen thousand men.[1277] A Mexican assault on the invaders would have potentially resulted in a rout of the Mexican forces, a fact that Carranza was well aware of but refused to acknowledge. In the end, Huerta's call to arms could not rally the Mexican masses to the banner of national defense, especially not those fighting his government. Carranza co-opted Huerta's tactics and openly chose to let his sense of nationalism prevail over the "Realpolitik" of Sommerfeld and the American government. Sommerfeld and Carothers' achievement in pushing Villa to distance himself from the rest of the military leadership of Mexico was the single most critical ingredient in averting larger hostilities between the U.S. and Mexico. For all the accusations of corruption and dilettantism, George Carothers for a few days became the most influential and successful diplomat Americans had in the field in Mexico.[1278]

Villa's decision to embrace U.S. foreign policy did much to endear him to the American government and public. Newspapers celebrated him as a potential savior for Mexico. President Wilson stood witness to Sommerfeld and Hopkins' Herculean efforts to promote the Mexican rebel before the American government: "...General Villa certainly seems capable of some good things and often shows susceptibilities of the best influences. He is hard to understand, however..."[1279] Villa in turn appreciated Carothers and Sommerfeld's advice. From April 1914 on until Villa's demise in 1915, the two men had unlimited access to the inner workings of Villa's organization. Carothers "had access to Villa anytime he wanted, and Villa assigned him a special carriage in which he traveled when on campaign." [1280] Sommerfeld was appointed Villa's top diplomat in the U.S., and chief arms buyer. Clearly, Sommerfeld and Carothers used Villa's tattered public image in the U.S. after the expulsion of the Spaniards from Torreon and the Benton murder to push him away from Carranza. As a result of promises from Carothers and Sommerfeld or as a result of his own imagination, Villa expected the U.S. to support him over Carranza if a break ever occurred. Only with that expectation in mind did he consider it expedient to risk further conflict with Carranza. Historian Edward Bell described the quid quo pro arrangement: "It remains to be said that on April 5 Villa was acquitted of all blame in the Benton affair, by Carranza's court of inquiry whose verdict was in accord with Secretary Bryan's frequently expressed belief. Though this decision carried little weight, it helped somewhat to make Villa a more possible figure in the design of the Washington government for the expulsion of Huerta."[1281] With Villa firmly on the side of the U.S., Carranza had to soften his stance. Unquestionably, this episode widened cracks in Villa's relationship with Carranza that could not be repaired. United in a common purpose - the ouster of General Huerta - Carranza and Villa would remain publicly aligned. The moment the common enemy was gone, however, the schism became unstoppable.

The final analysis of what can only be called a terribly flawed operation by the Americans is still outstanding. The timing of the invasion was badly chosen. It would have made more sense to ask the German government to halt the German supplies for Huerta and wait for the rebel forces to be closer. Within weeks of the U.S. intervention, the Constitutionalists had taken Tampico and pushed deep into the state of Veracruz. While von Hintze and others in the international community seemed sure that the Americans would take Huerta out themselves, the operation stayed limited to Veracruz. President Wilson and his advisors realized that a wider military action would have caused the Mexican rebel armies to unite with federal forces and fight. Without Sommerfeld and Carothers influencing Villa, the occupation of Veracruz would have turned into a catastrophe. In the spring of 1914, more than 130,000 Mexicans were in arms. Despite superior training and armament, the U.S. military would have had its hands full in a full-fledged Mexican war. Without further escalation, American forces stayed in Veracruz for the better part of 1914. They turned the city over to the Constitutionalists on November 23rd 1914.

Besides accelerating the downfall of Huerta, the European governments including Germany supported the U.S. occupation for another, obvious reason: International banks expected the seized customs revenue to be used for paying Mexican coupons. This the Americans did not do. Bleichröder wrote an infuriated letter to the German Foreign Office on June 19th 1914, alleging that the U.S. was stealing the customs revenue that by law had been pledged to Mexico's debtors.[1282] He was right. German-American relations cooled significantly in the wake of the American intervention. All the discussions in contemporary news coverage and in the subsequent historiography characterized Germany as a supporter of Huerta and the reason for the U.S. intervention in Mexico. In reality, the arms were purchased from French, German, and Belgian manufacturers via suspect channels completely outside of German government control. The U.S. could have stopped the shipments through diplomatic or military means but did not. In reality, the reasoning behind the intervention had nothing to do with the arms shipments. Historians have grappled with the fact of how and why the arms of the "Ypiranga," "Dania" and "Bavaria" ended in Huerta's hands anyway. Sometimes even a historian has to acknowledge that if something looks like a duck, quacks like a duck, and walks like a duck, it might just be a duck! By any objective measure, the U.S.' capture of the customs houses in Veracruz affair was messy in detail but achieved its ends: The U.S. captured the cash register of Mexico's government, kept the proceeds, and, in taking it away from Huerta (and the other creditors), the Usurper President was done for.

CHAPTER 21

ᔕ

THE BREAK-IN AT THE HIBBS

*H*uerta had hoped that the occupation of Veracruz would backfire badly for the Wilson administration. However, neither Mexican public opinion nor the Constitutionalist leaders fell in line behind the Usurper President. Huerta's strained attempts to rouse Mexican nationalism came to nothing. This failure was by no means a foregone conclusion. Carranza found himself in a delicate political position. While President Wilson undoubtedly saw the military intervention as a final nail into Huerta's coffin, the First Chief Carranza hesitated to publicly support the violation of Mexican sovereignty by the Americans. A perceived alignment of Carranza with the American invaders would have stood a realistic chance for Huerta to assume leadership in a fight against the northern neighbor. At the very least, the public could withdraw support from Carranza and throw it behind the dictator. When the First Chief voiced his outrage over the American intervention, Sommerfeld, Hopkins, and Wilson's special envoy, John Lind, sincerely hoped Carranza's statements to be a ruse to save his nationalistic, public image. When Sommerfeld found out that this assumption was false, he pushed Villa to declare his opposition to Carranza's belligerent tone. War now seemed averted. However, Wilson and his advisors decided that an international mediation effort would further quell the ill feelings of Carranza and Obregon and stabilize the situation. After all, observers in the Wilson administration as well as the diplomatic community expected the collapse of the Huerta government to be imminent. An orderly transfer of power to a Mexican administration sympathetic to U.S. interests was of tantamount importance.

On April 25th 1914, only a few days after the landing of marines at Veracruz and on the same day that Villa had sent a conciliatory letter of friendship to President Wilson, the U.S. government requested the ABC powers, Argentina, Brazil, and Chile, to mediate in the Mexican crisis.[1283] Both the Constitutionalists and the Huerta regime agreed to a conference to be held at Niagara Falls, Canada in May. The topic of discussion was the American intervention in Veracruz. However, it quickly became clear to Carranza and his advisors that the Wilson administration wanted to use the conference as a vehicle not only to resolve the occupation of Veracruz but also to settle questions concerning the political affairs of Mexico. This he could not support. Carranza was adamant that internal affairs of the country remained the domain of Mexico. On April 29th, President Wilson insisted on a prerequisite for the conference that Carranza flat-out rejected: The warring factions were to hold fire while the negotiations took place in Niagara Falls. Carranza withdrew his commitment to participate while Huerta excitedly welcomed the U.S. request. The Mexican dictator saw an armistice and drawn out negotiations as his last chance to remain in power. Militarily the federals stood before the abyss on all fronts. The final campaign to oust Huerta had picked up full speed after Villa's conquest of Torreon on April 2nd.

"Four armies were required to make a lasting success of the southward movement, and three of them were already in the field. To the east, in the Gulf of Mexico state of Tamaulipas, one large force had been operating for several weeks. It had taken Victoria, capital of the state, and had seriously menaced the port of Tampico which Villa now needed more than ever, for reasons which will presently appear. In the West a Constitutionalist force was active in the Pacific Coast state of Sinaloa, and the territory of Tepic. In the center, under Villa himself, was the remainder of the army which had captured and was now occupying Torreon. Another army must speedily be raised to act in concert with Villa's own forces in their campaign for possession of the cities on the two trunk lines of railway in Central Mexico. Recruiting seemed surprisingly easy for Villa. Immediately after Torreon he was able to send a force toward Monterrey in pursuit of the Federals, and start another southeastward in the direction of Saltillo."[1284]

It was unrealistic of the U.S. President to think that the Constitutionalists, while having the initiative, would agree to a cease-fire. The last thing commanders in the field fighting against Huerta needed was to give the federals time to rearm and reconstitute. As a result, Carranza rebuffed the U.S. effort to negotiate.[1285]

The conference officially started on May 20th, almost a full month after the initial proposal. In an endless back and forth the ABC diplomats and U.S. representatives battled the intransigence of the First Chief. To no avail! The conference proceeded with delegates from the Huerta government only. Without the attendance of the Carranza faction, Niagara became a farce of public relations entirely removed from the realities on the ground. Meanwhile, the Constitutionalists marched relentlessly toward Mexico City independent of any international effort.

To claim that the Constitutionalists played no part in the international negotiation in May 1914, however, would be incorrect. While Carranza had not empowered any delegates to participate at Niagara Falls on his provisional government's behalf, the press noted a flurry of diplomatic activity between Carranza and the U.S. government before and during the conference. Felix Sommerfeld engaged with consular agent George Carothers and Wilson emissary to Mexico, John Lind, in the effort to persuade the First Chief to agree to participate in the meetings in some fashion.[1286] The issues at hand far exceeded the topics discussed in the newspapers. Henry Clay Pierce, Charles Flint, and a host of U.S. financiers made their support of the Constitutionalists contingent on Carranza and Villa's support of their interests. On April 22nd 1914, Huerta with the stroke of a pen had ordered the firing of all American employees from the national railroads.[1287] The Mexican dictator correctly suspected collaboration between the American-run railroads and the U.S. government in the event of a full-scale invasion of Mexico.[1288] In addition to the fact that the railroads had not paid interest on their bonds under Huerta's government, this latest move increased the chances of nationalization or takeover of the railroads by the hated competitor, Lord Cowdray. Pierce and Flint were incensed. The big question that loomed on the horizon was who would take charge of the railroads once the Constitutionalists had taken power in Mexico City. Hopkins chaired the negotiations.

There was little danger that Carranza and Lord Cowdray would arrive at a deal. On May 12th, the Constitutionalists had arrested the Mexican chief of Cowdray's El Aguila Company, F. E. Teza, an Italian citizen. Carranza wanted $10,000 in "loans" from the company to free the executive. In charge of the negotiations in Ciudad Juarez on May 15th between Lord Cowdray's people and Carranza was Roberto Pesquiera, Carranza's secret service chief.[1289] Someone else who just "happened" to be present was Hopkins' eyes and ears, Felix Sommerfeld.[1290] The negotiations stalled, mainly because Carranza would not respond to any suggestions from the other side. Carranza proceeded to shut down El Aguila operations on June 5th forbidding the Cowdray concern to export any oil.[1291] The war was on.

On May 16th, Sommerfeld took the train to Washington to report to Hopkins. Either both of them or Sommerfeld by himself went on to New York to meet with Charles Flint. U.S. investors had yanked $1 million in financing from Carranza after the First Chief had instituted a tax increase on oil products of forty cents per ton.[1292] As a result of the cutting of funds and the reinstitution of the arms embargo, the Constitutionalists' badly needed support to finish off Huerta hung in the balance. Flint and Pierce demanded that Alberto Pani, a Carranzista disposed to Henry Clay Pierce, replace Villa's man, Eusebio Calzado, as director of the northern railways. In return, Flint would supply the Constitutionalists with arms and ammunition as well as the required finance. Villa, however, would not and could not agree to a Carranzista running the railroads. His army depended on controlling the operations of the railroads. If Pani had operational control, Carranza would be empowered to cut off Villa's advance from one minute to the next. Sommerfeld and Hopkins convinced Flint and Pierce that Carranza was committed to Pani becoming director once the Constitutionalists were in control of the capital. Initially, Carranza kept his word. In September 1914, Pierce received an offer to buy back the majority of shares in the Mexican railroads and on October 13th 1914, the new board of the national railways convened, chaired by Director Pani. However, the harmony between Carranza and Pierce lasted only a month. When Pierce refused the offer to buy the railways, Carranza confiscated the company, sacked the board, and brought the railroads under control of his military, which by then was engaged in a full-scale war against Villa. This latest move reinforced the determination of the powerful men who supported Villa, Army Chief of Staff General Scott, General Tasker Bliss, Henry Clay Pierce, Charles Flint, Sherburne Hopkins, and, of course Felix Sommerfeld. In their eyes Carranza simply was not a man of his word. [1293]

Mostly as a result of the disagreements between Villa and Carranza, the División Del Norte had to be supplied for its final push into Mexico City. Carranza had devastated the supply lines of Villa's army. The First Chief in his hasted letter to President Wilson had caused the U.S. reaction of placing a renewed embargo on arms importations. At the same time, Carranza refused to allocate munitions to Villa's army that arrived by sea through Tampico. Since the beginning of 1914, Carranza and his inner circle, which did not include Villa, had deliberately tried to push the División Del Norte to the sidelines. Carranza had ordered Villa to divert to Saltillo rather than pursuing the retreating federals into Zacatecas. Though irritated, Villa complied and took Saltillo in a resounding victory.[1294] When Carranza restricted the deliveries of coal to Villa's forces, the general's emotions boiled over. The First Chief effectively sabotaged Villa's advance to Zacatecas since the locomotives used north of Torreon were fueled by coal. Clearly Carranza tried everything in his power to push more loyal generals such as Alvaro Obregon to the fore and take Mexico City for the Constitutionalists. Villa, disgusted by Carranza's power play, tendered his resignation as a Constitutionalist general. Felipe Ángeles and the rest of the officer corps argued for Villa to withdraw his resignation, defy Carranza's orders, and proceed to attack Zacatecas, a strategic mountainous city considered nearly impregnable. Zacatecas was the source of much of Mexico's silver, and thus a supply of funds for whoever held it. Victory in Zacatecas meant that Huerta's chances of holding on to the remainder of the country would be slim. Villa accepted Ángeles' advice and cancelled his resignation. In the last week of June the División Del Norte defeated the federals at Zacatecas in the single bloodiest battle of the revolution, with the military forces counting approximately seven thousand dead and five thousand wounded, as well as unknown numbers of civilian casualties.

Before Villa could march on Zacatecas, the main objective was to fortify the vital military supplies lines from the U.S. Reestablishing and securing shipments to the División Del Norte thus became Sommerfeld's mission. According to Sommerfeld's statement in 1918, General Hugh Lenox Scott intervened with the Secretary of War, Lindlay Garrison, on Villa's behalf in early May 1914.[1295] Sommerfeld's negotiations in New York and Hopkins' parallel efforts in Washington had become a resounding success for the two. On May 2nd, Secretary of State Bryan as well as Secretary of War Garrison agreed to allow Villa's forces to supply through the Mexican-American border.[1296] While the embargo remained in place for everyone else, the Wilson administration suddenly seemed to wholeheartedly support Villa over Carranza. President Wilson and his advisors did not want to see Villa sidelined in the pending victory over Huerta. Villa was too powerful and his foreign policy too friendly to the United States as to risk his demise. At the same time, the Wilson administration attempted to glue together the cracks in Carranza and Villa's relationship. The backup solution in case of a failure of these attempts was to throw full support behind Villa, and, Hopkins and Sommerfeld hoped, to grant diplomatic recognition to their protégé. With Hopkins having moved the U.S. administration into this direction, Sommerfeld now could bring Flint and Co. back on board. Meetings between Carranza's envoy to the United States, Rafael Zubaran Capmany, and Flint took place on the 13th of May.[1297] Zubaran was a lawyer from Campeche and served in Carranza's provisional cabinet as

Secretary of the Interior. Zubaran apparently forwarded to Flint Carranza's agreement on the railroad directorship. Sommerfeld replaced Zubaran as a negotiator around the 18th of May 1914 and completed the agreements.[1298] The result of Sommerfeld's negotiations with Flint became immediately apparent to the agents of the Bureau of Investigation. From Remington Arms Company alone, Flint had ordered and shipped eight million cartridges to the border right around the time Sommerfeld was in New York.[1299]

The organization to supply Villa that Sommerfeld now built would stay in place for the next few years. The División Del Norte sourced their supplies through Lazaro De La Garza who had set up shop in El Paso. The orders came from Silvestre Terrazas, now Villa's director of the department of the hacienda. De La Garza forwarded the orders to the company Alberto, Alfonso, Salvador, and Ernesto Madero had founded in New York. Partial funding came from the División Del Norte but Frederico Stallforth, Sommerfeld's man in the New York office, handled the finances coming from Flint.[1300] Since Sommerfeld did not fully trust De La Garza, he installed an old and reliable friend in De La Garza's office. Sam Dreben headed the logistics of these shipments to Villa's army. The Madero brothers and De La Garza were suspicious of Sommerfeld's organization since they had little control over it.[1301] However, as the saying goes, 'don't look a gift horse in the mouth.' The suspicions were not helped when Sommerfeld purchased the wrong ammunition and, despite Secretary Bryan's promise, U.S. customs in New York confiscated munitions shipments to Villa.[1302] By the middle of June, New York authorities had confiscated $500,000 in supplies destined for Villa.[1303] The communications between New York and the State Department clearly lacked efficiency, unless Secretary Bryan somehow played a pressure tactic in his negotiations with Hopkins. The fact remains that for four weeks neither the customs in New York nor the BI seemed to be aware of the loosened embargo to support Villa.[1304] To Sommerfeld and Hopkins' credit, they resolved not only the issue of false and faulty deliveries, but also had the confiscated supplies released and shipped. Emotions on all sides ran high and one can only imagine the German agent reeling between blows. On May 29th, even Villa was ready to fire him, although, considering the consequences for his army, he more likely vented his frustrations to De La Garza than seriously considering Sommerfeld's dismissal. De La Garza and Alberto Madero did not trust the German either. While Flint held the finger on finances and Secretary Bryan seemed unable to direct the customs officials in New York, Sommerfeld earned every penny of his dynamite concession in those weeks!

Hopkins and Sommerfeld succeeded in shoring up Villa's supply lines in the U.S. But Carranza's people did not idly sit by and let their commander be sidelined. Since the beginning of the year, the First Chief had become highly suspicious of Hopkins' loyalty. Frequent disagreements on policy between the two accompanied the attempts of William Bayard Hale to negotiate with Carranza. As an immediate reaction, the First Chief signed a contract for legal representation and lobbying with Charles A. Douglas, a judge and intimate friend of William Jennings Bryan. Douglas' relationship with Bryan resembled that of Hopkins' and Knox in the previous administration. With a second lobbyist on the Carranza team, Hopkins watched almost helplessly as his influence on the First Chief and the State Department waned, and with it the sound foreign policy that he so believed would have led to an American recognition of the Constitutionalist government. Carranza disapproved of Hopkins' role in the Benton murder. Rather than following Carranza's rule to leave all foreign policy negotiations in his realm, Hopkins and Sommerfeld had intervened on Villa's behalf with Secretary Bryan and Hugh Lenox Scott. Another huge disagreement developed over the reaction to the American intervention at Veracruz. Rather than adopting Hopkins and Sommerfeld's recommendations, Carranza sent a belligerent message to President Wilson resulting in the renewed arms embargo. Sommerfeld told the German Naval Attaché Karl Boy-Ed that this "...telegram was a huge folly...He, Sommerfeld, fixed the issue with the help of Carothers by telegraphing immediately that the Carranza protest was 'b.s.'...[in a footnote Boy-Ed clarified to the German Foreign Secretary that that meant bull shit]."[1305]

Throughout the crises that Carranza seemed to bungle, Charles Douglas kept a back door communications channel open for the First Chief and the Wilson administration without Hopkins having any control over it. By the beginning of May, the cracks in the mortar that held together Carranza and Hopkins had developed into a massive rupture. Sherburne Hopkins, with Sommerfeld and his New York clients, now put all his clout behind the Centaur of the North, Francisco "Pancho" Villa. Villa's diplomatic recognition by the United States now became Hopkins' primary goal. It is not documented but highly likely that Villa forwarded Hopkins the customary fee of $50,000 to complete the switch. While Hopkins preserved the appearance of still working with Carranza, all intimate contact ceased around the middle of May 1914. Sommerfeld followed suit. "The last time I had a talk with him [Carranza] was after the Veracruz affair," Sommerfeld recalled in 1918.[1306]

Insurgency

The battle for Villa's recognition and America's favor was now in full swing and would intensify in the months to come. On May 9th, Pancho Villa's first movie, "The Life of General Villa," with the general starring himself premiered in New York. The silent movie with battle scenes from Ojinaga and Torreon became a huge success and one of the centerpieces of Villa's media campaign. On May 10th 1914, the New York Times published this telling poem about Villa's friends and his newfound friendship with the American President:

> Wilson (or Woodrow, if I may,)
> I blush to own that ere to-day
> I have described you as a "gringo";
> For you are now my loved ally;
> We see together, eye to eye;
> The same usurper we defy
> Each in his local lingo.
>
> Friends I have had in your fair land,
> Nice plutocrats who lent a hand
> (In view of possible concessions.)
> But still I lacked official aid,
> And lived, with that embargo laid
> Upon the gunning border trade,
> A prey to rude depressions.
>
> But when you let the barrier drop,
> And all the frontier opened shop
> To deal in warlike apparatus,
> Much heartened by your friendly leave
> To storm and ravage, slay and reave,
> I felt my fighting bosom heave
> As with a fresh afflatus.
>
> Thence here's my hand all warm and red,
> And we will march through fire and lead
> Waging the glorious war of Duty;
> Though impotent to read or write,
> I love the cause of Truth and Light,
> So God defend us in the fight
> For Villa, Home and Beauty![1307]

In a series of secret meetings paralleling the Niagara Conference the Wilson administration and the forces opposing Huerta decided on the modalities of the takeover of Mexico City. Participants included Charles Douglas, Rafael Zubaran Capmany, and Luis Cabrera, who joined in the end of May after his return from Spain.[1308] Sommerfeld and Hopkins officially negotiated on the Constitutionalists' behalf, but in reality represented Villa's faction.[1309] The Wilson administration participated through William Jennings Bryan in Washington, John Lind in Veracruz, and George Carothers who was embedded with Villa. Zubaran Capmany staunchly upheld Carranza's stance of obstructing any U.S. attempt to mingle in Mexico's internal affairs. As a result Secretary Bryan refused to talk to him directly and sent his communications via his personal friend turned Constitutionalist attorney Charles Douglas instead.[1310] Manuel Esteva, the Mexican Consul General in New York, who had been a personal friend of Sommerfeld for some time, as well as Enrique Llorente who Sommerfeld had recently established in New York to head the Villa junta, complemented Sommerfeld's team. According to the German agent, the takeover of Mexico City would be accomplished in a matter of weeks through a three-pronged assault. Once Huerta was gone, either General Villar (who had been wounded in the Decena Tragica defending Madero) or General Ángeles would take over the provisional government as dictator.[1311]

It seems that both Hopkins and Sommerfeld floated the idea of Ángeles becoming provisional President and dictator either as a trial balloon or without checking with the home office. Carranza's reaction was swift. On June 20th, when he heard rumors of Ángeles' potential ascendancy to power, he fired the general as his Secretary of War. Most Mexican military leaders including some of Villa's own generals opposed Ángeles potential candidacy, because he was a former federal officer. Villa and Ángeles quickly told their U.S. power brokers to retract the idea. In a telegram published in the New York Times on June 21st, Lazaro De La Garza instructed Sommerfeld to "...categorically deny the statements that Gen. Villa has issued a manifesto proclaiming Gen. Angeles First Chief. Therefore it is completely false."[1312] With or without Ángeles at the helm, Sommerfeld explained to Boy-Ed that after initiating changes in the Mexican Constitution, the provisional president would call for elections through which Carranza would be elected President. The "US government knows this plan and supports it," Sommerfeld reported to Boy-Ed.[1313] "The plan" that the German described to Boy-Ed realistically did not aim for the election of Carranza to become President of Mexico. The allusion to "dictatorship," and "changes in the constitution" allows for an interpretation of what Mexico would look like after Huerta if Hopkins and Sommerfeld had had their way: Carranza would never make it into a presidential contest. Villa and his huge military colossus would control the government through a puppet president named Felipe Ángeles. It would not take long for exactly that scenario to take shape with a minor change of personnel. On the 6th of November 1914, Villa chose General Eulalio Gutierrez Ortiz instead of Ángeles as his puppet. Hopkins and Sommerfeld had devised and executed yet another plan for Mexico - this time to benefit Pancho Villa (besides Flint and Pierce) the man they thought was Madero's rightful political heir.

The conferences in Niagara dragged on through June with Carranza publicly playing cat-and-mouse with the Wilson administration while privately negotiating. The war of the lobbyists in New York and Washington began to heat up and turn into open conflict. Carranza blamed Hopkins and with him Sommerfeld, Carothers, and Ángeles for inciting Villa against him. Carranza's opinion, which was well founded, played out in the American press. On the 27th of June, Carranza's secretary Alfredo Breceda publicly accused Secretary of State Bryan of favoring Villa. The New York Times reported: "An attack is also made by Breceda on Felix Sommerfeld, Villa's chief agent in this country. The statement alleges that Sommerfeld and Carothers were the principal outside agents engaged in the intrigue to foster Villa's attitude of insubordination toward Carranza, and to impress the people and the Government of the United States with the idea that Villa is the chief factor in the revolution."[1314]

On Sunday, June 28th 1914, a day after the public attacks of the Carranzistas on Sommerfeld, Hopkins, and the U.S. government, an exposé with wide ranging consequences exploded on the first page of the New York Herald. As unbelievable as it sounds today, this second volley by the Carranza people against U.S. lobbyists and Villa supporters was so significant that the details of the scandal competed for first page headlines with the assassination of the Austrian Archduke Franz Ferdinand and his wife on the same day. The scandal had its origin just around the beginning of May, the time when Sommerfeld and Hopkins shuttled between New York and Washington, trying to sideline Carranza, and arranging the finance for the final push against Huerta. According to Sherburne Hopkins, burglars entered his Washington D.C. offices at the Hibbs building on 725 15th Street, NW in the middle of the night and "stole a mass of correspondence from his desk." He suspected the burglars to be "Cientificos," people who wanted to turn the clock back to Porfirio Diaz' times.[1315] Hopkins naturally lumped all supporters of Huerta and any enemy of the Constitutionalist cause together under the "Cientifico" label. The

Washington lawyer denied knowing who in particular was to blame for the heist, but "had certain parties under suspicion."[1316] Clearly, he was implicating Huerta agents in the crime. Most astonishing is the fact that, despite the break-in and removal of not a few but hundreds of files from his office, Hopkins did not file a police report. At least such a report cannot be found. This is surprising since an earlier calamity concerning the prominent lawyer found its way into the local press on February 6th 1914, namely the apparent house fire in the Hopkins Residence caused by sparks from a fireplace.[1317] On November 18th 1914, the Washington Herald reported the theft of Hopkins' coat and trousers in an apparent robbery.[1318] No further detail was given leaving the reader with the impression of a hapless Washington lawyer making his way home in his skivvies. Considering that the theft of Hopkins' trousers made it into the paper, the burglary most certainly had not been reported.

Sommerfeld had his own suspicions as to the identity of the thieves and implied the Huerta faction.[1319] Certainly, Huertistas would have been the obvious choice. Huerta's grip on power in May was fading quickly. Money from Pierce and Flint flowed in dazzling amounts to his enemies. The attempt to rally his enemies to the flag and against the Americans had failed, mainly as a result of Hopkins and Sommerfeld's efforts. The last chance to either achieve an orderly retreat from power, or cling to it for another few months, presented itself in the Niagara Conference. However, without Carranza taking part and without a cease-fire the chances of any tangible results coming from the conference were slim. A scandal was needed. An issue needed to boil to the surface that would deeply divide the American government and the Constitutionalist coalition. If the Mexican public and the revolutionary soldiers would lose their faith in the cause, if it seemed that their idealism had been corrupted by big business and foreign interests, then Huerta and the remaining conservative forces in Mexico had a chance to reverse their fortunes. That exact possibility became reality the night a burglar rifled through Hopkins' desk. Hundreds of letters between Hopkins, Carranza, Flint, and Pierce told a story of foreign interests using the Constitutionalists as puppets for their greedy ends. When reading the letters it seemed that the whole revolution had become a competition between Lord Cowdray and Henry Clay Pierce. When the loot appeared on the first page of the New York Herald on June 28th, Huerta had his scandal. Whether a diversion or lame excuse, Huerta's delegates in Niagara immediately rejected any involvement and even asserted that the questionable correspondence had been offered to them for $100,000.[1320]

Naturally, they claimed that they did not take the offer for ethical reasons. They also refused to disclose who offered the papers to them.

The Hopkins papers revealed the extent to which American investors fronted by Pierce and Flint had been involved in the Mexican Revolution. Not much of the overall story should have been a surprise. For years American newspapers had reported on the financial dealings of the Maderos with Wall Street. When after President Madero's murder the rest of the family fled to the U.S., their support for Carranza was public knowledge. However, what made the Hopkins papers so combustible was the undeniable link between major parts of the U.S. government, oil and railroad interests headed by Flint and Pierce, and certain factions within the Constitutionalists headed by Pancho Villa. Sommerfeld defended the content and wrote that the letters told "the naked truth" and showed "ardent and intelligent support for the constitutionalist cause."[1321] However, the appearance of impropriety was undeniable. As late as April 1914, President Wilson's special envoy to Mexico, John Lind, negotiated with Hopkins and Carranza with regards to the Niagara Conference.[1322] The exposé suggested also a second, less favorable picture of the Carranza government. The mere fact of Carranza corresponding freely with Hopkins and Pierce seemed to suggest that Carranza was willing to sell Mexico's infrastructure and natural resources to American finance if they helped him win the revolution. In a sense, these revelations threatened to reduce Carranza to the level of Porfirio Diaz whose sell-out had precipitated the revolution. Carranza would not let this stand and quickly issued a categorical denial of his government ever having accepted any financing from U.S. interests.[1323] Like a pack of rats scurrying for cover, Hopkins, Pierce, Flint, Carranza, Cabrera, Vasconselos, Lind, Garrison, and Bryan all voiced public denials of ever having known anyone or dealt with anyone of the group. Only two parties smiled through the show: Senators Smith and Fall who loved to see the Wilson administration tumble, and Huerta's representatives in Niagara who only had to gain from the revelations.

As the Republican Senators Smith and Fall correctly assumed, Hopkins had driven a deep wedge of suspicion between President Wilson and his Secretaries Bryan and Garrison. The latter even publicly announced that he never met or dealt with Hopkins.[1324] The issue of both cabinet members surreptitiously relenting on the embargo, while publicly proclaiming its enforcement, smelled of intrigue and illegal influence. There are some clues as to why Huerta or agents of Lord Cowdray might not have been behind the break-in and theft after all. First of all, why did Hopkins not call the authorities if he even reported his coat and trousers stolen? The larger question is who could pull this off without getting caught? What would Alfred Hitchcock suggest? While it is not possible to interrogate the gardener or Hopkins' chauffeur, the distinct possibility exists that the culprits were the Constitutionalists themselves. Hopkins' offices in the Hibbs building contained not only his desk but also those of the entire Constitutionalist junta. At least until June 8th 1914, Hopkins was the official head of the junta.[1325] Not until August would the Carranzistas establish their separate offices in Washington D.C.[1326]

Those members included José Vasconcelos, like Hopkins on the payroll of Pierce and Carranza at the same time, Juan F. Urquidi, Mexican consul, Rafael Zubaran Capmany, Luis Cabrera, and Felicitos F. Villareal. Many others came and left as business necessitated. Roberto V. Pesquiera, Carranza's secret service chief, was a frequent visitor, as was Alfredo Breceda, Carranza's secretary. Anybody of that group could have taken the documents and sent them to the New York Herald for publication. The logic for someone like Urquidi or Pesquiera stealing and revealing the documents is obvious: Hopkins successfully promoted Villa over the First Chief especially since the intervention of Veracruz. The oil lobby as well was on a warpath with Carranza since the imposition of higher taxes. If Carranza allowed the New York financiers to back their own candidate for president in the person of Villa, his grip on power could take the same turn as Huerta's had. Carranza knew all too well about the power of Wall Street, especially in combination with the U.S. State Department and the U.S. military.

The campaign to promote Villa needed to be derailed. The main driver in the campaign was Hopkins. Once his true affiliations became public, his team of financiers and politicians would abandon him and run for cover. In a sense, that happened, although Hopkins simply stepped into the background and let Sommerfeld take the stage. In the best case for Carranza the revelations could also force Flint and Pierce to withdraw their unconditional support for Villa. While this did not happen, the correspondence clearly drove a wedge between Secretary Bryan and American high finance. Without a backdoor, Flint and Pierce had to make up with the Wilson administration and get in line behind whatever foreign policy was implemented. Propaganda became one of the most important tools of the Carranzistas. The American and Mexican public would hopefully find Pancho Villa aligning himself with the likes of Hopkins and Pierce distasteful or even corrupting. Again, this calculation did not add up. With the help of the propaganda of Sommerfeld and Hopkins, the charismatic

Villa remained the true hero of the revolution in America's public mind for at least another year. Only two days after the revelations became public, Carranza called Juan Urquidi back to Mexico. If Urquidi had been the thief, his trip to Mexico conveniently removed him from the public eye.[1327]

Whoever the culprits were, neither Hopkins, nor the Huerta faction, nor the New York Herald revealed their identities. Sommerfeld's actions as well as Hopkins' behavior between May 15th and the end of June indicated that both knew what would be revealed. Hopkins sent Sommerfeld to fess up to Pierce and Flint. By the time the scandal broke, the New York financiers and Hopkins had prepared a response. Sommerfeld stayed almost completely clear of the attention, which saved his relationships with Secretaries Bryan and Garrison. The scandal raged for several weeks. Newspapers from New York and Washington down to Miami, over to El Paso and Los Angeles, up to San Francisco, and back to St. Louis and Chicago ran daily updates on the situation until the middle of July. José Vasconcelos whose work for Pierce had been a complete secret was discredited. Carranza appointed him Secretary of Education in Mexico City, not a department of priority in the middle of the revolution. Their fragile relationship broke in the latter part of 1914 causing Vasconcelos to seek refuge in the United States. He did not return to Mexico until after Carranza's assassination in 1920 when Adolfo De La Huerta appointed him Secretary of Education. His links to Pierce and Hopkins had ruined his political career for almost a decade. Vasconcelos was one of Mexico's most formidable educators, a philosopher, politician, and scholar.

Hopkins took the heat but deflected questions and allegations very smoothly. After two weeks the public lost interest. A threatened proceeding in the U.S. Senate against Lind, Pierce, Hopkins, Sommerfeld, and Carothers for neutrality violations came to nothing.[1328] Villa and Carranza, at the urging of the American government, attempted to patch things up in a series of meetings at Torreon in July. They reached an agreement, which lasted just long enough to oust Huerta and take over Mexico City. On the 20th of July 1914, the Mexican dictator left his country via Puerto Mexico on the German naval cruiser SMS "Dresden."[1329] The "Dresden" delivered him and his family to Jamaica from where he went into exile to Spain. The Constitutionalists entered Mexico City on August 15th.[1330] The Villa agents in the U.S. could not prevent General Obregon from becoming the conqueror of the Mexican capital. Despite this setback, Villa remained the powerhouse in the north of Mexico for the next year. Franz von Papen, German military attaché for the United States and Mexico framed the high opinion with which the international community viewed Villa's military power on July 3rd 1914: "The Army and Navy Journal reported about Villa the following facts: According to the opinion of an American Army officer who had the opportunity to attend several battles, Villa's army is the best organized and best equipped fighting force Mexico has ever possessed. Villa himself is an outstanding commander, who is called the 'Napoleon' of Mexico..."[1331]

Hopkins also retained his influence as an influential broker of U.S. financial interests. Most historians have accorded the Washington lawyer a disreputable image, assigning to him the non-descriptive word of "shady." Not just Katz but others as well adopted the characterizations of his detractors in the press and the American government. Hopkins, like Sommerfeld, was a pragmatist. For all the negative press and historical reviews he received, the Washington lawyer worked for his clients loyally and tirelessly. Henry Clay Pierce and Charles Flint had been his clients before, during, and after the Mexican Revolution. They provided his main source of income. When in 1910 Hopkins met Gustavo Madero, he connected his clients in New York with the family of the future Mexican President for a fee. His work proved to be crucial for the success of Madero's revolution. Hopkins opened doors for the Mexican revolutionaries to the Taft administration. He also cultivated his connections to the U.S. Senate. When the Wilson administration took power, Hopkins did his best to support U.S. foreign policy as long as it coincided with his clients' interests. That is standard procedure in a legal practice that offers lobbying services. Hopkins was no different from most lobbyists scurrying up and down the hallways of Capitol Hill since.

After Madero's demise, Hopkins continued on the same path and supported the faction in Mexico that most likely favored his New York clients. The break with Carranza showed no sign of disloyalty or double play on the part of Hopkins. Carranza was impossible to work with not only for Hopkins but also for President Wilson, Secretary Bryan, William Bayard Hale, John Lind, General Scott, Felix Sommerfeld, and scores of others. Carranza biographers have pointed out the positive elements of Carranza's leadership style. The First Chief ultimately set in motion the evolution of relative political and financial independence for Mexico. However, this achievement should not distract from the carnage that Carranza's intransigence left on the international stage. Hopkins and the others had every right to be frustrated and abandon the Constitutionalists in 1914. In the years after Hopkins' break with the First Chief, Carranza did institute regulations that diametrically opposed the interests of

American high finance. Hopkins' decision to leave, therefore, was correct from this perspective.

The real failure of Hopkins was not the power brokering and influence peddling he undertook as part of his job. Both the Taft and the Wilson administrations gratefully used his service, as did anyone else who needed his connections. He failed to understand for himself and his clients that in the spring of 1914 the days of Dollar Diplomacy had come to an end. The intervention in Veracruz showed that Wilson's foreign policy had more depth than simply enforcing the interests of American corporations. The proceeds from the customs house of Veracruz ended in the hands of the U.S. government not international banks, which, as Bleichröder rightfully pointed out, had the legal rights to this revenue. Rather than using the customs revenue to pay down the Mexican debt, the U.S. government illegally appropriated the funds for itself. Secretary Bryan distrusted Hopkins mainly because of the latter's history. Again and again, Hopkins and his backers had involved the U.S. military in enforcing their schemes. While dealing with Veracruz, U.S. marines still occupied Nicaragua, another of Hopkins' projects. In August 1914, Bryan signed a contract with that country's President for the rights to another canal project. With the three million dollar proceeds for these rights, the U.S. government paid Nicaragua's foreign creditors, mainly American. Bryan blamed Hopkins and his clients for the Nicaraguan mess and, at the same token, suspected and disliked their motives for mingling in Mexican affairs.

It is thus no wonder that Charles Douglas took the lead in connecting Carranza with the State Department in the spring of 1914. Hopkins remained a solid soldier for the interests of Pierce and Flint. His political clout, however, had been on decline throughout the spring of 1914 and finally ended with the exposé of his stolen papers on June 28th. In a larger sense, the Hopkins papers confirmed to the American public and international observers alike just how deep the machinations of American finance reached into U.S. foreign policy and Mexican affairs. Suddenly, all the rumors and suspicions voiced for years in newspapers and Senate investigations lay on public display as fact. Hopkins' carefully crafted lobbying schemes, his financing of select revolutionary factions in Mexico, the pushing of his clients' interests while hurting their competitors, and his intricate network of whole layers of government that operated on a system of favors – all of it had broken to pieces. After the scandal, Hopkins remained in the background. His protégé Sommerfeld took the public stage. Throughout the coming world war, Hopkins gave information to the American government when asked. Off and on between 1914 and 1918, he acted as an informant and filed reports with the U.S. Military Intelligence Division.[1332] His influence on the Mexican Revolution never reached the heights of 1913 and 1914. When Pancho Villa self-destructed on the battlefield a year later, Hopkins had already faded into the background. He supported Villa's resurgence a few years later and supported the rise of Adolfo De La Huerta in the 1920s. When Hopkins died on June 22nd 1932, only one paper remembered the brilliant manipulator that had revolutionary chieftains move at his behest like marionettes.[1333]

If Carranza was behind the burglary, he emerged as the winner. The First Chief had rid the Mexican Revolution of a huge corrupting influence. Never again would the oil companies wield as much power on the Mexican government, although their battle for control and market share remained a headache for Mexican governments all the way to World War II.[1334] However, the eventual nationalization of Mexico's oil production saw its beginnings in this daring break-in. Hopkins tried his best to avert the inescapable, namely that this obstinate politician from Coahuila, who would not listen to his advice, and who, in Hopkins and Sommerfeld's opinion, sabotaged his own foreign policy, had check-mated him.

Astonishingly, Sommerfeld managed to stay out of the line of fire when the Hopkins scandal broke. The published letters mentioned him only in a few instances and did not reveal his true involvement in Hopkins' schemes. He, like his lawyer friend, had nothing but disdain for Carranza. By the time the letters graced the first pages of American dailies, Sommerfeld had fully aligned himself with Villa. The revolutionary chief granted him concessions and commissions, which paid him over $100,000 per month in today's value.[1335] How long he would last was a different question. Politics in the Villa camp forced Sommerfeld to constantly watch his back. He could not tell if he was friend or foe from one minute to the next. As to his true calling, Sommerfeld also drew consequences after he learned of the theft of Hopkins' papers in the beginning of May and after he had shifted his loyalties to Villa. He decided to move from El Paso to New York. There was no chance that he would play any role in the upcoming Constitutionalist government. There were several German agents surrounding Carranza, the likes of Arnold Krum-Heller and Newenham A. Gray.[1336] In May, the German government had dispatched one of their junior spymasters to Mexico to take account of von Hintze's secret service activities: Captain Franz von Papen. He stayed in Mexico City until the 7th of August, filing self-elevating reports on his trips to the revolutionary battle lines and his efforts to protect the German community, which had organized itself long before von Papen's arrival.[1337] Upon return he took the reigns as the German military attaché in the United States until his expulsion in December 1915.

For the German government there was lots of information to be gained in New York and Washington. Sommerfeld had developed much better contacts in the U.S. government than in Constitutionalist circles. For all practical purposes in May of 1914 Villa made Sommerfeld his ambassador with plenipotentiary powers, which he retained until 1916. Once more Sommerfeld's contacts made him a star agent for the German government. Meanwhile his friend Hugh Lenox Scott was Woodrow Wilson's Army Chief of Staff. Through him he had met and become closely acquainted with Lindlay Garrison, the Secretary of War. Secretary of State Bryan also called on Sommerfeld in matters of foreign policy that touched on Villa's realm. In addition, Sommerfeld wined and dined with the financial elites of New York.

On the 26th of May 1914, the German agent reported to German Naval Attaché Karl Boy-Ed in New York, leaving for good the services of Admiral von Hintze. Under the title "Conversation with Agent Sommerfeld," Boy-Ed reported to his superiors about a "chance meeting."[1338] In the report to his superiors Boy-Ed sounded relatively cool to Sommerfeld's entreaty. He even seemed to make fun of him, for example when he described that Sommerfeld "told him strictly confidentially in a whisper," what the American government was really negotiating with Carranza about.[1339] Boy-Ed did not agree with Sommerfeld and Admiral von Hintze's opposition to General Huerta. The German Naval Attaché wrote to Military Attaché von Papen on May 25th, within days of meeting Sommerfeld in New York, "In my opinion, Admiral von Hintze was not quite right in his estimate of him [Huerta]...I met a number of people in Mexico City who were in close touch with Huerta, and without exception they all spoke very highly of the President's patriotism, capacity, and energy."[1340] By July 1914, the disagreement about the "capacity" and "energy" of the Usurper President became moot points. Huerta stood defeated by his foes. The new powers in Mexico City were Venustiano Carranza, Pancho Villa, and Alvaro Obregon. Admiral von Hintze went on to his World War assignment in China. Boy-Ed took over von Hintze's protégé and hired Sommerfeld at the onset of the war. On August 13th, the German agent reported to the German embassy that he had now moved to the Astor Hotel in New York.[1341] Germany had invaded the neutral country of Belgium in an all-out assault on France. World War I had begun and Agent Sommerfeld started his new assignment as the highest-placed German intelligence asset in the American theatre of war.

EPILOGUE

ᴧ

Felix Sommerfeld's career in the Mexican Revolution is unsurpassed. No other foreigner had the influence or clout that the German agent amassed. He achieved prominence not because he was "shady," a "con-man," or otherwise untrustworthy, and of bad character. These characterizations emerged in reports of State Department officials who disliked him, such as Marion Letcher, American Consul at Chihuahua, and Zach Lamar Cobb, the customs agent at El Paso. Historians such as Katz have used his detractors' descriptions, many of which missed the true personality of this man. The Bureau of Investigation added their bleak assessments in the heat of World War I, and historians failed to account for the changed environment these comments were written in. Sommerfeld was a German spy. This occupation in itself implies deceit, manipulation, and hidden agendas. All of that holds true for Sommerfeld. However, if one accepts his occupation for what it was, the characterization of his personality has to be discerning. As his biography shows starting with his first trip to the United States, Sommerfeld was a complicated man who cannot be described in a few paragraphs as historians have attempted to do.

When analyzing a personality, two subjects contain the crucial questions: What features formed the core personality traits and what motivated that character? The ease with which the German agent moved between Mexican, German, and American business interests, his ability to connect with Chihuahuan society, and the ultimate success with which he catapulted himself into one of the most powerful positions in the Mexican government deserve analysis. Between 1908 and 1910 Sommerfeld shaped and honed his personality traits both natural and trained.[1342] People liked the man. He was confident, knowledgeable, and always portrayed an air of success. He did not drink or gamble. Throughout his life in Mexico and the United States not a single scandal came to the surface except for the one time he admitted making a "boyish mistake." He always dressed nicely. His physique told a story of regular exercise and health. Every morning, whether living in Chihuahua, Mexico City, El Paso, or New York City, Sommerfeld took a horseback ride. At five foot eight inches, barrel chested, stocky, broad shoulders, his muscular upper body stretched the buttons of his suit jacket. Low eyebrows emphasized the stern, powerful, discerning brown eyes. He smiled rarely but when he did his smoothly shaven, tanned face opened up and revealed sympathetic lines around his eyes and cheeks.

Although surrounding himself with "real friends," the man stayed intensely private.[1343] "I never had partners," Sommerfeld told investigators in 1918, "I don't believe in breaking in to [i. e. sharing] my work: the houses pull apart."[1344] No one, not even his roommate Leonard Worcester knew the full extent of his activities. Sommerfeld operated alone. Unlike his friend Frederico Stallforth, he always seemed to have money and if he did not, nobody would know. Historians such as Meyer, Katz, and Tuck have emphasized and mischaracterized Sommerfeld's income, portraying it as a main motivation. While he certainly never said no to a good commission, the real motivation was not the prospect of financial rewards. Sommerfeld thirsted for power and influence, which would provide his greatest source for energy: Adulation by others in order to make him feel more worthy. His obsession was his own image, his greatest fear that anything other than what he desired would be revealed. Sommerfeld built a cocoon of privacy around himself. This enigmatic persona that evolved in the years 1908 to 1910 insured that for the rest of his life, while in prominent positions, only five photographs of his have survived.

His perfect physical persona, impeccable clothing, haircut, and honed manners constituted the exterior shell of what he wanted to represent: control, over himself and others. Imperfections in the exterior shell including his appearance were manifestations of a loss of control. Sommerfeld did not show emotions, and, like Pancho Villa, he disdained lack of self-discipline. This is the reason why neither of them drank nor smoked or gambled. As a man whose life was a planned event, he played in his own script. Like a chess player, Sommerfeld allowed his friends and associates to see the part of his life movie he wanted them to see. He had a passion for strategy. As a deep thinker, Sommerfeld was a master in anticipating events. They were part of his own script, which he controlled. Sommerfeld rarely ever did anything without intent. As such he could not work with people who he considered stupid. His frustrations with Venustiano Carranza and Franz von Papen resulted from his impatience with people who he considered to not be strategic thinkers.

While his mind produced innovative and complicated strategies, Sommerfeld also had a proclivity for detail. Deeply analytical, he had an insatiable appetite for information. With a passion, Sommerfeld assimilated seemingly unrelated facts from many sources on all tiers of society. In order to either receive more or leave his peers indebted to him, he used and disseminated information as it fit his plans. His understanding of interpersonal relationships was a system of quid pro quo. Sommerfeld manipulated anyone around him by giving and taking information as well as favors. Most importantly, he kept minute score. Portraying sincerity, which in all fairness to him was real, Sommerfeld could quickly figure out what information his counterpart needed in order to receive what he was looking for. This pattern of networking and trading information clearly developed in those Chihuahua years of his professional life as a German master spy. Although telling his interrogators in 1918 that he never gambled, Sommerfeld was the bank in a lifelong game of roulette. On average he always ended up with the information others desperately needed. This ability gained him access to the highest echelons of power, the Mexican President, the American Secretary of War, Secretary of State, President Wilson's Army Chief of Staff, generals, and business leaders. Historian Friedrich Katz suspected him of being a double agent, Meyer even of being a triple agent, precisely because of his constant trading of information. However, Sommerfeld knew which information to volunteer and which to let only his German superiors see.

The spymaster was a formidable judge of character. Although he used men of disreputable character for his ends, to sometimes being briefly taken by them, he never counted them among his friends. Sommerfeld showed a great loyalty to people he liked. To his longtime friends, General Hugh Lenox Scott, Mexican Secretary of State Miguel Diaz Lombardo, Soldier-of-Fortune Sam Dreben, and lobbyist Sherburne G. Hopkins, Sommerfeld was the most honest, reliable, and loyal character they knew. He got things done. Failure, as he once wrote in Frederico Stallforth's diary, was not a word in his vocabulary. With tremendous goal orientation, the ability to conceive of a plan, and then do the detailed homework to implement it made the German a highly effective partner in any undertaking. He hated being controlled. Pursuing a goal based on his own plan, and in fact allowing no one else to see the whole plan, created his biggest successes. He could easily delegate, but a stickler for quality, he also had to supervise the activities of his subordinates. As a result, he caught deviations from his plan early and corrected them quickly.

People he disliked saw him as arrogant at best and a relentless and formidable enemy at worst. His view of the human character and the world was black and white. Forgiveness was not one of his traits. The appearance of arrogance illuminates another important part of his personality. Because of his work and because it helped him achieve the goals he had set for himself, Sommerfeld appeared to the people he considered players in "his movie" as a good communicator. However, networking and connecting with people was not natural. He had to acquire the ability to connect and relate to others. As opposed to Frederico Stallforth, for whom social interaction was like drinking water, Sommerfeld had to work hard on that personality feature. Every day of his professional life, Sommerfeld moved out of his comfort zone to build personal relationships and maintain the very effective social networks he had created. He faked it well but when he considered communication unnecessary he would revert to his natural, reserved, and lonely self. Thus appearing arrogant to people that did not have a "role in his movie."

Above all, Sommerfeld was not a fake. When referring to President Madero in 1918 as "the purest man I ever met in my life. When I spoke to him, he took my breath away..." he meant it. His loyalty to Madero's principles and character was absolute because Madero as an idea served as the vehicle to achieve self-worth. Sommerfeld did not reflect on himself too much. Because Madero died before the world war started, serving the Mexican cause did not interfere with an even deeper loyalty: The German fatherland. In the Chihuahua years, while starting to work clandestinely, Sommerfeld gave historians a brief glimpse into his feeling for Germany when he had a poem read in the honor of the emperor. Shortly after that, Sommerfeld ceased to associate in public with Germans, even refused to speak his mother language in public. "I have heard him rebuke waiters for attempting to converse with him in German," Sherburne Hopkins wrote to the Attorney General in 1919 about Sommerfeld's life before World War I.[1345] It is significant to note, that Sommerfeld stopped speaking his native language when he entered the services of von Hintze and Madero, not when the First World War started. One supporting piece of evidence for this fact is the entry in Stallforth's guest book in 1911. Despite knowing Stallforth who preferred speaking German, Sommerfeld signed the guest book in English.[1346] When the Great War started, he, like so many Germans, saw America's one-sided "neutrality" which advantaged the Entente against German interests as a black and white issue. Assisting Germany in this epic struggle for survival became a matter of honor and duty above any other loyalties. His lack of self-reflection explains his biggest failure towards the end of the Great War. Abandoned by his friends, American authorities finally arrested him in 1918. This was not the end to the movie script he had envisioned. In his opinion he had plenty of chips to cash from when he helped the American government. He never reflected on the possibility that his manipulation of others in the end might not work. World events had rendered his chips worthless.

Sommerfeld had no deep understanding of, nor did he attempt to reflect upon the idealistic ideas that motivated the Mexican masses to march into battle again and again with little hope of achieving a better life. He admired the ideals of Madero as a conservative reformer who could transform the country without sending it into the tailspin of a social revolution. Consul Letcher accused Sommerfeld of being a "convinced monarchist and absolutist."[1347] Friedrich Katz and others used Letcher's accusations as a basis to characterize Sommerfeld's true convictions. Nothing in Sommerfeld's biography, his letters and statements or in his actions supports this assertion. Having grown up in a middle class Jewish household in the eastern part of Prussia, a monarchist and absolutist mindset would not have led him to revolt against his parents and move to the United States. The opposite, the very bright kid from Schneidemühl would have accepted the imperial authority and tried to rise through the ranks of Prussian society either in a military, political, or entrepreneurial career.

Instead Sommerfeld chose to come to the United States. Abandoning Germany did not mean abandoning loyalty to the homeland. As the story of the Stallforth family showed, German colonialists clung to a strange type of patriotism while establishing themselves in foreign lands. A certain idealistic view of Germany created a surreal loyalty in which the tough realities of life in an absolute state transformed into an expectation of freedom of action while still professing to lead a Prussian way of life. The years of Stallforth's education in Germany with the move back to the frontier illustrate the difficulties, colonialists had in reintegrating into the Prussian state. Almost none succeeded. It is thus no accident that neither Stallforth nor Sommerfeld wanted to be repatriated after 1918. The taste of liberty, freedom of action, and democracy proved too strong for most Germans who had gone into the world. Making statements such as wishing for a "strong man" to take charge of Mexico or ruling the masses with an authoritarian regime cannot solely account for Sommerfeld's disposition towards democracy. Taken at face value, Senator Albert Fall and many of the conservative members of Congress who clamored for intervention against President Madero would all be absolutists.

As historians who have analyzed him agree, Sommerfeld's political orientation was certainly conservative. He supported the Madero government for exactly that reason. There was no option for Porfirio Diaz to remain in power. Of the next generation of potential leaders for Mexico, Madero was the most viable not only in the eyes of Sommerfeld but also of a broad coalition of Mexicans. True to his character, once the German became the head of

Madero's Secret Service, he pursued his goals with determination and precision. In return he bolstered the Mexican President's hold on power and stepped on various toes, including those of Letcher and Cobb. If Consul Letcher and historian Katz's assertions were correct, Sommerfeld could have easily abandoned the Madero camp, as did many of the President's erstwhile companions, and join with Reyes, Orozco, Felix Diaz, or finally with Huerta. Sommerfeld never even gave a thought to supporting any of the reactionary forces in Mexico. When the Madero government fell, it was Sommerfeld who made sure that the new American administration had all the pertinent information to develop a solid foreign policy. The German agent joined Carranza not because of expediency or expectation of financial gain. He saw in Carranza the rightful heir to Madero's ideology. Sommerfeld tried his best in promoting Carranza and his faction in front of William Bayard Hale and Secretary Bryan. Once more, the German spymaster activated his organization and, with the help of Hopkins, delivered to Carranza money, arms, ammunition, and political access. Sommerfeld and Hopkins' support was Carranza's to lose. Sommerfeld's switch of loyalty from Carranza to Villa was born out of pragmatism. Villa had shown a remarkable pragmatism when it came to furthering his aims. Both Hopkins and Sommerfeld were pragmatists. While idealism and ideology drove Francisco Madero and Carranza, it was the pragmatist behind the President, Gustavo Madero, who hired Hopkins and directed Sommerfeld. Villa accepted the advice of Sommerfeld and Hopkins. As a result, Wilson's foreign policy team had access to the revolutionary general. Generals Scott, Pershing, and Bliss saw in Villa a man that could evolve into a political leader for the battered Mexican state. For a while, Villa did almost everything right. The American intervention at Veracruz proved to Sommerfeld beyond any doubt that Villa had evolved into a responsible leader. Sommerfeld decided that Villa deserved his unfettered support. This decision had little or nothing to do with the financial reward Sommerfeld received from his new boss. Money did not motivate him. Power did.

The most important question that remains when analyzing Sommerfeld's true character is how he could have worked for the German government while serving Madero, Carranza, and Villa. Again, historians Katz, Meyer, Tuck, and others have used Sommerfeld's double life as proof for his insincerity and bad character. However, the German agent had no ethical problem with giving information to Germany. As a matter of fact, his intelligence was instrumental in changing German attitudes and foreign policy. Germany's support of Madero came as a surprise to many observers and historians. It was largely to Sommerfeld's credit that German Ambassador von Hintze had first-hand information about the revolutionary leadership. Sommerfeld extracted from Madero commitments, such as the pursuit of the murderers of Covadonga, which calmed German fears of mayhem under a revolutionary government. Katz and most of his American colleagues are mistaken in their assessments of von Hintze's hostility towards Madero. Sommerfeld insured that the German government would not support Huerta, a fact that only one German historian, Thomas Baecker, recognized.[1348] Until the World War broke out, German and American foreign policy largely coincided. Sommerfeld therefore served two masters who pursued the same goal: Help Mexico develop a stable and reliable government that would support foreign investment and commerce. Only when the war caused German and U.S. interests to diverge did Sommerfeld make a clear and logical decision to work for his fatherland. He would pursue his new responsibility in New York with the same vigor that made him the most influential foreigner in the Mexican Revolution. With his network of connections in the United States and Mexico, with other German agents such as Frederico Stallforth and Carl Heynen, and with his organization that remained in place along the Mexican-American border, Sommerfeld would become the highest placed German agent on the North American front during the war. He would deal devastating blows to the Entente supply lines and would deliberately plunge the United States into a virtual war with Mexico.

... to be continued in *In Plain Sight: Sommerfeld and Stallforth on the North American Front, 1914 to 1918*[1349]

ENDNOTES

~

[1] NA RG 60 Department of Justice, file 9-16-12-5305-19, Sommerfeld to Sherburne Hopkins, July 10, 1919.

[2] Stanley R. Ross, *Francisco I. Madero: Apostle of Democracy*, Columbia University Press, New York, NY, 1955, p. 175.

[3] Ibid.

[4] This is a personal theory of the author, namely that the first social revolution of the 20th century started in China (1899-1949), the second in Mexico (1910-1940), the third in Russia (1917-1953), finally the fourth in Cuba (1959). By definition a social revolution is a complete class upheaval and restructuring of the social and economic fabric of a people from the bottom up. It stands apart from political or military rebellions, revolutions that do not change existing property relations, or gradual social and economic reforms.

[5] Charles H. Harris III and Louis R. Sadler, *The Secret War in El Paso: Mexican Revolutionary Intrigue, 1906-1920*, University of New Mexico Press, Albuqerque, NM, 2009, p. 76.

[6] Ibid., p. 75

[7] Felix also had two sisters, Hedwig and Rosa, but their birth and death records probably disappeared in the flames of the "Endlösung," which wiped out the Jewish history of Schneidemühl in 1942.

[8] Felix Sommerfeld gave his residence as "Borkendorf" on his first trip to America in 1896. According to the Allgemeine Zeitung des Judentums, 1900, Heft 34 (August 24, 1900), Der Gemeindebote, p. 2. Borkendorf was half-an-hour from Schneidemühl (by horse).

[9] Schneidemühl is today the Polish city of Pila.

[10] History of Pila, official website, viewed 10-2010.

[11] Peter Simonstein Cullman, *History of the Jewish Community of Schneidemühl 1641 to the Holocaust*, Avotaynu, Bergenfield, NJ, 2006, p. 80.

[12] Ibid p. 81.

[13] www.kehilalinks.jewishgen.org, courtesy of Avotaynu Press.

[14] Ibid. p. 81, quoted from Markus Brann, *Geschichte des Jüdisch-Theologischen Seminars in Breslau*, pp. 3-5.

[15] Ibid p. 95 in the example of member of the school board and chairman of the city council Dr. Davidson.

[16] Ibid p. 81.

[17] Ibid, p. 101.

[18] For example NA RG 60 Department of Justice, file 9-16-12-5305-25, Interview agent Creighton with S.G. Hopkins, October 21, 1919.

[19] NA RG 60 Department of Justice, file 9-16-12-5305, Statement F.A. Sommerfeld June 21 to June 24, 1918 p. 1; his middle name is listed as Armand. Hereafter cited as Statement F.A. Sommerfeld.

[20] Simonstein Cullman, *History of the Jewish Community of Schneidemühl*, p. 100.

[21] Ibid., p. 98.

[22] „Allgemeine Zeitung des Judentums," 1900, Heft 34 (August 24, 1900), Der Gemeindebote, p. 2.

[23] The Prussian school system, one of the best at the time, had three distinct high school paths: The Volksschule (people's school) prepared kids for careers in the trades. One graduated after 9th grade and became an apprentice. The Realschule or Technical High School prepared kids for careers in technical fields or the government. Graduation after tenth grade did not allow students to enter regular university but instead one could go to technical schools and receive an engineering degree. The grammar school or Gymnasium offered the highest level of education. The Gymnasium required parents wealthy enough to support their children since one graduated only after 13th grade with a baccalaureate. Rather than paying school fees of 10 German marks per year, a grammar school student cost up to 100 Marks, a hefty burden and obvious deterrent for lower income families. Grammar school offered Latin and ancient Greek, Geography, Literature, History, Algebra, Geometry, Physics, Chemistry, Religion, and Music. With the "Abitur" or baccalaureate a graduate could enter University. One also qualified for officer career in the military.

[24] See Simonstein Cullman, *History of the Jewish Community of Schneidemühl*, pp. 75 to 79.

[25] See Heribert von Feilitzsch, "Wild West made in Germany," *Journal of Popular Culture*, Oct 1992, p. 179 for a description of German fascination with the American frontier.

[26] Ancestry.com. *Einbürgerungsgesuche New York* [Datenbank online]. Provo, UT, USA: Ancestry.com Operations, Inc., 2007. Ursprüngliche Daten: *Soundex Index to Petitions for Naturalization filed in Federal, State, and Local Courts located in New York City, 1792-1989*. New York, NY, USA: National Archives and Records Administration, Northeast Region.

[27] Statement F.A. Sommerfeld, June 22, 1918.

[28] In 1899 there is another entry record where he gave his occupation as shoemaker (maybe horseshoe maker?). NA RG 36 U.S. Customs Service, M237 Roll 537, Line 32.

[29] Ancestry.com. *Einbürgerungsgesuche New York* [Datenbank online]. Provo, UT, USA: Ancestry.com Operations, Inc., 2007. Ursprüngliche Daten: *Soundex Index to Petitions for Naturalization filed in Federal, State, and Local Courts located in New York City, 1792-1989*. New York, NY, USA: National Archives and Records Administration, Northeast Region.

[30] See www.ancestry.com, public family tree Felix A. Sommerfeld, author Heribert von Feilitzsch, 2010.

[31] For the keen analysis of an American observer of Prussian society around the turn of the century, see Ray Stannard Baker, *Seen in Germany*, Harper and Brothers, London, Great Britain, 1902.

[32] History of Schneidemühl www.schneidemuehl.de, viewed 8-2011.

[33] The Jewish cemetery, the Synagogue as well as all documents of the Jewish community were destroyed. For more details, see Simonstein Cullman.

[34] See Statement F.A. Sommerfeld, June 21, 1918.

[35] Ibid., he gave his highest rank as corporal. However, there are questions as to his service after the turn of the century. If Sommerfeld went to the Army Intelligence School in Charlottenburg between 1906 and 1908, and had converted to Christianity, which is unknown, the Prussian military listed a Lieutenant Sommerfeld. Because the army listing did not include first names, there is no proof whether Felix Sommerfeld was the Lieutenant in the "Rangliste."

[36] See statement of F.A. Sommerfeld, June 21, 1918.

[37] Staatsarchiv Hamburg, Bestand: 373-7 I, VIII (Auswanderungsamt I), Roll K 1754, Page 353.

[38] NA RG 85 Immigration and Naturalization, M237, Roll 658, Line 12.

[39] Statement F.A. Sommerfeld, June 24, 1918. He says in his statement to the BI in 1918 that he went to America without telling his parents.

[40] Both the manifest and the Ellis Island Immigration Records do not show another Sommerfeld on board.

[41] NA RG 85 Immigration and Naturalization, M237, Roll 658.

[42] www.norwayheritage.com, viewed September 1, 2010.

[43] Statement F.A. Sommerfeld, June 24, 1918.

[44] Ibid.

[45] NA RG 165 Military Intelligence Division, file 9140-1754-30, MID report for Department of Justice, June 27, 1918.

[46] NA RG 85 Immigration and Naturalization, M237, Roll 658; Also NA RG 165 Military Intelligence Division, file 9140-1754-73, September 24, 1917, interview with Jack Neville, wire editor, Daily News.

[47] NA RG 85 Immigration and Naturalization, M237 Roll 15.

[48] Ibid.

[49] Sam Dreben was born on June 1, 1878 in Poltava, Ukraine. See Art Leibson, *Sam Dreben, the Fighting Jew*, Westernlore Press, Tucson, AZ, 1996, p. 15.

[50] NA RG 36 U.S. Customs Service, T715, Roll 14.

[51] *New York in the Spanish-American War, 1898*, part of the report of the adjutant-general of the state for 1900. Volume II, Registers of organizations, p. 319.

[52] Ibid.

[53] The New York Times, October 28, 1915.

[54] Ibid.

[55] F.A. Sommerfeld statement, June 22, 1918.

[56] New York Times, October 28, 1915 claims that he stole $275, in his statement to the BI in 1918 he only talks about $250.

[57] New York Department of Health, *Deaths Reported in the City of New York, 1888-1965*, New York, NY, certificate number 3082.

[58] Statement F.A. Sommerfeld, June 22, 1918.

[59] Ibid.

[60] Siegfried became a successful businessman and turned the old mill into a factory for electric parts. See http://forum.sommerfeldfamilien.net/index.php, viewed 10-2010.

[61] Statement F.A. Sommerfeld, June 24, 1918.

[62] The New York Times, October 28, 1915.

[63] Statement F.A. Sommerfeld, June 22, 1918.

[64] NA RG 65 Records of the FBI, M1085, Roll 865, file 232-931, Memo E. B. Stone to Bielaski October 25, 1916.

[65] NA RG 65 Albert Papers, numbered correspondence, Box 1, Navy Attaché Boy-Ed to General Consul Hossenfelder, October 28, 1915, translated by the author.

[66] Ibid., General Consul Hossenfelder to Naval Attaché Boy-Ed, October 28, 1915, translated by the author.

[67] Statement F.A. Sommerfeld, June 22, 1918.

[68] Ibid.

[69] Ibid.

[70] Ibid.

[71] Ibid.

[72] NA RG 165 Military Intelligence Division, file 9140-1754-44, April 26, 1919, Hanna to van Deman; Harris and Sadler, *Secret War in El Paso*, p. 75; Sommerfeld's height in Harris and Sadler is given as 5feet, 6 inches, which is not correct.

[73] Stallforth Papers, Private Collection, Guestbook entry, March 11, 1911.

[74] Examples will be plentiful in this work, such as calling Senator Fall his "personal enemy" to his face, physically threatening Adolph Krakauer when he supplied arms to Orozco or corresponding with Hugh Lenox Scott and Lindlay Garrison about helping American citizens caught in the revolution.

[75] NA RG 165 Military Intelligence Division, file 9140-1754-4, report of Richmond Levering, member A-3700 of the American Protective League, July 23, 1917.

[76] Ibid., file 9140-1754-16, June 22, 1918.

[77] Statement F.A. Sommerfeld, June 22, 1918.

[78] www.worldwar1.com/biokais.htm, Trenches on the Web, Mike Iavarone, January 15, 2000.

[79] Diana Preston *The Boxer Rebellion: The Dramatic Story of China's War on Foreigners that Shook the World in the Summer of 1900*, Walker Publishing Company, New York, NY, 2000, p. xi Illustration "Spheres of Influence in China, c. 1900."

[80] Jennifer Rosenberg, "A rebellion in China against all foreigners," 2010 About.com, a part of The New York Times Company.

[81] According to Walter LaFeber 70% of the Boxers were peasants. Walter LaFeber, "The Boxer Rebellion," on PBS.org interviews.

[82] Preston, *The Boxer Rebellion*, p. 23.

[83] Paul H. Clements, *The Boxer Rebellion: A Political and Diplomatic Review*, Columbia University Press, New York, NY, 1915, p. 39.

[84] Ibid., pp. 70-71.

[85] Ibid., pp. 82-83.

[86] Ibid., p. 99 from U.S. Foreign Relations, 1900, Inc. 2 in no. 399, p. 190.

[87] The Chinese derogative description of their fellow countrymen that had converted to Christianity.

[88] Sir William Laird Clowes, *The Royal Navy: A History from the Earliest Times to the Present*, Volume VII, S. Low, Marston and Company, Limited, London, Great Britain, 1903, p. 551, Public Domain.

[89] Ronald Allen, *The Siege of the Peking Legations: Being the Diary of Rev. Roland Allen, M.A.*, Smith, Elder, and Co., London, Great Britain, 1901, p. 103.

[90] Ibid., p. 77.

[91] Ibid., p. 78.

[92] From the Berlin paper *Die Woche*, 1900, published by Rainer Dombrowsky, www.jadu.de, Berlin, 2001.

[93] „Allgemeine Zeitung des Judentums," Heft 34, August 24, 1900.

[94] From the Berlin paper *Die Woche*, 1900, published by Rainer Dombrowsky, www.jadu.de, Berlin, 2001.

[95] NA RG 165 Military Intelligence Division, file 9140-1754-20, MID report for Department of Justice, June 27, 1918, NA RG 59 Department of State, file 9687-73, statement dated September 24, 1917 from Jack Neville, wire editor of Daily News. NA RG 165 Military Intelligence Division, file 9140-1754-20, September 21, 1917, Senator McCherry to Robert Lansing: "Mr. Summerfeld [sic] stated that he was an officer in the German army."

[96] *Die Woche*, 1900, published by Rainer Dombrowsky, www.jadu.de, Berlin, 2001.

[97] Translated by the author from Wikipedia, "Die Hunnenrede," viewed October 2010.

[98] Clements, *The Boxer Rebellion*, p. 132.

[99] Kennedy Hickman, "The Boxer Rebellion: China fights imperialism," About.com, a part of The New York Times Company, 2010. The exact casualties were: 27 dead (97 wounded) British, 4 (25)

American, 1 (10) French, 12 (62) German, 5 (3) Italian, 2 (3) Japanese, 1 (1) Austrian and 10 (27) Russian, Clements, p. 134.

[100] For more information: Colin Narbeth, *Admiral Seymour's Expedition & Taku Forts, 1900*, Hyperion Books, December, 1987.

[101] Ada Haven Mateer, *Siege Days: Personal Experiences of American Women and Children During the Peking Siege*, Fleming H. Revell Company, New York, Chicago, Toronto, London, Edinburgh, 1903, p. 374.

[102] Minister Conger to Secretary Hay, U.S. Foreign Relations, 1900, pp. 161-167 as quoted in Clements, *The Boxer Rebellion*, p. 136.

[103] Leibson, *Sam Dreben, the Fighting Jew*, p. 32.

[104] Statement F.A. Sommerfeld, June 21, 1918.

[105] The Reiter Regiment was the only one to ship out to China, see Paul von Schmidt, *Der Werdegang des Preußischen Heeres*, Verlag von Karl Hermann Düms, Germany, 1903, p. 346.

[106] Admiralstab der Marine, *Die Kaiserliche Marine während der Wirren in China 1900 - 1901*, Volume 1, Ernst Siegfried Rittler und Sohn, Berlin, Germany, 1903, p. 172.

[107] www.boxeraufstand.com/1900/august_1900.htm: Wednesday, August 8, from *Tagebuch des Friedrich Neubert 19. Juli 1900 – 24. November 1901 (Privatbesitz Lambert Müller)*. Viewed 10-2010. This diary accurately reflects the journey of the Prussian fleet that had left Bremerhaven on July 27.

[108] Ibid., August 13.

[109] Ibid., August 18.

[110] www.boxeraufstand.com/dokumente/sbstempel/sb_stempel.htm, viewed 10-2010.

[111] Statement F.A. Sommerfeld, June 21, 1918.

[112] www.uglychinese.org; also Preston, *The Boxer Rebellion*, pp. 286-290

[113] http://www.mahalo.com/the-boxer-rebellion, viewed 10-2010.

[114] Admiralstab der Marine, p. 172. The Reiterregiment returned on SS "Silvia" and arrived on August 12, 1901 in Bremen.

[115] Statement F.A. Sommerfeld, June 21, 1918; Sommerfeld said that he was discharged in July, which was before his unit returned to Bremen. His memory might have been wrong, or he traveled home with another unit, which is not likely.

[116] NA RG 59 Department of State, file 862.20212/286, Agent Cobb to Counselor Polk, April 24, 1917.

[117] Jim Tuck, www.Mexconnect.com, 2006, "Though he had fought against the revolutionary Boxers in China, he came to Mexico and convinced Madero that he was a revolutionary democrat."

[118] Statement F.A. Sommerfeld, June 22, 1918.

[119] There are recent scholarly articles suggesting that the Boxer Rebellion of 1900 was actually more than that. However, maybe because of a lack of Chinese sources, no serious attempt has been made to date to study the Boxer movement in an ideological framework that links them to the Bolsheviks, Villistas, Zapatistas, Cuban revolutionaries and the like.

[120] F.G. Stapleton, "The unpredictable dynamo: Germany's economy, 1870-1918," *History Review*, December 2002.

[121] Statement F.A. Sommerfeld, June 21, 1918.

[122] Königliches Finanzministerium, *Jahrbuch für das Berg- und Hüttenwesen im Königreiche Sachsen, Jahrgang 1902 (Statistik vom Jahre 1901): Part B Mittheilungen über das Berg- und Hüttenwesen im Jahre 1901*, C. Menzel, Freiberg, Germany,1902, p. 85.

[123] Staatsarchiv Hamburg, 373-7 I, VIII A 1 Band 135, Seite 2251 (Mikrofilm Nr. K 177).

[124] Statement F.A. Sommerfeld, June 21, 1918.

[125] National Archives and Records Administration, Northeast Region, Soundex Index to Petitions for Naturalization filed in Federal, State, and Local Courts located in New York City, 1792-1989, Volume 158, Entry 72.

[126] Statement F.A. Sommerfeld, June 21, 1918.

[127] Ibid.

[128] Ibid.

[129] Ibid.

[130] Ibid.

[131] Ibid. Sommerfeld stressed on numerous occasions that he did not drink, smoke or gamble. He might have smoked, however, since his brother Julius sent him a box of cigars to his prison in 1918. If he was truthful and did not smoke, the cigars at Ft. Oglethorpe could also have functioned as currency.

[132] www.sedona.biz/jeromeaz.htm, 2006.

[133] Statement F.A. Sommerfeld, June 21, 1918.

[134] Ibid.

[135] Ibid.

[136] Ibid.

[137] William T. Greene received the title "Colonel" for leading some men in an Indian raid. He was never a soldier. See Bernstein, Marvin D., "Colonel William C. Greene and the Cananea Copper Bubble," *Bulletin of the Business Historical Society*, Vol. 26, No. 4 (December 1952), pp. 179-198.

[138] Statement F.A. Sommerfeld, June 21, 1918.

[139] Ibid.

[140] Ibid.

[141] Horace J. Stevens, *The Copper Handbook, A Manual of the Copper Industry of the World*, Vol. 6, Houghton, MI, 1906, p. 891.

[142] Statement F.A. Sommerfeld, June 21, 1918.

[143] Ibid.

[144] See Archivos Municipales Chihuahua, Fondo Porfiriato, Secretaria de Gobierno del Estado de Chihuahua, The Chihuahua Enterprise 1905 to 1910, Mines Register 1904, 1905, 1907, 1908, 1910.

[145] City Directory, Chicago, Illinois, 1905, page 1477.

[146] Staatsarchiv Hamburg, 373-7 I, VIII A 1 Band 187, Roll K179, page 237.

[147] NA RG 36 U.S. Customs Service, T715, Roll 830, Line 14.

[148] The National Archives of the UK, Board of Trade, Commercial and Statistical Department and successors, Inwards Passenger Lists, Kew, Surrey, England, BT26, number: 287, Element 3.

[149] NA RG 65 Records of the FBI, M1085, Roll 862, file 232-311, p. 5, E. B. Stone to Bruce Bielaski, October 22, 1916.

[150] Statement F.A. Sommerfeld, June 21, 1918.

[151] AA Politisches Archiv Berlin, Mexiko VI, Paket 45.

[152] Unknown source, 1910, Archivos Municipales Hidalgo del Parral, p. 58.

[153] Statement F.A. Sommerfeld, June 21, 1918.

[154] Archivos Municipales Chihuahua, Fondo Porfiriato, distrito Mina 1909, "La Abundancia- F. Stallforth – Baborigame -20 – oro y plata." The archives including distrito Hidalgo, distrito Iturbide, and distrito Mina show no listing for Felix Sommerfeld as a mine owner or registered mining engineer in 1908 or 1909.

[155] Staatsarchiv Hamburg, 373-7 I, VIII A 1 Band 187, Roll 179, Page 237 for the February trip to Montreal; For the trip from Montreal to Hamburg in August: The National Archives of the UK, Board of Trade, Commercial and Statistical Department and successors, Inwards Passenger Lists, Kew, Surrey, England, BT26, Part number 287, Element 3.

[156] Michael L. Hadley and Roger Sarty, *Tin-Pots and Pirate Ships: Canadian Naval Forces and German Sea Raiders, 1880-1918*, McGill-Queen's University Press, Montreal and Kingston, Canada, 1991, p. 34.

[157] See for example: Nauticus, *Jahrbuch für Deutschlands Seeinteressen, 10. Jahrgang*, Ernst Siegfried Mittler und Sohn, Berlin, Germany, 1908, p. 307.

[158] *Rangliste der Königlich Preußischen Armee und des XIII (Königlich Württembergischen) Armeekorps für 1907*, Ernst Siegfried Mittler und Sohn, Berlin, Germany, 1907, p. 752.

[159] Letter from Dr. Fleischer to author, Bundesarchiv Militärarchiv, Freiburg, March 11, 1991.

[160] James Creelman, "President Diaz, Hero of the Americas", *Pearson's Magazine*, Vol. 19, March 1908, pp. 231-277.

[161] Diaz did not run for reelection in 1880 but used a puppet government. In 1884 he had himself elected again and stayed in power until his ouster in 1911.

[162] Thomas Russell Lill, *National Debt of Mexico: History and Present Status*, Searle, Nicholson and Lill C.P.A.'s, New York, NY, 1919, p. 5.

[163] Ibid., p. 56.

[164] Russell Lill, *National Debt of Mexico*, p. 57.

[165] Katz, Friedrich, *The Life and Times of Pancho Villa*, Stanford University Press, Stanford, CA, 1998, p. 58.

[166] Henry F. Pringle, *Theodore Roosevelt: A Biography*, Cornwall Press, New York, NY, 1931, p. 289.

[167] New York Times, January 16, 1903, "Germany's friendly aims."

[168] Reinhard R. Doerries, *Imperial Challenge: Ambassador Count Bernstorff and German-American Relations, 1908-1917*, University of North Carolina Press, Chapel Hill, NC, 1989, p. 14. Doerries mentions the underlying tensions between Germany and the United States, which remained "still unresolved by 1914."

[169] Jalisco Lancer, "German-Mexican Relations Before the Revolution," *www.allempires.net*, December 22, 2005.

[170] Vincent P. Carosso, Rose C. Carosso, *The Morgans: Private International Bankers, 1854-1913*, Harvard Studies in Business History, Harvard University Press, Cambridge, MA, 1987, pp. 414-419. For a thorough analysis of German investment in Mexico also see Thomas Baecker, *Die Deutsche Mexikopolitik 1913/14*, Colloquium Verlag, Berlin, Germany, 1971, pp. 62-120.

[171] Carosso, *The Morgans*, p. 524.

[172] Russell Lill, *National Debt of Mexico*, p. 78.

[173] Werner Schieffel, *Bernhard Dernburg 1865 - 1937: Kolonialpolitiker und Bankier im wilhelminischen Deutschland*, Atlantis Verlag, Zürich, Switzerland, 1974, p. 22.

[174] Ibid., pp. 20, 21.

[175] NA RG 36 U.S. Customs Service, T715, roll 501, page 14, line 7; Rintelen arrival in New York, October 5, 1904; Rintelen departure record June 8, 1905 from New York to Liverpool, Rintelen departure record May 18, 1906 from New York to Plymouth; The National Archives of the UK (TNA). Series BT26, Board of Trade, Commercial and Statistical Department and successors, Inwards Passenger Lists, Kew, Surrey, England.

[176] The title to Rintelen's book about his spy activities in the U.S.

[177] There are on-going discussions with respect to magnitude since the Richter scale did not exist in 1906. Richter himself calculated 8.3 in 1958, which is disputed today. For more information see http://earthquake.usgs.gov/regional/nca/1906/18april/magnitude.php, viewed 05-2010.

[178] Abstract from Kerry A. Odell and Marc D. Weidenmier, "Real Shock, Monetary Aftershock: The 1906 San Francisco Earthquake and the Panic of 1907," *The Journal of Economic History*, 2005, vol. 64, issue 04, p. 1002–1027.

[179] Federal Reserve Bank of Boston, "The Panic of 1907," Boston, MA, 2002. For more detail see also Jon Moen, "Panic of 1907," *EH.Net Encyclopedia*, edited by Robert Whaples. August 14, 2001.

[180] Kevin J. Cahill, "The U.S. Bank Panic of 1907 and the Mexican Depression of 1908-1909," *The Historian*, Vol. 60, Issue 4, 1998, pp. 795 to 811.

[181] Jon Moen, "Panic of 1907," *EH.Net Encyclopedia*, edited by Robert Whaples, August 14, 2001.

[182] NA RG 165 Department of War, Holmdahl Papers, public domain.

[183] There is a dispute about when the run on the bank started. See Carosso, *The Morgans*, Drawing from information of the private papers of J.P. Morgan, Carosso concluded that the panic started on October 18 not 21 as other historians had claimed.

[184] Carosso, *The Morgans*, pp. 535-549.

[185] Robert F. Bruner, Sean D. Carr, *The Panic of 1907: Lessons Learned from the Market's Perfect Storm*, John Wiley and Sons, Hoboken, NJ, 2007, p. 143.

[186] Cahill, "The U.S. Bank Panic of 1907," pp. 795 to 811.

[187] Frank McLynn, *Villa and Zapata: A History of the Mexican Revolution*, Basic Books, New York, NY, 2000, p. 22.

[188] Lill, *National Debt of Mexico*, 1919, p. 80.

[189] Katz, *Life and Times of Pancho Villa*, 1998, pp. 48-49.

[190] McLynn, *Villa and Zapata*, 2000, p. 21.

[191] Katz, *Life and Times of Pancho Villa*, 1998, p. 50.

[192] Ibid., pp. 50-52.

[193] Katz, *Life and Times of Pancho Villa*, p. 49.

[194] William P. Filby, editor, *Passenger and Immigration Lists Index, 1500s-1900s*, Farmington Hills, MI, Gale Research, 2009, New York, NY, 1962, p. 142.

[195] www.hidalgodelparral.gob.mx; viewed 08-2010. Translated into English by the author.

[196] www.chihuahuamexico.com, viewed 10-2010.

[197] Ruben Rocha, *Galeria de Parralenses Ilustres*, 1985, pp. 31-33.

[198] Katz, *Life and Times of Pancho Villa*, p. 26.

[199] www.wikipedia.org/World's_Columbian_Exposition, viewed 01-2010.

[200] Mauricio Tenorio-Trillo, *Mexico at the World's Fairs Crafting a Modern Nation*, University of California Press, Los Angeles, CA, 1996, p. 184.

[201] Ibid.

[202] www.wikipedia.org/World's_Columbian_Exposition, viewed 01-2010.

[203] http://boards.ancestry.com/localities.northam.mexico.chihuahua/216/mb.ashx, Posted June 21, 1999.

[204] http://boards.ancestry.com/localities.northam.mexico.chihuahua/233.234.236/mb.ashx, Posted June 26, 1999; author visited the grave at the municipal cemetery of Parral in 1992.

[205] Stallforth Papers, Private Collection, diary, October 3, 1906, picture courtesy Mary Prevo Collection.

[206] Stallforth Papers, Private Collection, Letter to Anita, November 21, 1908.

[207] The Chihuahua Enterprise, December 5, 1908 "Mexico Consolidated Mining Co. Reorganized."

[208] Otis and Hough, *Red Manual of Statistics: Stock Exchange Handbook*, Cleveland, OH, 1910, p. 627.

[209] AA Politisches Archiv Berlin, Mexiko II, Paket 15.

[210] NA RG 36 U.S. Customs Service, T715, Roll 1102, Page 2, Line 12.

[211] NA RG 59 Department of State, file 341.112 M49/12; Walter Hines Page to Secretary of State, Statement of Andrew Meloy, August 14, 1915.

[212] Andrew Meloy became involved with Germany's sabotage agent Franz Rintelen in 1915, resulting in much publicity and legal troubles for the investment banker.

[213] NA RG 59, Department of State, file 341.112 M49/12; Walter Hines Page to Secretary of State, Statement of Andrew Meloy, August 14, 1915.

[214] ANDREW D. MELOY & CO. v. DONNELLY et al., (Circuit Court, D. Connecticut. December 30, 1902.),

No. 523, pp. 556 to 436.

[215] Walter Harvey Weed, The Mines Handbook, New York, NY, 1918, p. 1641; Bold letters added by author.

[216] Stallforth Papers, Private Collection, diary, 1908.

[217] NA RG 59 Department of State, file 341.112 M49/document 12, Statement of Andrew D. Meloy to Ambassador Walter Hines Page, August 14, 1915.

[218] Chihuahua Archivos Municipales, Secretaria de Gobierno del Estado de Chihuahua, Sección de Estadística, Chihuahua 1909; In 1909 in the district of Hidalgo, the Stallforths are listed in a host of mines as co-owner, such as Criosura, Sta. Antonia; in the Mina District the Stallforths own La Abundancia, Presidente, El Lucero, La Luz del Día, La Encerradora, San Fernando. As non-producing the mine register lists El Povenir.

[219] Stallforth Papers, Private Collection, Income and Expense statement, Mexico Consolidated Mining and Smelting Co., 1908.

[220] NA RG 59 Department of State, file 341.112 M49/document 12, Statement of Andrew D. Meloy to Ambassador Walter Hines Page, August 14, 1915.

[221] Stallforth Papers, Private Collection, Letter from Juan Creel to Stockholders of the Mexico Consolidated Mining and Smelting Company, October, 1910.

[222] See the official website of Parral, www.hidalgodelparral.gob.mx, viewed 10-2010.

[223] Stallforth Papers, Private Collection, diary entry, April 20, 1910.

[224] Ibid., illegible to Frederico Stallforth, October 11, 1910; letter confirms deposit of $50,000 from Paris to Stallforth Y Hermanos in Parral.

[225] Ibid., Memo from W. Schulze (manager of the Guanacevi, Durango office) to F. Stallforth, San Pedro, October 7, 1910.

[226] Ibid.

[227] Ibid., Juan Creel to Board of Directors, undated, around October 18, 1910.

[228] Ibid., Alberto to Frederico, undated telegram, around October 18, 1910.

[229] Ibid., Alberto to Frederico in a draft of pending letter to Board, October 18, 1910.

[230] Ibid., Letter from Frederico Stallforth to Wingate & Cullen in New York, October 18, 1910.

[231] Ibid., Telegram from Alberto Stallforth to Frederico, October 18, 1910.

[232] Ibid., guest book entry, November 2, 1910.

[233] Ibid., picture courtesy Mary Prevo Collection.

[234] Ibid., guest book entry, March 25, 1911, picture courtesy Mary Prevo Collection.

[235] Weed, *The Mines Handbook*, 1918, p. 1641.

[236] Statement F. A. Sommerfeld, June 21, 1918.

[237] Chihuahua Enterprise, August 15, 1908.

[238] Ibid., August 22, 1908.

[239] Ibid., September 5, 1908, September 19, 1908, October 3, 1908.

[240] Ibid., October 3, 1908, "German Charge d'Affairs Here. Baron von Radowitz is on visit to German colony here." The paper refers to Baron Wilhelm von Radowitz, Charge d'Affairs of the German embassy in Mexico City in 1908 until Count von Bernstorff officially was accredited as ambassador to Mexico and the United States.

[241] AA Politisches Archiv Berlin, Mexiko VI, Paket 45.

[242] Ibid., Mexiko II, Paket 5, Wangenheim to Bülow, September 30, 1905, number 125.

[243] Ibid., Mexiko VI, Paket 45.

[244] NA RG 65 Records of the FBI, M1085, Roll 862, file 232-296, copy of memo Zach Lamar Cobb to Counselor Frank Polk, April 24, 1917.

[245] Statement F.A. Sommerfeld, June 21, 1918.

[246] *The Mining World*, Volume 32, January 1 to June 25, 1910, Chicago, IL, p. 682.

[247] Ibid., p. 402.

[248] Archivos Municipales Chihuahua, Secretaria de Gobierno del Estado de Chihuahua, Sección de estadística, 1909.

[249] Statement F. A. Sommerfeld, June 21, 1918.

[250] NA RG 60 Department of Justice, file 9-16-12-18, Statement of Frederico Stallforth, April 22, 1917, p. 19.

[251] Statement F. A. Sommerfeld, June 21, 1918.

[252] In the records of mining properties 1907 to 1910 in the Archivos Municipales of Chihuahua he is nowhere listed either as a registered mining engineer, mine supervisor or mine owner. See also Horace J. Stevens, *The Copper Handbook 1908*, Chicago, 1909.

[253] Chihuahua Enterprise, January 30, 1909, p.7.

[254] In a crucial document dated May 10, 1915 to be discussed in In Plain Sight: Sommerfeld and Stallforth on the North American Front, 1914-1918, Dernburg mentions "meinen Freund, Herrn Felix A. Sommerfeld" to Admiral von Holtzendorff.

[255] Chihuahua 1910, Archivos Municipales Hidalgo del Parral, p. 58; Translation by the author.

[256] Statement F. A. Sommerfeld, June 21, 1918.

[257] Ibid.

[258] Ibid.

[259] Chihuahua Enterprise, June 12, 1909, p. 3.

[260] Sommerfeld was an accredited Associated Press reporter in the spring of 1911 in El Paso.

[261] Press Club of Chicago, Officers and Members 1913. Haggerty is spelled either with one "g" or two throughout the archival documentation. This author chose the spelling with a single "g."

[262] Only a few border registrations exist for Sommerfeld in 1912, none for the El Paso-Ciudad Juarez crossing, although there are many records showing his going back and forth. Also see United Sates Senate, *Revolutions in Mexico*, Hearing before the Subcommittee of the Committee on Foreign Relations, Government Printing Press, Washington D.C., 1912, Testimony of Felix A. Sommerfeld, p. 394.

[263] Martin Luis Guzman, *Memoirs of Pancho Villa*, translated by Virginia H. Taylor, University of Texas Press, Austin, TX, 1975, p. 22. Also in quoted from Reed in McLynn, *Villa and Zapata*, p. 68.

Also Tuck, *Pancho Villa and John Reed*, p. 38, and Randolph Welford Smith, *Benighted Mexico*, John Lane Company, New York, 1916, p. 291.

[264] Statement F.A. Sommerfeld, June 24, 1918.

[265] Ibid., June 22, 1918.

[266] http://www.gringorebel.com/interview-with-francisco-madero, viewed 10-2010.

[267] See story of two captured Germans in next chapter.

[268] Statement F. A. Sommerfeld, June 21, 1918; Kueck is also mentioned by German agent Horst von der Goltz as his contact to Franz von Papen in 1914; see Horst von der Goltz, *My Adventures as a German Secret Agent*, Robert M. McBride and Company, New York, 1917, pp. 121-125.

[269] AA Politisches Archiv Berlin, Mexiko II, Paket 5.

[270] Ibid.

[271] NA RG 65 Records of the FBI, M1085, Roll 862, file 232-296, copy of memo Zach Lamar Cobb to Counselor Frank Polk, April 24, 1917.

[272] Kueck arrived in New York with his wife Emilia and 2-year-old daughter Laura in April 1908 from Hamburg. He was 30 years old. As profession he listed "Consul." See Staatsarchiv Hamburg, Bestand: 373-7 I, VIII (Auswanderungsamt I). Mikrofilmrollen K 1701 - K 2008, S 17363 - S 17383, 13116 – 13183, Staatsarchiv Hamburg 373-7 I, VIII A 1 Band 200, page 387 (Mikrofilm Nr. K 1804). Frederico Stallforth arrived in May 1908, Sommerfeld sometime before October 1908, and Bruchhausen on October 6, 1908, see NA RG 36 U.S. Customs Service, T715, Roll 1152.

[273] AA Politisches Archiv Berlin, Mexiko II, Paket 5, Kueck to Richthofen, November 23, 1910 and November 28, 1910.

[274] Schlagende Gesellschaft is a fraternity where in the course of admission potential members had to fence without protection. Once the coveted wound in the face had been received the fraternity brothers would add salt to the wound to insure that the scar stood out. Many high-ranking officers of the German military had been members in such fraternities. The practice is outlawed in Germany but still existent.

[275] AA Politisches Archiv Berlin, Mexiko II, Paket 5, Sommerfeld to Bruchhausen, November 23, 1910.

[276] Ibid., Kueck to Richthofen, December 28, 1910.

[277] AA Ibid., Sommerfeld to Bruchhausen, November 23, 1910 and November 28, 1910.

[278] Ibid., Paket 6, German Ambassador to von Bülow, October 31, 1905.

[279] See for example NA RG 131, Alien Property Custodian, Box 67, Entry 195, Sommerfeld.

[280] AA Politisches Archiv Berlin, Mexiko II, Paket 5, Kueck to Rieloff, November 23, 1910, December 14, 1910.

[281] For example AA Politisches Archiv Berlin, Mexiko II, Paket 5, Rieloff to Richthofen, November 29, 1910.

[282] Von der Goltz, *My Adventures as a German Secret Agent*, p. 57.

[283] Charles H. Harris and Louis R. Sadler, *The Border and the Revolution: Clandestine Activities of the Mexican Revolution: 1910-1920*, High-Lonesome Books, Silver City, NM, 1988, pp. 71-98. Also Katz, *Secret War in Mexico*, pp. 339-344. Katz maintains that German agents could have been involved but shows no clear evidence.

[284] AA Politisches Archiv Berlin, Mexiko III, Paket 28; German Consul Unger of Mazatlan wrote Ambassador to Mexico von Magnus a summary of Bopp's legal troubles. The consul finally served four years in Ft. Leavenworth for hiring sabotage agents and violating the neutrality laws.

[285] NA RG 65 Albert Papers, Box 27, Grosser Generalstab Sektion IIIB to Papen, Document, March 31, 1914.

[286] NA RG 242 Captured German Documents, T141, Roll 19, Papen to Auswärtiges Amt, July 30, 1914, Document 147.

[287] For example Doerries, *Imperial Challenge*, p. 175.

[288] See Walter Nicolai, *The German Secret Service*, translated with an additional chapter by George Renwick, Stanley Paul and Co., London, Great Britain, 1924.

[289] Barbara Tuchman, *The Zimmermann Telegram*, Macmillan Company, New York, NY, 1958, pp.28-32.

[290] AA Bonn, Mexiko 10, vol. 1, Wangenheim to Bülow, 25 May 1907; quoted from Katz, *Secret War in Mexico*, p. 68.

[291] See Francisco I. Madero, *La Sucesión Presidencial en 1910 – El Partido Nacional Democrático*, San Pedro, Coahuila, Mexico, December, 1908.

[292] See story of Germans captured at Casas Grandes in the next chapter.

[293] Statement F. A. Sommerfeld, June 21, 1918.

[294] United Sates Senate, *Revolutions in Mexico*, Hearing before the Subcommittee of the Committee on Foreign Relations, Government Printing Press, Washington D.C., 1912, Testimony of Felix A. Sommerfeld, p. 393.

[295] Statement F. A. Sommerfeld, June 21, 1918.

[296] Ibid.

[297] NA RG 60 Department of Justice, file 9-16-12-5305, John Hanna, Memo for the Department Files, April 4, 1919.

[298] United Sates Senate, *Revolutions in Mexico*, Hearing before the Subcommittee of the Committee on Foreign Relations, Government Printing Press, Washington D.C., 1912, Testimony of Felix A. Sommerfeld, p. 392.

[299] NA RG 59 Department of State, file 312.11/752, Letter Marion Letcher to Secretary of State, July 15, 1912.

[300] The San Antonio Light, July 30, 1911, "How Mexican Revolt News was gathered."

[301] Turner remained one of the most well-known reporters on Mexico, Jimmy Hare went on to report on World War I for Colliers Magazine and is probably the most famous and daring photo journalist in the early 20th century. Willis became city editor of the New York Harold and David Lawrence went on to found the U.S. News and World Report. Both tried to help Sommerfeld be paroled in 1919.

[302] Katz, *Life and Times of Pancho Villa*, p. 317.

[303] Statement F.A. Sommerfeld, June 21, 1918.

[304] Stallforth Papers, Private Collection, guest book entry, March 25, 1911.

[305] El Paso Library, Otis Aultman Collection, B816; Other people depicted Francisco I. Madero Jr., Mrs. Frank Wells Brown, Francisco I. Madero Sr., Bryan Brown, Felix Sommerfeld, Ethel Brown, Giuseppe Garibaldi, Sara Madero, Frank Wells Brown, Gustavo Madero, Roque Gonzalez Garza.

[306] Von der Goltz, *My Adventures as a German Secret Agent*, p. 43.

[307] El Paso Public Library, Aultman Collection, B0763185. Other people depicted are Francisco I. Madero, Jr., Chris Haggerty, and Allie Martin.

[308] Garibaldi, *A Toast To Rebellion*, The Bobbs-Merrill Company, New York, NY, 1935, opposite page 268. Also *Collier's Magazine*, Volume 47, June 3, 1911, p. 22.

[309] El Paso Public Library, Aultman Collection, A1473190.

[310] Library of Congress, Bain Collection, Washington, D.C. (LC-DIG-ggbain-01887).

[311] There are questions as to Madero's middle name. His birth certificate shows Ignacio. His father's middle name was Indalecio which spurred confusion among Madero's biographers.

[312] Edith O'Shaughnessy, "Diplomatic Days in Mexico, Second Paper," *Harper's Magazine*, 10, 1917, p. 711.

[313] Ross, *Francisco I. Madero*, p. 4; "Thirteen children were to reach maturity: Francisco, Gustavo, Emilio, Alfonso, Raul, Gabriel, Carlos, Mercedes, Angela, Rafaela and Magdalena."

[314] Madero's Jewish ancestry has been disputed by biographer Stanley R. Ross.

[315] Ross, *Francisco I Madero*, p. 6.

[316] Quoted from Ross, *Francisco I. Madero*, p. 8.

[317] Ibid., p. 18.

[318] Ibid., p. 10.

[319] While Stallforth did not mention knowing the Maderos before 1910, it seems that San Pedro where Stallforth's mines were located is the same city where Madero's family estate existed.

[320] Ross, *Francisco I. Madero*, p. 11.

[321] Ibid., p. 12.

[322] Ibid., p. 14.

[323] Ibid., p. 12.

[324] Katz, *Life and Times of Pancho Villa*, p. 53.

[325] Dirk Raat "Madero and the Comet: Corrido," in *Twentieth Century Mexico*, edited by Dirk Raat and William Beezley, University of Nebraska Press, Lincoln, NE, 1986, p. 104.

[326] Ross, *Francisco I. Madero*, p. 105.

[327] Katz, *Life and Times of Pancho Villa*, p. 53.

[328] Ross, *Francisco I. Madero*, p. 109.

[329] Katz, *Life and Times of Pancho Villa*, p. 53.

[330] Ross, *Francisco I. Madero*, p. 116.

[331] Arthur Link, editor, *Woodrow Wilson and a Revolutionary World, 1913-1921*, New York, NY, 1982, Chapter 1: Lloyd C. Gardner, "Woodrow Wilson and the Mexican Revolution," p. 3.

[332] John Womack, Jr., *Zapata and the Mexican Revolution*, Alfred E. Knopf, New York, 1968, p. 90.

[333] McLynn, *Villa and Zapata*, p. 73, also see a detailed description in Ross, *Francisco I. Madero*, pp. 125-126.

[334] Quoted from Ross, *Francisco I. Madero*, p. 127.

[335] AA Politisches Archiv Berlin, Mexiko II, Paket 5, Sommerfeld to Bruchhausen, Nov. 23, 1910. Translated by the author. Due to the hand writing minor differences in wording are possible.

[336] Ibid., Kueck to Rieloff, Nov. 23, 1910. Translated by the author.

[337] This note is widely publicized online, for example on the Texas Historical Association Website (www.tshaonline.org/handbook/online/articles/for08). Whether Orozco actual wrote it cannot clearly be determined.

[338] Giuseppe Garibaldi, *A Toast To Rebellion*, p. 232. Garibaldi's account is to be taken with one, two or more grains of salt. His descriptions of the first campaigns in the revolution are slanted to his favor.

[339] Harris and Sadler, *Secret War in El Paso*, p. 40.

[340] Leibson, *Sam Dreben, the Fighting Jew*, p. 65.

[341] Ibid., p. 69.

[342] Douglas V. Meed, *Soldier of Fortune*, Halcyon Press, Ltd., Houston, TX, 2003, p. 55.

[343] *The Financial Review: Finance, Commerce, Railroads*, Annual 1912, p. 21.

[344] Diaz had been quoted as saying "poor little Mexico, so far from God, so close to the United States."

[345] Katz actually made the well-taken point that Pancho Villa's reputation as outlaw and bandit is more myth than fact. Before the revolution started Villa worked in construction and other honorable occupations where he stood out as an apt leader of men. However, shortly before the revolution started, Villa was a wanted man. See Katz, *Life and Times of Pancho Villa*.

[346] Katz, *Life and Times of Pancho Villa*, p. 7.

[347] For an exhaustive biography of Pascual Orozco see Michael C. Meyer, *Pascual Orozco: Mexican Rebel*.

[348] Harris and Sadler put the strength of Madero's forces to 550, while most other historians put his numbers to around 800.

[349] Garibaldi, *A Toast to Rebellion*, pp. 243-249.

[350] Ibid., p. 239.

[351] Ross, *Francisco I. Madero*, p. 147; also Harris and Sadler, *Secret War in El Paso*, p. 41.

[352] Harris and Sadler, *Secret War in El Paso*, p. 41.

[353] Quoted from Katz, *Life and Times of Pancho Villa*, p. 93.

[354] AA Politisches Archiv Berlin, Mexiko II, Paket 5, Reichskanzler to Rhomberg, April 6, 1911.

[355] Ibid., Kueck to Sommerfeld, April 24, 1911.

[356] Ibid., Kueck to Rhomberg, May 1, 1911.

[357] Ibid., Kueck to Hintze, April 24, 1911.

[358] Ibid., Kueck to Hintze, June 13, 1911.

[359] "All the newspaper correspondents who know anything of Mexico know Sommerfeld," NA RG 165 Military Intelligence Division, file 9140-1754, document 21, Agent Berliner report June 15, 1918.

[360] NA RG 60 Department of Justice, file 9-16-12-5305, Memorandum for John Lord O'Brian, May 27, 1919.

[361] Ibid.

[362] Garibaldi, *A Toast to Rebellion*, p. 292.

[363] A reference to them working together is contained in www.Mexfiles.net but without a source.

[364] Garibaldi, *A Toast to Rebellion*, opposite page 268.

[365] The El Paso Herald, May 19, 1911, "Capital Notes by Timothy Turner."

[366] Harris and Sadler, *Secret War in El Paso*, p. 29.

[367] NA RG 65 Records of the FBI, M1085, Roll 851, file 232, BI report "Investigation Violations Neutrality Laws – Mexico," April 25, p. 7.

[368] United States Senate, *Investigation of Mexican affairs*, Subcommittee of the Committee of Foreign Relations, Government Printing Office, 1920, Testimony of Sherburne G. Hopkins, p. 2543.

[369] NA RG 65Records of the FBI, M1085, Roll 851, file 232, BI Report "Investigation Violations Neutrality Laws – Mexico," April 25, p. 7.

[370] Ross, *Francisco I. Madero*, p. 128.

[371] Katz, *Life and Times of Pancho Villa*, p. 92.

[372] John Skirius, "Railroad, Oil and Other Foreign Interests in the Mexican Revolution, 1911 to 1914," *Journal of Latin American Studies*, Vol. 35, No. 1 (Feb. 2003), Cambridge University Press, p. 27.

[373] Alan Knight, *The Mexican Revolution: Volume 1: Porfirians, Liberals and Peasants*, Cambridge University Press, Cambridge, MA 1986, p. 185.

[374] Skirius, "Railroad, Oil and Other Foreign Interests in the Mexican Revolution, 1911 to 1914," p. 28; also Katz, *Secret War in Mexico*; Meyer and Morales, *Petroleo y nación*.

[375] United States Senate, *Investigation of Mexican affairs*, Subcommittee of the Committee of Foreign Relations, Government Printing Office, 1920, Testimony of Sherburne G. Hopkins, p. 2532.

[376] Harris and Sadler, *Secret War in El Paso*, p. 36.

[377] Skirius, "Railroad, Oil and other Foreign Interests in the Mexican Revolution, 1911-1914," p. 30; also United States Senate, *Investigation of Mexican affairs*, Subcommittee of the Committee of Foreign Relations, Government Printing Office , 1920, Testimony of Sherburne G. Hopkins, p. 2532.

[378] Harris and Sadler, *Secret War in El Paso*, p. 56; Referring to the same source almost the same numbers appear in Skirius, "Railroad, Oil and Other Foreign Interests in the Mexican Revolution, 1911 to 1914," p. 31; Hopkins testified to the same number stating in his U.S. Senate testimony "They [Madero family] had advanced huge sums out of their own pockets, of which I have personal knowledge." He further stated that the Maderos personally invested about 400,000 in the revolution which they wanted to have reimbursed. United States Senate, *Investigation of Mexican affairs*, Subcommittee of the Committee of Foreign Relations, Government Printing Office , 1920, Testimony of Sherburne G. Hopkins, p. 2530 and p. 2543.

[379] United States Senate, *Investigation of Mexican affairs*, Subcommittee of the Committee of Foreign Relations, Government Printing Office, 1920, Testimony of Sloan W. Emery, pp. 2222 to 2223.

[380] Skirius, "Railroad, Oil and other Foreign Interests in the Mexican Revolution, 1911-1914," p. 31, referring to a New York World article on January 9, 1914.

[381] Stallforth Papers, Private Collection, diary entry, March 25, 1911.

[382] Ibid., undated note (sometime in 1912), "Is Maderos [sic] conection [sic] to be lugrative [sic] for me?"

[383] United States Senate, *Investigation of Mexican affairs*, Subcommittee of the Committee of Foreign Relations, Government Printing Office, 1920, Testimony of Sherburne G. Hopkins, p. 2552.

[384] NA RG 60 Department of Justice, File 9-16-12-5305, Letter from Miguel Diaz Lombardo to Department of Justice, April 25, 1919.

[385] Ibid.

[386] Statement F.A. Sommerfeld, June 22, 1918.

[387] NA RG 165 Military Intelligence Division, file 9140-1754 document 43, Lieutenant Colonel G. F. Bailey to Captain George B. Lester, January 8, 1919.

[388] Azel Ames, *The May-Flower and Her Log, July 15, 1620-May 6, 1621*, Chiefly from Original Sources; Houghton, Mifflin, Boston and New York, 1907, p. 181.

[389] Louis H. Cornish, editor, *National Register of the Society of Sons of the American Revolution*, New York, NY, 1902, p. 441.

[390] Frederick Virkus, editor, *Immigrant Ancestors: A List of 2,500 Immigrants to America before 1750*, Genealogical Publishing Co., Baltimore, MD, 1964, p. 28.

[391] NA RG 165 Military Intelligence Division, Correspondence 1917 to 1941, Box 1266, File 2338-997.

[392] The Evening Bulletin, Maysville, Kentucky, "Almost beyond Belief," p. 1.

[393] Ibid.

[394] Ibid.

[395] The New York Sun, November 12, 1887 "The infernal machine hoax."

[396] The Batavia Daily News, January 6, 1888, p.1.

[397] Harris and Sadler, *Secret War in El Paso*, p. 33.

[398] The New York Times, April 8, 1915; also The Oakland Tribune, April 18, 1915.

[399] The New York Times, August 4, 1903 "Railway Earning Prospects."

[400] The New York Times, June 28, 1914.

[401] The St. Louis Republic, January 3, 1900, "State Department Addresses Britain."

[402] NA RG 165 Military Intelligence Division, Correspondence 1917 to 1941, Box 3692, files 10640-2413.

[403] The Times, Washington, October 10, 1898.

[404] United States Senate, *Investigation of Mexican affairs*, Subcommittee of the Committee of Foreign Relations, Government Printing Office, 1920, Testimony of Sherburne G. Hopkins, p. 2565.

[405] Official program, Admiral Dewey Reception, October 2 and 3, Washington, 1899.

[406] NA RG 165 Military Intelligence Division, file 10640-2413, document 2; Colonel Mathew Smith to General Nolan, December 21, 1920.

[407] Naval Militia Yearbooks 1901, 1902, 1903, 1904.

[408] Testimony of Henry Clay Pierce before the 8th Circuit Court, "The United States of America vs. Standard Oil Company of New Jersey et al defendants, Petitioner's Testimony," Volume 3, Washington Government Printing Office, 1908, p. 1066.

[409] Jonathan C. Brown, *Oil and Revolution in Mexico*, University of California Press, Berkeley, CA, 1993, pp. 14-15.

[410] Testimony of Henry Clay Pierce before the 8th Circuit Court, "The United States of America vs. Standard Oil Company of New Jersey et al defendants, Petitioner's Testimony," Volume 3, Washington Government Printing Office, 1908, p. 1070.

[411] Ibid., p. 1067.

[412] Brown, *Oil and Revolution in Mexico*, p. 23.

[413] The New York Times, February 2, 1913, "Pierce is in Control of Big Oil Company."

[414] Library of Congress Prints and Photographs Division Washington, D.C., Harris and Ewing Collection, H261- 2928, public domain.

[415] For a fascinating read of the 1840s, 50s and 60s upheaval in Nicaragua see the memoirs of William Walker: William Walker, *The War in Nicaragua*, S.H. Goetzel, New York, NY, 1860.

[416] Manzar Foroohar, *The Catholic Church and Social Change in Nicaragua*, State University of New York Press, Albany, NY, 1989, p. 11.

[417] United States Senate, *Investigation of Mexican affairs*, Subcommittee of the Committee of Foreign Relations, Government Printing Office, 1920, Testimony of Sherburne G. Hopkins, p. 2565.

[418] Ibid.

[419] Leibson, *Sam Dreben, the Fighting Jew*, p. 46.

[420] Meed, *Soldier of Fortune*, p. 39.

[421] Ibid., p. 41.

[422] The New York Times, November 23, 1909, "Zelaya broke Faith to Kill Americans."

[423] Meed, *Soldier of Fortune*, p. 42.

[424] Leibson, *Sam Dreben, the Fighting Jew*, p. 57.

[425] Meed, *Soldier of Fortune*, p.42.

[426] United States Senate, *Investigation of Mexican affairs*, Subcommittee of the Committee of Foreign Relations, Government Printing Office, 1920, Testimony of Sherburne G. Hopkins, p. 2565.

[427] Ibid., p. 2566.

[428] Ibid., p. 2565.

[429] NA RG 165 Military Intelligence Division, Correspondence 1917 to 1941, Box 1266, File 2338-692, Memorandum for Lieut. Dunn.

[430] Skirius, "Railroad, Oil and other Foreign Interests in the Mexican Revolution," p. 30; apparently he is referring to a not well-cited document in the Madero Archive, Biblioteca Nacional, Mexico City.

[431] NA RG 165 Military Intelligence Division, Correspondence 1917 to 1941, Box 1885, file 5761-409, Major Henry A. Barber to A. L. Mills, March 12, 1912.

[432] Charles H. Harris, III and Louis R. Sadler, *The Archeologist was a Spy: Sylvanus G. Morley and the Office of Naval Intelligence*, University of New Mexico Press, Albuquerque, NM, 2003, p. 8.

[433] Ibid., pp. 13-14.

[434] NA RG 165 Military Intelligence Division, Correspondence 1917 to 1941, Box 1266, File 2338-692, Hopkins to M. Churchill, November 7, 1918.

[435] Ibid., File 2338-997, Colonel John M. Dunn to Hopkins, February 13, 1919.

[436] NA RG 165 Military Intelligence Division, Correspondence 1917 to 1941, Box 3692, File 10640-2413; Memorandum for General Nolan, December 21, 1920.

[437] United States Senate, *Investigation of Mexican affairs*, Subcommittee of the Committee of Foreign Relations, Government Printing Office, 1920, Testimony of Sherburne G. Hopkins, p. 2535.

[438] NA RG 165 Military Intelligence Division, Correspondence 1917 to 1941, Box 1266, File 2338-692, Memorandum for Lieut. Dunn.

[439] United Sates Senate, *Revolutions in Mexico*, Hearing before the Subcommittee of the Committee on Foreign Relations, Government Printing Press, Washington D.C., 1912, Testimony of Felix A. Sommerfeld, p. 393.

[440] Ibid.

[441] The San Antonio Light, July 30, 1911, "How Mexican Revolt News was gathered."

[442] Garibaldi, *A Toast to Rebellion*, p. 273.

[443] The Washington Herald, "War Resolution still in Debate," April 22, 1914.

[444] Louis M. Teitelbaum, *Woodrow Wilson and the Mexican Revolution, 1913-1916*, Exposition Press, New York, NY, 1967, p. 63. It is a little known fact that Carranza was in New York in 1911 on behalf of Madero.

[445] Henry Lane Wilson, *Diplomatic Episodes in Mexico, Belgium, and Chile*, Kennikat Press, Port Washington, NY, 1971 (re-print of the 1927 print), p. 212.

[446] United States Senate, *Investigation of Mexican affairs*, Subcommittee of the Committee of Foreign Relations, Government Printing Office, 1920, Testimony of Sherburne G. Hopkins, p. 2562.

[447] Ibid.

[448] Peter V. N. Henderson, *In the Absence of Don Porfirio: Francisco Leon De La Barra and the Mexican Revolution*, Scholarly Resources, Wilmington, DE, 2000, p. 34.

[449] Ross, *Francisco I. Madero*, p. 157.

[450] AA Politisches Archiv Berlin, Mexiko III, Paket 24, Bernstorff to Auswärtiges Amt, April 4, 1911.

[451] Ibid., Madero to German Ambassador, February 15, 1911.

[452] The New York Times, "Steever to succeed Brush," May 7, 1912.

[453] The New York Times, "Taft adds to snarl in War Department," August 6, 1912.

[454] The New York Times, "Steever to succeed Brush," May 7, 1912.

[455] United Sates Senate, *Revolutions in Mexico*, Hearing before the Subcommittee of the Committee on Foreign Relations, Government Printing Press, Washington D.C., 1912, Testimony of Felix A. Sommerfeld, p. 394.

[456] Ibid.

[457] The New York Times, April 21, 1911 "Limit Reached Says Limantour."

[458] United Sates Senate, *Revolutions in Mexico*, Hearing before the Subcommittee of the Committee on Foreign Relations, Government Printing Press, Washington D.C., 1912, Testimony of Felix A. Sommerfeld, p. 394.

[459] Madero biographer Ross insists that Francisco Gomez was the one successfully urging Madero to hold fire.

[460] New York Times, May 21, 1911 "A vivid story of the battle of Juarez by a participant."

[461] United Sates Senate, *Revolutions in Mexico*, Hearing before the Subcommittee of the Committee on Foreign Relations, Government Printing Press, Washington D.C., 1912, Testimony of Felix A. Sommerfeld, p. 396.

[462] Henderson, *In the Absence of Don Porfirio*, p. 47.

[463] Garibaldi, *A Toast to Rebellion*, p. 286.

[464] Statement F.A. Sommerfeld, June 22, 1918.

[465] Harris and Sadler, *Secret War in El Paso*, p. 49.

[466] Garibaldi, *A Toast to Rebellion*, 291.

[467] Ibid., 289.

[468] The El Paso Herald, May 9, 1911, "Battle Rages between Federals and Insurrectos in C. Juarez."

[469] Ibid.

[470] Ibid.

[471] The New York Times, May 21, 1911, "A Vivid Story of the Battle of Juarez by a Participant."

[472] Katz, Life and Times of Pancho Villa, p. 110.

[473] The San Antonio Light, July 30, 1911, "How the Mexican Revolt News was gathered."

[474] Garibaldi, *A Toast to Rebellion*, p. 295.

[475] Ibid., p. 294.

[476] Ibid., p. 293.

[477] Ibid., p. 295.

[478] Katz, *Life and Times of Pancho Villa*, p. 118.

[479] Garibaldi, *A Toast to Rebellion*, 302.

[480] Ross, *Francisco I. Madero*, p. 131.

[481] The exact circumstances of Madero's run in with Orozco and Villa are disputed. For more information read Katz, *Life and Times of Pancho Villa*, p. 112 and Harris and Sadler, *Secret War in El Paso*, p. 51.

[482] www.elpasotimes.com/ci_16524568, viewed 01-2011.

[483] Skirius, "Railroad, Oil and other Foreign Interests in the Mexican Revolution, 1911-1914," p. 30.

[484] Katz, *Life and Times of Pancho Villa*, p. 115.

[485] *Chicago Daily News Almanac and Yearbook for 1912*, Chicago Daily News Company, Chicago, IL, 1911, p. 211.

[486] The El Paso Herald, June 1, 1911, "El Pasoans Give Insurrectos a Banquet."

[487] Library of Congress, Papers of Hugh Lenox Scott, Box 15, General Correspondence, Captain Harry Cootes to Hugh Lenox Scott, April 15, 1914.

[488] Katz, *Life and Times of Pancho Villa*, p. 117.

[489] NA RG 65 Records of the FBI, M1085, Roll 852, file 232, L. L. Ross to Department, August 4, 1911.

[490] Harris and Sadler, *Secret War in El Paso*, p. 53.

[491] United Sates Senate, *Revolutions in Mexico*, Hearing before the Subcommittee of the Committee on Foreign Relations, Government Printing Press, Washington D.C., 1912, Testimony of Felix A. Sommerfeld, p. 398.

[492] Ibid., p. 421.

[493] Katz, *The Secret War in Mexico*, p. 87.

[494] Robert Welles Ritchie, "The Passing of a Dictator," *Harper's Monthly Magazine*, April, 1912, p. 786.

[495] Ibid., p. 788.

[496] Ibid., p. 789.

[497] It seems that Wilhelm II gave the order of the red eagle to German ambassador to Mexico, Dr. Karl Gottlieb Buenz at the same time.

[498] AA Politisches Archiv Berlin, Mexiko III, Paket 24, von Treutler to Porfirio Diaz and Diaz to Wilhelm II, June 30, 1911.

[499] Anita Brenner, "The Wind that Swept Mexico: Part I. Fall of a Dictator," *Harper's Magazine*, November, 1942, p. 630.

[500] Ibid.

[501] Statement F.A. Sommerfeld, June 22, 1918.

[502] Anita Brenner, "The Wind that Swept Mexico: Part I. Fall of a Dictator," *Harper's Magazine*, November, 1942, p. 630.

[503] Edith O'Shaughnessy, "Diplomatic Days in Mexico," Harper's Magazine, October, 1917, p. 708.

[504] Link, *Woodrow Wilson and a Revolutionary World, 1913-1921*, Chapter 1: Lloyd C. Gardner, "Woodrow Wilson and the Mexican Revolution," p. 4.

[505] See The New York Times, February 20, 1913 "Why victors shot Gustavo Madero" for a discussion of Gustavo's power.

[506] United States Senate, *Investigation of Mexican affairs*, Subcommittee of the Committee of Foreign Relations, Government Printing Office, 1920, Testimony of Sherburne G. Hopkins, p. 2567.

[507] Ibid., p. 2561.

[508] The Washington Post, August 23, 1911 "Pearsons sell oil lands."

[509] See The New York Times, December 6, 1913.

[510] United States Senate, *Investigation of Mexican affairs*, Subcommittee of the Committee of Foreign Relations, Government Printing Office, 1920, Testimony of Sherburne G. Hopkins, p. 2249.

[511] Womack, *Zapata and the Mexican Revolution*, p. 91.

[512] Ross, *Francisco I. Madero*, p. 177.

[513] Womack, *Zapata and the Mexican Revolution*, p. 95.

[514] Ibid., pp. 95-96.

[515] Ibid., p. 98.

[516] David G. LaFrance, "Germany, Revolutionary Nationalism, and the Downfall of Francisco I. Madero: The Covadonga Killings," *Mexican Studies*, Vol. 2, No. 1 (Winter 1986), p. 59.

[517] Statement F.A. Sommerfeld, June 22, 1918.

[518] LaFrance, "Germany, Revolutionary Nationalism, and the Downfall of Francisco I. Madero: The Covadonga Killings," p. 70. Lawrence H. Officer, "Exchange Rates," in Susan B. Carter, Scott S. Gartner, Michael Haines, Alan Olmstead, Richard Sutch, and Gavin Wright, eds., *Historical Statistics of the United States*, Millennial Edition, Cambridge University Press, New York, NY, 2002.

[519] LaFrance, "Germany, Revolutionary Nationalism, and the Downfall of Francisco I. Madero: The Covadonga Killings," p. 78.

[520] Ibid., p. 70.

[521] Ibid., p. 77.

[522] Statement F.A. Sommerfeld, June 22, 1918.

[523] NA RG 242 Captured German Documents, T149, Roll 37, von Hintze to von Bethmann Hollweg, July 25, 1911.

[524] Ibid., Ernesto Madero to Felix Sommerfeld, July 22, 1911.

[525] Statement F.A. Sommerfeld, June 22, 1918.

[526] Katz, *The Secret War in Mexico*, p. 88.

[527] NA RG 131 Alien Property Custodian, Entry 199, Box 3306, Buenz retirement and award to the order of the Red Eagle, second class on January 14, 1911.

[528] LaFrance, "Germany, Revolutionary Nationalism, and the Downfall of Francisco I. Madero: The Covadonga Killings," p. 74.

[529] Ibid., p. 75.

[530] He was indicted in 1915 for sending freight under false manifests to German warships in 1914. He died in an Atlanta penitentiary on September 15, 1918. See The New York Times, September 16, 1918, "Karl Buenz dies in Atlanta Prison."

[531] Only one meager biography of von Hintze was ever published, von Hintze's papers are strewn among different archives and collections, whole episodes of his professional career, such as his World War I assignment in China are undocumented.

[532] Hadley and Sarty, *Tin-Pots and Pirate Ships: Canadian Naval Forces and German Sea Raiders 1880 – 1918*, p. 34.

[533] Ibid., p. 35; Also *Marine Crew Chronik*, Marineschule Mürwik, Flensburg, Deutschland, MIM620/CREW, 1891, pp. 159-160, autobiographic article by Karl Boy-Ed.

[534] Karl Boy-Ed's mother was Ida Boy-Ed. She published 70 novels and book size essays. One of her most famous protégés was Thomas Mann, who Karl Boy-Ed had met many times as a youth.

[535] The New York Times, "Liberals Resent Coup on Hintze," July 12, 1918.

[536] Johann Heinrich Count von Bernstorff, *My Three Years in America*, Skeffington and Son, London, Great Britain, unknown date, approximately 1940, p. 13.

[537] *Marine Crew Chronik*, Marineschule Mürwik, Flensburg, Deutschland, MIM620/CREW, 1891, pp. 159-160, autobiographic article by Karl Boy-Ed.

[538] Johannes Huertner, Editor, *Paul von Hintze: Marineoffizier, Diplomat, Staatssekretär, Dokumente einer Karriere zwischen Militär und Politik, 1903-1918*, Harald Boldt Verlag, München, Germany, 1998, p. 31, translated freely by the author.

[539] Reinhard R. Doerries, *Journal of Intelligence History*, Volume 4, Number 1, Summer 2004, Nürnberg, Germany.

[540] Hadley and Sarty, *Tin-Pots and Pirate Ships*, p. 106.

[541] Guoqi Xu, *China and the Great War: China's pursuit of a new National Identity and Internationalization*, Cambridge University Press, New York, NY, 2005, p. 111.

[542] Bancroft Library, University of California at Berkeley, M-B 12, German Diplomatic Papers, Box 7, Rohmberg to Salado Alvarez, May 25, 1911.

[543] Ibid., Manuel Calero to von Hintze, December 7, 1911; referring to request from von Hintze dated December 6, 1911.

[544] Statement F.A. Sommerfeld, June 24, 1918.

[545] See for example Katz and LaFrance.

[546] NA RG 242 Captured German Documents, T-149, Roll 378, von Hintze to von Bethmann Hollweg, February 6, 1912.

[547] Ibid., Guillermo Bach to von Hintze, December 15, 1913, "Lieferung der im Juni 1912 geschlossenen Vertrag....Mangels an Barmitteln noch nicht hat erfüllen können..."

[548] Ibid., von Hintze to von Bethmann Hollweg, July 8, 1912.

[549] Ibid.

[550] Ross, *Francisco I. Madero*, p. 179.

[551] Speech of Madero at Cuautla, August 18, 1911 as quoted in Ross, Francisco I. Madero, p. 194.

[552] Statement F.A. Sommerfeld, June 24, 1918.

[553] Ross, Francisco I. Madero, p. 183.

[554] El País, September 2, 1911 as quoted in Ross, Francisco I. Madero, p. 183.

[555] NA RG 65 Records of the FBI, M1085, Roll 868, file 232-2450, F.A. Sommerfeld to William Offley, December 9, 1917.

[556] Ibid.

[557] Edith O'Shaughnessy, "Diplomatic Days in Mexico, Second Paper," Harper's Magazine, 10, 1917, pp. 714, 715.

[558] For each 500 votes the states created one elector, meaning that the 20,000 electoral votes amounted to 10 million voters. The election results have often been misrepresented as Madero receiving only 19,000 votes out of a population of 15 million. This was started by American interventionists trying to discredit the Madero administration and sadly has been used as fact in history books.

[559] Edith O'Shaughnessy, "Diplomatic Days in Mexico, Second Paper," Harper's Magazine, 10, 1917, p. 716.

[560] Statement F.A. Sommerfeld, June 24, 1918.

[561] NA RG 165 Military Intelligence Division, file 9140-1754, Marion Letcher to Secretary of State, July 15, 1912; "...because of his position as head of the Mexican Secret Service force..." There are numerous acknowledgements of Sommerfeld's job with the Mexican government.

[562] NA RG 65 Records of the FBI, M1085, Roll 852, file 232-804, C. M. Williams to H. A. Thompson, November 21, 1911.

[563] Ibid., file 232, Lancaster to Department, February 15, 1912.

[564] United Sates Senate, Revolutions in Mexico, Hearing before the Subcommittee of the Committee on Foreign Relations, Government Printing Press, Washington D.C., 1912, Testimony of Felix A. Sommerfeld, p. 387.

[565] Statement F.A. Sommerfeld, June 24, 1918.

[566] NA RG 65 Records of the FBI, M1085, Roll 852, file 232, Memorandum to the Department, December 23, 1911; also Harris and Sadler, Secret War in El Paso, p. 76.

[567] United Sates Senate, Revolutions in Mexico, Hearing before the Subcommittee of the Committee on Foreign Relations, Government Printing Press, Washington D.C., 1912, Testimony of Felix A. Sommerfeld, p. 419.

[568] RG 65 Records of the FBI, M1085, Roll 852, file 232, Memorandum to the Department dated October 3, 1911.

[569] The World Almanac and Encyclopedia, 1902, Press Publishing Co, New York, NY, 1902, p. 425, foreign consuls in the United States. There are discrepancies as to Llorente's age because on some records his birth year as 1877 (which seems correct) on others 1872, possibly because he was only 26 when he first became a diplomat.

[570] The New York Times, November 10, 1914, "Aguilar no Match for Funston."

[571] NA RG 85 Immigration and Naturalization, M1769, Roll 9.

[572] See for example La Prensa, February 13, 1913.

[573] E. V. Niemeyer, "The Revolutionary Attempt of General Bernardo Reyes from San Antonio in 1911," The Southwestern Historical Quarterly, Volume 67, No. 2, October 1963.

[574] Harris and Sadler, The Border and the Revolution, p. 31.

[575] Governor Colquitt had established a Texas version of the neutrality laws in order to use the Texas Rangers against Madero in February 1911. For a in depth discussion see Harris and Sadler, *The Border and the Revolution*, pp. 26-50: "The 1911 Reyes Conspiracy: The Texas Side."

[576] Ibid., p. 31. The political supporters of Colquitt were Francisco A. Chapa, who worked for Colquitt, and Amador Sánchez, Sheriff at Laredo.

[577] Ibid., p. 35.

[578] Statement F.A. Sommerfeld, June 24, 1918.

[579] NA RG 65 Records of the FBI, M1085, Roll 852, file 232, Ross memorandum, November 17, 1911.

[580] Statement F.A. Sommerfeld, June 24, 1918.

[581] Harris and Sadler, *The Border and the Revolution*, p. 37.

[582] Charles H. Harris and Louis R. Sadler, *The Texas Rangers and the Mexican Revolution: The Bloodiest Decade 1910-1920*, University of New Mexico Press, Albuquerque, NM, 2004, p. 83.

[583] Ibid.

[584] Statement F.A. Sommerfeld, June 24, 1918.

[585] Harris and Sadler, *The Border and the Revolution*, p. 41.

[586] NA RG 65 Records of the FBI, M1085, Roll 852, file 232, Chamberlain to headquarters, December 22, 1911.

[587] Harris and Sadler, *The Texas Rangers and the Mexican Revolution*, pp. 84-85.

[588] NA RG 65 Records of the FBI, M1085, Roll 852, file 232, Chamberlain to headquarters, December 22, 1911.

[589] Harris and Sadler, *The Border and the Revolution*, p. 44.

[590] NA RG 59, Department of State, file 312.11/752, Lock McDaniel to Attorney General, July 16, 1912.

[591] Statement F.A. Sommerfeld, June 24, 1918.

[592] NA RG 36 U.S. Customs, T715, Roll 1785, Page 32, Line16; Hopkins went to England in the beginning of November and returned from Liverpool on the 15th of December, 1911 on the Lusitania.

[593] Harris and Sadler, "The 'Underside' of the Mexican Revolution," p. 74.

[594] Ibid, p. 72.

[595] United States Senate, *Investigation of Mexican affairs*, Subcommittee of the Committee of Foreign Relations, Government Printing Office, 1920, Testimony of Sherburne G. Hopkins, p. 2548.

[596] Charles Ghequiere Fenwick, *The Neutrality Laws of the United States*, Carnegie Endowment for International Peace, Washington D.C., 1913, p. 57.

[597] Statement F.A. Sommerfeld, June 24, 1918.

[598] Guy P.C. Thomson and David G. LaFrance, *Patriotism, Politics and Popular Liberalism in the late 19th Century Mexico: Juan Francisco Lucas and the Puebla Sierra*, Scholarly Resources Inc., Wilmington, DE, 1999, p. 283

[599] The New York Times, February 2, 1912, "Juarez in Revolt: Names a President."

[600] The El Paso Herald, February 7, 1912, "Vasquista Junta is active here."

[601] NA RG 65 Records of the FBI, M1085, Roll 852, file 232; F. H. Lancaster to BI office, February 21, 1912, "He told me that Madero was absolutely down and out..."

[602] Ibid., February 19, 1912.

[603] NA RG 65 Records of the FBI, M1085, Roll 852, file 232; F. H. Lancaster to BI office, February 16, 1912.

[604] Harris and Sadler, *Secret War in El Paso*, p. 69.

[605] The El Paso Herald, February 7, 1912, "Troops coming to hold Juarez."

[606] Statement F.A. Sommerfeld, June 24, 1918.

[607] Ibid.

[608] NA RG 65 Records of the FBI, M1085, Roll 852, file 232; F. H. Lancaster to BI office February 19, 1912.

[609] Ibid.

[610] Ibid., F. H. Lancaster to BI office, February 20, 1912.

[611] NA RG 65 Records of the FBI, M1085, FBI case files, case 8000-3089, footnote.com image 2039096, "Statement concerning the Madero Company."

[612] Stallforth Papers, Private Collection, diary entry February 27, 1912.

[613] NA RG 65 Records of the FBI, M1085, Roll 852, file 232; F. H. Lancaster to BI office, February 21, 1912.

[614] Stallforth entered the U.S. with his wife and older daughter on February 19, 1912. He left for New York on March 2, 1912 and did not return until May 14, 1912. See Stallforth Papers, Private Collection, diary entries February 26, 27, March 2, May14, 1912; also NA RG 85 Immigration and Naturalization, A 3365, Lists of Aliens Arriving at El Paso, entry February 19, 1912.

[615] Thornton Jones Blelock, "The Constant Villain," Unpublished manuscript courtesy of Mary Prevo, Woodstock Arts, 2008, p. 4.

[616] Ibid., pp. 1-21.

[617] Harris and Sadler, *Secret War in El Paso*, p. 69.

[618] The Washington Post, March 17, 1912, "Cut Woman to Pieces."

[619] These are the subsequent payments from Waters-Pierce Company to the Madero administration referred to earlier. Charles Flint had by now purchased the Madero robber plantations. Since the actual purchase price is unknown, Flint is suspected to have used this transaction as a vehicle to funnel money to the Maderos.

[620] United Sates Senate, *Revolutions in Mexico*, Hearing before the Subcommittee of the Committee on Foreign Relations, Government Printing Press, Washington D.C., 1912, Testimony of Felix A. Sommerfeld, p. 404.

[621] United States Senate, *Investigation of Mexican affairs*, Subcommittee of the Committee of Foreign Relations, Government Printing Office , 1920, Testimony of Sherburne G. Hopkins, p. 2524.

[622] United Sates Senate, *Revolutions in Mexico*, Hearing before the Subcommittee of the Committee on Foreign Relations, Government Printing Press, Washington D.C., 1912, Testimony of Felix A. Sommerfeld, pp. 387 to 448.

[623] Harris and Sadler, *Secret War in El Paso*, p. 82.

[624] United Sates Senate, *Revolutions in Mexico*, Hearing before the Subcommittee of the Committee on Foreign Relations, Government Printing Press, Washington D.C., 1912, Testimony of Felix A. Sommerfeld, p. 403.

[625] Harris and Sadler, "The Underside of the Mexican Revolution," p. 72.

[626] Harris and Sadler are probably the most prolific scholars on the border region. Their books are researched to unbelievable detail and yet, easy to read. It is hard to miss that this work has relied on many of their books and articles which this author considers must reads. See for example *The Secret War in El Paso, The Texas Rangers and the Mexican Revolution, The Archeologist was a Spy* and many more articles about El Paso, Fort Bliss, the attack on Columbus, NM etc.

[627] Meed, *Soldier of Fortune*, p. 85.

[628] William H. Beezley, *Insurgent Governor: Abraham Gonzalez and the Mexican Revolution in Chihuahua*, University of Nebraska Press, Lincoln, NE, 1973, p. 130.

[629] NA RG 65 Records of the FBI, M1085, Roll 852, file 232-1136; H. A. Thompson to BI office, February 28, 1912.

[630] Ibid.

[631] United Sates Senate, *Revolutions in Mexico*, Hearing before the Subcommittee of the Committee on Foreign Relations, Government Printing Press, Washington D.C., 1912, Testimony of Felix A. Sommerfeld, p. 419.

[632] NA RG 65 Records of the FBI, M1085, Roll 852, file 232, F. H. Lancaster to BI office February 19, 1912, reference to Agent Hughes, a Thiel detective in Chihuahua.

[633] United Sates Senate, *Revolutions in Mexico*, Hearing before the Subcommittee of the Committee on Foreign Relations, Government Printing Press, Washington D.C., 1912, Testimony of Felix A. Sommerfeld, p. 437.

[634] United States Senate, *Investigation of Mexican Affairs*, Subcommittee of the Committee of Foreign Relations, Government Printing Office, 1920, Testimony of Sherburne G. Hopkins, p. 2543.

[635] NA RG 65 Records of the FBI, M1085, Roll 851, file 232-1117, F.H. Lancaster to Department, March 4, 1912.

[636] Ibid., file 232-1200, Ross to Department, March 18, 1912.

[637] United States Senate, Investigation of Mexican Affairs, Subcommittee of the Committee of Foreign Relations, Government Printing Office, 1920, Testimony of Sherburne G. Hopkins, p. 2529.

[638] NA RG 65 Records of the FBI, M1085, Roll 851, file 232-1171, L. E. Ross to Department, March 11, 1912.

[639] Ibid., file 232-1265, L. E. Ross to Department, March 22, 1912.

[640] Ibid., March 30, 1912.

[641] Ibid., Roll 852, file 232, Ross to Department, May 15, 1912.

[642] Harris and Sadler wrote that a Peter S. Aiken was a locomotive engineer at the Northwestern railroads. While this author could not confirm the identity of Aiken, there is a Peter F. Aiken who was a British subject and arrived in San Francisco from Japan in October 1905. This could indicate that Aiken's story in his statement included kernels of truth.

[643] Harris and Sadler, *Secret War in El Paso*, p. 77.

[644] NA RG 65 Records of the FBI, M1085, Roll 852, file 232, Ross to Department, May 16, 1912.

[645] Ibid., Statement of Peter F. Aiken, May 9, 1912.

[646] Ibid.

[647] United Sates Senate, Revolutions in Mexico, Hearing before the Subcommittee of the Committee on Foreign Relations, Government Printing Press, Washington D.C., 1912, Testimony of Felix A. Sommerfeld, p. 432.

[648] NA RG 65 Records of the FBI, M1085, Roll 852, file 232-1931, Ross to Department, July 3, 1912.

[649] Ibid., Statement of Peter F. Aiken, May 9, 1912.

[650] Ibid., Ross to Department, May 2, 1912.

[651] United Sates Senate, *Revolutions in Mexico*, Hearing before the Subcommittee of the Committee on Foreign Relations, Government Printing Press, Washington D.C., 1912, Testimony of Felix A. Sommerfeld, p. 401.

[652] The Clearfield Progress, February 25, 1915, "Aeroplanes safe at Elevation of 4000 Feet in Air."

[653] Ibid.

[654] NA RG 65 Records of the FBI, M1085, Roll 852, file 232, Lancaster to Department, May 5, 1912.

[655] NA Ibid., Roll 851, file 232, C. D. Hebert to Department, April 25, 1912.

[656] United Sates Senate, *Revolutions in Mexico*, Hearing before the Subcommittee of the Committee on Foreign Relations, Government Printing Press, Washington D.C., 1912, Testimony of Felix A. Sommerfeld, p. 400.

[657] Harris and Sadler, "The Underside of the Mexican Revolution," p. 72.

[658] NA RG 65 Records of the FBI, M1085, Roll 852, file 232, L. E. Ross to Department, May 12, 1912.

[659] Ibid., Ross to Department, May 15, 1912.

[660] www.smithonianeducation.org, viewed June 2011, also The New York Times, August 17, 1895, "To Mexico for Revenge."

[661] Ibid.

[662] Harris and Sadler, *Secret War in El Paso*, p. 96.

[663] United Sates Senate, *Revolutions in Mexico*, Hearing before the Subcommittee of the Committee on Foreign Relations, Government Printing Press, Washington D.C., 1912, Testimony of Felix A. Sommerfeld, p. 417.

[664] For example NA RG 65 Records of the FBI, M1085, Roll 852, file 232, Thompson to Department, August 21, 1912.

[665] Ibid., Roll 851, file 232-1171, Ross to Department, March 11, 1912.

[666] Ibid., file 232-1043, Ross to Department, March 17, 1912.

[667] Ibid., March 18, 1912.

[668] Ibid., file 232-1205, Ross to Department, March 18, 1912.

[669] Ibid., file 232, Hebert to Department, April 25, 1912.

[670] Ibid., Roll 852 file, 232-1099, Hebert to Department, March 18, 1912.

[671] Ibid., file 232, Thompson to Department, May 7, 1912.

[672] Ibid., Ross to Department, May 16, 1912.

[673] Ibid., Roll 851, file 232-1205, Ross to Department, March 18, 1912.

[674] United Sates Senate, *Revolutions in Mexico*, Hearing before the Subcommittee of the Committee on Foreign Relations, Government Printing Press, Washington D.C., 1912, Testimony of Felix A. Sommerfeld, p. 429.

[675] Ibid., p. 427.

[676] NA RG 65 Records of the FBI, M1085, Roll 852, file 232-1628, Ross to Department, May 17, 1912.

[677] NA RG 59 Department of State, file 312.11/752, Adolph Krakauer to Marion Letcher, July 3, 1912.

[678] Ibid., Marion Letcher to Secretary of State, July 16, 1912.

[679] For an analysis of Gonzalez revolutionary program, see Beezley, *Insurgent Governor*.

[680] See Katz, *Life and Times of Pancho Villa*, pp. 165-169 for the best account of Villa's trouble with Huerta.

[681] Leibson, *Sam Dreben, the Fighting Jew*, pp. 82 -86.

[682] NA RG 65 Records of the FBI, M1085, Roll 852, file 232-1937, Ross to Department, July 5, 1912.

[683] See infiltration of juntas by Holmdahl, recovery of Captain Aguilar and other stories detailed later in the book.

[684] Meed wrote that Tracy Richardson claimed over 1,200 federals died, the actual number was around 500.

[685] NA RG 65 Records of the FBI, M1085, Roll 852, file 232-1937, Ross to Department, July 5, 1912.

[686] Quoted from Harris and Sadler, *Secret War in El Paso*, p. 79.

[687] NA RG 165 Military Intelligence Division, file 9140-3098-65, Summary, July 19, 1918.

[688] NA RG 65 Records of the FBI, M1085, Roll 853, file 232, Blanford to Department, February 27, 1913.

[689] NA RG 165 Military Intelligence Division, file 9140-3098-86, Curriculum vitae by Newenham A. Gray, July 10, 1914.

[690] Ibid., file 9140-3098-98, Agent Cantrell to Department, September 12, 1917.

[691] Ibid., Agent Cantrell to Department, September 12, 1917.

[692] Holmdahl Papers, Bancroft Library, C-B-921, Box 1.

[693] Ibid., various newspaper clips.

[694] Ibid., Box 1.

[695] Harris and Sadler, *Secret War in El Paso*, p. 127; Harris and Sadler write that Holmdahl appeared in El Paso in October as an employee of L.L. Hall.

[696] Ibid., p. 128.

[697] Holmdahl Papers, Bancroft Library, C-B 921, Box 1.

[698] NA RG 65 Records of the FBI, M1085, Roll 853, file 232, Breniman to Department, November 6, 1912.

[699] NA RG 165 War Department, Holmdahl Papers.

[700] NA RG 65 Records of the FBI, M1085, Roll 853, file 232, Sommerfeld to Thompson, September illegible date, 1912.

[701] The Washington Post, August 11, 1913, "Defy Order of Court."

[702] NA RG 65 Records of the FBI, M1085, Roll 853, file 232, Breniman to Department, November 2, 1912, "Confered [sic] with Mr. Hall and Mr. Ross of Mexican secret service..."

[703] United Sates Senate, *Revolutions in Mexico*, Hearing before the Subcommittee of the Committee on Foreign Relations, Government Printing Press, Washington D.C., 1912, Testimony of Felix A. Sommerfeld, pp. 441-443.

[704] Beezley, *Insurgent Governor*, p. 142.

[705] The New York Times, August 31, 1915, "Orozco was killed by an American Posse."

[706] United Sates Senate, *Revolutions in Mexico*, Hearing before the Subcommittee of the Committee on Foreign Relations, Government Printing Press, Washington D.C., 1912, Testimony of Felix A. Sommerfeld, p. 415.

[707] NA RG 165 Military Intelligence Division, file 9140-1754-43, G. F. Bailey to Captain George B. Lester, January 8, 1919.

[708] AA Politisches Archiv Berlin, Mexiko III, Paket 24, Sommerfeld to von Hintze, September 19, 1912.

[709] Ibid.,, von Hintze to Foreign Office, July 4, 1912.

[710] NA RG 165 Military Intelligence Division, file 9140-1754, Memorandum to the Department files, April 4, 1919.

[711] NA RG 65 Records of the FBI, M1085, Roll 853, file 232, Ross to Department, September 11, 1912.

[712] Arthur S. Link, *Wilson and the Progressive Era, 1910 to 1917*, Harper and Brothers, New York, NY, 1954, p. 14.

[713] Candice Millard, *The River of Doubt*, Broadway Books, New York, NY, 2005.

[714] www.nationalcowboymuseum.org, viewed 01-2011.

[715] Link, *Wilson and the Progressive Era, 1910 to 1917*, p. 18.

[716] Josephus Daniels, *The Life of Woodrow Wilson*, John C. Winston Company, Chicago, IL, Philadelphia, PA, 1924, p. 122.

[717] www.freeinfosociety.com, Roosevelt, Theodore - The Free Information Society, public domain.

[718] Woodrow Wilson and William Bayard Hale, *The New Freedom*, Doubleday, Page and Co., 1913.

[719] John F. Chalkley, *Zach Lamar Cobb: El Paso Collector of Customs and Intelligence During the Mexican Revolution, 1913-1918*, Southwestern Studies No. 103, Texas Western Press, El Paso, TX 1998, p. 14.

[720] Arthur D. Howden Smith, *Mr. House of Texas*, Funk and Wagnalls Company, New York, 1940, p.39.

[721] John Milton Cooper Jr., *Woodrow Wilson: A Biography*, Alfred A, Knopf, New York, 2009, p. 175.

[722] Link, *Wilson and the Progressive Era 1910 to 1917*, p. 20.

[723] United Sates Senate, *Revolutions in Mexico*, Hearing before the Subcommittee of the Committee on Foreign Relations, Government Printing Press, Washington D.C., 1912, Testimony of Felix A. Sommerfeld, p. 402.

[724] Smith, *Mr. House of Texas*, p. 55.

[725] Arthur S. Link, *The Papers of Woodrow Wilson*, Volume 25, Princeton University Press, Princeton, NJ, 1966, p. 124, "Address to the New York Press Club. September 9, 1912"

[726] AA Politisches Archiv Berlin, Mexiko III, Paket 24, Sommerfeld to Hintze, September 19, 1912; translated by the author.

[727] Katz, *Secret War in Mexico*, p. 93.

[728] Cole Blasier, *The Hovering Giant: U.S. responses to revolutionary change in Latin America*, University of Pittsburg Press, Pittsburg, PA, 1976, p. 39. Katz in *The Secret War in Mexico*, 13 cases had been linked to Madero's term. The November response from Madero clarified the error.

[729] RG 65 Records of the FBI, M1085, Roll 853, file 232, Ross to Department, November 11, 1912.

[730] Katz, *Secret War in Mexico*, p. 94.

[731] Ibid., p. 93.

[732] Von Bernstorff, *My Three Years in America*, p. 22.

[733] New Mexico achieved statehood in January and Arizona in February 1912. Alaska and Hawaii were not part of the union in 1912.

[734] For a most enthralling read on Roosevelt's expedition see Candice Millard, *The River of Doubt*, Broadway Books, New York, 2005.

[735] Smith, *Mr. House of Texas*, p. 67.

[736] Frederic William Wile, *Men around the Kaiser: The Makers of Modern Germany*, The MacLean Publishing Company, Toronto, Canada, 1913, p. 191.

[737] Von Bernstorff, *My Three Years in America*, p. 15.

[738] NA RG 76 Mixed Claims Commission, U.S. and Germany, 1922 to 1941, Box 6.

[739] Wile, Men around the Kaiser, p. 190.

[740] See Johann Count von Bernstorff, *Memoirs of Count Bernstorff*, Random House, New York, NY, 1936.

[741] See next volume of In Plain Sight.

[742] Von Bernstorff, *My Three Years in America*, pp. 21-22.

[743] Quoted in Smith, *Mr. House of Texas*, p. 70.

[744] Ibid.

[745] Von Bernstorff, *My Three Years in America*, pp. 23-24.

[746] Smith, *Mr. House of Texas*, p. 94.

[747] Ibid.

[748] Ibid.

[749] Ray Stannard Baker, *Woodrow Wilson: Life and Letters*, Volume 5, Doubleday, Doran and Company, New York, NY, 1938, p. 15.

[750] Smith, *Mr. House of Texas*, p. 94.

[751] As quoted in Baecker, *Die Deutsche Mexikopolitik 1913/14*, p. 18.

[752] Doerries, *Imperial Challenge*, p. 34.

[753] Henderson, *In the Absence of Don Porfirio*, p. 248.

[754] Karl B. Koth, *Waking the dictator: Veracruz, the struggle for federalism and the Mexican Revolution 1870 – 1927*, University of Calgary Press, Calgary, Alberta, Canada, 2002, p. 148.

[755] The New York Times, October 20, 1912, "Beginning of the end seen in New Revolt."

[756] Ibid.

[757] The New York Times, February 16, 1913, "The man who upset Mexico: Felix Diaz."

[758] The New York Times, October 20, 1912, "Beginning of the end seen in New Revolt."

[759] McLynn, *Villa and Zapata*, p. 150.

[760] The New York Times, October 18, 1912, "Madero unmoved by Diaz Uprising."

[761] McLynn, *Villa and Zapata*, p. 151.

[762] Ibid., p. 146.

[763] Emory R. Johnson, editor, *International Relations of the United States, The Annals of the American Academy of Political Science*, American Academy of Political and Social Science, Volume LIV, Philadelphia, PA, July 1914, pp. 148-161, "Errors with reference to Mexico and events that have occurred there," by Henry Lane Wilson.

[764] McLynn, *Villa and Zapata*, p. 152.

[765] The New York Times, March 11, 1911, "New Yorkers figure in Mexican Problem."

[766] Henderson, *In the Absence of Don Porfirio*, pp. 34-35.

[767] McLynn, *Villa and Zapata*, p. 152.

[768] Although it turns out that the actual size of the American colony was about half of the number given by the New York Times. In the State of the Union speech to Congress in December 1912, President Taft gave the number as "some thirty of forty thousand" at the beginning of the revolution.

[769] Many historians such as Katz and Doerries have described a strained relationship between Madero and von Hintze. A careful examination of the diplomatic reports Hintze wrote does not bear out this assessment.

[770] Von Hintze an von Bethmann Hollweg, No. 62, March 10, 1912 as printed in Huertner, *Paul von Hintze*, p. 309.

[771] Baecker, *Deutsche Mexikopolitik 1913/14*, p. 94.

[772] John S. D. Eisenhower, *Intervention! The United States and the Mexican Revolution, 1913-1917*, W.W. Norton and Company Inc., New York, NY, 1993, p. 20.

[773] German Diplomatic Papers, University of California at Berkley, M-B 12, Box 7, Calero to von Hintze, November 28, 1911.

[774] Ibid., Gonzalez Salas to von Hintze, November 29, 1911.

[775] Ibid., von Hintze to Schubert, February 13, 1912.

[776] AA Politisches Archiv Berlin, Mexiko IV, Paket 29, Calero to von Hintze March 11 and 12, 1912, multiple releases for German Hacienda owners to carry arms.

[777] Ibid., Rieloff to von Hintze, March 12, 1912.

[778] Ibid., Francisco Madero to von Hintze, March 11, 1912.

[779] Quoted in Baecker, *Deutsche Mexikopolitik 1913/14*, p. 55.

[780] Ibid.

[781] McLynn, *Villa and Zapata*, p. 149.

[782] Author photograph of the bronze medal participants in the German expeditionary forces received.

Endnotes

[783] Date 1919, Source "Mexico, Its Ancient and Modern Civilisation," Author Charles Reginald, public domain.

[784] *Collier's Magazine*, June 3, 1911, "The Man Who Ousted Diaz," by Timothy Turner, p. 22, P. F. Collier and Son, New York, NY.

[785] Von der Goltz, *My Adventures as a German Secret Agent*, p. 48.

[786] Ibid., p. 152.

[787] The New York Times, August 9, 1912, "Denies Tale about Mexico."

[788] Ibid.

[789] United Sates Senate, *Revolutions in Mexico*, Hearing before the Subcommittee of the Committee on Foreign Relations, Government Printing Press, Washington D.C., 1912, Testimony of Felix A. Sommerfeld, p. 441-443.

[790] As quoted in Edward I. Bell, *The Political Shame of Mexico*, McBride, Nast and Company, New York, NY, 1914, p. 170.

[791] Bell, *The Political Shame of Mexico*, p. 170.

[792] Von Hintze to von Bethmann Hollweg as quoted in Katz, *The Secret War in Mexico*, p. 90.

[793] Ibid.

[794] AA Politisches Archiv Berlin, Mexiko III, Paket 24, Stronge to von Hintze, March 5, 1912.

[795] As quoted in Blasier, *U.S. responses to revolutionary change in Latin America*, p. 39.

[796] Bell, *The Political Shame of Mexico*, p. 229.

[797] The New York Times, December 12, 1912, "Calero Quitting Madero."

[798] NA RG 242 Captured German Documents, T149, Roll 377, Report number 25, von Hintze to von Bethmann Hollweg, February 28, 1913.

[799] Bell, *The Political Shame of Mexico*, pp. 251-252.

[800] Blasier, *U.S. responses to revolutionary change in Latin America*, p. 40. Also Henry Lane Wilson, *Diplomatic Episodes*, p. 247.

[801] Bell, *The Political Shame of Mexico*, p. 252.

[802] Henry Morris, *Our Mexican Muddle*, Laird and Lee Publishers, Chicago, IL, 1916, p. 104, "Articles by Henry Lane Wilson."

[803] Ibid.

[804] Blasier, *U.S. responses to revolutionary change in Latin America*, p. 40.

[805] NA RG 65 Records of the FBI, M1085, Roll 853, file 232, P. A. Palmer to Department, January 4, 1913.

[806] Statement F.A. Sommerfeld, June 24, 1918.

[807] McLynn, *Villa and Zapata*, p. 149.

[808] As quoted in Blasier, *U.S. responses to revolutionary change in Latin America*, p. 41.

[809] Statement F.A. Sommerfeld, June 24, 1918.

[810] The New York Times, July 21, 1914, "Says we helped bring about Anarchy in Mexico."

[811] Ibid.

[812] Statement F.A. Sommerfeld June 24, 1918.

[813] NA RG 59 Department of State, file 812.00/7798 ½, William Bayard Hale to Woodrow Wilson, June 18, 1913.

[814] Ibid.

[815] McLynn, *Villa and Zapata*, p. 153.

[816] Bell, *The Political Shame of Mexico*, p. 271.

[817] Von Hintze to von Bethmann Hollweg, February 25, 1913 as printed in Huertner, *Paul von Hintze*, p. 316.

[818] Ross, *Francisco I. Madero*, p. 284.

[819] Von Hintze to von Bethmann Hollweg, February 25, 1913 as printed in Huertner, *Paul von Hintze*, p. 316.

[820] Ross, *Francisco I. Madero*, p. 284.

[821] Ibid.

[822] NA RG 59 Department of State, file 812.00/7798 ½, William Bayard Hale to Woodrow Wilson, June 18, 1913.

[823] Von Hintze to von Bethmann Hollweg, No. 64, January 3, 1913 as printed in Huertner, *Paul von Hintze*, p. 312.

[824] Von Hintze to von Bethmann Hollweg, February 25, 1913 as printed in Huertner, *Paul von Hintze*, p. 316.

[825] Katz, *The Secret War in Mexico*, pp. 96-97.

[826] Von Hintze to von Bethmann Hollweg, February 25, 1913 as printed in Huertner, *Paul von Hintze*, p. 316.

[827] See The New York Times and The Washington Post, February 10, 1913.

[828] The San Antonio Light, February 10th, 1913 is one of the many papers that claimed Zapata was advancing on Mexico City. The story originated in the American embassy.

[829] Von Hintze to von Bachmann Hollweg, No. 66, February 25, 1913, as printed in Huertner, *Paul von Hintze*, p. 317.

[830] Ibid.

[831] NA RG 59 Department of State, file 812.00/7798 ½, William Bayard Hale to Woodrow Wilson, June 18, 1913.

[832] Ibid.

[833] Ibid.

[834] Ibid.

[835] Katz, *Secret War in Mexico*, p. 96. Katz concluded from these contacts that Huerta was part of the conspiracy which is a leap given the evidence.

[836] Later in World War I, Berliner interviewed Sommerfeld clandestinely on many occasions. The quality of Berliner's information suggests that Sommerfeld, who was not careless when it came to his contacts with the American government, had no idea of the American agent's true occupation.

[837] Henry Lane Wilson, *Diplomatic Episodes*, p. 276.

[838] NA RG 59 Department of State, file 812.00/7798 ½, William Bayard Hale to Woodrow Wilson, June 18, 1913.

[839] McLynn, *Villa and Zapata*, p. 154.

[840] NA RG 59 Department of State, file 812.00/7798 ½, William Bayard Hale to Woodrow Wilson, June 18, 1913.

[841] McLynn, *Villa and Zapata*, p. 155.

[842] Baecker, *Die Deutsche Mexikopolitik 1913/14*, p. 122.

[843] As quoted in Baecker, *Die Deutsche Mexikopolitik 1913/14*, p. 123, translation by the author.

[844] Ibid.

[845] NA RG 59 Department of State, file 812.00/7798 ½, William Bayard Hale to Woodrow Wilson, June 18, 1913.

[846] NA RG 59 812.00/7798 ½, William Bayard Hale to Woodrow Wilson, June 18th 1913.

[847] Ross, *Francisco I. Madero*, p. 293.

[848] Katz, *Secret War in Mexico*, p. 100.

[849] Baecker, *Die Deutsche Mexikopolitik 1913/14*, p. 123.

[850] Ibid., p. 124.

[851] As quoted in Katz, *Secret War in Mexico*, p. 100.

[852] Ibid., p. 102.

[853] NA RG 60 Department of Justice, file 9-16-12-5305-6; Mrs. Harold Walker who knew Sommerfeld well while in Mexico testified to the Justice Department in 1918 that Sommerfeld "was the go-between between the Madero interests and the German Ambassador to Mexico."

[854] AA Politisches Archiv Berlin, Mexiko V, Paket 33.

[855] Ibid.

[856] See Katz, Ross, McLynn.

[857] AA Politisches Archiv Berlin, Mexiko V, Paket 33.

[858] Statement F.A. Sommerfeld, June 24, 1918.

[859] McLynn, *Villa and Zapata*, p. 156.

[860] Katz, Secret War in Mexico, wrote that on the 17th von Hintze "reversed himself," p. 104; Baecker, *Die Deutsche Mexikopolitik 1913/14*, wrote "a new situation presented itself for Hintze," p. 124.

[861] Katz, *Secret War in Mexico*, p. 104. Other than Baecker, there is not one history on Huerta's rule that doubts German support of the usurper president.

[862] Von Hintze diary as referenced in Baecker, *Die Deutsche Mexikopolitik 1913/14*, p. 124.

[863] AA Politisches Archiv Berlin, Mexiko V, Paket 33, hand-written diary of Ambassador von Hintze.

[864] Baecker, Die Deutsche Mexikopolitik 1913/14, p. 124.

[865] Von Hintze diary entry as quoted in Katz, *The Secret War in Mexico*, p. 105.

[866] NA RG 59 Department of State, file 812.00/7798 ½, William Bayard Hale to Woodrow Wilson, June 18, 1913.

[867] Statement F.A. Sommerfeld, June 24, 1918.

[868] Ibid.

[869] NA RG 59 Department of State, file 812.00/7798 ½, William Bayard Hale to Woodrow Wilson, June 18, 1913.

[870] Ibid.

[871] Ross, *Francisco I. Madero*, pp. 307-309. Ross used eye witness accounts and newspaper articles for this most detailed and authentic description of the events.

[872] As quoted in Ross, *Francisco I. Madero*, p. 310.

[873] NA RG 59 Department of State, file 812.00/7798 ½, William Bayard Hale to Woodrow Wilson, June 18, 1913. Also Henry Lane Wilson, *Diplomatic Episodes*, p. 275.

[874] AA Politisches Archiv Berlin, Mexiko V, Paket 33, von Haniel to von Bernstorff, August 14, 1914.

[875] NA RG 59 Department of State, file 812.00/7798 ½, William Bayard Hale to Woodrow Wilson, June 18, 1913.

[876] Von Hintze diary entry as quoted in Katz, *Secret War in Mexico*, p. 105.

[877] Henry Lane Wilson, *Diplomatic Episodes*, p. 278. Wilson claimed that Lascurain, Ernesto Madero and Hernandez had been arrested which is not true.

[878] In that meeting Wilson told Hintze that the coup would take place that day. See Katz, *Secret War in Mexico*, p. 105.

[879] AA Politisches Archiv Berlin, Mexiko V, Paket 33, hand written diary of Ambassador von Hintze.

[880] Ibid.

[881] Statement F.A. Sommerfeld, June 24, 1918.

[882] AA Politisches Archiv Berlin, Mexiko V, Paket 33.

[883] Statement F.A. Sommerfeld, June 24, 1918.

[884] The Washington Post, February 10, 1913.

[885] Isidro Fabela, *Historia diplomática de la Revolución Mexicana*, vol I. (1912-1917), México Ciudad, Fondo de Cultura Económica, Mexico D.F., Mexico, 1958, pp. 175-183. Interview of Sara Madero in 1916 by Robert Hammond Murray.

[886] Statement F.A. Sommerfeld, June 24, 1918.

[887] Katz, *Secret War in Mexico*, p. 106.

[888] NA RG 59 Department of State, file 812.00/6256, Huerta to Taft, February 18, 1913.

[889] Ross, *Francisco I. Madero*, p. 310.

[890] NA RG 59 Department of State, file 812.00/7798 ½, William Bayard Hale to Woodrow Wilson, June 18, 1913. Also Henry Lane Wilson, *Diplomatic Episodes*, p. 280.

[891] NA RG 59 Department of State, file 812.00/7798 ½, William Bayard Hale to Woodrow Wilson, June 18, 1913.

[892] Ibid.

[893] Ross, *Francisco I. Madero*, pp. 312-313. The same event is recounted in McLynn, *Villa and Zapata*, p. 157. The account seems slightly embellished and is not footnoted. The main differences in the stories are that in McLynn Felix Diaz personally led Gustavo to be executed. Also Gustavo was taken straight to the Ciudadela from the restaurant. General Mondragon is not mentioned but a businessman who allegedly presided over the court martial.

[894] NA RG 242 Captured German Documents, T149, Roll 378, von Hintze to von Bethmann Hollweg July 8, 1912.

[895] The New York Times, February 20, 1913.

[896] Ibid.

[897] Ross, *Francisco I. Madero*, p. 318.

[898] As quoted in Ross, *Francisco I. Madero*, p. 319 from Marquez Sterling, *Los Ultimos Dias*, pp. 510-17.

[899] As quoted in McLynn, *Zapata and Pancho Villa*, p. 159.

[900] Henry Lane Wilson, *Diplomatic Episodes*, p. 285.

[901] NA RG 59 Department of State, file 812.00/7798 ½, William Bayard Hale to Woodrow Wilson, June 18, 1913. Also Henry Lane Wilson, *Diplomatic Episodes*, pp. 283-284.

[902] NA RG 59 Department of State, file 812.00/7798 ½, William Bayard Hale to Woodrow Wilson, June 18, 1913. Also United States Senate, *Investigation of Mexican affairs*, Subcommittee of the Committee of Foreign Relations, Government Printing Office, 1920, Testimony of Ambassador Henry Lane Wilson, p. 2273.

[903] Fabela, *Historia diplomática de la Revolución Mexicana*, pp. 175-183. Interview of Sara Madero in 1916 by Robert Hammond Murray.

[904] As quoted in Katz, *Secret War in Mexico*, p. 109.

[905] Ibid., p. 110.

[906] As quoted in Ross, *Francisco I. Madero*, p. 326.

[907] Baecker, *Die Deutsche Mexikopolitik 1913/14*, p. 326.

[908] AA Politisches Archiv Berlin, Mexiko V, Paket 33, Manuel Esteva to Sommerfeld, February 23, 1913.

[909] The Coshocton Morning Tribune, February 23, 1913, "Troops revolt against Huerta."

[910] The Indianapolis Star, February 24, 1913, "Madero's Aid in Hiding."

[911] Statement F.A. Sommerfeld, June 24, 1918.

[912] Huertner, *Paul von Hintze*, p. 58. Also United States Senate, *Investigation of Mexican affairs*, Subcommittee of the Committee of Foreign Relations, Government Printing Office, 1920,

Testimony of Ambassador Henry Lane Wilson, p. 2264, in a letter to Ambassador Wilson dated March 8, 1913 Hintze himself described his affliction as „intestinal hemorrhage."

[913] NA RG 242 Captured German Documents, T149, Roll 377, Hintze to Bethmann Hollweg, February 28, 1913.

[914] Ibid.

[915] Ibid.

[916] NA RG 65 Records of the FBI, M1085, Roll 853, file 232, Blanford to Department, February 27, 1913.

[917] Katz, *Life and Times of Pancho Villa*, p. 206.

[918] Beezley, *Insurgent Governor*, p. 158.

[919] NA RG 59 Department of State, file 812.00/7798 ½, William Bayard Hale to Woodrow Wilson, June 18, 1913.

[920] The Washington Post, February 10, 1913.

[921] The San Antonio Light, February 10, 1913.

[922] The Washington Post, February 11, 1913.

[923] The Washington Post, February 12, 1913.

[924] Ibid.

[925] The San Antonio Light, February 13, 1913.

[926] The San Antonio Light, February 15, 1913.

[927] The San Antonio Light, February 18, 1913, The Washington Post, February 18, 1913.

[928] The Washington Post, February 19, 1913.

[929] The New York Times, February 16, 1913.

[930] The San Antonio Light at least felt sympathy for Gustavo Madero and reported on the question of Madero's safety. Other papers toned down their rhetoric, making the New York Times and Washington Post stand out as the most vicious of the interventionist mouth pieces.

[931] Fabela, *Historia diplomática de la Revolución Mexicana*, pp. 175-183. Interview of Sara Madero in 1916 by Robert Hammond Murray

[932] Quoted in Katz, *Life and Times of Pancho Villa*, p. 118.

[933] The New York Times, June 29, 1914, "Constitutionalists Deny." Hopkins admitted to the paper that he worked for the Constitutionalists since Madero's assassination but denied being paid for his services.

[934] Statement F.A. Sommerfeld, June 24, 1918.

[935] Staatsarchiv Hamburg, 373-7 I, VIII A 1 Band 255, Page 488, Microfilm K1827.

[936] NA RG 76 Mixed Claims Commission, Box 13, BI agent William Offley to Department, June 28, 1915.

[937] NA RG 36 U.S. Customs Service, T715, Roll 2006, Page 157, Line 3.

[938] AA Politisches Archiv Berlin, Mexiko V, Paket 33, Marinebericht Nr. 83, May 27, 1914.

[939] Committee of the American Colony, April 1913, Library of Congress call number F1234.M65. See also United States Senate, *Investigation of Mexican affairs*, Subcommittee of the Committee of Foreign Relations, Government Printing Office, 1920, Testimony of Ambassador Henry Lane Wilson, pp. 2266 to 2270.

[940] Henry Lane Wilson, *Diplomatic Episodes*, p. 318. Wilson's contract actually ended in November. De jure he was still employed until then.

[941] United States Senate, *Investigation of Mexican affairs*, Subcommittee of the Committee of Foreign Relations, Government Printing Office, 1920, Testimony of Ambassador Henry Lane Wilson, p. 2288.

[942] The exact date of Villa's re-entry is a matter of debate. The BI reports clearly indicate him leaving El Paso for the visit of Maytorena in Tucson on February 26. See NA RG 65 Records of the FBI, M1085, Roll 853, file 232, Agent Blanford to Department, February 28, 1913. Historian Katz put Villa's entry into Mexico on the night of March 6. However, Abraham Gonzalez was murdered that same night. According to Katz and others, Villa's decision to enter Mexico was prompted by fears of arrest and extradition in the U.S. Clearly Villa abandoned his plans to organize and fund his uprising in the U.S. when he heard of his mentor's death. See Katz, *Life and Times of Pancho Villa*, p. 198.

[943] For an exhaustive work on Carranza and the Constitutionalist movement see Charles C. Cumberland, *The Mexican Revolution: The Constitutionalist Years*, University of Texas Press, Austin, TX, 1974.

[944] McLynn, *Villa and Zapata*; This historian while accusing others of ignoring facts which put Carranza's credentials as a revolutionary in question, himself ignores the important role Carranza played in the ouster of Diaz.

[945] Cumberland, *The Constitutionalist Years*, p. 71.

[946] For a translated version of Carranza's decree, see Manuel Calero, *The Mexican Policy of Woodrow Wilson as it appears to a Mexican*, Smith and Thompson, New York, NY, 1916, pp. 95-97.

[947] As quoted in Edward P. Haley, *Revolution and Intervention: The Diplomacy of Taft and Wilson with Mexico, 1910-1917*, The MIT Press, Cambridge, MA, 1970, p. 84.

[948] As quoted in Haley, *The Diplomacy of Taft and Wilson with Mexico, 1910-1917*, p. 84.

[949] Ibid., p. 96.

[950] Ibid.

[951] NA RG 242 Captured German Documents, T149, Roll 377, von Hintze to von Bethmann Hollweg, February 28, 1913.

[952] Ibid.

[953] Statement F.A. Sommerfeld, June 24, 1918.

[954] The New York Times, June 30, 1914, "Need 50,000,000 to finance Mexico."

[955] New York Times, February 2, 1913, "Pierce is in Control of Big Oil Company."

[956] NA RG 60 Department of Justice, file 9-16-12-5305, Charles R. Flint to Mitchell Palmer, May 6, 1919.

[957] NA RG 65 Records of the FBI, M1085, Roll 853, file 232, G. R. Matthews to Department, May 6, 1913, U.S. vs. General Neutrality matters.

[958] Ibid. See various BI reports for April 1913.

[959] NA RG 65 Records of the FBI, M1085, Roll 853, file 232, Agent Thompson to Department, June 28, 1913.

[960] Ibid., Roll 856, file 232-98, J. A. Baker to Department, May 18, 1914.

[961] Leibson, *Sam Dreben, the Fighting Jew*, pp. 101-102. The story Leibson tells cannot be verified in the BI records and might be slightly embellished. However, the main point was that Dreben high jacked the arms as a result of the State Department's indecision on whether to allow the importation. This matches the conundrum Sommerfeld faced all along the border in April and May 1913.

[962] NA RG 65 Records of the FBI, M1085, Roll 853, file 232, Agent Barnes to Department, May 15, 1913.

[963] Ibid., Agent Thompson to Department, May 1, 1913.

[964] Ibid.

[965] Ibid., Agent Barnes to Department, May 15, 1913.

[966] Ibid., Agent Thompson to Department, May 1, 1913.

[967] Ibid., William Offley to Department, May 23, 1913.

[968] Ibid., Agent Barnes to Department, May 15, 1913.

[969] Ibid., file 232-11, Agent Barnes to Department, January 6, 1914.

[970] The Washington Post, August 11, 1913, "Defy Order of Court."

[971] NA RG 65 Records of the FBI, M1085, Roll 853, file 232, Agent Thompson to Department, June 28, 1913.

[972] Harris and Sadler, Secret War in El Paso, p. 121.

[973] Silvestre Terrazas Papers, University of California at Berkley, Bancroft Library, M-B-18, Box 83, outgoing letters; Molina receipt for $320 for beans, dated November 18, 1913.

[974] NA RG 65 Records of the FBI, M1085, Roll 853, file 232, William Offley to Department, May 23, 1913.

[975] Ibid., H. A. Thompson to Department, May 21, 1913.

[976] Library of Congress, Papers of General Scott, Box 15, General Correspondence, E. de la Sierra to Lieut. Col. A.C. Macomb, June 18, 1913.

[977] NA RG 60 Department of Justice, file 157013-537, breach of Neutrality Laws.

[978] Harris and Sadler, Secret War in El Paso, p. 145.

[979] Ibid., pp. 144/145. The historians detail how Krakauer first shipped bobbed wire to the federals then sold the badly needed wire cutters to the rebel forces.

[980] Silvestre Terrazas Papers, University of California at Berkley, Bancroft Library, M-B-18, Marion Letcher Correspondence, list of enemies of the state, undated but estimated to be 1913.

[981] AA Politisches Archiv Berlin, Mexiko II, Paket 5, Weber to Magnus, August 22, 1914; Villa supposedly ordered the expulsion of the consul that summer but Kueck stayed in Chihuahua until August 1914. It is not clear what exactly caused the expulsion. It seems that more was at issue because Kueck stayed in the city after Villa had control over it and Kueck's replacement was Ernst Goeldner, also a Ketelsen and Degetau executive. The German embassy only referred to the affair only once as "Kueck replaced because of irregularities."

[982] NA RG 60 Department of Justice, file 157013-537, breach of Neutrality Laws.

[983] Ibid.

[984] The Washington Post, April 16, 1905, "Mdme Johanna Gadski: The great singer's talent was discovered in the United States."

[985] Stallforth Papers, Private Collection, diary entry, October 13, 1912.

[986] Baecker, Die Deutsche Mexikopolitik 1913/14, pp. 86-87. Baecker correctly identified Historian Katz' claim that Germany sent loads of weapons to Huerta as myth. While the Mexican government requested quotes and concluded delivery contracts the majority of these arms were never delivered because of lack of funds. Japan had received orders from Madero and shipped those arms as late as summer 1914, again not ostensibly to support the Huerta government.

[987] NA RG 65 Records of the FBI, M1085, Roll 953, File 232, Offley to Department, May 23, 1913.

[988] His enlistment could not be verified. The only source is the von der Goltz' memoir.

[989] Von der Goltz, My Adventures as a German Secret Service Agent, p. 117. Von der Goltz does not mention Sommerfeld by name but the picture of him with Sommerfeld complements his description.

[990] Ibid., p. 43.

[991] NA RG 165 Military Intelligence Division, file 9140-676, Statement of Frederico Stallforth, February 23, 1918, p. 1.

[992] NA RG 131 Alien Property Custodian, Entry 199, Box 95, file 1955.

[993] NA RG 242 German Captured Documents, T149, Roll 378, von Hintze to von Bethmann Hollweg, October 27, 1913.

[994] NA RG 60, Department of Justice, file 9-16-12-18, Statement of Frederico Stallforth, April 22, 1917, p. 18; Von der Goltz came to New York in 1914 and when von Papen hired him, Frederico Stallforth cashed Papen's check for von der Goltz and kept the money Goltz owed him.

[995] Harris and Sadler, *Secret War in El Paso, pp. 151-153.*

[996] NA RG 242 Captured German Documents, T141, Roll 20, von Eckart to von Bethmann Hollweg, May 17, 1916.

[997] NA RG 165 Military Intelligence Division, file 9140-5773-18, March 24, 1920. The MID associates the first name Maximilian with him which does not seem to be correct.

[998] Ibid., file 9140-358, "Alphabetical list of subject of the Teutonic Powers," March 24, 1917.

[999] Ibid., file 9140-5773-1, December 1, 1917.

[1000] NA RG 242 Captured German Documents, T141, Roll 20, German ambassador in Switzerland (signature illegible) to Bethmann Hollweg, September 15, 1917. Krumm-Heller offered his services as a spy for South America.

[1001] NA RG 165 Military Intelligence Division, file 9140-5773-18, March 24, 1920.

[1002] Sabazius, "The Invisible Basilica: Dr. Arnoldo Krumm-Heller (1876 -1949 e.v.)," Ordo Templi Orientis, USA, 1997.

[1003] As quoted in Chalkley, *Zach Lamar Cobb*, p. 8.

[1004] Ibid., p. 16.

[1005] Statement F.A. Sommerfeld, June 24, 1918. By 1914, there are ample documents from Sommerfeld directly to President Wilson's cabinet members, which will be discussed in detail later.

[1006] Ibid.

[1007] Cumberland, *The Constitutionalist Years*, 279.

[1008] Ibid., p. 280.

[1009] Statement F.A. Sommerfeld, June 24, 1918.

[1010] Cumberland, *The Constitutionalist Years*, p. 280.

[1011] The El Paso Herald, November 11, 1913, "Sommerfeld to Meet WM. Hale at Tucson."

[1012] Statement F.A. Sommerfeld, June 24, 1918.

[1013] Stallforth Papers, Private Collection, letter to Anita, July 25, 1913.

[1014] Ibid., diary entries for 1912 and 1913. He testified to American authorities in 1917 that he moved in the summer of 1912 which in view of the violence and his diary entries does not seem likely.

[1015] Ibid., draft letter undated around October 1912.

[1016] Ibid., diary entries August 31 shows Stallforth to be in New York until October 13, when he traveled with the Tauschers on the Golden State Limited. Sommerfeld left for New York on the Golden State Limited on September 11.

[1017] Ibid., letter to Alberto, December 13, 1912.

[1018] Statement F.A. Sommerfeld, June 22, 1918.

[1019] Stallforth Papers, Private Collection, letter to Alberto, December 13, 1912.

[1020] Ibid.

[1021] Ibid.

[1022] Ibid., 1913 Correspondence, undated.

[1023] NA RG 165 Military Intelligence Division, file 9140-878, Memorandum of Nicholas F. Lenssen, September 11, 1918. Lenssen functioned mainly as a lawyer for the German embassy in WWI. He was born and raised in Germany. His law degree is from Heidelberg University;

[1024] NA RG 165 Military Intelligence Division, file 9140-878, Statement concerning the Madero Company.

[1025] Stallforth Papers, Private Collection, Letter to Anita, July 8, 1913.

[1026] Ibid., Letter to Anita, July 25, 1913.

[1027] University of Texas, Benson Library, Austin, Texas, Papers of Lazaro De La Garza, Box 9, Folder A; Letter De La Garza to Miguel Diaz Lombardo, April 15, 1915; translated from Spanish by the author.

[1028] United States Senate, *Investigation of Mexican Affairs*, Hearing before a Subcommittee of the Committee of Foreign Relations, Government Printing Office, Washington, D.C., 1920, Testimony of John Lind, p. 2324.

[1029] Statement F. A. Sommerfeld, June 24, 1918.

[1030] Baecker, *Die Deutsche Mexikopolitik 1913/14*, pp. 101, 102.

[1031] Alden Buell Case, *Thirty Years with the Mexicans: In Peace and Revolution*, Fleming H. Revell Company, New York, NY, 1917, p. 178.

[1032] Ibid., p. 135.

[1033] Ibid., p. 176, also quoted in Katz, *Life and Times of Pancho Villa*, p. 211.

[1034] From the diary of Pastor Rouaix as quoted in Katz, *Life and Times of Pancho Villa*, p. 214. Also see Consul Hamm to Secretary of State, June 21, 1913 as quoted in Cumberland, *The Constitutionalist Years*, p. 42.

[1035] Cumberland, *The Constitutionalist Years*, p. 28.

[1036] See for example NA RG 59 Department of State, file 812-00-9658, Carothers to Department of State, October 15, 1913 as quoted in Katz, *Life and Times of Pancho Villa*, p. 217.

[1037] Kathlene Scalise, "Surprising new information on Pancho Villa comes to light in obscure Wells Fargo files at University of California Berkeley," University of California at Berkley, Bancroft Library, http://berkeley.edu/news/media/releases/99legacy/5-3-1999.html.

[1038] Cumberland, *The Constitutionalist Years*, p. 35.

[1039] NA RG 242 Captured German Documents, T149, Roll 378, Hintze to Bethmann Hollweg, October 27, 1913. Freely translated by the author.

[1040] Ibid.

[1041] Katz, *Life and Times of Pancho Villa*, p. 213.

[1042] Hugh Lenox Scott, *Some Memoirs of a Soldier*, The Century Company, New York, NY, 1928, p. 497.

[1043] Meed, Soldier of Fortune, p. 101.

[1044] RG 65 Records of the FBI, M1085, Roll 853, file 232, Thompson to Chief, June 20, 1913, page 2.

[1045] Ibid., Thompson to Chief, July 5 1913, page 4.

[1046] Ibid.

[1047] Ibid., Blanford to Chief, June 20 1913, page 2-3.

[1048] Harris and Sadler, *Secret War in El Paso*, p. 141.

[1049] RG 65 Records of the FBI, M1085, Roll 854, file 232, Chief Bielaski to Thompson, October 7, 1913.

[1050] Ibid.

[1051] Ibid., Roll 855 file 232-37, Breniman to Chief, January 7 1914.

[1052] Katz, *Life and Times of Pancho Villa*, p. 214.

[1053] Historians vary on the actual number of men in Villa's army, estimates range for 6,000 to 10,000.

[1054] Holmdahl Papers, Bancroft Library, C-B 921, Agent Breniman to L. L. Hall, November 4, 1913.

[1055] Clarence Clendenen, *The United States and Pancho Villa: A Study in Unconventional Diplomacy*, Cornell University Press, Ithaca, NY, 1961, p. 36. Also McLynn, *Villa and Zapata*, p. 171. Also Katz, *Life and Times of Pancho Villa*, p. 222.

[1056] John Reed, *Insurgent Mexico: With Pancho Villa in the Mexican Revolution*, Red and Black Publishers, St. Petersburg, FL, 2009 (first published New York, 1914), p. 175.

[1057] Reed, *Insurgent Mexico*.

[1058] As quoted in Katz, *Life and Times of Pancho Villa*, pp. 314-315.

[1059] As quoted in Katz, *Life and Times of Pancho Villa*, p. 223.

[1060] McLynn, *Villa and Zapata*, p. 173.

[1061] Harris and Sadler, *Secret War in El Paso*, p. 150. The historians mentioned November 15 as the day of the attack. It seems that the attack occurred in the early morning hours of November 16.

[1062] The El Paso Morning Times, "By brilliant coup Villa takes Juarez from Federals," November 16, 1913.

[1063] Ibid., one little boy was shot through the hand.

[1064] For more detailed description see Harris and Sadler, Clendenen, McLynn, Cumberland, Katz.

[1065] Clendenen, *The United States and Pancho Villa*, p. 43.

[1066] Harris and Sadler, *Secret War in El Paso*, p. 150.

[1067] McLynn, *Villa and Zapata*, p. 173.

[1068] The El Paso Morning Times, November 16, 1913, "By a brilliant coup Villa takes Juarez from Federals."

[1069] Scott, *Some Memoirs of a Soldier*, p. 498.

[1070] Ibid., p. 499.

[1071] Ibid.

[1072] Harris and Sadler, *Secret War in El Paso*, p. 174.

[1073] Katz, *Life and Times of Pancho Villa*, p. 228.

[1074] Guzman, *Memoirs of Pancho Villa*, p. 122.

[1075] Ibid., p. 127.

[1076] Ibid., p. 140.

[1077] Manuel A. Machado Jr., *Centaur of the north: Francisco Villa, the Mexican Revolution, and northern Mexico*, Eakin Press, Austin, TX, 1988, p. 55.

[1078] Silvestre Terrazas Papers, University of California at Berkley, Bancroft Library, M-B-18, Part I, container 11, Accounts.

[1079] Statement F.A. Sommerfeld, June 24, 1918.

[1080] Ibid.

[1081] AA Politisches Archiv Berlin, Mexiko II, Paket 5.

[1082] J. Campana, *L'artillerie de campagne à tir rapide et à boucliers: Son Matériel, sa puissance, son organisation, son emploi*, Charles-Lavauzelle, Paris, France, 1909, pp. 62-91 as quoted in www.bulgarianartillery.it/Bulgarian Artillery 1/Testi/TB_Effect of fire.htm.

[1083] Thayer signed with Villa on January 5 to produce the Movie "And Starring Pancho Villa as himself."

[1084] Guzman, *Memoirs of Pancho Villa*, p. 129.

[1085] NA RG 65 Records of the FBI, M1085, Roll 854, file 232-16, Agent Wren to Chief, January 9, 1914.

[1086] Ibid., Agent Wren to Chief, January 7, 1914.

[1087] Villa took two brigades. In the Division del Norte a brigade consisted of 450 to 550 men. Some historians estimated Villa's reinforcements to have been between 1500 and 2000 troops. That seems to be exaggerated.

[1088] Guzman, *Memoirs of Pancho Villa*, p. 130.

[1089] Ibid., p. 131.

[1090] Glenn Willeford, "Ambrose Bierce, 'the Old Gringo': Fact, Fiction and Fantasy," http://ojinaga.com/bierce, viewed 3-27-2011.

[1091] NA RG 65 Records of the FBI, M1085, Roll 854, file 232-14, Agent Blanford to Chief, January 20, 1914.

[1092] Ibid, file 232-16, Agent Blanford to Chief, January 19, 1914.

[1093] Ibid.

[1094] Ibid., file 232-14, Agent Blanford to Chief, January 20, 1914.

[1095] Troy Taylor, "Can such Things be? The Riddle of the Orion Williamson & the Strange Mystery of Ambrose Bierce," www.prairieghosts.com/bierce.html, 2003-2008.

[1096] www.time.com/time/specials/packages/article/0,28804,1846670_1846800_1846845 ,00.html, Ambrose Bierce.

[1097] University of California at Los Angeles, Papers of William McWilliams, Box 1, Ambrose Bierce Correspondence, Scott to Sommerfeld, September 9 1914.

[1098] Ambrose Bierce Appreciation Society, "The Death of Bierce ," www.biercephile.com/death.cfm, 1994-2004.

[1099] Brad Steiger, "Ambrose Bierce and Strange Disappearances ," www.forteanswest.com, viewed March 28, 2011.

[1100] Ibid., quoted from Edward H. Smith, Mysteries of the Missing.

[1101] Troy Taylor, "Can such Things be? The Riddle of the Orion, Williamson & the Strange Mystery of Ambrose Bierce," www.prairieghosts.com/bierce.html, 2003-2008.

[1102] University of California at Los Angeles, Papers of William McWilliams, Box 1, Ambrose Bierce Correspondence, Sommerfeld to Carey McWilliams, May 12, 1930.

[1103] Ibid., Carey McWilliams to Sommerfeld, April 8, 1930.

[1104] Ibid., Sommerfeld to Carey McWilliams, May 12 1930.

[1105] The New York Times, February 23, 1914, "Villa shoots Diaz Emissary."

[1106] NA RG 65 Records of the FBI, M1085, file 232-134, Harvey Phillips to Department, March 3, 1915.

[1107] The Washington Post, July 4, 1914, "Big Aid to Rebels."

[1108] The New York Times, February 8, 1914, "Sandoval back in Havana."

[1109] Guzman, *Memoirs of Pancho Villa*, p. 329.

[1110] Silvestre Terrazas Papers, University of California at Berkley, Bancroft Library, M-B-18, Marion Letcher Correspondence, "The List of the Enemies of the People."

[1111] The New York Times, February 23, 1914, "Villa shoots Diaz Emissary."

[1112] Katz, *Life and Times of Pancho Villa*, pp. 220-221.

[1113] Scott, *Some Memoirs of a Soldier*, pp. 501-502.

[1114] Papers of Hugh Lenox Scott, Box 15, Villa to Scott February 12, 1914; translated by the author.

[1115] Silvestre Terrazas Papers, University of California at Berkley, Bancroft Library, M-B-18, Marion Letcher Correspondence.

[1116] The New York Times, February 21, 1914, "Execution of Benton may force hand of the Administration."

[1117] Katz, *Life and Times of Pancho Villa*, p. 327.

[1118] Ibid., p. 328.

[1119] The Terrazas papers do not show any order of confiscation being issued before and after Benton's murder. See Silvestre Terrazas Papers, University of California at Berkley, Bancroft Library, M-B-18, Container 111, accounts.

[1120] The New York Times, May 30, 1915, "Villa accused by former aide."

[1121] The New York Times, February 23, 1914, "Villa's own story of Benton killing."

[1122] Katz, Life and Times of Pancho Villa, p. 328. Katz quoted the British Vice Consul of Torreon as saying that Fierro killed Benton because he mistakenly thought Benton was reaching for a gun.

[1123] The New York Times, May 30, 1915, "Villa accused by former aide."

[1124] Guzman, Memoirs of Pancho Villa, p. 133; The New York Times, May 30, 1915, "Villa accused by former aide."

[1125] Katz, Life and Times of Pancho Villa, p. 326.

[1126] Ibid., p. 328.

[1127] Ibid., p. 327.

[1128] NA RG 65 Records of the FBI, M1085, Roll 854, file 232-14, Branford to Department, January 19, 1914.

[1129] Ibid.

[1130] The New York Times, February 21, 1914, "Execution of Benton may force hand of the Administration."

[1131] Ibid., "El Paso Citizens Condemn the Killing of W. S. Benton."

[1132] De La Garza Papers, Box 1, Folder B, William Jennings Bryan to Francisco Villa, undated, believed to be February 23, 1914, handwritten on the stationary of the Sheldon Hotel.

[1133] The New York Times, February 21, 1914, "Execution of Benton may force hand of the Administration."

[1134] NA RG 65 Records of the FBI, M1085, Roll 855, file 232-51, Branford to Department, February 13, 1914.

[1135] The El Paso Herald, February 24, 1914, "Bauch missing; Maybe Benton's Fate befell him."

[1136] Sausalito News, Vol. 30. Number 9, February 28, 1914.

[1137] The New York Times, March 1, 1914, "Carranza inquires about Benton case."

[1138] Ibid.

[1139] Ibid.

[1140] The Oakland Tribune, December 15, 1913, "Fletcher holding Federals in check." Also, The El Paso Herald, December 15, 1913, "Carranza Directs Villa to Respect Foreigners; Losses May be Made Good."

[1141] NA RG 65Records of the FBI, M1085, Roll 857, file 232-134, Agent Scully to Department, December 16, 1914.

[1142] Statement F.A. Sommerfeld, June 24, 1918.

[1143] Ibid.

[1144] NA RG 65 Albert Papers, Box 22, Proclamation by the President of the United States, February 3, 1914.

[1145] Papers of Hugh Lenox Scott, Box 16, General Correspondence, Sommerfeld to Hugh Lenox Scott, July 6, 1914.

[1146] Statement F.A. Sommerfeld, June 24, 1918.

[1147] A thorough search of the accounts of the state (Silvestre Terrazas Papers) as well as the accounts of the division of the north (Lazaro De La Garza Papers) has yielded no results.

[1148] The Washington Post, July 6, 1914, "Rebel Cash held up."

[1149] Statement F.A. Sommerfeld, June 24, 1918.

[1150] The Washington Post, July 6, 1914, "Rebel Cash held up;" see also De La Garza Papers, Benson Library, University of Texas at Austin.

[1151] Ibid.

[1152] Statement F.A. Sommerfeld, June 24, 1918.

[1153] Ibid.

[1154] NA RG 60, Department of Justice, file 9-16-12-97, letter from F. Stallforth to Col. Robertson, October 24, 1917.

[1155] De La Garza Papers, Box 5, Folder A.

[1156] NA RG 165 Military Intelligence Division, file 9140-878, Statement concerning the Madero Company.

[1157] NA RG 242 Captured German Documents, T149, Roll 378, Huerta to von Hintze, January 13, 1914.

[1158] Ibid., Bondholders to Foreign Office, January 16, 1914.

[1159] The New York Times, February 25, 1914, "Villa defies the United States and Britain."

[1160] Baecker, Die Deutsche Mexikopolitik 1913-14, p. 169.

[1161] To his immense credit, only historian Baecker correctly came to the conclusion that this alleged support for Huerta was false based on the facts.

[1162] Ambassador von Hintze reported on the arrival of a 7 million-cartridge shipment from Germany on March 12 that had been funded. However, this seems to be one of the only deals that were actually consumed.

[1163] De La Garza Papers, Box 5, Folder A, Alberto Madero to De La Garza March 6, 1914.

[1164] Ibid.

[1165] Ibid., Tauscher to Alfonso Madero, February 27, 1914.

[1166] Ibid.

[1167] NA RG 242 Captured German Documents, T149, Roll 378, Guillermo Bach to von Hintze , September 18, 1913.

[1168] As quoted in Michael Meyer, "The Arms of the Ypiranga," Hispanic American Historical Review, Vol. L, No. 3, 1970, p. 547.

[1169] NA RG 242 Captured German Documents, T149, Roll 378, Guillermo Bach to von Hintze, September 9, 1913.

[1170] Ibid., von Hintze to von Bethmann Hollweg, December 4, 1913.

[1171] De La Garza Papers, Box 5, Folder A, Alberto Madero to De La Garza March 6, 1914; this document is the best available indication that the Maderos had a large contract which included the listed shipments.

[1172] NA RG 242 Captured German Documents, T149, Roll 378, von Bernstorff to Auswärtiges Amt, February 14, 1914.

[1173] Ibid.

[1174] NA RG 65 Records of the FBI, M1085, Roll 853, file 232, Agent Barnes to Department, May 15, 1913 and Agent Matthews to Department, May 20, 1913.

[1175] NA RG 242 Captured German Documents, T149, Roll 378, Hintze to Bethmann Hollweg, December 4, 1913.

[1176] De La Garza Papers, Box 5, Folder A, Payments to F. Stallforth, February 9, 1914, February 28, 1914, March 4, 1914.

[1177] Ibid., Tauscher to Alfonso Madero February 9, 1914. Tauscher advised Madero that he shipped 300 cases of 7mm Mauser cartridges by SS "El Norte" to De La Garza most likely with the Gans

Steamship Line, which was one of the German-owned freight lines Tauscher and later Commercial Attaché Albert used frequently. US authorities eyed Gans with suspicion since the summer of 1913. United Fruit steamers also were suspected to smuggle arms and ammunition from New York via New Orleans to Mexico.

[1178] Baecker, *Die Deutsche Mexikopolitik 1913/14*, pp. 86-87.

[1179] Statement F.A. Sommerfeld, June 24, 1918. Sommerfeld testified that he dealt with Western Cartridge Company around February 1914 when he sent used Mauser rifles to the company to have them tested.

[1180] Guzman, *Memoirs of Pancho Villa*, p. 181.

[1181] Villa's endearing name for De La Garza while they worked together.

[1182] De La Garza Papers, Box 1, Folder D, De La Garza to Villa, April 14, 1914.

[1183] Jim Tuck, "Pancho Villa as a German Spy," www.mexconnect.com/articles/1853-pancho-villa-as-a-german-agent, viewed May 10, 2011.

[1184] NA RG 165 Military Intelligence Division, file 5761-1091/2, Hopkins to MID, April 10, 1916.

[1185] De La Garza Papers, Box 5, Folder A, De La Garza to Alfonso Madero, February 18, 1914.

[1186] Ibid., Alfonso Madero to De La Garza, February 20, 1914.

[1187] Ibid., Box 1, Folder C, De La Garza to Villa, April 12, 1914.

[1188] Ibid., Box 1, Folder B, De La Garza to Villa, February 27, 1914. Translated by the author.

[1189] Ibid.

[1190] Ibid., De La Garza to Villa, February 28, 1914. Translated by the author.

[1191] Ibid., Folder C, Villa to De La Garza March 2, 1914, March 5, 1914, March 12, 1914.

[1192] Statement F.A. Sommerfeld, June 24, 1918.

[1193] De La Garza Papers, Box 1, Folder C, De La Garza to Villa, March 12, 1914. Translated by the author.

[1194] Ibid.

[1195] For a vivid description see Reed, *Insurgent Mexico*, Chapters 13 and 14.

[1196] De La Garza Papers, Box 1, Folder C, Villa to De La Garza, April 14, 1914. Translated by the author.

[1197] Ibid., Box 5, Folder B, Sommerfeld to Flint, May 30, 1914. Translated by the author.

[1198] Ibid., Sommerfeld to De La Garza, May 31, 1914.

[1199] AA Politisches Archiv Berlin, R 16873, Bl. 59-65, von Hintze to von Bethmann Hollweg, April 14, 1914, as printed in Huertner, *Paul von Hintze*, p. 351.

[1200] Ibid.

[1201] Guzman, *Memoirs of Pancho Villa*, p. 190.

[1202] http://militaryhistory.about.com/od/battleswars1900s/p/veracruz.htm; viewed 10-2011.

[1203] Daniels, *The Life of Woodrow Wilson*, p. 181.

[1204] Ibid.

[1205] Ibid., p. 182.

[1206] Thomas Baecker, "The Arms of the Ypiranga: The German Side," *The Americas*, Vol. 30, No. 1 (Jul., 1973), pp. 5-6.

[1207] www.freepages.genealogy.rootsweb.ancestry.com/~katloregen/FtCrockett.htm, Fort Crockett and the occupation of Veracruz, Mexico, viewed 5-11-2011.

[1208] Baecker, "The Arms of the Ypiranga: The German Side," p. 7.

[1209] Ibid.

[1210] AA Politisches Archiv Berlin, Mexiko V, Paket 33, Hintze to Auswärtiges Amt, April 18, 1914.

[1211] United States Senate, *Investigation of Mexican affairs*, Subcommittee of the Committee of Foreign Relations, Government Printing Office, 1920, p. 783.

[1212] *Fuel Oil Journal*, Volume 5, May 1914, Houston, TX, p. 7.

[1213] The New York Times, May 7, 1914, "Gerard thanks Germany."

[1214] NA RG 65 Albert Papers, Box 32, file 822, Wilson to Kohler [sic], August 25, 1914.

[1215] The New York Times, May 8, 1914, "The Ypiranga Carries Refugees;" Also Meyer, "The Arms of the Ypiranga," p. 554.

[1216] Baecker, "The Arms of the Ypiranga: The German Side," p. 9.

[1217] The New York Times, April 30 1914, "Reichstag debates Mexican Affairs."

[1218] Baecker, "The Arms of the Ypiranga: The German Side," p. 15.

[1219] NA RG 65 Albert Papers, Box 27, Papen to War Department, May 28, 1914.

[1220] The New York Times, May 31, 1914, "Fines German Ships Total of $200,000."

[1221] AA Politisches Archiv Berlin, Mexiko V, Paket 33, Hintze to Auswärtiges Amt, April 18, 1914.

[1222] Ibid., von Hintze to von Jagow, April 26, 1914.

[1223] Meyer, "The Arms of the Ypiranga," p. 548.

[1224] The New York Times, May 9, 1914, "Arms for Huerta on German Ships."

[1225] United States Senate, *Investigation of Mexican Affairs*, Subcommittee of the Committee of Foreign Relations, Government Printing Office, 1920, p. 782.

[1226] The New York Times, May 31, 1914, "Fines German Ships Total of $200,000."

[1227] The HAPAG representative became a German secret service agent in the United States in World War I.

[1228] The New York Times, April 30, 1914, "Brazil takes Charge."

[1229] NA RG 60 Department of Justice, file 9-16-12-5, Memorandum for Department, file on Carl Heynen, October 6, 1919.

[1230] Meyer and others cited Rasst as vice consul of Mexico City. Immigration files with his own statements show that he was vice consul in Puebla in 1913. See NA RG 85 Immigration and Naturalization, M237, Roll 2230, Page 2 Line 26.

[1231] http://cdigital.dgb.uanl.mx/la/1080089135/1080089135_49.pdf, viewed May 2011, El Delito de Quiebra, published around 1888, pp. 529-535.

[1232] Ibid.

[1233] Leticia Gamboa, *Los empresarios de ayer: El grupo dominante en la industria textil de Puebla, 1906-1929,* Puebla, Mexico, 1985, UAP, cuadro 7, p. 65.

[1234] Secretaría de Comunicaciones y Obras Públicas, Estadística de ferrocarriles de jurisdicción federal año de 1918. México, Talleres Gráficos de la Nación, 1924.

[1235] NA RG 165 Military Intelligence Division, file 9140-1754-39, Agent Doyas to Department, September 25, 1918.

[1236] Ibid., file 9140-1754-40, Agent Berliner to Department, August 3, 1918. Berliner was of Jewish descent himself, making his characterization of Rasst a matter of opinion but not anti-Semitism.

[1237] NA RG 59 Department of State, file 812.00/10235, as quoted in Meyer, "The Arms of the Ypiranga," p. 547.

[1238] NA RG 65 Records of the FBI, M1085, Roll 856, file 232-94, Agent Scully to Department, April 29, 1914.

[1239] Meyer, "The Arms of the Ypiranga," p. 548. He quoted from a report New York BI Agent Scully filed after he had seen the Brinkhorn manifest.

[1240] Baecker, "The Arms of the Ypiranga: The German Side," p. 5.

[1241] Meyer, "The Arms of the Ypiranga," p. 547.

[1242] NA RG 36 U.S. Customs Service, T715, Roll 2230, Page 3, Line 26.

[1243] NA RG 65 Records of the FBI, M1085, Roll 856, file 232, Agent Scully to Department, April 29, 1914.

[1244] NA RG 165 Military Intelligence Division, file 9140-1754-40, Agent Berliner to Department, August 3, 1918.

[1245] Statement F.A. Sommerfeld, June 24, 1918.

[1246] NA RG 131 Alien Property Custodian, Entry 195, Box 67, BI card catalogue of Alien enemies.

[1247] The New York Times, December 12, 1910, "De Kay's 'Judas' a new Conception."

[1248] Jeffrey M. Pilcher, *The Sausage Rebellion: Public Health, Private Enterprise, and Meat in Mexico City, 1890–1917*, University of New Mexico Press, Albuquerque, NM, 2006. Reviewed by William Schell Jr., www.hbs.edu/bhr/archives/bookreviews/81/wschell.pdf, viewed May,12, 2011.

[1249] The New York Times, November 13, 1915, untitled.

[1250] The New York Times, December 30, 1910, "Judas a Lover in John De Kay's Play."

[1251] The New York Times, February 21, 1910, "De Kay tells of lavish gifts."

[1252] The New York Times, December 18, 1910, "Bernhardt to Present a Millionaires First Play."

[1253] The New York Times, February 21, 1914, "J. W. De Kay tells of Lavish Gifts."

[1254] Baecker, "The Arms of the Ypiranga: The German Side," p. 5.

[1255] The New York Times, December 18, 1910, "Bernhardt to Present a Millionaires First Play."

[1256] Baecker, "The Arms of the Ypiranga: The German Side," p. 3.

[1257] NA RG 242 Captured German Documents, T149, Roll 378, von Hintze to von Bethmann Hollweg, March 12, 1914.

[1258] Ibid.

[1259] There are slight disagreements between the numbers of the two historians. It seems that Baecker double counted several hundred cases.

[1260] NA RG 65 Albert Papers, Box 27, Papen to War Department, May 28, 1914.

[1261] Ibid.

[1262] NA RG 59 Department of State, file 812.00/11547, Canada to Bryan, April 18, 1914.

[1263] Meyer, "The Arms of the Ypiranga," p. 551.

[1264] Statement F.A. Sommerfeld, June 24, 1918.

[1265] Ibid.

[1266] Carothers to Secretary of State, April 22, 1914, Wilson Papers, Ser. 2, as quoted in Haley, *The Diplomacy of Taft and Wilson with Mexico, 1910-1917*, p. 135.

[1267] AA Politisches Archiv Berlin, Mexiko V Paket 33, Marinebericht Nr. 88, May 27, 1914.

[1268] Papers of Hugh Lenox Scott, Box 15, General Correspondence, Hopkins to Carranza, April 24, 1914.

[1269] De La Garza Papers, Box 1 Folder E, De La Garza to Villa, May 3, 1914.

[1270] Ibid.

[1271] AA Politisches Archiv Berlin, Mexiko V Paket 33, von Hintze to von Jagow, April 30, 1914.

[1272] Carothers to Secretary of State, April 23, 1914, Wilson Papers, Ser. 2, as quoted in Haley, *The Diplomacy of Taft and Wilson with Mexico, 1910-1917*, p. 135.

[1273] The New York Times, May 8, 1914, "Villa urges US to lift Embargo."

[1274] De La Garza Papers, Box 1, Folder E, De La Garza to Villa, May 29, 1914.

[1275] The New York Times, April 29, 1914, "Pershing takes Command."

[1276] The New York Times, April 30 1914, "Army of 13,000 men guards the border."

[1277] AA Mexico V Paket 33, Marinebericht Nr. 88, Boy-Ed to Auswärtiges Amt, May 27, 1914.

[1278] See Katz, *Life and Times of Pancho Villa*, pp. 314-315 for examples of the harsh treatment Carothers received in the historiography of the Mexican Revolution.

[1279] Papers of Hugh Lenox Scott, Box 15, General Correspondence, Woodrow Wilson to Scott, April 16, 1914.

[1280] Katz, *Life and Times of Pancho Villa*, p. 314.

[1281] Bell, *The Political Shame of Mexico*, pp. 385-386.

[1282] NA RG 242 Captured German Documents, Roll 378, file 14, Bleichröder to Secretary of State, June 19, 1914.

[1283] Cumberland, *The Constitutionalist Years*, p. 142.

[1284] Bell, *The Political Shame of Mexico*, pp. 383-384.

[1285] The New York Times, May 7, 1914, "Fear Conference will fail."

[1286] AA Mexico V, Paket 33, Marinebericht Nr. 88, Boy Ed to Auswärtiges Amt, May 27, 1914.

[1287] Skirius, "Railroad, Oil and Other Foreign Interests in the Mexican Revolution, 1911 to 1914," p. 48.

[1288] Ibid.

[1289] The El Paso Herald, "Rebels hold oil man for big ransom," May 15, 1914.

[1290] Ibid.

[1291] NA RG 242 Captured German Documents, T141, Roll 19, von Hintze to von Bethmann Hollweg, June 25, 1914.

[1292] Skirius, "Railroad, Oil and Other Foreign Interests in the Mexican Revolution, 1911 to 1914," p. 47. Also The Times-Picayune, "Money Bag String Pulled and Swift Action Follows," July 6, 1914.

[1293] Papers of Hugh Lenox Scott, Box 15, Bliss to Scott, August 26, 1914.

[1294] The New York Times, April 30, 1914, "Villa Joins his Army."

[1295] Statement F.A. Sommerfeld, June 21, 1918.

[1296] De La Garza Papers, Box 1, Folder E, Alfredo Farias to Villa, May 3, 1914.

[1297] The El Paso Herald, July 1, 1914 with transcripts of the following letters: Pierce to Hopkins, May 7 and May 12, Hopkins to Carranza, May 13 1914.

[1298] See The El Paso Herald, May 15, 1914 and De La Garza Papers, Box 1, folder E, De La Garza to Villa, May 20, 1914.

[1299] NA RG 65 Records of the FBI, M1085, Roll 856, file 232-98, Agent Baker to Department, May 18 and May 22, 1914.

[1300] Evidence for Flint's money is the fact that Villa sent Sommerfeld $75,000 via Hanover Bank but two weeks later $500,000 worth of shipments were impounded. See De La Garza Papers, Box 1, Folders E and F.

[1301] De La Garza Papers, Box 1, Folder E, De La Garza to Villa and Villa to De La Garza, May 29, 1914.

[1302] The New York Tribune, "Bryan again bans Arms for Mexico," May 31, 1914. Secretary Brian re-instituted the weapons ban after the Ypiranga and Bavaria discharged their cargo in Puerto Mexico. He then rescinded the order. Bryan's waffling on the issue seriously interrupted the supply lines for the Constitutionalist armies trying to finish off Huerta.

[1303] De La Garza Papers, Box 1, Folder E, De La Garza to Villa, June 14, 1914.

[1304] NA RG 65 Records of the FBI, M1085, Roll 856, file 232-98, Agent Baker to Department, May 18 and May 22, 1914.

[1305] AA Mexico V, Paket 33, Marinebericht Nr. 88, Boy Ed to Auswärtiges Amt, May 27, 1914.

[1306] Statement F.A. Sommerfeld, June 21, 1918.

[1307] The New York Times, May 10, 1914.

[1308] NA RG 36 U.S. Customs Service, T715, Roll 2324, Page 73, Line 12; also The New York Times, "Cabrera awaiting Carranza's Orders," May 29, 1914.

[1309] See newspaper clips in the New York Times and others papers in that time. Hopkins is always mentioned as a lobbyist for the Constitutionalists.

[1310] AA Mexico V, Paket 33, Marinebericht Nr. 88, Boy Ed to Auswärtiges Amt, May 27, 1914.

[1311] Ibid.

[1312] The New York Times, "General Villa denies naming Angeles," June 21, 1914.

[1313] AA Mexico V, Paket 33, Marinebericht Nr. 88, Boy-Ed to Auswärtiges Amt, May 27, 1914.

[1314] The New York Times, "Carranza asks Delay; His Agent Accuses Ours," June 28, 1914.

[1315] The Washington Times, "Captain Hopkins Charges Letters Were Stolen As Part Of Conspiracy," June 28, 1914.

[1316] Ibid.

[1317] The Washington Herald, February 6, 1914, "Fire in Sherburne Hopkins' House."

[1318] The Washington Herald, November 18, 1914, "Robberies of Yesterday."

[1319] De La Garza Papers, Box 5, Folder B, Sommerfeld to De La Garza, undated (probably June 30, 1914).

[1320] The New York Times, "Deny Cowdray's Financing," June 28, 1914.

[1321] De La Garza Papers, Box 5 Folder B, Sommerfeld to De La Garza, undated (probably June 30, 1914).

[1322] The Nation Magazine, July 2, 1914, Volume 99, "Intriguers and Mexico."

[1323] The New York Times, "Carranza denies railway deal; No American Financial Aid," June 30, 1914.

[1324] The Times-Picayune, "Said Embargo Applied Only to Land Boundary," July 4, 1914.

[1325] The Washington Times, June 8, 1914

[1326] Carranza organized the PANS, a propaganda arm counteracting Hopkins' and Sommerfeld's publicity campaign.

[1327] The New York Times, June 30, 1914, "Need 50,000,000 to Finance Mexico."

[1328] See Skirius, "Railroad, Oil and Other Foreign Interests in the Mexican Revolution, 1911 to 1914," p. 47. Skirius mentioned a Mexican archives document. However, no U.S. documents are available that would support actual proceedings against the five. A congressional inquiry is mentioned in newspapers but also seems to not have materialized. Hopkins, Lind, and Pierce did answer questions in the Fall Committee in 1919. However, there was no direct link to the Hopkins' papers.

[1329] NA RG 242 Captured German Documents, T141, Roll 19, Hintze to German Consul Veracruz, July 13, 1914, requesting service. Affirmative response, Dresden to von Hintze, July 14, 1914. Actual departure was reported on July 21, 1914, Panselow to Auswärtiges Amt.

[1330] Cumberland, The Constitutionalist Years, p. 149.

[1331] NA RG 242 Captured German Documents, T141, Roll 19, Militärbericht Nr. 1, July 3, 1914.

[1332] NA RG 165 Military Intelligence Division, Box 1266 to 1269, files 5761, 2338, 9700, 10270, 10640.

[1333] The New York Times, June 23, 1932, "S.G. Hopkins Dead; Lawyer in Capital."

[1334] For a thorough analysis and the perspective of the British side see Peter Calvert, The Mexican Revolution 1910-1914: The Diplomacy of Anglo-American Conflict, Cambridge University Press, New York, NY, 1968. Calvert argued that Henry Clay Pierce was severely weakened by the end of 1913 and stood to lose his power and influence in Mexico. It is against this background, Calvert argued, that Hopkins promoted Pierce with Carranza. When it all came to light, Pierce retreated and Cowdray gained significantly in a 50-50 market share agreement between the two competitors.

[1335] The Times-Picayune, July 6, 1914, "Money Bag String Pulled and Swift Action Follows."

[1336] Gray's true name remained a secret to American investigators. He was suspected to be a German spy but not convicted. See NA RG 165 Military Intelligence Division, file 9140-3098.

[1337] NA RG 65 Albert Papers, Box 27, Military Reports 15-21, May 22 to July 23, 1914.

[1338] AA Mexiko V, Paket 33, Boy-Ed to Auswärtiges Amt, Marinebericht Nr. 88, May 27, 1914.

[1339] Ibid.

[1340] NA RG 65 Albert Papers, Box 45, Falmouth Papers, Boy-Ed to von Papen, May 25, 1914. See also Karl Boy-Ed, *Verschwörer?* Verlag August Scherl GmbH, Berlin, Germany, 1920, pp. 80ff.

[1341] AA Mexiko V, Paket 33, Haniel to German Legation, Mexico City, August 13, 1914.

[1342] The following analysis of Sommerfeld's personality is based on a simulation that the author performed with Alaina Love and Marc Cugnan. Based on all available letters and statements of Sommerfeld, a passion profile was developed. Sommerfeld appears to have been a conceiver and processor with the learned skills of connector and builder. His reflective score was on the low side. The results of Sommerfeld's simulated personality were validated with actions and reactions known from available original sources. For more information see Love, Alaina and Marc Cugnon, *The Purpose Linked Organization: How passionate leaders inspire winning teams and great results,* McGraw Hill, New York, NY, 2009.

[1343] Statement F. A. Sommerfeld, June 21, 1918.

[1344] Ibid.

[1345] NA RG 60 Department of Justice, file 9-16-12-5305-13; S. G. Hopkins to Attorney General, April 2, 1919.

[1346] Stallforth Papers, Private Collection, Guest book entry, March 25, 1911.

[1347] As quoted in Katz, *Life and Times of Pancho Villa,* p. 317.

[1348] See Baecker, *Die Deutsche Mexikopolitik, 1913/1914.*

[1349] For more information on this volume and the next, please visit www.in-plain-sight.info.

BIBLIOGRAPHY

~

Secondary Literature

Allen, Ronald, *The Siege of the Peking Legations: Being the Diary of Rev. Roland Allen, M.A.*, Smith, Elder and Co., London, Great Britain, 1901.

Ames, Azel, *The May-Flower and Her Log, July 15, 1620-May 6, 1621, Chiefly from Original Sources*; Houghton, Mifflin, Boston and New York, NY, 1907.

Baecker, Thomas, *Die Deutsche Mexikopolitik 1913/14*, Colloquium Verlag, Berlin, Germany, 1971.

Baker, Ray Stannard, *Seen in Germany*, Harper and Brothers, London, Great Britain, 1902.

Baker, Ray Stannard, *Woodrow Wilson: Life and Letters*, seven volumes, Doubleday, Doran and Company, New York, NY, 1938.

Beezley, William H., *Insurgent Governor: Abraham Gonzalez and the Mexican Revolution in Chihuahua*, University of Nebraska Press, Lincoln, NE, 1973.

Bell, Edward I., *The Political Shame of Mexico*, McBride, Nast and Company, New York, NY, 1914.

Blasier, Cole, *The Hovering Giant: U.S. responses to revolutionary change in Latin America*, University of Pittsburg Press, Pittsburg, PA, 1976.

Brann, Markus, *Geschichte des Jüdisch-Theologischen Seminars in Breslau*, unknown publisher and year.

Brown, Jonathan C., *Oil and Revolution in Mexico*, University of California Press, Berkeley, CA, 1993.

Bruner, Robert F., Carr, Sean D., *The Panic of 1907: Lessons Learned from the Market's Perfect Storm*, John Wiley and Sons, Hoboken, NJ, 2007.

Calero, Manuel, *The Mexican Policy of Woodrow Wilson as it appears to a Mexican*, Smith and Thompson Press, New York, NY, 1916.

Bibliography

Calvert, Peter, *The Mexican Revolution 1910-1914: The Diplomacy of Anglo-American Conflict*, Cambridge University Press, New York, NY, 1968.

Campana, J. *L'artillerie de campagne à tir rapide et à boucliers: Son Matériel, sa puissance, son organisation, son emploi*, Charles-Lavauzelle, Paris, France, 1909.

Carosso, Vincent P., Carosso, Rose C., *The Morgans: Private International Bankers, 1854-1913*, Harvard Studies in Business History, Harvard University Press, Cambridge, MA, 1987.

Carter, Susan B., Gartner, Scott S., Haines, Michael, Olmstead, Alan, Sutch, Richard, and Wright, Gavin, eds., *Historical Statistics of the United States*, Millennial Edition, Cambridge University Press, New York, NY, 2002.

Case, Alden Buell, *Thirty Years with the Mexicans: In Peace and Revolution*, Fleming H. Revell Company, New York, NY, 1917.

Chalkley, John F., *Zach Lamar Cobb: El Paso Collector of Customs and Intelligence During the Mexican Revolution, 1913-1918*, Southwestern Studies, No. 103, University of Texas Press, El Paso, TX, 1998.

Clements, Paul, H., *The Boxer Rebellion: A Political and Diplomatic Review*, Columbia University Press, New York, NY, 1915.

Cooper, John Milton Jr., *Woodrow Wilson: A Biography*, Alfred A. Knopf, New York, NY, 2009.

Clendenen, Clarence, The United States and Pancho Villa: A study in Unconventional Diplomacy, Cornell University Press, Ithaca, NY, 1961.

Cullman, Peter Simonstein, *History of the Jewish Community of Schneidemühl – 1641 to the Holocaust*, Avotaynu, Bergenfield, NJ, 2006.

Cumberland, Charles C., *Mexican Revolution: Genesis under Madero*, Greenwood Press, New York, NY, 1969.

Cumberland, Charles C., *Mexican Revolution: The Constitutionalist Years*, University of Texas Press, Austin, TX, 1974.

Daniels, Josephus, *The Life of Woodrow Wilson*, John C. Winston Company, Chicago, IL, Philadelphia, PA, 1924.

De Bekker, Leander Jan, *The Plot against Mexico*, Alfred A. Knopf, New York, NY, 1919.

Bibliography

Doerries, Reinhard R., *Imperial Challenge: Ambassador Count Bernstorff and German-American Relations, 1908-1917*, University of North Carolina Press, Chapel Hill, NC, 1989.

Doerries, Reinhard R., Editor, *Diplomaten und Agenten: Nachrichtendienste in der Geschichte der deutsch-amerikanischen Beziehungen*, Universitätsverlag C. Winter, Heidelberg, Germany, 2001.

Ecke, Heinz, *Four Spies Speak*, John Hamilton Limited, London, Great Britain, 1933.

Eisenhower, John S. D., *Intervention! The United States and the Mexican Revolution, 1913-1917*, W. W. Norton and Company Inc., New York, NY, 1993.

Fabela, Isidro, *Historia diplomática de la Revolución Mexicana*, vol I. (1912-1917), México Ciudad, Fondo de Cultura Económica, México D.F., Mexico, 1958.

Fenwick, Charles Ghequiere, *The Neutrality Laws of the United States*, Carnegie Endowment for International Peace, Washington D.C., 1913.

Foroohar, Manzar, *The Catholic Church and Social Change in Nicaragua*, State University of New York Press, Albany, NY, 1989.

Gamboa, Leticia, *Los empresarios de ayer: El grupo dominante en la industria textil de Puebla, 1906-1929*, UAP, cuadro 7, Puebla, México, 1985.

Gould, Lewis L. and Greffe, Richard, *Photojournalist: The Career of Jimmy Hare*, University of Texas Press, Austin, TX, 1977.

Greever, William S., *Bonanza West: The Story of the Western Mining Rushes, 1848-1900*, University of Idaho Press, Moscow, ID, 1990.

Griggs, Jorge, *Chihuahua Mines*, 1907.

Hadley, Michael L., Sarty, Roger Flynn, *Tin-Pots and Pirate Ships: Canadian Naval Forces and German Sea Raiders 1880 – 1918*, McGill-Queens University Press, Montreal, Canada, 1991.

Hale, William Bayard, *Woodrow Wilson: The Story of his Life*, Doubleday, Page and Company, New York, NY, 1911, 1912.

Haley, Edward P., *Revolution and Intervention: The Diplomacy of Taft and Wilson with Mexico, 1910-1917*, The MIT Press, Cambridge, MA, 1970.

Hanrahan, Gene Z., *The Bad Yankee: American Entrepreneurs and Financiers in Mexico*, volume 1, Documentary Publications, Chapel Hill, NC, 1985.

Harris, Charles H., III and Sadler, Louis R., *The Archeologist was a Spy: Sylvanus G. Morley and the Office of Naval Intelligence*, University of New Mexico Press, Albuquerque, NM, 2003.

Harris, Charles H., III and Sadler, Louis R., *The Border and the Revolution: Clandestine Activities of the Mexican Revolution : 1910-1920*, High Lonesome Books, Silver City, NM, 1988.

Harris, Charles H., III and Sadler, Louis R., *The Secret War in El Paso: Mexican Revolutionary Intrigue, 1906-1920*, University of New Mexico Press, Albuqerque, NM, 2009.

Harris, Charles H., III and Sadler, Louis R., *The Texas Rangers and the Mexican Revolution: The Bloodiest Decade, 1910-1920*, University of New Mexico Press, Albuqerque, NM, 2004.

Hart, Albert Bushnell, *The Monroe Doctrine: An Interpretation*, Little, Brown, and Company, Boston, MA, 1916.

Henderson, Peter V. N., *In the Absence of Don Porfirio: Francisco Leon De La Barra and the Mexican Revolution*, Scholarly Resources, Wilmington, DE, 2000.

Huertner, Johannes, Editor, *Paul von Hintze: Marineoffizier, Diplomat, Staatssekretär, Dokumente einer Karriere zwischen Militär und Politik, 1903-1918*, Harald Boldt Verlag, München, Germany, 1998.

Jeffreys-Jones, Rhodri, *Cloak and Dollar: A History of American Secret Intelligence*, Yale University Press, New Haven, CT, 2002.

Jensen, Joan M., *The Price of Vigilance*, Rand McNally and Company, Chicago, New York, NY, 1968.

Johnson, Emory R., ed., *International Relations of the United States, The Annals of the American Academy of Political Science*, American Academy of Political and Social Science, Volume LIV, Philadelphia, PA, July 1914.

Jones, John Price, *The German Spy in America: The Secret Plotting of German Spies in the United States and the Inside Story of the Sinking of the Lusitania*, Hutchinson and Co., London, Great Britain, 1917.

Katz, Friedrich, *The Secret War in Mexico: Europe, the United States, and the Mexican Revolution*, The University of Chicago Press, Chicago, IL, 1981.

Katz, Friedrich, *The Life and Times of Pancho Villa*, Stanford University Press, Stanford, CA, 1998.

Kauze, Enrique, *Francisco Madero: Mistico de la Libertad*, Fondo de Cultura Económica, Mexico D.F., Mexico, 1987.

Knight, Alan, *The Mexican Revolution: Volume 1: Porfirians, Liberals and Peasants*, Cambridge University Press, Cambridge, MA, 1986.

Knight, Alan, *The Mexican Revolution: Volume 2: Counter-revolution and Reconstruction*, Cambridge University Press, Cambridge, MA, 1986.

Koenig, Louis W., *Bryan: A Political Biography of William Jennings Bryan*, G.P. Putnam's Sons, New York, NY, 1971.

Koenig, Robert L., *The Fourth Horseman: One Man's Mission to Wage the Great War in America*, Public Affairs, New York, NY, 2006.

Koth, Karl B., *Waking the dictator: Veracruz, the struggle for federalism and the Mexican Revolution 1870 – 1927*, University of Calgary Press, Calgary, Alberta, Canada, 2002.

Leibson, Art, *Sam Dreben, the fighting Jew*, Westernlore Press, Tucson, AZ, 1996.

Lemke, William, *Crimes Against Mexico*, Great West Publishing Company, Minneapolis, MN, 1915.

Lill, Thomas Russell, *National Debt of Mexico: History and Present Status*, Searle, Nicholson and Lill C.P.A.'s, New York, NY, 1919.

Link, Arthur S., editor, *Woodrow Wilson and a Revolutionary World, 1913-1921*, New York, NY, 1982.

Link, Arthur S., *Wilson and the Progressive Era, 1910 to 1917*, Harper and Brothers, New York, NY, 1954.

Link, Arthur S., *The Papers of Woodrow Wilson*, vols. 23-26, Princeton University Press, Princeton, NJ, 1966.

Love, Alaina and Marc Cugnon, *The Purpose Linked Organization: How Passionate Leaders Inspire Winning Teams and Great Results*, McGraw Hill, New York, NY, 2009.

Mateer, Ada, Haven, *Siege Days: Personal Experiences of American Women and Children During the Peking Siege*, Fleming H. Revell Company, New York, NY, 1903.

Mauch, Christoff, *The Shadow War Against Hitler: The Covert Operations of America's Wartime Secret Intelligence Service*, Columbia University Press, New York, NY, 1999.

McKenna, Marthe, *My Master Spy: A Narrative of the Secret Service*, Jarrolds Publishers Ltd., London, Great Britain, 1936.

McLynn, Frank, *Villa and Zapata: A History of the Mexican Revolution*, Basic Books, New York, NY, 2000.

Meed, Douglas V., *Soldier of Fortune*, Halcyon Press, Ltd., Houston, TX, 2003.

Millard, Candice, *The River of Doubt*, Broadway Books, New York, NY, 2005.

Morris, Henry, *Our Mexican Muddle*, Laird and Lee Publishers, Chicago, IL, 1916.

Mowry, Sylvester, *Arizona and Sonora: The Geography, History, and Resources of the Silver Region of North America*, Harper and Brothers, New York, NY, 1864.

Mueller, Lambert, *Tagebuch des Friedrich Neubert 19. Juli 1900-24, November 1901*, www.boxeraufstand.com, viewed September 21, 2010.

Narbeth, Colin, *Admiral Seymour's Expedition and Taku Forts, 1900*, Hyperion Books, December, 1987.

Nauticus, *Jahrbuch für Deutschlands Seeinteressen, 10. Jahrgang*, Ernst Siegfried Mittler und Sohn, Berlin, Germany, 1908.

Newman, Bernard, *Secrets of German Espionage*, The Right Book Club, London, Great Britain, 1940.

Otis and Hough, *Red Manual of Statistics: Stock Exchange Handbook*, Cleveland, OH, 1910.

Pilcher, Jeffrey M, *The Sausage Rebellion: Public Health, Private Enterprise, and Meat in Mexico City,1890–1917*, University of New Mexico Press, Albuquerque, NM, 2006.

Bibliography

Powell, Fred Wilbur, *The Railroads of Mexico*, The Stratford Co., Boston, MA, 1921.

Preston, Diana, *The Boxer Rebellion: The Dramatic Story of China's War on Foreigners that Shook the World in the Summer of 1900*, Walker Publishing Company, New York, NY, 2000.

Pringle, Henry F., *Theodore Roosevelt: A Biography*, Cornwall Press, New York, NY, 1931.

Quirk, Robert E. *An Affair of Honor: Woodrow Wilson and the Occupation of Veracruz*, University of Kentucky Press, Lexington, KY, 1962.

Quirk, Robert E. *The Mexican Revolution, 1914-1915*, University of Indiana Press, Bloomington, IN, 1960.

Raat, W. Dirk and Beezley, William H., editors, *Twentieth Century Mexico*, University of Nebraska Press, Lincoln, NE, 1986.

Reed, John, *Insurgent Mexico: With Pancho Villa in the Mexican Revolution*, Red and Black Publishers, St. Petersburg, FL, 2009 (first published New York, 1914).

Reiling, Johannes, *Deutschland: Safe for Democracy?* Franz Seiner Verlag, Stuttgart, Germany, 1997.

Rocha, Ruben, *Galeria de Parralenses Ilustres*, Hidalgo del Parral, México, 1985.

Ross, Stanley R., *Francisco I. Madero: Apostle of Democracy*, Columbia University Press, New York, NY, 1955.

Schieffel, Werner, *Bernhard Dernburg 1865 - 1937: Kolonialpolitiker und Bankier im wilhelminischen Deutschland*, Atlantis Verlag, Zürich, Switzerland, 1974.

Skaggs, William H., *German Conspiracies in America*, T. Fisher Unwin Ltd., London, Great Britain, 1916 (estimated).

Small, Michael, *The Forgotten Peace: Mediation at Niagara Falls, 1914*, University of Ottawa Press, Canada, 2009.

Smith, Arthur D. Howden, *Mr. House of Texas*, Funk and Wagnalls Company, New York, NY, 1940.

Bibliography

Smith, Arthur D. Howden, *The Real Mr. House*, George H. Doran Company, New York, NY, 1918.

Smith, Randolph Welford, *Benighted Mexico*, John Lane Company, New York, NY, 1916.

Stevens, Horace J., *The Copper Handbook 1908*, Chicago, IL, 1909.

Stroher, French, *Fighting Germany's Spies*, Doubleday Page and Company, Garden City, NY, 1918.

Synon, Mary, *McAdoo: The Man and his Times: A Panorama in Democracy*, The Bobbs-Merrill Company, Indianapolis, IN, 1924.

Tenorio-Trillo, Mauricio, Mexico at the World's Fairs Crafting a Modern Nation, University of California Press, Los Angeles, CA, 1996.

Teitelbaum, Louis M., *Woodrow Wilson and the Mexican Revolution, 1913-1916*, Exposition Press, New York, NY, 1967.

Thomas, William H. Jr., *Unsafe for Democracy: World War I and the U.S. Justice Department's Covert Campaign to Suppress Dissent*, The University of Wisconsin Press, Madison, WI, 2008.

Thomson, Guy P.C. and LaFrance, David G., *Patriotism, Politics and Popular Liberalism in the late 19th Century Mexico: Juan Francisco Lucas and the Puebla Sierra*, Scholarly Resources Inc., Wilmington, DE, 1999.

Tuchman, Barbara, *The Zimmermann Telegram*, Macmillan Company, New York, NY, 1958.

Tuck, Jim, *Pancho Villa and John Reed: Two Faces of Romantic Revolution*, University of Arizona Press, Tucson, AZ, 1984.

Turner, John Kenneth, *Hands off Mexico*, Rand School of Social Science, New York, NY, 1920.

Volkman, Ernest, *Espionage: The Greatest Spy Operations of the 20th Century*, John Wiley and Sons Inc., New York, NY, 1995.

Volkman, Ernest and Baggett, Blaine, *Secret Intelligence: The Inside Story of America's Espionage Empire*, Doubleday, New York, NY, 1989.

Von Schmidt, Paul, *Der Werdegang des Preußischen Heeres*, Verlag von Karl Hermann Düms, Germany, 1903.

Weed, Walter Harvey, *The Mines Handbook*, New York, NY, 1918.

Bibliography

Whitcover, Jules, *Sabotage at the Black Tom*, Algonquin Books of Chapel Hill, Chapel Hill, NC, 1989.

Wile, Frederic William, *Men around the Kaiser: The Makers of Modern Germany*, The MacLean Publishing Company, Toronto, Canada, 1913.

Womack, John, Jr., *Zapata and the Mexican Revolution*, Alfred A. Knopf, New York, NY, 1968.

Xu, Guoqi, *China and the Great War: China's pursuit of a new National Identity and Internationalization*, Cambridge University Press, New York, NY, 2005.

Young, William, *German Diplomatic Relations, 1871-1945*, iUniverse, Inc., New York, NY, 2006.

Bibliography

Newspapers, Bulletins and Magazines

Allgemeine Zeitung des Judentums, Heft 34, August 24, Berlin, 1900.

The American Historical Review, Vol. 83, No. 1 (Feb., 1978), "Pancho Villa and the Attack on Columbus, New Mexico," by Friedrich Katz.

The Americas, Vol. 30, No. 1 (Jul., 1973), "The Arms of the Ypiranga: The German Side," by Thomas Baecker, pp. 1-17.

The Americas, Vol. 32, No. 1 (Jul., 1975), "The Muddied Waters of Columbus, New Mexico," by E. Bruce White and Francisco Villa.

The Americas, Vol. 39, No. 1 (July, 1982), "The Underside of the Mexican Revolution: El Paso, 1912," by Charles H. Harris, III and Louis R. Sadler.

Bancroft Library News Release, "Surprising new information on Pancho Villa comes to light in obscure Wells Fargo files at UC Berkeley," by Kathlene Scalise, University of California at Berkley, http://berkeley.edu/news/media/releases/99legacy/5-3-1999.html.

Batavia Daily News, Batavia, NY, January 6, 1888.

Bulletin of the Business Historical Society, Volume 26, Number 4 (December 1952), "Colonel William C. Greene and the Cananea Copper Bubble," by Marvin D. Bernstein.

Chicago Daily News Almanac and Yearbook for 1912, Chicago Daily News Company, Chicago, IL, 1911.

Chihuahua en 1910, Álbum del Centenario, Ayuntamiento de Chihuahua, 1994

Collier's Magazine, Volume 47, June 1911.

The Copper Handbook: A Manual of the Copper Industry of the World, Volume 6, Houghton, MI, 1906.

Coshocton Morning Tribune, Coshocton, OH, February 1913.

Die Woche, Berlin 1900, published by Rainer Dombrowsky, www.jadu.de, 2001.

The Evening Bulletin, Maysville, KY, "Almost beyond Belief," November 6, 1887.

Bibliography

EH.Net Encyclopedia, Moen, Jon: "Panic of 1907," edited by Robert Whaples, August 14, 2001.

El Paso Herald, El Paso, TX, 1910-1920.

The Financial Review: Finance, Commerce, Railroads, Annual 1912.

Fuel Oil Journal, Volume 5, May 1914, Houston, TX.

The Gazette Times, Pittsburgh, PA, October 7, 1913.

Harper's Magazine, September, October, November 1917, "Diplomatic Days in Mexico, First, Second, Third Papers," by Edith O'Shaughnessy.

Harper's Magazine, November 1942, "The wind that swept Mexico: Part I, II, and III, by Anita Brenner.

Harper's Monthly Magazine, April, 1912, "The Passing of a Dictator," by Robert Welles Ritchie.

Hispanic Historical Review, Vol. L, No. 3, August 1970, "The Arms of the Ypiranga," by Michael C. Meyer, pp. 543-556.

The Historian, Vol. 60, Issue 4, "The U.S. Bank Panic of 1907 and the Mexican Depression of 1908-1909," by Kevin J. Cahill, 1998.

History Review, December 2002: "The unpredictable dynamo: Germany's Economy, 1870-1918," by F.G. Stapleton.

Journal of Intelligence History, Volume 4, Number 1, Summer 2004, Reinhard R. Doerries.

The Journal of Economic History, vol. 64, issue 04, "Real Shock, Monetary Aftershock: The 1906 San Francisco Earthquake and the Panic of 1907," Kerry A. Odell and Marc D. Weidenmier, 2005.

Journal of Latin American Studies, Vol. 35, No. 1 (Feb. 2003), "Railroad, Oil and Other Foreign Interests in the Mexican Revolution, 1911 to 1914," by John Skirius, Cambridge University Press.

La Prensa, San Antonio, TX, February 13th, 1913.

Lancer, Jalisco, "German-Mexican Relations Before the Revolution," *www.allempires.net*, viewed December 22, 2005.

Bibliography

Mexican Studies, Vol. 2, No. 1 (Winter 1986), "Germany, Revolutionary Nationalism, and the Downfall of Francisco I. Madero: The Covadonga Killings," by David G. LaFrance.

Mexican Studies, Vol. 17, No.1 (Winter, 2001), "Exiliados de la Revolución mexicana: El caso de los villistas (1915-1921)," by Victoria Lerner.

The Mining World, Volume 32, Chicago, IL, January 1 to June 25, 1910.

The Nation, volumes 99 to 109, July 1, 1914 to December 31, 1919, The Nation Press, NY 1919.

New York in the Spanish-American War, 1898, Volume II, Registers of Organizations, New York, NY, 1900.

New York Sun, New York, NY, November 12, 1887.

The New York Times, New York, NY, Archives 1896-1942.

The New York Tribune, New York, NY, 1910-1918.

The Oakland Tribune, Oakland, CA, April 18, 1915.

Pearson's Magazine, Vol. 19, March 1908, James Creelman: "President Diaz, Hero of the Americas."

Sabazius, "The Invisible Basilica: Dr. Arnoldo Krumm-Heller (1876 -1949 e.v.)," Ordo Templi Orientis, USA, 1997.

The San Antonio Light, San Antonio, TX, February, 1913.

The San Francisco Call and Post, San Francisco, CA, October 9, 1913.

Southwestern Studies, Monograph number 47, "Luther T. Ellsworth: U.S. Consul on the Border During the Mexican Revolution," by Dorothy Pierson Kerig, Texas Western Press, El Paso, TX 1975.

The St. Louis Republic, St. Louis, MO, January 3rd, 1900.

The Southwestern Reporter, Volume 118, Containing all the current decisions of the supreme and appellate courts of Arkansas, Kentucky, Missouri, Tennessee, and Texas May 19 – June 9, 1909, "Maury et al. v. McDonald et al., Court of Civil Appeals of Texas, April 3, 1909," West Publishing Co., St. Paul, MN 1909.

Bibliography

The Southwestern Historical Quarterly, Volume 67, No. 2, October 1963, E. V. Niemeyer, "The Revolutionary Attempt of General Bernardo Reyes from San Antonio in 1911."

The Times, Washington, D.C., October 10, 1898.

The Times-Picayune, New Orleans, LA, July 1 to July 6, 1914.

The Washington Herald, Washington, D.C., 1910-1922

The Washington Post, Washington, D.C., 1911-1922.

The Washington Times, Washington, D.C., 1910-1914

The World Almanac and Encyclopedia, 1902, Press Publishing Co, New York, NY, 1902, p. 425, foreign consuls in the United States.

Bibliography

Original Sources/Archival Sources

Admiralstab der Marine, *Die Kaiserliche Marine während der Wirren in China, 1900-1901*, Volume I, Ernst Siegfried Rittler und Sohn, Berlin, 1903.

ANDREW D. MELOY & CO. v. DONNELLY et al., (Circuit Court, D. Connecticut. December 30, 1902.), No. 523.

Archivos Municipales Chihuahua, Fondo Porfiriato, Secretaria de Gobierno del Estado de Chihuahua, Chihuahua Enterprise 1905-1910, Mines Register 1904-1910.

Auswärtiges Amt, Politisches Archiv Berlin, Mexiko Volumes I to X.

Carey McWilliams Papers, University of California at Los Angeles, 277.

Chihuahua Archivos Municipales, Secretaria de Gobierno del Estado de Chihuahua, Sección de Estadística, Chihuahua 1909.

Federal Reserve Bank of Boston, "The Panic of 1907," Boston, MA, 2002.

German Diplomatic Papers, University of California at Berkley, Bancroft Library, M-B 12.

Holmdahl Papers, University of California at Berkley, Bancroft Library, C-B-921.

Immigrant Ancestors: A List of 2,500 Immigrants to America before 1750, Frederick Virkus, editor; Genealogical Publishing Co., Baltimore, MD, 1964.

Königliches Finanzministerium, *Jahrbuch für das Berg- und Hüttenwesen im Königreiche Sachsen*, Jahrgang 1902 (Statistik vom Jahre 1901, C. Menzel, Freiberg, 1902.

Lazaro De La Garza Collection, University of Texas, Benson Library, Austin, TX.

Marine Crew Chronik, Marineschule Mürwik, Flensburg, Deutschland, MIM620/CREW, 1891, pp. 159-160, auto-biographic article by Karl Boy-Ed.

National Archives of the United Kingdom, BT26, Board of Trade: Commercial and Statistical Department and successors: Inwards Passenger Lists, Kew, Surrey.

National Archives of the United States of America, NARA, Washington D.C.

Bibliography

Record Group 36	Records of the U.S. Customs Service, Vessels arriving in New York 1820-1897 and 1897-1957
Record Group 38	Office of Naval Intelligence, 1913 to 1924
Record Group 45	Naval Records Collection, Caribbean File 1911 to 1927
Record Group 59	Department of State 1908 to 1927
Record Group 60	Records of the Department of Justice, Straight Numerical Files; Specifically file 9-16-12 Statement of F.A. Sommerfeld June 21, 1918 to June 24, 1918.
Record Group 65	Records of the FBI, specifically Papers of Heinrich Albert, Bureau of Investigation Case Files, 1908-1922, "Old German Files," and "Old Mexican Files."
Record Group 76	Mixed Claims Commission, 1922 to 1941
Record Group 80	General Records of the Navy, 1916 to 1926
Record Group 85	Records of the Immigration and Naturalization Service
Record Group 87	Records of the U.S. Secret Service, Daily Reports, 1875 to 1936
Record Group 131	Records of the Alien Property Custodian, Records seized by the APC
Record Group 165	Records of the War Department, Military Intelligence Division; Specifically file 9140-1754: Felix A. Sommerfeld
Record Group 242	German Captured Documents, Foreign Office, Mexico Book 1 to 10.
Record Group 395	Records of the Army Overseas Operations, Mexican Punitive Expedition.

National Register of the Society Sons of The American Revolution; Compiled by Louis H. Cornish, New York, NY, 1902.

Naval Militia Yearbooks 1901, 1902, 1903, 1904.

Bibliography

New York Department of Health, *Deaths reported in the City of New York, 1888-1965.*

Official Program, Admiral Dewey Reception, October 2 and 3, 1899, Washington, D.C., 1899.

Papers of Hugh Lenox Scott, Library of Congress, Washington, D.C.

Rangliste der Königlich Preußischen Armee und des XIII (Königlich Württembergischen) Armeekorps für 1907, Ernst Siegfried Mittler und Sohn, Berlin, Germany, 1907.

Secretaría de Comunicaciones y Obras Públicas, Estadística de ferrocarriles de jurisdicción federal año de 1918. México, Talleres Gráficos de la Nación, 1924.

Silvestre Terrazas Papers, University of California at Berkley, Bancroft Library, M-B-18.

Staatsarchiv Hamburg, Hamburger Passagierlisten, 1850-1934.

Stallforth Papers, Private Collection

Testimony of Henry Clay Pierce before the 8th Circuit Court, The United States of America vs. Standard Oil Company of New Jersey et al defendants, Petitioner's Testimony, Volume 3, Washington Government Printing Office, Washington, D.C., 1908.

United States Senate, Hearing before a Subcommittee of the Committee on Foreign Relations, *Revolutions in Mexico*, Government Printing Office, Washington D. C., 1913.

United States Senate, *Investigation of Mexican affairs*, Subcommittee of the Committee of Foreign Relations, Government Printing Office, Washington, D.C., 1920.

United States Senate, *Papers Related to the Foreign Relations of the United States*, Government Printing Office, Washington D.C., 1919.

Autobiographical Works

Boy-Ed, Karl, *Verschwörer?* Verlag August Scherl GmbH, Berlin, Germany, 1920.

Count von Bernstorff, Johann Heinrich, *My Three Years in America*, Skeffington and Son, London, Great Britain, unknown date, approximately 1940.

Count von Bernstorff, Johann Heinrich, *Memoirs of Count Bernstorff*, Random House, New York, NY, 1936.

Garibaldi, Giuseppe, *A Toast To Rebellion*, The Bobbs-Merrill Company, New York, NY, 1935.

Gerard, James W., *My first eighty three years in America: Memoirs of James W. Gerard*, Doubleday and Company Inc., Garden City, NY, 1951.

Hale, William Bayard, *The Story of a Style*, B. W. Huebsch Inc., New York, NY, 1920.

Guzman, Martin Luis, *Memoirs of Pancho Villa*, translated by Virginia H. Taylor, University of Texas Press, Austin TX, 1975.

Madero, Francisco I., *La Sucesión Presidencial en 1910 – El Partido Nacional Democrático*, San Pedro, Coahuila, México, December, 1908.

Nicolai, Walter, *The German Secret Service, translated with an additional chapter by George Renwick*, Stanley Paul and Co., London, Great Britain, 1924.

Von Papen, Franz, *Memoirs*, E. P. Dutton and Company Inc., New York, NY, 1953.

Rintelen, Franz, *The Dark Invader: Wartime Reminiscences of a German Naval Intelligence Officer*, Lovat Dickson Limited, London, Great Britain, 1933.

Rintelen, Franz, *The Return of the Dark Invader*, Peter Davies Limited, London, Great Britain, 1935.

Scott, Hugh Lenox, *Some Memories of a Soldier*, The Century Company, New York, NY, 1928.

Steffens, Lincoln, *The Autobiography of Lincoln Steffens*, Harcourt, Brace and Company, New York, NY, 1931.

Von der Goltz, Horst, *My Adventures as a German Secret Agent*, Robert M. McBride and Company, New York, NY, 1917.

Von der Goltz, Horst, *Sworn Statement*, Presented to both Houses of Parliament by Command of His Majesty, London, Great Britain, April 1916.

Walker, William. *The War in Nicaragua*, S.H. Goetzel, New York, NY, 1860.

Wilson, Woodrow and Hale, William Bayard, *The New Freedom*, Doubleday, Page and Co., New York, NY, 1913.

Wilson, Henry Lane *Diplomatic Episodes in Mexico, Belgium and Chile*, Kinnikat Press, Port Washington, NY, 1971, reprint of original 1927.

Wilson, Henry Lane "Errors with Reference to Mexico and Events that have occurred there," *International Relations of the United States: The Annals*, Vol. LIV, July, 1914.

INDEX